AF606001

TOSA MITSUNOBU AND THE SMALL SCROLL IN MEDIEVAL JAPAN

UNIVERSITY OF WASHINGTON PRESS SEATTLE AND LONDON

MELISSA McCORMICK

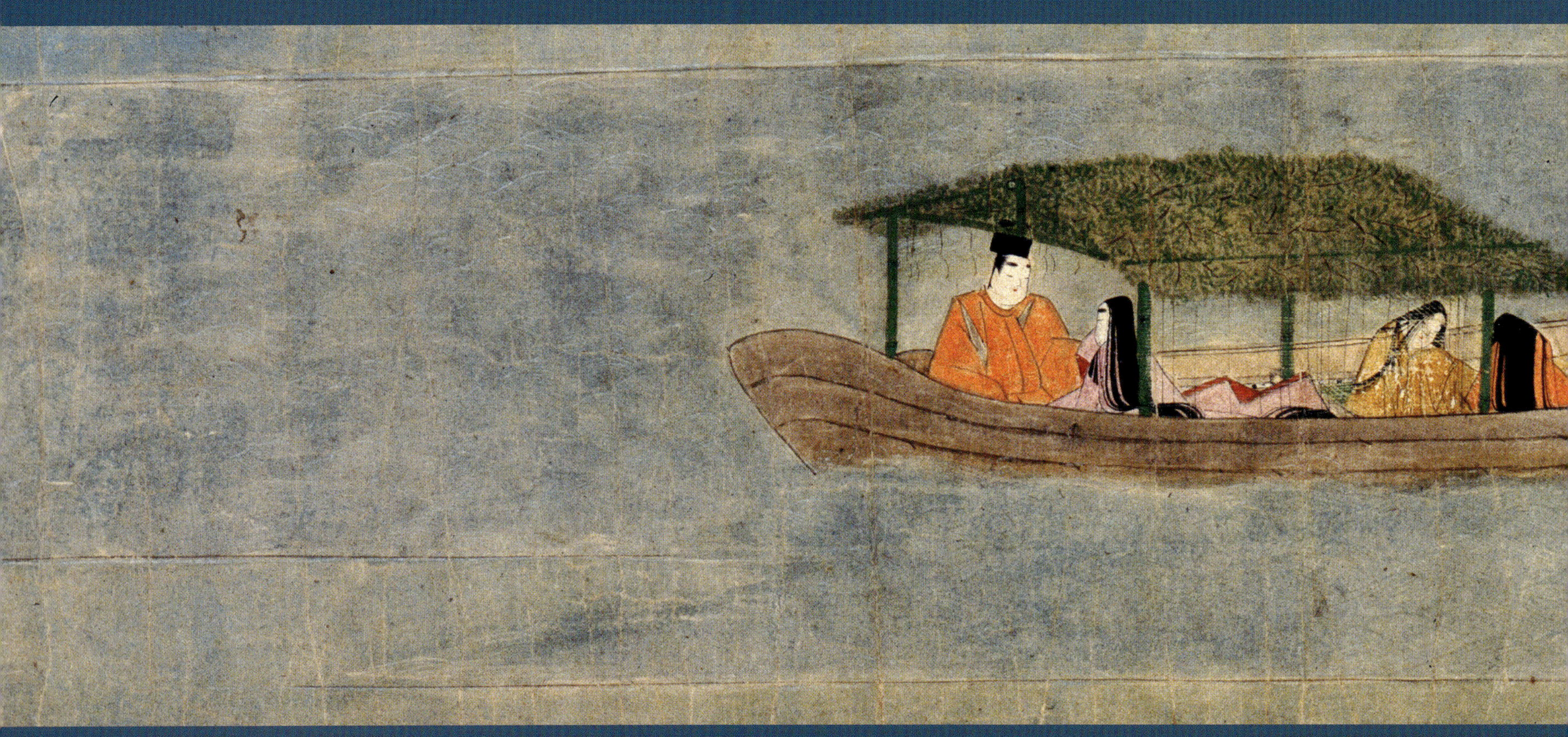

TOSA MITSUNOBU

AND THE SMALL SCROLL IN MEDIEVAL JAPAN

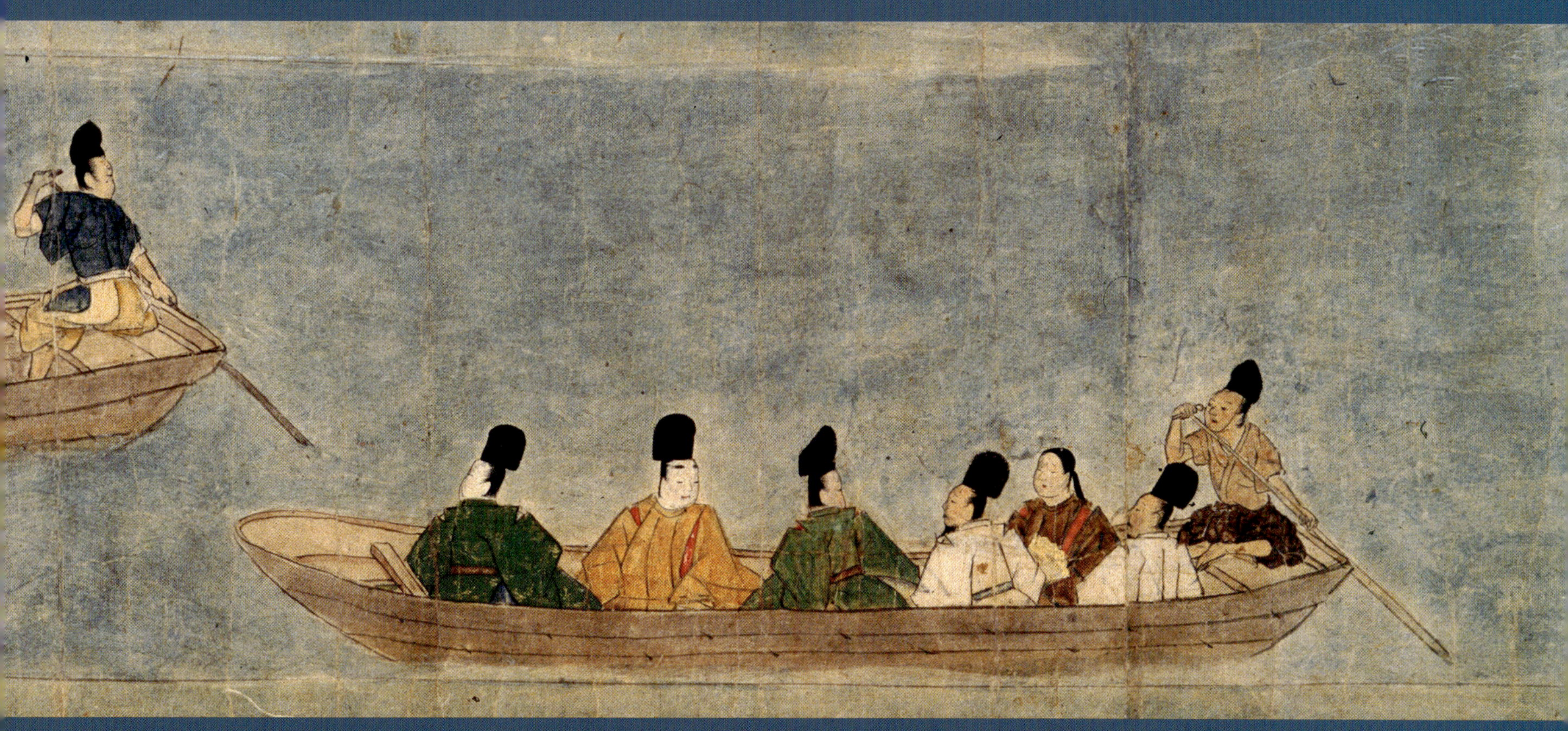

Tosa Mitsunobu and the Small Scroll in Medieval Japan is published with the assistance of the Getty Foundation.

The book also received generous support from the Publications Committee, Department of Art and Archaeology, Princeton University, and from the Reischauer Institute of Japanese Studies, Harvard University.

Printed in Singapore
Design by Ashley Saleeba
14 12 11 10 09 5 4 3 2 1

UNIVERSITY OF WASHINGTON PRESS
P.O. Box 50096, Seattle, WA 98145 U.S.A.
www.washington.edu/uwpress

The paper used in this publication meets the minimum requirements of American National Standard for Information Sciences—Permanence of Paper for Printed Library Materials, ANSI Z39.48–1984.

LIBRARY OF CONGRESS CATALOGING-IN-PUBLICATION DATA
McCormick, Melissa, 1967–
Tosa Mitsunobu and the small scroll in medieval Japan / Melissa McCormick.
p. cm.
Includes bibliographical references and index.
ISBN 978-0-295-98902-0 (hardback : alk. paper)
1. Scrolls, Japanese—Kamakura-Momoyama periods, 1185–1600.
2. Narrative painting, Japanese—Kamakura-Momoyama periods, 1185–1600. 3. Tosa, Mitsunobu, 1434?–1525—Criticism and interpretation. I. Title.
ND1053.4.M43 2009
759.952—dc22 2008050723

ILLUSTRATION DETAILS:
pp. ii–iii: Fig. 1. Tosa Mitsunobu, *A Wakeful Sleep* (*Utatane sōshi emaki*); p. viii: Fig. 32. *Legends of Kitano Tenjin* (*Kitano Tenjin engi emaki*); p. x: Fig. 5. *Lives of the Founders of the Kegon Sect* (*Kegonshū soshi eden*); p. 278: Fig. 32. *Legends of Kitano Tenjin* (*Kitano Tenjin engi emaki*); p. 280. Fig. 59. Mitsunobu, calligraphy by Sanjōnishi Sanetaka, *Legends of Kitano Tenjin* (*Kitano Tenjin engi emaki*)

FOR AZUSA

CONTENTS

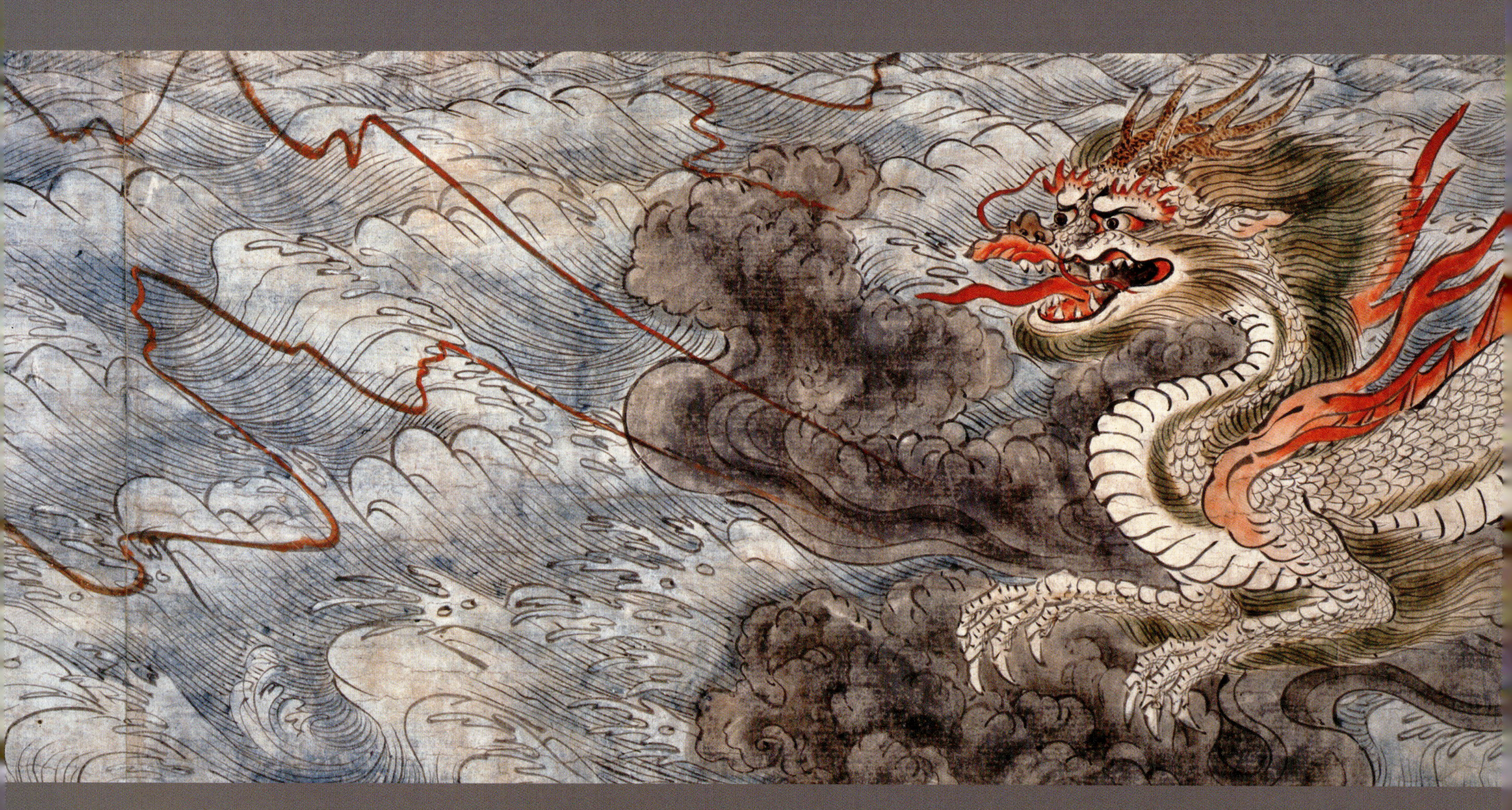

NOTE TO READERS

All Japanese names appear in the traditional Japanese order, surname followed by given name. Months and days appear according to the lunar calendar. Years are given by traditional Japanese era name (*nengō*) and an equivalent year in the Western calendar: Meiō 8 (1499) 3.15 thus indicates the fifteenth day of the third month of the eighth year of the Meiō era, 1499. Ages of individuals are rendered according to Western count.

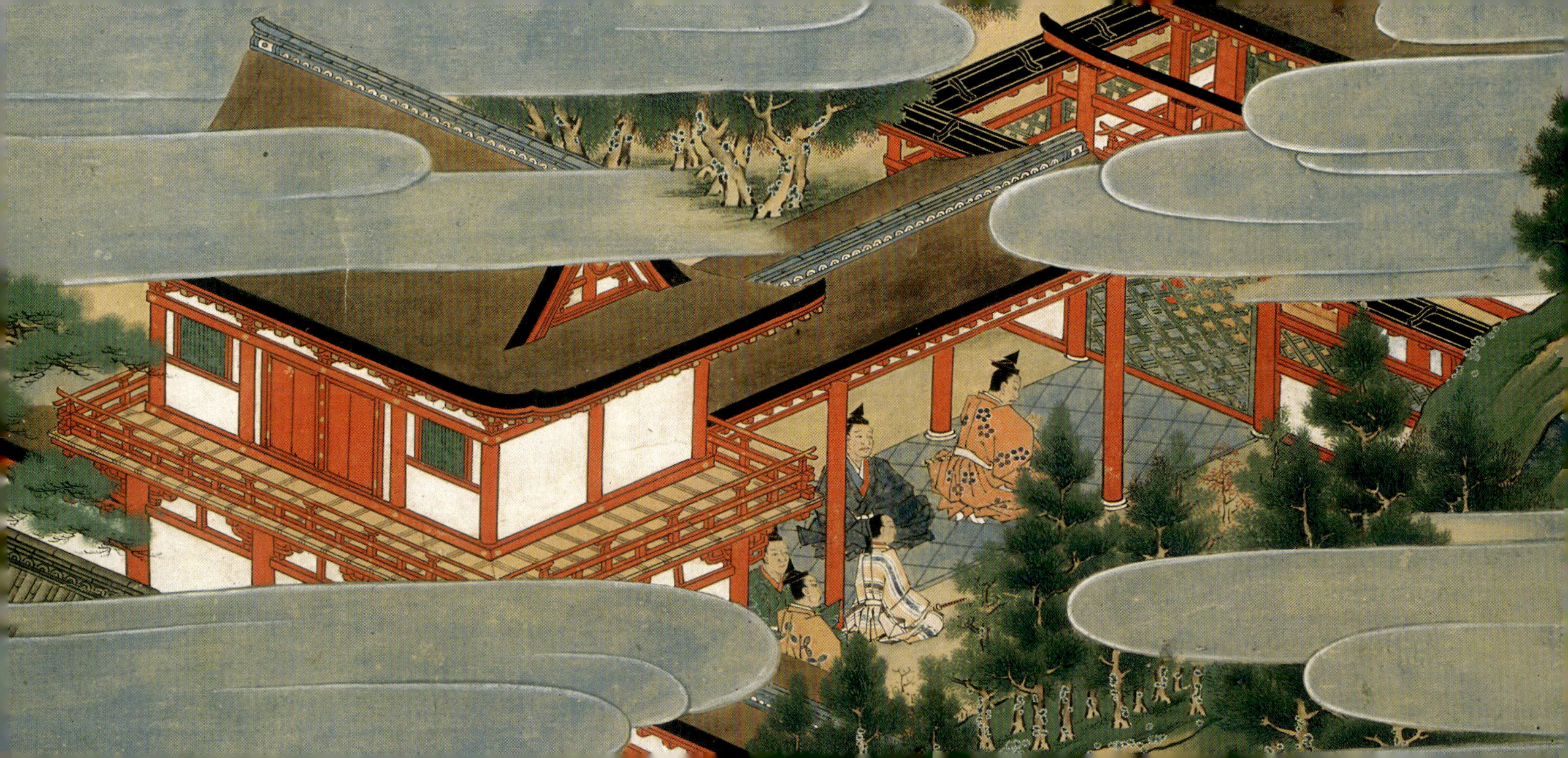

ACKNOWLEDGMENTS

This book evolved out of my doctoral research and therefore owes much to numerous scholars who have helped shape my ideas on this topic, beginning with my thesis adviser at Princeton University, Professor Yoshiaki Shimizu, whose scholarship on narrative painting inspired me early on, and my mentors in history, Professor Martin Collcutt, and in Japanese literature, Professor Richard Okada. In Japan I am indebted to the late Professor Chino Kaori, who oversaw my studies at Gakushūin University in Tokyo and who accompanied me to view firsthand many of the scrolls reproduced here; her insightful comments during those viewings were ever in my mind as I wrote this book. I am also indebted to the former members of Professor Chino's seminar for their friendship, feedback, and helpful skepticism, especially Estelle Bauer, Kamei Wakana, Mizuno Ryōko, Narihara Yuki, and Melanie Trede. Professor Tokuda Kazuo and the members of his seminar on medieval handscrolls at Gakushūin University opened my eyes to new ways of reading narrative picture scrolls.

I am pleased finally to be able to thank the many colleagues whose comments on this manuscript and whose own scholarship in related fields have had an influence on this project, including Mikael Adolphson, Aizawa Masahiko, Karen Brock, Ikeda Shinobu, Itakura Masa'aki, Kasashima Tadayuki, Kobayashi Tadashi, Matthew McKelway, Joshua Mostow, Quitman Eugene Phillips, Sano Midori, Suzuki Hiroyuki, Melinda Takeuchi, Mimi Yiengpruksawan, and Yonekura Michio. I owe a special debt to Christine Guth, Gregory Levine, and Andrew Watsky, who read drafts of the complete manuscript and offered insightful comments and criticisms on virtually every page. And a personal thanks goes to Takagishi Akira and Yamamoto Satomi, who helped make the study of Mitsunobu an adventure—

including a memorable road trip to the artist's land holdings in the countryside of old Tanba Province. Access to picture scrolls large and small was crucial for this study and was made possible through the generous assistance of Hosomi Ariko and Hosomi Yoshiyuki, Anne Rose Kitagawa, Kobayashi Yūko, Kuroda Taizō, Mito Nobue, Senkai Yoshiyuki, Shimatani Hiroyuki, Tamamushi Satoko, Taniguchi Kōsei, Wakasugi Junji, Masako Watanabe, and Watanabe Yūji. Talia Andrei, Akiko Walley, and Fujiki Masumi provided invaluable assistance in acquiring the photographs for this book. I was fortunate to complete this book while in the company of brilliant and kindhearted colleagues at Columbia University and at Harvard University; I am grateful to all of them, especially Ryūichi Abé, Edwin Cranston, Robert Harrist, Susan Pharr, Michael Puett, Haruo Shirane, and Eugene Wang. At the University of Washington Press, I wish to extend my deep thanks to Michael Duckworth for his enthusiasm about this project, and to Pamela J. Bruton, Ashley Saleeba, John Stevenson, and Marilyn Trueblood.

Generous grants from numerous institutions have supported the research for this book from the earliest stages. A Japan Foundation Dissertation Fellowship, a Fulbright-Hays Doctoral Dissertation Fellowship, and a Metropolitan Center for Far Eastern Art Studies Doctoral Grant enabled two years of research in Japan, while a Mellon Fellowship in the Humanities, a Princeton University Fellowship, and an Ittleson Predoctoral Fellowship from the Center for Advanced Study in the Visual Arts at The National Gallery of Art provided support during the final years of thesis writing. A yearlong sabbatical from the Department of Art History and Archaeology at Columbia University, supported by a J. Paul Getty Postdoctoral Fellowship in the History of Art and Humanities, gave me the time to reconceptualize the dissertation. The book's current physical form is indebted to generous subvention grants from the Publications Committee of the Department of Art and Archaeology, Princeton University, and the Reischauer Institute of Japanese Studies, Harvard University.

Significant portions of this book were revised and rewritten during winter vacations and summer breaks while staying with friends and family, where I was sustained by love and encouragement and many wonderful home-cooked meals. I will be forever grateful to my families in Japan and the United States for their emotional and intellectual support. My deepest gratitude goes to my husband, Yukio Lippit, for his tireless attention to this manuscript, which improved the book in countless ways. This book is dedicated to our daughter, Azusa, whose first four years coincided with its completion and who has done more to deepen my understanding of narrative, history, and humanity than I ever could have imagined.

TOSA MITSUNOBU AND THE SMALL SCROLL IN MEDIEVAL JAPAN

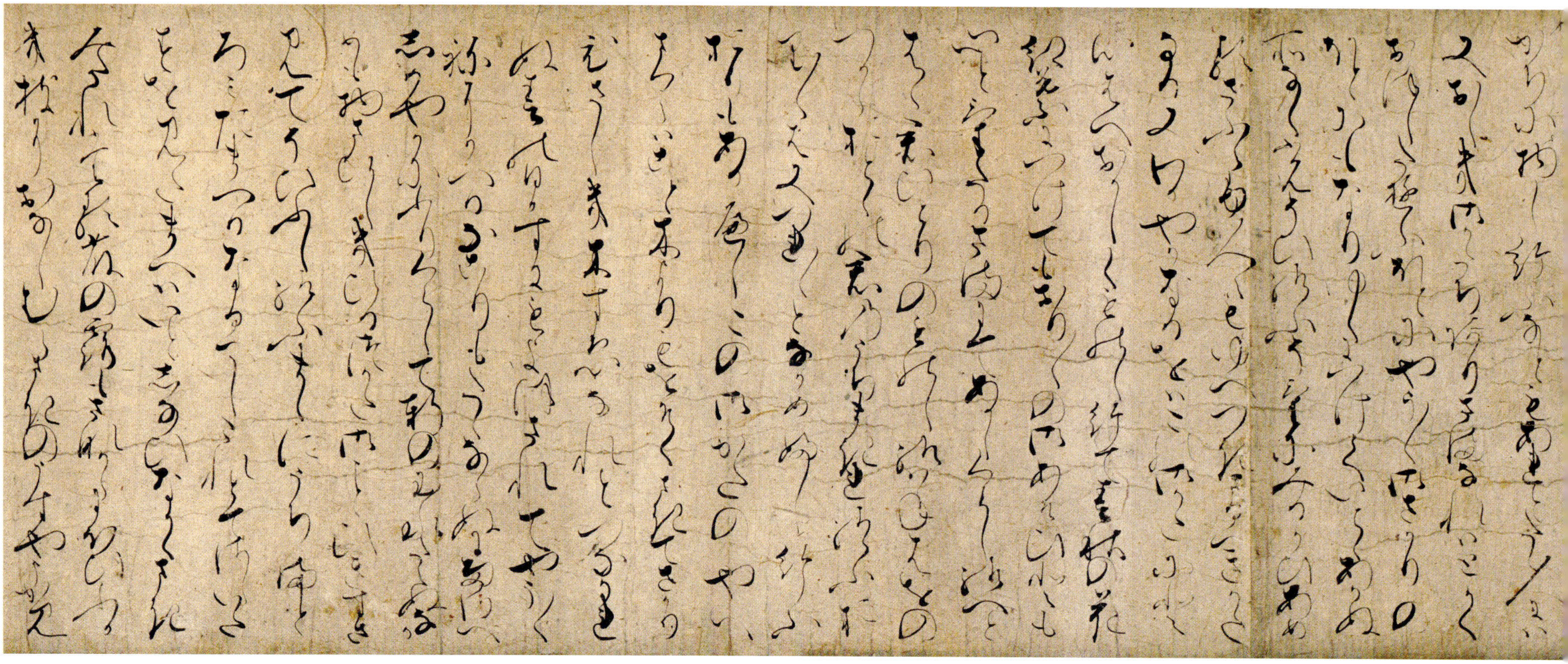

TEXT TWO

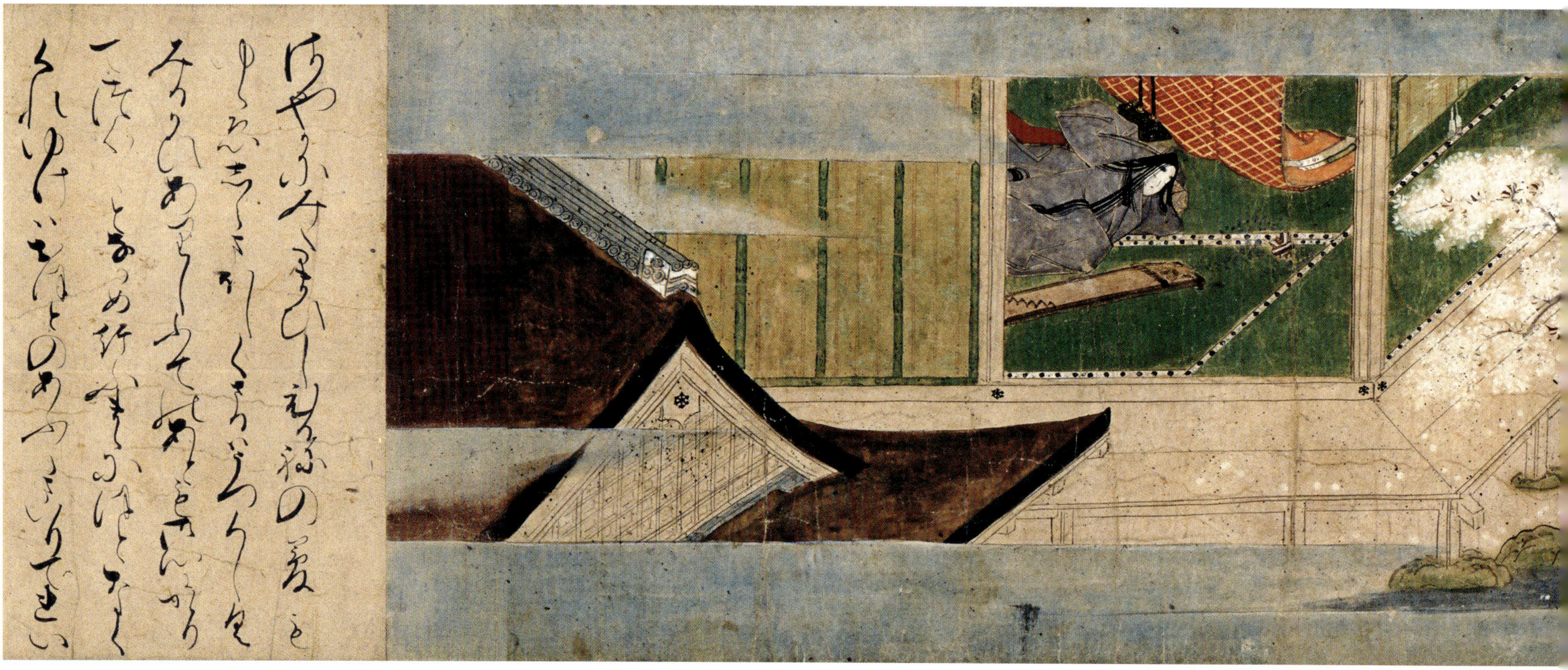

A

1 Tosa Mitsunobu, *A Wakeful Sleep* (*Utatane sōshi emaki*). Late fifteenth to early sixteenth century. One handscroll; ink, color, and gold on paper, 16.5 x 929.6 cm. National Museum of Japanese History, Chiba Prefecture.

TEXT ONE

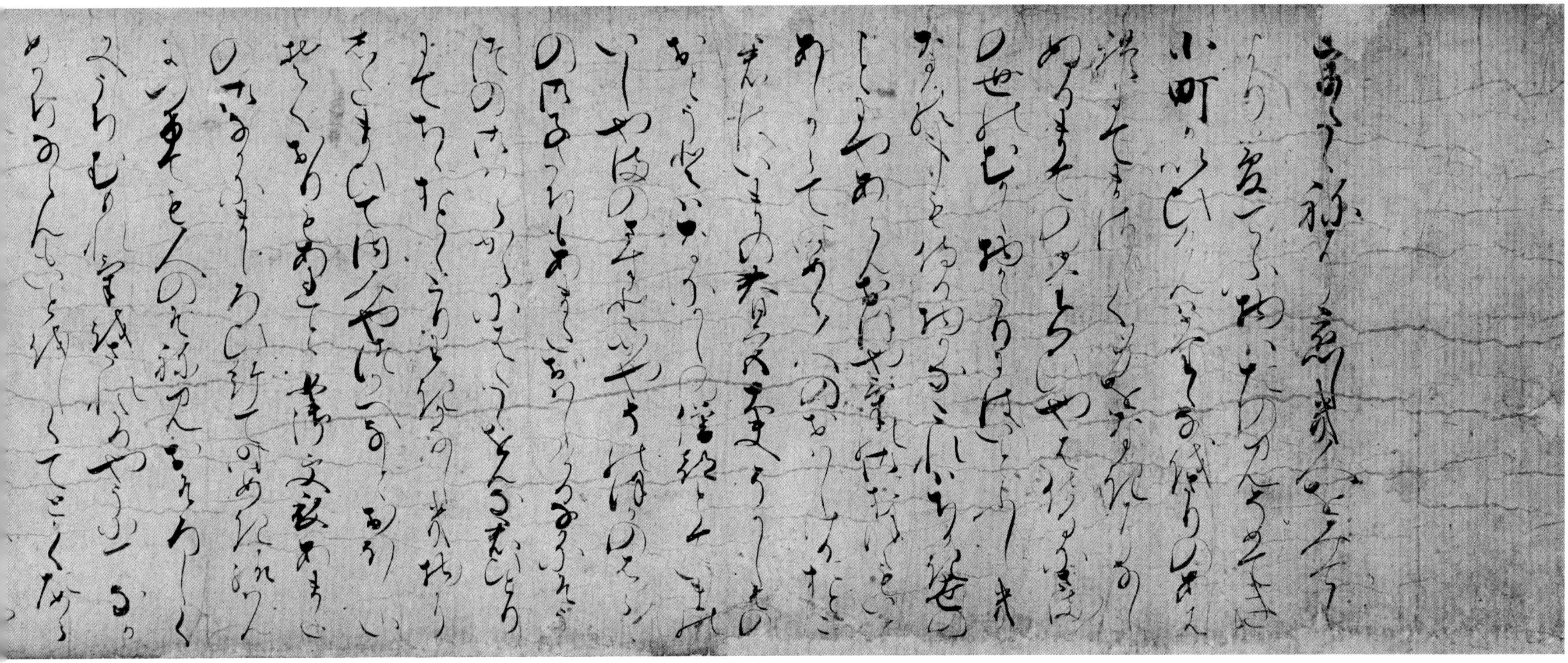

PAINTING ONE

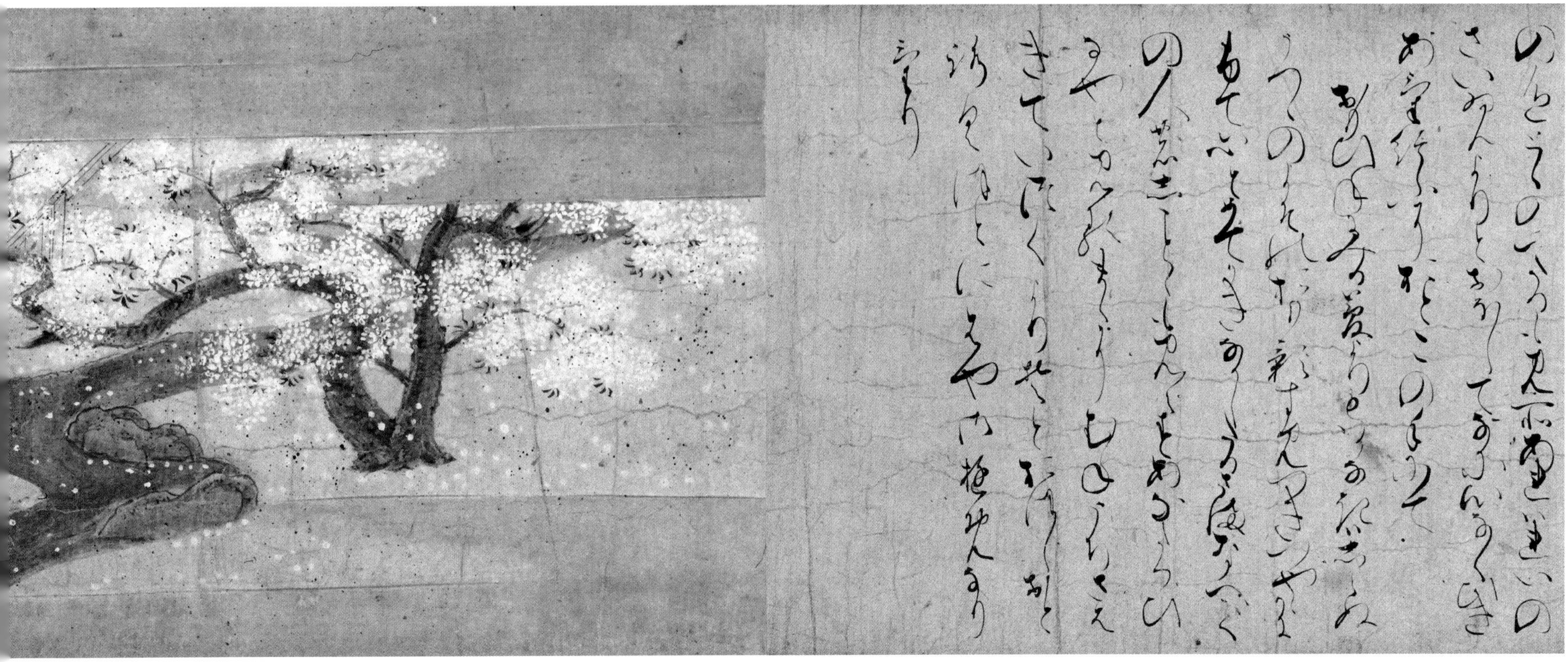

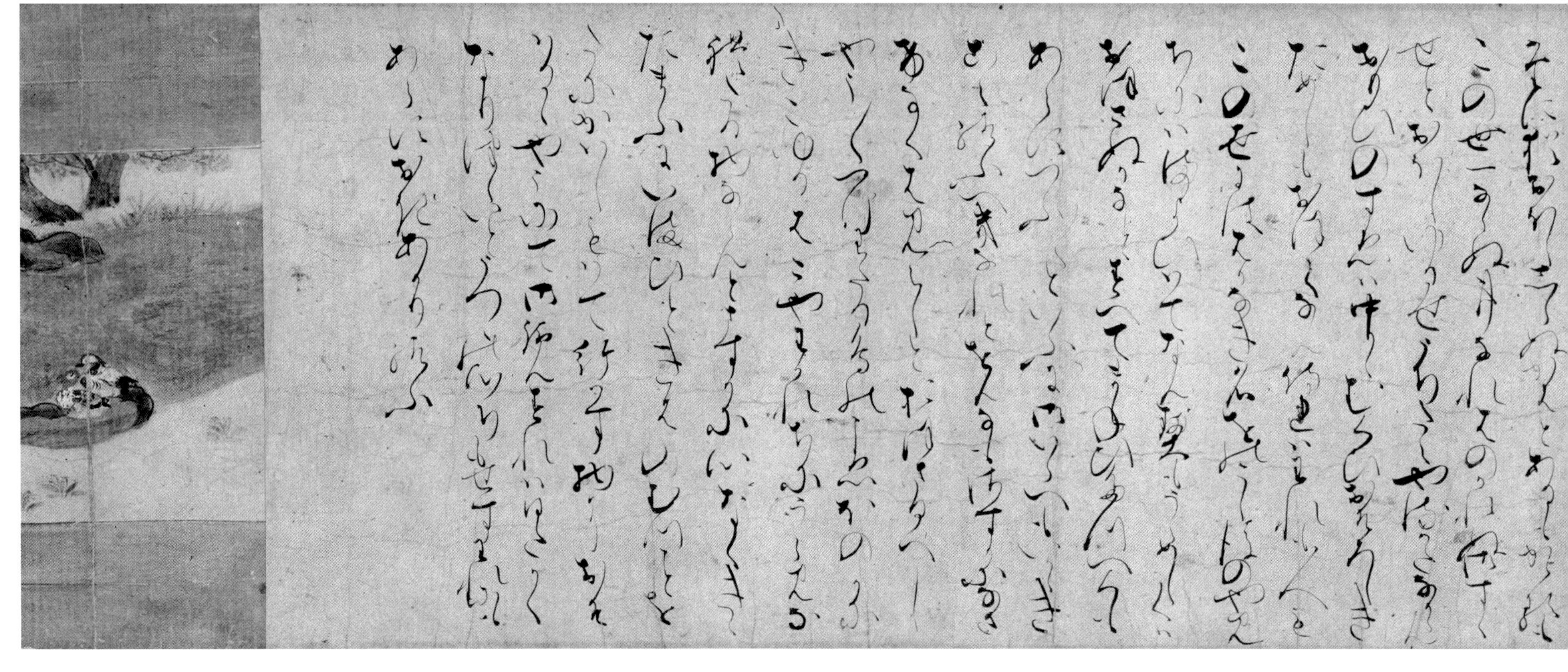

TEXT THREE

TEXT TWO (CONTINUED)

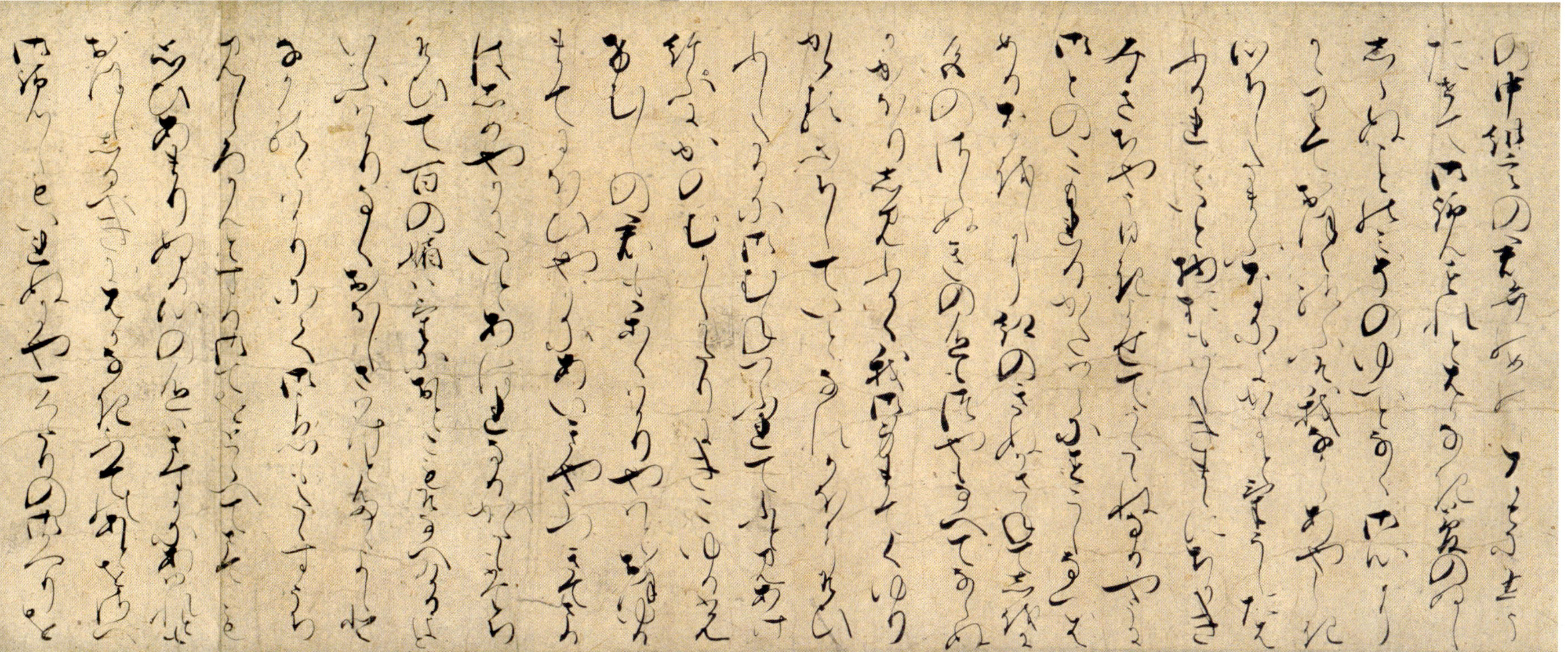

PAINTING TWO

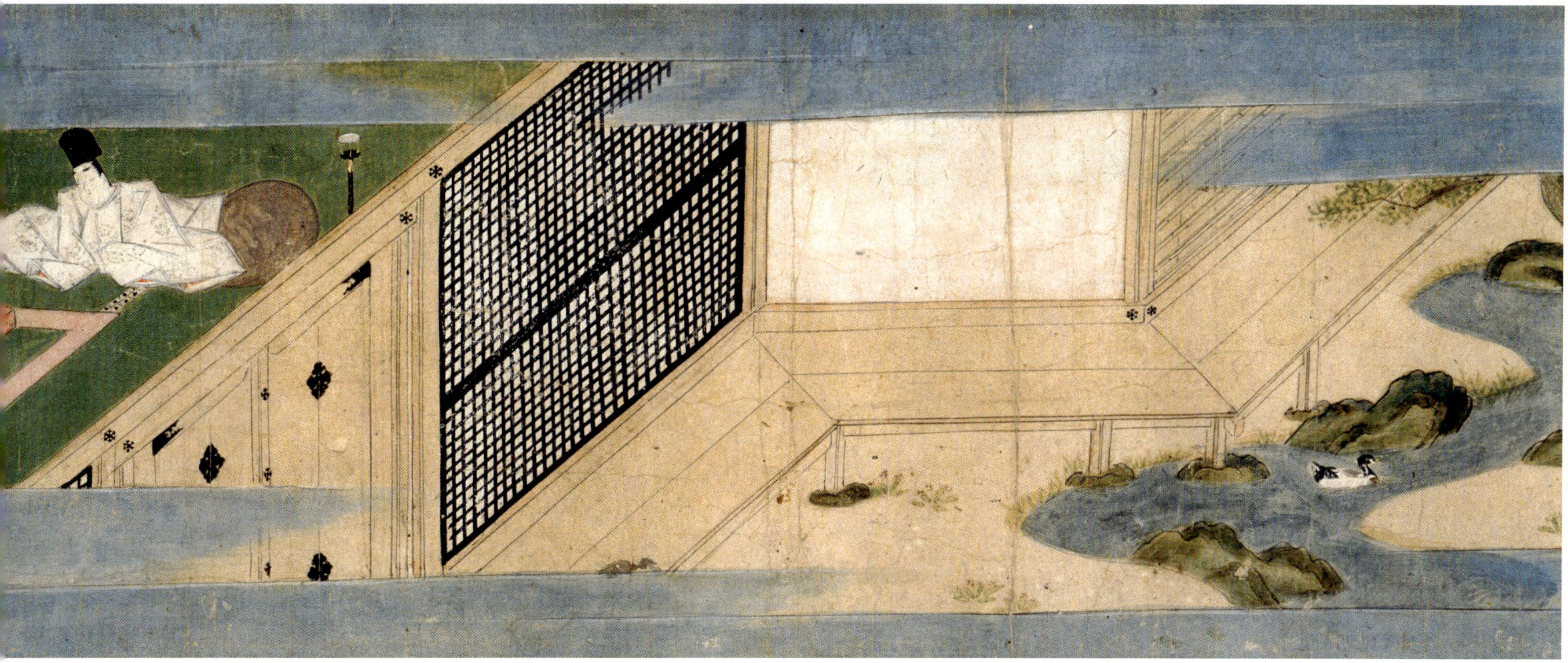

B

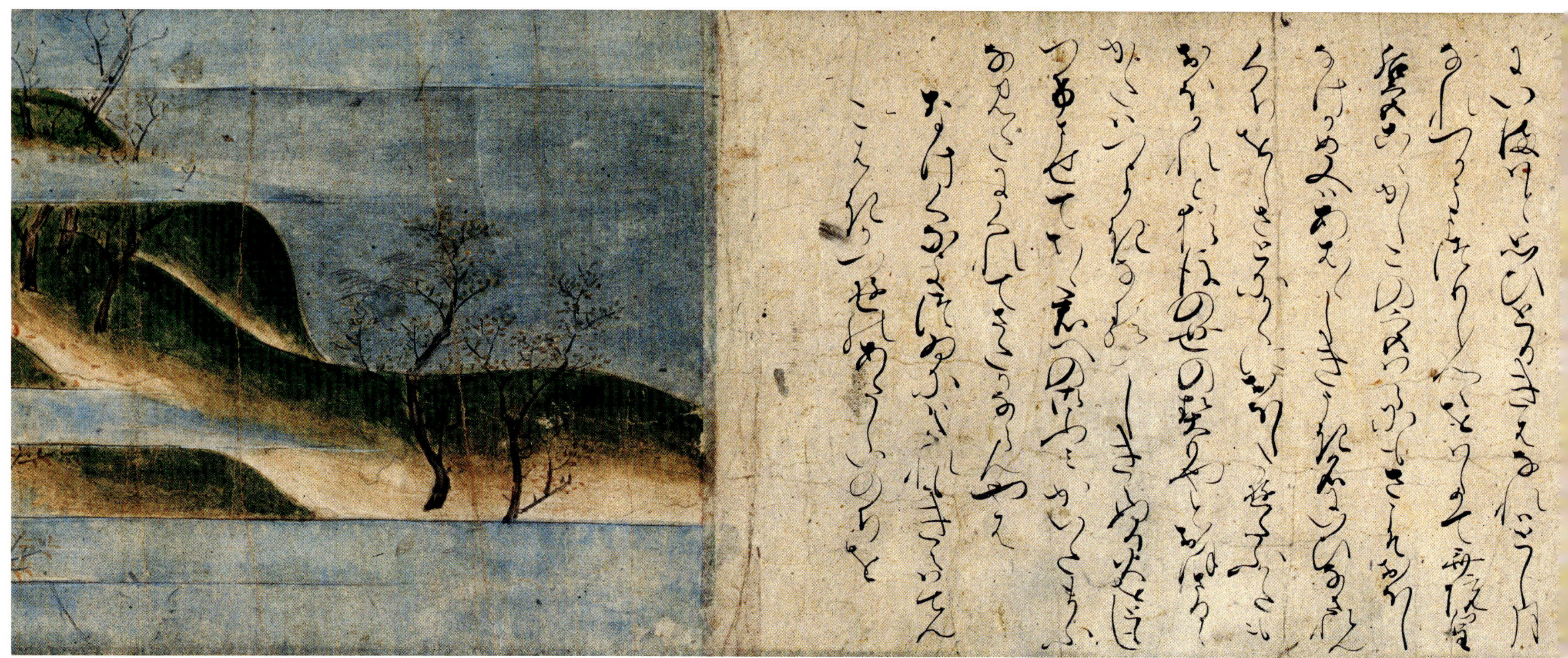

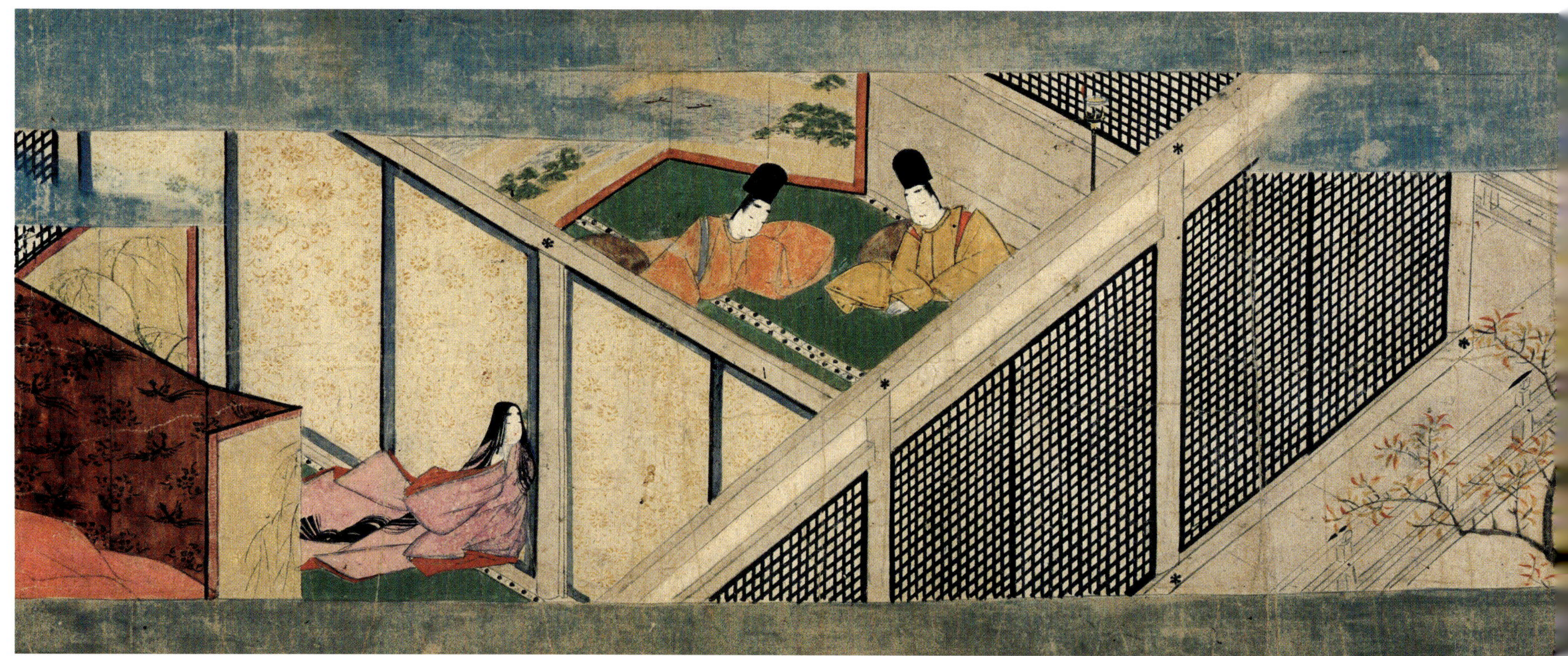

D

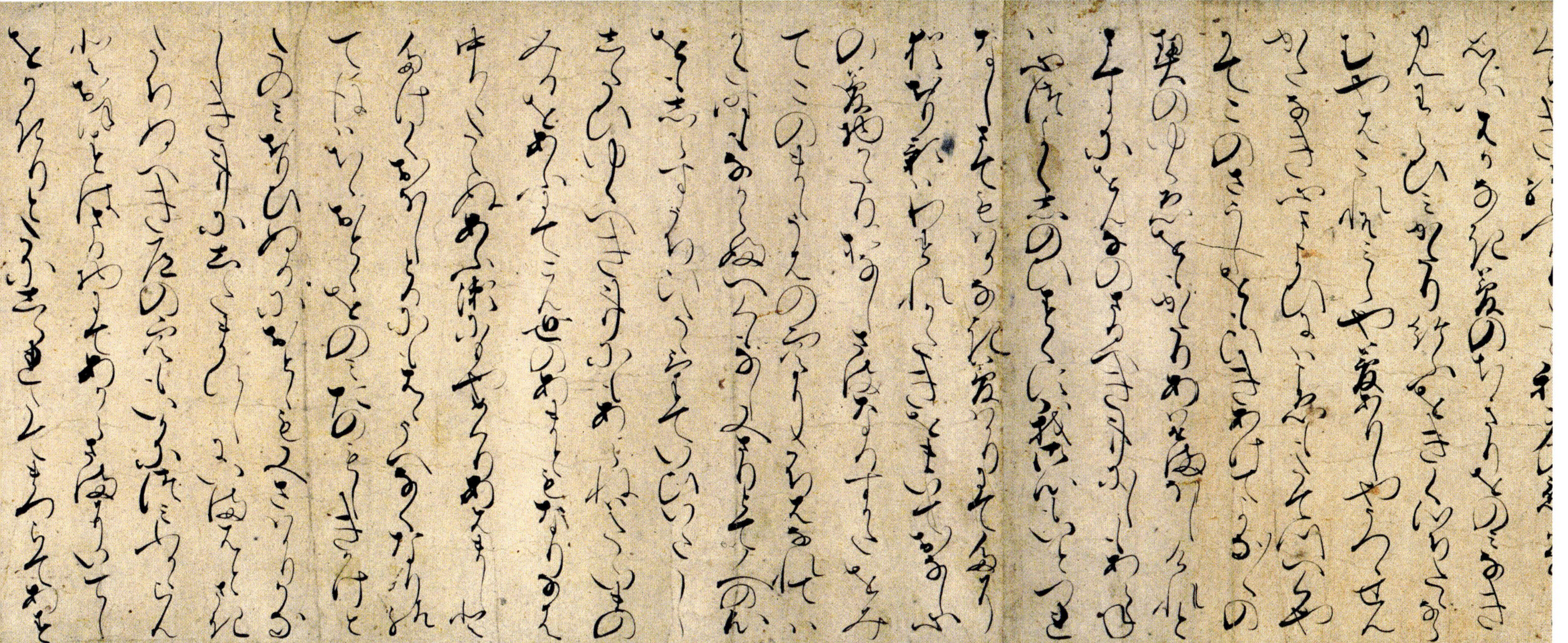

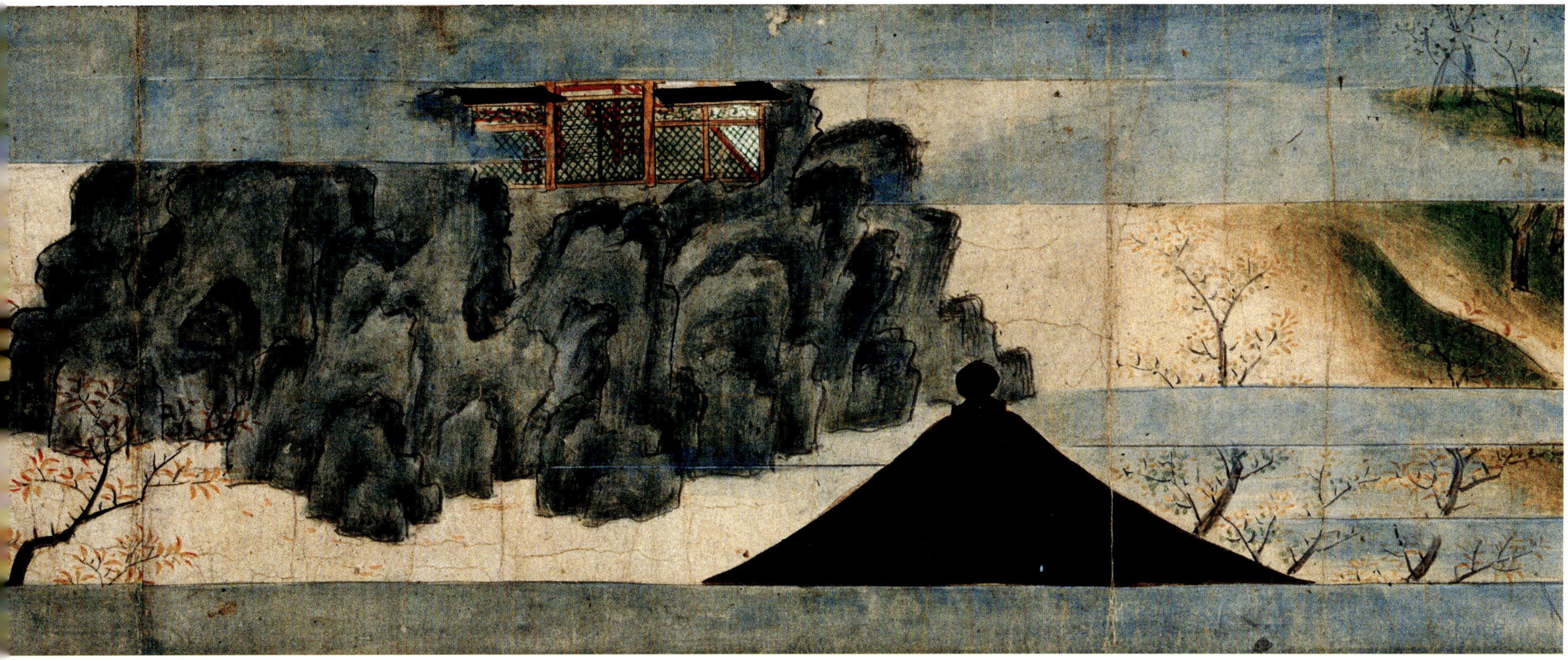

C

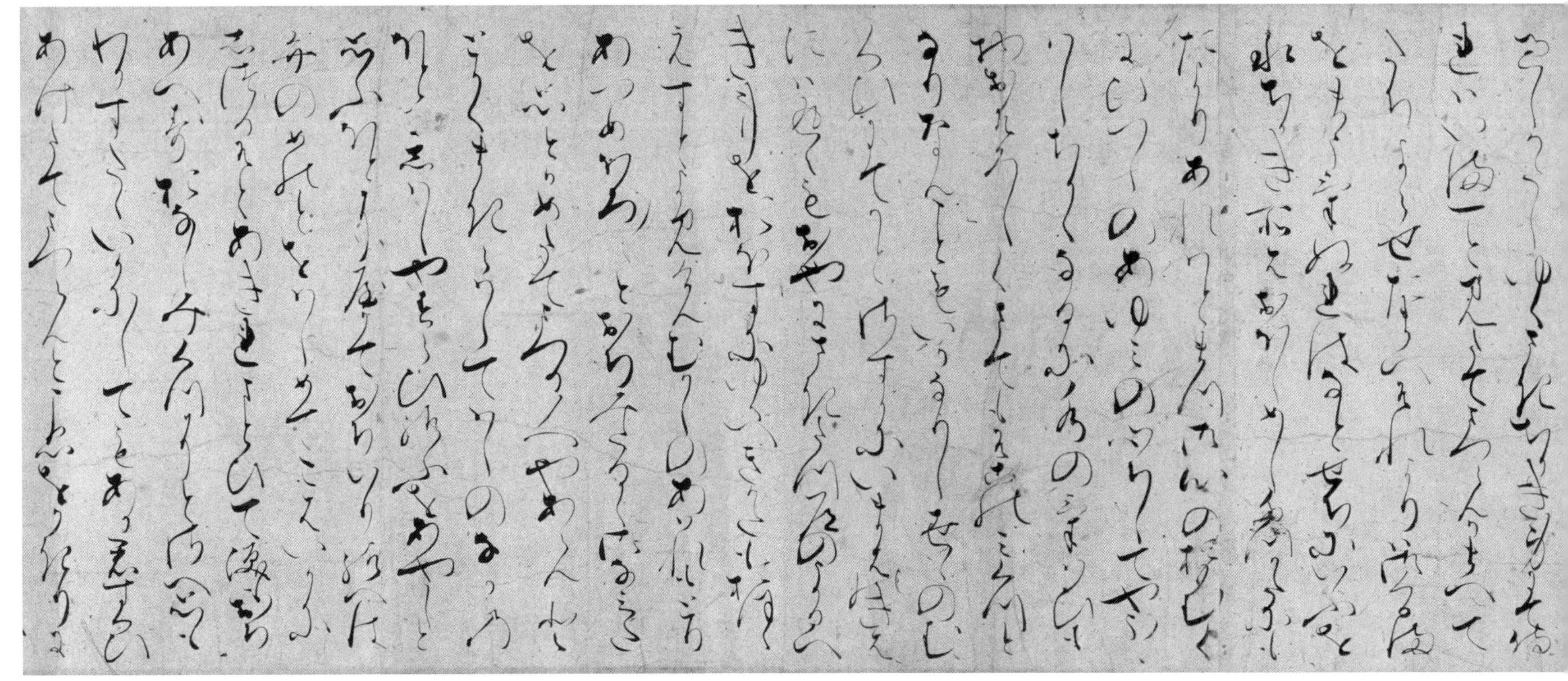

PAINTING FOUR

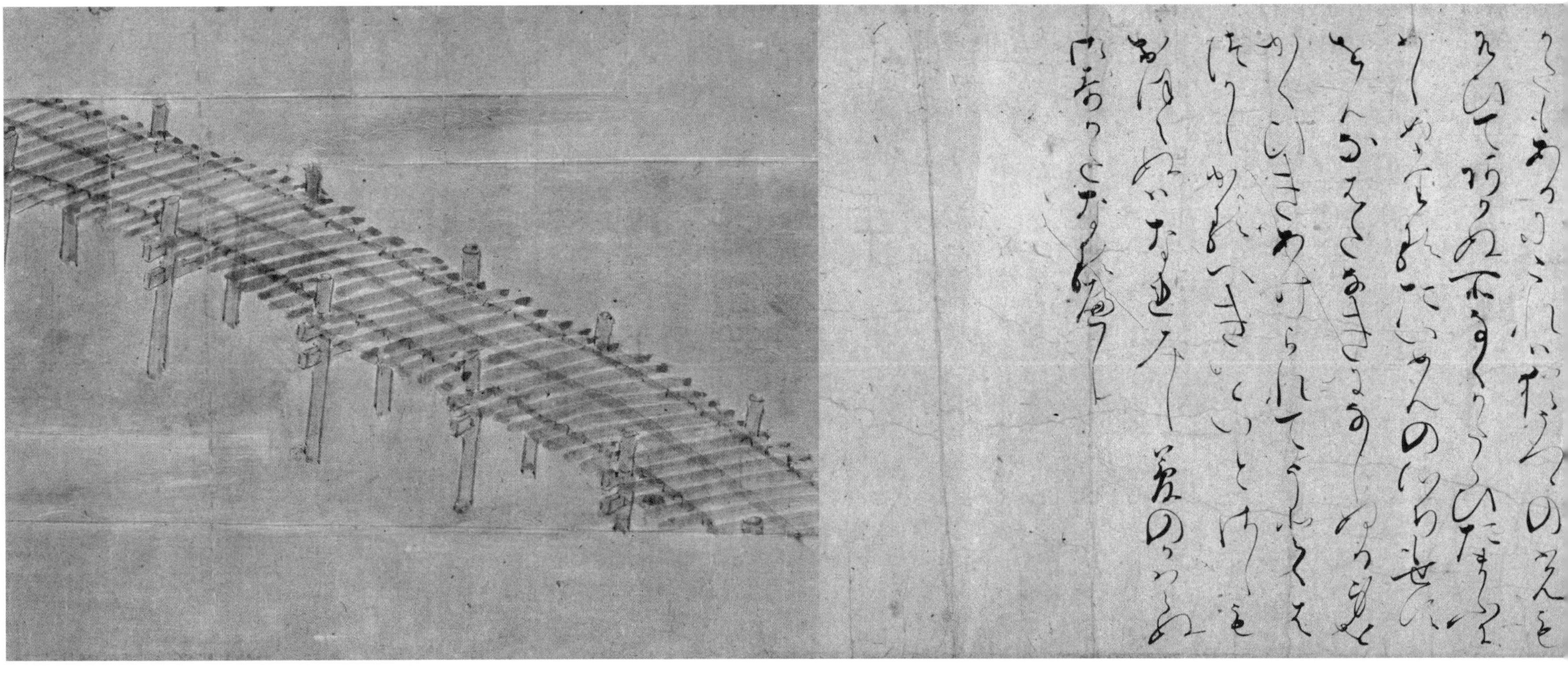

E

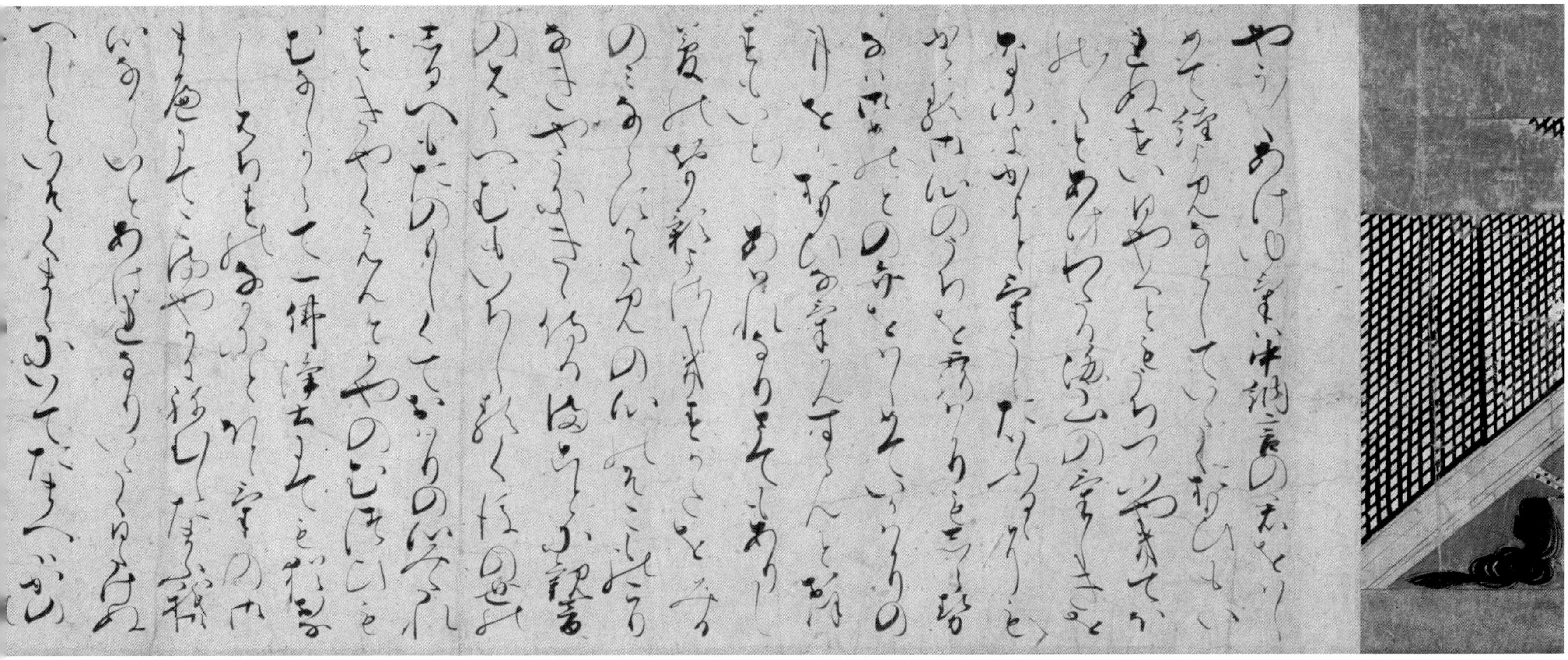

TEXT FOUR

TEXT FOUR (CONTINUED)

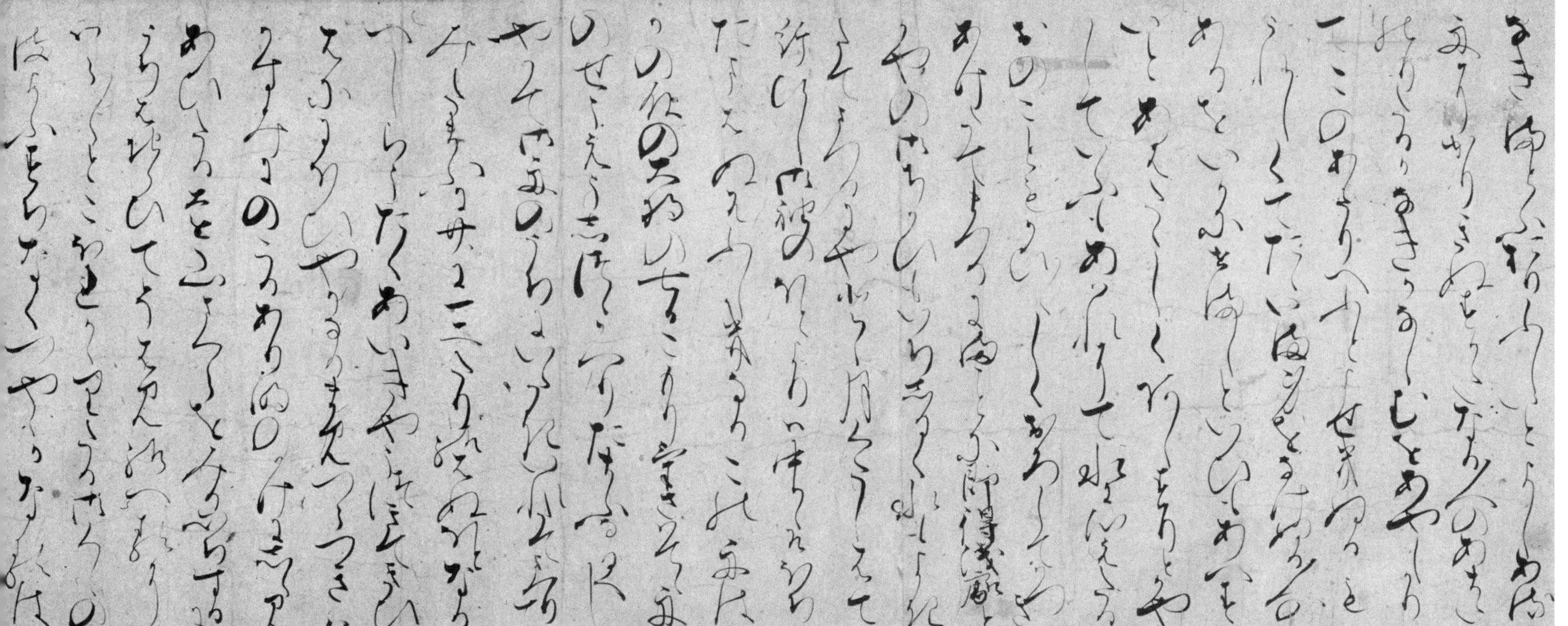

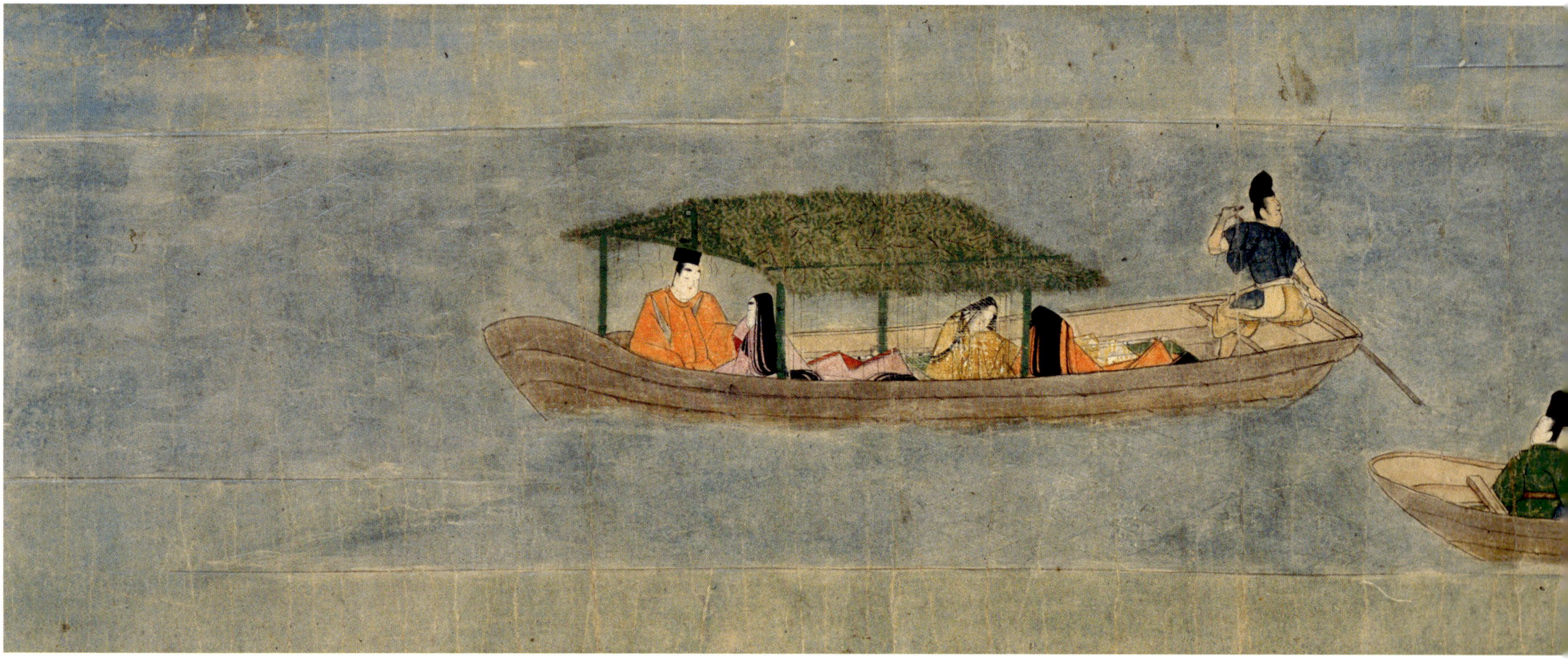

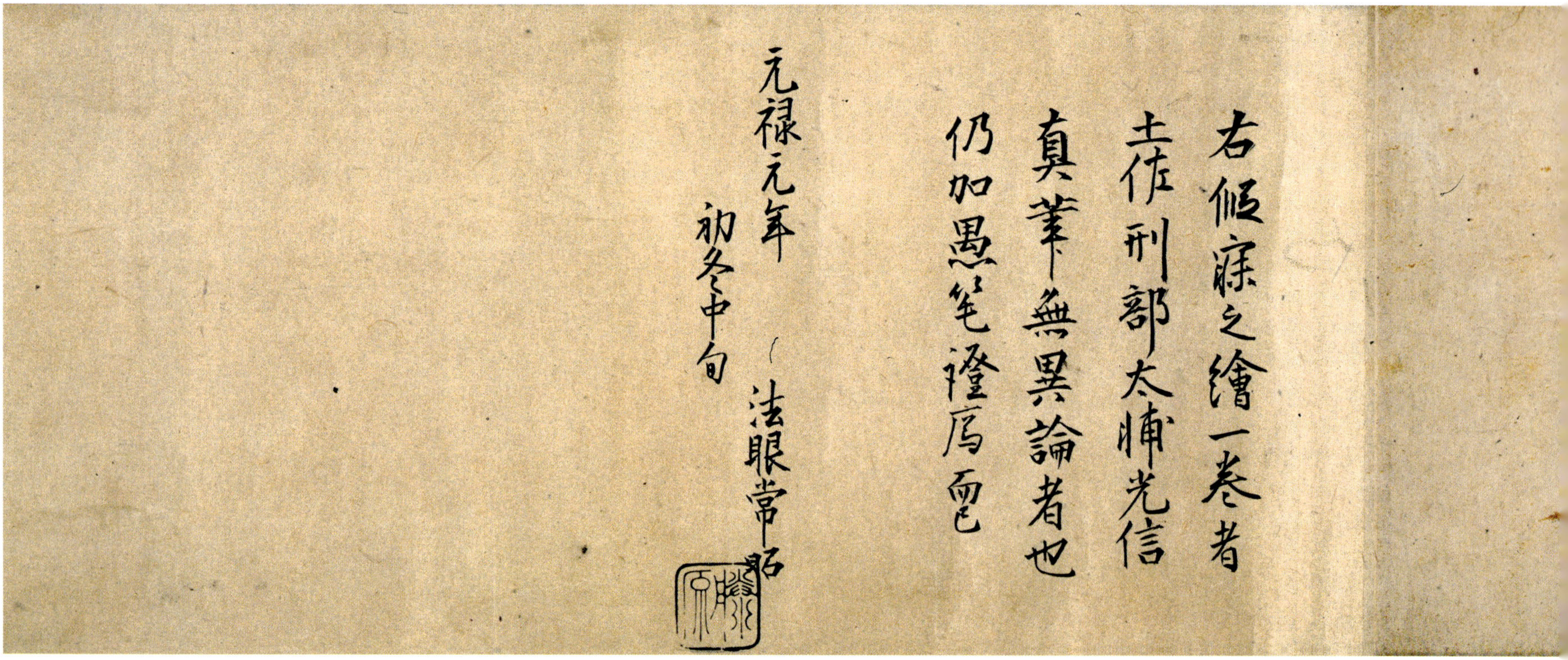

右假寐之繪一巻者
土佐刑部太輔光信
真筆無異論者也
仍加愚筆證爲[illegible]

元禄元年
初冬中旬　法眼常昭

G

F

TEXT FIVE

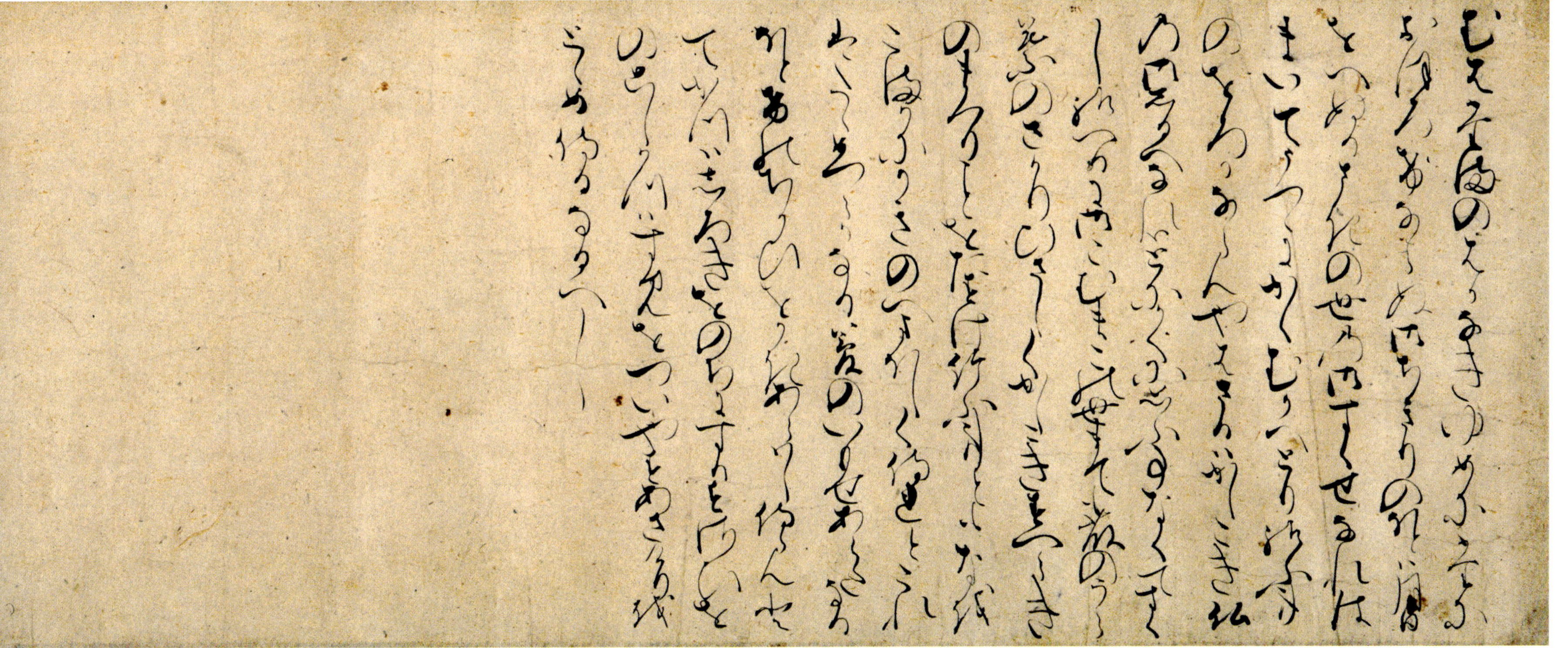

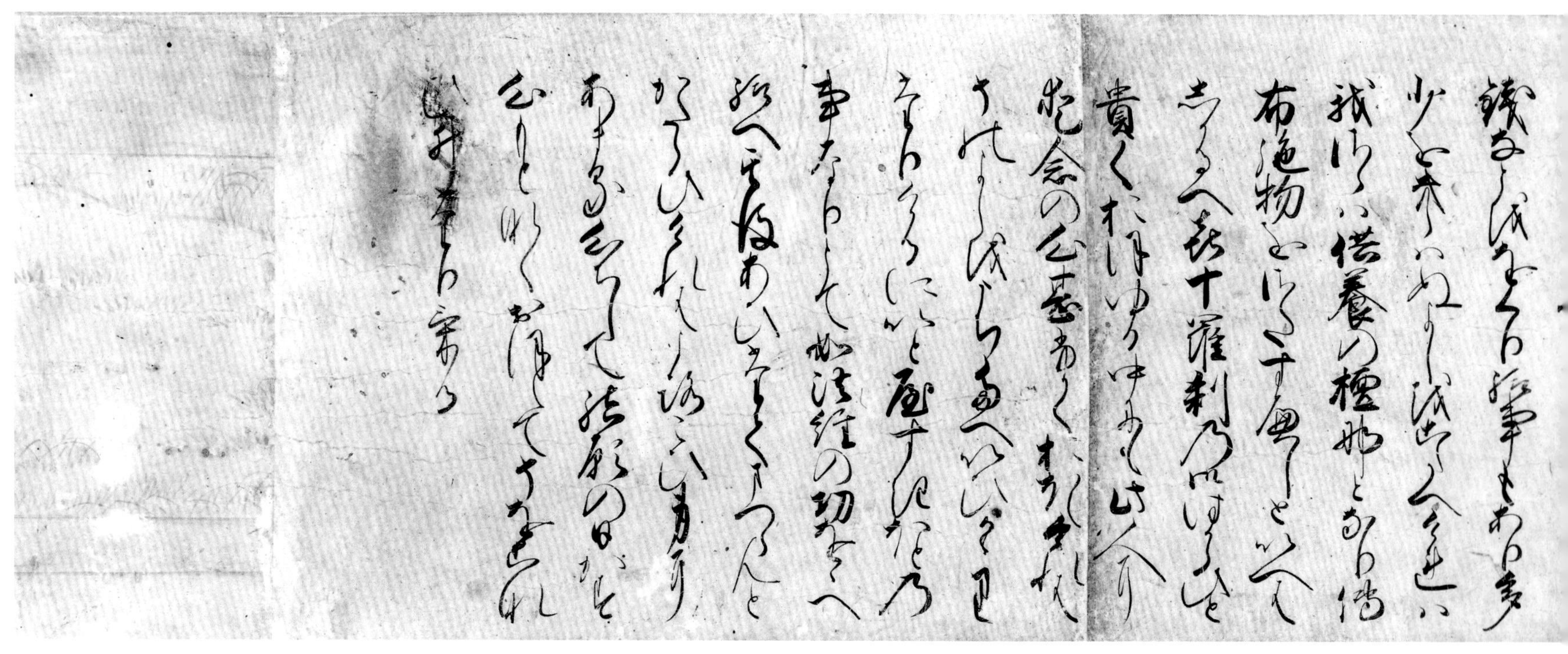

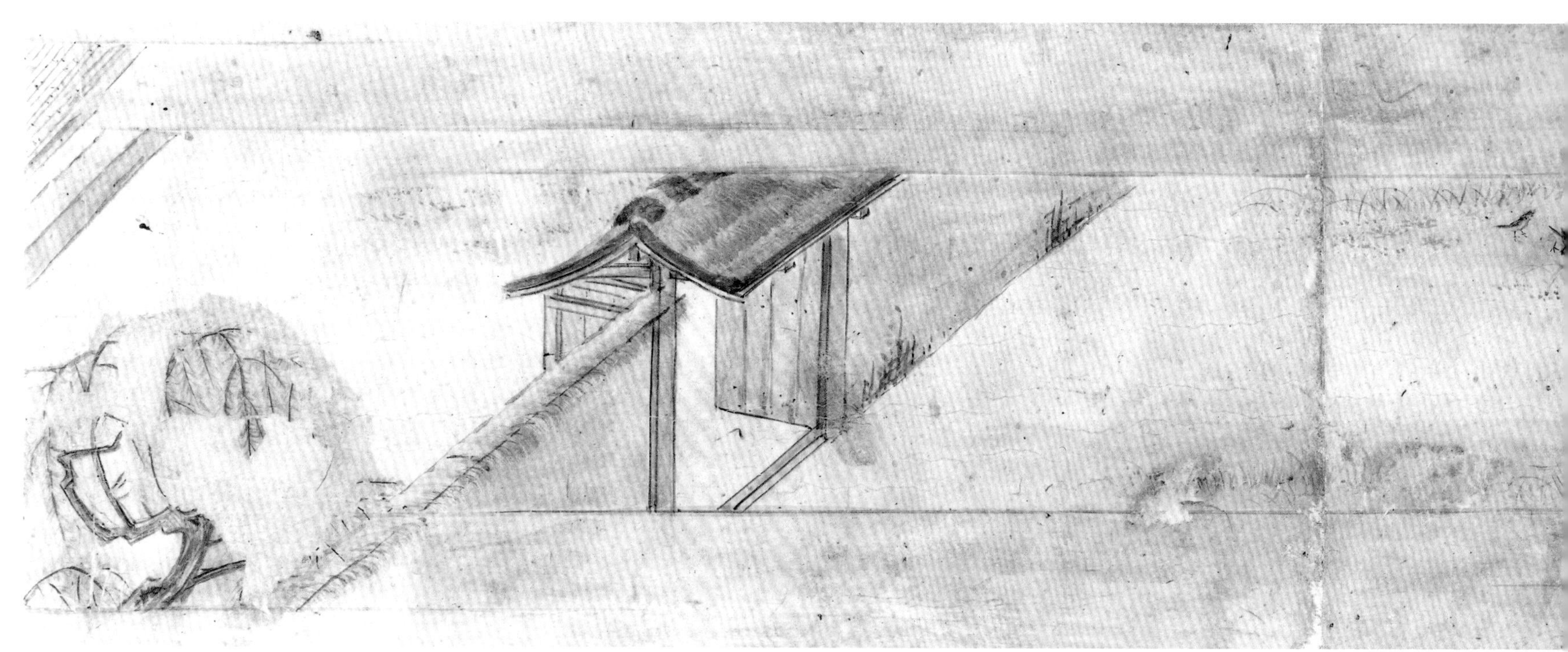

2 Tosa Mitsunobu, calligraphy by Sanjōnishi Sanetaka, *The Jizō Hall* (*Jizōdō sōshi emaki*). Late fifteenth century. One handscroll; ink, color, and gold on paper, 17.2 x 1586.7 cm. Private collection.

TEXT ONE

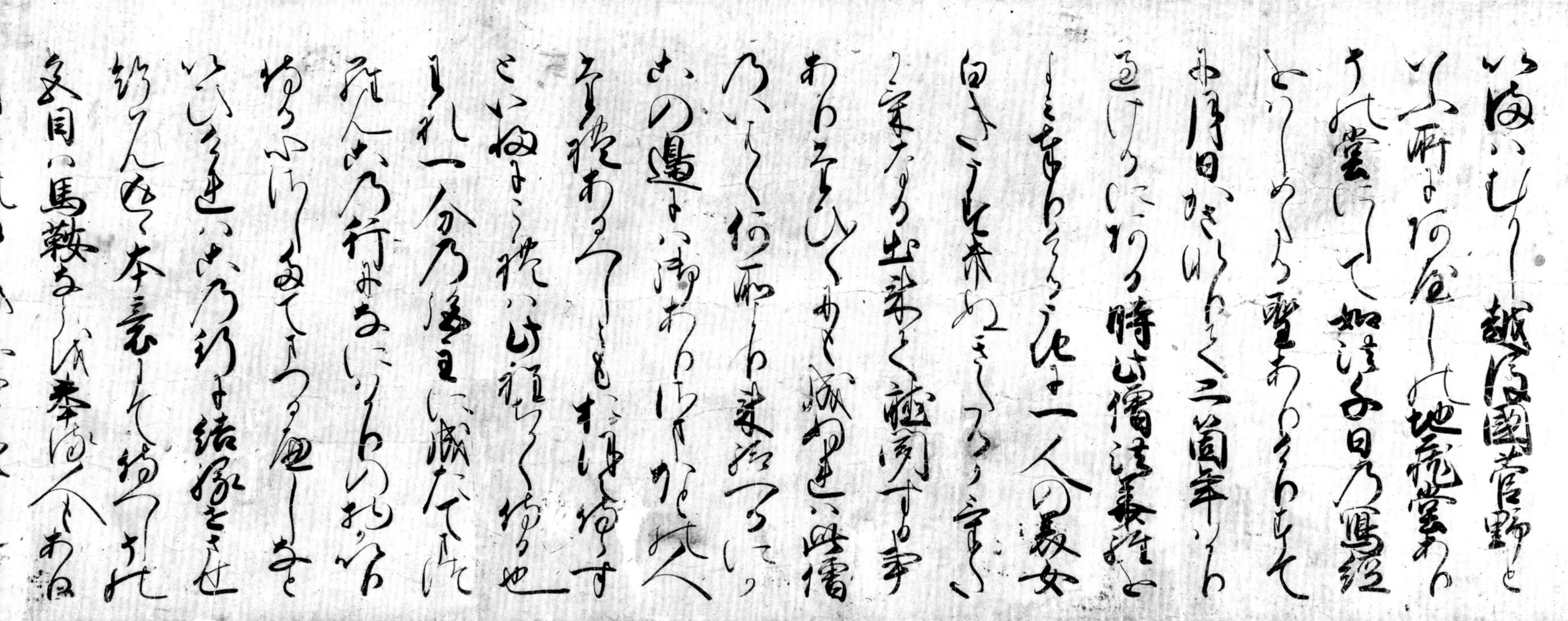

PAINTING ONE

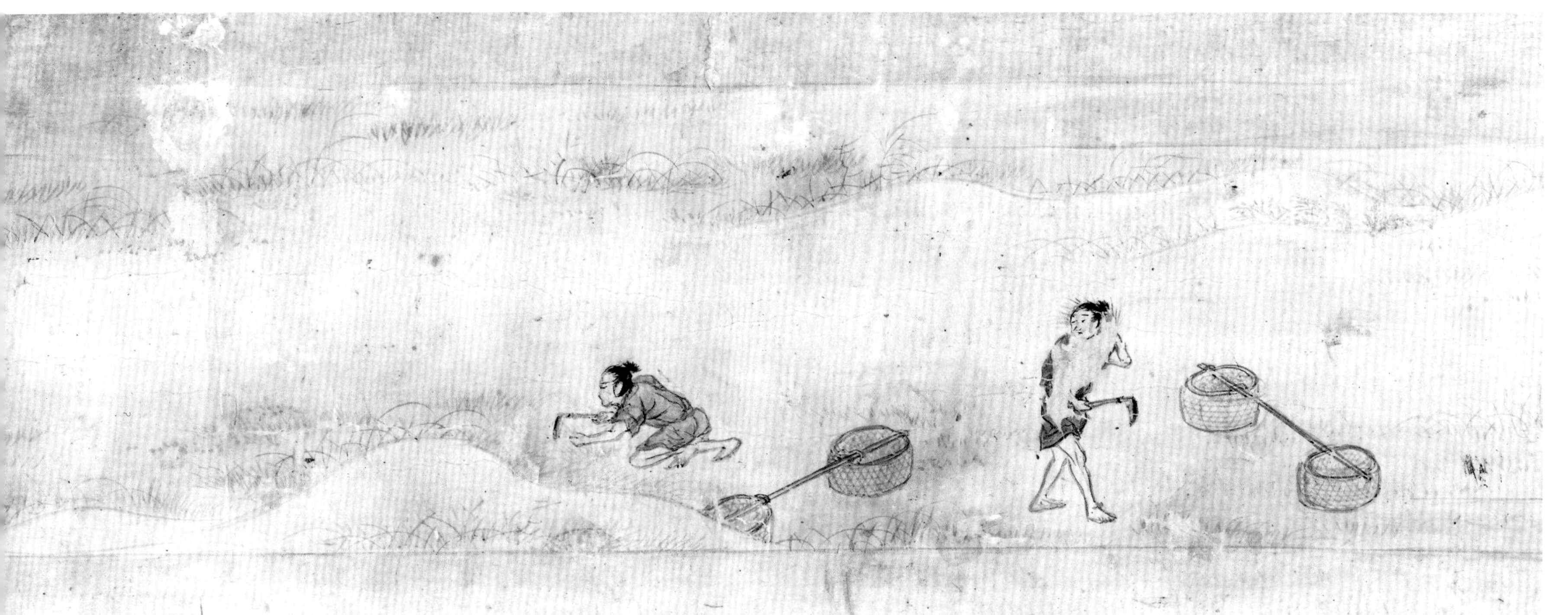

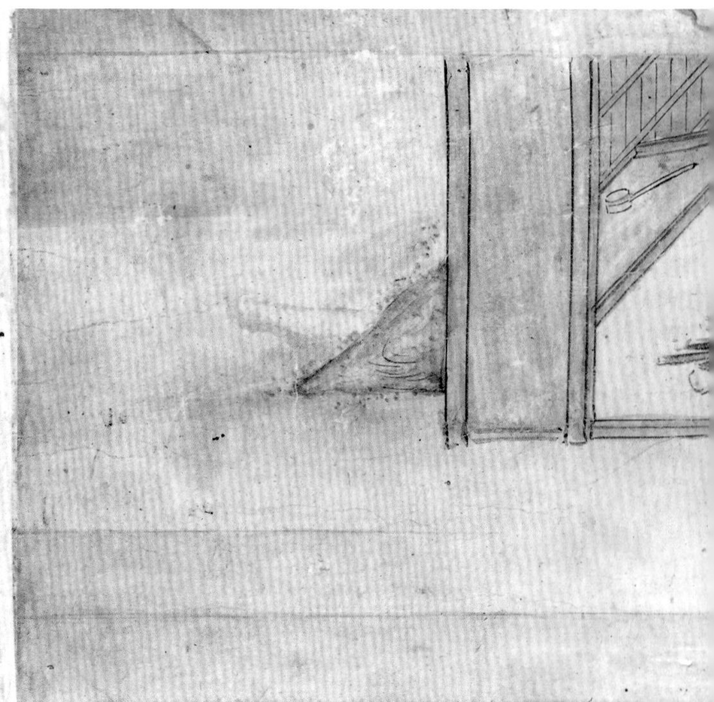

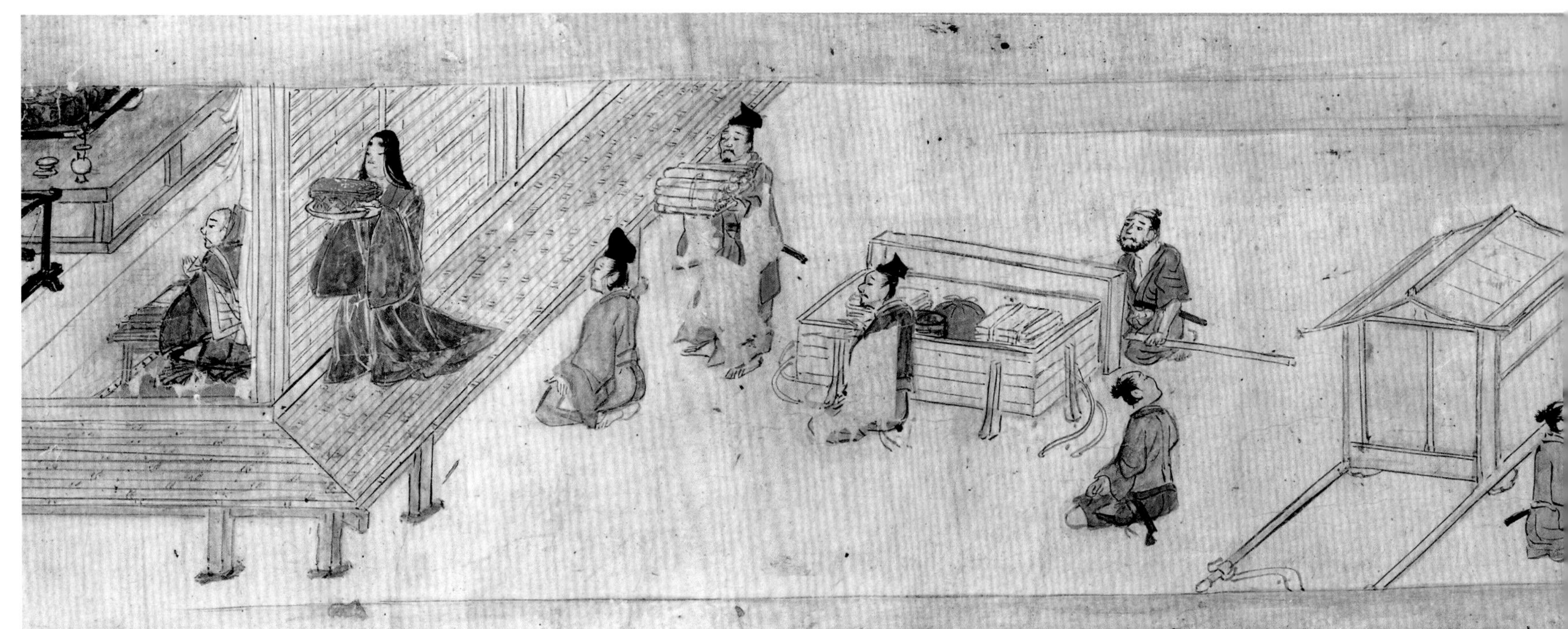

B

PAINTING ONE (CONTINUED)

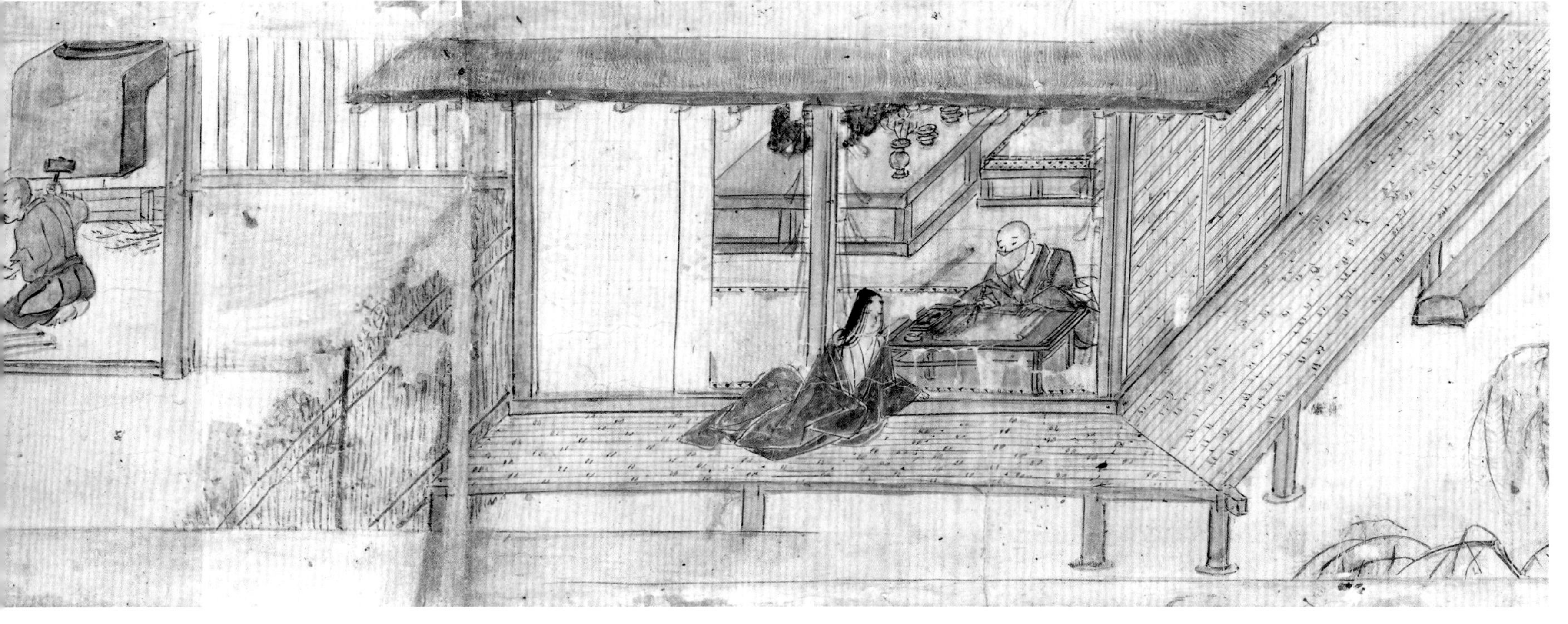

A

PAINTING TWO

TEXT TWO (CONTINUED)

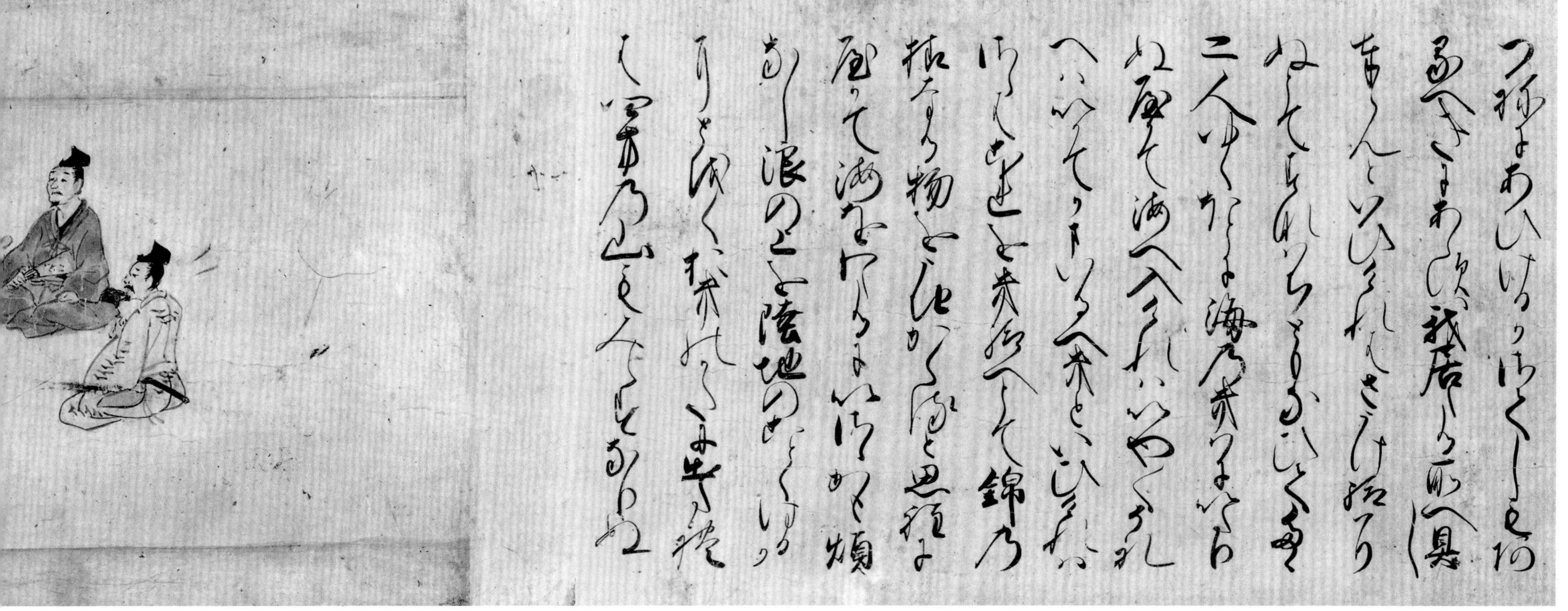

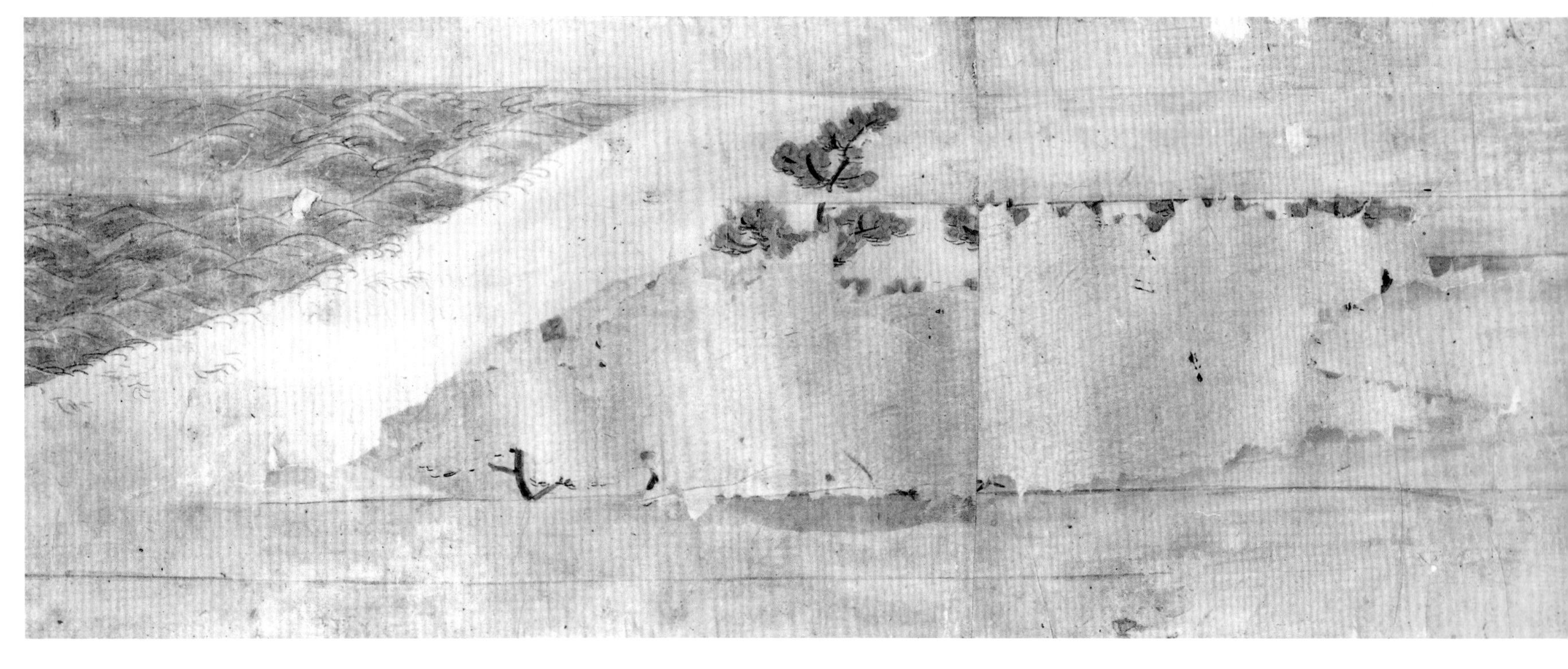

PAINTING THREE

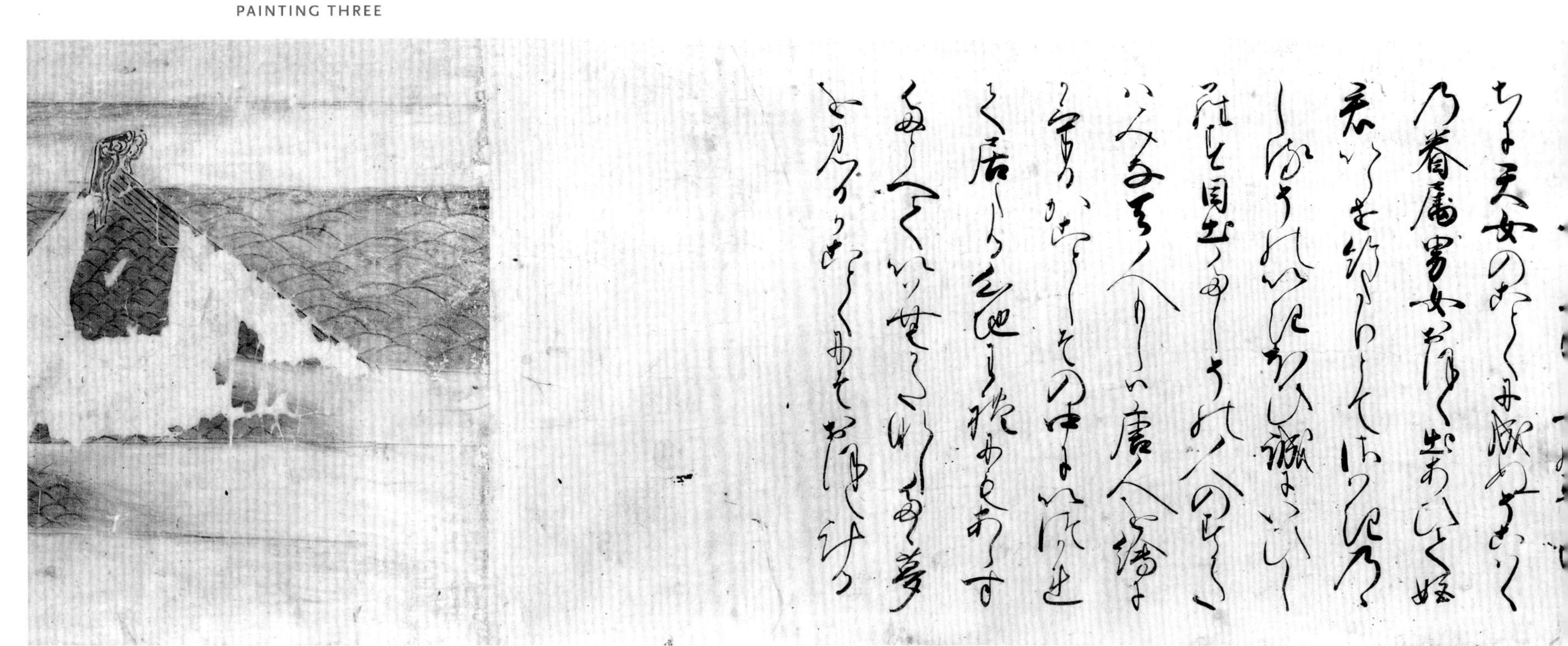

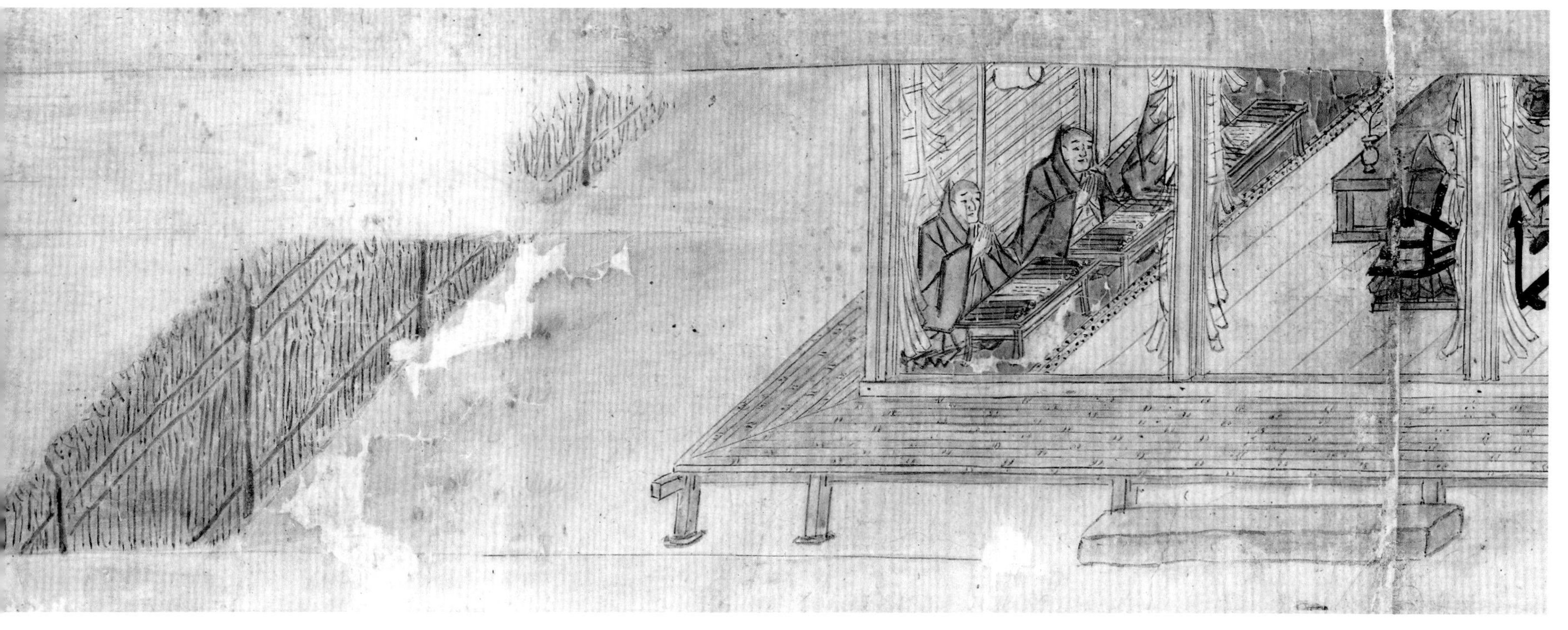

TEXT THREE

PAINTING TWO (CONTINUED)

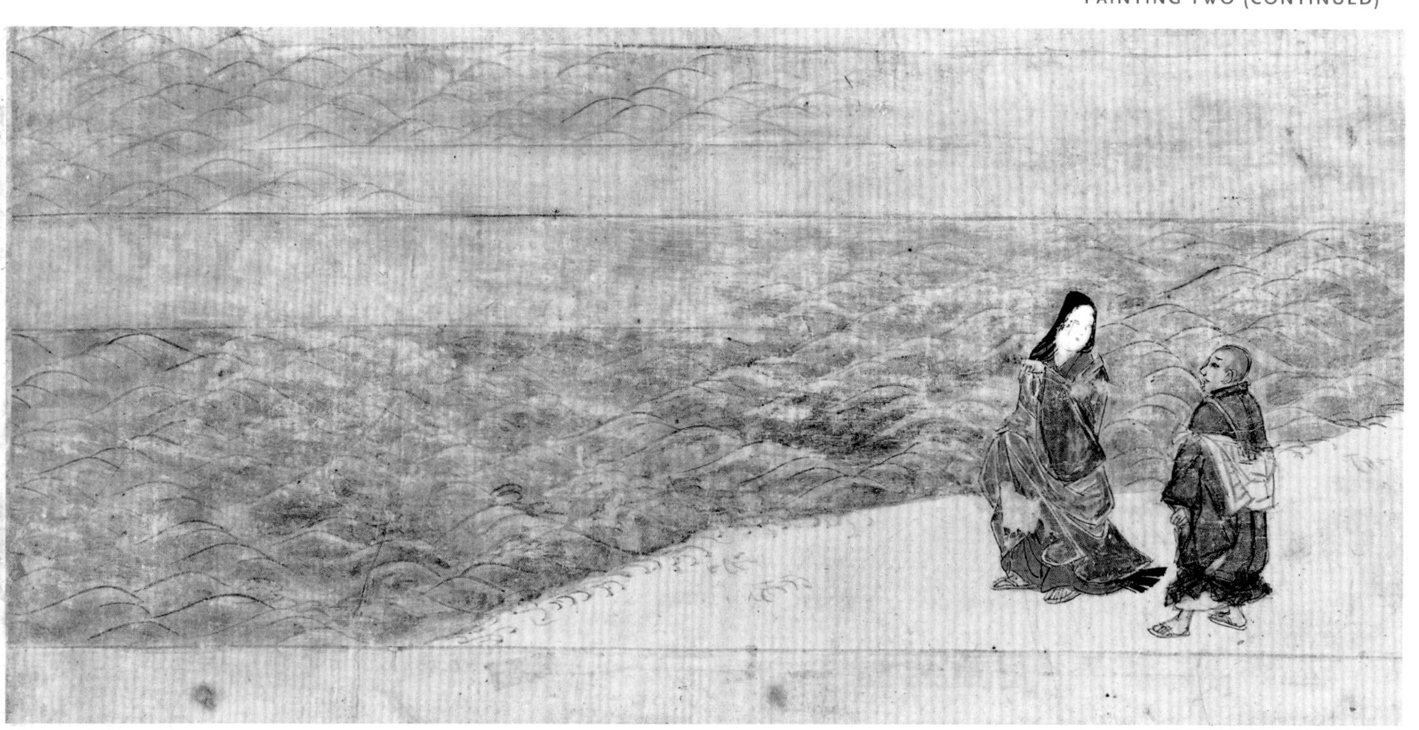

c

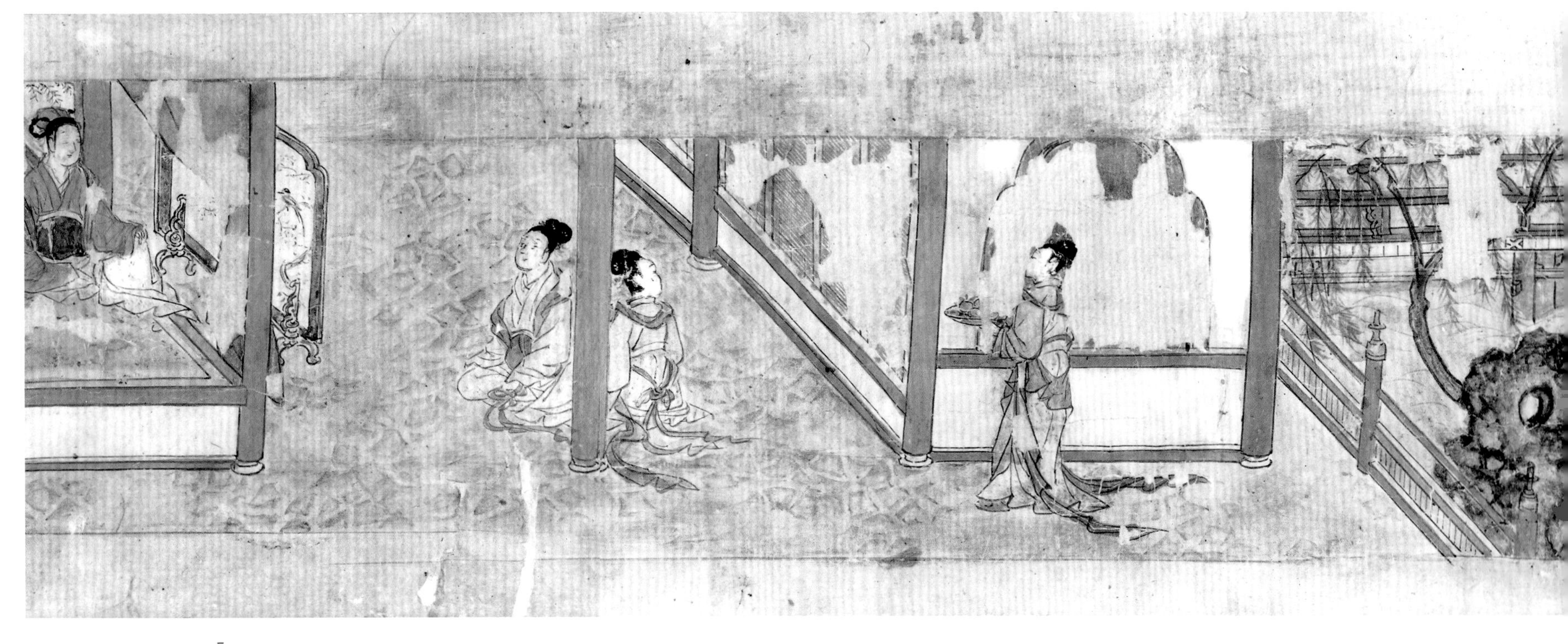

E

PAINTING FOUR

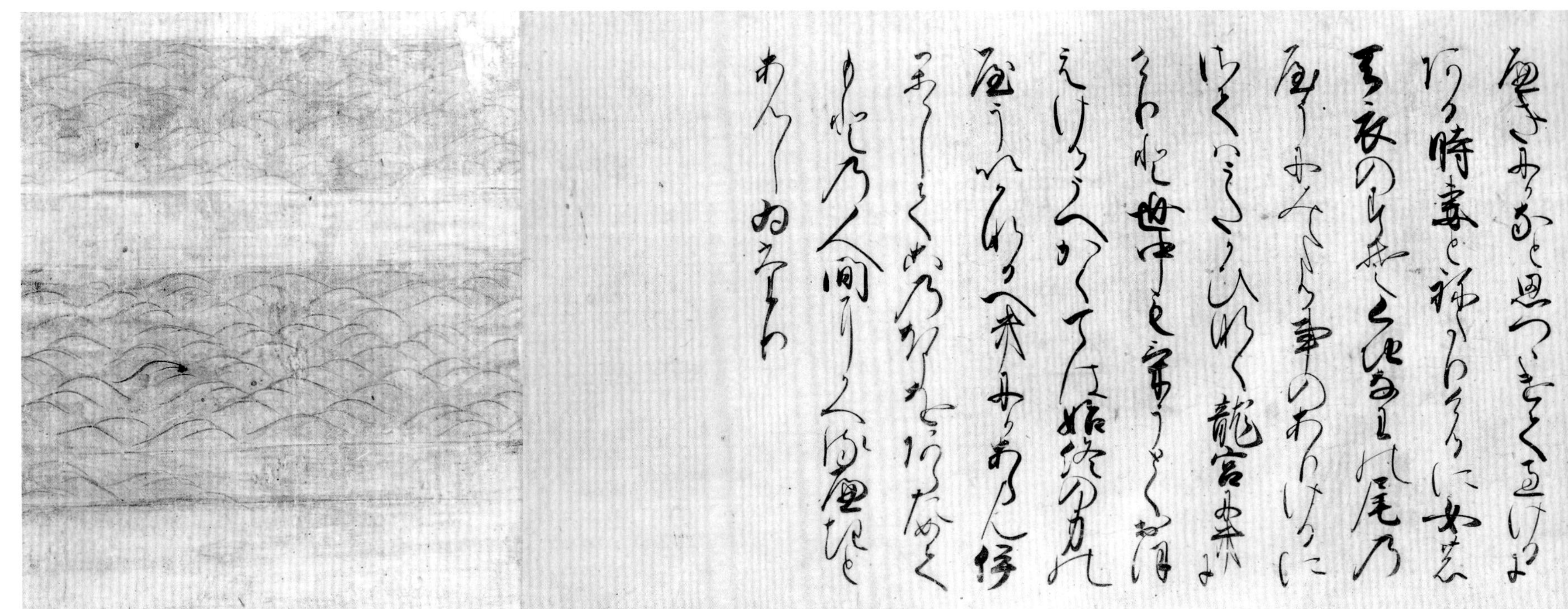

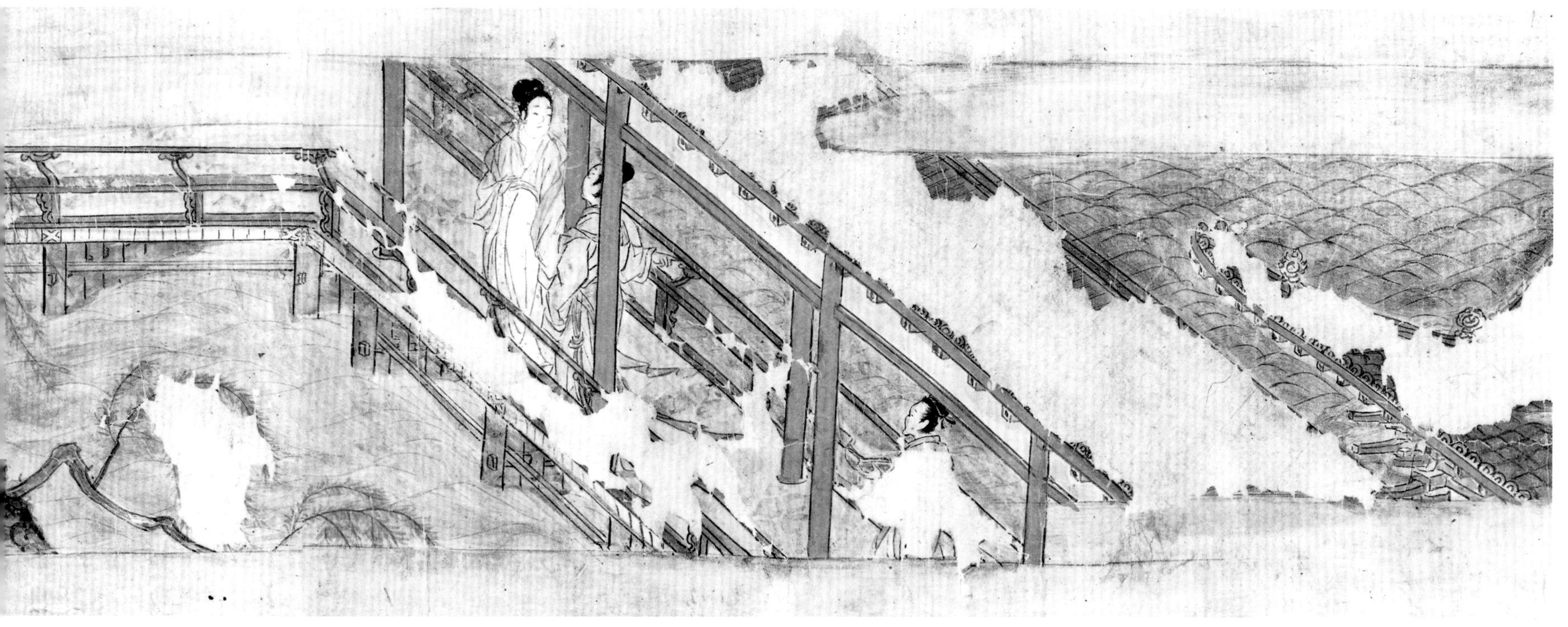

D

TEXT FOUR

PAINTING THREE (CONTINUED)

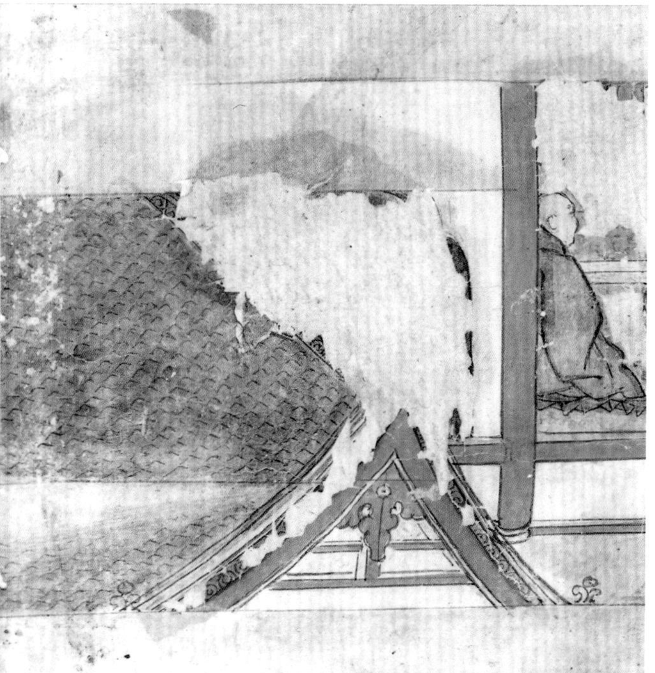

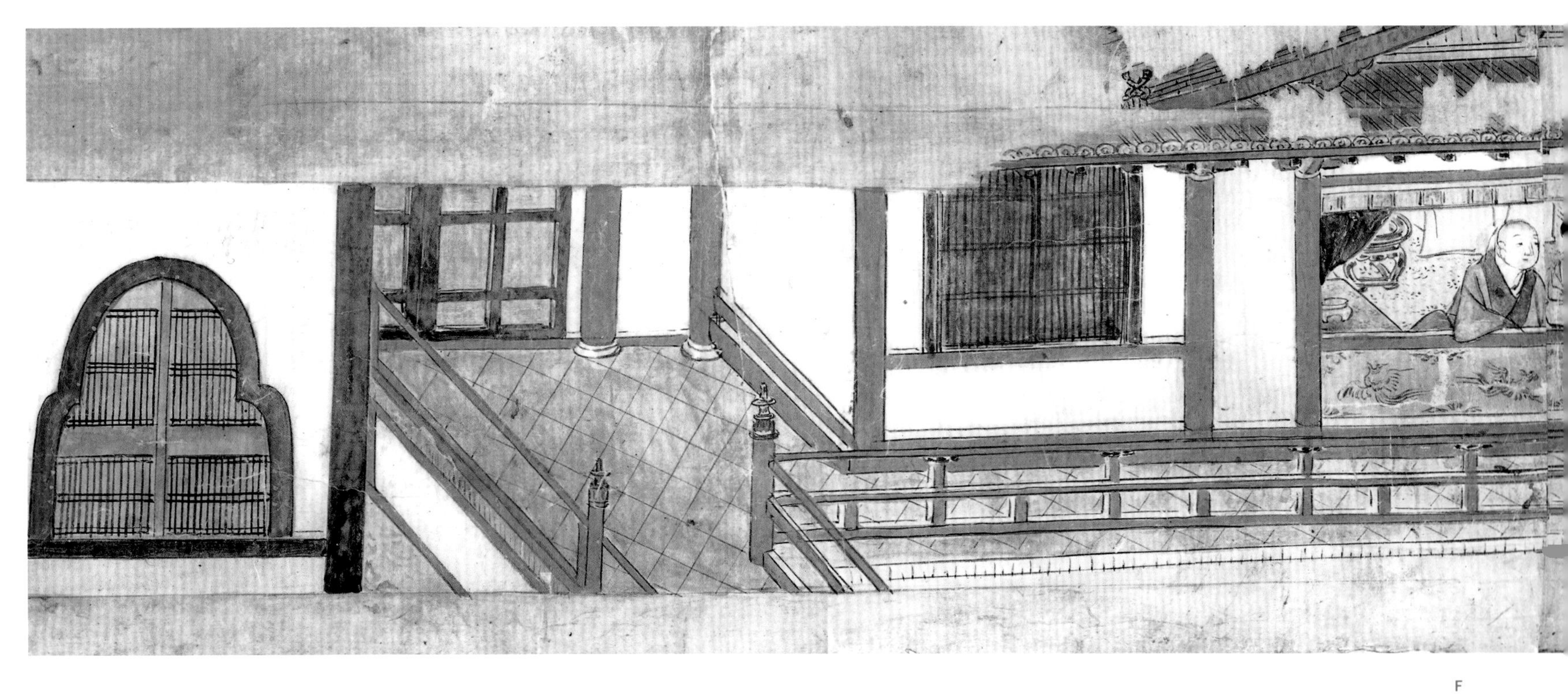

F

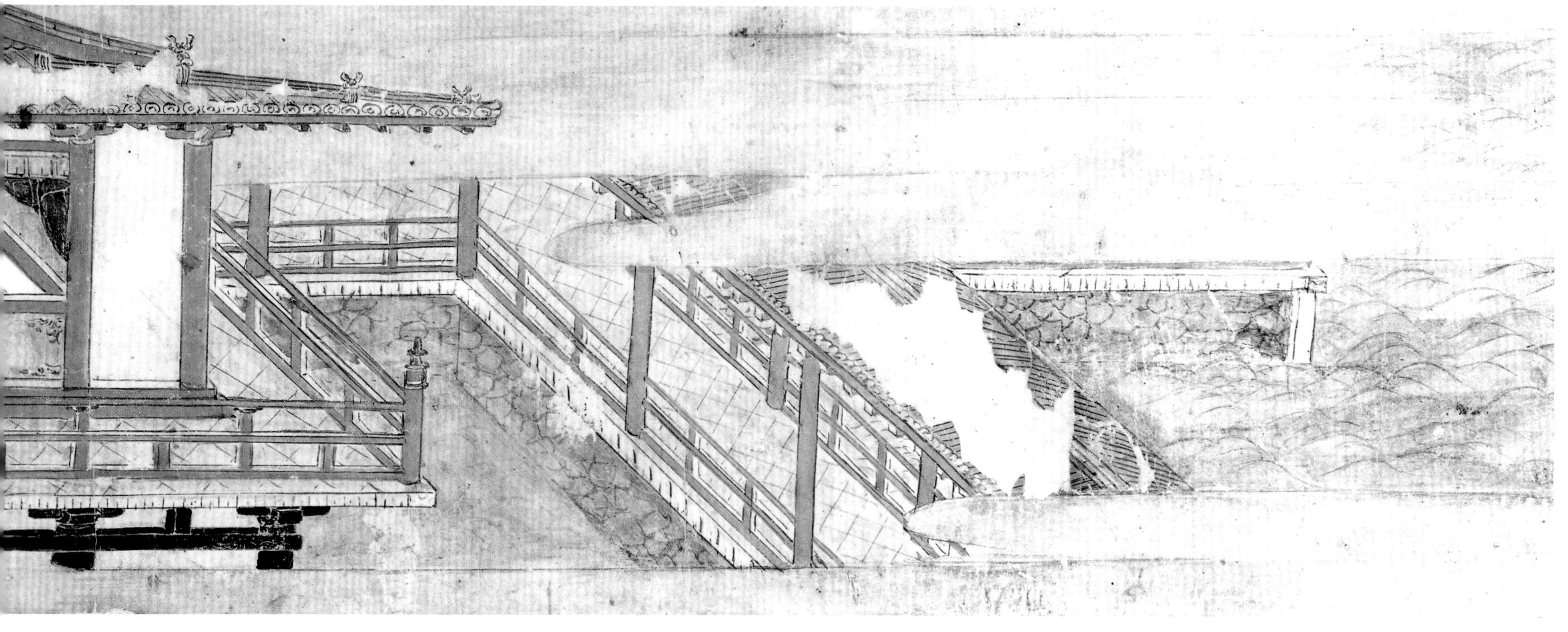

TEXT FIVE

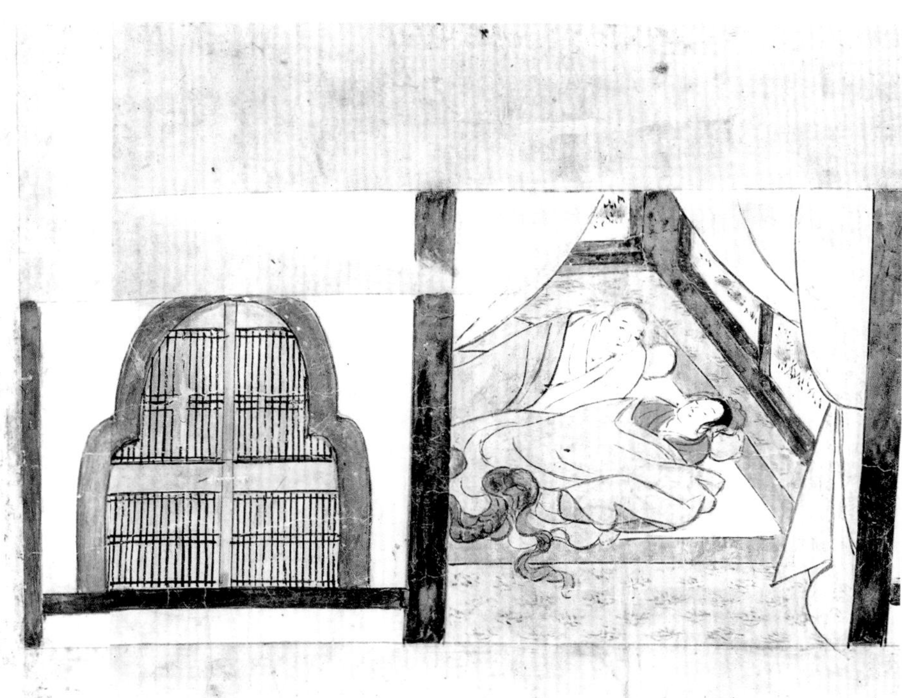

G

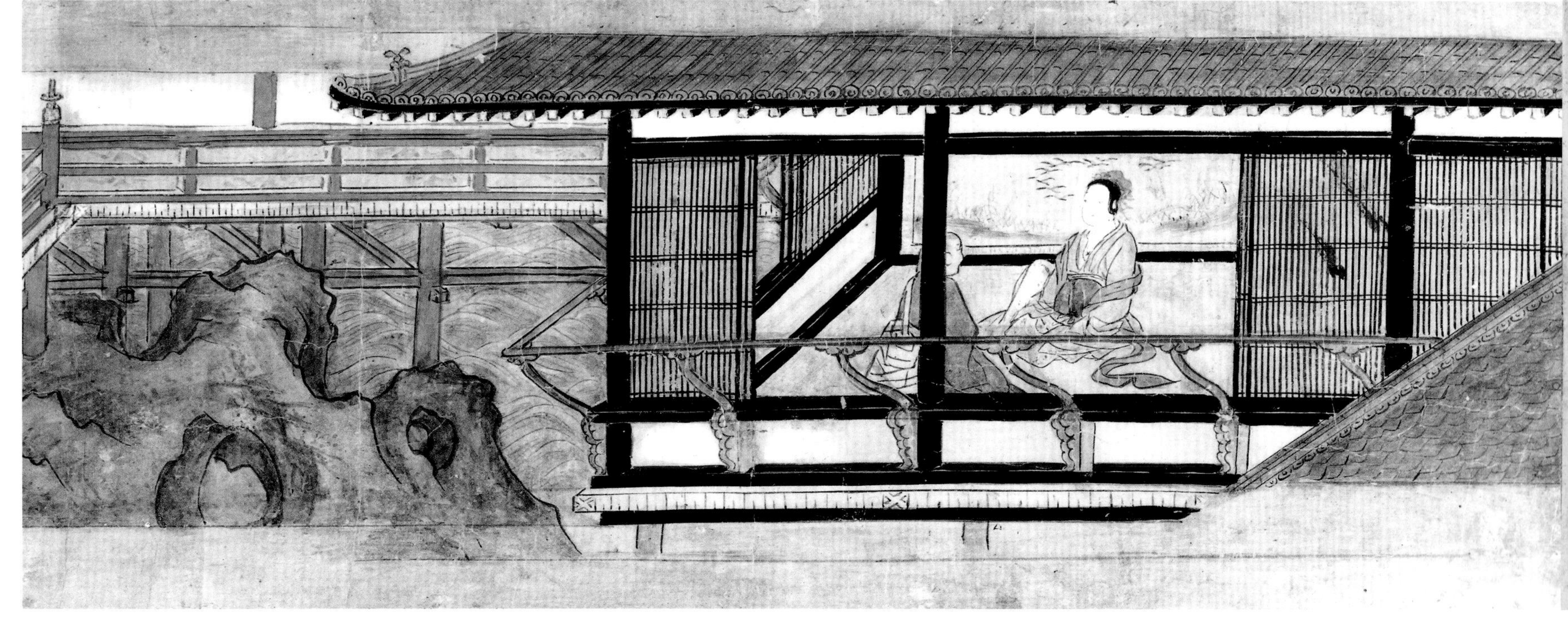

H

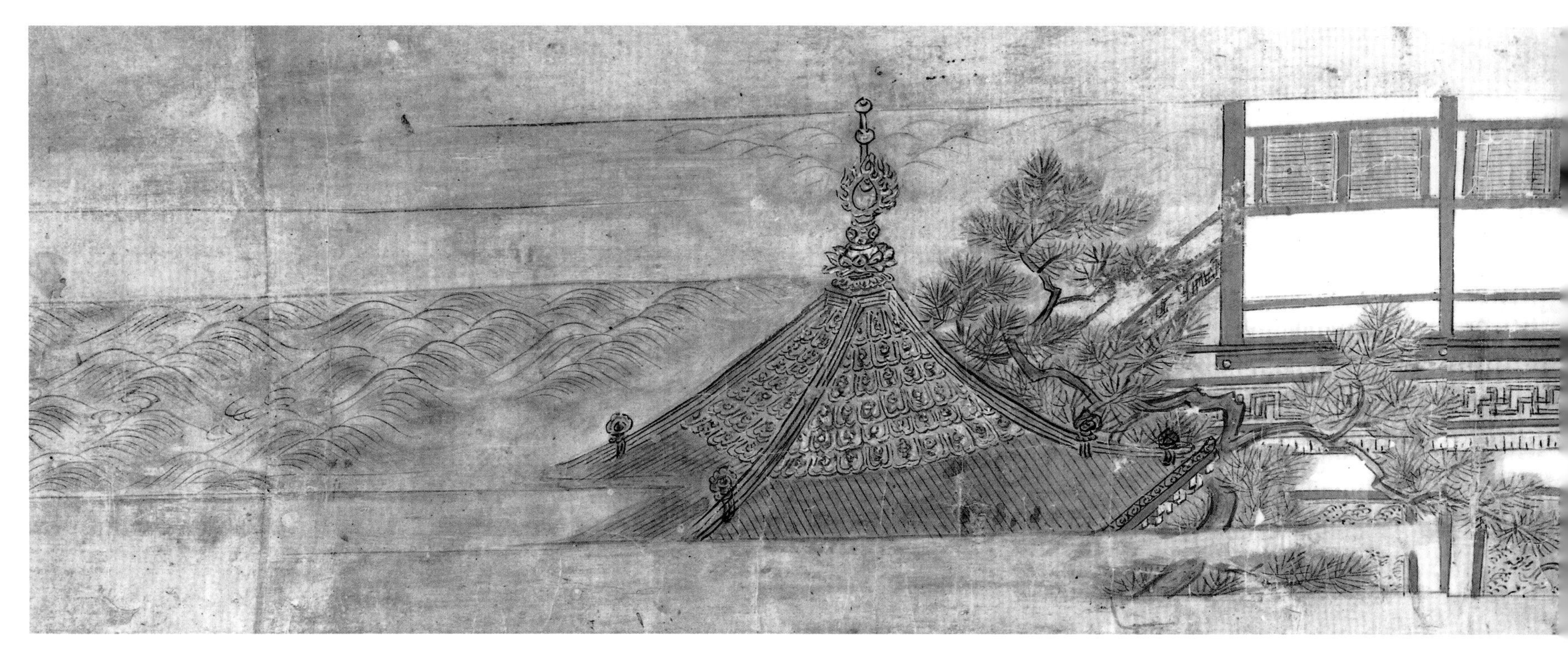

J

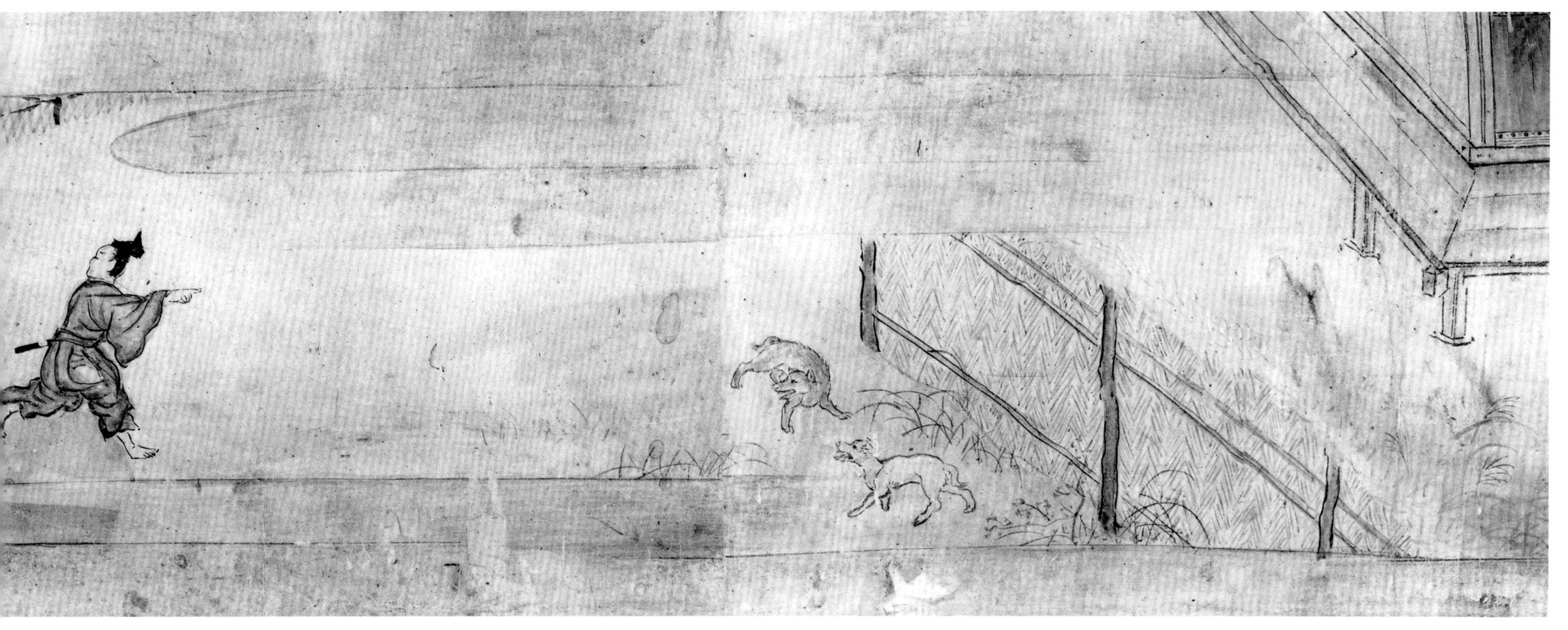

TEXT SEVEN

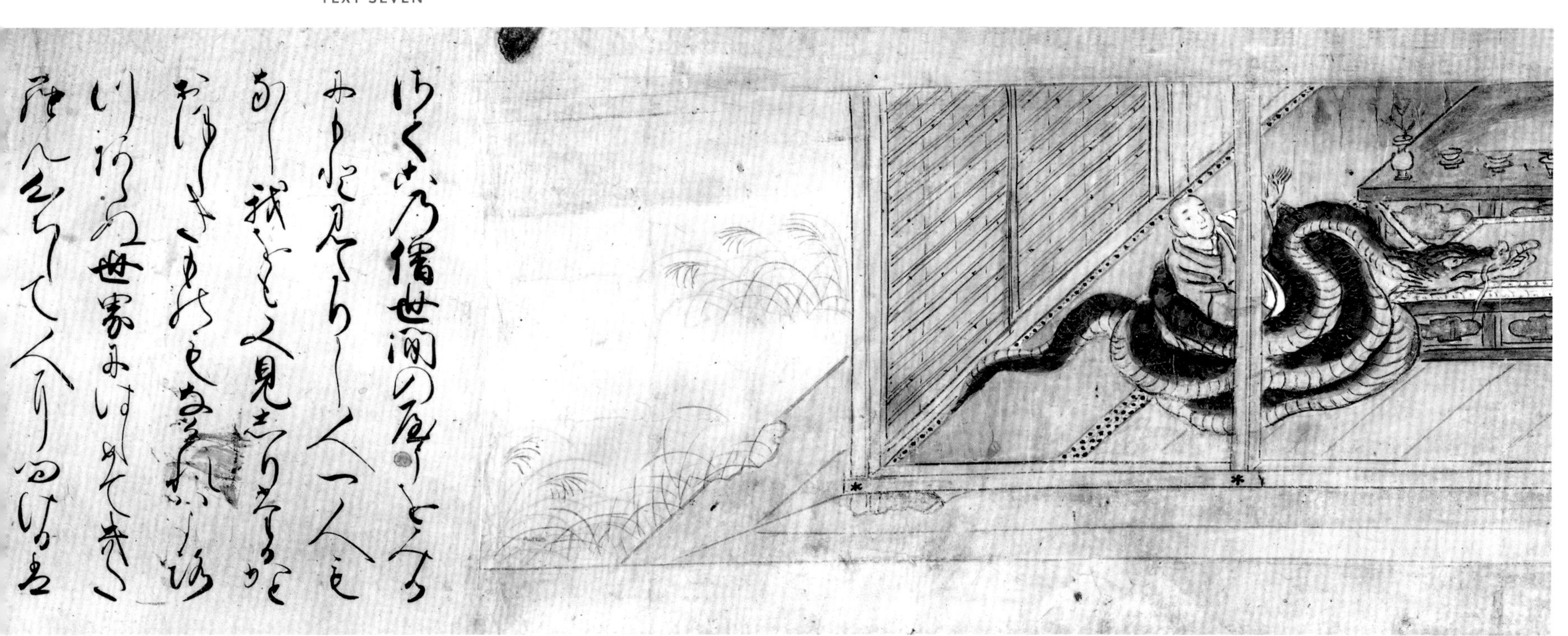

N

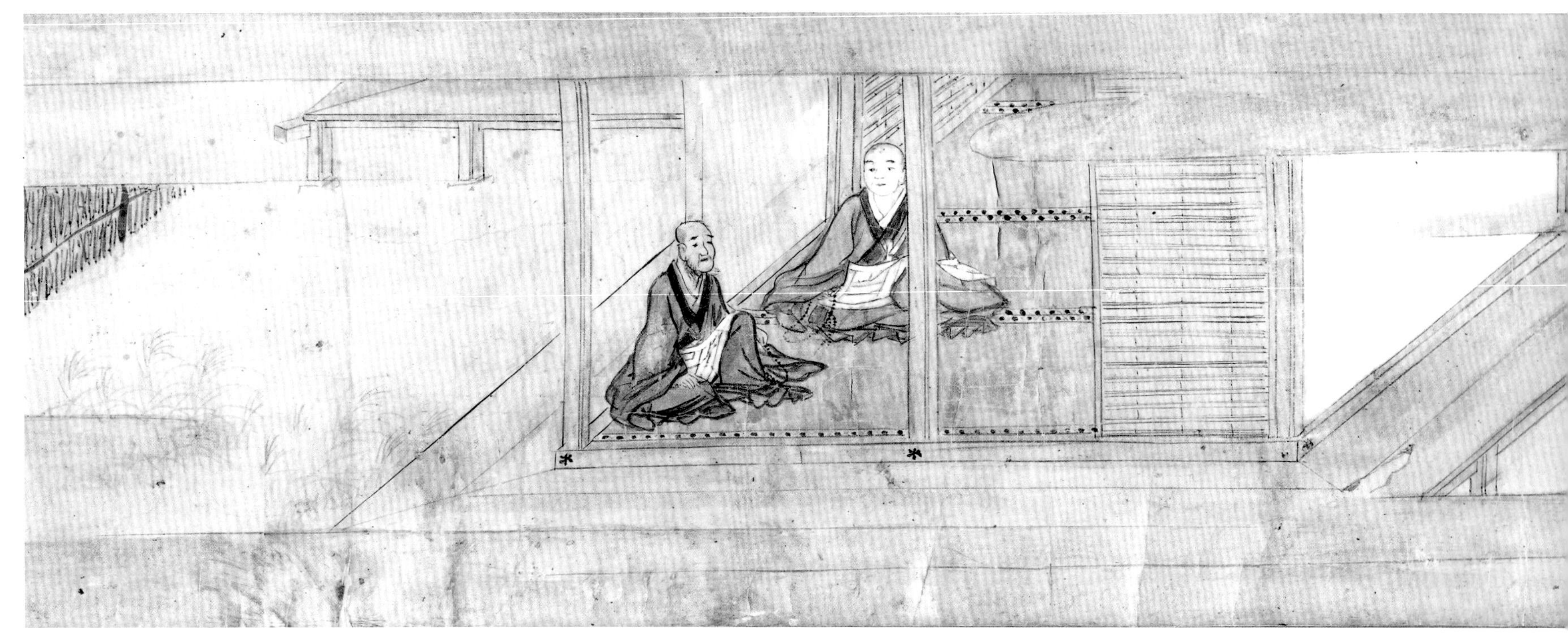

P

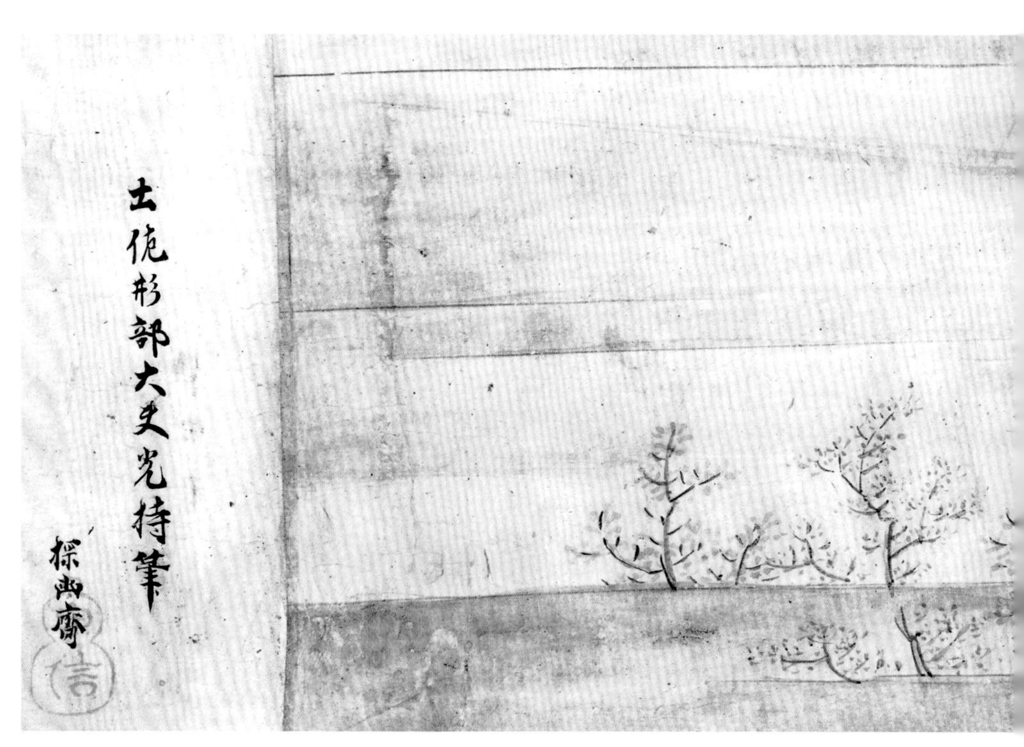

R

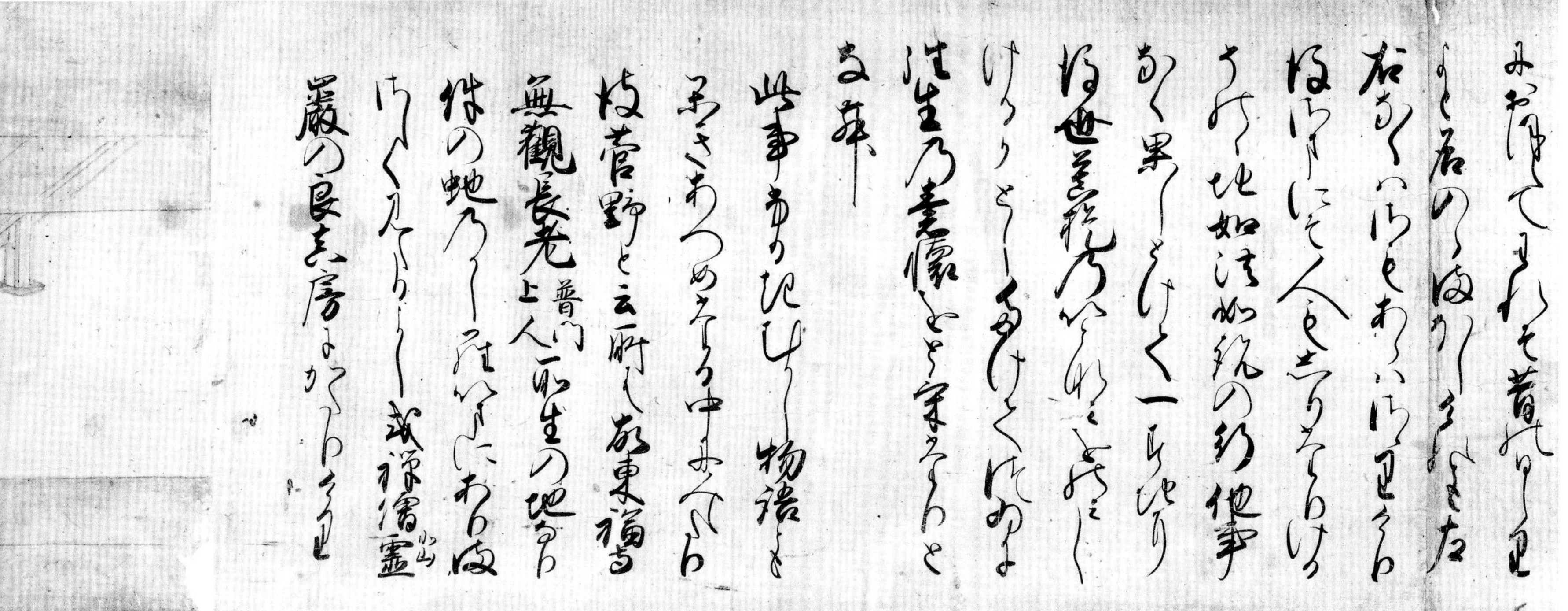

O

PAINTING SEVEN (CONTINUED)

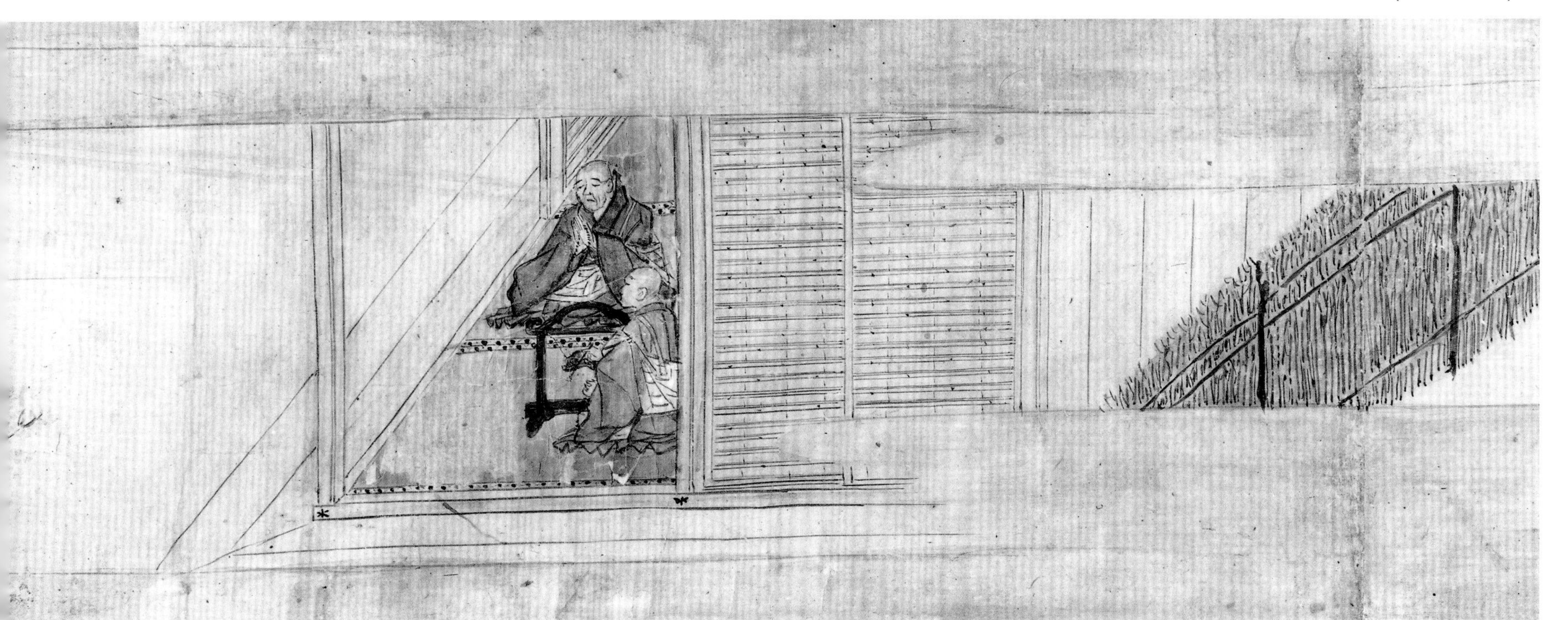

Q

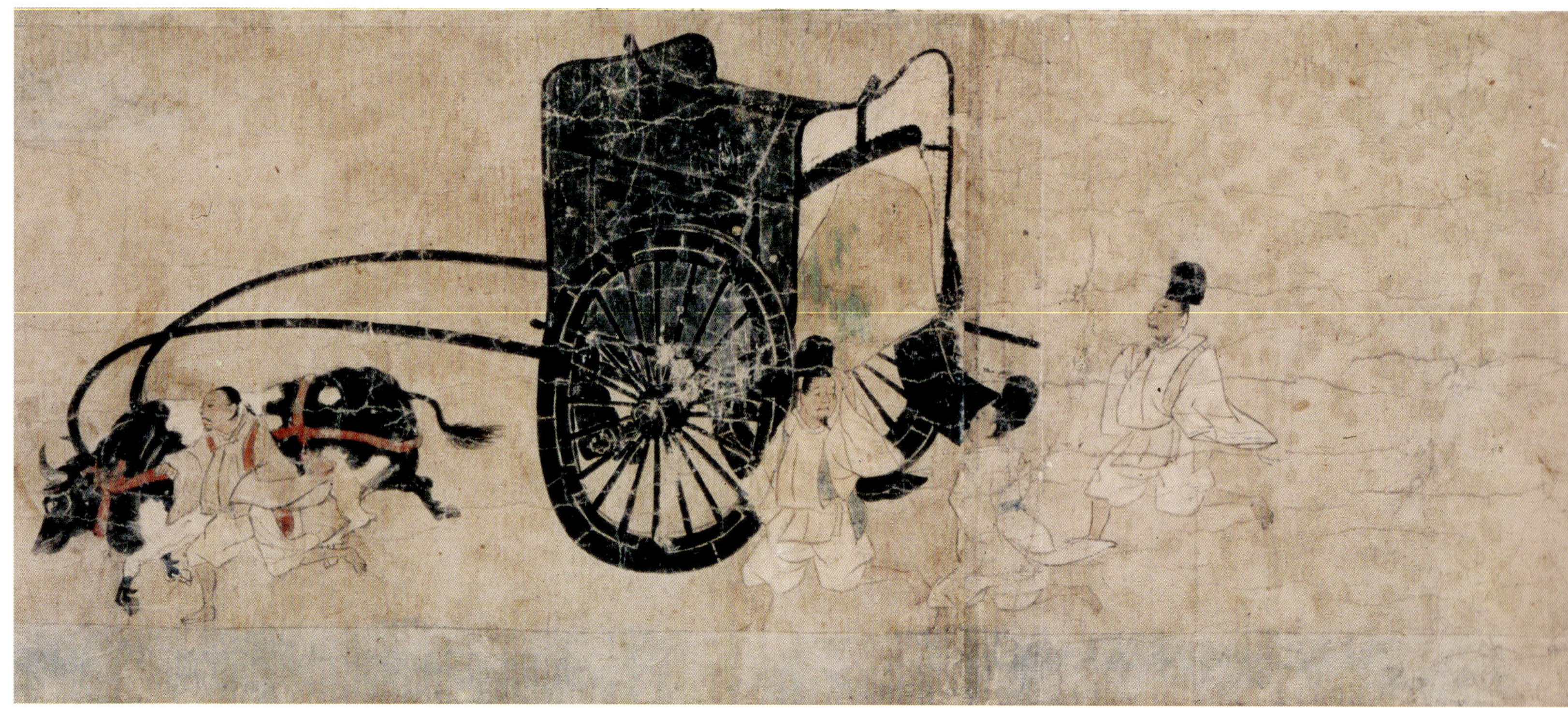

A

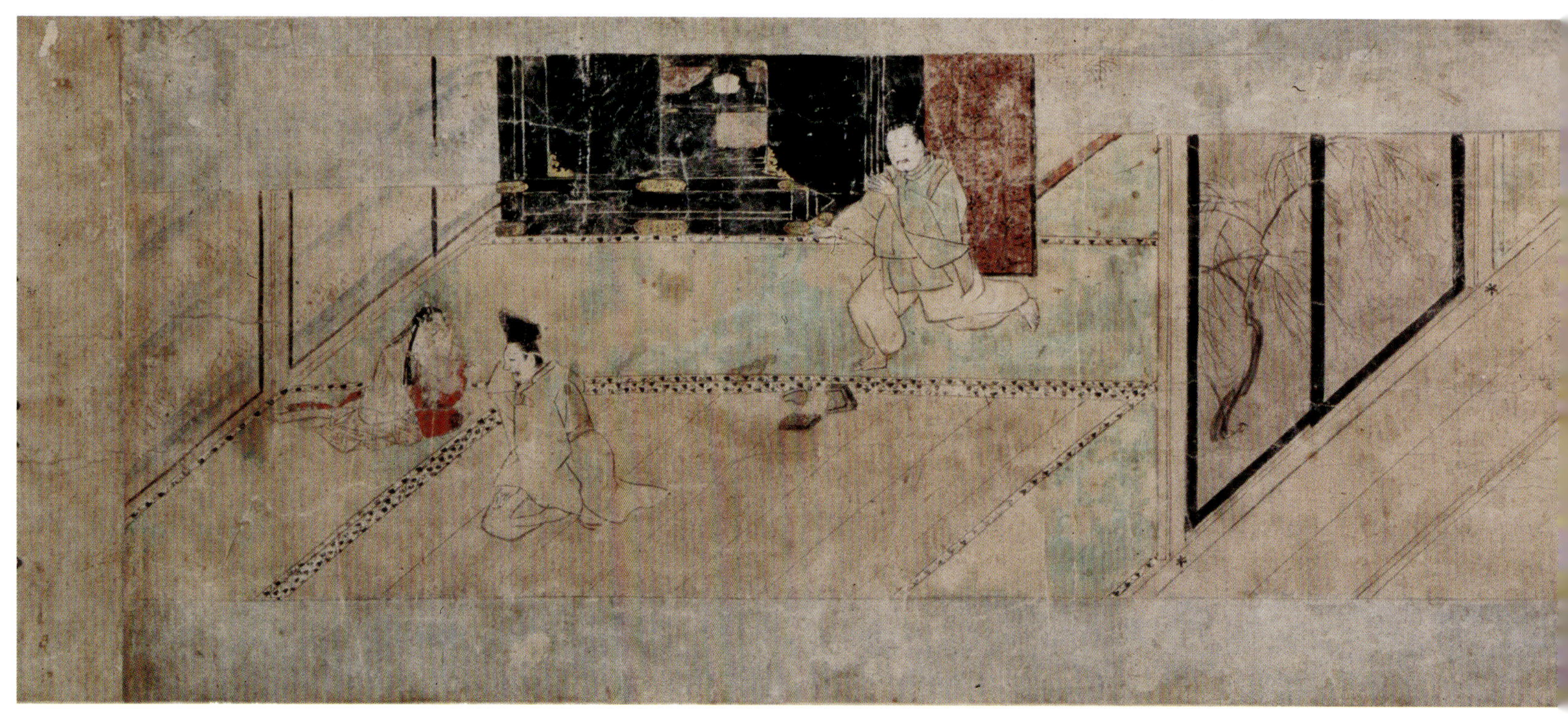

B

3 Tosa Mitsunobu, *Breaking the Inkstone* (*Suzuriwari sōshi emaki*). Dated 1495. One handscroll; ink, color, and gold on paper, 14.9 x 459.8 cm. Hosomi Museum, Kyoto.

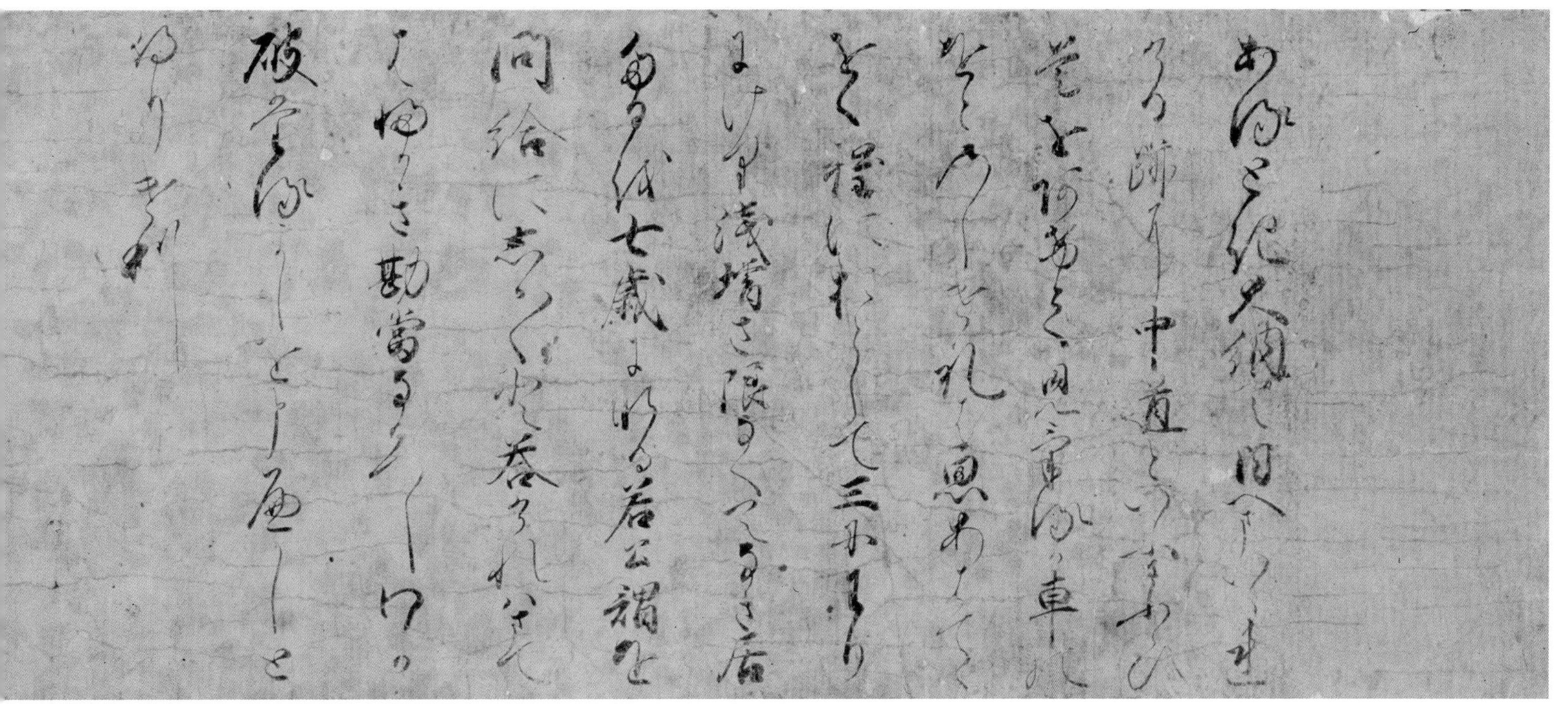

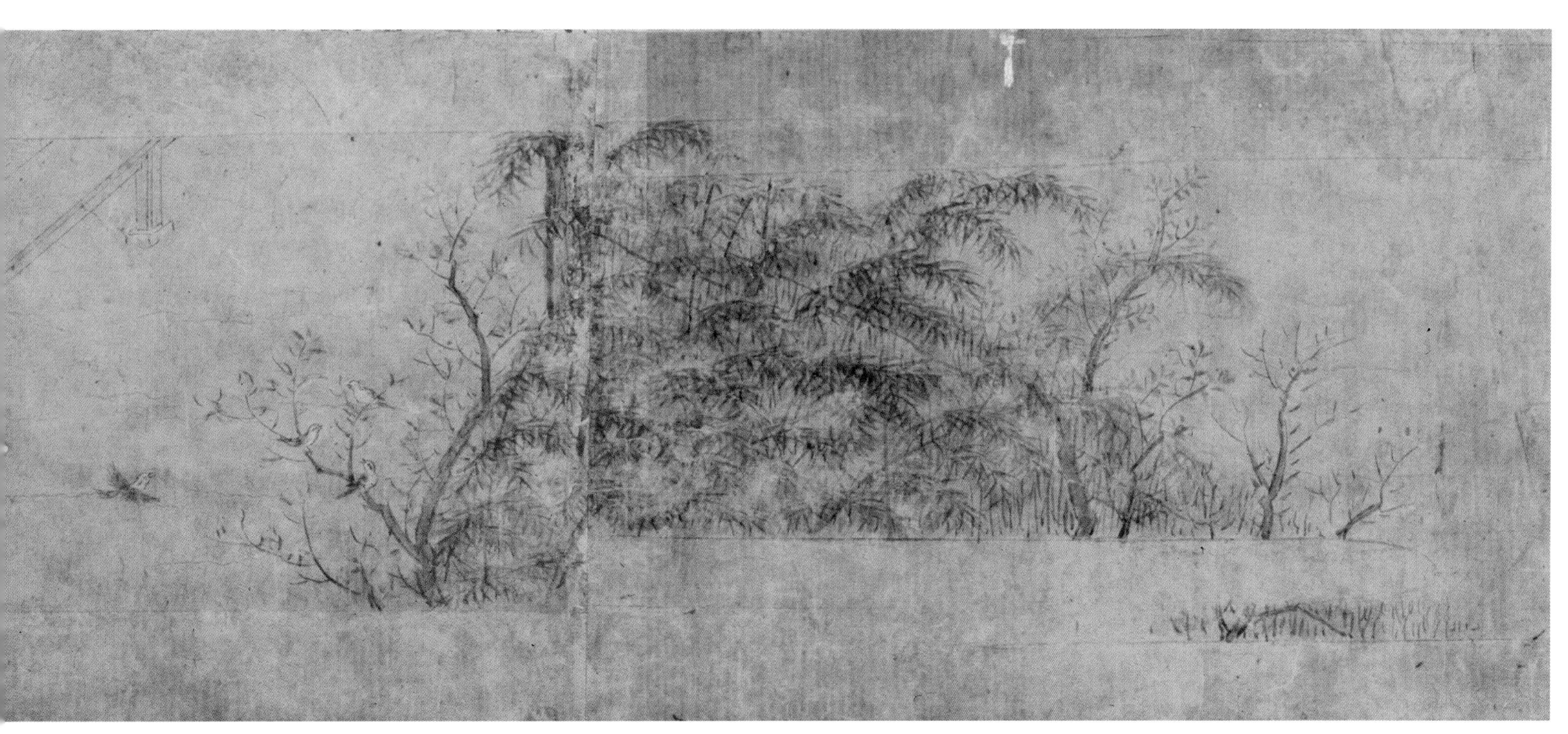

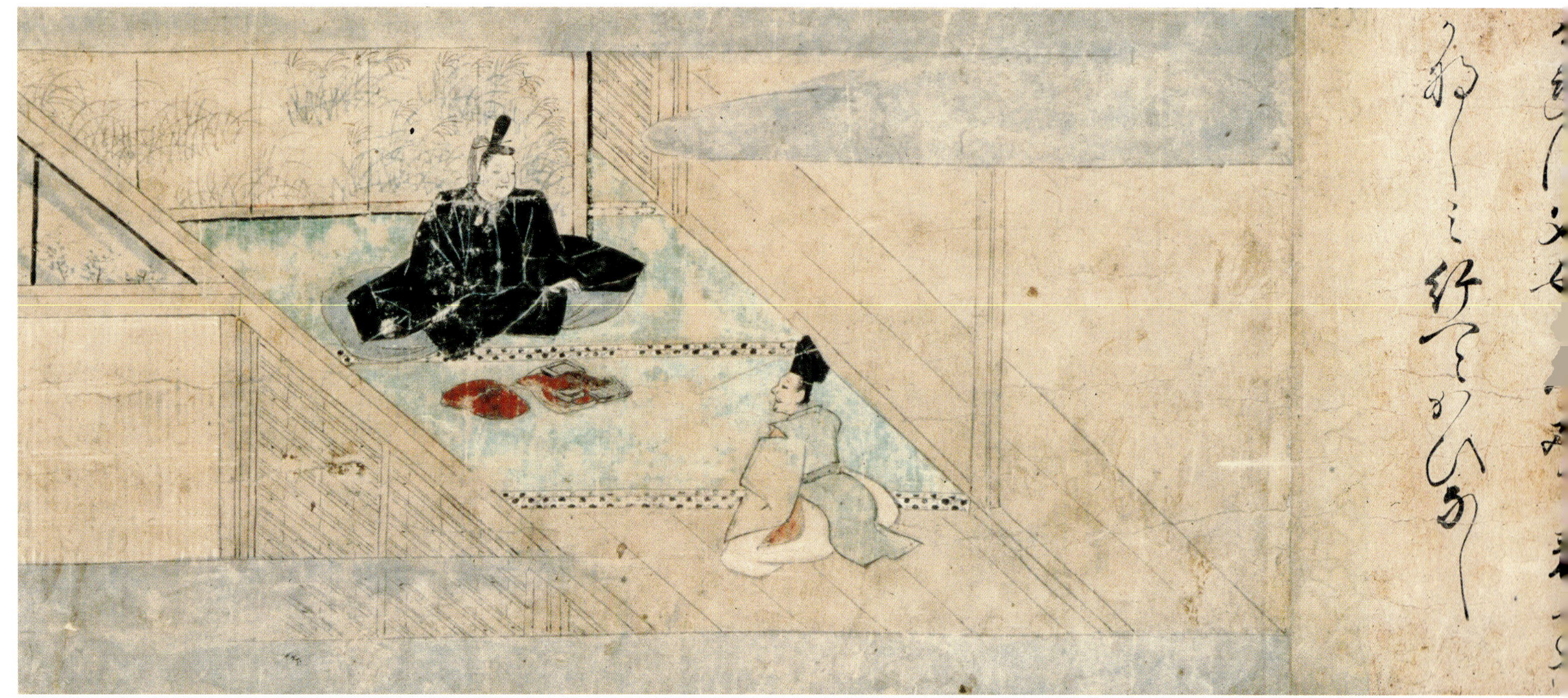

C

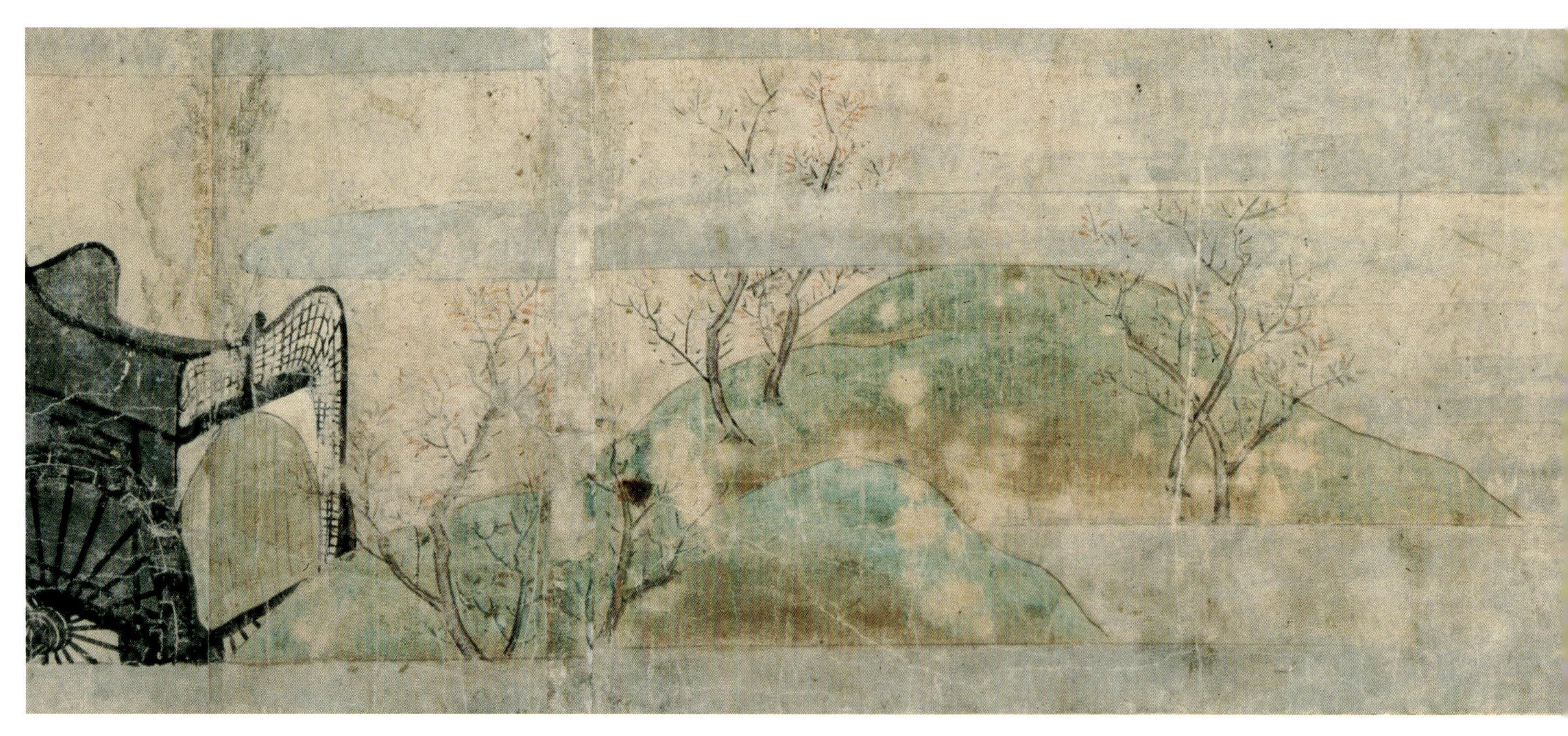

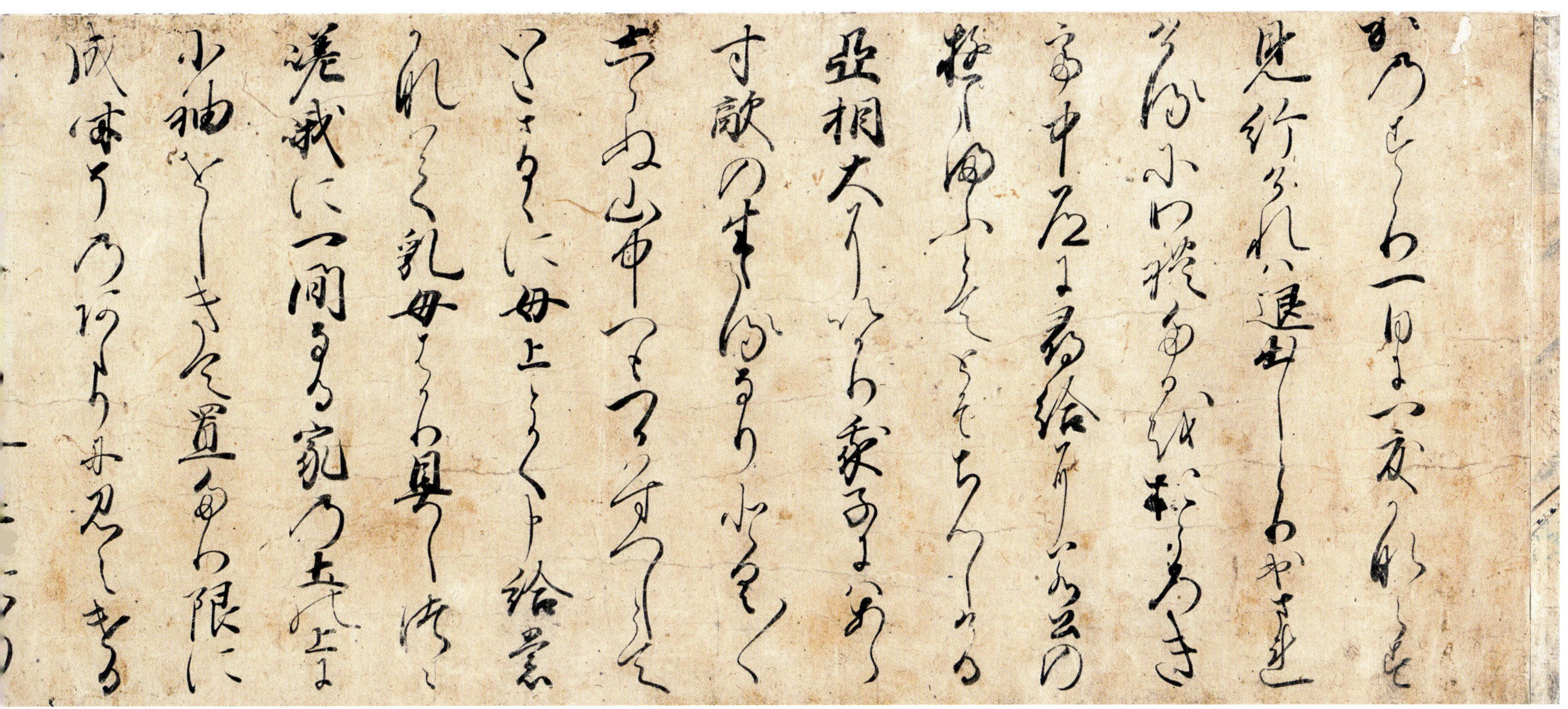

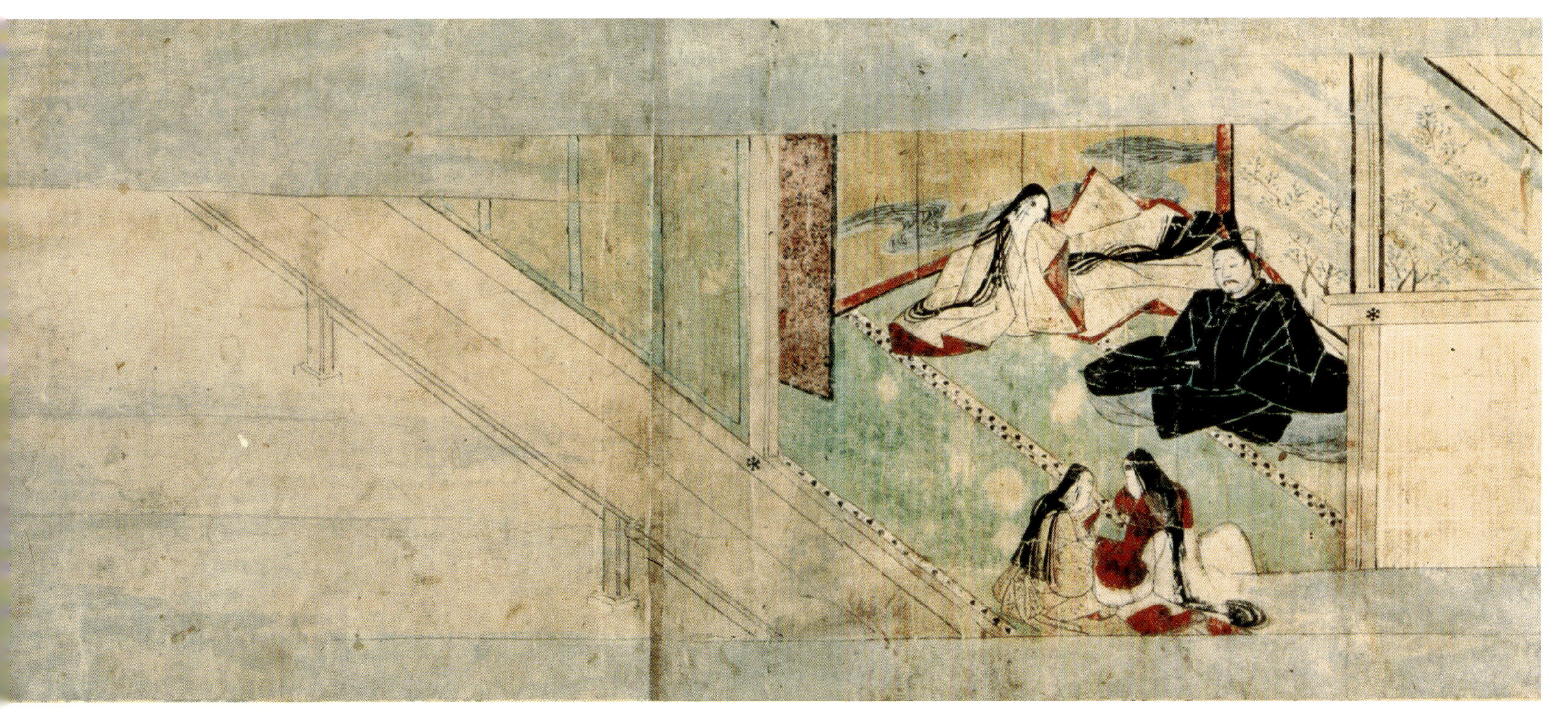

D

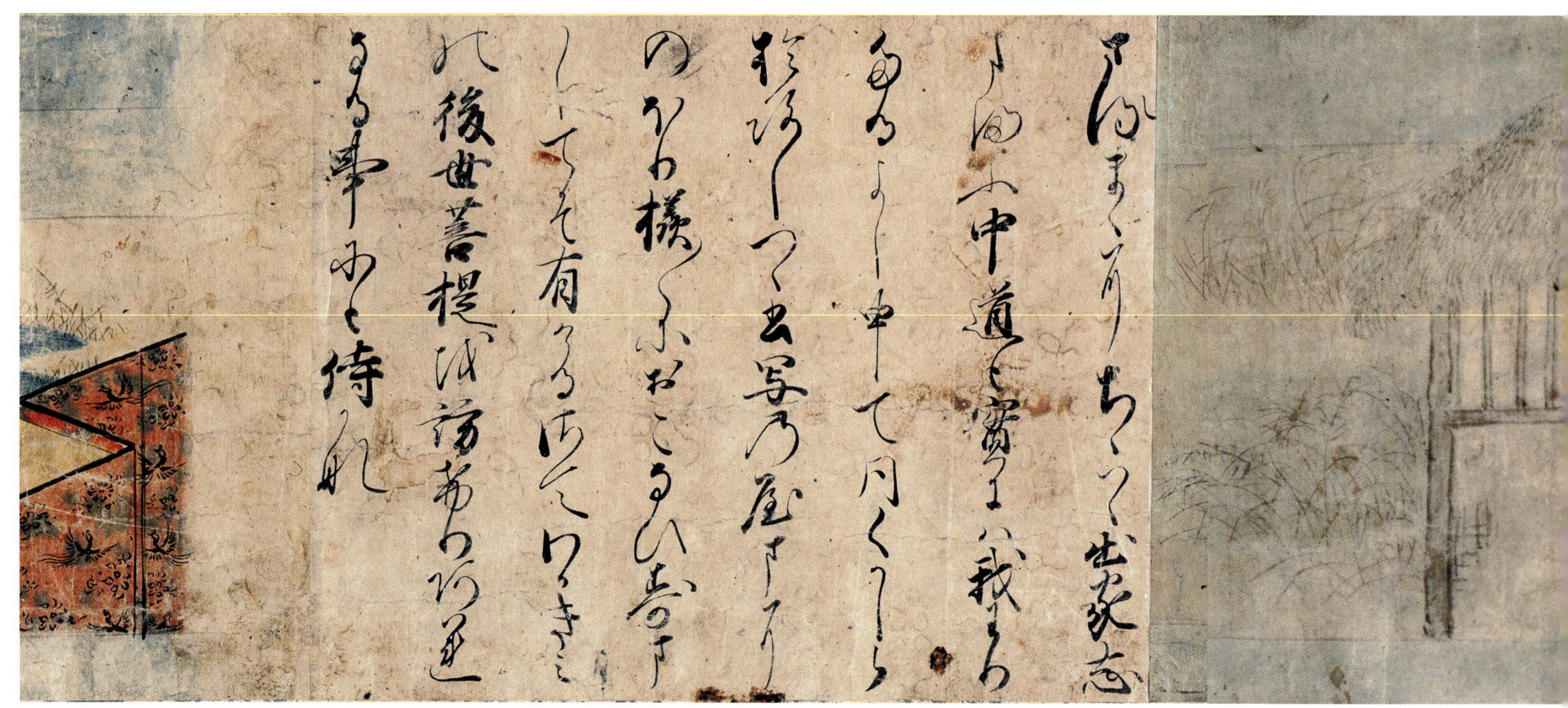

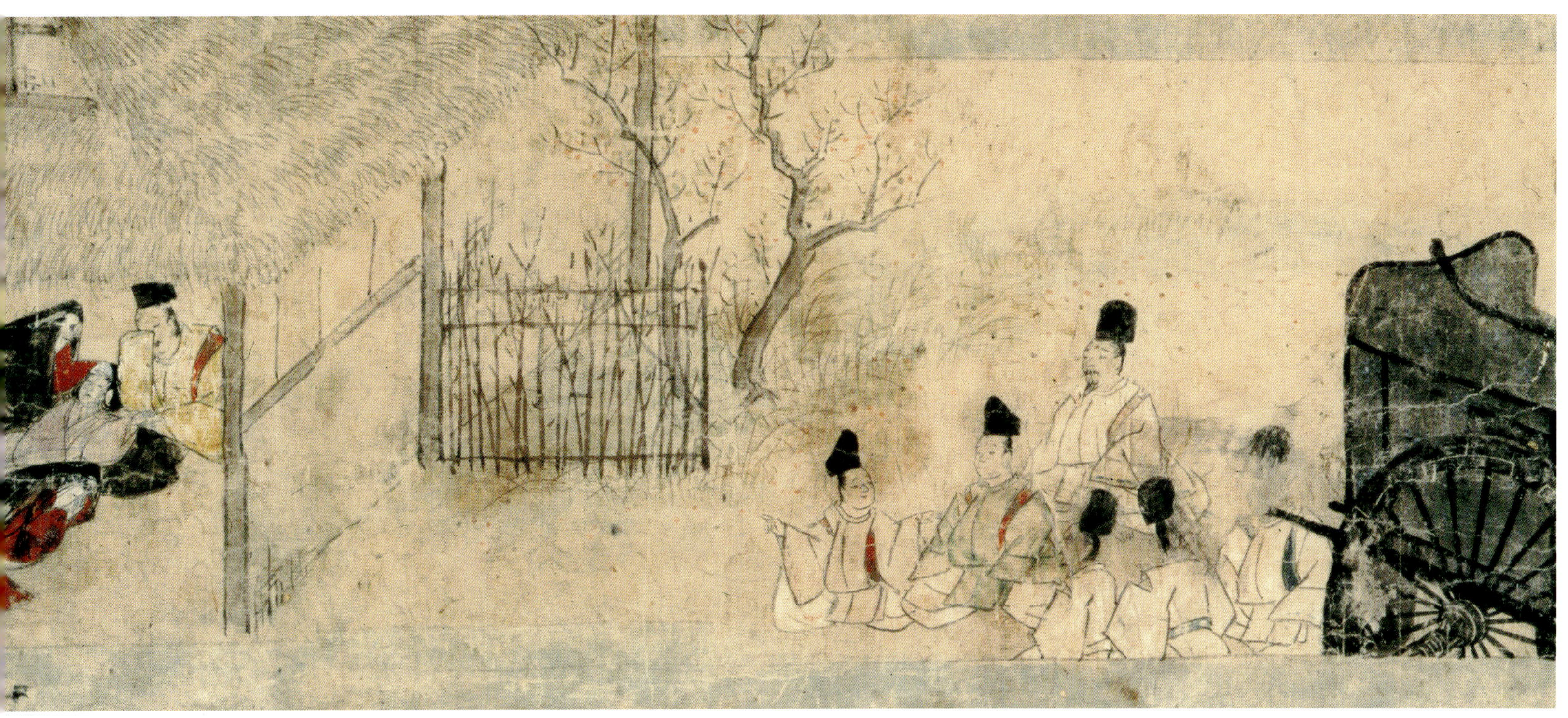

F E

PAINTING THREE (CONTINUED)

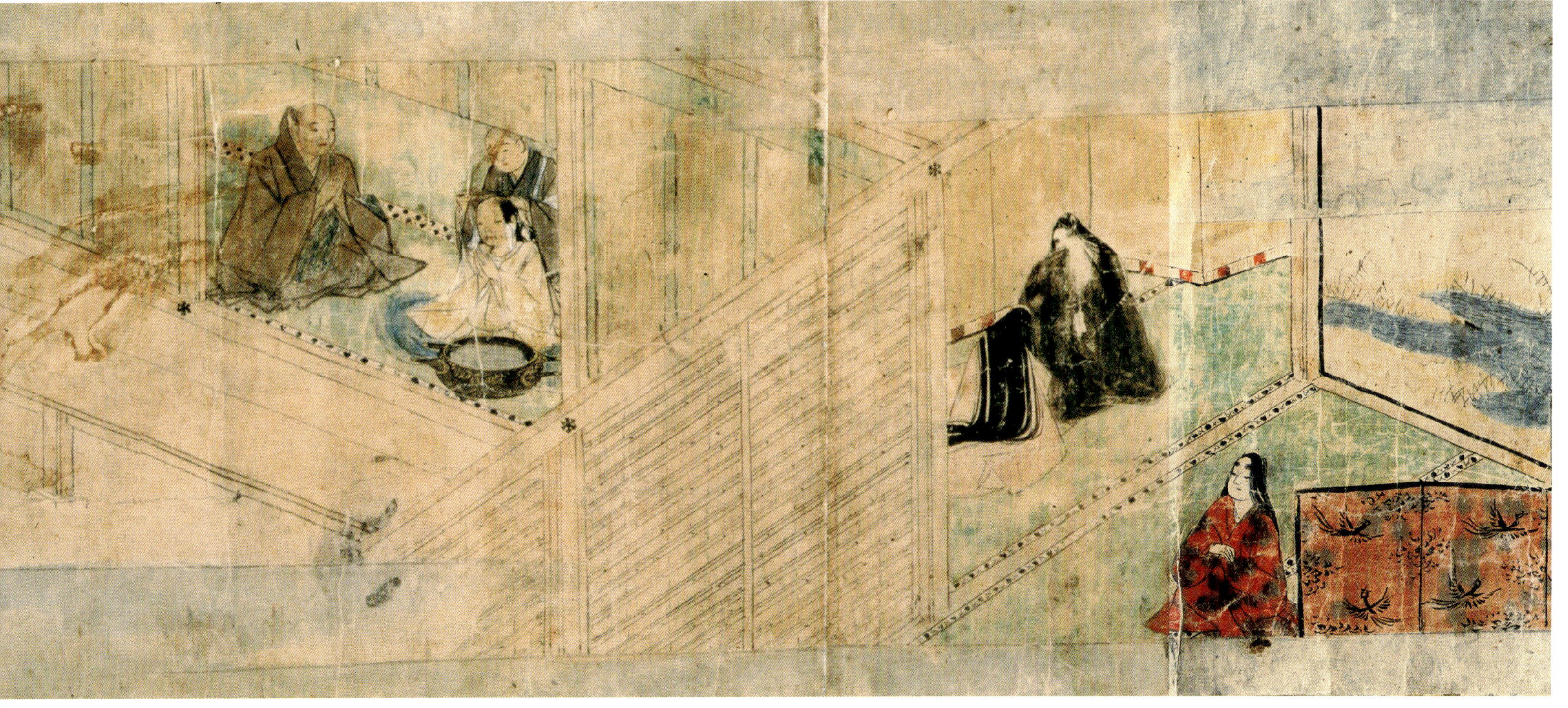

G

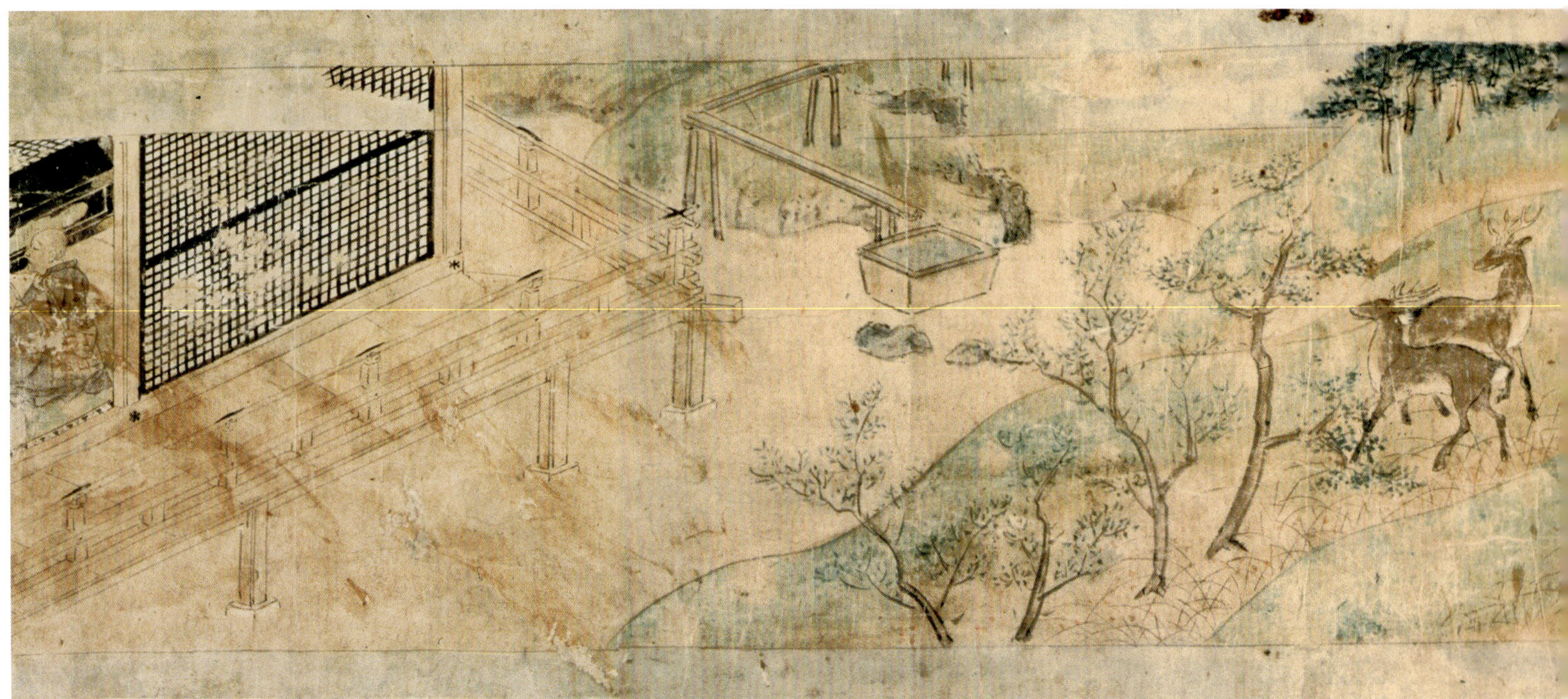

H

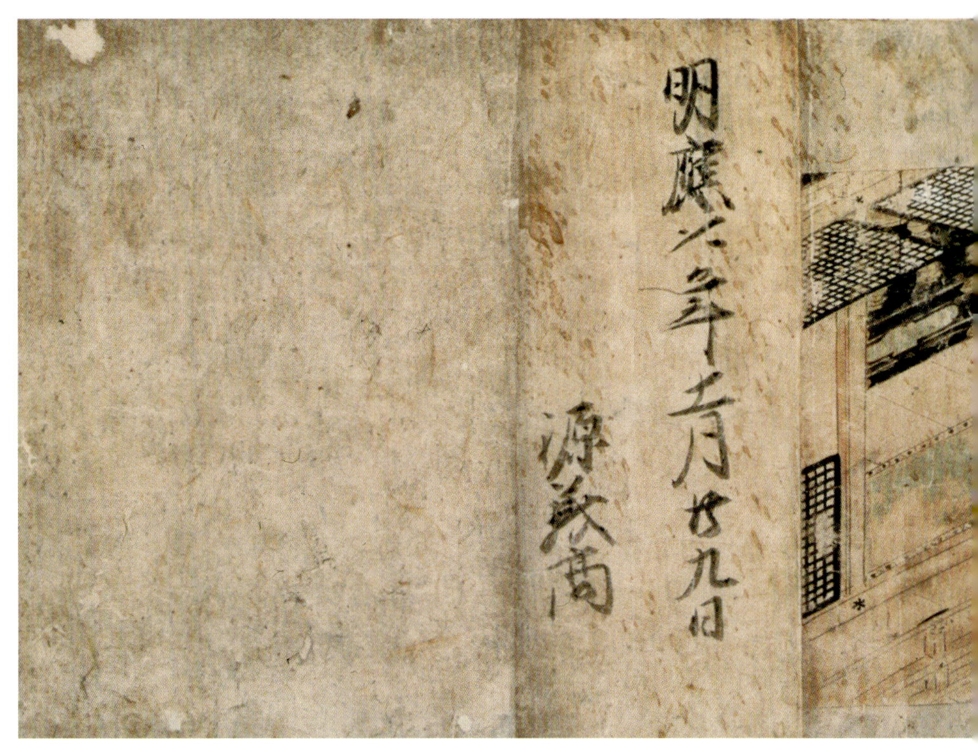

J I

INTRODUCTION THE SMALL SCROLL AND JAPANESE PICTORIAL NARRATIVE

This book takes as its subject a new type of painting, the small-format handscroll, which emerged among Japanese aristocrats during the medieval era. "Small scrolls" (*ko-e*), as they were referred to at the time, were diminutive in scale—approximately fifteen centimeters in height, or half the height of traditional handscrolls—and pictorialized short literary tales for a select group of readers. Typically they required only a handful of paintings to do so, interspersed among brief passages of text, all of which were easily viewed and read in one sitting. Despite the seeming simplicity of their status as pictorial objects, however, small scrolls were anything but simple. In many cases they were based upon short stories that were newly authored by the most able litterateurs at court, who drew upon a vast knowledge of literary tradition to compose tales of subtle complexity and wide-ranging allusive variation. These tales were then pictorialized by the leading court artists of the era, who mobilized the full technical repertoire of Japan's narrative painting tradition to accommodate the new format. The result was a pictoliterary object of unusual sophistication that provided customized viewing experiences for its audiences. As such, small scrolls mark a historically significant transition in the focus of pictorial narrative from institutions to individuals.

To better appreciate the implications of this shift, it is helpful to place the emergence of the small scroll within the development of Japanese picture scrolls more broadly. Horizontal picture scrolls, or *emaki*,[1] were adopted early on by Buddhist monasteries and the imperial court to enhance the stature and appeal of a select group of texts, often ones closely related to institutional identity, such as narratives recounting the miraculous origins of temples and shrines or legendary episodes about court culture. By the twelfth century,

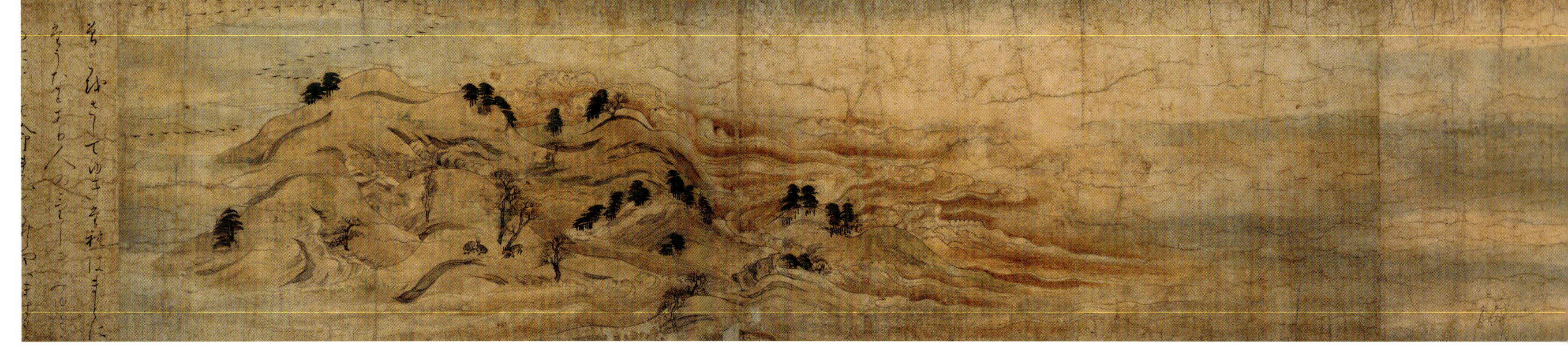

4 *Miraculous Origins of Mt. Shigi* (*Shigisan engi emaki*). Twelfth century. Three scrolls; ink and color on paper, 31.7 x 897.9 cm. Chōgosonshiji, Nara Prefecture. National Treasure. Detail, scroll 3.

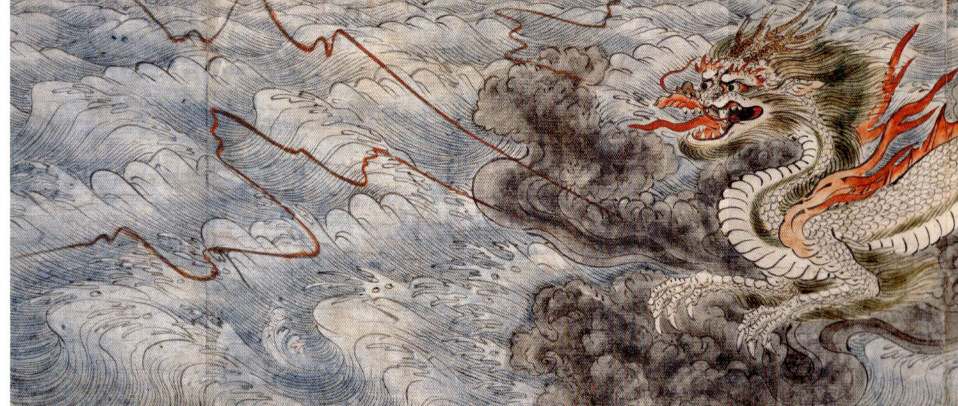

5 *Lives of the Founders of the Kegon Sect* (*Kegonshū soshi eden*). Thirteenth century. Seven scrolls; ink and color on paper, H. 31.7 cm. Kōzanji, Kyoto. National Treasure.

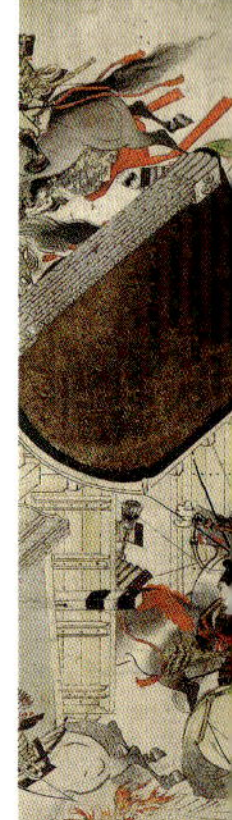

emaki had engendered a remarkably sophisticated language of pictorial narrative. Although China had a much earlier tradition of handscroll painting and was the source of its earliest models and techniques for the East Asian region, it was only in the Japanese court environment that this particular pictorial surface became the premier vehicle for advanced artistic expression. This was especially the case during the reign of the imperial sovereign GoShirakawa (1127–92), when *emaki* came to be characterized by sustained painterly experimentation and unique and virtuoso pictorial effects.[2] Single narrative episodes came to be depicted in elaborate, lingering fashion across great expanses of the paper surface—but were witnessed only piecemeal as viewers scrolled forward—or conversely, multiple narrative threads were condensed into a single view. During these and subsequent years court painters developed techniques of pictorial narrative uniquely suited to the horizontal-scroll format, making it the surface of choice for some of the most memorable moments in Japanese painting history: an elderly nun praying in front of the Great Buddha at Tōdaiji for the whereabouts of her brother (fig. 4); a Chinese maiden's transformation into a giant dragon to save the monk who had forsaken her (fig. 5); the night sky filled with iridescent flames and billowing smoke from the burning Sanjō Palace (fig. 6).

Such scenes, and the narratives to which they belong, are often conceptualized in terms of an intimate viewing experience, but the overwhelming majority of Japanese picture scrolls during the premodern period did not presuppose individual viewing subjects. Rather, *emaki* most often served imperatives that had little to do with the prerogatives of individuals. The case of "dependent-origin" scrolls (*engi-e*), which constituted a significant genre of picture scroll, illustrates this point.[3] In early Japan, unillustrated dependent-origin texts simply referred generically to temple histories, whose submission to the imperium was mandated by the Yamato state as a way of maintaining control over religious institutions.[4] Increasingly, however, these origin narratives became pretexts for the recounting of miracles associated with founding monks and main icons. Illustrated picture scrolls furthered their legitimacy by facilitating

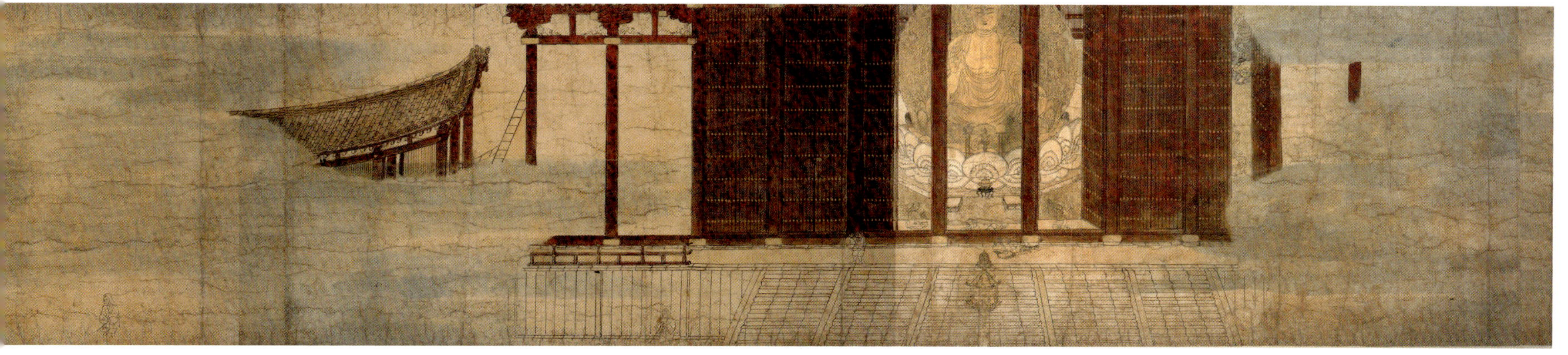

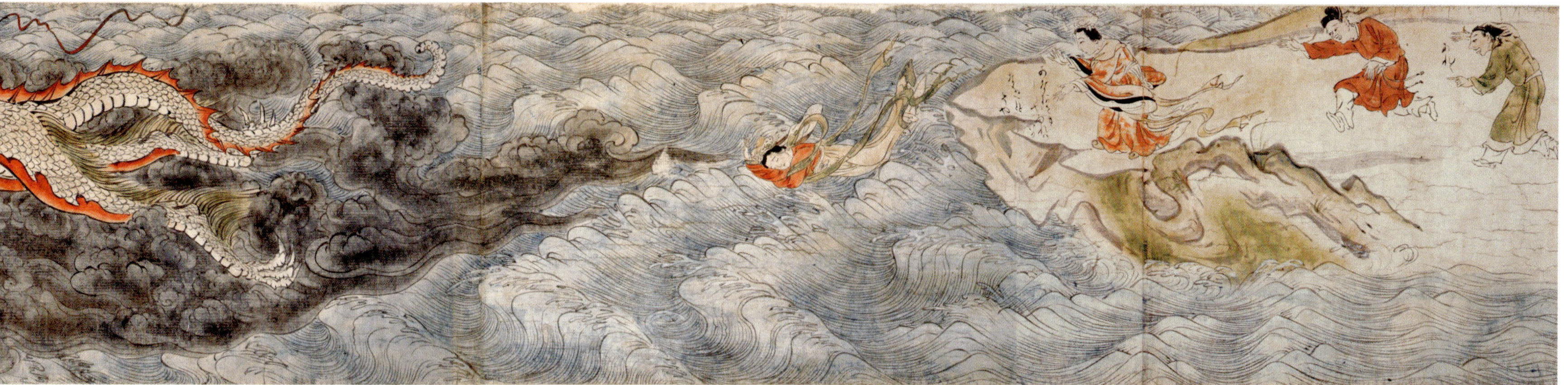

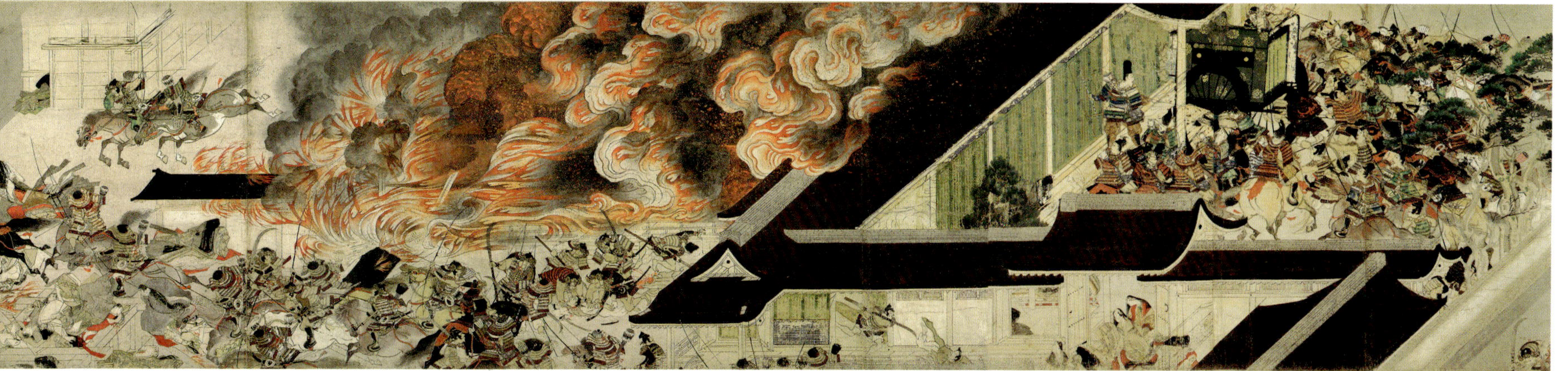

6 "Night Attack on the Sanjō Palace," from *Events of the Heiji Era* (*Heiji monogatari emaki*). Second half of the thirteenth century. One handscroll; ink and color on paper, H. 41.3 cm. Museum of Fine Arts, Boston. Fenollosa-Weld Collection. Photograph © 2009 Museum of Fine Arts, Boston.

a communal imagining of their legendary accounts. Indeed, the communal dimension of origin paintings was crucial to their function as deeds of institutional identity. Accordingly, they were enshrined in religious halls in a manner similar to icons, as living embodiments of deities. The auratic status of *engi-e* ensured that they were rarely viewed privately by individuals. As discussed in a later chapter, there are documented instances in which a recitation of textual passages was arranged at court, during which the scroll was viewed by a select audience. At the very least, such scenarios complicate the idea of origin scrolls as scaled to singular, personalized engagement in this period.

The same caution applies to early picture scrolls of seemingly more "literary" subject matter that illustrated courtly works such as *The Tale of Genji*. While it is difficult to understand with any precision how, for example, the twelfth-century *Genji Scrolls* were viewed, one of its own paintings (fig. 7) suggests that even pictorialized works of fiction, often executed on a slightly smaller scale and with more staid templates for composition and figuration, were viewed and experienced in group settings. More meaningful to an assessment of their significance, perhaps, was the process by which elaborate fiction scrolls came into being. These works were mostly the products of cultural competition in imperial circles, in which the sensitivities and resources of courtiers were put to the test.[5] In the manner in which texts were joined to highly crafted paintings, decorated papers, and skillful calligraphy, these projects were similar to decorated sutras, absent the karmic benefits. The results were adjudicated but not necessarily read or experienced in the manner associated with later formations of the subject presupposed by literature.

Fiction scrolls, like dependent-origin scrolls, were produced and circulated within corporate spaces of readership and in this regard were consistent with the economy of early literary circulation in general.[6] The arrival of the small scroll, and the short-story small scroll in particular, represented a considerable shift in the way picture scrolls were experienced, however. These small scrolls were created over approximately one hundred years, from the middle of the fifteenth to the sixteenth century. They were made primarily for the Kyoto aristocracy in the generations following the Ōnin War (1467–77) and accompanied a new type of literary genre, the short story, which had achieved maturation approximately one generation earlier. These short stories skillfully mixed and matched established literary genres to narrate courtly and didactic tales closely calibrated to the social and cultural contingencies of their time. Small scrolls, as I will argue, provided a visual corollary to this phenomenon by distilling conventions of picture scroll practice into condensed, gemlike paintings of a highly abbreviated and allusive nature.

The pictorial and narrative qualities of small scrolls are striking considering the scrolls' apparent simplicity. In most cases they consisted of tales focused on a single protagonist and a single, short plotline. As few as three or four textual passages and accompanying paintings

7 *The Tale of Genji Scrolls* (*Genji monogatari emaki*), chapter 50, "The Eastern Cottage I" (*Azumaya I*). Twelfth century. Ink and color on paper, 21.5 x 39.2 cm. Tokugawa Art Museum, Nagoya. National Treasure.

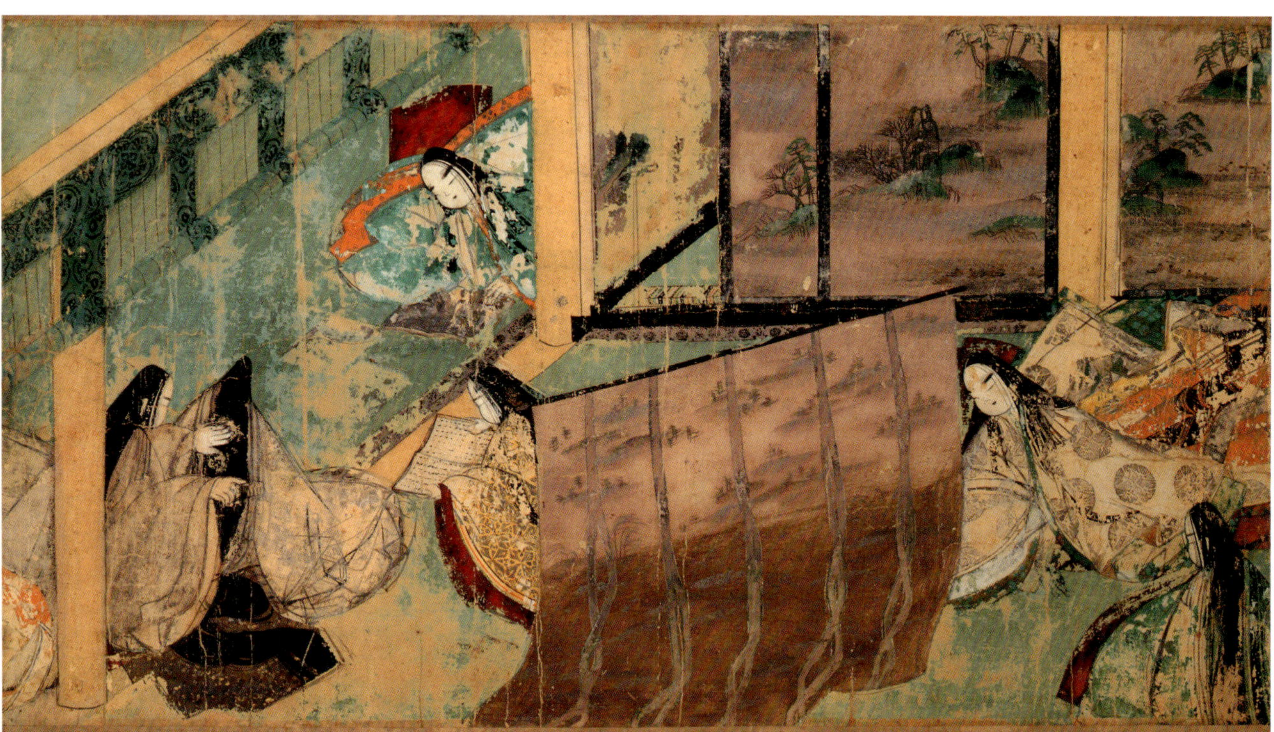

could suffice to do the telling. The economy of representation mandated by these reduced circumstances, however, proved an impetus for new forms of figuration in picture scroll painting. Complex, multilayered characterizations could be enfolded into a singular but resonant protagonist. Paintings could add inflections that introduced understated but nevertheless notable new dimensions to a character. Sometimes these figures were amalgamations of multiple character types whose complexity emerged only when the scroll was viewed from differing perspectives, like crystal turned in the hand. And in the most extraordinary instances, the pictorial complements to textual passages could allow a spare and simple story to accommodate numerous points of engagement simultaneously, anticipating a multiplicity of widely differing subject positions, each of which derived a separate meaning from the narrative. Visual figuration of this kind was not unknown in earlier picture scrolls, but despite the wide-ranging technical repertoire and the many dynamic modes of painterly representation that had been developed in the late Heian (794–1185) and Kamakura (1185–1333) periods, pictorial accomplishment in this format generally came at the expense of a deepening of "literary" characterization. *Emaki* picture making tended to encourage attention to spectacle in any given scene, whether it be a moment of poetic encounter or high drama in a work of fiction or a miraculous occurrence in a dependent-origin painting. Small scrolls contained their share of spectacle but their paintings focused more on characterization than on impersonation.

The argument set forth in this study is that small scrolls enabled a new mode of viewer engagement within the handscroll tradition because they were made for specific individuals in particular contexts, customizing representation of their subject tales accordingly. These individuals cannot always be identified in the documentary archive, as the production contexts of the overwhelming majority of small scrolls are poorly recorded, if at all. But in many cases the circumstances surrounding the creation of a *ko-e* can nevertheless be excavated through historical research, at the very least delineating a likely context for a work's initial reception. Moreover, it is the qualities internal to a small scroll that best suggest the context in which it might have been initially viewed. In the chapters that follow, therefore, a great deal of attention will be devoted to understanding the literary and pictorial inner mechanics by which these complex works anticipate their subject positions.

An analysis of representation in small scrolls requires two main areas of inquiry. The first concerns the narratives. These tales, as this study demonstrates, were often created during the medieval period and represented a previously unknown literary form. Short tales (*setsuwa*) had been authored and compiled in Japan for centuries, but the ones chosen for illustration were mostly characterized by ambient story lines with multiple subplots, in which the focus shifted easily from character to character. The narratives treated in small scrolls, on the other hand, were sparse and forward driven, focusing on single protagonists and episodes that directly advanced the story line, and ended with a firm sense of closure. Despite their compactness and economy of representation, however, these short stories were crafted with a great deal of care. They drew widely and freely upon earlier tale literature, often modeling themselves primarily upon one genre but borrowing elements from others in order to complicate and nuance all aspects of the story, first and foremost the dramatis personae. Indeed, a close reading of the texts of small scrolls reveals that much of what is enabled by the paintings is already latent in the narratives. And in some cases stories were newly authored for small scrolls, indicating the degree to which their authorship was symbiotic with the conditions of pictorial production.

In coming to terms with the representational complexity of small scrolls, the second area of inquiry is the paintings themselves. Sustained analyses of small-scroll paintings demonstrate the degree to which they are attuned to and shape the experience of their accompanying textual passages. Needless to say, in Japanese picture scrolls, paintings were never slavish illustrations of companion texts but thoroughly mediated the experience of the "underlying" story. In the case of an enormously popular text such as *Legends of Kitano Tenjin* (*Kitano Tenjin engi emaki*), of which some sixty illustrated scroll examples survive, each pictorial iteration of the parent text constitutes a significant variation.[7] Yet small-scroll paintings represent a qualitatively different type of relationship between word and image. The agendas of both components can be so calibrated one to the other, so mutually in attunement, that the paintings interpret their texts with great sensitivity. This interpretive engagement goes beyond a selective focus on certain elements of the narrative for dramatic emphasis, which is common in the picture scroll tradition. Rather, it actively shapes and promotes the latent multidimensionality of the texts, imbuing meaning to each scene through composition, detail, coloration, and figuration. The paintings demonstrate a similar combinatory logic and historical awareness as the text, accommodating traditional techniques and habits of representation to the more fine-grained mandate of small-scroll picture making.

Certainly size plays a crucial role in the pictorial dynamics of *ko-e*. The dimensions of small scrolls were somewhat less than half that of standard picture scrolls. Traditional *emaki*, even on the smaller end of the spectrum, could measure anywhere from twenty to twenty-five centimeters in height, but most examples were around thirty to thirty-five centimeters in height. The dimensions were usually dictated by conventions in paper size, which during the classical era of picture scroll production was typically thirty by fifty centimeters per sheet. Such papers were mounted one after the other horizontally to produce scrolls of considerable length, as long as twenty-three meters. Some surviving scrolls, however, such as *Legends of Kitano Tenjin* (1219) in Kyoto's Kitano Tenmangū and *Origins of the Taima Mandala* (thirteenth century) in the temple Kōmyōji, sought such grandeur of effect that papers were mounted to each other along the longer dimension to achieve a height of fifty centimeters for the pictorial surface. Short-story small scrolls did not attempt to transfer all of the pictorial effects associated with such large-scale works to their own dimensions; they were not, in other words, miniature versions of traditional picture scrolls. Created for new short stories, these *ko-e* adapted long-established modes of pictorial representation to radically new ends.

The comparatively confined surfaces of small scrolls forced painters to eschew the lengthy panoramas and dynamic action sequences of larger scrolls and to focus more on scenes of figural interaction, on intimate encounters between characters. This did not mean, however, that they abandoned all efforts at monumentality. The small-scroll genre developed a unique sense of internal scale, a sort of spatial shorthand that allowed for the suggestion of vastness beyond the pictorial field. Proportional and relational values were gauged in such a way as to suggest great expanses and crowds through the most indirect and allusive of methods. Small scrolls demonstrate as well as any pictorial genre that monumentality is an effect of pictorial representation and not of absolute size or scale. Nevertheless, ultimately the greatest emphasis in small-scroll pictures was necessarily placed not upon interludes and transitional scenes—pictorial infill—but rather upon core episodes of encounter and engagement between characters. Traditional techniques were applied with greater concentration to distill action and content. The sum total of adaptations amounted to what might be called a "small visuality," a pictorial idiom uniquely suited to the prerogatives of small scrolls. This visual language demanded from the viewer a mode of attention that was fine-tuned to the minutiae of pose, gesture, countenance, and formal interaction, as well as to the precision planning of composition and architectural interiors. Oftentimes, it was in these details that the parallel representational agendas of text and painting could be discerned with greatest insight.

The deep imbrication of pictorial and narrative surfaces in small scrolls can be traced to the circle of the court painter Tosa Mitsunobu (active ca. 1469–1522) and the courtier Sanjōnishi Sanetaka (1455–1537). Sanetaka was a leading literary scholar and left a sixty-one-year-long diary documenting his cultural activity in a number of spheres. Mitsunobu, who collaborated with Sanetaka on numerous scroll projects over a decades-long association, was the head of the official Painting Bureau (*edokoro*) and the leading artist of classical imagery in his generation. Although their status was incommensurate and it may be more proper to refer to Mitsunobu as a member of Sanetaka's circle, I will treat them as equals as a way of acknowledging the agency of a painter who has not been given sufficient recognition for his role in small-scroll production. Mitsunobu was a figure of considerable cultural accomplishment, well versed in poetry and a regular participant in rarefied cultural circles of the period. An avid student of earlier painting who nevertheless was highly innovative in numerous pictorial genres, he provided the ideal artisanal counterpart to Sanetaka's literary prowess. Their partnership, documented in later chapters, was crucial to the generation of a new approach to picture scroll production. Historically, the greatest concentration of small scrolls can be mapped onto their period of active collaboration, during the last two decades of the fifteenth and first two decades of the sixteenth century.

To demonstrate the pictorial intelligence of small scrolls associated with the Sanetaka-Mitsunobu sphere, I will subject three examples to sustained analysis. *A Wakeful Sleep* (*Utatane sōshi emaki*) (fig. 1) recounts the miraculous union of a man and a woman who had previously encountered each other only in their dreams; *The Jizō Hall* (*Jizōdō sōshi emaki*) (fig. 2) tells the story of a wayward monk who achieves enlightenment with the help of a dragon princess; and *Breaking the Inkstone* (*Suzuriwari sōshi emaki*) (fig. 3) narrates the sacrifice of a young boy for his household servant and its tragic consequences. These three works are easily among the most artistically accomplished and sophisticated small scrolls to have survived, and this alone merits their inclusion here. At the same time, the case studies demonstrate various ways in which small scrolls could tell stories according to their own delicate narratology. *A Wakeful Sleep* celebrates the Fujiwara lineage and uses pictorial sleight-of-hand to generate an aura of sanctity around its matrimonial union. Its young female protagonist, however, is marked by a high degree of ambivalence, caught between her proactive characterization in the tale and the conservative agenda of the small scroll itself. The narrative of *The Jizō Hall*, meanwhile, appears to have been uniquely authored for the small scroll. Within the same simple tale, two very different stories are told regarding male and female salvation. This twinning of stories is accomplished through the remarkable duality exhibited by the monk's benefactress, a dragon princess. The most virtuosic pictorial narration is found in *Breaking the Inkstone*, however, in which a tragic tale of a young boy's loyalty and redemption is somehow made to accommodate three equally compelling subject positions with which to identify.

As these scrolls show, the collaboration of Mitsunobu and scholar-calligraphers such as Sanetaka did not always lead to a unity of style. Underneath the compactness and seeming unidirectionality of small-scroll narratives lurked dissonances and surprising contradictions. These fissures were to some degree the result of a syncretic and accretive mode of production. But they were also the inevitable outcome of attempting to mold narratives to the contingencies of specific individuals or groups of individuals, as was the case with the small scrolls investigated here. As I argue in the following chapters, each scroll can be associated with historical figures of the late fifteenth century. *A Wakeful Sleep* was made for someone like Sanetaka's own daughter as she prepared to marry into one of the most powerful political families in the aristocracy. *The Jizō Hall* was likely intended for Emperor GoTsuchimikado (1442–1500) himself but also anticipated that his ladies-in-waiting would be among its audience. Finally, *Breaking the Inkstone* was certainly commissioned by the warlord Hosokawa Masamoto (1466–1507), at the time the most powerful figure in Japan, for the young shogun Ashikaga Yoshizumi (1480–1511), who was politically controlled by Masamoto and was even living in the Hosokawa household at the time. Yet Masamoto himself appears to be figured into the tale, as is a newly adopted seven-year-old son, his heir apparent. For all of these historical figures, small scrolls were intended to resonate in ways that far exceeded the relevance of traditional picture scrolls to individual circumstances.

A lack of awareness of this individuation in small scrolls may have been the most important factor in their exclusion from traditional accounts of the history and development of *emaki*. But in fact picture scrolls from the late medieval period in general have not been the beneficiaries of sufficient scholarly attention. While scholars have begun to redress this imbalance, general accounts of the long view of *emaki* history describe a trajectory that stops in the fourteenth century.[8] This type of narrative tends to proceed according to the following outline: after the emergence of the *emaki* format from illustrated Buddhist handscrolls imported from the Chinese mainland in the eighth century, its development proceeded along two lines during the ensuing Heian period (794–1185): (1) the compartmentalized mode, in which painting and text were syncopated one after the other, best embodied by a work such as the *Genji Scrolls*, and (2) the continuous mode, characterized by long passages of continuous visual narrative, famously exemplified by scrolls such as *Miraculous Origins of Mt. Shigi* (*Shigisan engi emaki*) (figs. 4, 17, 26) and *Major Counselor Ban* (*Ban Dainagon ekotoba*) (fig. 18). The golden age of picture scroll production during the Kamakura period (1185–1333) would witness a development of these two pictorial modes within a handful of established genres—courtly tales, priestly hagiographies, military chronicles, and records of the miraculous origins of temples and shrines. Increasingly, during the fourteenth century, the handscroll format would become the means by which religious institutions would attempt to legitimize their own genealogical claims amid fierce sectarian conflict, leading to both a proliferation in the number of *emaki* produced and a precipitous decline in their quality. The Muromachi period (1333–1573) oversaw the growing popularization of the medium in the form of "Nara picture books" (*Nara ehon*), or popular handscroll tales, and by the early modern era (1600–1868), *emaki* had taken a permanent backseat to other painting formats as vehicles for advanced painterly expression.

Small scrolls reveal the shortcomings of this narrative. One source of this deficiency lies in a misrecognition of the patronage base of later picture scrolls, which in turn stems from insufficient historical excavation. It is usually assumed that the primary community of sponsors shifted during the fourteenth century from established monasteries (of the Shingon and Tendai sects), aristocrats, and elite military houses to newly emerging religious sects based on Pure Land Buddhist belief. These Amidist institutions took advantage of the prestige and efficacy of *emaki* to embody their own lineal claims, which in turn abetted efforts to establish sectarian space within a populated religious landscape. This phenomenon typically took the form of founder hagiography, and picture scrolls illustrating such themes were sent from sectarian headquarters out to the growing number of provincial monasteries being established by the new Buddhist sects. Thus, the fourteenth century witnessed a remarkable increase in the number of handscrolls illustrating the legendary biography of the monk Shinran (1173–1262), founder of the expanding True Pure Land Sect (Jōdo Shinshū). As Akiyama Terukazu has argued, this shift in sponsoring institutions left an indelible mark on handscroll production.[9] It tended to conventionalize the format, which in the most blatant examples became marked by repetition and lower standards of pictorial expression.

Yet the predictability of hagiographic scrolls has conditioned many commentators to turn a jaundiced eye upon the numerous picture scrolls that postdate the so-called Amidist shift. General surveys of medieval Japanese painting tend to follow suit by turning at this point from a discussion of polychrome handscrolls to other types of painting, such as the monochrome painting prevalent in the Zen monastic community. Picture scrolls of high quality, however, continued to be produced in large numbers. The institutions that supported handscroll production during its ostensible peak era continued to commission picture scrolls throughout the fifteenth and sixteenth centuries. Although facing pecuniary hardship, aristocratic families of all kinds remained heavily invested in this particular painting format.[10] Literary tales and poetic themes were pictorialized as before; official pictorial records, in scroll form, of shrine and temple origins were offered by the courtly community in practically every generation of the medieval period. Women in service at the imperial court developed unique traditions of handscroll painting revolving around *The Tale of Genji* and the ink-line (*hakubyō*) mode of representation in particular.[11] Old monastic centers were resensitized to the effectiveness of the horizontal-scroll format, perhaps under pressure from the emergence of rival sects. The monks of Tōji, the headquarters of Shingon, or Esoteric, Buddhism in Kyoto, enthusiastically encouraged the pictorialization of the life story of their sect's founder, Kūkai, at subtemples.[12] Meanwhile, Enryakuji, the center of Tendai Buddhism, did the same for painted legends of its sister institution, the Hie Shrine. And when its Great Buddha Hall burned to the ground in the early sixteenth century, the venerable Nara monastery Tōdaiji employed its own painters to create a scroll pictorializing its own history to be used in fundraising efforts.[13]

Yet the greatest elite patrons of picture scroll production during the late medieval period were the Ashikaga shoguns. Their role in the creation of picture scrolls has only recently begun to be understood.[14] The patronage activities of the Ashikaga shoguns had previously been viewed exclusively through the lens of Zen Buddhist sponsorship, which in terms of painting referred primarily to the subdued, monochromatic mural décor of shogunal palaces. Nevertheless, the Ashikaga were closely involved with *emaki* production from the outset. The first shogun, Takauji (1305–58), upon assuming control of the government, immediately began to order the creation of scrolls commemorating victorious battles of the Minamoto shoguns, thus implying a link between himself and earlier paragons of military rule. Subsequent shoguns actively sponsored production of the pictorial biographies of Pure Land monks, primarily to commemorate death anniversaries of their ancestors. As demonstrated by Karen Brock, the sixth shogun, Yoshinori (1394–1441), used handscrolls to further his self-aristocratizing ambitions vis-à-vis the imperial family.[15] *Emaki* could also play a highly intimate role in the spiritual life of a shogun, as in the case of Ashikaga Yoshiharu's personal (and personalized) copy of *Miraculous Origins of Hasedera* (*Hasedera engi emaki;* fig. 12).[16] And when he was in temporary exile from Kyoto during the mid–sixteenth century, Yoshiharu commissioned the *Miraculous Origins of Kuwanomidera,* (*Kuwanomidera engi emaki*) which poignantly embodies his own claims to sovereignty.[17]

The example of the Ashikaga would inspire other warrior leaders of the Muromachi period. Hosokawa Masamoto, a shogunal regent who usurped power from the Ashikaga at the turn of the sixteenth century, embraced the *emaki* format both as an instrument of political puppeteering and as a means of supporting religious institutions with which he was personally affiliated.[18] The Hōjō family of northeastern Japan, meanwhile, would take advantage of its Kyoto connections to sponsor the production of one of the most impressive handscrolls to have survived from this era, the *Drunken Ogre Scroll* (*Shūten dōji emaki;* fig. 8).[19]

Indeed, not only did handscroll patronage *not* decline in the late medieval period, but it increased to a remarkable degree, spreading to all sectors of elite society during the fifteenth and sixteenth centuries. One might even argue that this period was the true golden age of the handscroll format. Small scrolls were simply one manifestation—albeit a unique and highly sophisticated one—of a much larger and richer *emaki* culture that infused Japanese society during this period. They have until now rarely been the objects of sustained scholarly attention. Although introduced decades ago by Umezu Jirō as intriguing miniature variations on the standard format, most small scrolls were thought to lack the art historical gravitas that merited in-depth analysis.[20] Indeed, in his early study of small-format handscrolls, Umezu famously designated them as "playthings for women and children," effectively banishing small scrolls from the domain of serious art.[21] As the following chapters demonstrate, *ko-e* in fact addressed multiple constituencies across the elite spectrum, men and women, old and young.

To build a new historical and analytical framework for an appreciation of the small scroll, the present study is divided into five chapters and an epilogue. Chapter 1, "A Brief History of Small Scrolls," offers a detailed discussion of the development of small scrolls from the fourteenth through the sixteenth century. This overview of the entire population of small scrolls clarifies the distinction between scrolls that are simply reduced-size versions of larger handscrolls and "short-story small scrolls" that bear sufficiently new visual and literary traits to be meaningfully recognizable as a separate

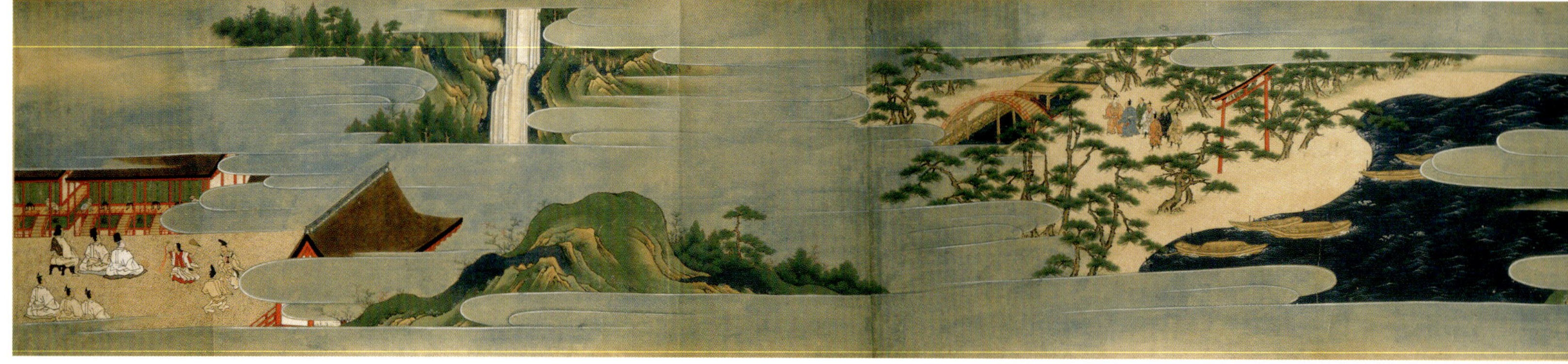

8 Kanō Motonobu (1477–1559), *The Drunken Ogre* (*Shuten dōji emaki*). Early sixteenth century. Three scrolls; ink, color, and gold on paper, H. 33.1 cm. Suntory Museum of Art, Tokyo. Detail, scroll 4.

medium. Nearly all examples of the latter category can be linked to the circle of Mitsunobu and Sanetaka, thereby reinforcing the idea that these two figures played a central role in the emergence of this art form. The survey of small scrolls in this initial chapter also allows for a more fully developed articulation of their relationship to the larger body of literary forms that traversed the medieval cultural landscape. As I will show, small scrolls consistently illustrated short stories of one main type: tales of personal transformation, in which the protagonist experiences a realization by the end of the tale, usually an awareness related to the Buddhist notion of the illusory nature of worldly desires.

Chapter 1 also tackles the issue of the relationship of *ko-e* to child readers, a connection that almost every previous commentator has emphasized. Although it is indisputable that certain privileged youths of the upper classes read and owned small scrolls, I propose instead that the format engaged a wide variety of age-groups. The argument presented here draws on studies of children's literature in the medieval West to problematize the notion of children's fiction in general and to readdress the issue of readership by providing a more nuanced account of reading practices in late medieval Japan. Indeed, the kinds of stories illustrated in small scrolls were commonly found in literary collections read by adults of the period, including the emperor himself. The chapter concludes with an overview of the unique literary and pictorial characteristics of Mitsunobu's corpus of small scrolls.

In chapter 2 I concentrate on the collaborative relationship between the painter Tosa Mitsunobu and the scholar Sanjōnishi Sanetaka. More specifically, two areas of their activity are most germane to my thesis: their study of older handscrolls and their joint production of small scrolls. Both Mitsunobu and Sanetaka were thoroughly familiar with early courtly painting. Mitsunobu based his practice on the careful study of classical paintings, which he was occasionally called upon to repair or supplement. Sanetaka, meanwhile, was an avid student of the treasured handscrolls stored in temples and shrines, which he was at times requested to read aloud before the imperial court. Through a study of their engagement with a famous work, *Miracles of the Kasuga Deity* (*Kasuga Gongen genki-e,* 1309), I relate their scholarly proclivities with the intrinsic properties of the small scroll itself. Also examined is one small-scroll project on which Mitsunobu and Sanetaka collaborated from its inception. The scroll in question, *Clouds of Mt. Kōya* (1474–79), which was intended for the emperor, no longer survives; by tracing its production process as documented in Sanetaka's diary, however, it is possible to understand the manner in which small scrolls offered new spaces for the pictorialization of hybrid literary and pictorial genres.

The first of the three chapters on individual works, chapter 3, studies *A Wakeful Sleep*, a scroll by Mitsunobu depicting what appears to be a classical courtly romance. A close reading of the paintings and texts, however, reveals that the work takes an oblique and ambivalent

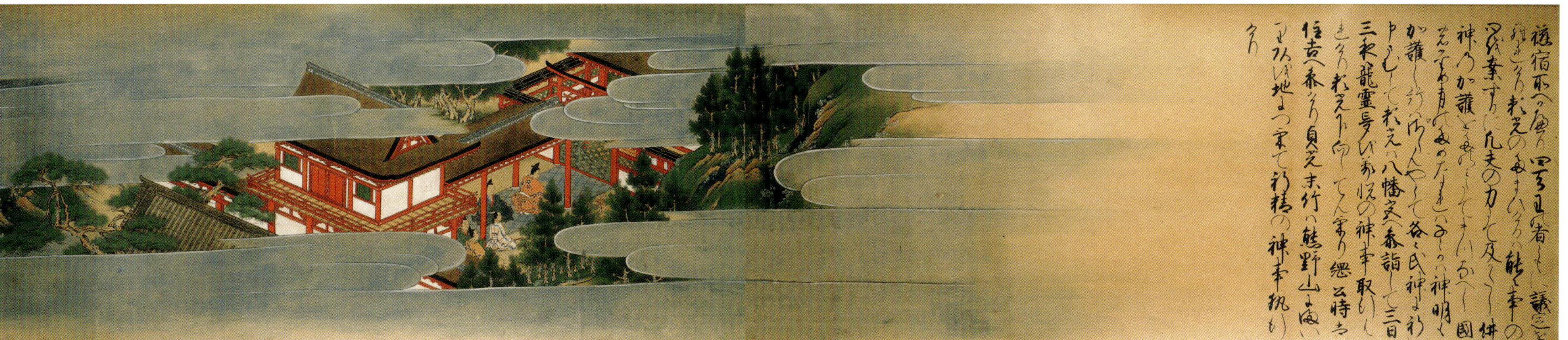

position toward tradition, revealed most dramatically in its subversion of numerous visual tropes that were by then entrenched in courtly picture making. This ambivalence, most evident in the young female protagonist, reflects the protocols of earlier genres upon which the scroll drew. In addition, I argue that *A Wakeful Sleep* can be understood as an allegory for patrilocal marital practice, newly prevalent among aristocrats in this period, and was possibly intended for Sanetaka's own daughter as she prepared to marry into the prestigious Kujō family.

In chapter 4, I examine *The Jizō Hall*, a work by Mitsunobu bearing Sanetaka's calligraphy. I explore the work's formal properties through an exposition of its sequential mode of pictorial representation and forms of visual experimentation with earlier conventions. These properties are linked to the literary structure of the accompanying tale, which appears to have been an expansive variation on the "tale of rebirth" (*ōjōden*), a distinct genre of Buddhist texts. Although the genre was thought to have died out by the fifteenth century, *The Jizō Hall* demonstrates its revival in the circle of Emperor GoTsuchimikado. Here it reemerges in narrativized form as a genre capable of accommodating simultaneously the subject positions of dissimilar court viewers. This capacity is most evident in the figure of the dragon woman, a benefactress who helps the monk-protagonist achieve awakening but who also seeks her own salvation.

Chapter 5 then examines *Breaking the Inkstone*, a work dated to 1495 and owned by the shogun Ashikaga Yoshizumi (1480–1511). I show that the scroll blends two distinct literary categories: the "acolyte tale" (*chigo monogatari*) and the "religious conversion" (*shukke*) tale. The pictorial and literary features associated with the acolyte tale were employed here to relate a story of self-sacrifice and loyalty by a young boy toward an older male figure. The entire scroll revolves around not only the inkstone of the title but other object motifs that are equal in significance to its cast of characters. It proceeds according to a complex strategy of metonymic representation whereby these objects frequently stand in for characters, and vice versa. This economy of representation and replacement lends itself to the effective narration of a story line charged with political and ideological importance, for Yoshizumi as well as for those who made up the community of readers around him. The most important figure in the production context of *Breaking the Inkstone*, Hosokawa Masamoto, appears to have commissioned the work for Yoshizumi and his own seven-year-old son, and traces of Masamoto's political and religious circumstances in the scroll itself provide insights into the spaces in which it circulated.

The epilogue discusses the fate of the small scroll in the sixteenth century and the reasons for its gradual disappearance. *Miraculous Origins of Hasedera*, a work painted around 1523 by Mitsunobu's son for a boy shogun, represents the continuation of a type of small-format handscroll that is simply a reduced-size version of larger scrolls. I also describe the process by which the small-format picture scroll was adopted by diverse communities to imagine literary texts in a more vernacular pictorial idiom. These later trends highlight the contingent nature of the short-story small-scroll genre, namely its dependence on a highly erudite milieu in which to achieve meaning and its ties to the historical circumstances of the post–Ōnin War generation.

1 A BRIEF HISTORY OF SMALL SCROLLS

> If any literary work is too long to be read at one sitting, we must be content to dispense with the immensely important effect derivable from unity of impression—for, if two sittings be required, the affairs of the world interfere, and every thing like totality is at once destroyed.
> —Edgar Allan Poe, *"The Philosophy of Composition," Graham's Magazine,* April 1846

During the medieval period in Japan a new type of narrative picture scroll emerged that dramatically reduced the size of the standard format. These scrolls typically measured half the height of the standard scroll and ranged from ten to roughly eighteen centimeters in height (fig. 9). More than fifty small scrolls dating to before 1600 survive today, the earliest one from the fourteenth century. It was not until the fifteenth century, however, that textual sources, primarily diaries, began to refer to *ko-e,* or "small scrolls" (literally, "small pictures"). Medieval diary entries rarely offer detailed descriptions of picture scrolls and typically list only a work's title, the number of scrolls in a set, and, occasionally, the collection from which the scroll emerged. When viewed against such limited documentation, the deliberate characterization of certain scrolls as "small" suggests an understanding that these works were distinct from their larger counterparts. The increase in the number of small scrolls in the fifteenth century thus coincides with a consciousness of the format as a separate category of handscroll. This awareness did not, however, simply concern the size of these works; indeed, small scrolls began to represent more than reduced-scale versions of traditional handscrolls. In the late fifteenth century a unique understanding emerged of the potential of small dimensions that would result in the birth of a new pictoliterary genre.

It was at this time, between the final years of the Ōnin War (1467–77) and the first quarter of the sixteenth century, that artists such as Tosa Mitsunobu and the circle of scholar-calligraphers and patrons with which he was acquainted transformed what had simply been a smaller alternative to the regular scroll format into a new pictoliterary mode of representation. In the hands of these individuals, small-format handscrolls departed from the conventional themes, representational practices, and functions that had characterized Japanese handscrolls throughout their six-hundred-year history. For the first time the format was paired with brief narratives, resulting in "short-story small scrolls." Nearly a dozen small scrolls from this period, by Mitsunobu and his studio or by unknown artists, demonstrate the ways in which the format became a space for literary and pictorial experimentation.

Many of the short stories illustrated in the small-scroll format were newly created literary works that shared several formal characteristics, the most important being a plot that revolves around a single dilemma faced by the protagonist. In contrast to the open-ended quality of many early Japanese narratives, specifically courtly ones, these tales arrive at a swift resolution in which the moral of the story reinforces the importance of a Buddhist path toward salvation. In a dramatic departure from earlier scrolls, painters such as Mitsunobu took advantage of the compact medium to present a condensed and intergeneric pictorialization of these tales, allowing the kind of unity of effect on the reader lauded by Poe in the quotation above. In both the text and images of short-story small scrolls, brevity itself is used to illustrate tales about the ephemerality of life. The result is a distinctive body of horizontal picture scrolls (*emaki*) that constitutes a brief but telling chapter in the history of painting and literature in premodern Japan.

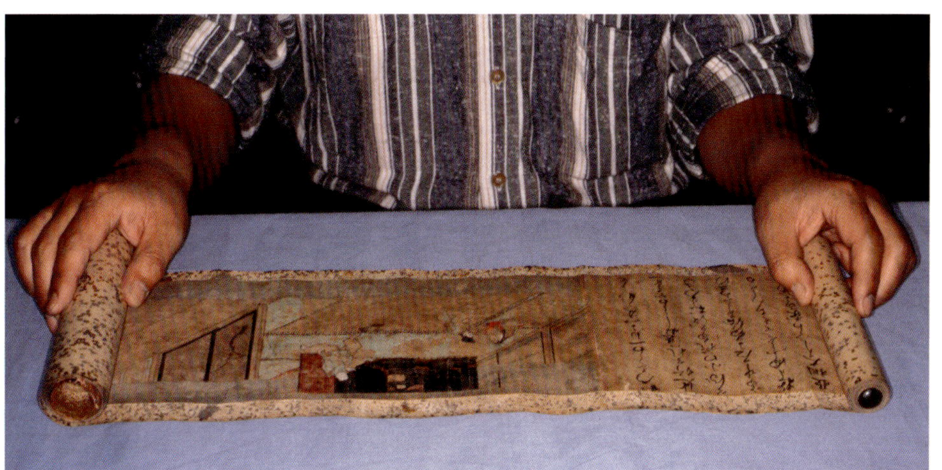

9 Reading the small scroll, *Breaking the Inkstone*. Photograph by the author.

FOURTEENTH-CENTURY EXAMPLES

Previous studies of small scrolls have examined them as a phenomenon of the fifteenth and sixteenth centuries without acknowledging any earlier examples, focusing instead on the perceived connection of small scrolls to adolescent readers in later years. In fact, the small scroll has a history prior to the Muromachi period, and the format clearly served a wide variety of functions throughout the medieval era. The history of the small scroll suggests that the format's origins have more to do with intimacy, informality, and personalization than with the age of the audience. A survey of the early examples will demonstrate the personal nature of *ko-e* and the degree to which later small scrolls by Mitsunobu represent a significant representational departure from the previous tradition.

The earliest extant dated *ko-e*, *Life of Prince Shōtoku* (*Shōtoku Taishi den-e*, 1324; figs. 10–11), illustrates in ten scrolls the entire biography of Shōtoku Taishi, the seventh-century statesman posthumously revered as the founder of Buddhism in Japan.[1] Measuring just 15.9 centimeters in height, the work provides a compact version of sixty-four episodes from Shōtoku's life, represented in polished polychrome paintings.[2] Unlike the small scrolls of later vintage, the paintings of *Life of Prince Shōtoku* do not accommodate either individual compositions or overall pictorial structure to the frame of the small format. Rather, these paintings resemble standard-size works at a reduced scale. Battle scenes, for example, are panoramic and employ a fore-, middle, and background (fig. 10). Other paintings project a sense of great distance across bodies of water or misty valleys and mountaintops (fig. 11). This segmentation of depth within a limited pictorial field was avoided in the later

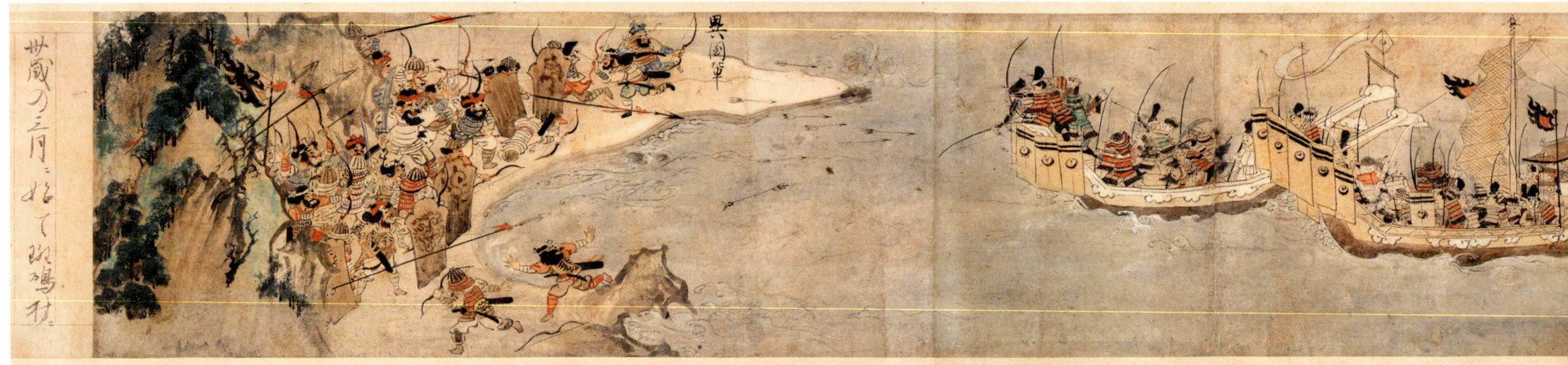

10 *Life of Prince Shōtoku* (*Shōtoku Taishi den-e*). Fourteenth century. Ten scrolls; ink and color on paper, H. 15.9 cm. Private collection. Detail, scroll 6.

11 *Life of Prince Shōtoku* (*Shōtoku Taishi den-e*). Fourteenth century. Ten scrolls; ink and color on paper, H. 15.9 cm. Private collection. Detail, scroll 10.

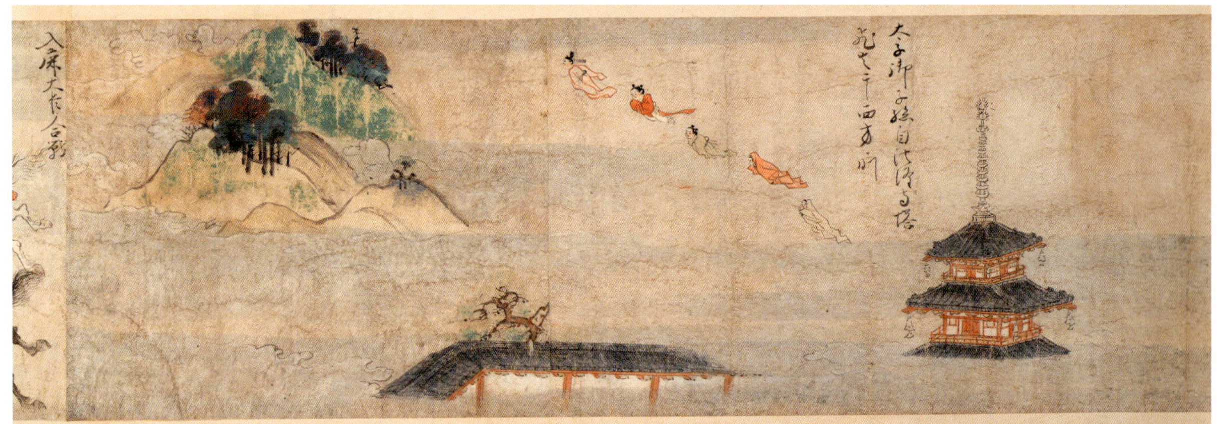

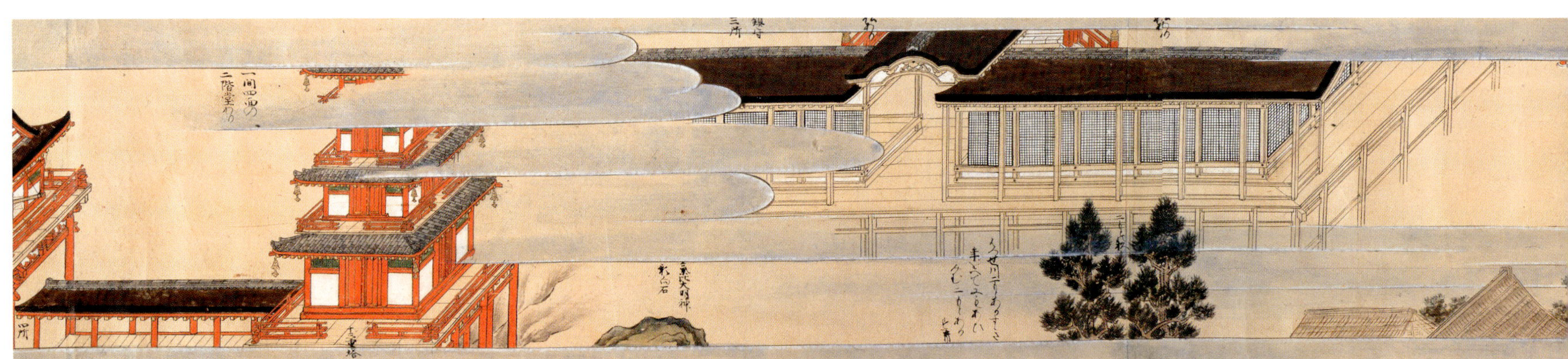

12 Tosa Mitsumochi (1496–ca. 1559), *Miraculous Origins of Hasedera* (*Hasedera engi emaki*). Six handscrolls; ink, color, and gold on paper, H. 17.9. Hasedera, Nara Prefecture.

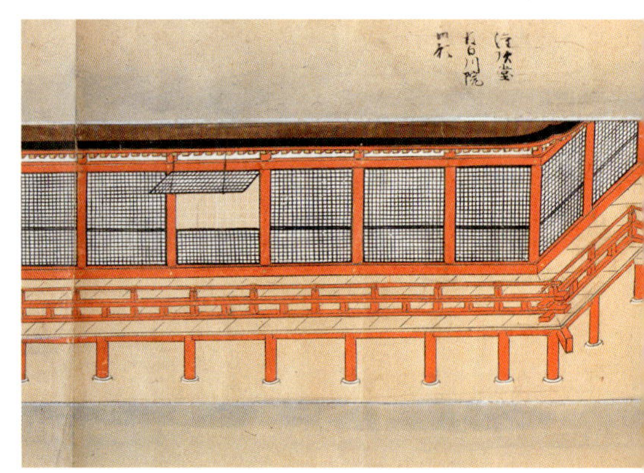

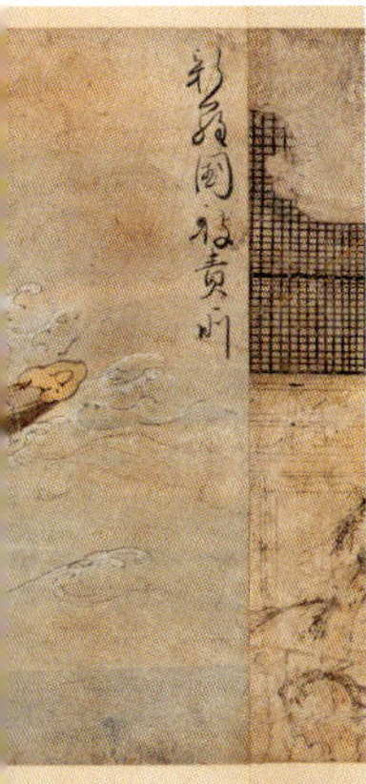

small scrolls associated with Mitsunobu, where the focal point is strategically confined to the foreground and where distance or depth of field is merely intimated.

Life of Prince Shōtoku is an early example of a *ko-e* apparently created in order to make a lengthy work more manageable for its reader. This functional aspect of *ko-e* never went out of favor; unabridged versions of long texts in the small format continue to appear into the fifteenth and sixteenth centuries. In *Miraculous Origins of Hasedera* (ca. 1523) for example, the artist Tosa Mitsumochi (active ca. 1522–69), son of Tosa Mitsunobu, included all thirty-three episodes of the Hasedera origin legend.[3] This small-format work consists of six scrolls that were copied from a large, three-scroll version.[4] Rather than abbreviating the architectural imagery, paring down the number of figures, reducing motifs, or otherwise employing more suggestive ways to convey meaning—all techniques common to Mitsunobu's small scrolls—Mitsumochi's paintings are all-inclusive (fig. 12). In terms of the representation of architecture, for example, the paintings include buildings in their entirety and an abundance of rooftops, conjuring up a sense of panorama exceeding that of even larger-format versions of the same subject.

The other two extant examples of small-format scrolls from the fourteenth century were executed in the ink-line (literally "white drawing," *hakubyō*) mode, a mode of representation crucial to the development of the small format. *Heike Courtiers* (*Heike kindachi sōshi emaki*) illustrates various anecdotes about members of the Taira clan during the brief period in the late twelfth century when the family ruled the country and held sway over the imperial court.[5] *Recollections of In no Dainagon* (*In no Dainagon ekotoba*) depicts courtiers conversing about courtly events.[6] The pairing of *hakubyō* paintings and small scrolls exemplified by these two works was well suited for two reasons. First, the *hakubyō* mode, which forgoes the complicated process of color application, was often associated with amateur, rather than professional, artists. A number of *hakubyō* paintings are attributed to courtiers and court ladies, suggesting that the paintings were the products of private salons. Most early *hakubyō* handscrolls from the thirteenth and fourteenth centuries are smaller than other handscrolls and measure between twenty-three and twenty-five centimeters in height.[7] The genre's most famous examples, such as *Lord Takafusa's Love Songs* (*Takafusa-kyō tsuyakotoba emaki*), *Resplendent Light*

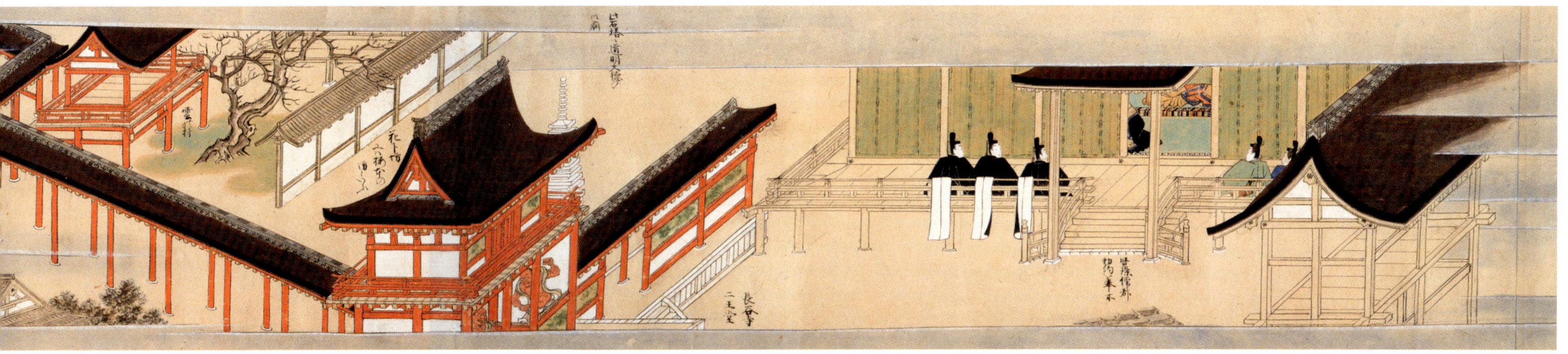

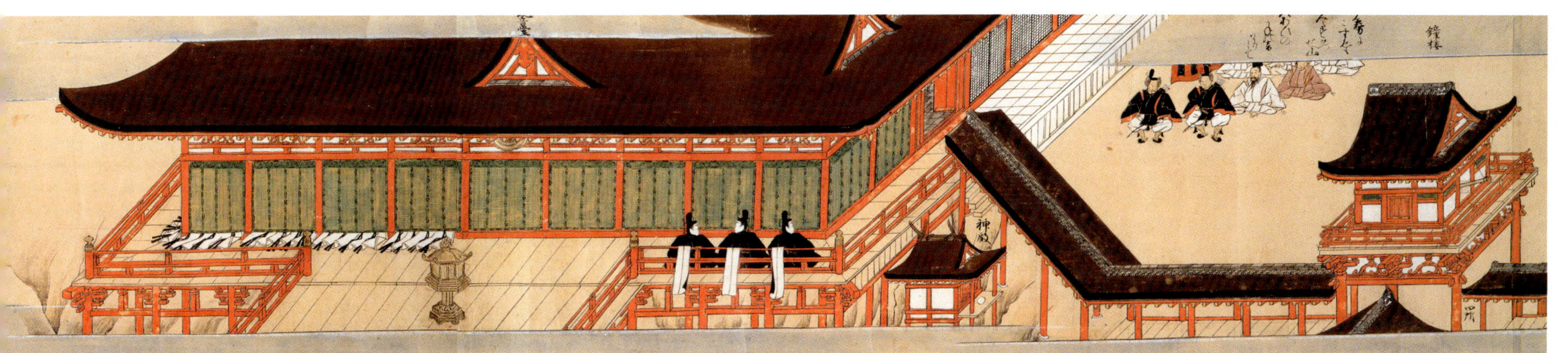

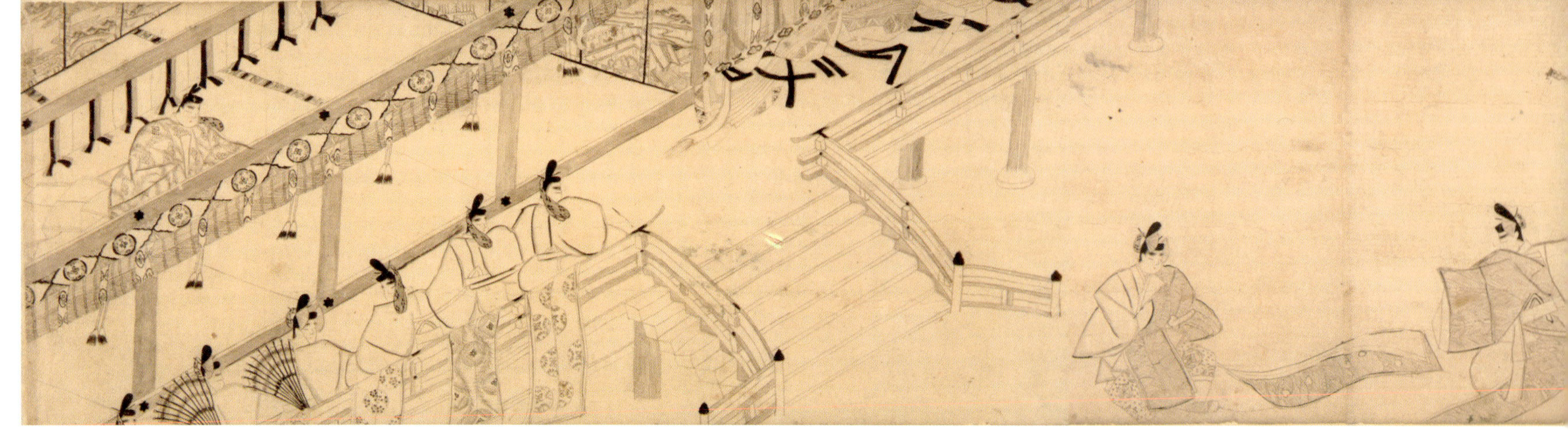

13 *Heike Courtiers* (*Heike kindachi sōshi emaki*). Fourteenth century. One scroll; ink on paper, 16.0 x 622.7 cm. Fukuoka Art Museum, Matsunaga Collection.

(*Toyo no akari-e sōshi*), and the *Pillow Book* (*Makura no sōshi ekotoba*), all fall within this range. These *hakubyō* narrative scrolls most commonly depict scenes of a perceived golden era of court life and are characterized by a nostalgic tone. The ink-line mode itself, with its fine, gossamer outlines, contributes to the dreamlike quality of the evanescent, bygone era being depicted.

Second, like their more famous ink-line counterparts, early *ko-e* in the *hakubyō* mode tend to represent a celebrated courtly past through the literary device of personal recollection. When the small-scale scroll emerged as a pictorial option, it must have seemed an appropriate medium for *hakubyō* works, in keeping with the aura of intimacy and connotations of the amateur painter that surrounded these monochrome depictions of courtly themes. In *Heike Courtiers*, one of the protagonists in the story narrates several of the episodes as a remembrance of things past.[8] In a striking contrast to the sense of impending doom surrounding the Taira clan's downfall in *Tales of the Heike* (*Heike monogatari*, mid–thirteenth century), the vignettes in the small scroll focus on the sanguine courtly activities of the Taira as they engage in life at the imperial palace. The first illustration (fig. 13) depicts Taira no Koremori's performance of the "Waves of the Blue Sea" dance at the celebration of Emperor GoShirakawa's fiftieth birthday, which was said to remind all of the Shining Genji's famous performance of the same dance in the "Beneath the Autumn Leaves" chapter of *The Tale of Genji*. The account of Koremori's dance in the small scroll differs dramatically from that found in *The Tales of the Heike*, in which the same performance is described in the con- text of a poignant remembrance of Koremori's fleeting life at court just before he takes his own life.[9] Likewise, Taira Shigehira, infamous for his violent siege of Nara in 1180, which led to the destruction of Tōdaiji's colossal state of Vairocana, appears in *Heike Courtiers* as the instigator of a lighthearted prank; he and Fujiwara no Takafusa break into the ladies' quarters of the imperial palace disguised as robbers and steal the women's robes, only to return them the next day (fig. 14). This monochrome small scroll thus casts the characters from *The Tales of the Heike* as debonair members of a fanciful courtly world, told through the language of recollection.

Stylistically, *Heike Courtiers* closely resembles other works from the Kamakura period (1185–1333) executed in the *hakubyō* mode, displaying the most salient features of the genre such as the emphatic representation of the long flowing hair of the female figures, depicted with glossy black ink, and an elaboration of the details of interior décor. Yet even though it measures a mere sixteen centimeters in height, the work does not tailor its compositions to a narrow pictorial field. Instead, relatively panoramic views of exteriors appear as they would in a scroll of standard size. The scene of Koremori's dance encompasses a view of a veranda filled with female spectators on the right and another veranda and

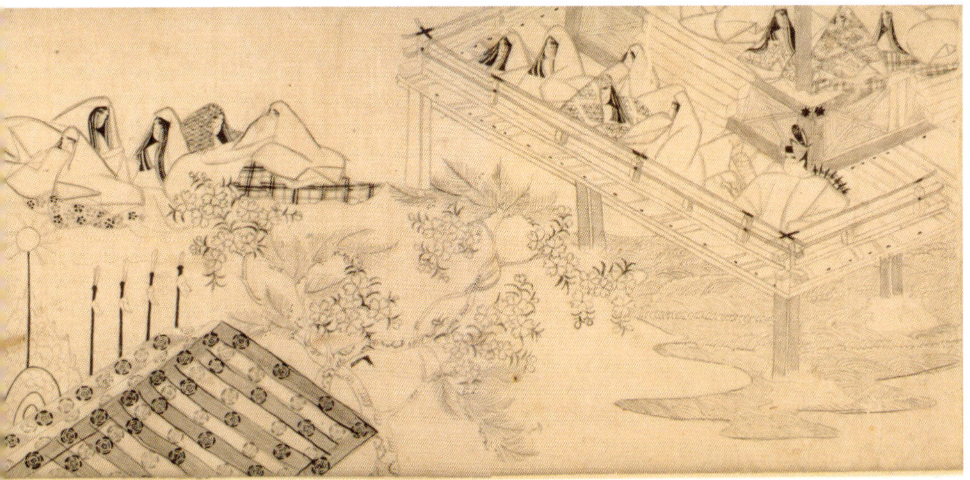

14 *Heike Courtiers* (*Heike kindachi sōshi emaki*). Detail.

15 *Recollections of In no Dainagon* (*In no Dainagon ekotoba*). Fourteenth century. One of two scrolls; ink on paper, 19.2 x 107.3 cm. Fukuoka Art Museum, Matsunaga Collection.

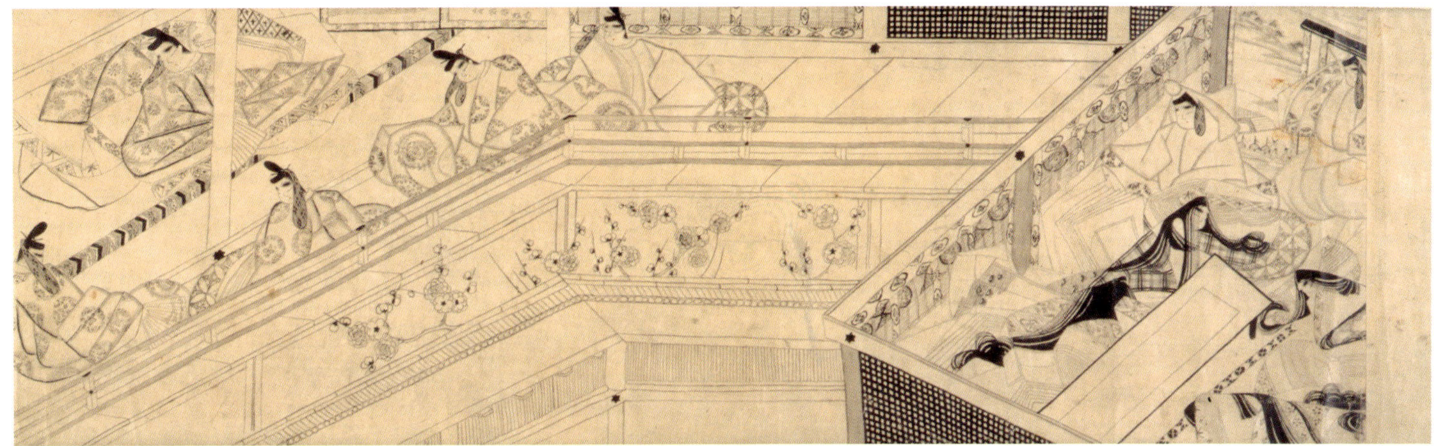

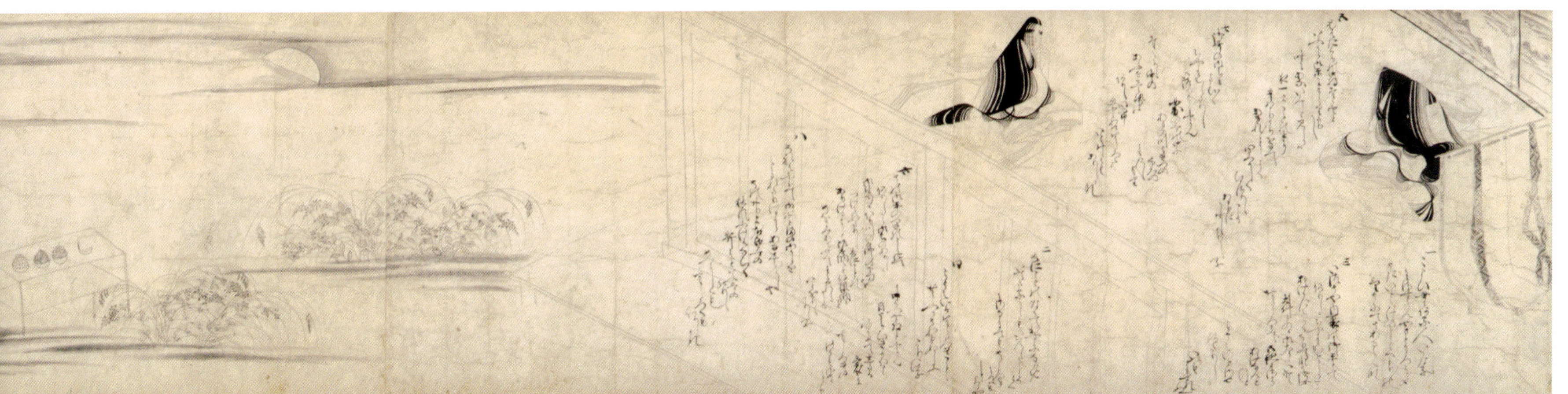

an interior view of the imperial palace on the left. In the middle stands the musicians' tent and Koremori in midperformance, all viewed from a high perspective. The interior scenes afford a bird's-eye view into the rooms of the ladies-in-waiting through the "blown-off roof" (*fukinuki yatai*) technique, a staple of the handscroll tradition, replicating the compositions of larger scrolls.

Recollections of In no Dainagon (*In no Dainagon ekotoba*, 1326–32) similarly reminisces about courtly life through the words of characters who possess intimate knowledge of its events. Here the text is inscribed on the surface of the paintings and takes the form of dialogues between court ladies (fig. 15) or male courtiers (fig. 16). On a moonlit night the men reflect back on a poetry gathering held by Emperor GoDaigo (1288–1339) in 1321

16 *Recollections of In no Dainagon* (*In no Dainagon ekotoba*). Fourteenth century. One of two scrolls; ink on paper, 19.2 x 80.4 cm. Fukuoka Art Museum, Matsunaga Collection.

and the highlights of the occasion: the emperor's poetic composition, the tears shed in response to it by the participants, and Tanba Tadamori's spontaneous dance of joy after his poem was praised by the celebrated poet Nijō Tameyo (1250–1338).[10] The women, depicted against a backdrop of the Tanabata festival, also reminisce about court gatherings, both poetic and musical, and comment on the performances of particular individuals. Singled out for praise is the beautiful voice of Minister of the Left Tōin Saneyasu (d. 1327) as he sang a poem during an evening of musical entertainment at the palace, and for criticism, Fujiwara Fuyusada's contorted expression as he attempted to regale his audience with song.

Recollections of In no Dainagon adopts the authorial conceit of an eyewitness to the events mentioned in the dialogues, which are cast in the nostalgic tone of someone who can no longer visit the palace. The melancholy mood of the dialogues and the work's small format and simple drawings suggest a kind of personal sketchbook.[11] The sparse images in and of themselves suggest very little, but when experienced through the words exchanged, they become thoroughly infused with the atmosphere of bygone events at GoDaigo's court. In this case the small-format scroll provides an intimate space for the communication of reminiscences and "inside conversations" about male and female courtiers prominent in the early fourteenth century. The priority for these compositions, therefore, is to accommodate the inscription of dialogue.

Although *Heike Courtiers* and *Recollections of In no Dainagon* are the only extant small scrolls in the *hakubyō* mode from the fourteenth century, references to other early *ko-e* can be found in medieval diaries. Sanjōnishi Sanetaka (1455–1537) recorded viewing a three-scroll *ko-e* of Sei Shōnagon's *Pillow Book* (*Makura no sōshi*) executed in the ink-line mode, the texts of which he read aloud for Emperor GoTsuchimikado (1442–1500).[12] In addition to praising the work as "marvelous," Sanetaka noted that the scrolls were by an "ancient hand" (*kojin hisseki*), a characterization typically reserved for works dating from the previous century or earlier.[13] Another early small scroll is referred to by the Fushimi prince Sadafusa in his diary: "Today I received a small picture in one scroll from the imperial palace. It was by the brush of Lay Monk Former Minister Tōin and depicted the annual courtly events of the twelfth month. I was told that it had been commissioned by the emperor. Never before had I seen the brush traces of Lord Tōin."[14] In this entry Sadafusa expresses excitement at encountering the brush traces of the well-known courtier Tōin Kinkata (1291–1360), who served the emperors of the Northern Court in the early fourteenth century, among them Sadafusa's grandfather, Emperor Sukō (r. 1349–51). Kinkata was renowned for his treatises on court protocol, and the small scroll must have been a valuable example of this genre, preserving for posterity imperial ceremonies of the past.[15] Illustrated scrolls had been crucial for documenting ceremony and precedent since at least the late twelfth century; GoShirakawa (1127–93) commissioned *Annual Court Events* (*Nenjū gyōji emaki*) as part of his

initiative to reinstate court ceremonies in the wake of the Hōgen and Heiji Disturbances.[16] GoShirakawa's set is thought to have originally encompassed sixty scrolls that were extra tall in height.[17]

The unusually large scale of GoShirakawa's *Annual Court Events* scrolls renders the diminutive scale of the Kinkata scroll all the more conspicuous. The latter's dimensions, however, can be related to Kinkata's authorship of manuals on protocol. These were likely passed down as secret texts intended to provide certain privileged families with a specialized knowledge of court protocol that would ensure their continued prominence at court. The small scale may have been appropriate for a cherished family treasure in light of its anticipated limited viewership. And while Sadafusa's account provides no details about the pictorial properties of the scroll, if the courtier Kinkata was both artist and calligrapher of the work, he most likely executed it in the ink-line mode.

None of the five known examples of early small scrolls discussed thus far illustrate short tales, nor do the extant examples employ a visual vocabulary that distinguishes them from standard-format handscrolls. *Heike Courtiers* transposes the classical pictorial vocabulary of the *hakubyō* genre onto the small format rather than responding to the limitations of the pictorial field in an inventive manner. In *Recollections of In no Dainagon* the texts and images are more symbiotic, as the images shape the dialogues and provide figures for the voices that articulate the text. The scroll's relationship to the small format is found in its nature as a private, amateur work. *Life of Prince Shōtoku* defies the small space of the format to present sweeping vistas and grand battle scenes. The subject matter of the two other recorded scrolls, the one depicting courtly events and the *Pillow Book*, would argue against their role as precedents for short-story small scrolls as well. The former was no doubt created to convey as much factual information about court ceremony as possible and thus would not have been motivated to explore an elliptic visual language. As a series of short, separate vignettes, the *Pillow Book* would not have exhibited the unilinear narrative characteristic of later small scrolls. In this early phase, the small format did not seem to function as a space for the representation of short narratives.

Already latent in the small-format picture scroll of the fourteenth century, however, is a sense of the quality of viewing experience entrusted to this medium. The large number of small scrolls executed in the ink-line mode, for example, is striking. Aside from *Life of Prince Shōtoku* and possibly the courtly events scroll, all of the fourteenth-century small scrolls examined above were executed in monochrome. This suggests that the small format was already conceptualized as an informal space appropriate for the representation of texts that strike a personal and nostalgic tone and for the work of nonprofessional artists. There is, in other words, an emerging link between private reading and ownership and the small format. This association would become fundamental once the format was paired with the short story.

LARGE SCROLLS AND SHORT NARRATIVES

While small-format handscrolls provided a precedent for the scale of late medieval small scrolls, other types of *emaki* offered equally important precedents as pictorializations of short narratives. A group of scrolls from the twelfth and thirteenth centuries known as "short-tale picture scrolls" (*setsuwa emaki*) pictorialize sequences of relatively brief texts. Many of these handscroll texts were lifted from larger compilations of tale literature, or *setsuwashū*. To understand the unique properties of small scrolls, it is important to consider *setsuwa emaki* and to understand how their short narratives and illustrations differ from those of later medieval *ko-e*.

Two of the most celebrated scrolls of the handscroll tradition, and indeed of the history of Japanese painting, *Miraculous Origins of Mt. Shigi* (*Shigisan engi emaki*) and *Major Counselor Ban* (*Ban Dainagon ekotoba*), were derived from early short-tale anthologies. Both stories appear in *A Collection of Tales from Uji* (*Uji shūi monogatari*, early thirteenth century), while the story represented in the *Mt. Shigi* scrolls also appears in *Old Collection of Tales* (*Kohon setsuwashū*, twelfth century).[18] The texts of these famous Heian period (794–1185) *emaki* were singled out for illustration from among a large

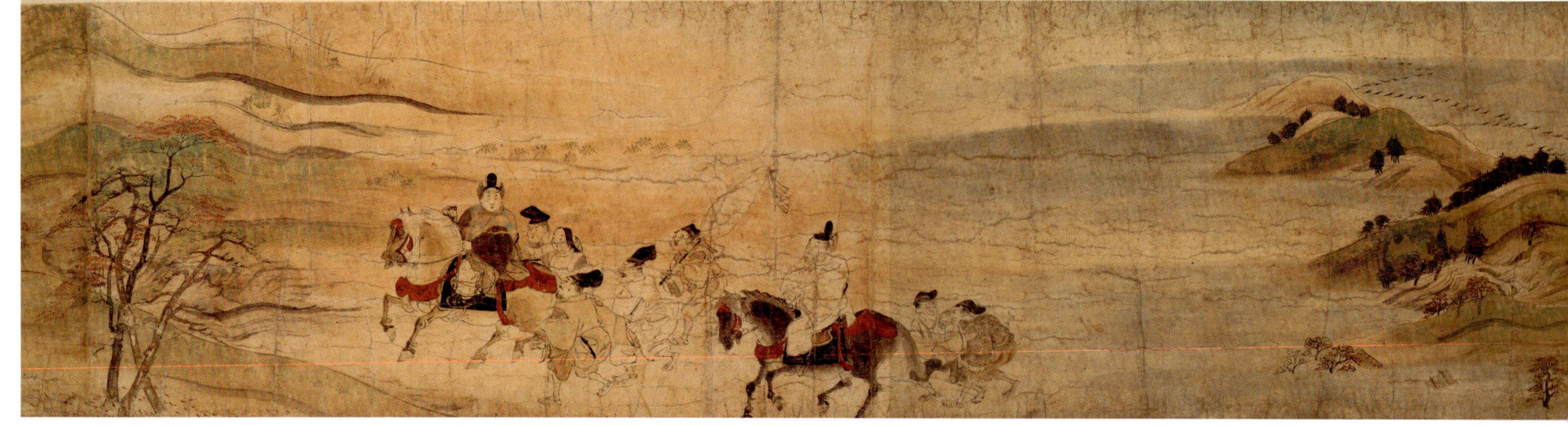

17 *Miraculous Origins of Mt. Shigi* (*Shigisan engi emaki*). Twelfth century. Three scrolls; ink and color on paper, 31.7 x 897.9 cm. Chōgosonshiji, Nara Prefecture. National Treasure. Detail, scroll 2.

number of tales in these collections.[19] Although some later small scrolls also draw from anthologies, the kinds of narratives selected for large and small scrolls were quite different; the Heian period scrolls illustrate stories of greater complexity, multiple story lines, and larger casts of characters.

Both *Miraculous Origins of Mt. Shigi* and *Major Counselor Ban* contain at least three story lines, which are presented sequentially in the illustrations.[20] The *Mt. Shigi* scrolls relate three separate episodes, each compelling in its own way. There is the story of the monk Myōren's miraculous alms bowl, which elevates a storehouse off its foundation, forcing its miserly owner to donate the building to the monk; the second tale tells of Myōren's supernatural ability to heal the ailing emperor by sending a deity to the palace; and the third relates the story of an old nun, Myōren's sister, and her journey in search of her long-lost brother, whom she discovers with the help of the Great Buddha at Tōdaiji (fig. 4). Expansive, contiguous pictorial fields illustrate these three tales and embellish them with details, from magnificent panoramic landscape scenery (fig. 17) to women washing clothes, workers in fields, and the minutiae of everyday village life.

Although the tale of *Major Counselor Ban* about the arson of the Ōten Gate at the imperial palace (fig. 18) is a short one, its telling requires a host of characters to move the plot forward. Major Counselor Ban is revealed to be the arsonist, for example, only through an episode involving secondary characters of lower rank and their sons: when a steward to Counselor Ban mercilessly beats a young boy who has gotten into a scuffle with his own son, the injured boy's father, who happens to have witnessed Ban setting fire to the Ōten Gate, retaliates by exposing him. The angered father relates his eyewitness account of the crime and takes the reader back in time to the night of the fire, beyond the temporal frame of the illustrations. Meanwhile, the representation of the trials and ultimate redemption of the courtier wrongly accused of the crime, Minamoto no Makoto, occupies a substantial portion of the work. In this way, both *Major Counselor Ban* and *Miraculous Origins of Mt. Shigi* illustrate compact tales, but ones that involve a multitude of characters and a certain complexity and thickness of action.

Another Heian period scroll illustrating a tale from a *setsuwa* collection, *Minister Kibi's Trip to China* (*Kibi Daijin nittō emaki*), comes closest to the narrative structure of a short-story *ko-e* by focusing on a solitary protagonist and a single plotline. The scroll narrates the story of an eighth-century minister who travels to the Tang capital and passes a variety of intellectual tests posed by his Chinese hosts, including an interrogation on his knowledge of the sixth-century anthology of Chinese literature *Wen xuan* and his skill at the game

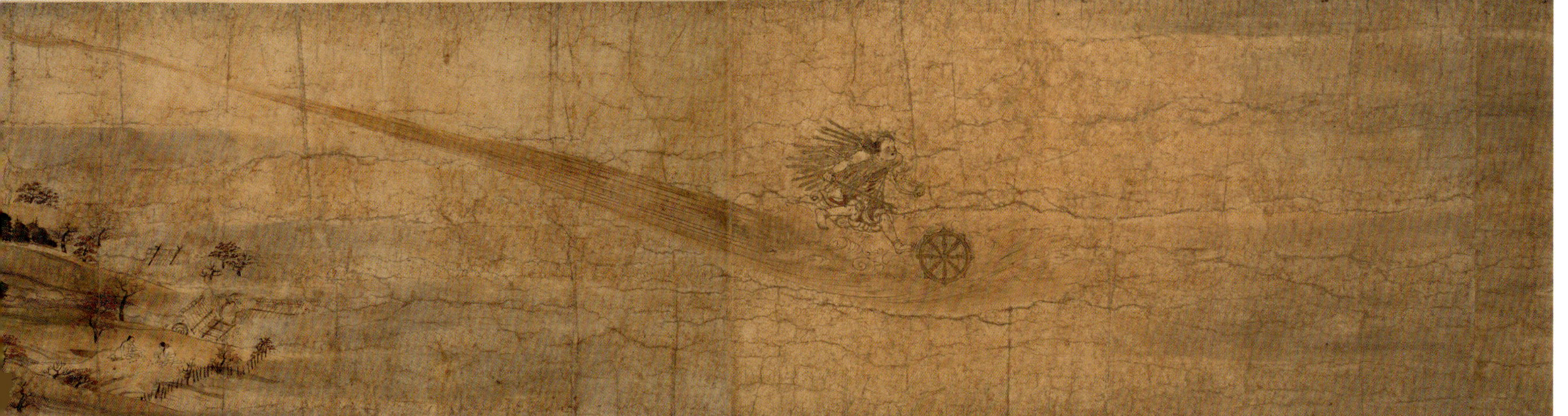

of *go*, and then returns victorious to his homeland. The scroll begins with an image of Minister Kibi arriving on the mainland.[21] From that point each of his encounters is imagined according to the same general compositional template. Thus, the viewer sees a series of identical architectural structures—tall tower, palace gate, and palace interior—repeated in each of the six painting sections of the scroll (fig. 19). The relentless pictorial repetition complements the narrative premise in which Chinese officials present Kibi with one intellectual challenge after another in an effort to outwit him, only to be outwitted themselves by this remarkable envoy from Japan.

In *Minister Kibi's Trip to China* the emphasis on a single protagonist overcoming obstacles against long odds resembles the narrative structure of several later small-scroll tales, such as *The Jizō Hall*, *Breaking the Inkstone*, and *A Wakeful Sleep*, as well as *Tale of the Fox* and other scrolls attributed to Tosa Mitsunobu. All of these *ko-e* are moved forward by the process of overcoming a predicament or a series of trials. In the majority of these pictorial tales, however, a religious epiphany is the device by which the narrative achieves resolution; the protagonist either takes the tonsure or comes to realize the power of a particular Buddhist deity through his or her awareness of the transience of human existence. These closures constitute something of an ethos of small-scroll narratives and, while found in early *setsuwa* as well, were not pictorialized in the Heian period. The illustrated *setsuwa* tales from the twelfth century conclude with grander events—the successful establishment of a Buddhist temple (*Mt. Shigi*), the resolution of a wrongful accusation (*Major Counselor Ban*), and the triumphant return of a Japanese minister from China (*Kibi*)—and transcend their origins as didactic anthologized tales. The *setsuwa* of Heian period handscrolls also tend to focus in some way on life at court. While the very premise of the *Ban* tale is rooted in court intrigue, both *Major Counselor Ban* and *Miraculous Origins of Mt. Shigi* feature prominent scenes of the emperor's private residence, the Seiryōden (Hall of Cool and Refreshing Breezes) of the imperial palace. Minister Kibi is of course a representative of the Japanese court, and that work too presents the viewer with palace images, albeit the palace of the Chinese court.

Large-format picture scrolls of *setsuwa* literature continued to be popular during the thirteenth and fourteenth centuries and also maintained their emphasis on the imperial court. A notable example is *Imperial Visit to View the Snows of Ono* (*Ono no yukimi gokō emaki*, late thirteenth century), the text of which appears in the *setsuwa* collection *Stories Selected to Illustrate Ten Maxims* (*Jikkinshō*, 1252).[22] Grouped with other tales that illustrate the maxim "Carefully Consider Everything," this story relates how an imperial guard informed the former empress Yoshiko (1021–1102), who was living in seclusion in Ono, of an impending visit by Emperor Shirakawa (1053–1129) to view the famous snowscape there. Although lacking in resources, the former empress managed to provide the emperor with a proper recep-

18 *Major Counselor Ban* (*Ban Dainagon ekotoba*). Twelfth century. Three scrolls; ink and color on paper, H. 31.5 cm. Idemitsu Museum of Arts, Tokyo. National Treasure. Detail, scroll 1.

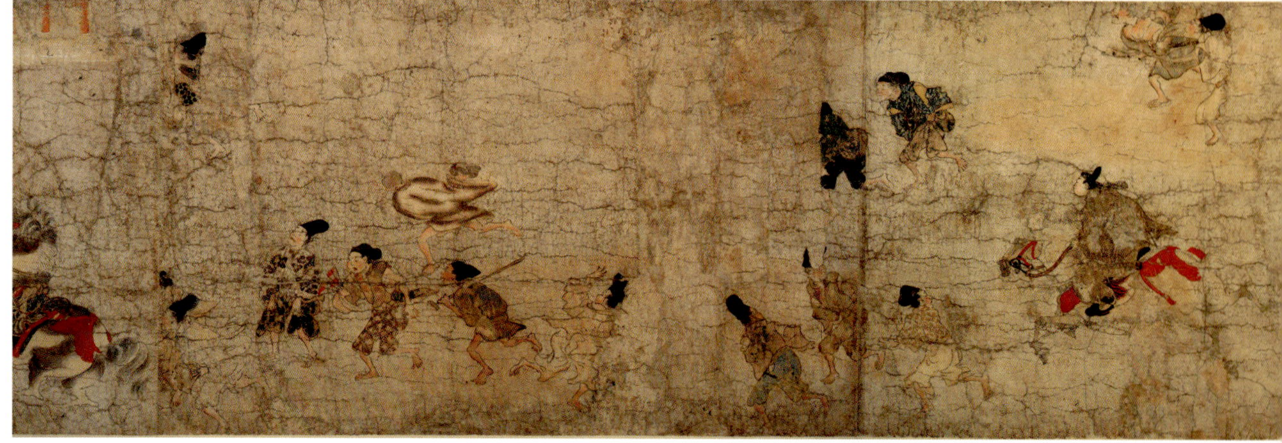

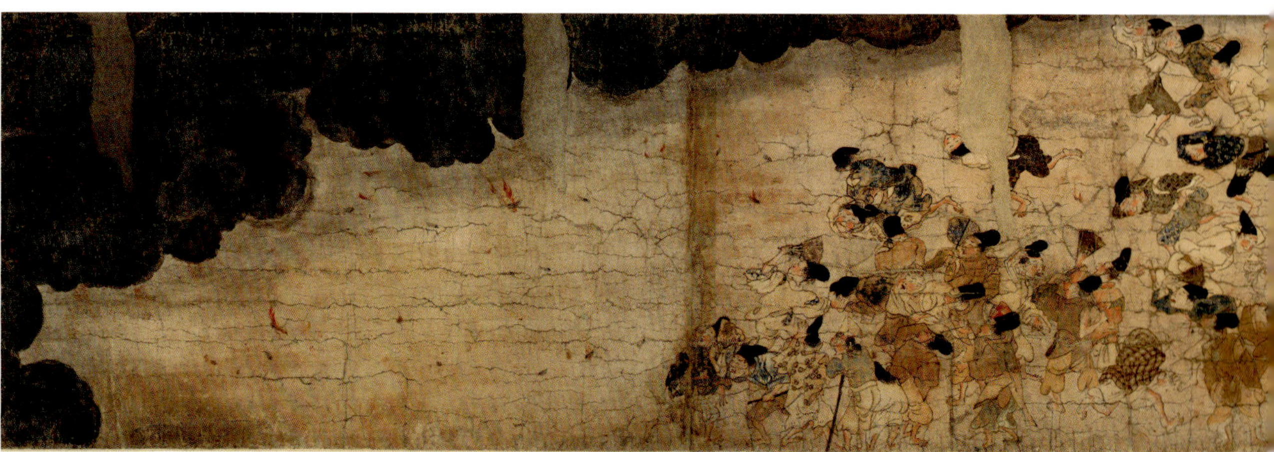

19 *Minister Kibi's Trip to China* (*Kibi Daijin nittō emaki*). Late twelfth century. Four handscrolls; ink, color, and gold on paper, H. 32.0 cm. Museum of Fine Arts, Boston. William Sturgis Bigelow Collection, 1932. Photograph © 2009 Museum of Fine Arts, Boston. Detail, scroll 3.

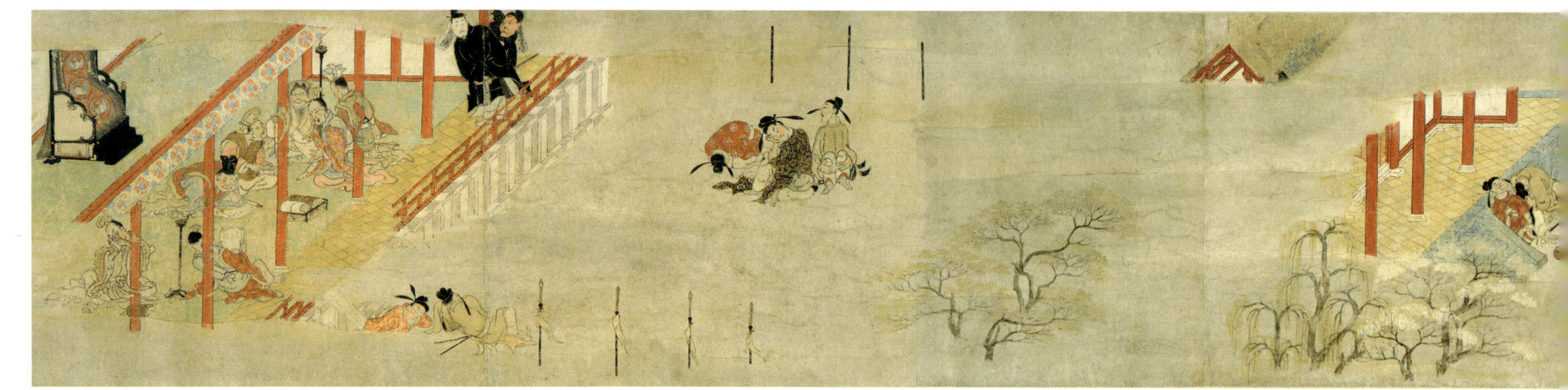

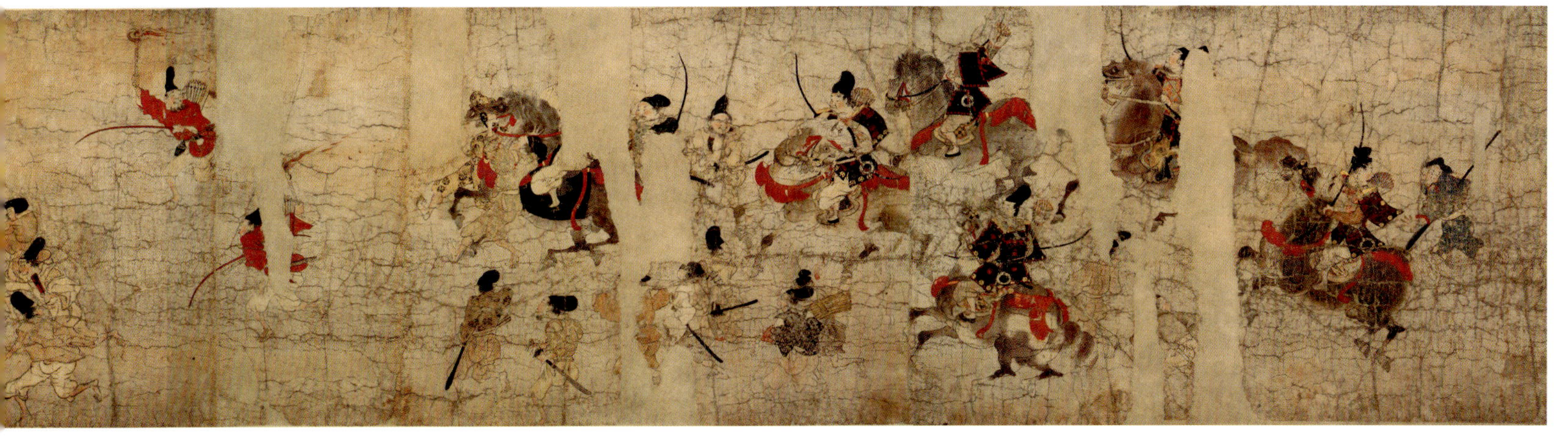

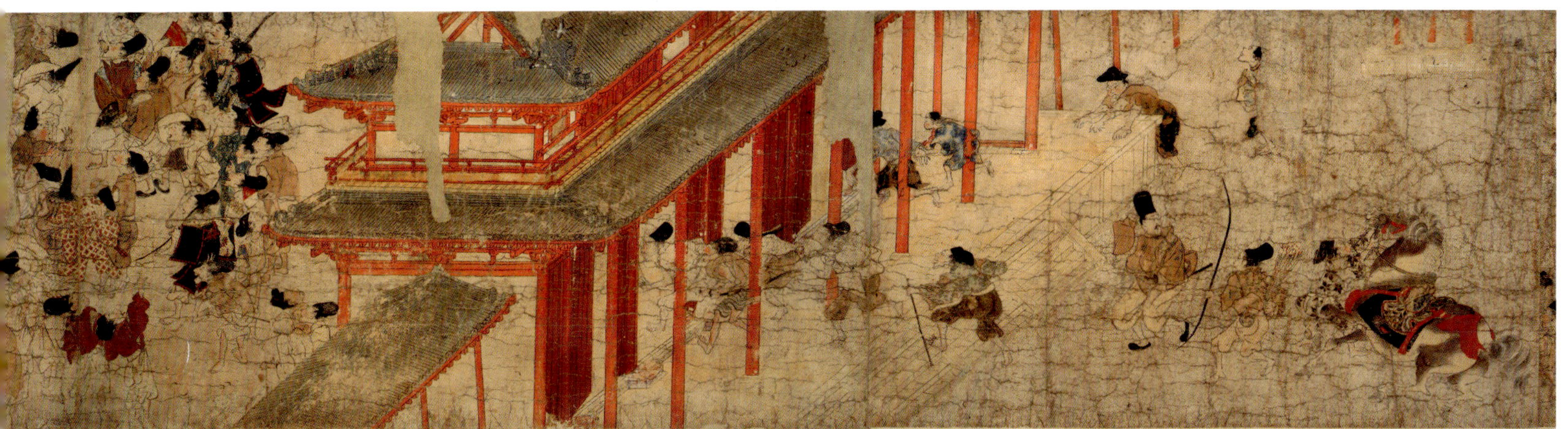

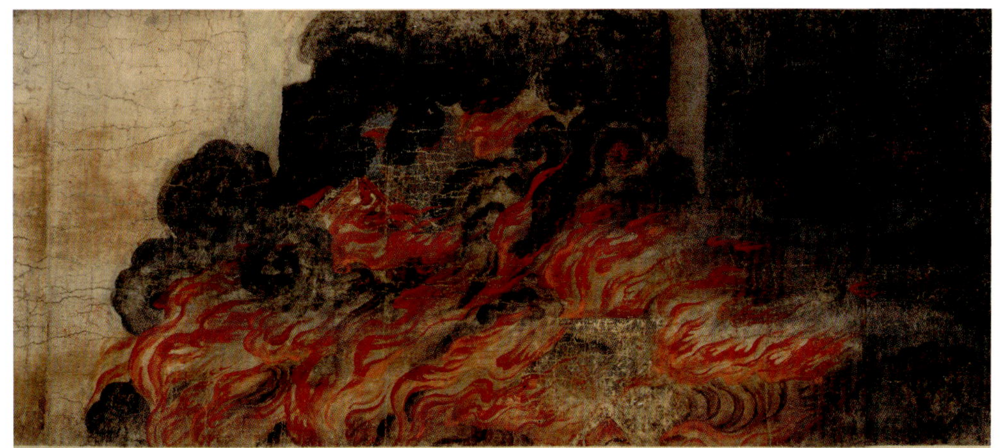

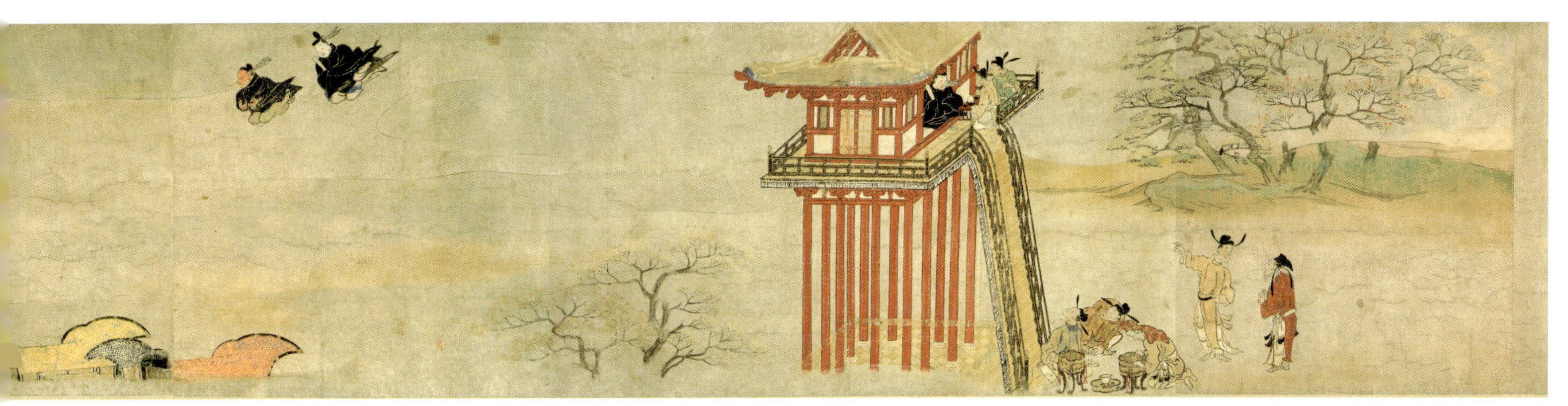

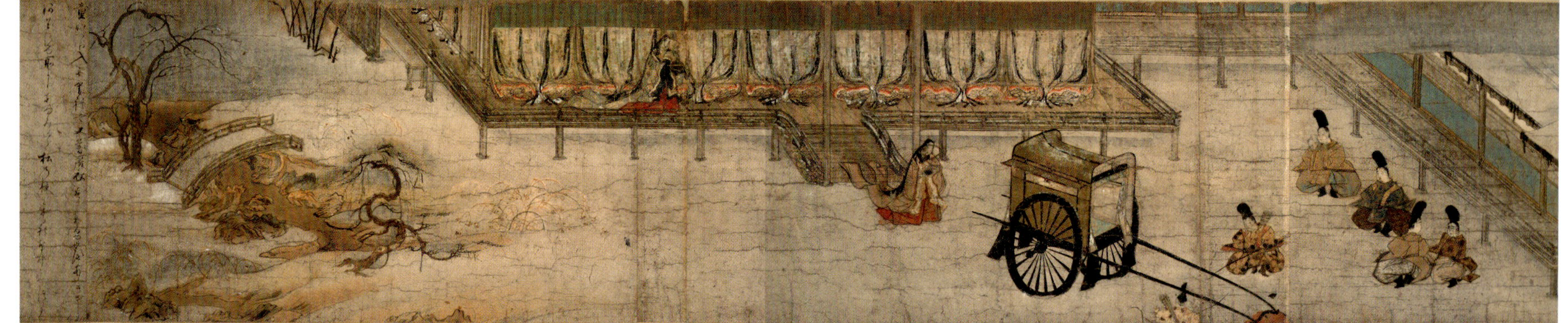

20 *Imperial Visit to View the Snows of Ono* (*Ono no yukimi gokō emaki*). Thirteenth century. One handscroll; ink and color on paper, 29.1 x 854.8 cm. the Tokyo University of the Arts. Important Cultural Property.

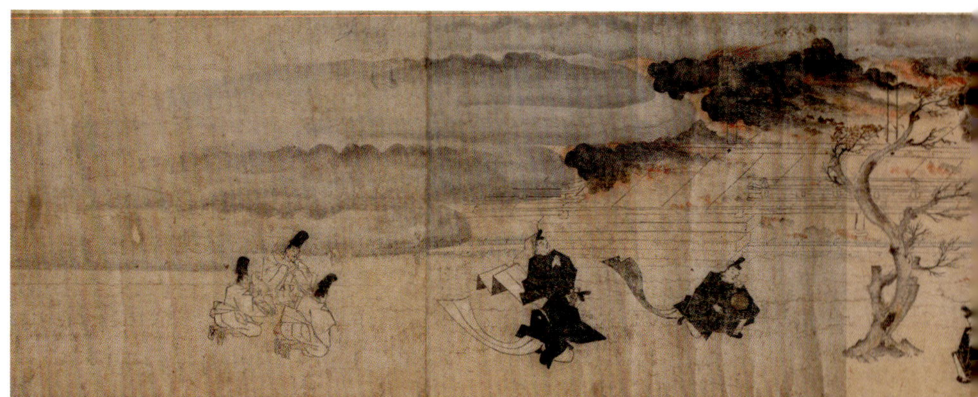

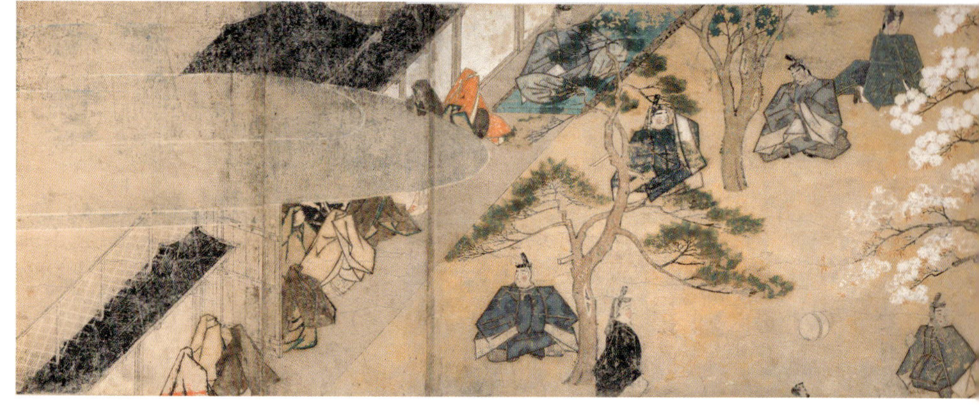

tion, including the all-important "display of robes" (*uchide*), for which she chopped up the meager robes in her possession to create the appearance of full garments flowing out from beneath the blinds (fig. 20). The emperor was so pleased that he rewarded her with a parcel of land, which she then promptly bestowed upon the thoughtful guard who had warned her of the imperial visit. Both the former empress and the guardsman exemplify the above-mentioned maxim by exercising prudent forethought. The painting, however, emphasizes above all else the imperial presence. The emperor's procession en route to Ono encompasses the longest painting passage in the scroll, and his representation is privileged to the point of redundancy, as two virtually identical paintings depict his reception at the empress's abode.[23]

Naomoto's Memorial to the Throne (*Naomoto mōshibumi ekotoba*, late thirteenth century) weaves together two separate *setsuwa* into one scroll to illustrate instances of imperial grace.[24] The scroll relates how the courtier Tachibana Naomoto authored a petition to Emperor Murakami (926–67) seeking an elevation in rank. Although he had the final copy brushed by the celebrated calligrapher Ono no Michikaze (894–966), Naomoto's pedestrian language infuriated the emperor. No one spoke of the matter again for fear of the emperor's wrath, but when the palace burned in the year 960, the emperor inquired as to whether Naomoto's petition had been safely removed, an action that the people of the time are said to have found "most elegant."[25] The picture scroll depicts the palace fire but also uses it as the backdrop for another *setsuwa*. During the same fire, so the reader is told, the building that housed the sacred mirror—one of the three sacred symbols of imperial rule—burned to the ground. The mirror was feared to have been destroyed, but Fujiwara Saneyori (900–970) spotted it shimmering in the branches of the cherry tree in front of the Shishinden (Ceremonial Hall) and prayed to Amaterasu, whereupon the sacred mirror flew down from the tree into his open sleeve (fig. 21).[26]

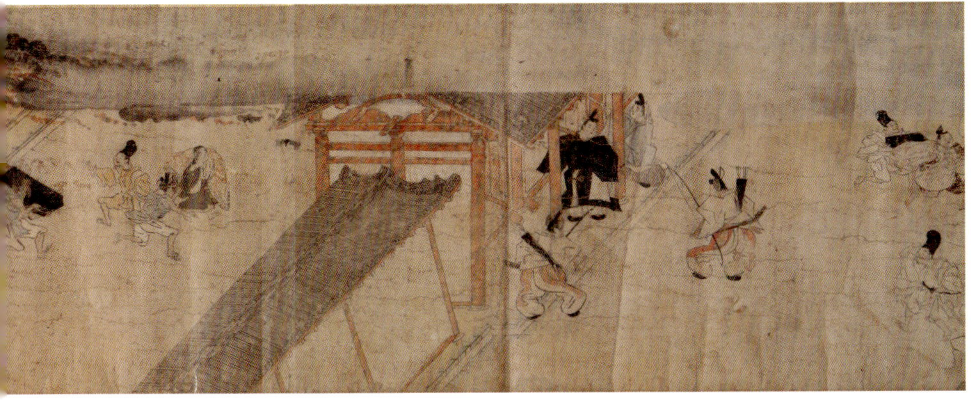

21 Tachibana Naomoto's *Memorial to the Throne* (*Naomoto mōshibumi ekotoba*). Thirteenth century. One scroll; ink and color on paper, 30.5 x 1076.1 cm. Idemitsu Museum of Arts. Important Cultural Property.

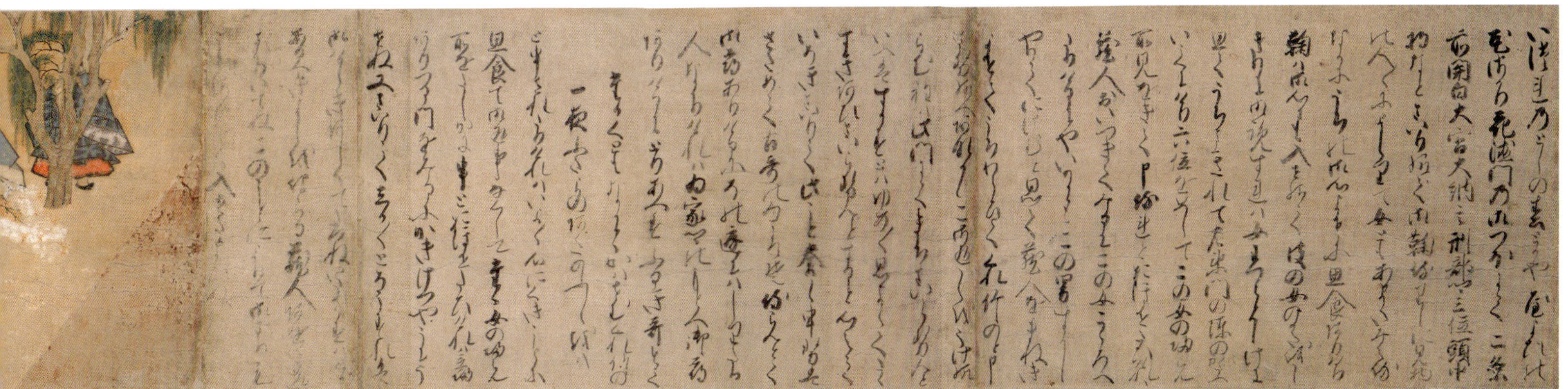

22 *Supple Bamboo* (*Nayotake monogatari emaki*). Fourteenth century. One scroll; ink and color on paper, 31.4 x 1317.4 cm. Kotohiragū, Kagawa Prefecture. Important Cultural Property.

Supple Bamboo (*Nayotake monogatari emaki*), a handscroll from the fourteenth century, similarly illustrates a tale about imperial privilege. When Emperor GoSaga falls in love with the wife of a courtier after catching a glimpse of her at a kickball match, the woman's husband eventually encourages her to join the emperor at the palace. The sovereign subsequently raises the rank of the husband in recognition of his loyalty and selfless act. Several scenes focus on the grandeur of courtly life, from the landscaped surroundings of the palace kickball courtyard, featuring the emperor himself obscured by the branches of a willow tree (fig. 22), to an image of a formal reading of *Sovereign Kings of the Golden Light Sutra* (*Konkōmyō saishō'ō kyō*) at the palace, to scenes of the elegant female attendants who serve the emperor in his residential quarters.[27]

These short-tale scrolls from the Kamakura period uniformly emphasize a courtly setting, both in their compositions and in their selection of court-based tales from hundreds of available *setsuwa*. All of their stories appear in the *setsuwa* anthology *Tales Heard from Writers Old and New* (*Kokon chomonjū*, 1254), a vast collection of over seven hundred tales popular among aristocrats and military elite, who were also the most likely patrons of these handscrolls. The scrolls can be understood as idealized representations of rulership combined with a pretense of didacticism. The pageantry of these early tale scrolls, however, clearly distinguishes them from later short-story small scrolls. While *ko-e* could also be about the court, their settings were secondary to their moralistic telos.

A THEORY OF THE SHORT-STORY SMALL SCROLL

Although large-scale scrolls illustrating short fiction continued to be made throughout the medieval period, their literary dispositions remained relatively distinct from their smaller counterparts. A number of small-scroll stories have their origins in *setsuwa* collections—*Breaking the Inkstone,* for example, illustrates a story found in *Tales of Times Now Past* (*Konjaku monogatari shū*, late eleventh–early twelfth century)—but unlike the large *setsuwa emaki* examined above, they do not excerpt the most courtly anecdotes for illustration. Instead, the narratives of these small scrolls are united by their relentless focus on a single protagonist who achieves a personal epiphany by the end of the tale. Most commonly this realization involves an awareness of the impermanence of life, conceptualized according to the Buddhist concept of transience (*mujō*). This theme infuses medieval literature of all kinds. Stories of religious awakening (*hosshindan*) or of renouncing the world (*shukke*) motivated by a character's insight into the illusion of permanence, usually through a tragedy of some kind, dominate late medieval fiction.[28]

These short stories, characterized by sparse and inexorably forward-moving story lines and suffused with a moral urgency, were paired with the small format during the fifteenth century, resulting in a new pictoliterary genre that, for the first time, made brevity its defining characteristic. This abbreviation of both form and content, text and image, represented a departure from all previous handscrolls, even those that illustrated short tales, because it was an issue of quality as well as of quantity. The long expanses of landscape scenery in the *Miraculous Origins of Mt. Shigi* paintings, which unfold at a leisurely pace, contradict the *setsuwa* origins of the text. Both *Mt. Shigi* and *Major Counselor Ban*, with their continuous visual fields, present their stories pictorially as if they were of epic proportions. Similarly, thirteenth- and fourteenth-century scrolls of short tales, although they illustrate brief, almost anecdotal tales from *setsuwa* collections, maintain the scale and objecthood of imperially sponsored picture scrolls. They betray little interest in accommodating their images to their anecdotal source texts. *Imperial Visit to View the Snows of Ono* includes a lengthy (more than ten sheets long) processional in painting 1 and repetitive scenes of the emperor's reception in Ono that do not, in the strictest sense, facilitate plot progression. In *Naomoto's Memorial to the Throne*, an abundance of visual details of village life in the first painting reveals an artist unconcerned with concision. The illustration of these texts in effect decelerates them temporally and disguises their brevity. In contrast, short-story small scrolls of the next century directly acknowledge succinctness as structurally intrinsic to their presentation.

Until now, accounts of small scrolls have not ventured beyond a discussion of what might be referred to as their *spatial* brevity—their height, which measures half the size of the standard scroll. No attention has been paid to their *temporal* brevity—the short length of their narratives and how this quality is enhanced by the small format. Such an inquiry, however, prompts a consideration of the implications of scale and duration in the experience of reading and viewing picture scrolls. Essential in this context is an analysis of the narratological impact of concision. There are, in other words, important formal and experiential implications stemming from the length of a work and specific characteristics associated with short prose tales that can provide a meaningful comparative framework for the new pictoliterary format being studied here.

Small scrolls, unlike many others from the premodern period, allow for a reading in one sitting. In other contexts this quality has been understood as a crucial element in the ability of a literary work to achieve a sense of "totality." Indeed, the latter effect was a keyword in the theoretical writings of Edgar Allan Poe, one of the earliest champions of the American short story.[29] Without the distractions of everyday life that enter into the experience of reading a long text, a short literary work heightens the concentration of the reader and enables the "contemplation of the picture as a whole."[30] In the case of picture scrolls, only a format that condenses the image-text throughout the work would allow for such a mode of cognition, in which the entire scroll is held in the mind at once. The short-story *ko-e*, typically a single scroll with as few as three painting sections, is the only handscroll format that privileges this kind of holistic cognition. Not only does the small-scroll format allow for a self-enclosed reading, but it also facilitates perusal by a single viewer, as opposed to the communal reading practice so prevalent in the premodern period. Standard-size picture scrolls were frequently read out loud before groups of people (see chapter 2) and were at the center of one common form of social interaction; the unrolling of a scroll and the reading of its texts brought its audience into both physical and psychological proximity as they communed over the stories at hand. In its drastically reduced form, however, the small scroll stood in opposition to this practice. The small format presupposed a personal, even silent reading experience. This quality conditioned the kind of stories represented in small scrolls, stories that involved single protagonists and encouraged an empathetic response in the reader.

The small scroll in its conciseness holds out to the reader the promise of narrative enthrallment followed by a quick resolution. The pictorial techniques of Heian picture scrolls were designed to compel the reader to continue unrolling lengthy scrolls, and the prolonged processional scenes in many works, particularly temple legends, are intended to impress upon the viewer the grandeur and spectacle of a given occasion. In this sense a scroll painted in such a manner "subjugates the reader to the domination of length."[31] In contrast, the small scroll enables mastery over the material, both in the physical handling of the object and in the reading and comprehension of the texts and images. These conditions were conducive to experiences that were more informal, intimate, and personal in nature.

For Poe, the ability of a short prose tale to be read in one sitting was most important, in that it allowed for the creation of a "unity or totality of effect," whereby artists so honed their tales that not a single word or phrase detracted from the whole.[32] In the case of small scrolls, this effect was most successfully achieved in works associated with Mitsunobu. The small scroll bears several traits in common with the short story, particularly in the way it "condenses 'much in little' through selectivity, ellipsis, foreshortening, and synecdoche."[33]

All of the short-story small scrolls examined in the chapters that follow share a distinct emphasis on the ending, specifically a closing revelation that retroactively structures the narrative and reinforces the sensation of a linear progression toward itself. Short-story small scrolls share general tendencies found in the forms of short fiction in that they are "constructed on the basis of a contradiction or incongruity" in order to generate momentum toward a resolution.[34] The "incongruities" that initiate small scrolls include a phantasmagorical letter delivered to a girl in her dreams (*A Wakeful Sleep*), the shattering of a precious heirloom (*Breaking the Inkstone*), and the appearance of a mysterious woman on a monk's veranda (*The Jizō Hall*). By demanding explanations, these openings embark the viewer on a linear trajectory toward endings that both transform their characters and decipher the unusual events of the narratives' opening sequences. But the revelatory endings of these small-scroll stories, typically Buddhist in nature, require a process of mental review of the entire preceding story to achieve maximum effect. Upon conclusion, prior events in the tale take on a new import, and the tale can be reexperienced on a second register. This effect of secondary revision tinges the entire narrative with a sense of retroactive preordination that is particularly effective within the limited purview of small scrolls.

SHORT-STORY SMALL SCROLLS IN THE FIFTEENTH CENTURY

Approximately fifty small scrolls survive from the mid–Muromachi period.[35] Although they illustrate diverse subjects, several share enough literary and

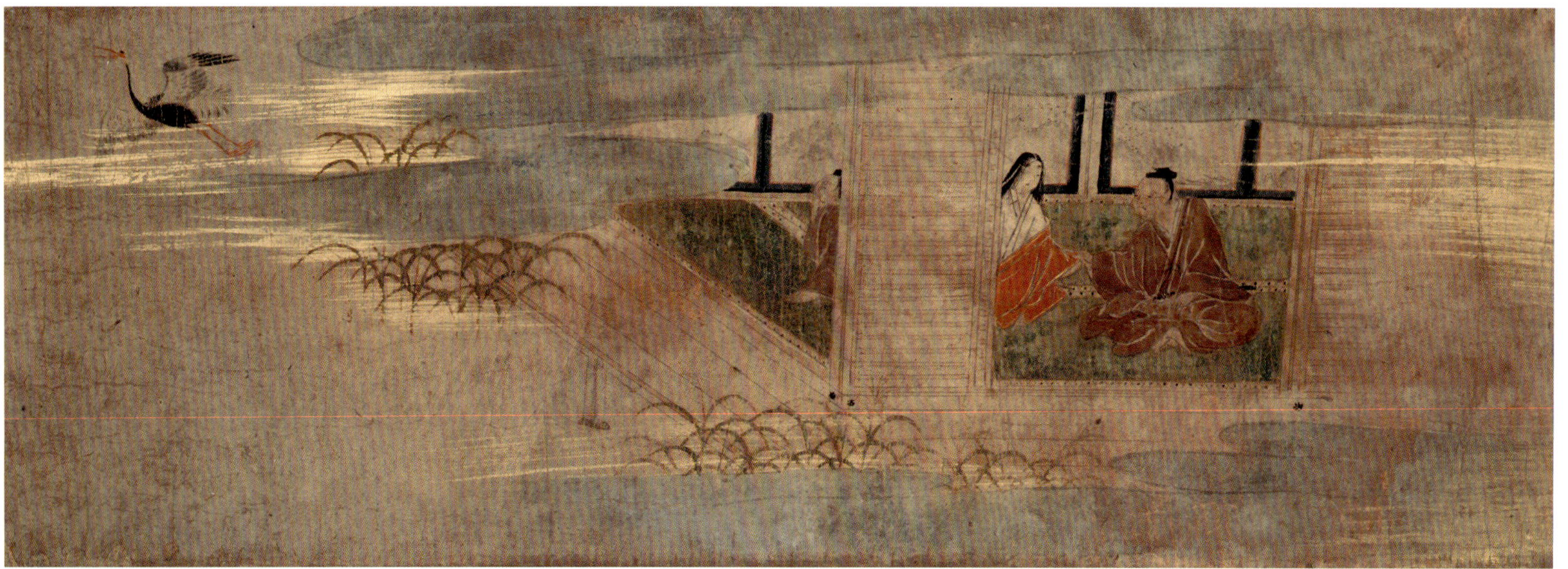

23 *Tale of the Crane* (*Tsuru sōshi emaki*). Muromachi period, mid- to late fifteenth century. One handscroll; ink, color, and gold on paper, 17.3 x 986.4 cm. Kyoto National Museum.

pictorial characteristics to be considered a distinct corpus. Among them is a group of six short-story scrolls, dated stylistically to the late fifteenth century, that are the best subjects for analysis due to their quality, sophistication, shared association with Mitsunobu, and proximity of production contexts. They include the three small scrolls examined in depth in the following chapters: *A Wakeful Sleep* (fig. 1), *The Jizō Hall* (fig. 2), and *Breaking the Inkstone* (fig. 3). The other three are *Tale of the Fox* (*Kitsune sōshi emaki*), *Tale of the Crane* (*Tsuru sōshi emaki*), and *Tale of the Rat* (*Nezumi sōshi emaki*), which were painted by artists contemporary with Mitsunobu and possibly connected to his studio. *Tale of the Fox* illustrates the story of an older lay monk who succumbs to the wiles of a shape-shifting fox in the guise of a beautiful woman but who is eventually saved by the beneficence of the bodhisattva Jizō.[36] In *Tale of the Crane* a lonely widower saves the life of a crane, who returns his kindness by reappearing as a beautiful woman who lives with him as his wife and comes to his aid until she eventually reverts to her original form (fig. 23).[37] *Tale of the Rat* recounts the tale of a woman who falls in love with a handsome stranger until she realizes that he is nothing but a rodent in disguise.[38] All three of these latter scrolls illustrate tales of relationships between humans and others, which scholars have categorized as "tales of nonhuman marriage" (*irui kon'intan* or *kaikontan*).[39] Such subject matter differentiates these works from the three small scrolls by Mitsunobu; nevertheless, the similarity in date, narrative structure, and pictorial language of all six merits their analysis as a group.

Before progressing further, a brief word about the connoisseurship of these scrolls is in order, especially because the three latter scrolls have all been at some point attributed to Tosa Mitsunobu. Close examination of *Tale of the Fox* and *Tale of the Crane*, however, reveals the hand of the artist who also executed *Tales of the Heike* (fig. 24), a small-format scroll in the ink-line mode.[40] All three scrolls (*Heike, Fox*, and *Crane*) bear a strikingly similar figure style that is markedly different from that of Mitsunobu's handscrolls. The mist bands in these three scrolls, which are executed with a tremulous outline and rounded edges, stand in contrast to those in Mitsunobu's works. In *Breaking the Inkstone*, *The Jizō Hall*, and *A Wakeful Sleep*, as well as in *Legends of Kitano Tenjin* (*Kitano Tenjin engi emaki*, 1503) and *Miraculous Legends of Kiyomizudera* (*Kiyomizudera engi emaki*, 1517–20), sharp, ruler-drawn ink lines, highlighted by a thin line of shell white, outline the mist bands. And, rather than ending with hard,

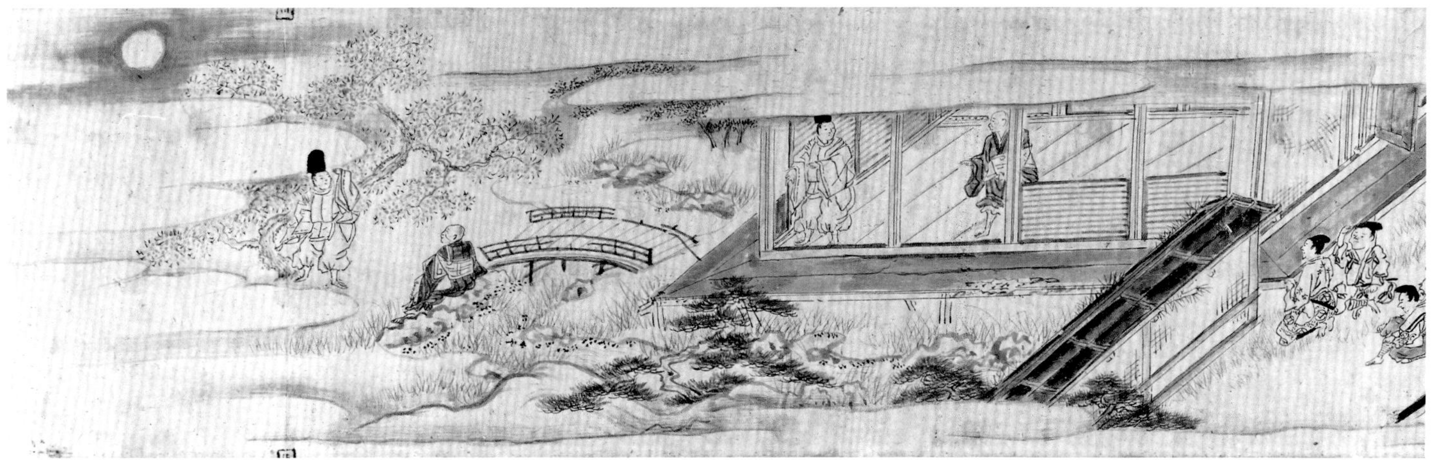

24 *Tales of the Heike* (*Heike monogatari emaki*). Muromachi period, mid- to late fifteenth century. One handscroll; ink on paper, H. 15.5 cm. Private collection.

rounded edges, Mitsunobu's mists employ a wash of pale blue pigment, which makes them appear to dissolve into thin air. *Tale of the Rat* (fig. 25), on the other hand, bears a close stylistic relationship to Mitsunobu's works and even employs his characteristic mist bands. Aizawa Masahiko, one of the most recent commentators on this scroll, considers it a Mitsunobu studio work, noting that the poses of several figures, particularly the female attendants in painting 3 (25g–h) are nearly identical to those in Mitsunobu's *Legends of Kitano Tenjin* (*Kitano Tenjin engi emaki*, 1503).[41] The paintings-within-paintings (*gachūga*) on panels, sliding doors, and folding screens are also similar in placement, scale, and subject matter to those in other scrolls by Mitsunobu. Certain aspects of the painting, however, such as the exaggeratedly unsteady hill line (fig. 25b), as if in deliberate imitation of Mitsunobu's characteristic wavering line for the depiction of rocks and landscape elements, as well as the excessively striated mist bands in the same scene, indicate a different artist at work. In all likelihood *Tale of the Rat* represents a close copy of a Mitsunobu original, while *Tale of the Fox*, *Tale of the Crane*, and *Tales of the Heike* were executed by a contemporary of Mitsunobu, possibly even someone in his studio. All six scrolls can be dated stylistically to the late fifteenth century or early sixteenth century and were executed for a similar constituency, members of the nobility and the military elite.[42]

Viewed as a group, these six small scrolls offer the most promising basis for understanding the way in which the small-format handscroll accommodated a specific type of short story in the late medieval period. The unity of literary agendas in this group is telling. The master theme of impermanence and the foolishness of worldly attachments appears in almost every short-story small scroll by Mitsunobu. Since the endings involve a character's newly found understanding of impermanence, the scrolls begin by portraying characters who conspicuously lack this insight, most commonly with scenarios that involve romantic or sexual desire on the part of the protagonist. *The Jizō Hall* begins, for example, with a monk's longing for a liaison with a beautiful woman, while events in *A Wakeful Sleep* stem from a woman's desire to be with a man who has appeared in her dreams. The plot of *Breaking the Inkstone* is initiated by another kind of worldly attachment, a servant's desire to possess his master's inkstone, while *Tale of the Fox* opens with an overture by a woman, via her beautiful female messenger, to an eager older monk. *Tale of the Rat* begins when a handsome young man suddenly calls upon a young woman desperate to find a husband. And although not the sole focus of the narrative, in *Tale of the Crane* a widower's romantic involvement with a beautiful woman who appears one day sets the main plot in motion.

Small scrolls inevitably begin, then, as narratives of desire but at their endings encourage retroactive

PAINTING ONE

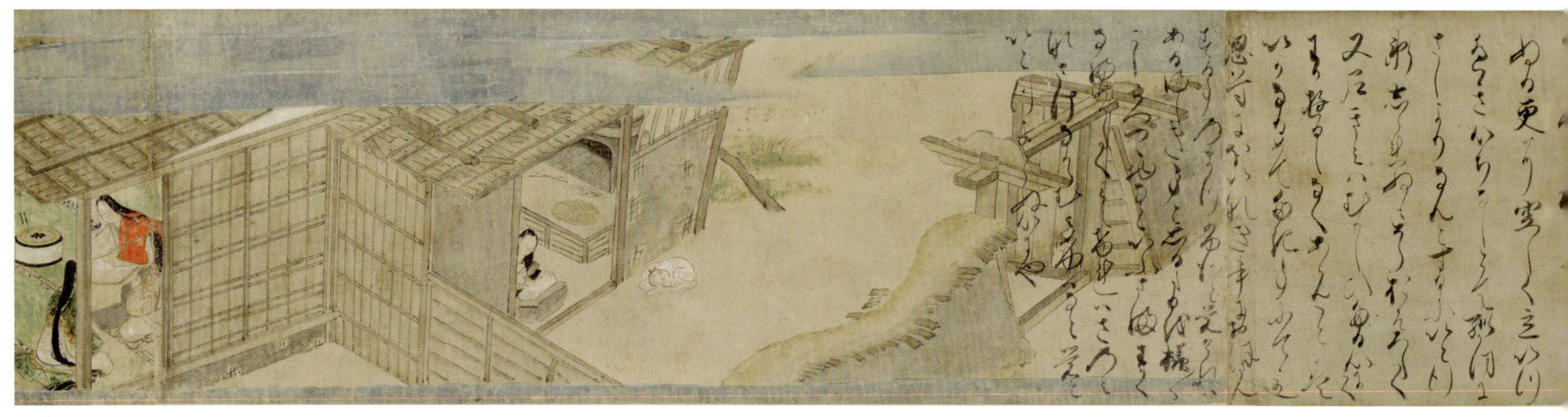

A

PAINTING TWO

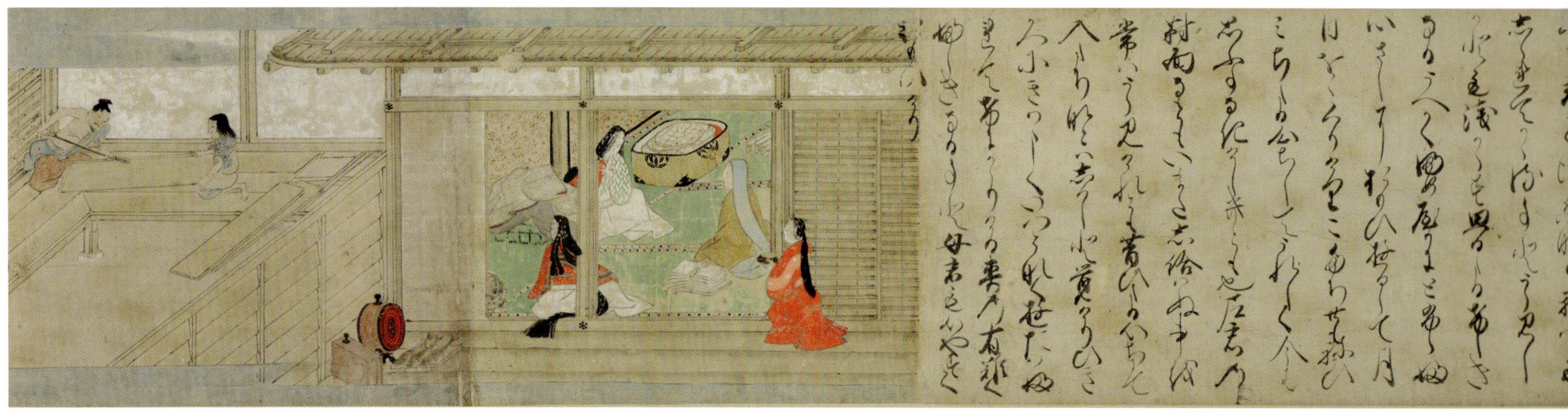

D

C

PAINTING THREE

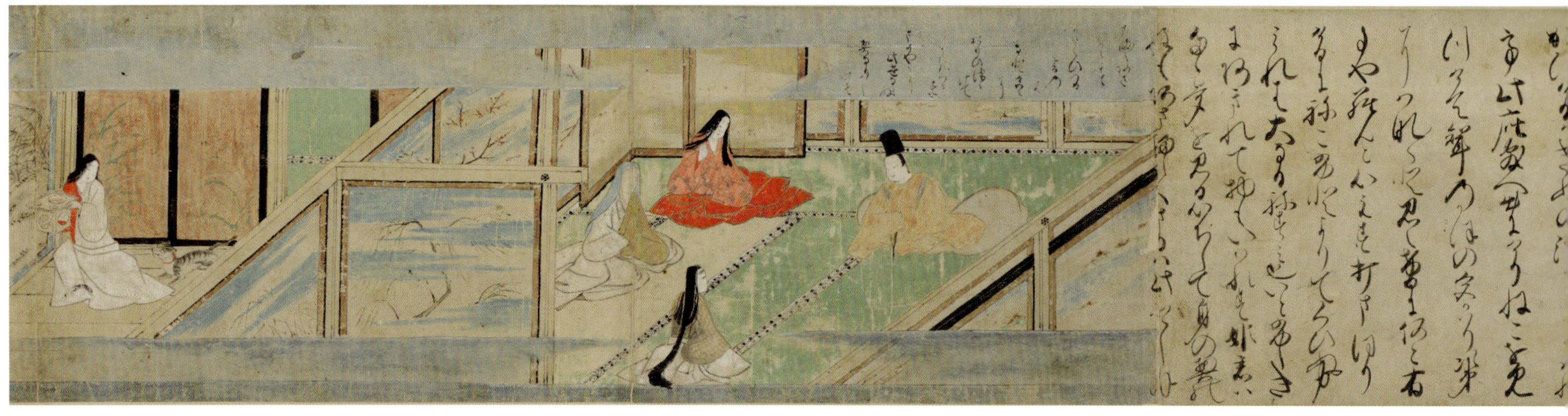

F

25 *Tale of the Rat* (*Nezumi sōshi emaki*). Late fifteenth century. One handscroll; ink, color, and gold on paper, 16.7 x 431.0 cm. Harvard Art Museum, Arthur M. Sackler Museum, Bequest of the Hofer Collection of the Arts of Asia, 1985. Photograph by Katya Kallsen © President and Fellows of Harvard College.

TEXT ONE

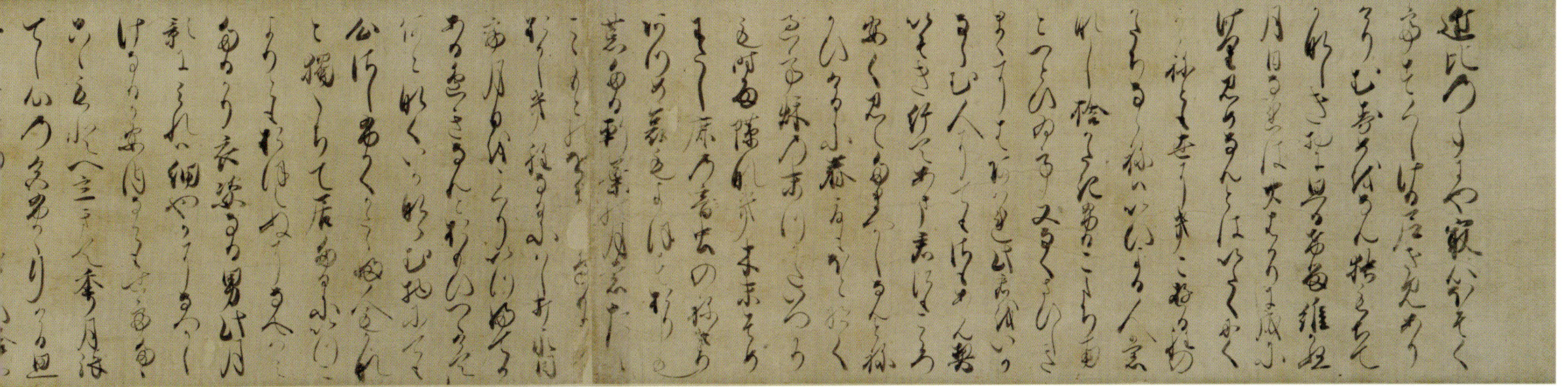

TEXT TWO

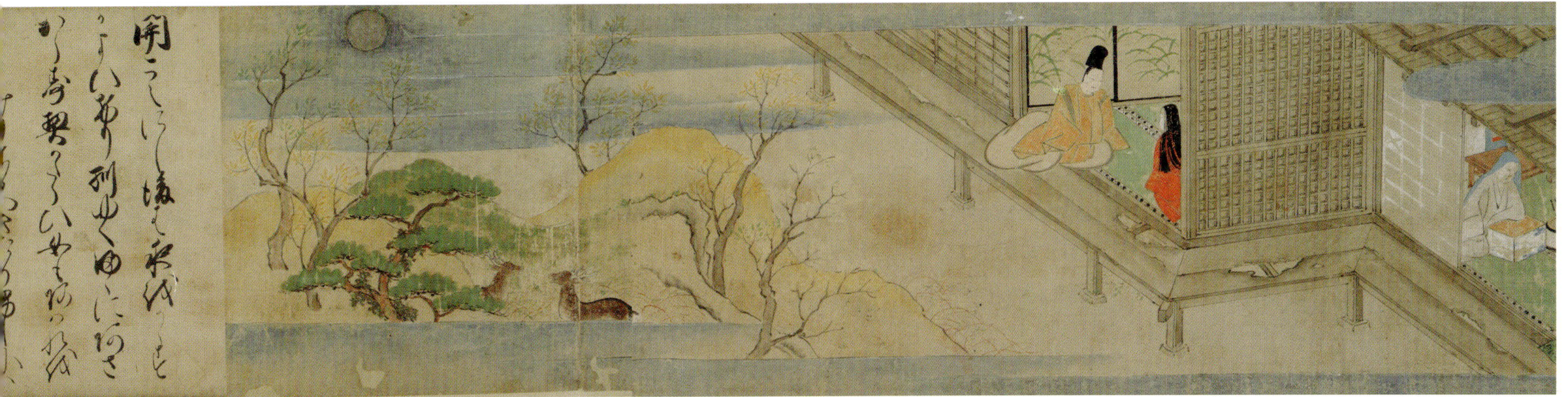

B

TEXT THREE

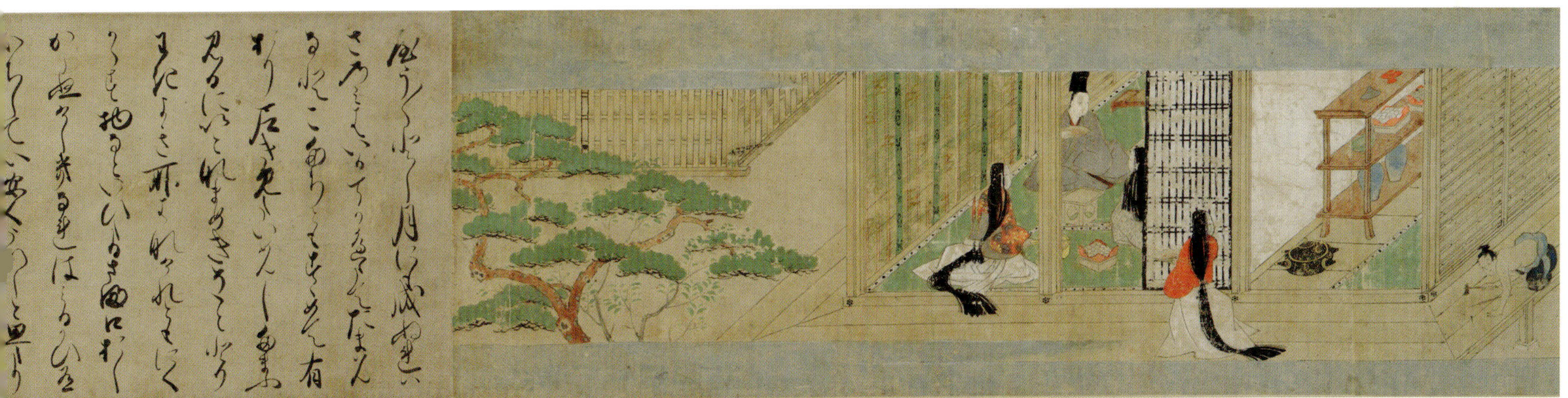

E

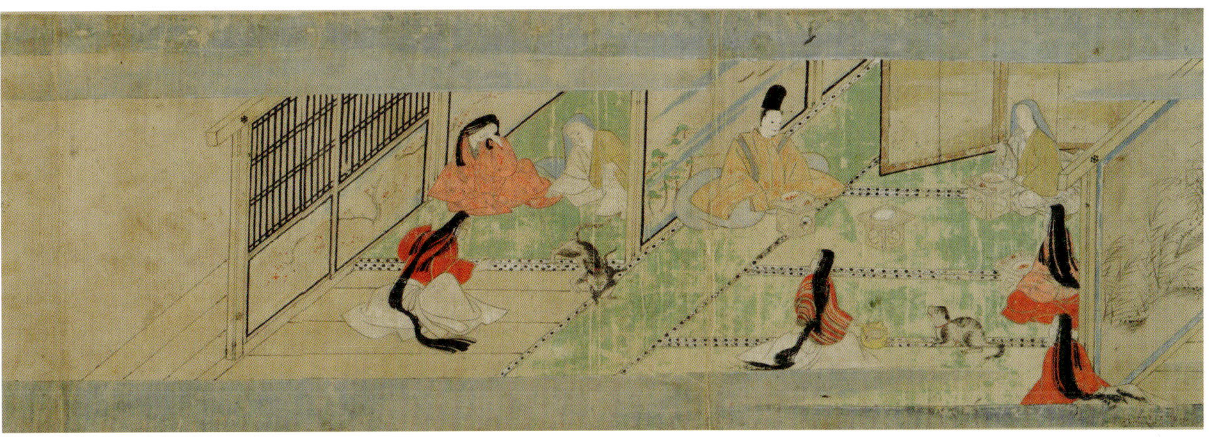

H G

reinterpretations of initial temptations as expedient means toward religious awakening. The narratological structure of these tales builds rapidly in intensity and places its greatest emphasis on the moment of closure. The servant's desire in *Breaking the Inkstone* leads ultimately to the death of a young boy, whose short life drives home the fleeting nature of existence and sets the man on the proper path. Similarly, the monk's escapade in the dragon woman's abode in *The Jizō Hall* nearly costs him his long-sought salvation, until he realizes the error of his own ways and pursues his religious practice with diligence. In *Tale of the Fox*, the monk's hedonistic life in the luxurious residence of the fox woman turns out to be an illusion, vividly expressed in the final paintings, which show him dressed in rags and seated amid the bones of corpses (see fig. 76). And finally, in *Tale of the Rat*, the rise in the family's fortunes is as fleeting as the woman's happiness, when it is discovered that her suitor is less than human (fig. 25g–h). The protagonists are thus followed at close range as they traverse a familiar arc of temptation, ecstasy, humiliation, and realization, and as works intended to be experienced from start to finish in one sitting, small scrolls are structured around a narrative drive toward resolution.

In each instance the protagonist leads an isolated or lonely existence, and is portrayed in a mood of alienation that sets the stage for the inevitably peculiar incidents that premise the tales. These lonely figures are stock characters and include monks removed from society and living either in reclusion (*Tale of the Fox*) or in a desolate provincial temple (*The Jizō Hall*); a widower spending his days in a humble abode (*Tale of the Crane*); a young woman soon to surpass a marriageable age and living a sheltered existence with her mother, an old nun (*Tale of the Rat*); and, finally, a motherless young girl who spends countless hours alone idling away her time gazing upon her garden or playing the zither (*A Wakeful Sleep*). In *Breaking the Inkstone*, although the servant does not live in isolation, his fateful viewing of the inkstone occurs when all other members of the household are away or occupied in other rooms. Small-scroll protagonists are emotionally susceptible beings whose loneliness drives them to succumb to the alluring figures or enticing objects that lead them astray. They are characters to whom "something oddly happened," Henry James's defining characteristic of the anecdote.[43]

THE VISUAL LANGUAGE OF SHORT-STORY SMALL SCROLLS

In small scrolls the stories in which "something oddly happened" were portrayed according to new techniques drawn from long-standing traditions of classical Japanese picture making. These features were closely related to the contingencies of their small, single-scroll format, as well as the texts they illustrated. But, at the same time, short-story small scrolls evince a sensitivity to pictorial narrative that is qualitatively different from that of larger-format handscrolls. The paintings of larger and longer scrolls tend not to engage in a formal way with the paintings that precede them in the scroll. This is especially the case with temple legend scrolls, in which a single work can contain over thirty painting sections, the majority of which illustrate separate vignettes with little formal relationships between them. Even most prose narrative scrolls illustrating a single tale do not coordinate their pictorial compositions to create a unified whole. It seems that for most artists and viewers this was not a priority. The interrelationship between paintings is clearly not the point of Heian period handscrolls such as *Miraculous Origins of Mt. Shigi* and *Major Counselor Ban*. There, the lengthy, continuous pictorial sequences form discrete visual worlds into which the viewer is absorbed as he or she moves through the scroll.

In *Miraculous Origins of Mt. Shigi*, for example, the artist represents both a totalizing effect, in which the sense of a vast cohesive world is depicted, as well as intimate personal encounters. To this end the artist employs what might be called a zoom, or close-up mechanism, whereby pictorial compositions anticipate and encourage focusing in on specific parts of a scene. When the storehouse owner meets Myōren to discuss the return of his property (fig. 26), for example, the artist places landscape elements in the foreground that are well out of proportion to the architecture of the

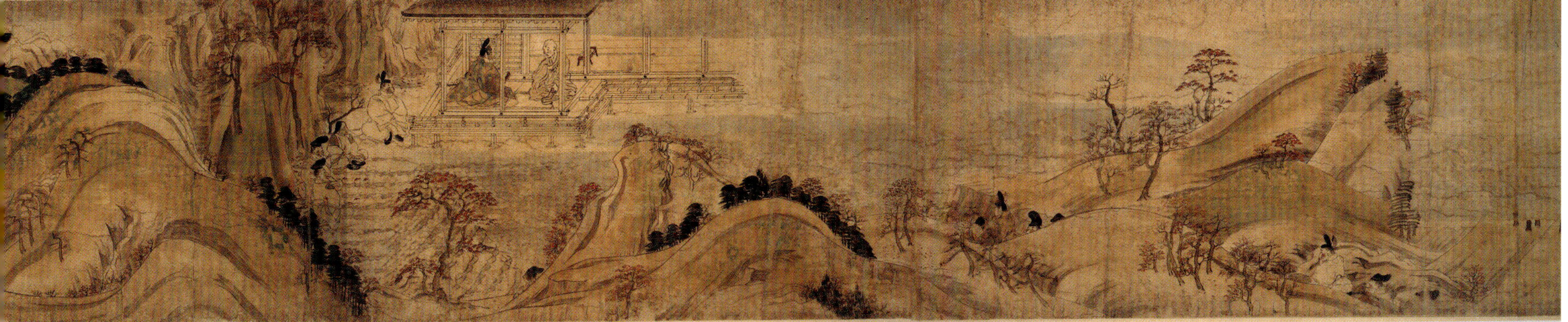

26 *Miraculous Origins of Mount Shigi* (*Shigisan engi emaki*). Twelfth century. Three scrolls; ink and color on paper, 31.7 x 897.9 cm. Chōgosonshiji, Nara Prefecture. National Treasure. Detail, scroll 2.

monk's abode. Small pine trees covering the hills in the foreground of this scene suggest that they are being viewed from a great distance. The juxtaposition of minuscule trees with the larger-scale architecture of Myōren's residence creates a telescopic effect; the viewer understands these two elements to be noncontiguous and thus focuses on the meeting between the two characters. By panning to the left or right, however, the distant landscape comes back into view. Another kind of totalizing effect appears in the first painting of *Major Counselor Ban*, where individuals from nearly every stratum of Heian period society make an appearance (fig. 18). The crowd scene teems with people of different ages, professions, and ranks, each with a unique pose and facial expression, suggesting the diversity and vastness of the capital's population. The absence of background elements here implies the large, limitlessness of the imperial palace. In both *Miraculous Origins of Mt. Shigi* and *Major Counselor Ban* each painting stands on its own and presents a total visual world that sustains the viewer's interest across a long horizontal expanse.

By contrast, small scrolls are constrained by length, the height of the pictorial field, and the number of paintings—usually between three and seven—in a single scroll. The best examples, however, turn these seeming limitations into strengths, enlisting each image in the creation of an integrated and unified pictorial effect. The manner in which this is achieved will be elaborated in the following chapters, but a brief description of the pictorial structure of *The Jizō Hall* and *Tale of the Rat* here will provide an introduction to small-scroll visuality. Both of these works effectively visualize their tales through the use of paintings that build upon one another as they depict the progressive transformation of the protagonist.

In *The Jizō Hall* (fig. 2) architectural motifs are abbreviated and employed as framing devices for close encounters between the two main characters; these encounters are arranged in a sequence to engender the narrative and visually structure it according to what can be termed a sequential mode. Of the scroll's seven paintings, five depict the monk's experience at the underwater residence of the woman with whom he has fallen in love. The scroll orchestrates this subaqueous adventure through a series of five intimate exchanges between the monk and the woman (fig. 2e–i), each depicted within a slightly different architectural frame. The first shows the pair seated between red columns on a dais (fig. 2e), and the second presents the couple through a window as they gaze lovingly into each other's eyes (fig. 2f). In the third scene, blue pillars, orange curtains, and mist bands above and below frame the image of the monk observing the sleeping woman (fig. 2g). By the fourth scene, which follows the monk's realization of his whereabouts, black columns, beams, and shutters and blue-tiled roofs help transform the mood to an ominous one (fig. 2h). In the final scene of the undersea sequence the couple is framed again between red columns as they peruse the monk's miscopied sutra together (fig. 2i).

In all five underwater scenes, the viewer gazes through a window or an opening at the figures inside from a relatively uniform distance. This constancy of viewpoint contrasts with the zooming technique and the totalizing effect of earlier, large-scale handscrolls but also solicits an empathetic response, creating a pictorial structure that emphasizes the perspective of the monk. The number of other figures in the paintings is kept to a minimum—in *The Jizō Hall* the man and woman are entirely alone in most of the scenes—which encourages the viewer to focus on the protagonist and his subjective state. The carefully designed architectural features and mist bands create frames within which the monk is consistently shown gazing upon the woman, in slightly different configurations, often with his own body partially obscured. His sideways glances entice the viewer to gaze with the monk's eyes and marvel at this wondrous world with him.

In *Tale of the Rat* (fig. 25) the sequential mode is also employed, and its narrative development too works in tandem with the presentation of its protagonist's experience. The visual interest of its paintings again centers on staged indoor encounters, set within the young woman's residence, modified in composition and details according to the contingencies of each scene. The reader of the scroll looks through close-cropped architectural frames of columns and partially open doors to glimpse the protagonist gazing upon the male suitor. As with the monk in *The Jizō Hall*, the woman in *Tale of the Rat* is frequently shown in three-quarter view as she looks at the man who is the focus of her attention and, by extension, that of the scroll's viewer. In this way, the reader sympathizes with the female protagonist and comprehends the story as being told from her perspective.[44] The visual emphasis on the perspectives of individual protagonists in small scrolls, facilitated through a sequential progression of indoor scenes, represents an important aspect of the new artistic response to narratives of personal realization.

The sequential mode of representation and the interdependent quality of the painting sections also imbue the scrolls with a coherent rhythm. In his analysis of *Tale of the Rat* (fig. 25), for example, Miya Tsugio noted the scroll's pace, which begins slowly with the scene of the couple courting in painting 1, then quickens as gifts are bestowed on the household and workers busily refurbish the residence in painting 2, until, in the third and final painting section, the same characters are shown multiple times, creating a temporal crescendo when the man is exposed as a rodent (fig. 25h). Miya interpreted this structure as a pictorial equivalent of the *jo-ha-kyū* (literally, "introduction-breaking-rapid") pattern in music and Nō theater, which starts slowly, builds in complexity, and then reaches a fast-paced conclusion.[45] This rhythmic structure was theorized by the Nō playwright Zeami (ca. 1363–1443) in the fifteenth century and appears in several of his treatises. In *Finding Gems and Gaining the Flower* (*Shūgyoku tokka*, 1428), for example, Zeami describes *jo-ha-kyū* as integral to the audience's experience of "fulfillment," an essential element of which is a "sense of completion."[46] In *Tale of the Rat* the architectural compositions build on each other from painting to painting to shape the rhythm of the scroll. For example, barriers between the viewer and the figures are progressively eliminated, from the opening of the scroll and its representation of the house's exterior, to the second painting, which presents the building at ground level, to the third painting, in which the roofs are removed and the viewer may stare down directly into the building's interior. In this last painting all is revealed, a fitting pictorial conclusion to the revelation of the man's true identity. While not all short-story small scrolls build temporally from slow to fast, they do seem to strive for organic unity, even a totality of effect, that Zeami argues for in his notion of a sense of completion.

SMALL SCROLLS AS "PICTURE BOOKS" FOR CHILDREN

Until now, the only attempt to explain the appearance of small scrolls has connected the format to a juvenile audience, equating smallness of scale with smallness of stature. The art historian Umezu Jirō first proposed a separate function or identity for small scrolls, particularly those by Tosa Mitsunobu and his circle, in an article on *Breaking the Inkstone* published in 1961.[47] He suggested that Mitsunobu's refined scrolls "were read to young people of the court and military aristocracy," and he speculated that small-format scrolls in the *hakubyō* mode were popular among women and children (*shijo*) of these same upper classes. Although Umezu's tone was speculative, his suggestion about the audience for small scrolls reified over the years so that no mention of *ko-e* could be complete without a statement concerning their female and juvenile audience.[48] As a result small scrolls and their readers have been grouped together in an ahistorical manner, as though "women and children" constitute a unified category of readers.

Although never articulated explicitly, what seems to underscore the modern scholarly reception of small scrolls is the idea that these works collectively constitute a children's literature of the medieval period. The very concept of a children's literature in this context, however, is in need of questioning. The idea presupposes a fixed notion of childhood in Muromachi period Japan, in which childhood is conceptualized not only as a unique stage of life but also as one that required specialized material objects, such as small scrolls. The status of children in premodern Japan is a site of increasing scholarship among cultural historians, who view childhood—indeed, all stages of the life cycle—as constructs shaped by the myriad contingencies of society in particular historical contexts.[49] Art historians in postwar Japan, however, in conceptualizing small scrolls as tales for children, appear to have been subscribing to a universalized notion of children's literature that achieved one mature form in Victorian England and was introduced to Japan, along with other well-established European and Euro-American literary genres, in the late nineteenth century.[50]

While the idea that small scrolls have been marginalized by the imposition of a problematically universal notion of "children's literature" is not without merit, the actual discursive framework within which many forms of medieval tale literature were imagined is older and more complex. Around the year 1700, the bookseller Shibukawa Seiemon compiled and published a set of twenty-three medieval tales under the title *The Companion Library* (*Otogi bunko*); in a colophon, Shibukawa advertised the printed book as ideal for wedding gifts and guides for women and children. Following the example of this anthology, many such truncated and deceptively simple tales from a bygone era came to be referred to in the modern era as "companion tales" or "fairy tales" (*otogi-zōshi*).[51] The category, which had no obvious precedent in medieval taxonomies of tale literature, was a symptom of the inexorable emergence of a national print culture during the early Edo period (1615–1868).[52] The rapid rise of printed texts did not efface manuscript culture, however, but led to various forms of coexistence, and indeed, the early Edo period witnessed not only the ongoing production of traditional *emaki* by professional painters but also a great efflorescence of more simple types of picture scrolls misleadingly known as "Nara picture books" (*Nara ehon*).[53] Nevertheless, under these circumstances publishers and booksellers in urban centers such as Kyoto, Osaka, and Edo sought to introduce printed versions of literary forms that had previously circulated only as manuscripts. This process entailed not only a transcription from the manual into the xylographic but also a parallel reframing of content to be more carefully calibrated with the niche markets that developed within early modern print culture.[54] The "companion tale," then, can be understood as a willful misprision of medieval short stories under commercial prerogatives. The modern misrecognition of small scrolls as children's literature can be viewed as an extension of this process, and indeed, Mitsunobu's *ko-e* themselves were oftentimes directly described as companion tales.[55] While the value of this term is minimal in reference to Muromachi period picture scrolls, its use has resulted in the neglect of scores of works as unworthy of scholarly consideration.[56]

Adding to the complexity of the issue is the fact that young people *did* constitute a significant readership for small scrolls. In fact, the stories pictorialized in small scrolls could resonate with readers of many different backgrounds and age-groups, a function of the multivalency and range of social roles such tales fulfilled. As recent scholarship on children's literature in medieval Europe has shown, fairy tales, folktales, and medieval

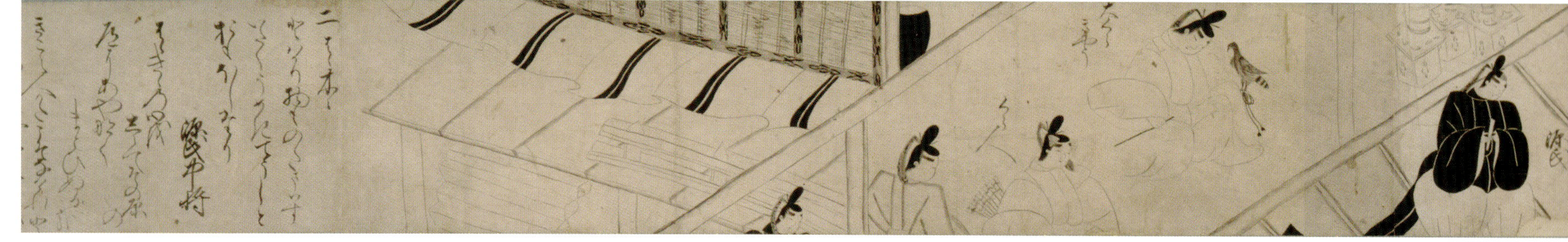

romances were read by and produced for mixed audiences, in addition to those tailored specifically to the young.[57] In Japan, tale literature was almost never intended *solely* for an audience of children, but it could be modified, particularly in the small-scroll format, to suit a youthful audience, as in the case of *Breaking the Inkstone*, examined in chapter 4. Certain medieval tales do employ elements that tend to distinguish modern children's literature, such as child or animal protagonists and simple language, including the substitution of *kana* for Chinese characters, but their open-endedness and nuanced, even complex moral messages suggest a more sophisticated audience. The child readership of such tales, however, deserves further explanation, as does the relationship between juveniles and small scrolls, which can provide new insight into the role picture scrolls played in the process of early education and the inculcation of social values.

It is not difficult to imagine why small scrolls would have appealed to young people, or to those responsible for educating them. Small scrolls were more easily manipulated than standard-size works twice their size and would have fit more comfortably into the hands of an adolescent, while offering the young person a sense of mastery over the object. As we have seen, unwieldy texts of great length, such as temple legends (fig. 12), *Life of Prince Shōtoku* (figs. 10–11), or *Tales of the Heike* (fig. 24), could be subdivided into multiscroll sets, so that individual scrolls might serve as convenient installments to be read over a number of days. And small scrolls provided a more manageable and economical medium for writing and drawing practice, an integral component of a young person's education.

Small scrolls that illustrate *The Tale of Genji*, knowledge of which was crucial for entry into the ranks of the well educated, constitute one of the largest categories of extant small scrolls.[58] These numerous *Genji* scrolls, which date primarily from the sixteenth century, attest to the use of the small format in transforming lengthy canonical texts into a more readable form (fig. 27). Although small *Genji* scrolls commonly contain scenes from all fifty-four chapters of the tale, they do not transcribe the entire lengthy narrative text but offer digests of key prose passages or, more frequently, famous poems from each chapter. Such digests could be heuristic devices for prompting further inquiry into the poetry or for familiarizing a reader with the complex *Genji* narrative. It is safe to assume that these small *Genji* scrolls, executed in the *hakubyō* mode and in a nonprofessional style, were not only read but also copied and created by readers, including young people.[59] The very small size of such works (one example measures only ten centimeters in height) was no doubt easier for an inexperienced artist to grapple with than the larger format.

Small scrolls that presented a large of amount of material, such as the thirty-three episodes of a temple origin tale, in a more convenient form were another category of small scrolls associated with young people. Such was Tosa Mitsumochi's *Miraculous Origins of Hasedera* (fig. 12), very probably made for the personal use of the thirteen-year-old shogun Ashikaga Yoshiharu.[60] Although the size was reduced, nothing was eliminated in terms of content; both the texts and the paintings contain the identical content of larger versions of the same subject. The six small scrolls thus offered the boy shogun the famous temple legend in a format that was easier to manipulate and study. Another example of a multivolume small scroll with a connection to a child is the fourteenth-century *Life of Prince Shōtoku* (figs. 10–

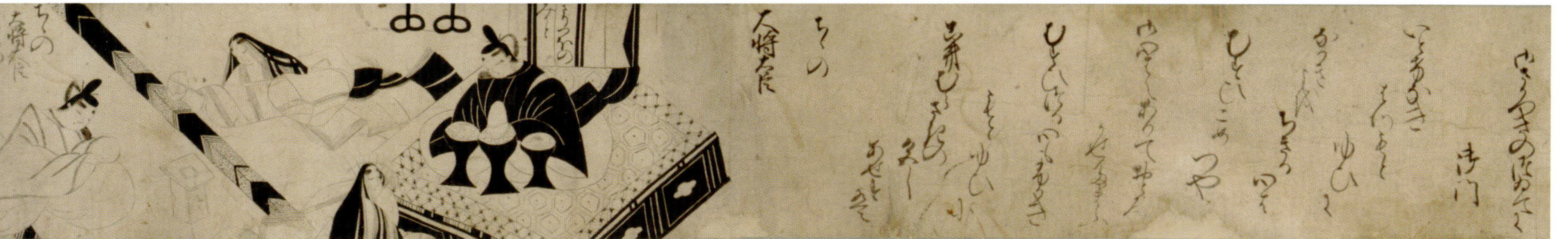

27 *Paulownia Pavilion* (*Kiritsubo*), *Monochrome Tale of Genji Scrolls* (*Hakubyō Genji monogatari emaki*). 1554. Spencer Collection, New York Public Library. Astor, Lenox, and Tilden Foundations.

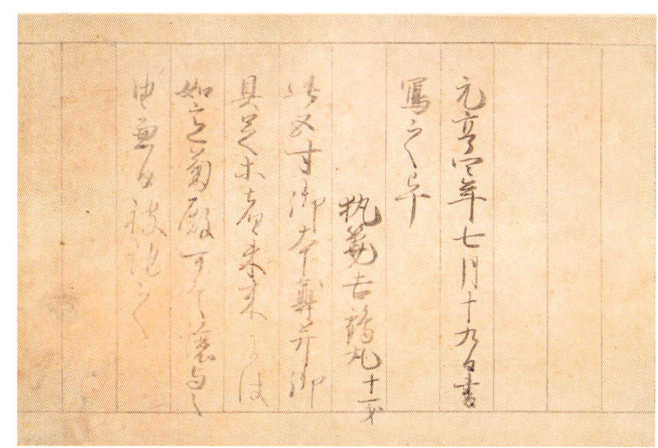

28 *Life of Prince Shōtoku* (*Shōtoku Taishi den-e*). Fourteenth century. Ten scrolls; ink and color on paper, H. 15.9 cm. Private collection. Colophon at the end of scrolls 5 and 10, dated 1324.

11), also mentioned above. This work contains a colophon signed by an eleven-year-old boy by the name of Kichitsurumaru (fig. 28), who claims to have executed the calligraphy for all ten scrolls of the work.[61] While the precise circumstances for the production of this scroll are unknown, the colophon clearly suggests that it was created for a religious ceremony, perhaps one commemorating an important date from the life of Shōtoku.[62] In this context the transcription of all sixty-four episodes of Shōtoku's biography may have served as a kind of religious exercise or as writing practice for young Kichitsurumaru. The lined paper of the text (unusual for narrative scrolls) and the small format must have made it easier for the young calligrapher to maintain consistently straight columns of characters.[63] In this case too, the texts were not altered for the sake of a young reader or writer but are identical to other manuscript versions. In other words, accommodations of subject matter were not deemed necessary for young audiences in these instances, which again problematizes the notion of a distinct children's literature.

Yet other evidence suggests that certain children not only read small scrolls but possessed their own collections. In 1438 Prince Sadafusa heard that the shogun Ashikaga Yoshinori was looking for small scrolls to borrow, "even amusing ones."[64] Although Sadafusa had no small scrolls to offer, the young Fushimi prince Sadatsune, Sadafusa's second son, sent three works to the shogun.[65] What the shogun meant by "amusing" one can only imagine, but he most likely referred to scrolls that were less than elevated, containing bawdy humor or topics of a scatological nature.[66] It cannot be assumed that this kind of subject matter was for juveniles alone; even Sadafusa himself was known to have enjoyed the occasional off-color picture scroll.[67] But the specific reference to Sadatsune sending the scrolls suggests that the young prince may have had his own library of *ko-e*.

Small scrolls of a more orthodox nature played a role in the education of the young imperial crown prince Katsuhito, who would become emperor GoKashiwabara (1464–1526), and are alluded to in the diary of Sanjōnishi Sanetaka (1455–1527). As a high-ranking courtier, man of letters, and accomplished calligrapher, Sanetaka frequently advised the prince's father, Emperor GoTsuchimikado (1442–1500), on literary matters during his regular service at the palace. His duties included examining the emperor's poetry, reading texts aloud, copying classical works, performing as a lecturer during poetry gatherings, annotating texts, such as the emperor's copy of the *Collection of Ancient and Modern Poems* (*Kokinshū*), and collaborating on the production of small scrolls at the imperial court.[68] Sanetaka, especially as a young man in his early twenties, also served as the private tutor of Prince Katsuhito. On one occasion Sanetaka received a small scroll from the prince, who was eleven years old at the time.[69] Judging from Sanetaka's other activities, he probably received this scroll from the prince in order to copy its text or to create a new text from the work. Sanetaka also frequently instructed the crown prince on poetry and poetic composition, and he presented the prince with a small-format booklet (*ko-sōshi*) of his own poems.[70]

The crown prince's education in poetry may also have been aided by the use of small scrolls. In 1479, nine days before the then-sixteen-year-old crown prince hosted a seasonal (*tsukinami*) poetry gathering at the palace, Sanetaka added his calligraphy to a small scroll depicting a fictional poetry contest (*ko-e utaawase*) and submitted it to the imperial court.[71] Sanetaka composed three pairs of poems for the scroll. He also added judgments that declared which poem of each pair was better and explained the reasoning behind the choice. Within the context of the crown prince's literary activities and role as poetry-gathering sponsor, a small scroll depicting a fictional poetry match would have been an ingenious heuristic device for instilling the rules or aesthetic principles of Japanese poetry. By enacting the exchanges of a poetry competition, round by round, a poetry-match scroll would have prepared the novice poet for an upcoming gathering by showing him what to expect. The poems cited in the scroll, whether newly created (as in the case of Sanetaka's additions) or famous classical verse, could have served as exemplars in themselves or as the springboard for a discussion of the process of poetic composition. Of the two poems of each match, one could have been an inferior example deliberately included to demonstrate for an aspiring poet what to avoid, while the judgments that followed each pair offered straightforward instruction on the elements of a superior poem. Although Sanetaka does not specify for whom at court the competition *ko-e* was made, its appearance within the context of the prince's instruction in poetry, his sponsorship of an upcoming poetry gathering, and his increasingly frequent participation at such literary events suggests that he, above all others at the palace, would have benefited from such a work.[72]

Evidence also suggests that *ko-e* were especially favored by the Ashikaga shoguns in their youth. The most well known example is Tosa Mitsunobu's *Breaking the Inkstone*, which bears the colophon of the sixteen-year-old Ashikaga Yoshizumi. But the collecting and reading activities of the shogun Ashikaga Yoshihisa (1465–89) provide further examples. Yoshihisa is known to have borrowed eleven small scrolls for viewing in 1481 at the age of sixteen.[73] And he owned a *Tale of the Fox* scroll, which scholars believe corresponds to the extant small scroll attributed to Mitsunobu.[74] The stories of *Breaking the Inkstone* and *Tale of the Fox* do seem appropriate for youthful audiences; in the former a young boy accepts the blame for a crime committed by a household servant who subsequently becomes a monk, while in the latter, the bodhisattva Jizō rescues an elderly monk who has been lured into a life of debauchery by a fox in the guise of a beautiful woman. Both contain a moralistic message that would have fit into the general pedagogical agenda for young boys in the fifteenth century.

An example of the materials used in the formal education of boys in the Muromachi period comes by way of the *Mirror of Society* (*Sekyōshō*), which describes the typical curriculum of a Buddhist temple school.[75] After a full day of sutra reading, writing practice, and studying Chinese historical and literary texts, boys (typically between the ages of seven and fifteen) would in the evening be encouraged to enjoy poem tales (*uta monogatari*) and narratives of valor (*giri monogatari*). This was also the time allotted for playing the flute and other musical instruments. Boys tutored at home (the other common manner of education in this period) might have followed a similar schedule or at least have been allotted some time for reading tale literature, if available. Both *Breaking the Inkstone* and *Tale of the Fox* seem perfect candidates for the kind of reading that young boys engaged in during the less mentally strenuous evenings. Fast-paced, entertaining, and containing Buddhist didactic messages, these two tales (along with other stories, such as *Tale of the Crane*, which specifically instructs against taking the life of any living creature) seem intended to instill a didactic message in young readers.

Even such homiletic small scrolls, however, should not be considered strictly on the basis of their didacticism as stories illustrated for children. Adults too were avid readers of moralistic short stories, and the emperor himself was a known auditor of similar tales.[76] In many ways, the subject matter of small scrolls reinforces what we already know about reading practice in this period in general: adults and children shared texts, and reading was a communal and social activity. Young people, or more precisely boys of the highest social classes, received rigorous training in reading with the ultimate goal of enabling them to participate in adult society by sponsoring or leading poetry gatherings and to attain fluency in the poetic, literary, and philosophical references that made up the common parlance of the day. For this reason, young people were necessarily educated using the same texts read by adults, such as excerpts from the *Collection of Ancient and Modern Poems*, *The Tale of Genji*, and Chinese classical and historical texts such as the *Classic of Filial Piety* and the Confucian *Analects*. Sanetaka taught his son Kin'eda (1487–1563) the latter two texts at the ages of six and seven respectively.[77] There were of course primers made just for children, such as the *Thousand Character Classic*, which Kin'eda was introduced to at age four.[78] But even adults were known to use such introductory works—in the creation of new literary texts, for example.[79] In other words, it is virtually impossible to find texts read exclusively by young people in the medieval period.

Children, adolescents, and adults also all read the same kinds of picture scrolls; *emaki* depicting military battles, which scholars do not tend to associate with children, provide a good example. In 1204, one year after assuming the position of shogun, the thirteen-year-old Minamoto no Sanetomo (1192–1219) was presented with *Rebellion of Taira Masakado* (*Masakado kassen-e*).[80] In 1245 another set of picture scrolls depicting the Masakado rebellion was presented to the seven-year-old Fujiwara no Yoritsugu (1239–56), who had become shogun in Kamakura in 1244.[81] The scrolls were commissioned by the shogunate from artists in Kyoto and read aloud for the young shogun by a retainer named Kiyohara Nori- taka the day after their arrival in Kamakura. A drinking party followed the viewing and recitation. Like Sanetomo before him, Yoritsugu received these scrolls and listened to the account of the battles one year after being designated shogun. The performance of this ancient battle tale thus resembles an initiation rite, marking the beginning of the boys' tenure as military leaders (albeit as figureheads), as well as their education in the country's military history.[82] While illustrated scrolls of battles seemed to have had a key role in the education and indoctrination of young puppet shoguns, they were by no means geared solely toward a young audience. The illustrated scrolls of *The Later Three Years' War* (*Gosannen kassen-e*, 1347, depicting an eleventh-century battle), for example, were highly praised by Sanjōnishi Sanetaka, who viewed them after they had been seen by Emperor GoKashiwabara.[83] Battle scrolls thus demonstrate how *emaki* suited audiences of varying ages.

In fact, adults and young people in the upper echelons of society frequently exchanged both large and small picture scrolls. Karen Brock has thoroughly documented such exchanges between the boy emperor GoHanazono and the shogun Ashikaga Yoshinori and demonstrates how viewings of specific titles could be deliberately orchestrated and motivated by political, lineal, or educational concerns.[84] Such exchanges of course continued in the late fifteenth century. In 1479 the fourteen-year-old Ashikaga Yoshihisa requested to see Emperor GoTsuchimikado's newly created two-volume picture scroll of *Holy Man Myōe of Toganoo* (*Toganoo Myōe Shōnin-e*), and two years later he lent the emperor twenty-three scrolls of his own.[85] Yoshihisa's receipt of eleven small scrolls from Hosokawa Shigeyuki in 1481 has already been mentioned, but the young shogun also borrowed fifteen large-size *emaki* on the same occasion.[86] The titles of scrolls borrowed in such large groups do not appear in the diary entries, making interpretations about the motivations behind the exchanges impossible. The numbers alone, however, confirm that a young person's reading material was in no way circumscribed by format, nor did it consist primarily of small-format works.

There are also descriptions of adults viewing, reading, and commissioning small scrolls. Two examples of fourteenth-century works being read and praised by grown men have already been observed: Prince Sadafusa viewing the *Activities of the Twelfth Month* scroll and Sanjōnishi Sanetaka viewing and reading aloud from Sei Shōnagon's *Pillow Book*. Still other examples in Sanetaka's diary demonstrate that "short-story small scrolls" were made for adults, such as *Clouds of Mt. Kōya* (*Takano gumo-e*) made for GoTsuchimikado in 1474–79 and a Buddhist "tale of rebirth" (*ōjōden*) made for the same emperor in 1498.[87] Both of these examples complicate the reigning hypothesis about the nature of small scrolls as objects intended for young people, and this is perhaps why these two works have not factored into any prior discussion of small scrolls.

By simply attributing the appearance of small scrolls to a juvenile audience, an opportunity to examine other factors related to scale has been overlooked. One of these issues, the importance of brevity and its relationship to readerly experience and to the pictorial representation in small scrolls has already been discussed. Another aspect related to scale that has been obscured by the acceptance of *ko-e* as children's possessions is the broader cultural context surrounding the sudden popularity of the small format, including the metaphorical meaning of smallness in the fifteenth century.

SMALLNESS IN LATE MEDIEVAL CULTURE

Given the long-standing view of small scrolls as diminutive objects produced for a juvenile readership, one might wonder whether there was something intrinsically childish about things described by the prefix *ko*. While the nuances of any term can change according to context, an examination of other words to which *ko* was attached demonstrates that the prefix did not necessarily infantilize the noun it preceded. When the term was used in reference to works from an earlier age, as we have seen, it seems to have simply suggested a format that branched off from a preexisting tradition of larger scrolls. In reference to works produced in the fifteenth century, the term may have conveyed a sense, not of childishness, but of intimacy and informality.

The era in which short-story small scrolls first appeared coincided with the emergence of other new forms of art and architecture characterized by a reduction in both scale and formality. Although several of these new forms were similarly described as *ko*, they were not necessarily associated with youth. Rather, the term in these instances appears to connote small, unofficial, and private. A prime example is a type of building within the imperial palace compound referred to as the "Small Palace" (*kogosho*). From the Ōei period (1394–1428) onward, the Small Palace measured four by five bays, significantly smaller than the size of the Small Palace in the previous Nanbokuchō period (1336–92).[88] After the Ōnin War, the Small Palace, in contrast to the formal spaces of the imperial complex such as the Ceremonial Hall (*shishinden*) and the Daily Palace (*tsune no gosho*), functioned as a meeting space (*kaisho*) for unofficial social events.[89] The Small Palace became the setting for *renga* and *waka* gatherings, flower-arranging sessions, moon and snow viewings, and for individual meetings with the emperor, on which occasion, in keeping with the private nature of the space, he wore unofficial attire.[90] With respect to the emperor's Small Palace, the term *ko* seems to denote a relatively intimate social space.

An even more intimate space was codified in architectural practice in the late fifteenth century in the form of the *kozashiki*, literally the "small room," which became a popular setting for tea gatherings in the sixteenth century. Sanjōnishi Sanetaka purchased a *kozashiki* (from another architectural compound) in 1502; it was a six-mat room for which he constructed a small viewing garden.[91] The interior of Sanetaka's *kozashiki* was covered in tatami, adorned with Chinese paper on its walls, and outfitted with a built-in desk (*oshi-ita*), shelves (*tana*), and other features of the *shoin* style.[92] This type of architectural setting facilitated cultural gatherings of individuals from different social strata and led to the development of small-scale tearooms.[93] But Sanetaka's *kozashiki*, where he could work in solitude, contemplate the rocks and small trees in his new viewing garden, or host a small group of friends or acquaintances, might also be seen as an architectural equivalent of the small scroll. Like the *ko-e*, with its intimate physical relationship to the viewer and its nature as a personal, private possession, the small room was a personalized alternative to the main residence.

Coinciding with these developments in architecture is the increasing use of a type of painting format that was also referred to in period texts as a *ko-e:* the small vertical hanging scroll. Examples of such usage appear in the *Record of the Shogunal Attendant* (*Kundaikan sōchōki*), a manual on the display of Chinese artworks compiled by the cultural advisers to the shogun Ashikaga Yoshimasa (1436–90).[94] Amid the directives for displaying precious Chinese objects such as tea bowls, incense burners, and flower vases, the manual suggests that *ko-e* should be hung on *ko-kabe*, small walls above the staggered shelves (*chigaidana*) found in the alcoves of *kaisho* meeting rooms. These *ko-e* were Chinese works, and as paintings hung in the shogunal residence they evoke a viewership antithetical to the stereotypical one of *ko-e* handscrolls, that is, adult male leaders of the government. The prefix in this fifteenth-century context conveys no hint of a minor art form or juvenile content. Rather, the small format worked in conjunction with the miniaturized architectural features of the *kaisho*. If anything *ko-e* here participated in fashioning an environment that conveyed a sense of private privilege. In this regard the term *ko* again connotes the personal and, in the case of its use for a work in the shogunal art collection, exclusivity.

But small vertical scrolls were also owned and used by individuals besides the shogun. Sanetaka possessed a small picture of *Shaka Descending from the Mountain* (*Shussan Shaka*), a hanging scroll in ink by a Chinese artist named Ke Shan (dates unknown).[95] It is likely that he occasionally hung the scroll in a display alcove, perhaps even in the *kozashiki* that he purchased and outfitted in 1502.[96] On one occasion, this small picture of Shaka was referred to as a "small figure" (*kozō*), a term that evokes a genre of small portraits (*xiaoxiang*) by Chinese literati of the Yuan period (1206–1368). Such portraits were smaller than those used in mortuary rituals, and their size pointed to a private mode of appreciation; the paintings circulated within scholar-official networks and were inscribed by their members.[97] Although *ko-e* hanging scrolls in Sanetaka's circle were far removed from the context in which such likenesses were inscribed and exchanged in fourteenth-century China, nuances of individual appreciation that attended the Chinese tradition of small figure paintings may have been transferred to the Japanese context.

The small-format scroll began to permeate the upper echelons of Muromachi society, not only in the form of the vertical hanging scroll but for a variety of other functions related to new cultural trends specifically associated with this period, such as the art of flower arranging. Masters of "flower presentation" (*tatebana*) began to appear in the fifteenth century in the context of the decoration of the *zashiki* and *shoin* spaces, which focused on the display of the so-called three implements (*mitsu-gusoku*): an incense burner, a candleholder, and a flower vase.[98] Flower-arranging manuals (*kadensho*) were passed down within the lineages of flower-arranging masters as closely guarded secrets. The format of choice for illustrated versions of these manuals was the small-format handscroll. At 15.3 centimeters in height, the oldest such manuscript, *Flower Arranging Manual* (*Kaō irai kadensho*, 1499, fig. 29), is typical, and the small size seems to have been in keeping with the private nature of the transmitted texts.

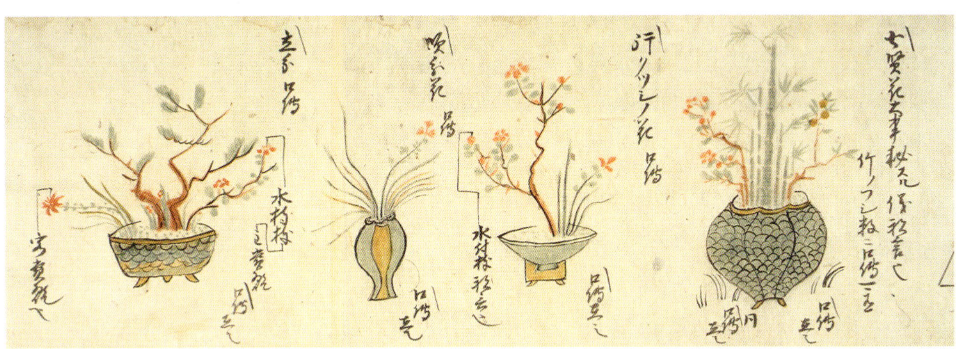

29 *Flower Arranging Manual* (*Kaō irai kadensho*). 1499. H. 15.3 cm. Kadō Iemoto, Ikenobō Sōmusho, Kyoto.

Another example of particular relevance to both Mitsunobu and Sanetaka is the use of the small format for transcriptions of linked verse (*renga*). Verses composed during *renga* gatherings were often recorded on full-size sheets of paper (roughly thirty centimeters in height) that had been folded in half lengthwise, creating a recto and verso with the fold at the bottom, and were subsequently bound. The term *renga kaishi*, literally "*renga* sleeve papers," suggests that the small folded papers could be placed inside one's garment. Given Mitsunobu's frequent participation in linked-verse gatherings (to be discussed in chapter 2) and Sanetaka's engagement with the poetic form, both men would have been familiar with small-format *renga kaishi*, official copies of which employed decorative dyed papers and underdrawings over which calligraphy was inscribed (fig. 30). Mitsunobu's studio may even have designed and painted the underdrawings of *renga kaishi*, as it did for calligraphic excerpts from *The Tale of Genji*.[99]

It is tempting to imagine that the sudden increase in small-scroll narrative paintings in the fifteenth century bears a direct connection to the circulation of small-format scrolls made for the purposes described above, all of which connote privacy, intimacy, and exclusivity. At the very least, painters and their collaborators may have been encouraged to look at the materials at their disposal in a new light. Consciousness of the small format and its connotations of personalization may have prompted its use for certain kinds of narratives, rather than simply for young readers. An important though overlooked distinction between Mitsunobu's regular and small-format handscrolls is their subject matter. All of Mitsunobu's extant standard-

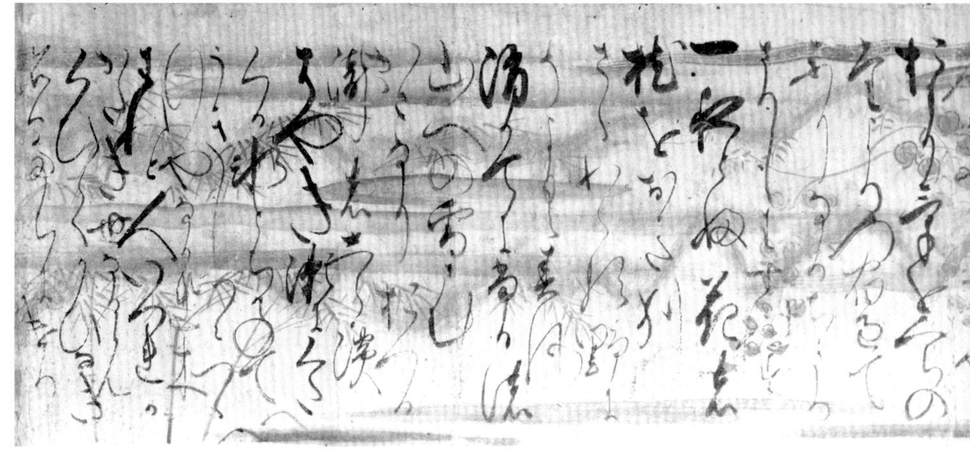

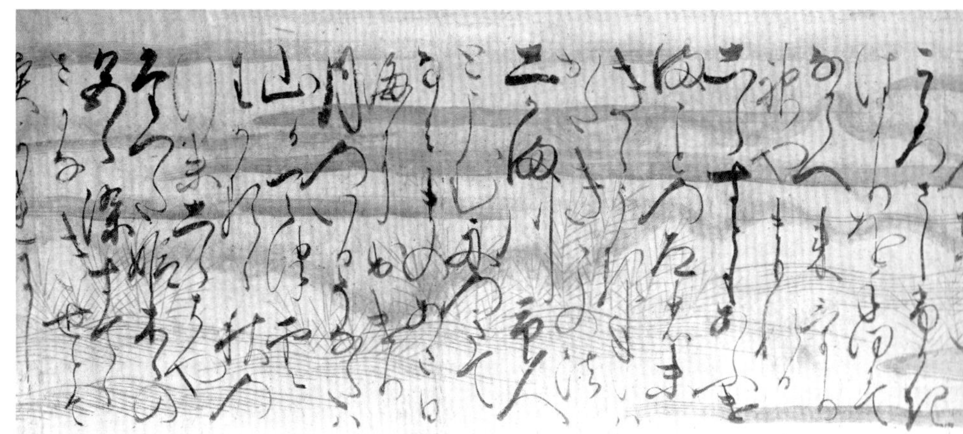

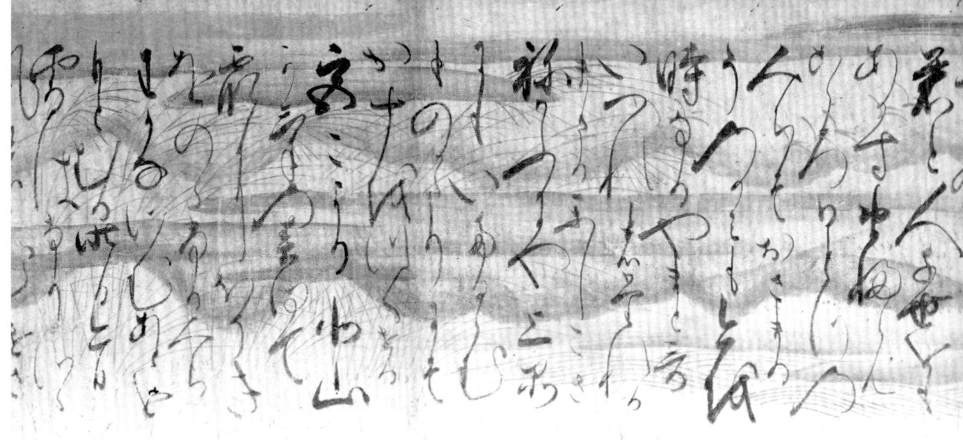

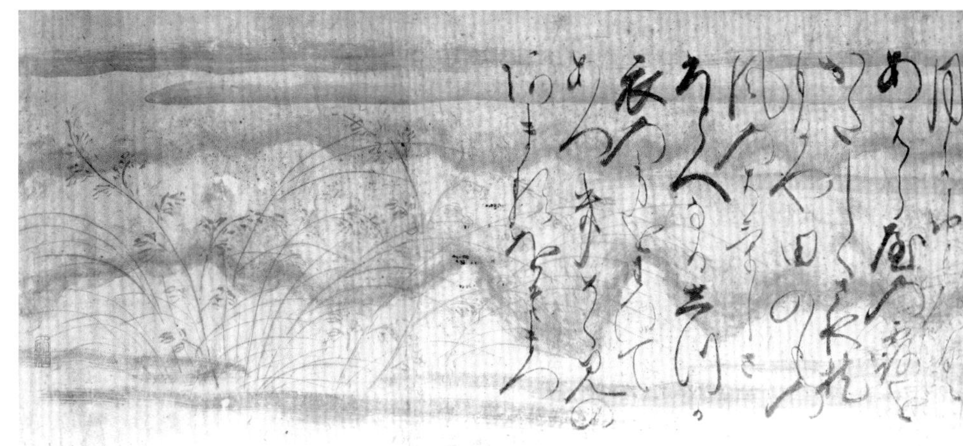

30 Linked verse on the topic "What Boat?" Dated 1474. Poems by Senjun (1418–89). One handscroll; ink, gold, and silver on cloud-pattern dyed paper, H. 17.7 cm. Harvard Art Museum, Arthur M. Sackler Museum, Gift of the Hofer Collection of the Printed and Graphic Arts of Asia in honor of Miss Louise A. Cort, 1973.67. Photograph by Rick Stafford © President and Fellows of Harvard College.

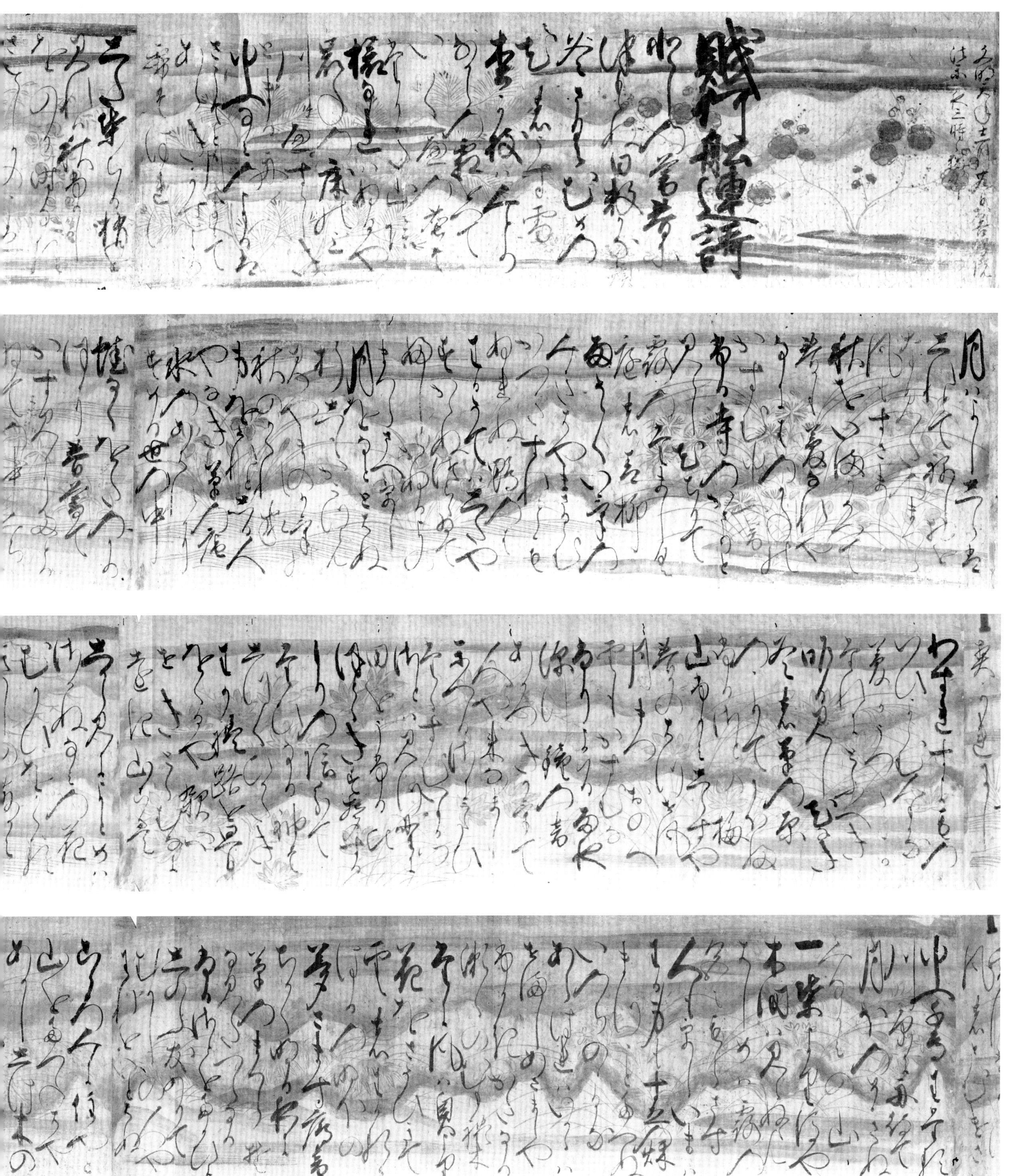

size scrolls illustrate official temple or shrine histories, while his small-format handscrolls illustrate short stories; his handscrolls that no longer survive seem to have been similarly divided.[100] Mitsunobu's illustrated temple legends were official, sacred works, made in lavish multivolume sets of great length, often dedicated to the institution, and only brought out for special occasions or for viewing by socially prominent individuals, such as the emperor, before whom they were seen by large groups while their texts were read aloud.

As informal, single scrolls owned by individuals and read alone or in intimate groups, Mitsunobu's *ko-e* clearly stand at the other end of the spectrum of handscroll production. Having witnessed the use of small-format scrolls to decorate the *zashiki* alcove, to illustrate private instructional texts, or to transcribe *renga* verse, artists seem to have considered this medium as another option, not simply for illustrating a miniaturized version of a given subject, but for depicting certain kinds of stories. This would have represented a break from the long-standing tradition of *emaki*, in which never before had there been a distinct representational site for the illustration of short stories. Such a new approach was predicated upon two historical conditions: the rich handscroll tradition against which it could define itself and the unusually proximate collaboration between a scholarly editor, Sanetaka, and a literate and talented painter, Mitsunobu. Both seem to have recognized that the small-format picture scroll, previously used sparingly out of convenience, in fact had the potential to suit handsomely the literary and social contingencies of a new mode of cultural consumption in late medieval Kyoto. The following chapter maps out the historical, intellectual, and cultural context in which these two individuals, so crucial to the small-scroll moment, pursued their mutual endeavors.

2 THE CULTURAL MILIEU OF SANJŌNISHI SANETAKA AND TOSA MITSUNOBU

Small scrolls can be understood as an extension of—or, rather, the epitome of—mutualistic artistic relationships that characterized most cultural production in the military and aristocratic circles of late medieval Kyoto. The environment itself demanded works of great sophistication, works that accommodated religious rituals of the most abstruse kind or visually distilled the merits of highly allusive literary texts. To meet the ambitious communicative agendas of these works, the preparatory process had to be informed by one or more knowledgeable consultants. Craftsmen were thus brought into contact with *renga* poets, Buddhist monks, and scholar-courtiers, who not only served as the gatekeepers of precedent but also functioned as sounding boards and go-betweens for the patron. Every high-level artistic commission brought together a unique constellation of such figures that communicated regularly for the duration of the project, only to disperse upon its completion. Within this ever-shifting environment, the professional bond between Sanjōnishi Sanetaka and Tosa Mitsunobu was unique in its staying power: seven collaborations over forty years have been recorded, or exist to this day, but given the lacunae of the archival record during this period, this figure surely fails to represent the full measure of their mutual endeavors.

Aside from the regularity and endurance of this collaboration, however, the Sanetaka-Mitsunobu relationship was also notable for its quality. The success of their teamwork stems from the fact that both had the ability to meet their partner halfway. Sanetaka was intimately informed about the history of painting and its menu of subjects and was himself the creator of aesthetic objects in the form of literary works; Mitsunobu was a poet in his own right, with the capacity for an extra-painterly appreciation of literary tales. The resulting

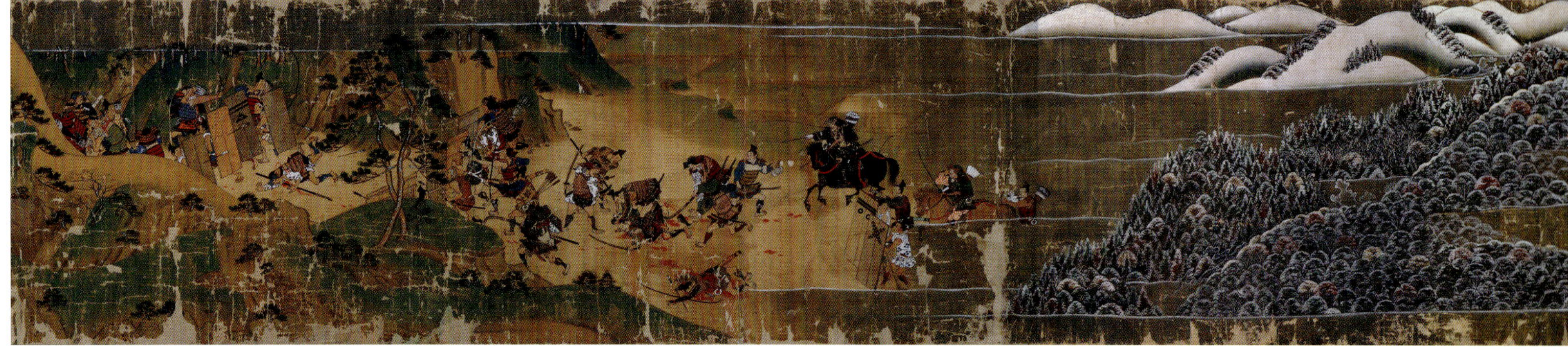

31 *Miracles of the Kasuga Deity* (*Kasuga Gongen kenki-e*). Dated 1309. Twenty scrolls; ink and color on silk, H. 41.0 cm. Museum of the Imperial Collections (Kunaichō Sannomaru Shōzōkan), Tokyo. Detail, scroll 19.

symbiosis was manifested in the artifacts they mutually created, first and foremost the small scrolls. Each worked with other collaborators, but often only on one occasion. During the same period, other such relationships are known, but they lacked the quality of engagement that characterized interactions between the Tosa artist and the Sanjōnishi scion.

Examining this relationship provides the best possible framework for an exploration of the context out of which small scrolls emerged. Thanks in large part to Sanetaka's magisterial diary, fastidiously maintained for sixty-one years, we know that Sanetaka and Mitsunobu collaborated in the production of a wide range of artworks—Buddhist ritual icons, mortuary portraits, official temple and shrine legends, as well as small scrolls—some of which still survive. This exploration also provides a context for the picture scroll culture of the period. Viewed from the perspective of the many different narrative handscrolls being produced in late medieval Japan, small scrolls occupy one extreme end of the spectrum, based upon the intimacy of the viewing environments they presupposed. At the other end are situated the pictorialized origin tales (*engi*) upon which Sanetaka and Mitsunobu also brought their energies to bear. Although these colorful and meticulously crafted works lie outside the purview of this study, they nevertheless highlight the specificity of small scrolls, and I will touch upon them here accordingly. Also significant are the social circles and subjectivities of these two figures; given the longevity of their professional relationship over several generations, its nature can be better understood by sketching what is known about the other activities and relationships in which they participated. This is all the more crucial considering that both Sanetaka and Mitsunobu have been the subject of only minimal attention in English.[1] The profiles that follow, then, serve as a social history of small scrolls from the perspective of their paired creators. It is motivated by the assumption that the unique representational qualities of short-story small scrolls derive to no small extent from the unique synergy of the collaboration between Sanetaka and Mitsunobu.

THE RECEPTION OF *MIRACLES OF THE KASUGA DEITY*

Let us begin, then, with Sanetaka the courtier. An episode from 1490 concerning a recitation of the famous *Miracles of the Kasuga Deity* scrolls at the imperial court provides a good introduction to Sanetaka's role in the cultural production of his day. According to Sanetaka's diary entry for Entoku 2 (1490) 7.22:

> Clear skies. Rose early, bathed, and, after eating breakfast, went to the palace. Recited the picture scroll text in the emperor's private Buddhist hall [*kurodo-no-gosho*]. I read scrolls one through ten, Major Counselor Nakamikado read scrolls eleven through thirteen, and then I read again from scrolls fourteen to twenty. The highest-ranking nobles came

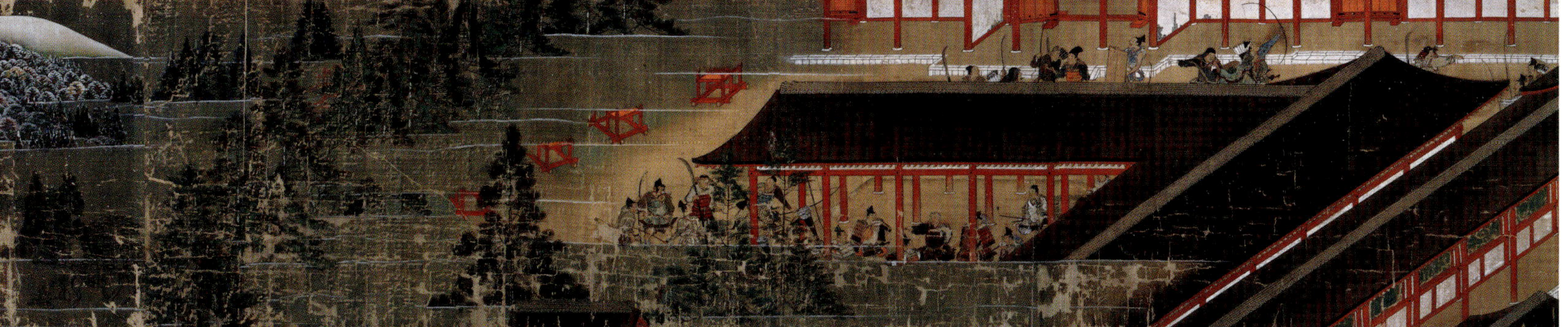

in great numbers to behold the work. The paintings portrayed the profound miraculous workings of the deity; they are sacred and mysterious. The great benevolence of the deity moved people to shed tears of gratitude.[2]

Sanetaka's testimony chronicles a gathering that took place at the imperial palace on the twenty-second day of the seventh month of the year 1490. On that occasion Emperor GoTsuchimikado (1442–1500; r. 1464–1500), who was approaching his fiftieth birthday, gathered his highest-ranking courtiers around him to view and read all twenty of the felicitous scrolls of *Miracles of the Kasuga Deity* (fig. 31). Created in 1309 and later donated to the Kasuga Shrine in Nara, these sacred treasures depicted the miracles performed by the Kasuga Gongen—the tutelary deity of the Fujiwara clan—in rich pigments on rolls of silk.[3] The court painter Takashina Takakane (fl. 1309–30) had executed the paintings, while the former head of the Fujiwara clan and his three sons, one of them the current regent, had brushed the calligraphy.[4] The project was conceived and sponsored by Saionji Kinhira (1264–1315), apparently in thanks for his appointment to the post of minister of the left (*sadaijin*) in the same year.[5] In terms of physical appearance, sacral content, and symbolic significance vis-à-vis their celebration of Fujiwara heritage, the scrolls set a standard to which all later painted shrine offerings would aspire. The work was rarely seen and even more rarely removed from the shrine; only a personal request from the likes of the emperor or a shogun could elicit its transference to Kyoto.[6] Thus, the courtiers who gathered on this day in 1490 understood this to be a once-in-a-lifetime opportunity to see the renowned paintings and to hear their texts read aloud in the presence of the emperor and their peers.

A few days before the event, the emperor sent word to Sanjōnishi Sanetaka that he should be in attendance at the palace for the viewing, and that he would be called upon to read aloud from the twenty scrolls.[7] In preparation, Sanetaka fasted, bathed the night before, and cleansed himself again on the morning of the event. Sanetaka understood the scrolls themselves to be a sacred manifestation of the Kasuga deity, and his belief in their power reveals itself in a telling episode a few days later. During the scrolls' temporary stay in Kyoto the emperor lent them to Kajūji Norihide, a well-connected courtier who also happened to be Sanetaka's father-in-law.[8] When Sanetaka heard that the scrolls would be viewed at the Kajūji household, he sent his wife there to see the work, making a point to mention in his diary that her menstrual cycle was eight days late and thus that she would not defile the scrolls.[9] Sanetaka's preoccupation with the state of his wife's body when she encountered the scrolls further illustrates his belief in the sacredness of the objects and his concern over paying the deity proper respect. But his deliberate mention of her menstrual cycle hints at other motives at work as well. In the third month of the following year Sanetaka's wife gave birth to a daughter; Sanetaka may have suspected his wife's pregnancy and sent her to view the *Kasuga* scrolls in the hopes that the deity would bless them with a child, a healthy childbirth, and a prosperous family line.[10]

The communal appreciation of *Miracles of the Kasuga Deity* at the imperial palace raises several issues concerning the status of the picture scroll during this period. The first concerns the dual nature of the *Kasuga*

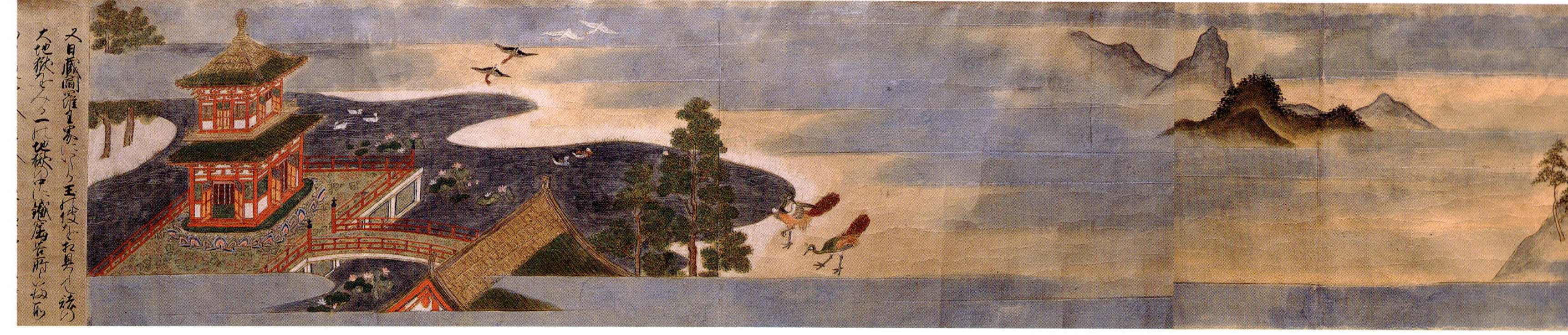

32 Tosa Mitsunobu, *Legends of Kitano Tenjin* (*Kitano Tenjin engi emaki*). Dated 1503. Three scrolls; ink, color, and gold on paper, H. 36.3 cm. Kitano Tenmangū, Kyoto. Important Cultural Property.

scrolls. While depicting the miraculous deeds of the Kasuga deity, the object itself was also thought to represent a manifestation of that deity. In other words, the set of scrolls was both a visual record of this numinous entity and its sacred embodiment. The former function is well understood, but it is through the latter capacity that the significance of the *Kasuga* scrolls for its medieval readers can be fully grasped. It was in the productive oscillation between these two roles—representation and embodiment, visuality and materiality, art and object—that *Miracles of the Kasuga Deity* acquired its efficacy. The ado surrounding the reading—Sanetaka's purification rituals, the anxiety over defilement, the hope for conception through divine intercession—all reflect a consciousness of the auratic presence of the deity, both represented in but also *dwelling within* the scrolls.

A second issue raised by the 1490 reading concerns the aural component of picture scroll viewing. The *Miracles of the Kasuga Deity* scrolls were in a sense performed at the imperial palace through the vocalization of their texts by Sanetaka and Nakamikado Nobutane. A special viewing dais had been constructed for the work at the time of its creation in the early fourteenth century.[11] Roughly two meters in width, the viewing platform opens in the manner of a folding screen to lie flat and prevent the scrolls from touching the floor. The width of the platform would have accommodated the unrolling of long portions of the scrolls to reveal both a complete text section and a corresponding painting. Thus, a relatively large group of viewers could have examined the paintings while listening to a simultaneous voice-over narration as the text was read aloud. This combination of visual and aural experience must have heightened the theatricality of the event; Sanetaka describes the audience as being moved to tears. The *Kasuga* scrolls, however, were not unique in being read aloud; oral recitations of picture scrolls occurred throughout the medieval period and sustained the popularity of the format.

The reading of the *Miracles of the Kasuga Deity* scrolls consisted of a cultural activity that provided one way of defining an aristocratic social body in this period. The event brought together the leading aristocrats in the capital, where they witnessed the past glory of the Fujiwara house and the miraculous powers of the protective deity of their clan. In fact, the reading and viewing of picture scrolls until the fifteenth century was for the most part a communal experience. The objects themselves were a pretense for social interaction, and the acquisition of a picture scroll, whether borrowed or created anew, inspired social gatherings in a variety of contexts. As the passage from Sanetaka's diary demonstrates, however, even officious handscrolls of the "miraculous origins" variety could function in multiple capacities for diverse constituencies. The Kajūji household viewing, for example, while still communal, nevertheless represented a much smaller audience with a somewhat differently invested readership. As one of the prominent family lines descended from Fujiwara aristocracy, the Kajūji no doubt thought

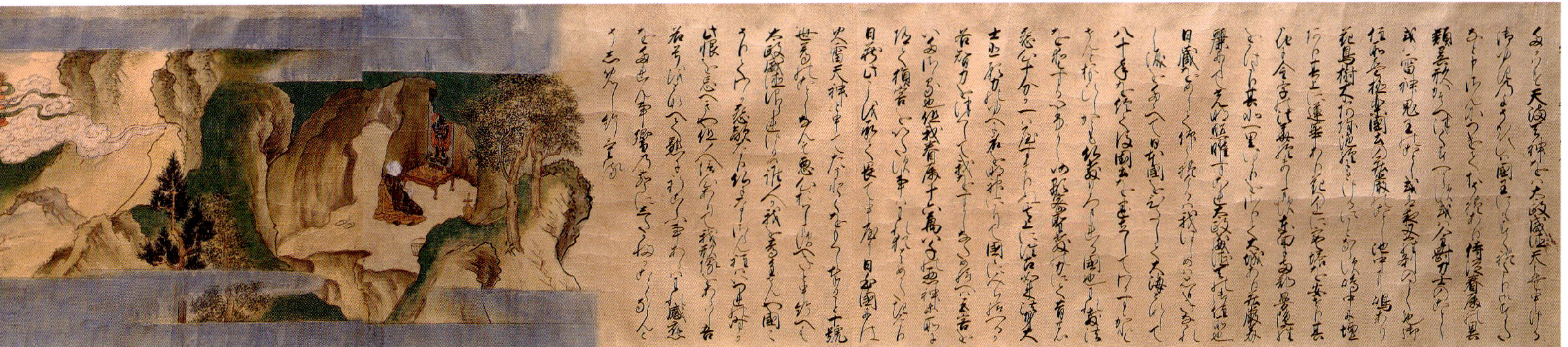

of the *Kasuga* scrolls as a shared family treasure and the protagonist as their own tutelary deity; yet the structure of their viewing—based upon an imperial loan and in a residential setting—indicates a literary and historic interest as much as a ritual engagement. Nonpublic viewing experiences were much more the norm for those historically significant picture scrolls that were not associated with a religious institution. *Emaki* pictorializing tale literature and classics from the Heian period were often kept in the possession of elite aristocratic clans and discretely circulated for reasons that might be described as primarily social and pedagogical.[12] In these cases the audiences for the scrolls need to be conceptualized at the level of the clan, family, or household rather than at the extreme poles of the court or individual. By the fifteenth century, the Ashikaga shogunate and certain elite warrior houses had so penetrated the fabric of Kyoto aristocracy that they had become enmeshed in the networks within which these objects circulated. It is against the background of this medieval picture scroll culture that the new cultural work of small scrolls needs to be understood.

A final issue highlighted by the viewing of the *Kasuga* scrolls concerns the role of material objects in the communion with and preservation of the past courtly tradition. Emperor GoTsuchimikado ascended to the throne in 1464, just three years before the outbreak of the Ōnin War (1467–77), which devastated the capital and destroyed a large portion of the precious manuscripts in the imperial archive.[13] Immediately after the war GoTsuchimikado instituted a movement to replenish this archive, resulting in a surge in the copying of a wide range of texts, from classical works of Japanese prose to Chinese poetry anthologies and Buddhist legends.[14] Sanetaka was one of the courtiers at the very center of this initiative. The diligence with which these men undertook this project, as glimpsed in period diaries, suggests a unified effort to reassemble for future generations a textual tradition that was in danger of eradication from the political unrest of the late fifteenth century. Manuscripts that had survived the ravages of battle became even more valuable as objects with a visceral connection to the past and from which new works could be birthed. To Sanetaka and his peers, *Miracles of the Kasuga Deity* was the most sacred and splendid symbol of Fujiwara heritage, but these scrolls were also artifacts that had transcended the recent conflagrations to link these men to their forebears.

As a member of what was by then an enormous Fujiwara lineage, Tosa Mitsunobu also had a stake in the symbolic currency of the *Kasuga* scrolls, but as a painter, he had even more interest in the scrolls as a representational model. Mitsunobu discussed the scrolls and their preparatory drawings with Sanetaka in 1501, while in the midst of creating another sacred handscroll, *Legends of Kitano Tenjin* (*Kitano Tenjin engi emaki*) (fig. 32).[15] The process by which this later work came into being sheds light on the way both men approached their cultural collaboration. Sanetaka and Mitsunobu were asked to work on the *Kitano Tenjin* scrolls in order to replace a celebrated version belonging to the shrine from the thirteenth century (the "Jōkyū" version), which had recently been lost.[16] Like the *Kasuga* scrolls, this work would be consecrated as a sacred manifestation of the shrine deity, reflected in the unusual gravitas with which Sanetaka carried out his inscription of the calligraphy.

Sanetaka had accepted the task with a degree of solemnity not usually recorded in his diary for other, similar responsibilities, and he made sure to bathe before executing the calligraphy on each of the four separate occasions that it took him to complete the text of the three scrolls.[17]

Sanetaka frequently acted as editor or coordinator of projects in which texts and images were involved, including narrative handscroll projects and compendia of calligraphy and paintings.[18] Mitsunobu visited Sanetaka on several occasions to receive advice on how to interpret pictorially the texts that were to accompany his paintings and to hear what the patron may have had in mind, conveyed through Sanetaka. When Mitsunobu had nearly completed the preparatory drawings for the *Kitano* scrolls, he went to see Sanetaka at the request of the patron to discuss the paintings. During their first meeting for the *Kitano* scrolls project they discussed, among other things, Takashina Takakane's preparatory drawings for *Miracles of the Kasuga Deity* scrolls, which Sanetaka referred to as "Takakane's divinely inspired designs."[19] Takakane had executed the full set of preparatory drawings and texts for the scrolls, which was itself regarded as a great treasure. Although donated along with the finished scrolls to the Kasuga Shrine in the early fourteenth century, the sketches had become heirlooms of the Fushimi family and were therefore in circulation in Kyoto, where Sanetaka could have had access to them.[20] While the details of the discussion between Sanetaka and Mitsunobu are unrecorded, it is certain that Takakane's work was held up as an ideal for the pictorialization of sacred subject matter.

The two episodes concerning the *Kasuga* scrolls just described—the court recitation and the Sanetaka-Mitsunobu collaboration on a new set—provide a context for understanding small scrolls, despite the fact that religious *emaki* and small scrolls were experienced in different ways. Small scrolls were largely informal works read more frequently than religious scrolls, which required special permission and important occasions to be removed from their temple or shrine collections. In many ways, the small scroll is defined in opposition to the large-scale temple or shrine legend work.

Even a cursory glance at the six works that make up Mitsunobu's extant oeuvre of handscrolls reveals a telling distinction: three standard-size handscrolls illustrate temple or shrine legends, while three small-format handscrolls depict short stories in single scrolls. It seems as though Mitsunobu distinguished between categories of handscroll painting in terms of subject matter and format, suggesting a consciousness of picture scroll genre that had not existed before. This is not surprising considering that it was during the Muromachi period that the genre of *engi-e* (dependent-origin scrolls) first took shape as a distinct category of painting.[21] Mitsunobu's awareness of handscroll genres may have contributed to the sharp distinction between *ko-e* and *engi-e* in his body of work and certainly suggests that in his workshop practice the execution of small scrolls was approached in a unique manner.

Small scrolls were intended for intimate reading experiences, although this still means that a variety of scenarios need to be envisioned. As we have seen, even the *Kasuga* scrolls could have a private audience of a single household's members, while small scrolls might also have been read aloud, albeit for a much smaller audience of one or two viewers. As objects that allow for communing with the past, works like the *Kasuga* scrolls or the numerous temple and shrine legend scrolls that Mitsunobu created differ greatly from small scrolls. A central premise of this study is that small scrolls were not copies of existing scrolls that had been lost or damaged but new Muromachi period stories that were often illustrated for the first time in these works. Small scrolls still drew upon past literary and painting traditions but became a uniquely visual distillation of the knowledge of past classics that men like Sanetaka and Mitsunobu were acquiring through their many encounters with older scrolls and their work in rebuilding the "lost archive." For men like Mitsunobu and Sanetaka immersed in their study and manual reproduction of older works, the small format, being relatively new to the fifteenth century, became a site for experimentation with genre and traditional literary and pictorial forms.

In the remainder of this chapter I will examine the roles played by the painter Mitsunobu and the courtier

Sanetaka in the facilitation of a "small-scroll culture." Their collaborative projects demonstrate the new types of interrelationality that were symptomatic of the communities anticipated by *ko-e* and, along with their independent projects, illustrate the depth of knowledge that they brought to bear on small-scroll production. An important place to begin is with Mitsunobu's position as "Painting Bureau director," a title and role that gave him access to a wide range of artifacts and to individuals who would be crucial to his survival as a professional artist and his identity within Kyoto society.

MITSUNOBU, PAINTING BUREAU DIRECTOR

The only pictorial image of Tosa Mitsunobu (fig. 33) that survives, an anonymous copy of a portrait sketch of the artist, encapsulates his identity as Painting Bureau director. He is dressed in formal court attire, with a sword at his waist and holding a wooden baton (*shaku*), and a folding fan lies before him on top of a lacquered tray. The inclusion of the fan points to his responsibility, as director of the Painting Bureau, of presenting fans both to the imperial court and the shogunate in the first month of the New Year, as well as to the countless fans his studio executed for individuals throughout the year.[22] The portrait sketch most likely dates to the Edo period, a time when hereditary painting studios were engaged in new strategies to legitimize their status, including the authorship of Japan's first histories of painting, within which a given painting school could be systematically presented as the natural successor to a vaunted predecessor.[23] Members of the Kanō School have been duly recognized as masters of these methods of self-promotion, but Tosa School artists also made bold lineal claims through a variety of discursive practices. One strategy to bolster the reputation of Tosa Mitsunobu as an illustrious predecessor and possessor of the *azukari* (director) title was to attribute to him a large number of existing works.[24]

As a result, modern scholars attempting to pin down Mitsunobu's oeuvre were confronted with many (dubious) Edo period attributions, and a clear understanding of a "Mitsunobu style" was not achieved until the mid-1990s.[25] Although it may at first seem difficult to break through the layers of discourse that have accumulated around the name of Mitsunobu, extant paintings and contemporary documents reveal a great deal concerning his artistic practices. An examination of period documents alone, for example, shows that Edo period artists were not unique in their preoccupation with lineage. The construction of Mitsunobu begins, not in the Edo period, but with the artist himself in the fifteenth century. A few concrete examples will demonstrate Mitsunobu's self-awareness of being part of a lineage of Painting Bureau directors, a consciousness of tradition that informs his painting practice as well.

In 1517, toward the end of his career, Tosa Mitsunobu himself claimed to have descended from the fourteenth-century artist Fujiwara no Yukimitsu (active

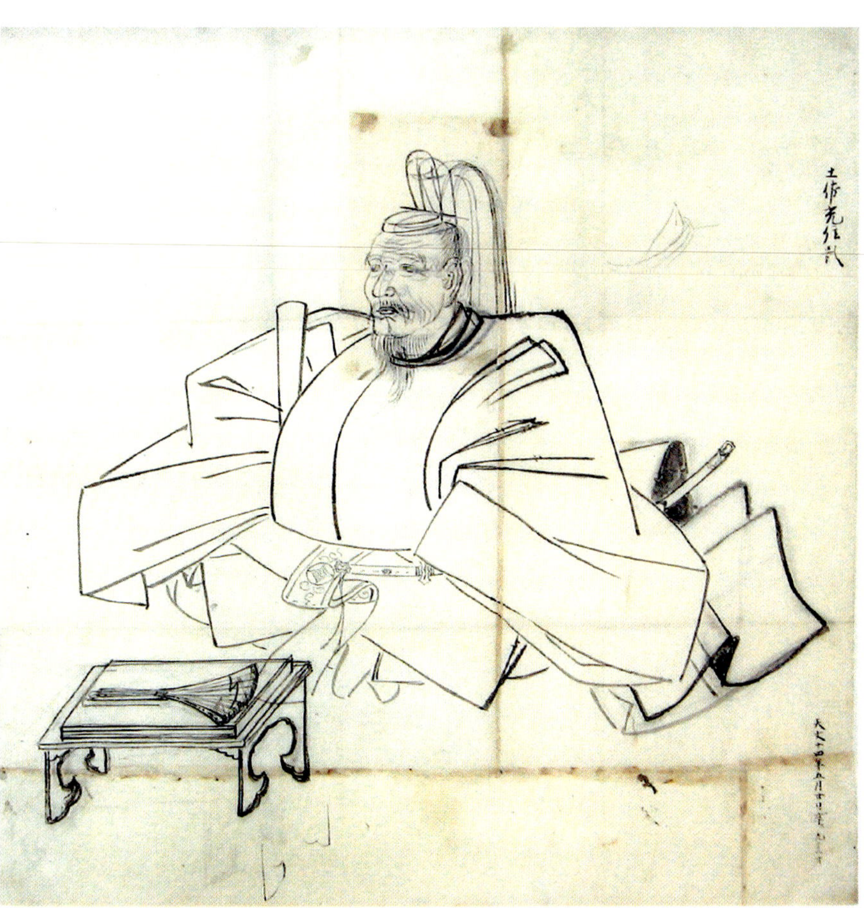

33 Portrait sketch of Tosa Mitsunobu. Undated. Single sheet; ink on paper, 49.3 x 47.2. Archives of the Kyoto City University of Arts.

mid- to late fourteenth century), whom scholars consider the founder of the Tosa School.[26] Mitsunobu made this connection while in the process of attributing an ancient folding-screen painting belonging to the courtier Nakamikado Nobutane (1442–1525) to Yukimitsu, whom he described as his "ancestor" (*senzo*).[27] Nobutane mentions the attribution in his diary, where he explains that the screen most likely depicts a gathering at the imperial court that took place in 1367, as described in the fourteenth-century historical epic *Taiheiki* (*Chronicle of Great Pacification*), and was painted soon afterward to commemorate the event.[28] Yukimitsu most likely received the title of *edokoro azukari* (Painting Bureau director) in 1352 and thus would have been the artist in that position when Nobutane's screen was painted.[29] Although there is no reason to doubt Mitsunobu's assertion, by claiming Yukimitsu as his ancestor the artist placed himself within a long line of illustrious Painting Bureau directors. Moreover, the subject matter of this screen made it a particularly desirable object with which to associate one's painterly lineage, since the extent to which a painter's own ancestors had served the imperial court could be crucial in determining an artistic career. The screen included actual portraits of aristocrats in attendance at an exclusive courtly gathering from one hundred and fifty years in the past and thus implied an intimate familiarity on the part of the painter of these likenesses with an ancient regime glorified in the *Taiheiki*.

A telling example of the importance of claiming an illustrious painterly pedigree is Mitsunobu's attempt to acquire the most prestigious commission at court: the painting of the displays for the Daijōe, or Harvest Festival, which marked the reign of a new emperor.[30] In 1466 Mitsunobu, the head of the Kasuga Studio (*Kasuga edokoro*), petitioned the court for the right to paint the mountain displays for the Daijōe ceremony for the accession of Emperor GoTsuchimikado (1442–1500; r. 1464–1500).[31] Although numerous painting studios (*edokoro*) populated the city of Kyoto, only one studio head possessed the officially designated *azukari* title, and it was this artist who customarily received the privilege of executing the Daijōe displays.[32] At that time the *azukari* was Rokkaku Masutsugu (active ca. 1451–77), head of the Rokkaku painting atelier.[33]

Mitsunobu attempted to disrupt the standard procedure and secure this commission for his studio by citing past precedent. He argued that the Kasuga Studio had executed the folding-screen paintings for the 1430 Daijōe ceremony of Emperor GoHanazono (1419–70; r. 1428–64) and should therefore be allowed to undertake the task again.[34] Rokkaku Masutsugu countered by citing another precedent, that of the 1383 Daijōe ceremony, for which a Rokkaku painter received the commission, and furthermore stressed the importance of the job going to the artist who currently held the *azukari* position.[35] The Muromachi *bakufu* apparently agreed with Rokkaku and decided that, all things being equal, it was only fair that the current *azukari* be designated the Daijōe painter.[36] A couple of months later the privilege was bestowed upon Rokkaku Masutsugu.[37] The Kasuga Studio clearly thought they had a chance at winning the commission. Certainly, things might have turned out differently if Masutsugu had not been able to cite a previous example of a Rokkaku painter performing the work.

The attempt by the head of the Kasuga Studio to usurp the Daijōe commission from the reigning *edokoro azukari* within the context of this rigidly structured society was clearly motivated by the high stakes. Aside from the prestige and status it awarded the painter, the Daijōe commission was a lucrative endeavor. When Rokkaku was selected for the commission, he received the hefty sum of 5,000 *hiki* for painting the *yuki* province portion of the display.[38] The payments did not end there, however. Roughly three months later, the studio received another 5,000 *hiki* for the remaining costs of this display, and one month after that it received another 4,000 *hiki* for work on the *suki* province displays, putting the grand total at 14,000 *hiki*.[39] Even if the production of the Daijōe displays entailed great expense, this staggering sum must have provided the artists with a considerable profit, at least enough to subsist on without having to pursue other projects.

Although the Kasuga Studio lost the bid for GoTsuchimikado's 1466 Daijōe ceremony, a mere three years

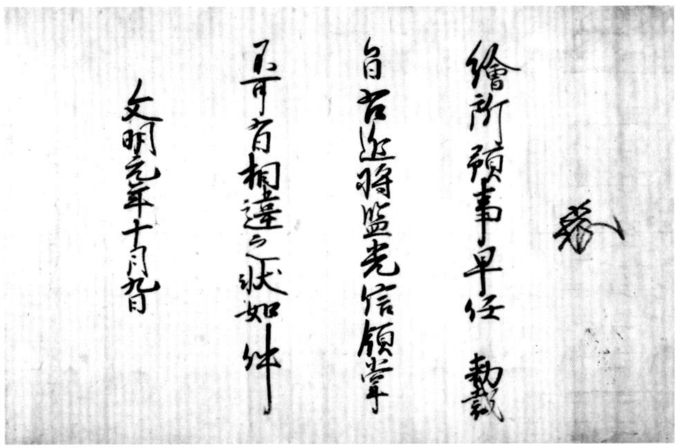

絵所預事早任勅裁
自右近将監光信領掌
不可有相違之状如件
文明元年十月九日

34 Letter signed by Ashikaga Yoshimasa confirming Mitsunobu as Painting Bureau director, from the *Tosa House Documents* (*Tosa ke monjo*). Dated Bunmei 1 (1469) 10.9. Scroll; ink on paper, 33.2 x 52.5 cm. Tokyo National Museum.

later the emperor bestowed upon Mitsunobu the *edokoro azukari* title, which he would hold for over fifty years. The appointment was confirmed by the shogun Ashikaga Yoshimasa (1436–90) in a document dated to Bunmei 1 (1469) 10.9 (fig. 34).[40] The longevity of Mitsunobu's tenure, spanning the reigns of two long-lived emperors, was unprecedented. The traditional practice had been to appoint a new *azukari* with each new imperial reign.[41] Although this system had already become less rigid in the early Muromachi period, Mitsunobu's ability to monopolize the title for so long is remarkable. He may have benefited from the uncertain political circumstances of his times and the decision by many other painters to seek work outside the capital. Nevertheless, his hold on the *azukari* title and his receipt of it so soon after the rejection in 1466 have inspired scholars to characterize him as politically shrewd and adept at advancing his career. While it is difficult to determine the depth of Mitsunobu's savvy, an array of documents reflects his proactive stance toward estate ownership, as well as his fraternizing with individuals who could potentially enhance his career and financial situation. A brief look at Mitsunobu's sources of income will serve as a way to begin examining the social dynamics that shaped the culture and artistic projects of this period.

The Painting Bureau director's income derived primarily from landholdings, but these could not be reaped passively; the proprietor constantly faced tenants and farmers who withheld payments, illegal usurpation, and individuals claiming ownership with falsified documents. In most instances, such disputes could be resolv- ed only through the intervention of the court, the *bakufu*, or both, a situation that required an owner to be on good terms with those in power. This was certainly the case with Mitsunobu's landholding history, even with the Okumosha estate, a land parcel that belonged to the office of the Painting Bureau director (*edokoro azukari-ryō*). Mitsunobu received the rights to this estate, located in Tanba Province (present-day Hyōgo Prefecture), immediately following his appointment.[42] Although it was an officially designated parcel, the income derived from it could be unreliable if local clan heads and farmers did not relinquish the proprietor's percentage of the yield. This was the case in 1484, when a series of documents reveal that local leaders and farmers refused to recognize Mitsunobu's right to dedicated income and absconded with the annual rice tax.[43] The conflict was resolved only when the *bakufu* instructed a group of provincial families to assist Mitsunobu's representative in the use of force against those who resisted returning to the estate.[44] Mitsunobu lost control over the estate income at least one other time, in 1506, when an individual by the name of Zui'a falsified documents in an attempt to usurp the lands, with the result that the local clan heads, residents, and farmers withheld their annual stipend payment to Mitsunobu. Letters from both court and *bakufu* attesting to Mitsunobu's rights appear to have put an end to the problem.[45]

The Okumosha estate was Mitsunobu's most consistent source of income, but there were at least four others in his portfolio, and at least one of them was even more difficult to manage.[46] The Kokubunji estate, also in Tanba Province, was granted to Mitsunobu sometime before 1492 and seems to have been particularly hard to control, even though the income from this land parcel was specifically designated to pay for the production of fan paintings that the *edokoro* routinely presented to the court and *bakufu*.[47] In 1492 local farmers on the Kokubunji estate withheld Mitsunobu's portion of the annual yield, and in 1503 the land was usurped and payments ceased to be made to Mitsunobu.[48] The land was again seized unlawfully in 1507.[49] Two years later the *bakufu* ordered that Mitsunobu share the income from this estate with a Buddhist sculptor who had produced documents attesting to his rights.[50] The land was yet again illegally seized in 1511 by someone named Niki Tarō, who continued his unlawful intrusion onto the estate for another three years despite orders from the *bakufu*.[51]

Although laconic sources of information, the numerous letters related to Mitsunobu's estate holdings in the *Tosa House Documents* provide a unique view of the difficulty with which Kyoto aristocrats and painters like Mitsunobu procured their income.[52] The official documents from members of the military government that were required to confirm land rights were not necessarily easy to come by; in one of the early examples regarding the Okumosha estate, for example, a letter was obtained from Hosokawa Masamoto's office only after two provincial governors entreated Masamoto on the artist's behalf.[53] Similar personal appeals to military rulers must have been necessary for each of the twenty extant letters affirming his landholdings. In all of these cases it was helpful if the Hosokawa governors of Tanba Province knew and thought favorably of the court artist.

One way for Mitsunobu to fraternize with men of this class was to participate in *renga* (linked-verse) gatherings attended or sponsored by them. In this way, Mitsunobu was a man of his age; *renga* is commonly thought of as the representative poetic form of the Muromachi period, as the two most important *renga* anthologies, the *Tsukuba Collection* (*Tsukuba Shū*, 1356) and the *New Tsukuba Collection* (*Shinsen Tsukubashū*, 1495), which was imperially recognized by GoTsuchimikado, were produced during this period.[54] As a collaborative poetic form, *renga* was in part responsible for ushering in a new kind of interaction between individuals of different social strata, and Mitsunobu clearly took advantage of this opportunity. Renga, as Mack Horton has put it, "*was* linking: of verses, of people, and of poetic traditions."[55] As early as 1465, Mitsunobu participated in a linked-verse gathering sponsored by the shogunal administrator Hosokawa Katsumoto (1430–73); fourteen men were present, including the most prominent *renga* poets of the day, Sōgi (1421–1502) and his teacher Senjun (1411–76).[56] Mitsunobu's appearances at these events betray a pattern: his participation immediately precedes requests to the *bakufu*. In this light, the upcoming Daijōe commission likely prompted Mitsunobu to join the *renga* gathering in 1465 and the one sponsored by Katsumoto in 1466, just a few months before the artist petitioned the court for the commission.[57] The *bakufu* partially oversaw the Daijōe ceremony preparations and weighed in on the debate between the Kasuga and Rokkaku studios, making the shogunal administrator a potentially key ally in the case. Although the shogunate in the end decided to maintain the custom of awarding the commission to the reigning *azukari*, Mitsunobu's personal interaction during these *renga* gatherings surely emboldened him to propose his own studio for the job.

Hosokawa Katsumoto's 1465 gathering was also important to Mitsunobu because the artist expected to rise to the rank of *azukari* in the very near future, and Katsumoto, who was the governor of Tanba Province (home to the Okumosha estate), would be responsible for confirming Mitsunobu's future landholdings. In later years when Mitsunobu needed assistance in bringing the estate back under his control, he participated in *renga* gatherings sponsored by the newly appointed governor Hosokawa Masamoto (1466–1507). It was only after Mitsunobu joined the *renga* session that the *bakufu* threatened the tenants of his land with force if they did not restore Mitsunobu's income. The timing of Mitsunobu's socializing was surely not coincidental. Clearly, the *renga* gatherings offered a unique opportunity for Mitsunobu to fraternize with the guardians of his financial interests. His appearances at warrior-sponsored poetry gatherings cease, however, after the mid-1480s, when his poetic acquaintances shift to the sphere of *renga* masters and aristocrats.[58] As with

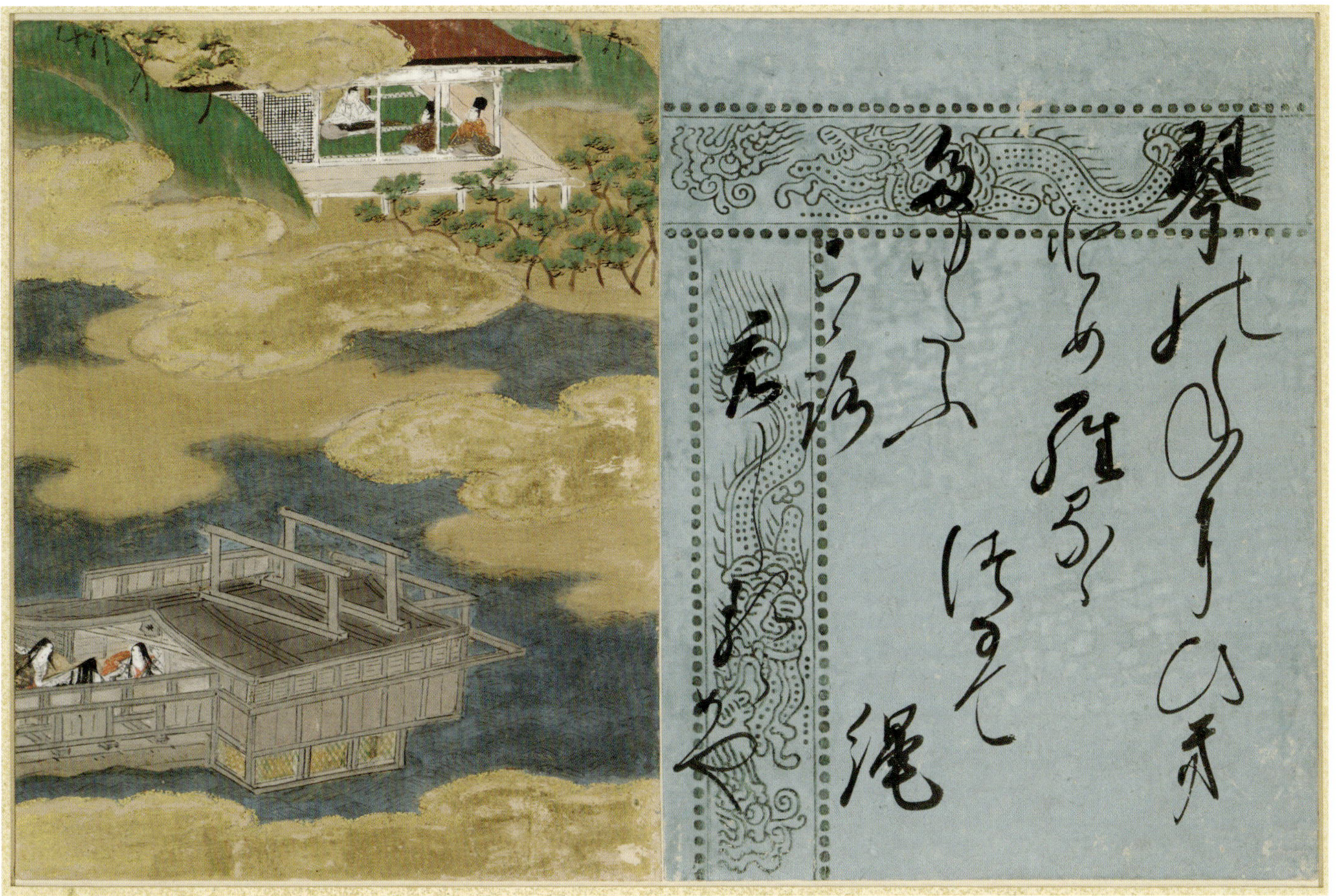

35 Tosa Mitsunobu, calligraphy by Shōren'in Son'ō Jugō, chapter 12, "Suma," from the *Tale of Genji Album*. 1509–10. 108 leaves of painting and calligraphy; ink, color and gold on paper, 23.3 x 18.1 cm. Harvard Art Museum, Arthur M. Sackler Museum, Bequest of the Hofer Collection of the Arts of Asia, 1985.352.12.A. Photograph by Katya Kallsen © President and Fellows of Harvard College.

the previous examples, Mitsunobu's attendance at *renga* sessions in his later years is far from arbitrary but reveals instead the opportunism and occasionality that governed the social habits of elite artisans in his day.

POETRY GATHERINGS AND ARTISTIC PROJECTS

Mitsunobu participated in at least thirty separate poetry and linked-verse gatherings over the course of his career, a frequency that makes it difficult to characterize his involvement as solely motivated by financial or political gain. For one thing, the opportunity to compose poetry alongside the most celebrated versifiers of the day would have been an invaluable experience for the artist. Many of the artistic projects that Mitsunobu engaged in required a close calibration between word and image. This is obviously the case with his narrative picture scrolls and *Genji* poem cards (*shikishi*), but other objects—including fans and even sake cups—could be inscribed with texts intended to create a symbiotic relationship with the pictorial images on their surfaces.[59] For such projects Mitsunobu worked closely with *renga* masters, who sometimes acted as coordinators, and with scholar-calligraphers, such as Sanjōnishi Sanetaka. The well-documented production of the 1509–10 *Tale of Genji Album* (fig. 35) exemplifies this process, whereby men such as Sanetaka and the poet Gensei, working as a go-between for the patron, selected the textual excerpts and organized the distribution of the calligraphy sent to six different aristocrats.[60] Although not involved in the process of selecting the texts, Mitsunobu made sure that the pictorial image resonated with the chosen passage. The more the artist knew of the classical literary canon and was able to interpret the text at hand, the more successful his finished product.

Mitsunobu's poems composed for some of the *renga* gatherings he attended bear the traces of the literary knowledge that would be important for his painting. For Hosokawa Katsumoto's *One Thousand Votive Verses for Kumano* in 1466, Mitsunobu's line of verse appears in the fifth sequence after a line by a poet named Morinaga:

Morinaga:
If only there were someone to ask after me in times of trouble (*ika ni tomo / tofu hito arena / mono omohi*)
Mitsunobu:
separated from home, the sadness of Suma
(*sato hanarenaru / suma no awaresa*) [61]

Mitsunobu's contribution refers to the "Suma" chapter of *The Tale of Genji*, a text with which he had a lifelong engagement. In addition to the 1509–10 *Genji Album* (fig. 35), for which he painted leaves depicting one scene for each of the fifty-four chapters in the tale, Mitsunobu created book covers for separately bound chapters of the *Genji* that each depicted two scenes from the chapter enclosed within, on the front and back. Two of these booklets survive in the Tenri University Library Museum and in the Idemitsu Museum of Arts (fig. 36a–b). There must have been countless other *Genji* paintings executed by Mitsunobu that no longer survive, and it was for one of these, or perhaps in preparation for a poetry session, that the artist went to the home of the courtier and *Genji* scholar Nakanoin Michihide (1428–94) in 1486 to discuss Murasaki's tale.[62] Besides references to the *Genji*, other turns of phrase appear in Mitsunobu's poetry that relate to his later projects,[63] suggesting that the artist's participation in these poetry sessions was intimately connected to his ability to create images that responded in a sophisticated manner to their accompanying texts.

Ultimately, however, Mitsunobu's involvement in *renga* should be viewed as integral to the social network that supported his painting commissions. Whereas in earlier years Mitsunobu participated in poetry sessions sponsored by members of the *bakufu* perhaps related to land rights, Mitsunobu joined gatherings in later years that included people with whom he was involved in producing paintings. Between 1486 and 1500 nearly all of the poetic gatherings Mitsunobu attended were sponsored by the *renga* master Sōgi.[64] One of these events even centered on a painting by Mitsunobu: a *waka* (thirty-one-syllable poetry) gathering in 1491 intended

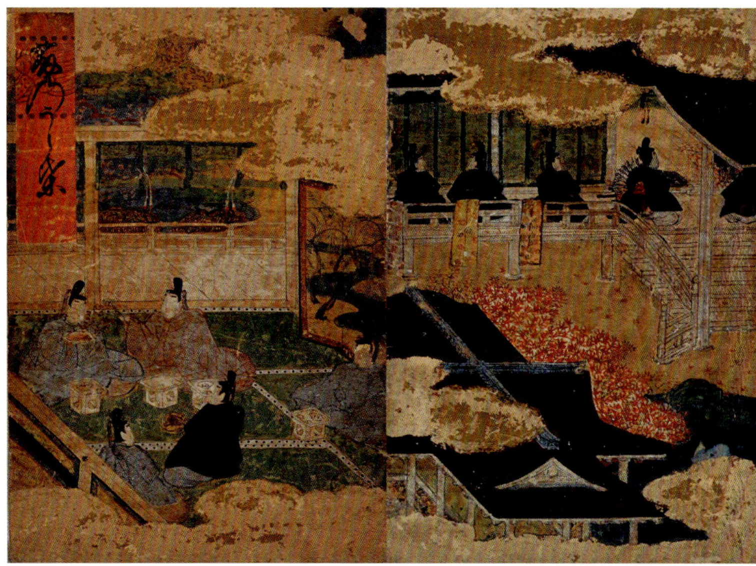

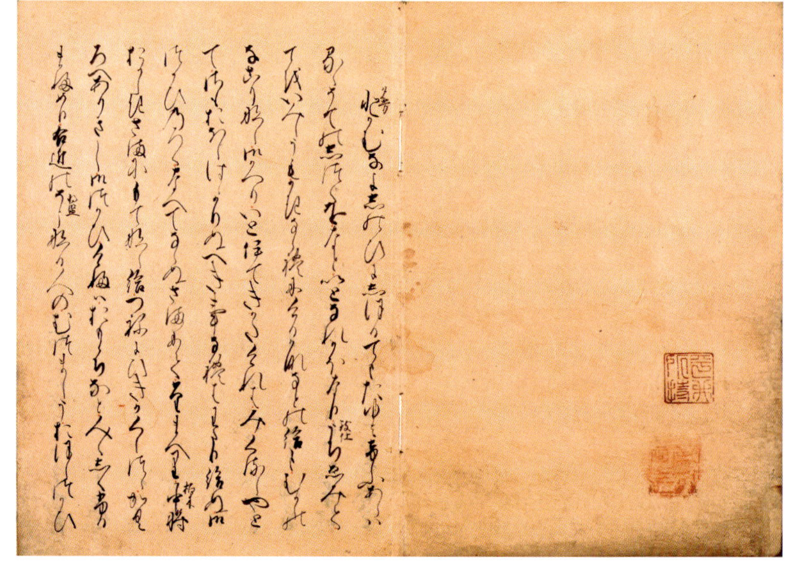

36a–b Tosa Mitsunobu, calligraphy attributed to Kanroji Motonaga (1457–1527), *Tale of Genji* chapter covers. "Wisteria Leaves" (*Fuji no uraba*). Late fifteenth to early sixteenth century. Ink, color, and gold on paper, 25.3 x 17.2 cm. Idemitsu Museum of Arts, Tokyo.

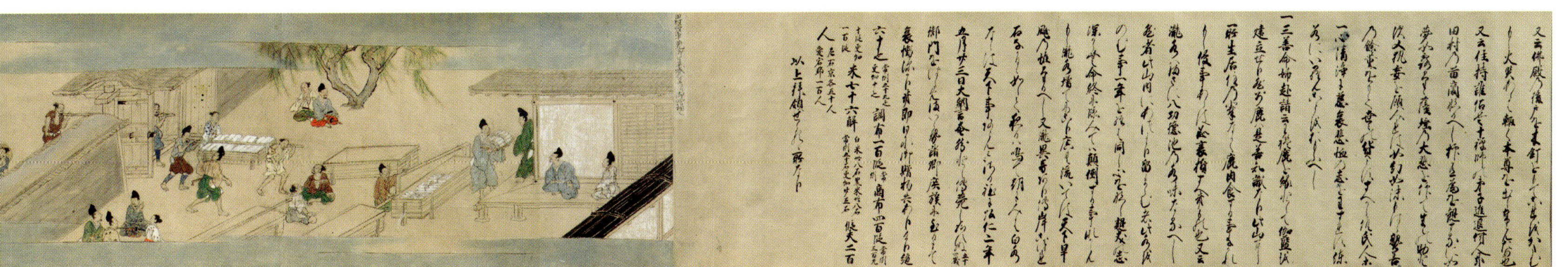

37 Tosa Mitsunobu, calligraphy by Kanroji Motonaga (1457–1527), *Miraculous Legends of Kiyomizudera* (*Kiyomizudera engi emaki*). Dated 1517. Three scrolls; ink, color, and gold on paper, 34.6 x 2299.6, 34.6 x 1912.2, 34.1 x 2146.4 cm. Tokyo National Museum. Important Cultural Property.

to commemorate a new portrait of the "patron saint" of poetry, Kakinomoto no Hitomaro (fl. ca. 680–700).[65] Sōgi commissioned Mitsunobu to execute the painting based on an earlier example by Fujiwara no Nobuzane (ca. 1176–1245), which bore a calligraphic inscription by Fujiwara no Teika (1162–1241). Sōgi lent the painting to the courtier Konoe Masaie (1444–1505) roughly one year later for a fifty-verse poetry gathering and "offering ceremony to Hitomaro" (*Hitomaro eigu*).[66] Portraits of Hitomaro figured prominently in the *waka* culture of the late fifteenth and sixteenth centuries; the paintings were frequently hung at poetry gatherings and were handed over, like certificates, when someone completed an "initiation" (*denju*) into the secret interpretations of the *Collection of Ancient and Modern Poems* (*Kokinshū;* tenth century).[67] As the highest-ranking painter in Kyoto, Mitsunobu's services were in great demand among the aspiring poets in the capital, and it is no surprise to find him among those who gathered frequently at Sōgi's residence.

His presence at Sōgi's home also reveals another pattern: individuals who had hired Mitsunobu as a painter invited him to participate in *renga* gatherings before, during, or after the projects' completion. Less than a year after finishing the illustrated handscroll *Miraculous Legends of Kajūji* (*Kajūji engi-e*) in 1512, Mitsunobu attended a poetry gathering at the home of Kanroji Motonaga (1445–1527), who had overseen the project.[68] Between 1517 and 1520 Mitsunobu appeared at the monthly *renga* sessions held by a group of aristocrats that included Yamashina Tokitsuna (1486–1530) and Nakamikado Nobutane. It is unclear whether Tokitsuna had commissioned anything from Mitsunobu at the time, but his family had called upon Mitsunobu's studio to paint a funerary sculpture of Tokitsuna's brother, who died in 1494.[69] Mitsunobu's relationship with Kanroji Motonaga and Nakamikado Nobutane may have developed around the production of the *Miraculous Legends of Kiyomizudera* (*Kiyomizudera engi emaki;* fig. 37), a set of scrolls that all of these men worked on in 1517.[70] Thereafter, Mitsunobu attended *renga* sessions at Nobutane's home almost monthly before painting an Amida icon for the courtier.[71] While some of this socializing might have been motivated by ulterior concerns on the part of both Mitsunobu and his hosts, in other cases a genuine friendship may have developed. Whatever the case may be, the diversity of Mitsunobu's *renga* companions reflects a shifting coterie that surrounded the artist as he moved from project to project.

BUDDHIST ICONS, MORTUARY PORTRAITS, AND THE COURT ARTIST

By far the majority of Mitsunobu's private commissions, including those for Nobutane, were for Buddhist icons and mortuary portraits that his patrons needed to conduct funerary rites. While Mitsunobu's Buddhist paintings have always been included in surveys of his work, the tendency has been to divorce these works from their ritual contexts and to view them as something of an anomaly within his oeuvre. For this reason his portraits have always been studied under the separate category of "portraiture," when in fact virtually all of them were intended to function in a mortuary capacity. Relatively

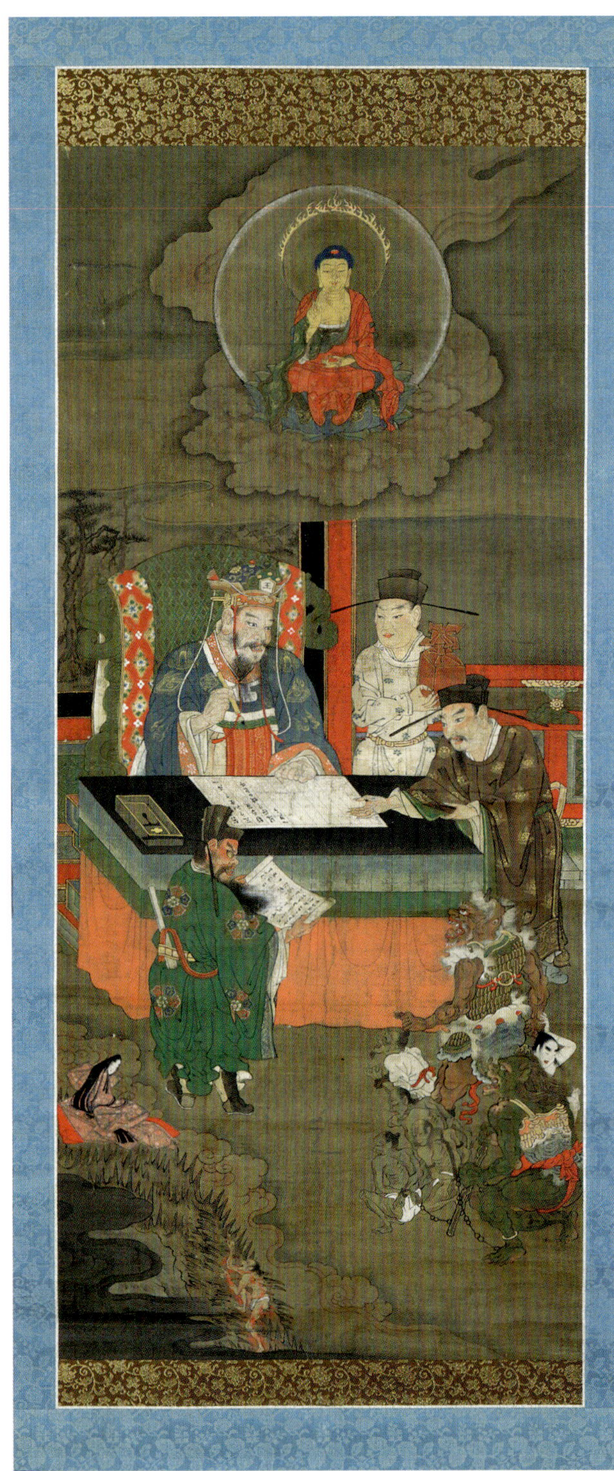

38 Tosa Mitsunobu, *Godō Tenrin Ō* (*The Tenth King*) from *The Ten Kings* (*Jūōzu*). Dated 1489. One of a set of ten hanging scrolls; ink and color on silk, 99.0 x 42.8 cm each. Jōfukuji, Kyoto. Important Cultural Property.

few of Mitsunobu's Buddhist icons and mortuary portraits survive (or, at least, have been identified), but diary references to this aspect of his work abound and reveal much about his familiarity with Buddhist iconography and the visual culture of Buddhist ritual in late medieval Japan.

Clearly, Buddhist icons and mortuary portraits made up a significant part of Mitsunobu's studio practice. In contrast to a professional "Buddhist painter" (*ebusshi*), however, he never painted icons on behalf of large Buddhist institutions, nor did he focus exclusively on such works but executed them at the request of the same patrons who asked for small scrolls, *Genji* paintings, and folding screens. Given the technical and iconographical expertise Buddhist images demand, it may be surprising that Mitsunobu's range included them, but his patrons' needs took precedence, prompting him to execute whatever they required, which was of course true of his Tosa predecessors as well.[72] Mitsunobu thus created Buddhist paintings for aristocrats, warriors, and, as one of his responsibilities as director of the Painting Bureau, for the emperor. What all of these projects have in common is their intended use within the residences or family chapels of their owners. As such, they illustrate the visual culture of private Buddhist ritual and how late medieval aristocrats outfitted their homes for mortuary rites.

The majority of Mitsunobu's Buddhist images were painted for Emperor GoTsuchimikado. Several of these were done for a specific ceremony conducted by the emperor in 1489, a "reverse-rites," or *gyakushu,* ceremony, a funerary ceremony conducted while the person was still alive.[73] The ritual was held in the Fushimi imperial-family temple known as the Hanjūzanmai'in and required a number of paintings by Mitsunobu. Scrolls depicting the "Ten Kings" (fig. 38) were crucial for premortem rites, and Mitsunobu made these for GoTsuchimikado, completing seven of them in time for the ceremony on 12.23.[74] Mitsunobu used as his model a set of Ten Kings paintings done by his most eminent predecessor, Fujiwara no Yukimitsu (active mid- to late fourteenth century). For Mitsunobu to copy them, the palace borrowed Yukimitsu's set from the temple

Nison'in (where they are still preserved) roughly seven months before the ceremony.[75] Sanetaka saw the ancient set at the imperial palace the day after they were borrowed and marveled at the work; he was told it was by "Kasuga Painting Bureau Director Yukimitsu, a work executed one hundred and forty to one hundred and fifty years in the past."[76] Mitsunobu's ten paintings are virtually identical to the earlier set attributed to Yukimitsu, in size, subject, and style.

The *gyakushu* rite also included a now-lost portrait of the emperor, which was consecrated on 12.23, as well as a mandala painting.[77] The emperor's portrait was no doubt created to be his future mortuary portrait, and it was literally at the center of the ritual: it may have hung in the center of the wall, flanked by the Ten Kings, five of whom face right and five left, thereby accommodating such an arrangement. The portrait bore an inscription, brushed by Sanetaka, of the emperor's own *waka* poem, a poetic vow to Amida.[78] This portrait of the emperor was likely painted by Mitsunobu, as commentators since the sixteenth century have assumed.[79] The previous year, Mitsunobu had executed a portrait of GoTsuchimikado's mother, Karakumon'in Nobuko (1411–88), which was installed in the Hanjūzanmai'in soon after her death on Chōkyō 2 (1488) 4.28, and before which mourners burned incense.[80] Mitsunobu's imperial portrait commissions continued with one of Emperor GoEn'yū (1358–93) executed in 1492 (fig. 39) and now in the collection of the Unryū'in subtemple at Sennyūji.[81] Although it was the abbot of Unryū'in who requested the painting for GoEn'yū's one-hundredth death anniversary, members of the imperial family such as GoTsuchimikado, who inscribed the work in 1499, may also have venerated the portrait.[82] One of Mitsunobu's main responsibilities as Painting Bureau director, then, was to reproduce likenesses of the imperial family specifically for the purpose of mortuary rituals.

The numerous Buddhist ceremonies at court demanded more than portraits, however, and Mitsunobu was asked to execute a variety of icons. A year after Mitsunobu had painted the emperor's portrait and *Ten Kings* scrolls, GoTsuchimikado called upon him to draw images of Bishamonten, one of the four guardian deities

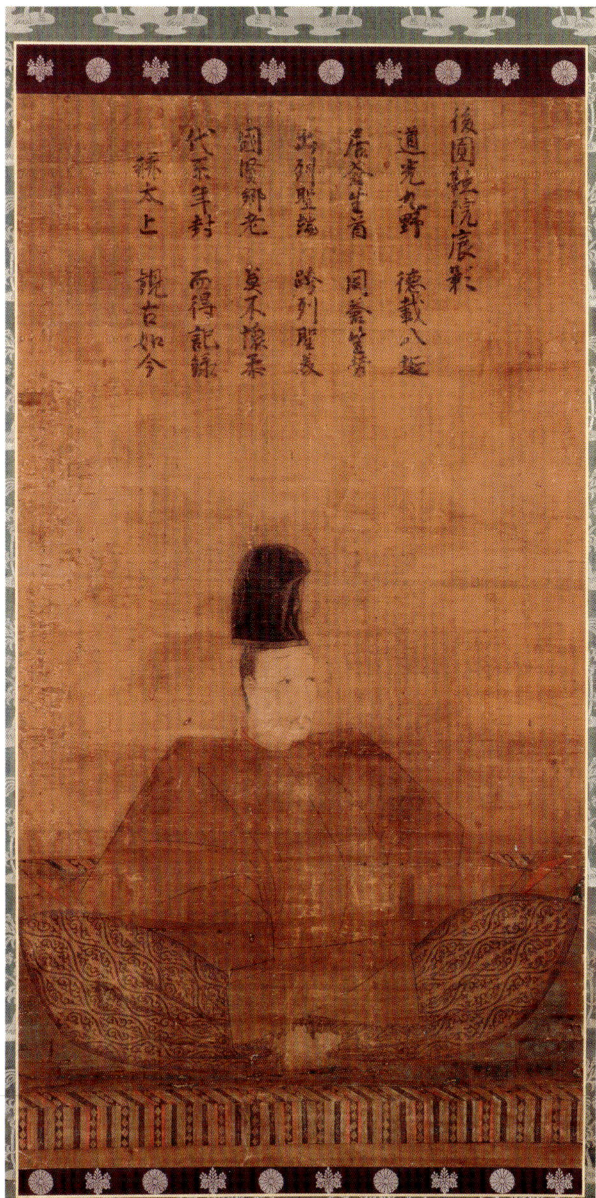

39 Tosa Mitsunobu, Portrait of Emperor GoEn'yū (1358–93). 1492. Hanging scroll; ink and color on silk, 105.4 x 55.1 cm. Unryū'in, Kyoto. Important Cultural Property.

of the four directions, and Daikokuten, a fierce incarnation of Dainichi, based upon a vision manifested in one of the emperor's dreams.[83] Subsequently, in 1495, Mitsunobu executed a painting of the bodhisattva Fugen for GoTsuchimikado for use in the "Samantabhadra rite for longevity" (*Fugen enmei hō*).[84] The emperor's request for such an image that year, along with the predeath ceremonies he had arranged, may

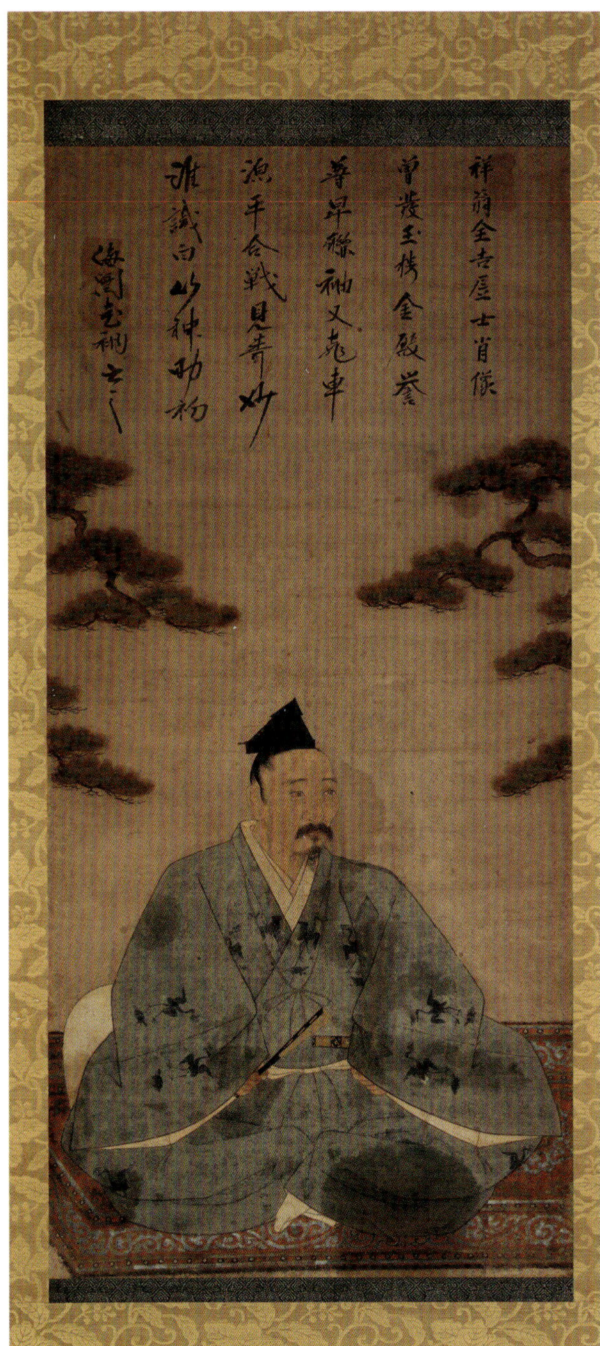

40 Tosa Mitsunobu, *Portrait of Momonoi Naoakira* (1393/1403–1470/1480). Late fifteenth century. Hanging scroll; ink and color on paper, 89.7 x 41.8 cm. Tokyo National Museum. Important Cultural Property.

reflect a growing preoccupation with his own afterlife, an issue which will appear again in the following chapter in relation to his commissioning of a "tale of rebirth" scroll. Such an icon was traditionally used as part of the "Three Altar" (*sandan*) ceremony conducted to mark the onset of a new imperial reign, involving rites directed toward Nyōrin Kannon, Fudō Myōo, and Fugen Enmei for the prosperity, safety, and longevity of the new emperor and his reign.[85] Perhaps GoTsuchimikado's Fugen painting was intended for his son GoKashiwabara's Three Altar ceremony, held in 1502, for which Mitsunobu provided at least one of the three icons.[86]

Imperial family members were not the only individuals who were able to employ Mitsunobu as their portrait painter; he worked for members of the warrior class, Buddhist monks, and, of course, aristocrats. The earliest extant portrait by Mitsunobu is of Momonoi Naoakira (1393/1403–1470/1480) (fig. 40), the reputed founder of *kōwakamai*, a form of chanted narrative accompanied by music and dance popular during the Muromachi period.[87] Having been born into the Seiwa branch of the Minamoto clan, Momonoi was essentially of military stock, although the performer had been given court rank. It comes as no surprise that Mitsunobu executed the portrait during the period when he was participating in the *renga* gatherings held by the Hosokawa and other military retainers. Soon after painting Momonoi's image, the courtier Nakanoin Michihide singled out Mitsunobu's skills for praise and recommended him for the task of executing the portrait of the monk Honkaku Daishi of Ninnaji.[88] Thus, by the 1480s Mitsunobu was servicing a wide range of patrons and commanding a certain acclaim as a portrait artist.

The most intriguing extant portrait by Mitsunobu is a portrait sketch of the scholar-courtier Sanjōnishi Sanetaka (fig. 41), the artist's closest collaborator on his narrative scroll projects. A hastily drawn sketch on paper, the image exposes the hand of the artist in a way that none of the finished paintings are able to, due to their heavy pigments, which obscure the original underdrawings. In 1501 while Sanetaka and Mitsunobu were collaborating on the new version of the *Legends of Kitano Tenjin* scrolls, the artist visited Sanetaka to discuss the project and, as already noted, one of their conversations touched upon the ancient underdrawings of Takakane's *Kasuga* scrolls. During a subsequent visit

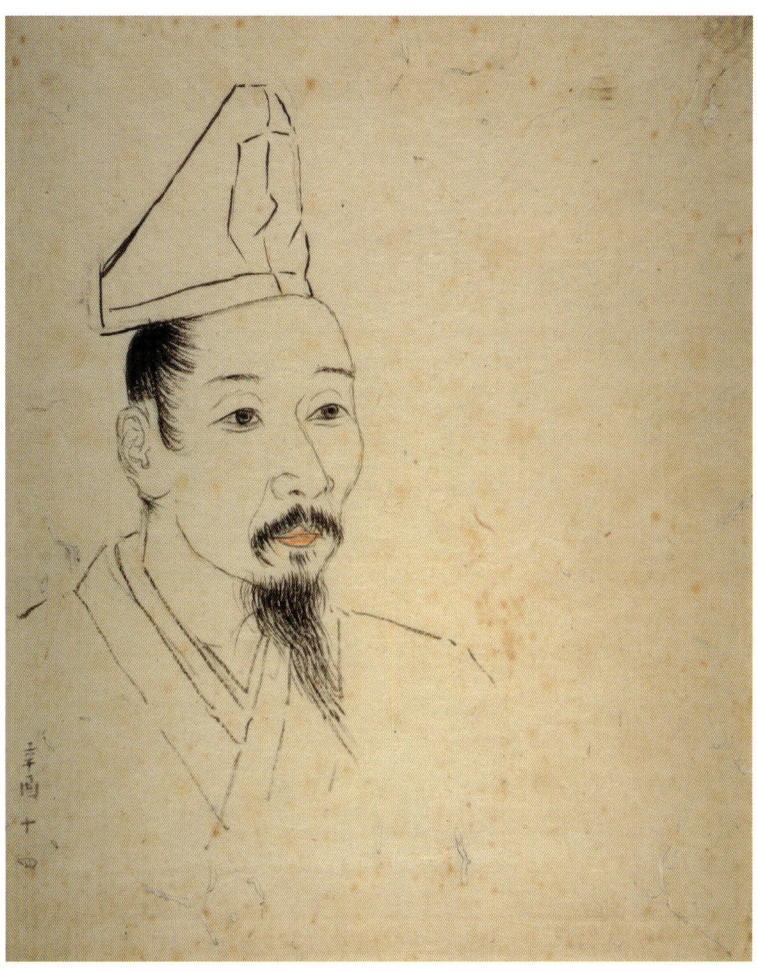

41 Tosa Mitsunobu, Portrait sketch of Sanjōnishi Sanetaka. 1501. Single sheet; ink on paper, 41.2 x 25.8 cm. Historiographical Institute, The University of Tokyo.

recorded in Sanetaka's diary (fig. 42), Mitsunobu sketched the face of the forty-seven-year-old courtier at his request. Apparently, Sanetaka deemed the impromptu rendering to be of insufficient resemblance and promptly tucked the small sheet of paper away in his reading material that day.[89] Four hundred and fifty years later, the sketch was found folded between the pages of a fifteenth-century text on court protocol that was once in the Sanjōnishi library, with a date in the lower-left corner that corresponds to the entry in Sanetaka's diary.[90] The image survives as a record of that day in 1501 when Sanetaka and Mitsunobu discussed their handscroll project and as a fragment of a long-standing collaborative relationship.

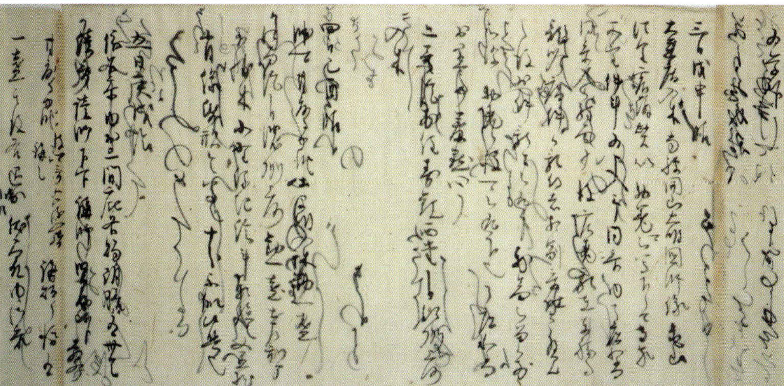

42 Sanjōnishi Sanetaka (1455–1537), *Diary of Sanjōnishi Sanetaka* (*Sanetaka-kō ki*). Ink on paper, H. 26.4 cm. Historiographical Institute, The University of Tokyo. Entry from Bunki 1 (1501), referring to Mitsunobu sketching Sanetaka's portrait.

The art historical scholarship on Mitsunobu has tended to emphasize his identity as a "court painter," taken to mean a painter of courtly subjects or traditional court-sponsored formats, such as picture scrolls, rather than religious works. Mitsunobu's Buddhist paintings were therefore all but ignored, and until only recently none had been reproduced in color. Buddhist rituals, and the paintings made for them, however, were an integral part of court life, and Tosa paintings were finely crafted works that illustrate a thorough knowledge of Buddhist iconography. As an artistic heir to painters such as Fujiwara no Yukimitsu and other Tosa artists who executed a wide range of Buddhist paintings in the past, Mitsunobu had access to the models, sketches, and "trade secrets" for producing these specialized works that enabled him to meet his patrons' needs. When it came to Buddhist painting, Mitsunobu's knowledge and technical expertise earned him the highest praise from Sanetaka.

MITSUNOBU, SANETAKA, AND THE COLLABORATIVE PROCESS

Sanetaka was by no means the only scholar-courtier whom Mitsunobu consulted regarding his artistic projects, especially ones with accompanying texts. As already noted, courtiers such as Kanroji Motonaga and Nakanoin Michihide oversaw picture scroll and *Genji*

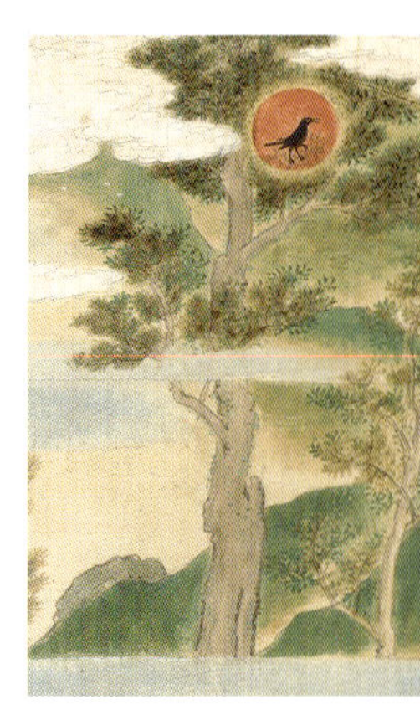

projects for which Mitsunobu was the lead painter, and they engaged in direct conversations with the artist. The former organized the production of the *Miraculous Legends of Kiyomizudera* (fig. 37), while the latter gave Mitsunobu explicit instructions on at least one *Genji* project as well as more general advice on Murasaki's narrative. Documentation concerning most of Mitsunobu's other handscroll projects no longer survives, but for works such as the *Miraculous Origins of Seikōji* (1487)[91] and *Origins of Religious Austerities at Tsukiminedera* (*Tsukiminedera konryū shugyō engi emaki*, 1495; fig. 43), a coordinator must have played a crucial role in counseling the painter on the vagaries of the parent texts. In many cases the coordinator of a project also executed its calligraphy. This was the case in the production of the *Legends of Kitano Tenjin* scrolls, for which Sanetaka brushed all of the text and took an active role in advising Mitsunobu on the paintings. Hashimoto Kinnatsu (1454–1538), who brushed both of the *Tsukiminedera* scrolls, may have performed a similar role in the production of this work, most likely produced in the circle of the shogunal administrator Hosokawa Masamoto. As Takagishi Akira has argued, Kinnatsu's knowledge of classical Japanese poetry, prose narratives, and Chinese texts makes him a likely candidate as both the author and calligrapher of this new temple legend.[92]

Although Mitsunobu benefited from the input of a variety of well-educated scholar-calligraphers of the late fifteenth and early sixteenth centuries, his relationship with Sanetaka is the best documented and provides the best insight into the emergence of the short-story small scroll. Sanetaka was clearly at the center of efforts to reproduce the numerous texts lost in the Ōnin War, not only on behalf of the imperial palace but for his own family's library as well. He copied texts and also authored new ones, works that included temple legends, Nō libretti, and, most importantly, short stories. It is this aspect of Sanetaka's career and his role in the production of several small scrolls for the emperor and the crown prince that make him the most logical figure to examine for an understanding of how small scrolls came to flourish in Mitsunobu's circle. A brief look at the production of paintings with which they were both involved will help to flesh out the collaborative process of these two men.

Sanetaka mentions in his diary twelve separate artistic projects involving Mitsunobu's studio over the course of some forty years, projects that show a wide variety of interaction between the two men, as well as a wide variety of types of paintings, from Buddhist icons to *Genji* albums and narrative scrolls. Sanetaka's engagement with these projects ranged from calligrapher, to coordinator, and, despite his relatively unpredictable income, to sponsor.[93] In his role as patron Sanetaka commissioned at least three paintings from Mitsunobu, all of them Buddhist images. The most pressing need for icons arose from the calendar of death anniversary rituals held on behalf of one's relatives. In this regard, Sanetaka was one of a number of courtiers, such as Nakamikado Nobutane, who called upon the *edokoro azukari* to supply them with the paintings needed for specific familial religious rituals.

Sanetaka began preparing for his mother's thirty-third death anniversary services in 1504, for example, by speaking to Mitsunobu about a new painting of the Thirteen Buddhas six months in advance of the memorial.[94] The single *Thirteen Buddhas* scroll by Mitsunobu no longer survives, but extant examples of this popular Muromachi Buddhist painting genre provide a sense of its appearance (fig. 44).[95] Mitsunobu delivered the painting to Sanetaka roughly two months after their initial conversation, and Sanetaka was delighted with the outcome, describing the work as "beautiful and marvelous" (*birei shushō*).[96] The painting was the central image of the memorial service conducted in Sanetaka's residence, during which the abbot of Nison'in and eight monks chanted sutras and lectured upon the sacred texts.[97] Sanetaka was equally pleased with the painting *Five Original Buddhas of the Kasuga Deity* (*Kasuga Honji goson*), produced by Mitsunobu's studio in 1506, which he also described as a "marvelous" (*shushō*) work.[98] The success of the *Thirteen Buddhas* painting in 1504 no doubt led Sanetaka to request yet another painting of this subject in 1508, this time on behalf of his fifteen-year-old son, Keiyō (1494–1526).[99] At the time, Keiyō,

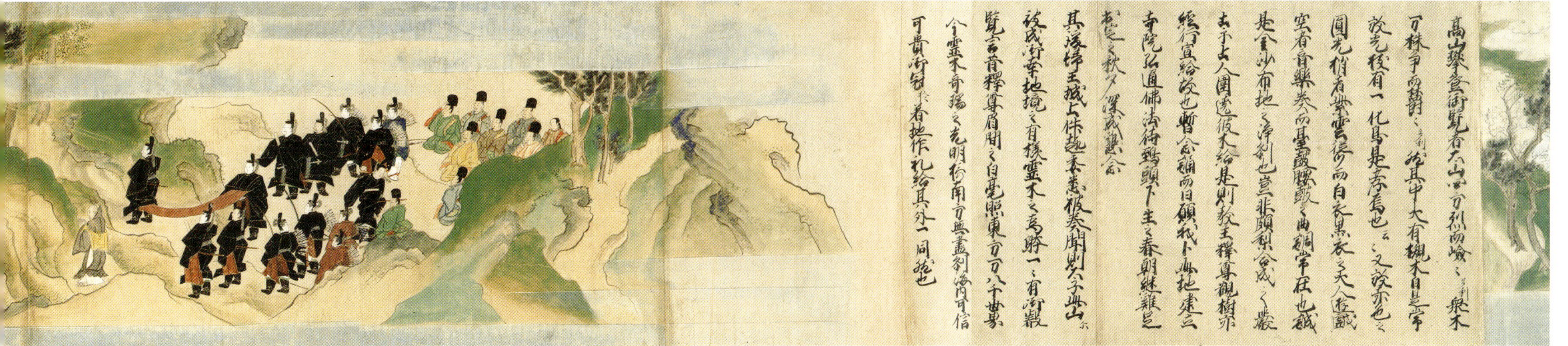

43 Tosa Mitsunobu, calligraphy by Hashimoto Kinnatsu (1454–1538), *Origins of Religious Austerities at Tsukiminedera* (*Tsukimindera konryū shugyō engi emaki*). 1495. Two scrolls; ink, color, and gold on paper, H. 34.3 cm. Freer Gallery of Art, Smithsonian Institution, Washington, DC. Detail, scroll 1.

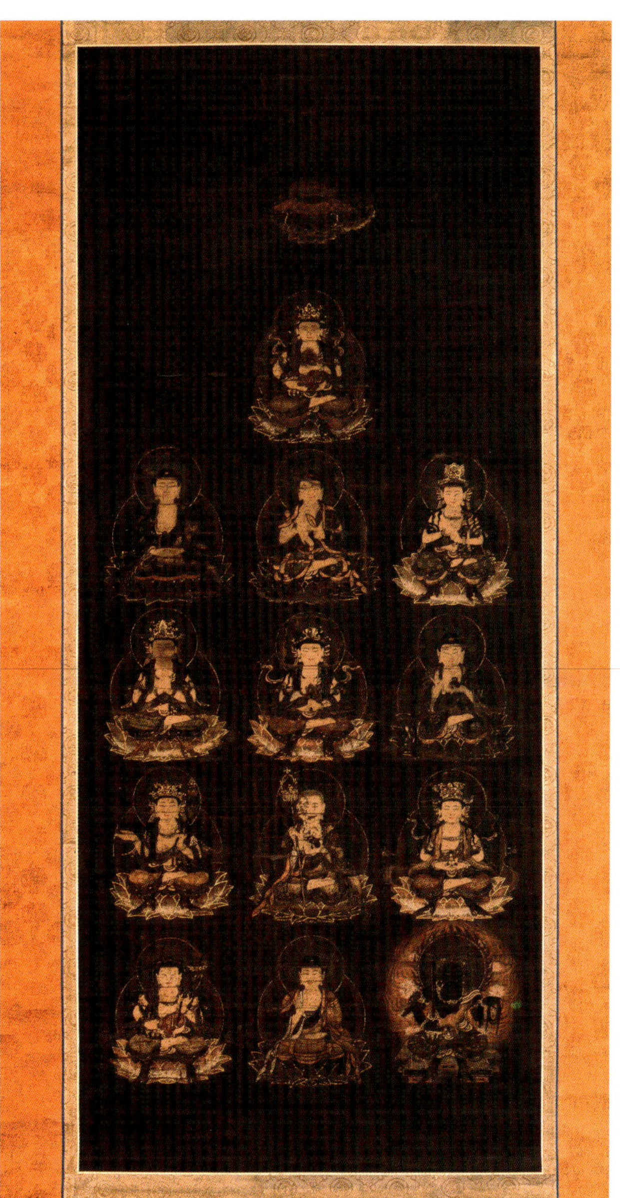

44 *Thirteen Buddhas (Jūsan-butsu zu)*. Fifteenth century. Hanging scroll; ink, color, and gold on silk. Private collection, Japan.

who was a disciple of the venerable monk Ryōan Keigo (1425–1514) of Tōfukuji, was in western Japan with his master en route to China.[100] The precise services for which his *Thirteen Buddhas* painting was commissioned are unknown, but it is easy to imagine a number of scenarios for its use by either Ryōan Keigo or Keiyō while on their journey. Sanetaka promptly had the painting mounted and sent to his son, along with a letter and several poems.[101]

The three Buddhist images requested of Mitsunobu required minimal input from Sanetaka. Aside from the initial conversation that he had with the artist concerning his mother's memorial image, he seems to have left Mitsunobu to his own devices to produce the icons. They were fairly straightforward tasks, requiring only that Mitsunobu follow a template for this particular type of Buddhist painting, which presumably he had done before. As with the *Ten Kings* scrolls, Mitsunobu's Buddhist paintings tended to be based on preexisting models; an Amida painting that he made for Nobutane, for example, was based on another Amida image owned by Sanetaka.[102] Sanetaka was especially taken with Mitsunobu's Buddhist paintings and felt no need to make suggestions. Not only did the courtier bestow unusually high praise on the *Thirteen Buddhas* and the *Kasuga* painting in his possession, but he expressed equal admiration for the Amida image that Mitsunobu painted for Nobutane.[103] Of course, Sanetaka's demonstrative reactions to these paintings could have derived as much from their spiritual content as their aesthetic qualities, to the extent that the two can be disentangled. The elegant pigmentation and use of gold in Mitsunobu's and Yukimitsu's *Ten Kings*, as well as a number of other Muromachi Tosa Buddhist paintings, such as Tosa Yukihiro's *Twenty-five Descending Bodhisattvas* (fig. 45) in the Nison'in Collection, go a long way toward explaining Sanetaka's reaction. As a layman with no particular expertise in Buddhist iconography, Sanetaka apparently felt no need to discuss the Buddhist paintings that he commissioned from Mitsunobu or those that he worked on for the emperor, such as the *Ten Kings*.[104]

This was not the case, however, when it came to literary projects or paintings accompanied by texts. These were the kinds of projects that Sanetaka was asked to oversee, and several examples provide a glimpse of how the courtier's erudition and literary insights helped to enhance Mitsunobu's paintings. For the set of fifty-four *Genji* texts and paintings of the *Tale of Genji Album* (1509–10) (fig. 35) in the collection of the Harvard Art Museum, Sanetaka selected the textual excerpts and distributed the decorated papers and detailed instructions to the six men chosen to execute the calligraphy. He may also have had some say in the final selection of paintings or how they should relate to the textual passages. Of course, the content of the paintings would have had to be discussed with the patron or the patron's proxy (the *renga* poet Gensei), as well as the artist. One strong possibility is that Sanetaka sent the calligraphers sketches of the proposed paintings, as a way of orchestrating the nuanced interrelationship that appears between text and image in this work.[105]

A much more modest project than the *Genji* album—a sake cup and stand for Hino Tomiko—illuminates even more clearly how Sanetaka, and other men of letters like him, influenced Mitsunobu's paintings down to the smallest detail. In 1488, Tomiko, the wife of the former shogun Ashikaga Yoshimasa and the mother of the current shogun, Yoshihisa (1465–89), requested Mitsunobu to draw the designs for a sake cup and stand. The cup and stand were each to have a different poem from *New Collection of Ancient and Modern Poems* (*Shinkokinshū,* ca. thirteenth century) inscribed on their surfaces, along with a minimal number of motifs to pictorialize the verse.[106] When Mitsunobu's preparatory drawings did not accord with Tomiko's wishes, she sent Kai'a, a cultural facilitator (*dōbōshū*) employed by the shogun, along with the artist to consult with Sanetaka. The expectation was that Sanetaka's familiarity with the verse would allow him to suggest a more pleasing pictorial and graphic expression for the two poems.

The cup's design was meant to represent the following poem:

Though mountain paths lead this way and that,
there are no friends to spur me on, back to the capital.
(*Ashihiki no konata kanata ni michi wa aredo*
miyako he iza to ifu hito zo naki)[107]

According to Sanetaka, Mitsunobu had drawn overlapping hills, a meandering road, and a wheel of a cart on the exterior of the cup in order to pictorialize the first half of the poem. The interior of the vessel was to be inscribed with the entire first line of the second part of the poem: *miyako he iza to*, "spur me on, back to the capital." Mitsunobu, in other words, conceived of a design that maintained a distinction between exterior and interior and the first and second half of the poem.

This two-part design scheme was not to Tomiko's liking. Sanetaka understood her concerns and suggested that they leave the design for the cup divided but use only three syllables from the second half of the poem: *iza to* (spur me on). He argued that the poem would still be recognizable and that in this way the cup could also be made to harmonize better with the stand. Kai'a agreed on behalf of Tomiko, and Sanetaka subsequently wrote the three syllables as requested. Mitsunobu later consulted Sanetaka about the design of the stand in order to confirm with the courtier that the type of garb for the figure he had painted was appropriate.

While Sanetaka did not alter Mitsunobu's images for the cup design, he did edit the text to create a more

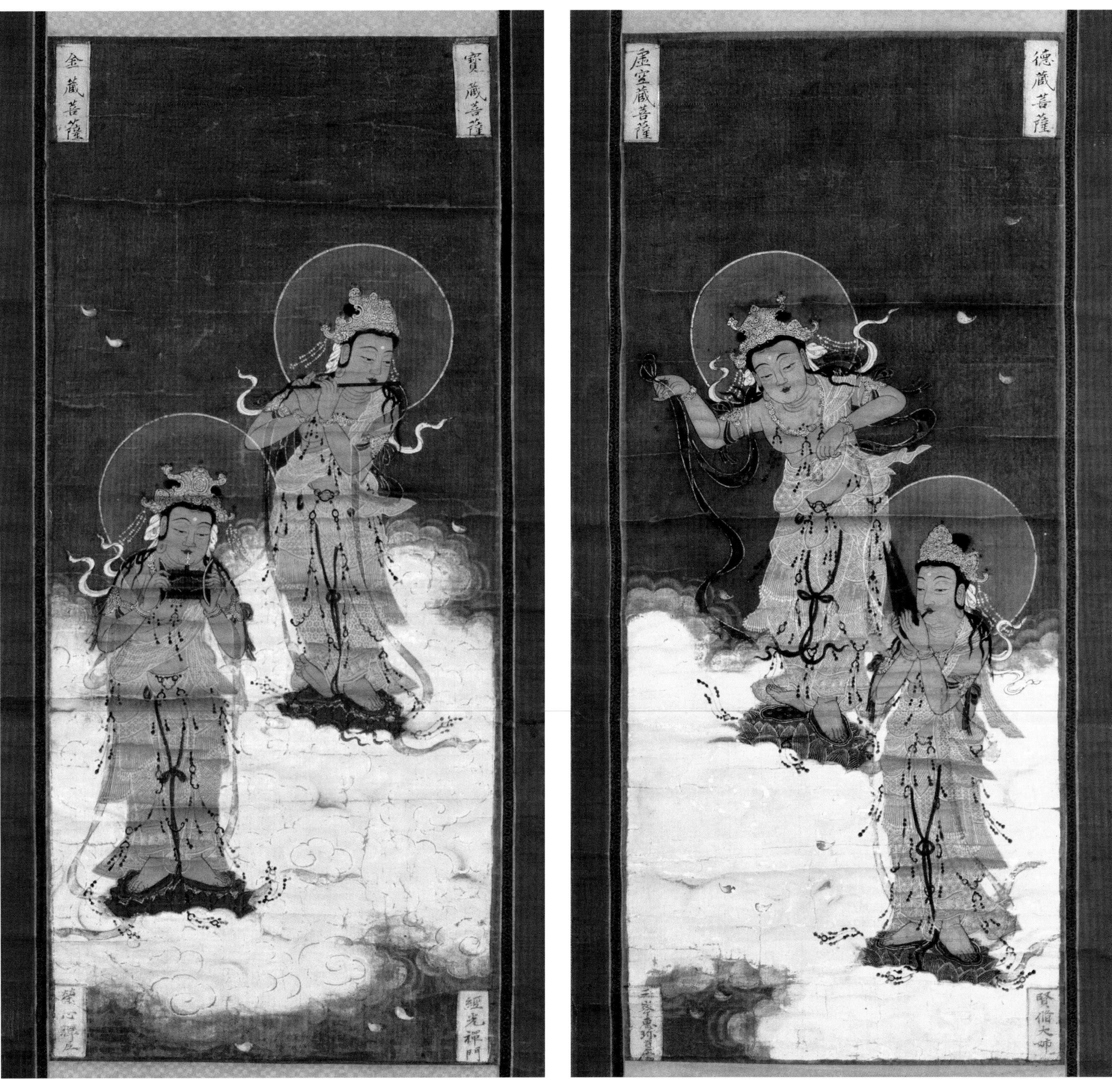

45 Tosa Yukihiro (fl. 1406–34), *Twenty-five Descending Bodhisattvas (Nijūgo Bosatsu raigō zu)*. Two of twenty-five hanging scrolls. Nison'in, Kyoto.

subtle representation of the poem. He eliminated the words "back to the capital," which he assumed would not be necessary to identify the verse and would in fact make the reference too obvious, while crowding the interior surface unnecessarily. In making this decision Sanetaka understood the level of sophistication of the patron and also that the primary person using the cup and appreciating the subtle suggestion of the poem on its interior would be her son, the shogun Yoshihisa. Tomiko intended to bring the cup with her to visit her embattled son in Ōmi Province, where he was engaged in a military campaign against the insurgent daimyo Rokkaku Takayori (d. 1520). It is easy to imagine Tomiko presenting her son with the cup, an object from the capital that would please him but that would also lend a certain poignancy to his own situation: the poem chosen for representation epitomized the classic sense of "loneliness while away from the capital" and was composed by the Heian period's most famous exile, Sugawara no Michizane (845–903). This small, personal object would have imbued Yoshihisa's own time away from the capital with poetic sentiment, and Sanetaka was surely correct in assuming that a three-syllable line would be enough to evoke the famous poem in Yoshihisa's mind.[108]

The sake cup for Hino Tomiko demonstrates that most, if not all, artworks in the aristocratic milieu from this period—no matter how seemingly trivial—should be viewed as collaborative projects.[109] The creation of the cup involved the types of figures who played important roles in most major commissions of the period: the patron (Hino Tomiko), the artist (Tosa Mitsunobu), the facilitator or go-between (Kai'a), and the scholar-calligrapher (Sanetaka). It can be assumed that Tomiko herself, or perhaps with Kai'a, conceived of the object and selected the poem to adorn its surface. Then the artist was charged with interpreting the poem and translating its words into pictorial motifs placed within a schematic design that would enhance the poetic meaning and conform to the shape of the vessel. In the end, however, the patron turned to the scholar to make minor adjustments to enhance the presentation of the poem and the sophistication of the final artwork. All the while, the cultural facilitator, Kai'a, seems to have acted as Tomiko's surrogate, accompanying the painter to the courtier's residence and approving the design changes on Tomiko's behalf. While few projects were documented in such detail, these kinds of figures operated, some behind the scenes, in the production of Muromachi artworks, including small scrolls.

The production of a small scroll entitled *Clouds of Mt. Kōya* (*Takano gumo-e*), which was made for Emperor GoTsuchimikado by Mitsunobu and Sanetaka in the 1470s but no longer survives, is the most well documented. An examination of how this work came about provides important insights into the process of making a small scroll, the emergence of the short-story small scroll within the sphere of the imperial court in the late fifteenth century, and how the small format was conceptualized as an alternative narrative space for experimentation with literary and pictorial genres.

CLOUDS OF MT. KŌYA: A SMALL SCROLL BY MITSUNOBU AND SANETAKA

In the hands of artists like Mitsunobu and scholar-calligraphers like Sanetaka, the small-format handscroll became a venue that privileged the illustration of recently authored short stories. *Clouds of Mt. Kōya* was a small scroll that illustrated a short narrative newly authored by Sanetaka himself. With paintings by Mitsunobu and the patronage of GoTsuchimikado, this work offers numerous insights into the cultural context out of which the new short-story *ko-e* emerged.

Thirteen separate references to *Clouds of Mt. Kōya* appear in Sanetaka's diary, several of which mention personal meetings between Sanetaka and the emperor to discuss both the paintings and the texts for his small scroll. These references describe a small-scroll project to which patron, artist, and calligrapher devoted considerable thought and energy. The creation of *Clouds of Mt. Kōya* occupied roughly three months in late 1474 and early 1475, and then after what appears to have been a four-year hiatus, it was completed over four months in 1479. Sanetaka's diary entries reveal a substantial amount of negotiation between all parties involved in the production, which is understandable for the creation of a new scroll as opposed to a copy of a preexisting work. In addition to the numerous discussions involved in the preparation of the work, other clues that suggest this was a new story authored by Sanetaka emerge through a close analysis of the language he used in the diary entries related to the scroll.

There is, for example, the issue of the title of the story. In his first reference to the piece, Sanetaka provides a working title: referring to it as the "small-scroll text," he adds a parenthetical comment stating that "it is to be called *Clouds of Mt. Kōya*" [*takanogumo gō su*].[110] He also describes his work on the text by using a word that often means "to compose" (*sō*), rather than the more common verbs to "write" (*kaku*) or "copy" (*shosha*). These are sure signs that Sanetaka was writing a new story.

This was all at the request of the emperor, who emerges from the records as an exacting and engaged patron. Sanetaka had several direct meetings with the emperor concerning the scroll text, including one that lasted well into the night.[111] The emperor demanded copies of the text in various states of completion and also requested that Sanetaka make certain corrections, implying that he had strong ideas about the kind of story he wanted illustrated. When Sanetaka was just beginning to compose the tale, he consulted the scholar-courtier Nakanoin Michihide.[112] Although Sanetaka's diary never delves into the nature of these conversations, they must have discussed details of language and meaning, which would be important elements in determining the illustrations for the work.

As the figure with the greatest insight into the text, Sanetaka provided feedback to the artist concerning the paintings for *Clouds of Mt. Kōya*, albeit through intermediaries and indirectly through his meetings with the emperor. In the early stages of the scroll's production, for example, Sanetaka went to the palace to examine Mitsunobu's preliminary sketches for the paintings and suggested that Mitsunobu make additions in a few areas.[113] Intermediaries then conveyed Sanetaka's advice to Mitsunobu. Although Sanetaka conversed directly with Mitsunobu on other scroll projects, he does not record such interaction concerning *Clouds of Mt. Kōya*. Mitsunobu had attained the position of *azukari* in 1469, but in the 1470s was still of relatively low standing. It may have been beneath Sanetaka to meet with the painter at this point, or he may simply have not known him well enough yet, this being the first record of a collaboration. While it is possible that the two met during the years that it took to complete the scroll, it is clear that other individuals, such as palace ladies, communicated instructions on Sanetaka's behalf.

The female attendants serving the emperor played an important role as intermediaries in many artistic projects at the palace. Traces of their participation survive in the form of letters they wrote to the various parties involved, to convey precise instructions, to arrange meetings that helped orchestrate the projects, or simply to express the emperor's satisfaction with the outcome. Most of these letters were preserved by chance when Sanetaka received them and used their blank reverse sides as paper for his diary. Thus, in 1479, a few months before the completion of *Clouds of Mt. Kōya*, Sanetaka received a letter from a palace lady announcing that Tosa Mitsunobu had delivered the paintings to the imperial palace.[114] Soon thereafter Sanetaka went to the palace to discuss the paintings again. The letter from the female attendant demonstrates how information was conveyed between palace, artist, and calligrapher-author. Other letters by female attendants, concerning, for example, the small scroll of a tale of rebirth to be discussed in chapter 4, contain more details and step-by-step instructions for Sanetaka concerning the emperor's desires. The women who served the emperor were highly educated and politically well connected, and their potential role in artistic projects at the palace should not be dismissed.

Although *Clouds of Mt. Kōya* does not survive, Tokuda Kazuo has suggested that two identical Edo period copies of a picture scroll in the small format were based on the Mitsunobu and Sanetaka original.[115] The copies in the Tokyo National Museum (figs. 46–48) and the Literature Department of Gakushūin University are now called *Legends of Kokawadera* (*Kokawadera engi*) and the *Tale of Kokawa* (*Kokawa no sōshi*), respectively, titles created by later connoisseurs. (For convenience, the story in the copies will be referred to here as *Tale of Kokawa*.) The title of the original scroll upon which both copies were based, however, could well have been *Clouds of Mt. Kōya*; as Tokuda has pointed out, the text contains the words "the clouds of Mt. Kōya" (*Takano gumo*) both in a poem and in a phrase toward the end of the narrative. The presence of these words and the stylistic and compositional similarity of the copied paintings to Mitsunobu's works (fig. 47), as well as the small format of the copies, make for a compelling argument that it does indeed represent Sanetaka's and Mitsunobu's *Clouds of Mt. Kōya*.

The narrative relates a tangled love triangle between a married couple and the husband's childhood friend that ends with all three characters renouncing the secular world and eventually achieving Buddhist salvation (fig. 48). The point at which the protagonists decide to withdraw from the world marks a climax in this and similar tales. In this story the wife returns home to find that both her husband and her husband's friend, who had pursued her romantically without realizing her identity, have renounced the secular world to devote the remainder of their lives to Buddhist practice. The woman finds a poem left for her by the husband's friend that links the tale's opening and conclusion, as it announces his intention to practice on Mt. Kōya. At the same time, the poem recalls his chance encounter with the woman depicted in the first scene (fig. 46):

Even amid the clouds of Mt. Kōya, I will not forget
The faint vision of that flowering spring
(*Wasuremeya takano no gumo ni majiru tomo*
Honomishi hana no haru no omokage)

In some ways the entire story could have been woven from this particular poem, and it is interesting to consider this in light of the references in Sanetaka's diary in which he names the work *Clouds of Mt. Kōya*, as though he began his composition with this poem.

This would not be the only time that Sanetaka authored a narrative handscroll text. Fragments of narratives composed by Sanetaka are preserved on the reverse side of his diary in 1475, the same year that *Clouds of Mt. Kōya* was created.[116] These fragments contain notations that divide the texts into sections to accommodate the format of a picture scroll. They also reveal that Sanetaka wove one of the stories around a popular poem, thus further suggesting that this may have been his approach in the creation of *Clouds of Mt. Kōya*. He even authored a dependent-origin tale (*engi*) for a statue of Jizō donated by his wife's family to a local temple, and he was a playwright as well, coauthoring a Nō play based on *Tale of Sagoromo,* or literally *Tale of Narrow Robes* (*Sagoromo monogatari*), at the request of the shogun Ashikaga Yoshihisa (1465–89) in 1481.[117]

The process of prose authorship in this era was in many ways a process of citation, which helps to account for the distinct intertextuality of Muromachi period tales. Prose narratives, Nō plays, and Buddhist origin tales from this period are dense in literary allusions; they incorporate narrative patterns, poems, and scenarios from previous works and use these citations in creative ways: as the premises of new tales, as efficient means to enrich a setting or character, or to play upon the expectations of a reader and even to subvert the source text. The key to the successful creation of any literary work in such a context was access to other texts. As a high-ranking courtier and close adviser to three successive emperors, virtually every genre of literature passed through Sanetaka's hands, whether as a copyist, a reader, or an editor. With his remarkable knowledge of poetry and his many years of studying classical texts,

46 *Tale of Kokawa* (*Kokawadera engi*). Edo-period copy of Muromachi scroll, possibly of *Clouds of Mt. Kōya* (*Takano gumo-e*). One scroll; ink, color, and gold on paper. Tokyo National Museum.

47 *Tale of Kokawa* (*Kokawadera engi*). Edo-period copy of Muromachi scroll, possibly of *Clouds of Mt. Kōya* (*Takano gumo-e*). One scroll; ink, color, and gold on paper. Tokyo National Museum.

48 *Tale of Kokawa* (*Kokawadera engi*). Edo-period copy of Muromachi scroll, possibly of *Clouds of Mt. Kōya* (*Takano gumo-e*). One scroll; ink, color, and gold on paper. Tokyo National Museum.

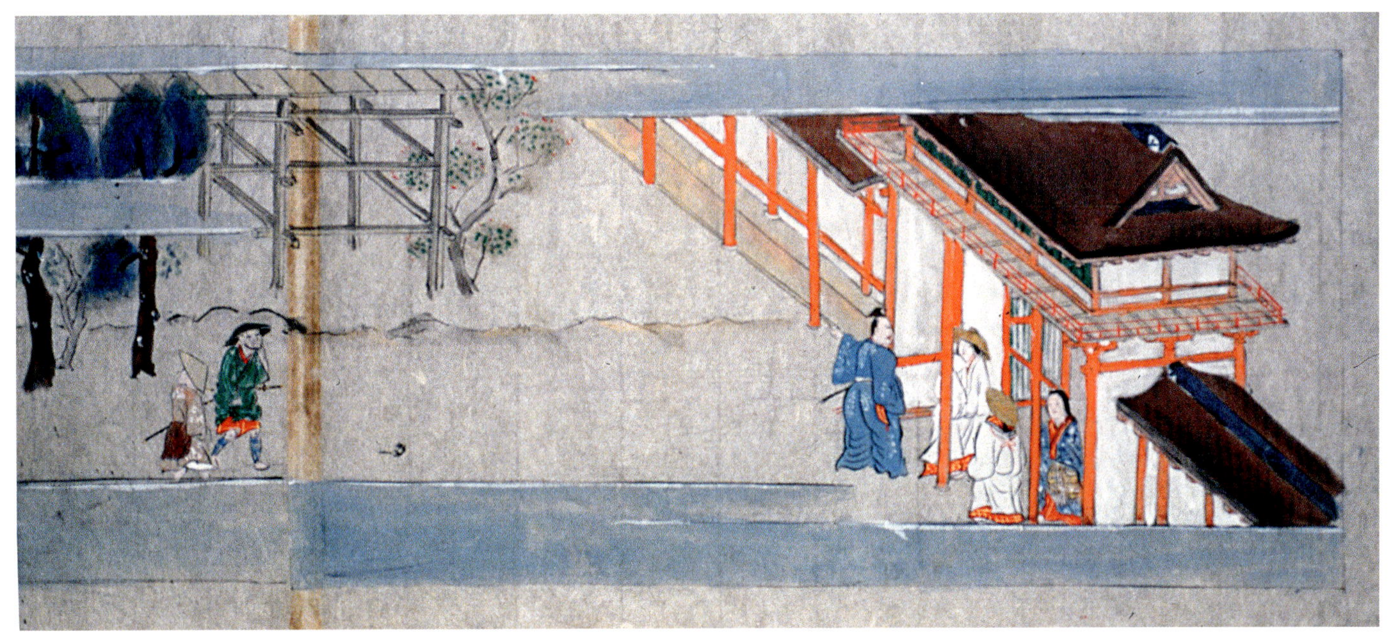

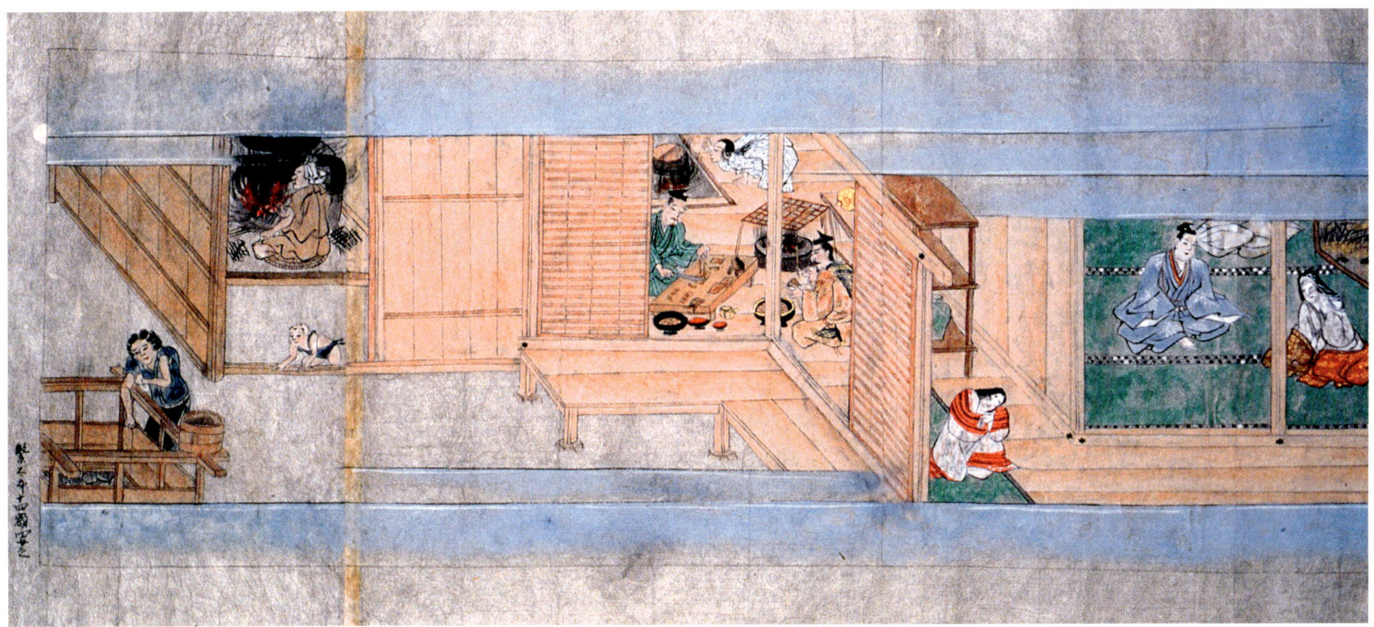

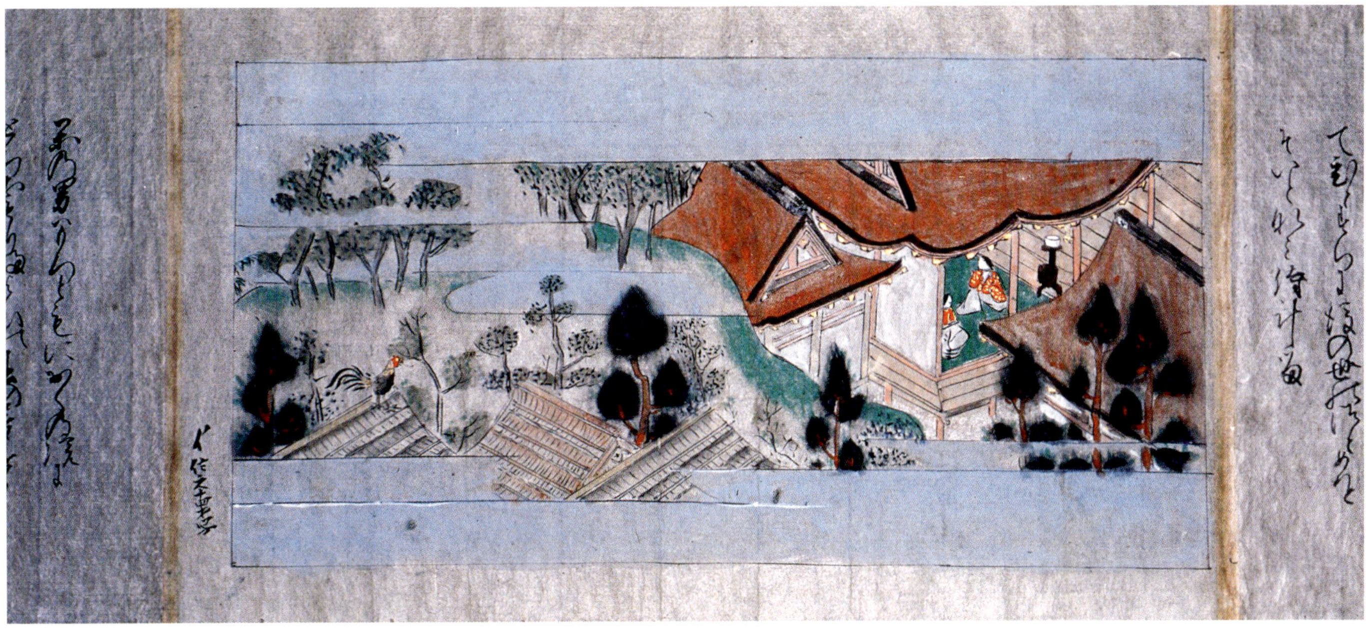

Sanetaka was certainly capable of authoring scroll texts, such as the one found in the possible Edo-period copy of *Clouds of Mt. Kōya, Tale of Kokawa.*

The story found in the Edo period copy resembles tales popular at court in the late fifteenth century, ones avidly read by Sanetaka and GoTsuchimikado. More precisely, the tale consists of a pastiche of different narrative genres read at the imperial court in this period. *Tale of Kokawa* skillfully combines a frame narrative based on the genre of the *engi*, or the "origin tale of a temple and shrine," with the central story being a "tale of renunciation." The story begins as many other origin tales do by describing the setting and history of a temple or shrine (in this case, Kokawadera), the sacred nature of its site, how it was founded, and the miraculous origins of its main icon, albeit in a brief manner. This opening passage no doubt prompted later connoisseurs to title the copy in the Tokyo National Museum *Kokawadera engi*. It becomes clear in the second text, however, that the temple serves only as the setting for the fateful encounter between the man and the wife of his friend and is not itself the subject of the scroll. Yet the *engi*-like opening and the conclusion, in which the woman takes the tonsure at Kokawadera, lend this short story an epic tone. Moreover, these two scenes at Kokawadera are represented by images of the temple site that allude to painted *engi* (fig. 48), the genre of picture scroll most frequently read at the imperial court in the late fifteenth century. The producers of *Tale of Kokawa*, clearly familiar with the tradition of painted *engi*, framed the tale (in both word and image) with references to this genre of picture scroll.

But while *Tale of Kokawa* utilizes the elements of the origin tale to frame the story, the work belongs primarily to the category of renunciation tales, which relate the circumstances behind an individual's decision to leave the world. *Tale of Kokawa* describes a confluence of events that prompt three people to take Buddhist vows and thus falls well within the scope of this genre. Such tales of renunciation were found in collections of anecdotes and short stories in the medieval period, many of which date to the thirteenth century but continued to be read in the fifteenth century.

GoTsuchimikado was an avid reader of origin tales and tales of renunciation; the palace frequently borrowed *engi* from temples and shrines, and there were several *setsuwa* (short-story) collections in the imperial library.[118] The emperor had both kinds of texts read aloud for him by his attendant courtiers. Around the time of the production of *Clouds of Mt. Kōya*, Sanetaka read from a three-scroll set of *Miraculous Origins of Zenkōji* (*Zenkōji engi-e*) for GoTsuchimikado.[119] Tales of renunciation were frequently read to the emperor at night, in his sleeping chamber or in his study, as in 1476 when Sanetaka read aloud from *Stories of Spiritual Awakening* (*Hosshinshū*), compiled by Kamo no Chōmei (1155–1216).[120] Such renunciation narratives were also at the heart of a number of short-story *ko-e*, and *Clouds of Mt. Kōya*, if it is the short story represented in the Edo period copy, fits well within the characteristics of this genre.

The preceding account of the cultural milieu of Mitsunobu and Sanetaka in the late fifteenth and early sixteenth centuries is offered as a means of explaining the rather sudden appearance of the short-story small scroll, which flourished in the same time period. As discussed in chapter 1, at no other point in the history of Japanese narrative painting had the small format been exploited as a venue for the illustration of short stories. Not until the fifteenth century did artists and their collaborators realize the creative possibilities of matching the brevity of the short story with a diminutive pictorial counterpart. The full potential of this new pictoliterary genre was achieved by a group of individuals who possessed not only a thorough knowledge of but also a critical distance from the classical forms of the past.

As *edokoro azukari* for roughly fifty years, Mitsunobu had access to an astounding array of paintings and was called upon to paint an equally large range of subjects, formats, and styles. This experience added to his store of knowledge, and this visual literacy made it possible for him to create small scrolls dense with pictorial allusions to past *emaki* genres. On the other hand, Mitsunobu's paintings must always be seen as group-authored works, with men such as Sanetaka advising him behind the scenes. The sensitivity to language and graphic representation by the scholar-calligraphers who collaborated with artists in this period clearly enhanced the sophistication of the relationship between word and image in small scrolls. Equally important, however, was the atmosphere at GoTsuchimikado's court, which should be recognized as a contributing factor to the emergence of the short-story small scroll; it was this milieu, steeped in the preservation of ancient texts, that became the epicenter for the creation of short-story small scrolls.

Three scrolls produced in this environment, *A Wakeful Sleep*, *The Jizō Hall*, and *Breaking the Inkstone*, were created by artists, patrons, and scholar-calligraphers who concerned themselves with the most minute details of relationships between word and image and, as a result, reward close textual and pictorial analysis. In the following chapters I examine the multifaceted nature of these scrolls while connecting them to their historical contexts, beginning with a work that embodies the atmosphere just described, a small scroll steeped in references to the classical past, *A Wakeful Sleep*.

3

A WAKEFUL SLEEP PAINTING THE DREAM TALE

Utatane ni	In a brief slumber
koishiki hito o	I caught sight of my beloved
miteshi yori	and now I cling
yume chō mono wa	to each passing dream
tanomisometeki	

Komachi's words express but a trifling fancy in comparison to the passion that rejects even life itself. Among the many tales of long ago is one extraordinary account of such a love.
—*A Wakeful Sleep* (*trans.* Skord)

The ninth-century poetess Ono no Komachi was considered the archetypal femme fatale in the medieval Japanese imaginary. Her remarkable beauty, haughtiness, lyrical intensity, and heartlessness, especially toward would-be lovers, marked her as worthy of inclusion in the pantheon of larger-than-life poets along with Hitomaro, Izumi Shikibu, Ki no Tsurayuki, Saigyō, and others, all of whom continuously inspired new forms of versification and literary reproduction during the Muromachi period. The karmic retribution that was thought to have been visited upon Komachi in her old age, the direct result of her cruelty toward hapless suitors, ensured that she would be a proper protagonist for the morality lessons of Nō plays and a suitable subject for the admonitions of hosts of literary commentaries. As with many of the legendary authors apotheosized in medieval Japan, however, very little was actually known about Komachi's life, and her qualities were almost entirely imagined from a handful of poems that had been immortalized in personal and imperial anthologies centuries earlier. It was the perceived intensity of expression in her love poetry from which everything else was imagined. In the thirty-one syllables of the classical *waka* form, this otherwise obscure court lady managed to record testimonies of her own longing and amorous experiences that distinguished her from her contemporaries and later *waka* practitioners. And it was Komachi's rhetorical passion that made her such an effective voice for the poetic epigraph to *A Wakeful Sleep*, the first of the three small scrolls examined in this study.

A Wakeful Sleep was painted by Tosa Mitsunobu (fig. 1) in the late fifteenth or early sixteenth century and the handscroll is now preserved at the National Museum of Japanese History in Chiba Prefecture.[1] The story concerns a young woman of the courtier class who falls in love with a man who visits her in her dreams; pining for him, she falls ill and is cured only through the intercession of the Kannon deity at Ishiyamadera; while visiting the temple to thank her savior icon, she glimpses the man of her dreams, and knowing she cannot approach him without breaking social taboos, she attempts to commit suicide by throwing herself in the river; yet she is saved by her dream lover, and the remainder of their lives pass in conjugal bliss. *A Wakeful Sleep* is characterized by an intensity of mood and expression seldom rivaled in prose works of the Muromachi period. This condensation of emotion is enhanced by the austere and linear progression of the narrative. Like other small scrolls, *A Wakeful Sleep* conveys its story in compact, highly economical fashion. Only four paintings suffice to provide a rich visual counterpart to the tale. Indeed, minimalism of word and image is crucial in maintaining the story line at a highly attenuated level. Komachi's poem establishes with forceful immediacy the tenor of the text; by describing the longing in Komachi's verse as a mere "trifling fancy" in comparison to what is to come, the narrator sets the stakes high for a work that otherwise appears to have all the trappings of an elegiac courtly romance.

Yet there was another side to the medieval reception of Komachi, also invoked in the opening salvo of the tale, that is even more germane to the establishment of setting and atmosphere at the outset, and that highlights even more the pictorial qualities of *A Wakeful Sleep*. Komachi was recognized as perhaps the most important dream poet of the classical *waka* canon. Much of her most memorable poetry emerged from the territory of dreams or, even more evocatively, from the terra incognita between dream and reality, sleep and wakefulness, a state of in-betweenness that allowed her to question and hope for the validity of surreptitious encounters and amorous experiences.

yumeji ni wa	though my feet never
ashi mo yasumezu	cease running to him on the
kayoedomo	byways of my dreams
utsuutsu ni hitome	such meetings do not equal
mishi goto wa arazu	one waking glimpse of my love[2]

omoitsutsu	in love-tormented
nureba ya hito no	sleep I saw him beside me—
mietsuran	had I known my love's
yume to shiriseba	visit was but a dream I
samezaramashi o	should never have awakened[3]

It is in this capacity, as the voice that hovers between states of consciousness, that Komachi raises the curtain on the ethereal, dreamy world of *A Wakeful Sleep*: for the entire tale unfolds in a condition of prolonged suspension between dream and reality, with characters that inhabit both worlds and are equally visceral in both states. This suspension affects the voice that narrates, instilling a skepticism of tone that hangs over the entire story and is even exacerbated by the otherworldly intervention of the Ishiyamadera Kannon and the haunting presence of Murasaki Shikibu, the author of *The Tale of Genji,* who is invoked at a key moment in the narrative. And this condition of irreality is captured perfectly in the Japanese term *utatane* used in Komachi's opening poem, which serves as the title and is translated here as "wakeful sleep." No English translation of *utatane* is adequate to it, for *utatane* designates a peculiar condition of semiconsciousness. It is not quite one of sleepwalking, nor of insomnia, catnapping, or the "brief slumbers" with which *utatane* is occasionally translated. Rather, this state can only be articulated oxymoronically as one of "alert somnolence" or "drowsy cognition." The literary appeal of *A Wakeful Sleep* is precisely the atmosphere of wakeful sleepiness that it manages to capture with so few words.

Mitsunobu's achievement in *A Wakeful Sleep* lies in the carefully calibrated moods of his pictorial complements to the tale. As in his other small scrolls examined in this study, the paintings here appear to follow the technical conventions that had governed courtly narrative painting (*yamato-e*) for centuries, which included the three-stage delineation and coloration of motifs, the application of mineral pigments, and the use of mist bands to structure the lateral leftward progression of the picture plane. The precise attunement and interpretive sophistication of each picture to its corresponding textual moment, however, distinguishes this work from the overwhelming majority of Japanese narrative handscrolls. The result is greater than the sum of its parts, a unity of reading-viewing experience that marks *A Wakeful Sleep* as in many ways the archetypal small scroll of medieval Japan.

The primary aim of this chapter is to introduce *A Wakeful Sleep* as one of the most significant examples of the small-scroll genre and through its close reading to understand the interpretive potential of the format. It offers an exemplary case study of how small scrolls could individuate tales newly authored in the medieval period and mold them through pictorial expression to suit the normalizing prerogatives of the aristocracy. This process necessarily includes a full introduction of the story and its relationship to the genre of the courtly tale or romance from which it emerges. It will also include a scene-by-scene analysis of each of Mitsunobu's four paintings. The paintings are permeated by a highly self-conscious approach to courtly narrative painting, resulting in subtle displacements of familiar techniques, several instances of direct citations, and, in one dramatic instance, a complete overturning of the rules governing aristocratic representation. The contexts and communities presupposed by *A Wakeful Sleep* are also carefully analyzed. Even though the initial production and reception context of the scroll is undocumented, visual analysis and a careful reading of the text are more than sufficient to flesh out the concerns of the scroll. I will argue that the narrative functions as an allegory for the newly prevalent practice of patrilocal marriage among aristocratic communities in the late medieval period and sketch the profile of the scroll's anticipated readers. Ultimately, however, the didactic nature of the scroll is compromised by the ambivalence of its characterization of the young female protagonist. Her pictorial interpretation generates a tension between romantic heroine and feminine and filial exemplar, a figure betwixt and between two figural topoi. This figure directly reflects the multiple layers of pictoliterary characterization enabled by the representational mandate of the small scroll.

A MUROMACHI PERIOD DREAM TALE

The author and date of the literary tale *A Wakeful Sleep* are unknown, but most literature scholars believe that it was written sometime during the Muromachi period and most likely by someone of the courtier class.[4] Ten recensions survive, including four small-format handscrolls (the Mitsunobu scroll, a polychrome scroll in the National Institute of Japanese Literature, and two ink-line scrolls in the collections of the Museum of Fine Arts, Boston, and the Freer Gallery of Art).[5] These texts are all nearly identical, with no dramatic differences in plot, structure, or characters.[6] The biggest differences among the recensions exist between the two ink-line handscrolls, which include inscribed dialogue amid their illustrations (*gachūshi*), and all other versions.[7] The text of the Mitsunobu handscroll is the oldest surviving example of the story, but scholars have assumed that the tale's authorship predates its production.[8] Given the erudition of Mitsunobu's cultural circle, however, the possibility should at least be entertained that the story's creation was contemporaneous.

Utatane sōshi was not the scroll's original title but was applied by seventeenth-century painting and calligraphy authenticators, who tended to name untitled handscrolls according to their opening lines.[9] Thus, in 1688 when Tosa Mitsuoki (1617–91) appended a colophon to *A Wakeful Sleep* attributing the scroll to Mitsunobu (fig. 1g), he took the first word from Komachi's poem and titled the piece "Utatane no e."[10] While this is certainly an appropriate and poetic title for the story, evidence suggests that the scroll's original title may have referred explicitly to dreams, as in one later, unillustrated manuscript of the tale called *Dream Travels* (*Yumeji monogatari*).[11] Such a title would have evoked the nocturnal wanderings of both the man and the woman in the story and recalled the literary precedents for lovers who travel to and from each other's dreams.[12]

A *ko-e* illustrating a story about dreams entitled *A Tale of Dreams* (or literally "Dream Telling," *Yumegatari*) was in the possession of GoTsuchimikado in 1474, the text of which Sanetaka was asked to copy.[13] Tokuda Kazuo has suggested that this *Tale of Dreams* corresponds to Mitsunobu's *A Wakeful Sleep* and is yet another example of collaboration between the artist and the courtier.[14] Unlike *The Jizō Hall*, however, *A Wakeful Sleep* does not bear Sanetaka's calligraphy, nor does his diary contain any other references to *Yumegatari*. Moreover Sanetaka did not "draft" (*sō*) or "write" (*kaku*) the text, his usual terms for executing the calligraphy on a new small scroll, but rather "copied" (*shosha su*) an existing text. That text may even have been an ancient tale, now lost, such as the *Yumegatari* mentioned in *Tale without a Name* (*Mumyōzōshi*, ca. 1200).[15]

Regardless of whether or not *A Wakeful Sleep* relates directly to *A Tale of Dreams* of 1474, Sanetaka's diary entry points to the potential importance of manuscript recensions as source texts and inspiration for new narratives, especially for the short stories of small scrolls. The narrative of *A Wakeful Sleep*, with its numerous allusions to *The Tale of Genji*, imperial poetry anthologies, and plot points from past narratives, demonstrates above all its mastery, and adroit manipulation, of literary tradition. This type of prose fiction could be called "accretive," as H. Mack Horton has characterized the approach of Sanetaka and his fellow critics to literary scholarship.[16] Sanetaka's own commentaries on *The Tale of Genji*, especially two texts known as *Delighting in the Blossoms* (*Rōkashō*, 1504, 1510) and *Slender Currents of "The Tale of Genji"* (*Genji monogatari sairyūshō*, 1513), for example, build on past commentaries and contain lengthy quotations as well as annotations from other scholars.[17] In a similar way, *A Wakeful Sleep* builds on older narratives, citing classical texts, quoting extensive passages from well-known anecdotes, and in general shaping the narrative in response to a shared and intimate knowledge of the literary canon. While the authorship of *A Wakeful Sleep* remains unknown, the tale was perfectly suited to those men and women in Mitsunobu's and Sanetaka's circle intent not only on preserving their courtly patrimony but also on reshaping it according to current ideas and concerns.

The opening lines of *A Tale of Wakeful Sleep*, cited at the beginning of the chapter, set the tone for a narrative that interweaves a multitude of classical allusions into the fabric of a new story. The tale begins with Komachi's famous poem from *Collection of Ancient and Modern Poems* (*Kokinshū*), thrusting the reader into the world of Heian period verse. Such beginnings, which announced that the story was taking the literary past as its point of departure and would reward those readers well versed in traditional texts, was common to many medieval tales that imitated the structure and character types of the perceived golden age of the Japanese court.[18] These tales were collectively known as *giko monogatari*, literally "archaic tales," a Meiji period term that refers to courtly narratives from the late Heian and Kamakura periods.[19] In the past, scholars have used the word *giko* pejoratively to describe narratives perceived as unoriginal in their reliance on the language and scenarios of past texts.[20] Seeking to remove the negative value judgments unjustly associated with these narratives, Ōtsuki Osamu advocated using the term *chūsei ōchō monogatari*, or "medieval court tales."[21] However, if the "imitation" is viewed not as an act of perfunctory emulation but as a form of expression based on the intertextuality inherent in manuscript culture, the term *giko monogatari* need not be negative; it can call attention to a self-consciousness of the literary past that underwrites these texts. In their straightforward admission of a relationship to canonized works, these stories expose their own processes of creation and encourage us to consider the historical contexts of their production.

As a medieval tale that draws heavily from *The Tale of Genji* and classical poetry, *A Wakeful Sleep* would seem to fall within the category of *giko monogatari*.[22] Technically however, when most scholars speak of *giko monogatari*, they refer specifically to tales from the late Heian period such as *Tale of Sagoromo* (*Sagoromo monogatari,* ca. 1180), *Wakefulness at Night* (*Yoru no nezame,* ca. 1045–68), and *Parting at Dawn* (*Ariake no wakare;* twelfth century), or those from the early Kamakura period such as *The Princess in Search of Herself* (*Wagami ni tadoru himegimi,* mid–thirteenth century) and *Tale of Unspoken Yearning* (*Iwade shinobu monogatari,* first half of thirteenth century), to name but a few.[23] These relatively well known post-*Genji* works, all of which date before the late thirteenth century, are long pieces of fiction usually spanning multiple volumes each, with complicated plots and large casts of characters. *A Wakeful Sleep,* with its later date and dramatically shorter length, does not fit within the rubric of "classic" *giko monogatari*. Indeed, *A Wakeful Sleep* is conscious not only of *Genji* but of post-*Genji* fiction and draws upon this body of texts as well for aspects of its plot.

A Wakeful Sleep is one of a number of Muromachi period works of courtly fiction that interweave aspects from earlier *monogatari* into new short tales. While scholars of Heian and Kamakura period *giko monogatari* rightly point out the lack of attention that field has received, studies of Muromachi period courtly fiction outside the rubric of *otogi-zōshi* are nonexistent in the English language. As discussed in chapter 1, courtly literature did not cease after the Ōnin War; rather, the destruction of the war served as an impetus for cultural revival under the reign of GoTsuchimikado. And although the imperial court of this period lacked the conditions that enabled the literary production of female salons in earlier times—specifically, an empress or excessively wealthy fathers of consorts to act as patrons—it continued to be populated by many educated, highborn women. Although poorly documented, these women could be accomplished litterateurs, such as GoTsuchimikado's high-ranking secretary Yotsuji Haruko (d. 1504).[24] Haruko attended imperial poetic gatherings, had poems included in the *renga* anthology *New Tsukuba Collection* (*Shinsen Tsukubashū,* 1495), and owned copies of classical manuscripts that she regularly lent out upon request.[25]

Yotsuji Haruko's literary activities suggest that she and other women like her, both female attendants and women of the courtier class, were engaged in the reading and writing of courtly fiction in this period and were likely the authors of many of the anonymous Muromachi period tales centered on courtiers.[26] One such tale attributed to Yotsuji Haruko and written before 1497, *Tale of Hanyū* (*Hanyū mongatari*), reflects the direct influence of *A Wakeful Sleep*.[27] *Tale of Hanyū* features a female protagonist who is a beautiful and intelligent daughter of a court minister and yearns to take Buddhist vows. To avoid marriage she negotiates an agreement with her parents that she will marry only the man who succeeds in sending her a love letter containing a poem that she cannot identify, which she considers an impossibility due to her impressive erudition. Otherwise, she will be allowed to become a nun. The story's similarity to *A Wakeful Sleep* occurs in episodes such as the woman's pilgrimage to Ishiyamadera, where she dreams about and then actually encounters the young man who wrote the only letter that she found moving. The young man's subsequent suicidal jump from the Seta Bridge and similarities in the poetic references further reflect the close relationship between the two tales.[28] Like *A Wakeful Sleep*, *Tale of Hanyū* ends happily when the youth is rescued from the waters of the Uji River and is eventually reunited with his female admirer.

Many court-centered tales of the Muromachi period were illustrated as ink-line, or *hakubyō,* handscrolls, which became the privileged medium for women's writing and illustration in the fifteenth and sixteenth centuries.[29] Illustrated *hakubyō* scrolls such as *Lady Chūgū* (*Chūgū monogatari emaki*), *The New Chamberlain* (*Shin kurōdo emaki*), and *The Lavender Robe* (*Fuji no koromo monogatari emaki* aka *Yūjo monogatari emaki*) relate stories of romance, family intrigue, and Buddhist salvation among the sons and daughters of the aristocracy. The narratives of these works are undated, but they probably range from the fourteenth to fifteenth centuries, making them earlier than most short works about aristocrats that tend to be categorized as *otogi-zōshi*.[30] The two identical copies of *A Wakeful Sleep* in the ink-line mode place the reception of this tale likewise within a medieval culture of writing, drawing, and copying aristocratic tales. In this regard, Mitsunobu's polychrome rendition of *A Wakeful Sleep* is an anomaly among Muromachi *emaki* in general and Mitsunobu's oeuvre in particular since no other polychrome handscroll of a courtly romance in his hand survives. The apparently unique status of his ren- dition of this aristocratic romance raises the intriguing question of why the Painting Bureau director would be asked to illustrate the kind of tale that was usually the preserve of the amateur *hakubyō* illustrator. The answer lies in the details of the work itself, which differs in significant respects from the monochrome versions. This highly polished *emaki* imbued its source text with an aura of supernatural inevitability, thereby presenting the tale as something closer to a fantasy of aristocratic matrimony. This recasting, in turn, is suggestive of significant social changes in the aristocracy at the time, especially the newly established practice of patrilocal marriage.

The deeply referential nature of *A Wakeful Sleep* reflected more than just nostalgia. Rather, within the larger context of cultural production at GoTsuchimikado's court, it may be understood as the beginning of a concerted and robust emphasis on the authority of the imperial position itself through literary representation. The scholarly tendency to dismiss the imperial institution in this period as politically feeble and economically impoverished remains prevalent to this day; most cite GoKashiwabara's postponed enthronement ceremony due to lack of funds as a prime example of the court's impotence. Wakita Haruko has suggested, however, that it was precisely during this period when scholar-courtiers disseminated classical courtly texts and other imperially centered art forms to the provinces that the emperor's authority as a political symbol increased.[31] *A Wakeful Sleep*, which concerns the union of an ideal aristocratic couple, should be situated within the numerous activities that celebrated imperial authority in the Muromachi period. At the story's core are important members of the court hierarchy: its female protagonist is the daughter of a court minister, and her future husband is the major captain of the left (*sadaishō*). When the couple reunite at the end of the tale, the narrator links their good fortune to the benevolence of the imperial reign. Conspicuous wisteria (*fuji*) motifs valorize the Fujiwara clan, members of which still occupied the highest-ranking court offices during the Muromachi period.[32]

Although *A Wakeful Sleep* pays its respects to precedent, it also attempts to outdo its prototypes. A surprising sense of one-upmanship, for example, can be found in the citation of the Komachi poem at the beginning of the tale. This poem sets the tone of the story but is also a foil that underscores the new story's "superior" qualities. Immediately following the poem, the narrator identifies its author, Ono no Komachi, and then proceeds to criticize its sentiment. The narrator boasts, "Komachi's words express but a trifling fancy in comparison to the passion that rejects even life itself," the kind that is displayed in *A Wakeful Sleep*. The "rejection of life itself" refers to the willingness of the protagonist of *A Wakeful Sleep* to risk her life for love. The woman's leap from the Seta Bridge at the close of the tale, in the hopes of meeting her lover in the next world, displays the "genuine passion" to which Komachi's sentiment does not measure up. The opening lines thus provide the first of many examples in the narrative where a past text is quoted only to be subverted. A close reading of the texts and images demonstrates that pictorial techniques were crucial in enabling this impious mode of reference.

REWORKING THE COURTLY ROMANCE IN TEXT AND IMAGE

The opening textual passage of *A Wakeful Sleep* introduces the female protagonist and recounts her initial dream encounter with her amorous counterpart (fig. 1):

The story I am about to tell occurred in the not-too-distant past. There was once a prominent minister well regarded at court. Of his many children born to several consorts, one son was the Master of the Crown Prince's Household; another

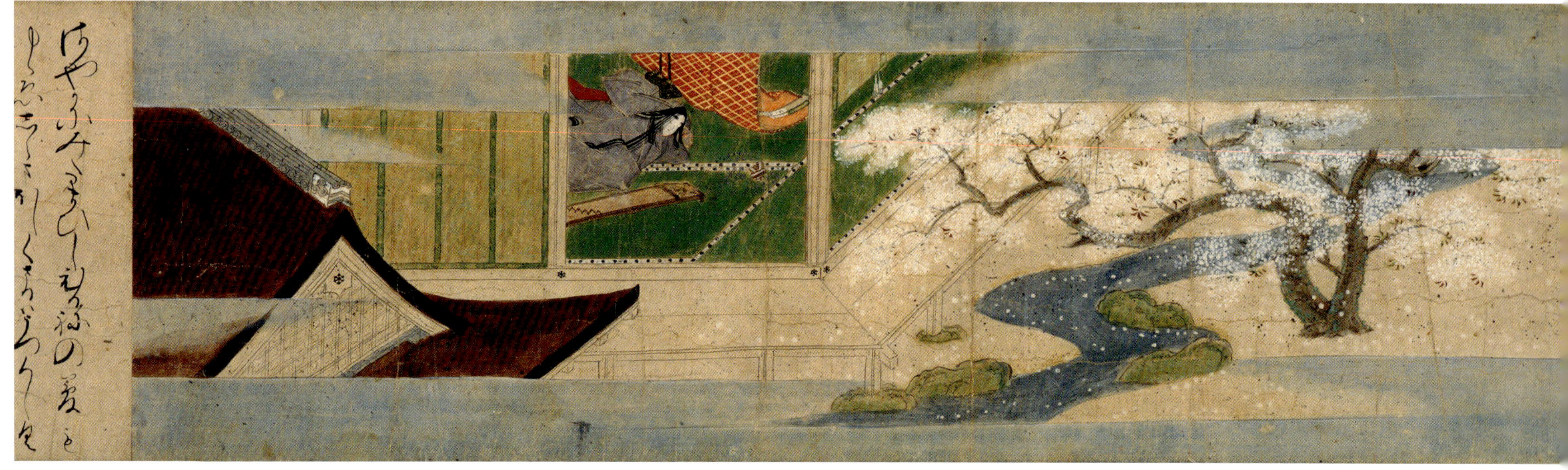

49 Tosa Mitsunobu, *A Wakeful Sleep*. National Museum of Japanese History, Chiba Prefecture. Painting 1.

younger son held the rank of prelate and was head priest of Ishiyama Temple. The Minister had but a single daughter, sister to the Prelate, whom he cherished beyond measure. He considered sending her to serve at court and had already begun making preparations for her presentation when he realized that she would be surrounded by a bevy of imperial consorts and ladies of the bedchamber. In such an atmosphere, even if she were to receive imperial favor, she would be subjected to fierce jealousy, and he feared lest she become withdrawn and sink into depression. As he vacillated over the decision, certain presentable suitors called with offers to marry and care for her, but he was reluctant to give his precious daughter to anyone at all.

Soon the girl blossomed into the full flower of maidenhood and radiated such an array of charms that she was a pleasure to behold. Her father treated her with special consideration, inviting ladies of excellent qualities to serve her. At times she lived happily, deriving amusement from the many diversions afforded by the spring flowers and autumnal foliage. Other times, however, the weight of her father's duties led him to neglect her, and, her mother having passed away, the girl perforce spent long hours in lonely idleness.

Near her rooms grew a late-blooming wild cherry tree, adorned with blossoms far outlasting those of other flowering trees. As the spring days slipped away, she found solace in these flowers and lamented their final descent to earth. One lonely afternoon, as the long rains gently fell and droplets ceaselessly pattered on the eaves, she left off her aimless plucking at the koto and lay down, falling off into a deep sleep.

Suddenly, it seemed that someone appeared before her, proffering a branch of flowering wisteria deeply fragrant despite the dew still clinging to it. Attached to the branch was a slip of paper tinted in the same pale lavender hue as the wisteria. Assuming that this lovely offering was a message from the Kamo Priestess,[33] the girl casually picked it up. In a man's hand was written:

Omoine ni	Yet more fleeting than a daydream
miru yume yori mo	from the slumbers of love—
hakanaki wa	the vision of another
yoso no omokage	a reality yet unknown.

The traces of ink were well modulated and the hand remarkable, revealing that the poem had been written by no ordinary person. She gazed at it with admiration, her heart in turmoil, wondering who might have sent it. This was a most unexpected dream!

This first passage of text evokes numerous scenes from classical romances, placing its protagonist in a lineage of well-known heroines. The image of a beautiful, isolated heroine plucking at her *koto* strings, for example, and the evocation of mood through the sound of the rain droplets upon the eaves, an apparent reference to a poem from *New Collection of Ancient and Modern Poems*, prepare the role of longing female courtier.[34] Most important, however, the first text invokes the legendary misfortune that befell Genji's mother, the Kiritsubo Consort, in the opening chapter of *The Tale of Genji*, especially through its reference to the "bevy of imperial consorts and ladies of the bedchamber," whose jealousy might lead to the girl's demise should she be sent to court. While Kiritsubo lacked a father to guide her at court, this young girl is motherless, but her father averts disaster by keeping her at home, enabling a different kind of outcome for our heroine.

The accompanying painting (figs. 1a and 49) opens with an image of the flowering cherry tree described in the text. The moss-covered tree with its profusion of white flowers stands on the bank of a gently winding stream in a garden. The wafting petals, whose descent to the ground was lamented by the protagonist, stand out against the blue water. One limb of the cherry tree extends leftward over the stream and leads the viewer's eye to the focal point of the painting, the girl languishing in her room. Mist bands further direct the viewer's focus with their sharp black outlines and pale blue pigment that fades away softly. The line of the veranda and vertical architectural posts create an emphatic frame around the woman lying next to her *koto*, a convention that recalls similar figures from past romances and illustrations such as the "Maiden at the Bridge" (*Hashihime*) scene from the *Genji Scrolls* (twelfth century) or the image of Murasaki at her *koto* in *Illustrated Diary of Murasaki Shikibu* (*Murasaki shikibu nikki ekotoba*, early thirteenth century, fig. 50). Here, however, the hipped and gabled roof of a building projecting into the foreground, a signature motif in the work of Mitsunobu, places the viewer at more of a remove.

The interior of the room is executed in the classical layered painting technique (*tsukuri-e*); for example, thickly applied pigments on the girl's face are supplemented with short, razor-thin ink lines that convey details of her countenance (fig. 51). The application of gold pigment to many of the objects in the girl's room further enhances the crafted quality of the picture. The

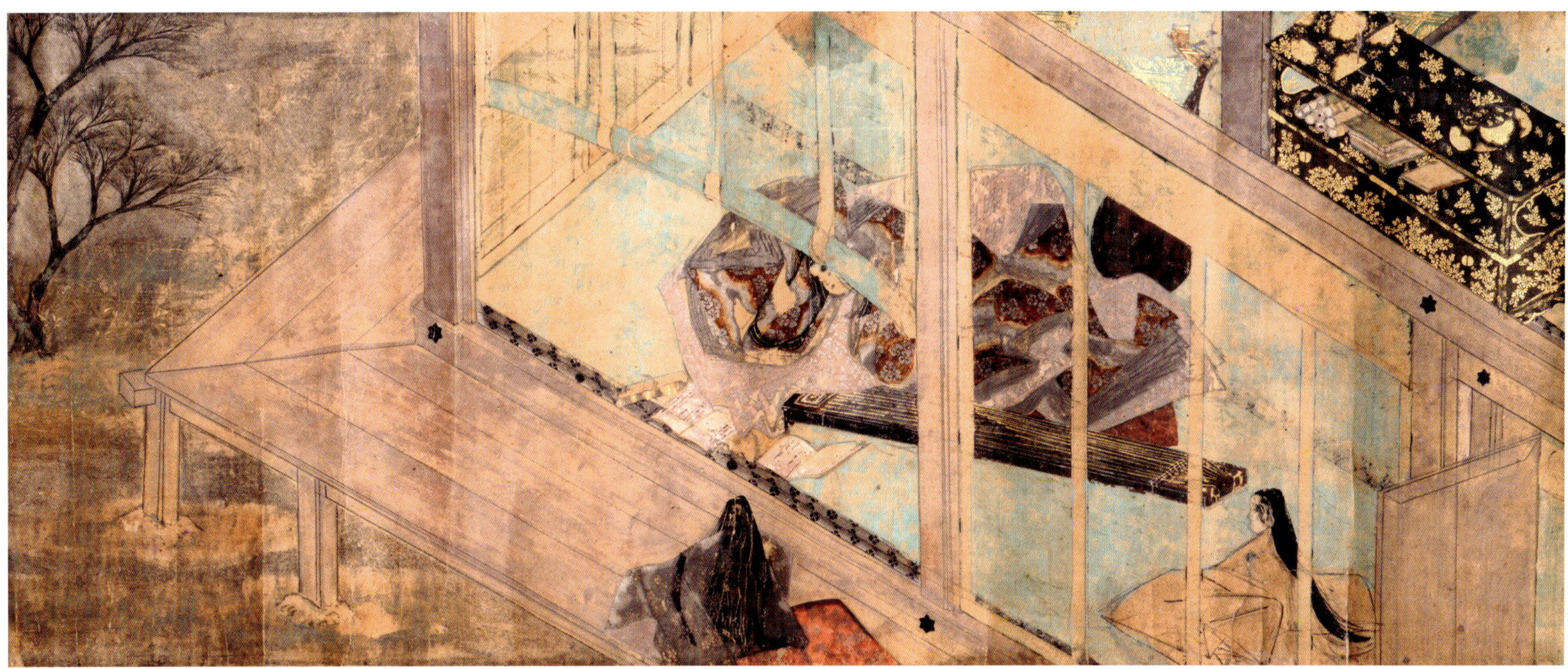

50 *Illustrated Diary of Murasaki Shikibu.* Early thirteenth century. Ink and color on paper; 20.9 x 50.0 cm. Private collection. Murasaki at her *koto*.

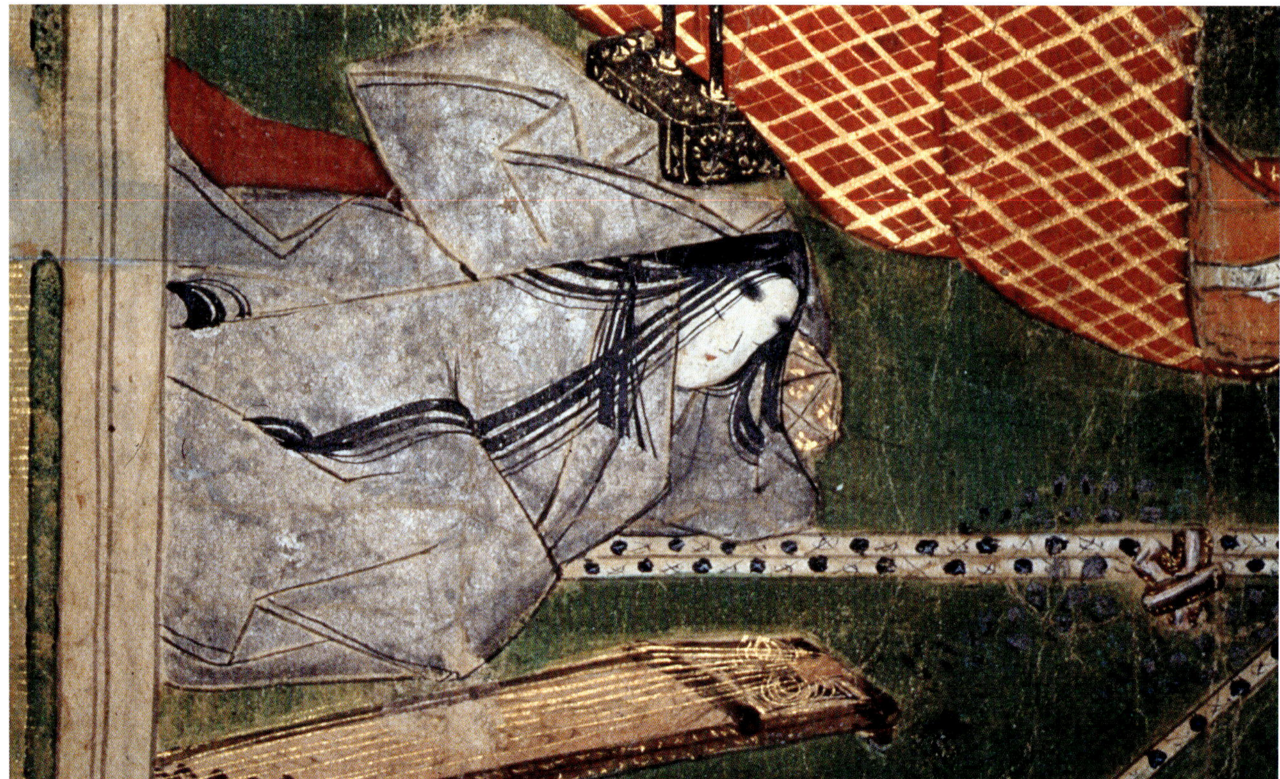

51 Tosa Mitsunobu, *A Wakeful Sleep*. Detail, painting 1.

large orange curtain that forms a diagonal line above the girl's head is decorated with a crisscross pattern in gold and supported by a black stand meant to evoke decorated lacquer through its delicate gold flower design. Gold details also appear on the rectangular pillow beneath the girl's head and on the fine strings of her *koto*. Underneath these strings, curved ink lines imitate the pattern of wood grain on a *koto*. Finally, the main motif of the love letter appears front and center, highlighted with gold touches and attached to a wisteria branch, the numerous purple flowers of which radiate toward the girl as if awakening her with their deep fragrance as described in the text.

While the first section of text offered an indirect reference to *The Tale of Genji* through an implicit contrast with the Kiritsubo opening, the second text, in which the woman meets her dream counterpart the following night, makes the *Genji* allusions explicit:

There at her side was a figure wearing a soft courtier's robe layered over a crimson robe and trousers of pale lavender lined with green. The color and quality of his dress were so elegant and his fragrance so profoundly penetrating that she was quite entranced. They lay together with an intimacy of long association. When she cast a glance at his face, her heart throbbed wildly. So radiantly handsome and charming was he, possessed of such refinement and a host of appealing features, that he brought to mind the shining Prince Genji of tales of old.

The man then claims that he was forced to come when the woman did not answer his previous missive and that theirs is a bond fated from past lives, one that should not go unconsummated. In this vein, he pours his heart out to her through the night until the sun rises and the girl awakens feeling a sense of "utter unreality" and being "not at all herself."

The painting corresponding to this text opens, like painting 1, with an exterior view showing the stream that runs through the woman's garden (figs. 1b and 52). A pair of mandarin ducks, a long-standing symbol of lovers, are perched on a rock at the water's edge, echoing the presence of the two lovers in the building's interior. Over the top of the wall of the residence the viewer sees into the room through the device of the blown-off roof (*fukinuki yatai*). The girl lies face down, her head resting on a rectangular orange pillow, her hair falling over her robe. A movable curtain, a folding screen decorated with golden bamboo, and the lines of the mats on the floor delineate the space of the sleeping girl. The man is depicted directly above her, outside her demarcated space, as if hovering above her in her dream. He gazes down and is positioned so that the viewer can see his face, the features of which had set the girl's heart aflutter.

The comparison of the male to Prince Genji in the text finds its visual counterpart in the exaggerated use of the "lines for eyes and hooks for noses" (*hikime kagihana*) technique (fig. 53). The exaggeration of convention witnessed here is unusual for the artist. Although depictions of courtiers with white faces, red lips, and hooked noses appear in other scrolls by Mitsunobu, almost none have the simple pupil-less line for an eye seen in *A Wakeful Sleep*. Indeed, among extant works, the only other instance in which Mitsunobu can be found to employ such a stark line for the eye is in his depiction of Genji in the Harvard *Genji Album* of 1509–10 (fig. 54). The dream man in *A Wakeful Sleep*, furthermore, is dressed in a white robe decorated with an ink-outlined cherry blossom pattern frequently worn by Genji in the *Genji Album*. It is as if the male protagonist is being pictorially twinned with the über-courtier Genji in order to accommodate the description in the textual passage.

Although paintings 1 and 2 make use of classical techniques, they fashion hybrids of courtly narrative painting by juxtaposing *tsukuri-e* painted interiors with more thinly pigmented exteriors. The compositions of paintings 1 and 2 (and, to a certain extent, of paintings 3 and 4) each consist of two parts: one depicting a secondary scene, an exterior view on the right, and the other depicting the main narrative event on the left. Such thick pigments and finely executed gold details and patterns in the interior scenes here were not traditionally associated with Mitsunobu.[35] The exterior areas on the right are more "Mitsunobu-like"; that is, they employ pale, almost-translucent colors, coarse brush strokes, and trembling ink outlines, resulting in a style that some have interpreted as an attempt to infuse narrative scrolls with a Sino-Japanese ink-painting aesthetic.[36] The differing levels of opacity found in different zones of the painting suggest the degree to which Mitsunobu was conscious of returning to earlier pictorial conventions

52 Tosa Mitsunobu, *A Wakeful Sleep*. Painting 2.

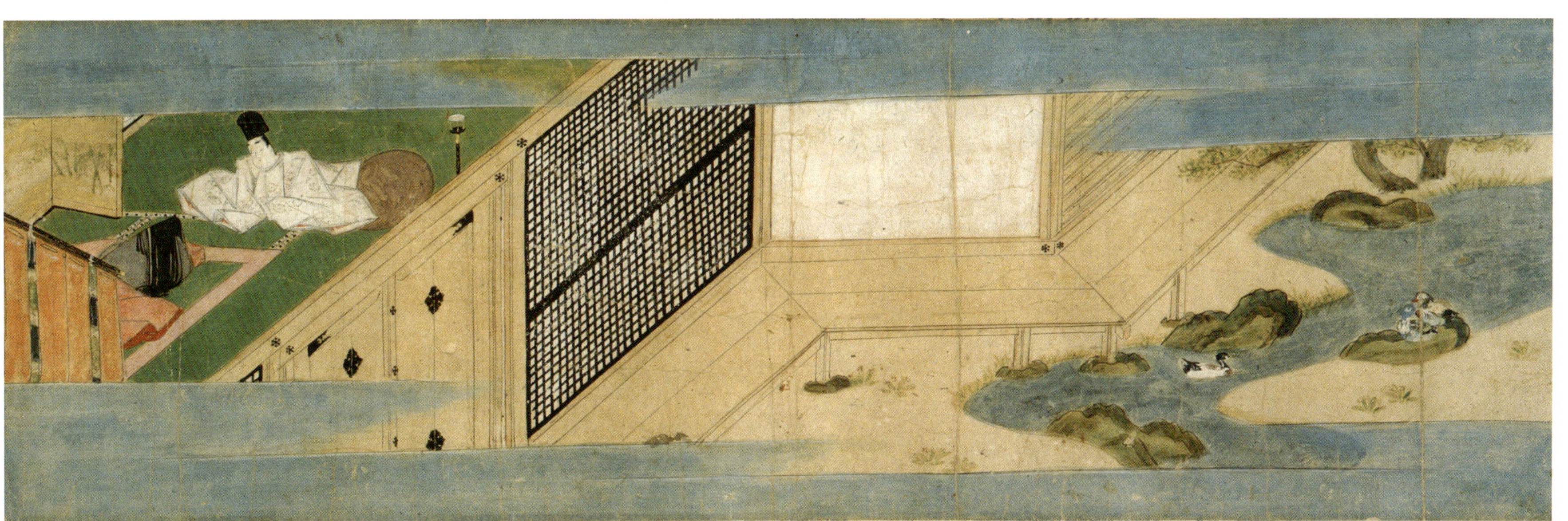

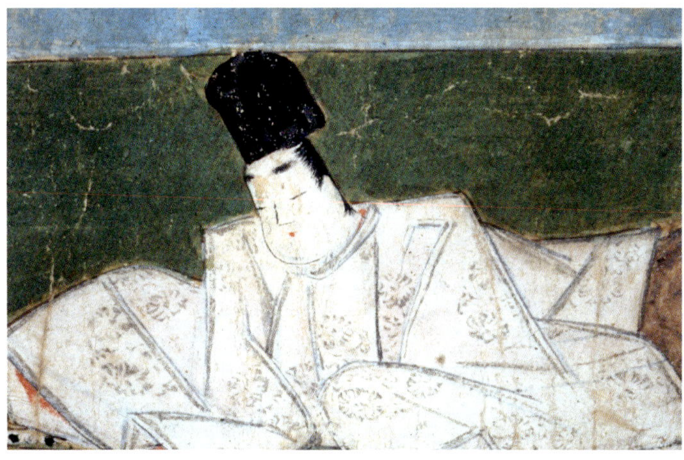

53 Tosa Mitsunobu, *A Wakeful Sleep*. Detail, painting 2.

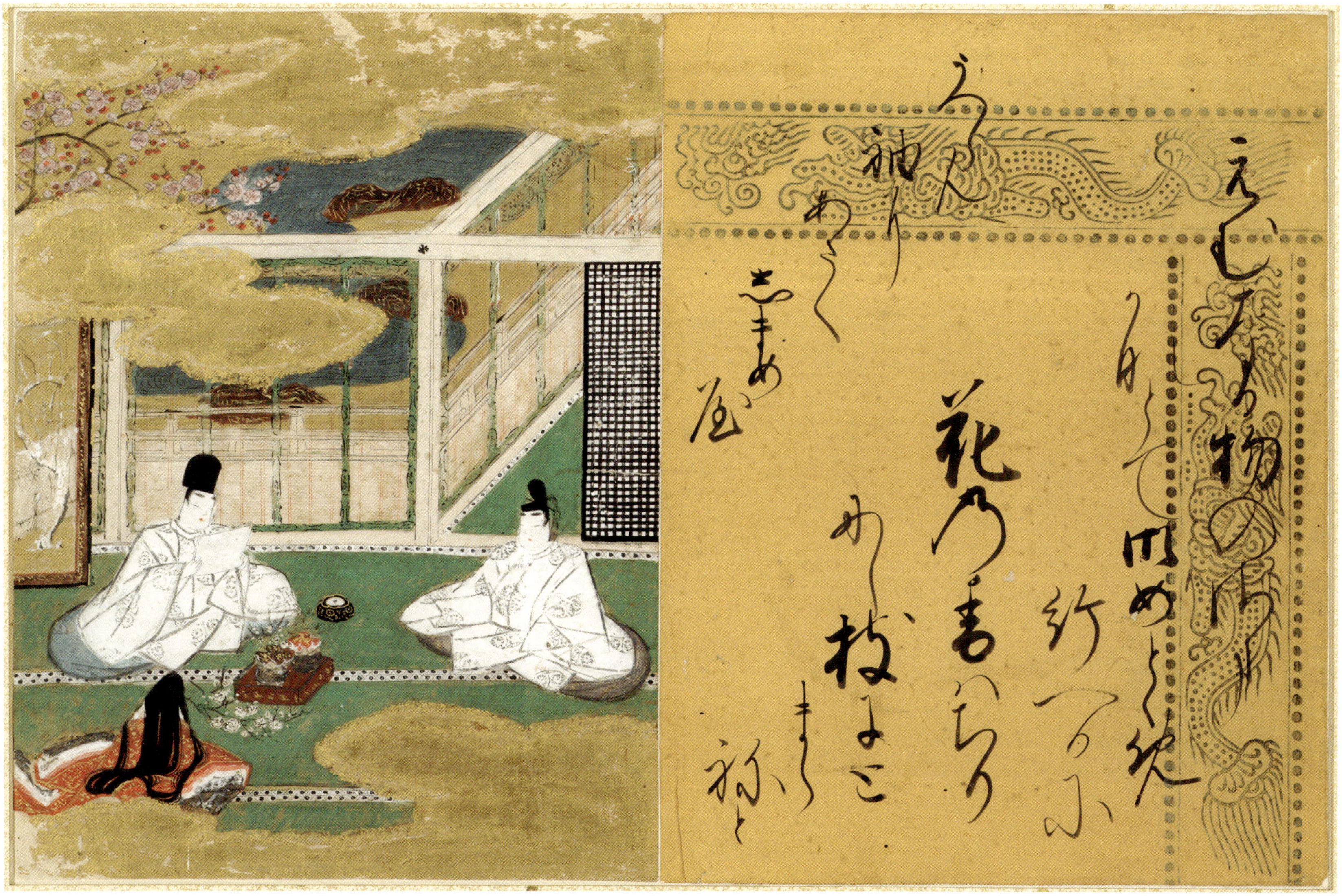

54 Tosa Mitsunobu, *Tale of Genji Album*. 1509–10. Chapter 32, "A Branch of Plum" (*Umegae*). Harvard Art Museum, Arthur M. Sackler Museum, Bequest of the Hofer Collection of the Arts of Asia, 1985.352.32A. Photograph by Katya Kallsen © President and Fellows of Harvard College.

to sustain the classicizing aspirations of the tale. The selective, compartmentalized manner in which he does so reflects the historicist conditions of cultural production in the late fifteenth century.

The third text section in *A Wakeful Sleep* continues the allusions to *Genji* and other previous early tale literature, as well as *waka* from *Collection of Ancient and Modern Poems* (*Kokinshū*). Here, however, the protagonist is taken outside her cloistered residence. After the girl's lover fails to reappear in her dreams, she falls seriously ill and recovers only when her brother the prelate prays to the Ishiyamadera Kannon and promises that she will make a pilgrimage in gratitude. The girl does recover, and her visit to Ishiyamadera resembles a literary pilgrimage to the legendary birthplace of Murasaki's tale. Initially, the text likens her journey to that of Tamakazura, the long-lost daughter of Genji's rival Tō no Chūjō from *The Tale of Genji*.

Soon she was making hurried preparations for a journey to Ishiyama. She chose to travel without carriage or fanfare, limiting her retinue to Chūnagon, her nurse, and four or five close attendants, for her petition was just as weighty as that of Lady Tamakazura, who had traveled on foot to Hatsuse Temple.

When she arrived she was impressed by the singular beauty of the place. From the foot of the cliffs stretched a moon-bathed expanse of rippling waves; the cliffs were covered by deep layers of moss—untold aeons must have passed since they were mere pebbles. The ancient garden was suffused with the silence of another world, and all the hardships of her journey were forgotten as she gazed at it. She prayed fervently and prostrated herself in supplication. Entreating that her many afflictions be vanquished, intoning loudly the prayer, "Thy great vow is as deep as the seas," she paid homage with all her soul.

By likening the girl's pilgrimage to Tamakazura's visit to Hasedera, the text invokes a classical precedent for female travel, but one specifically related to a chance encounter—Ukon, the attendant to Tamakazura's deceased mother, Yūgao, just happened to be at Hasedera at the same time and afterward brought this long-lost daughter of Yūgao and Tō no Chūjō to Genji's attention, changing her life forever.[37] *A Wakeful Sleep* draws upon this well-known episode to lend the girl's pilgrimage a sense of pedigree and to foreshadow the fateful encounter with her dream lover.

Ishiyamadera, one of the thirty-three sacred sites of Kannon located in the province of Yamato, was the destination of numerous female pilgrims from the literary past, including famous examples by the authors of the *Kagerō Diary* (*Kagerō nikki,* tenth century) and the *Sarashina Diary* (*Sarashina nikki,* eleventh century).[38] Such pilgrimages were undertaken for a variety of reasons, including preparation for renouncing the world and, as in *A Wakeful Sleep*, in thanks for recovery from illness; the latter was the motivation behind the annual trip made by Fujiwara Michinaga's sister Senshi in *A Tale of Flowering Fortunes* (*Eiga monogatari*, eleventh century).[39] The Kannon deity enshrined at Ishiyamadera was deemed especially helpful in matters of childbirth, in terms of both conception and safe delivery. Ishiyamadera was also a common setting for meetings between lovers or potential lovers, as in *Tale of Nezame*, *Tale of Hanyū*, and *A Wakeful Sleep*. The aura associated with its main icon was so powerful that pilgrimage to worship it could trigger strange and portentous dreams as in the case of the diarists mentioned above.

Yet the cultural significance of Ishiyamadera took on a new order of meaning during the medieval period, when it came to be known as the site where Murasaki wrote *The Tale of Genji*. This legend, first mentioned in a tale anthology known as *Collection of Old Tales* (*Kohon setsuwashū*), had hypostasized into fact by Mitsunobu's era. Depictions of Murasaki at the temple begin to appear around this time, none more important than the one included in *Miraculous Origins of Ishiyamadera* (*Ishiyamadera engi emaki*, fig. 55a–b), which shows Murasaki in a well-appointed room at the temple, pulling back a bamboo blind and gazing out in the direction of the moonlit Lake Biwa. While this scene makes official the association between author and temple, of direct relevance here is the fact that it appears in the fourth scroll of the set, made in 1497 with calligraphy by Sanjōnishi Sanetaka and with paintings most likely executed by a member of Tosa Mitsunobu's studio.[40] Thus, the Sanetaka-Mitsunobu circle was not only well versed but possibly played an active role in promoting the fanciful legend of *Genji*'s site of creation. This primal scene of female authorship figures prominently in *A Wakeful Sleep*; during her stay at the temple, the protagonist has the urge to investigate her surroundings and Murasaki's famous room:

Late at night, she finally completed her worship. The room adjoining her own was said to have sheltered Murasaki Shikibu when writing *The Tale of Genji*, and the girl was curious to see this unusual place. Suddenly she heard a refined voice from within. It seemed that a certain general of the left [*sadaishō*] was summoning a middle captain [*chūjō*].

Here the story reveals most explicitly its awareness of literary predecessors, in a way that even surpasses twelfth- and thirteenth-century *giko monogatari,* in which citations to *Genji* are overt but less acknowledged. The story here, in comparison, establishes a more ironic distance from its source texts.

Painting 3 of *A Wakeful Sleep* begins with a scene of the landscape surrounding the temple that resembles a painting in *Miraculous Legends of Ishiyamadera* and, more generally, temple and shrine legend paintings (fig. 1c). A glimpse of the "moon-bathed expanse of rippling waves" mentioned in the text and reminiscent of the scene of Murasaki at the temple is in the upper-right corner, where a patch of blue water appears through bands of pale blue mist. Verdant green hills rise above the water and suggest the elevation of the temple site. A brown temple roof in the foreground orients the viewer's perspective high above the buildings of the complex. Higher still on the site is a cluster of the temple's famous volcanic rocks, also evoked by the text's description of "cliffs covered by deep layers of moss." The same strangely shaped rocks appear in *Miraculous Origins of Ishiyamadera*, suggesting that they are motifs that mark the site. The landscape here reminds the viewer of the protagonist's journey away from the capital.

Having heard men's voices in the *Genji* room (*Genji no ma*), the woman decides to peek in through a crack in the door, whereupon she sees her dream lover (fig. 1d). He is in the middle of revealing to his companion that he and a woman have been visiting each other's dreams nightly for two years. Realizing that this is the man of her dreams but that she cannot simply barge in on him, she decides that her only recourse is to hope for a reunion in the afterlife. The fourth text section in the scroll begins with a description of the woman's great inner conflict as she struggles with her decision to kill herself and thus to die before her father, which was considered the gravest of sins. As she begins her journey home and crosses the Seta Bridge, however, her resolve strengthens:

In the middle of the bridge, she paused, wavered indecisively, then leaped into the waters below.

"What has she done!" screamed her nurse in shock, standing transfixed in utter horror. Unable to restrain her tears, lacking even the presence of mind to jump in after her, her only thought was somehow to rescue her mistress, and she screamed for help at the top of her lungs.

Just then there appeared an elegant boat bearing a number of gentlemen dressed in hunting costume, who wondered at her hysterical sobbing. Overjoyed to see them, the nurse wildly screamed out, "Someone has just jumped in. Can you help?" stamping her feet in the frenzy of her emotion. Moved by pity for her, they resolutely let down some men familiar with the ways of the water, who dragged up the girl.

That the girl should be rescued from the watery depths was indeed a true witness to the message of the Lotus Sutra. Miraculously, her robes bore not a trace of moisture, as if they had been dry for many a long year.

The boat bore none other than the General, who, having completed his seven days of prayer, was on his way home. . . . One might expect that a woman of such tender years would be embarrassed at having been pulled up in this manner, but she felt not a trace of reserve, for this was the same man dear to her in her dream life.

Following this passage, the fourth and final painting in the scroll depicts an empty Seta Bridge (fig. 1e) stretching from the lower-right corner of the composition into a patch of mist bands in the upper portion of the painting. Further left, the boat of the general's companions comes into view (fig. 1f), and finally the vessel of the general, in which he gazes down at the woman who has been pulled aboard.

Taken as an aggregate, the four paintings reflect the degree to which Mitsunobu has mastered, and is able to manipulate, time-honored protocols for compositional engineering in the horizontal-scroll format. Mitsunobu accomplished this by combining two traditional modes of handscroll painting, the "monoscenic" and the "continuous," in one work.[41] The first two paintings in *A Wakeful Sleep* are in the monoscenic mode, which refers to a type of pictorial representation in handscroll painting in which self-contained pictorial compositions that can usually be visually apprehended in one "view" are interspersed among textual passages.[42] Such monoscenic paintings were never very large; the paintings

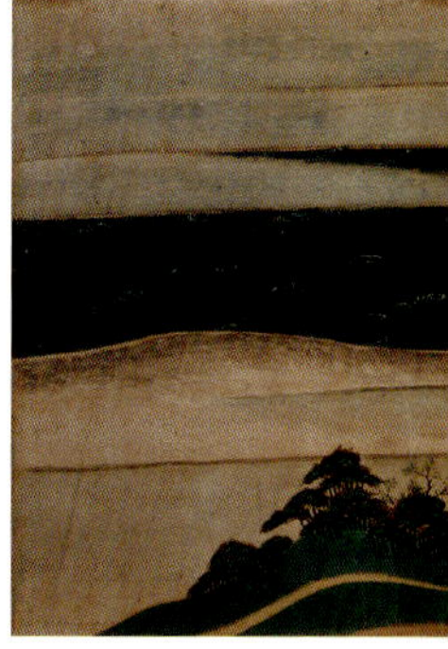

from the twelfth-century *Genji Scrolls* (fig. 7), which exemplify this mode, never exceed fifty centimeters in length, the typical size of a single sheet of paper used in early Japanese handscrolls. Paintings 1 and 2 in *A Wakeful Sleep* both measure fifty centimeters in width and consist of only one sheet of paper. Neither *Breaking the Inkstone*, *The Jizō Hall*, nor any of the other small scrolls attributed to Mitsunobu employ only one sheet of paper for an entire painting section. This size proved suitable, however, for the relatively quiet, static scenes that first show the girl asleep and then being visited by the man in her room.

While conforming to the monoscenic format, these initial paintings have recourse to another common technique of the handscroll tradition, that of the exterior/interior composition. The scene is divided into a view of the exterior of a residence on one side of the pictorial surface (usually including a garden and the peripheral zone of the architecture itself—veranda, eaves, latticed doors, and bamboo blinds) and the interior of a residence on the other side.[43] The latter usually presents one or several individuals at the center of the story and thus the core action of the narrative. The two halves are thoroughly symbiotic and equally weighted, however, in the sense that the garden is often symbolic of the psychic or emotional states of the figures inside the building. Meanwhile, the goings-on inside help interpret the symbolism of the state of nature outside. In this regard, "monoscenic" can be a misleading term, for even with small-scale paintings, the composition can structurally dictate a progression or oscillation between exterior and interior. Such is the case for paintings 1 and 2 of *A Wakeful Sleep*. Motifs in the exterior spheres of the scenes of these paintings set the tone for the events occurring in the interior spheres. The extra-large flowering cherry tree with its luminescent white blossoms in the first painting invites the viewer into a poetic realm. The white petals softly floating to the ground and the spots of ink indicating rain on the painting surface evoke the sleeping, dreamy state of the girl inside. In the second painting, the pair of male and female mandarin ducks echo the pair of lovers inside. Judging by the other versions of *A Wakeful Sleep*, which do not include the ducks or even an exterior scene (fig. 56), such pictorial flourishes were precisely the kind of classicizing touches that patrons expected from a Painting Bureau director.

Paintings 3 and 4 similarly make use of an exterior/interior compositional scheme. In the former, the depiction of the Ishiyamadera landscape precedes the scene of the protagonists inside the temple, while in the latter, the image of the Seta Bridge precedes that of the Sadaishō's entourage and the couple. These resemblances are ultimately superficial, however, as the exterior scenes that preface the interiors in the last two paintings are radically expanded in scope. The paintings consist of two sheets each, double the size of the first two. The resulting compositions resemble the continuous mode of pictorial representation used in early handscrolls. In continuous handscrolls, the scene cannot be grasped in one view but requires scrolling leftward to be fully comprehended as a narrative unit. The deferment of meaning structurally necessitated by this arrangement results in a more dynamic pictorial surface filled with effects that can range from panoramic movement to drama and suspense. In painting 3,

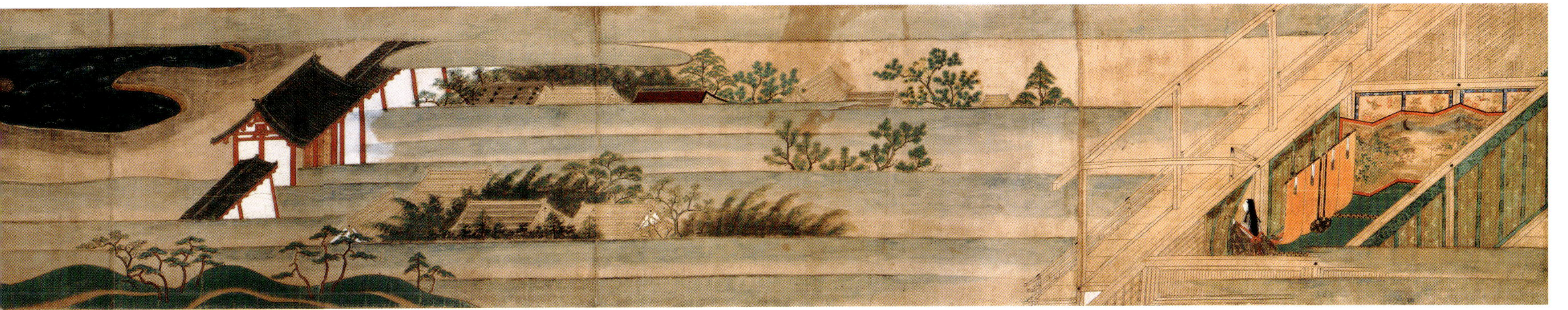

55 *Miraculous Origins of Ishiyamadera* (*Ishiyamadera engi emaki*). Fifteenth century. One of seven handscrolls; ink, color, and gold on paper. Ishiyamadera, Ōtsu. Important Cultural Property. Detail, scroll 4.

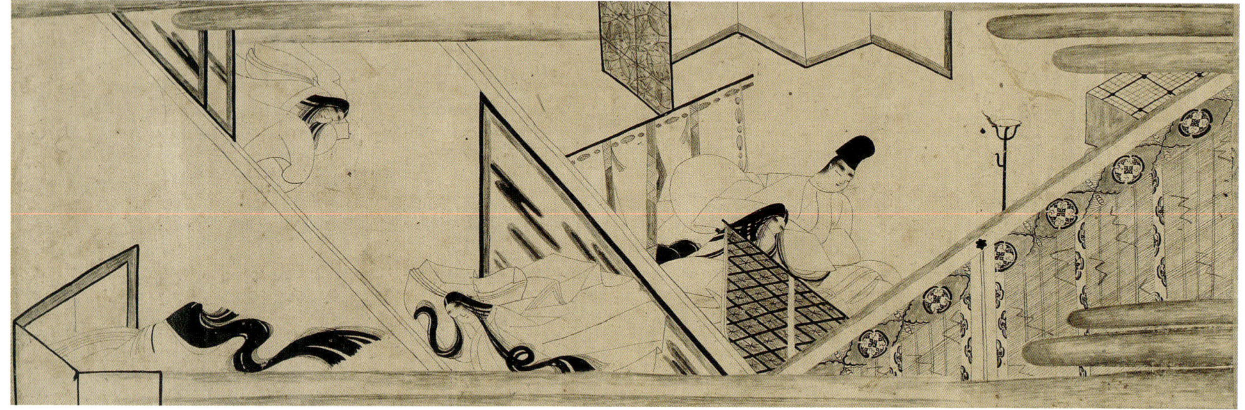

56 *A Wakeful Sleep* (*Utatane sōshi emaki*). Sixteenth century. Two handscrolls, ink on paper, H. 12.5 cm. Museum of Fine Arts, Boston. William Sturgis Bigelow Collection. Photograph © 2009 Museum of Fine Arts, Boston. Painting 2.

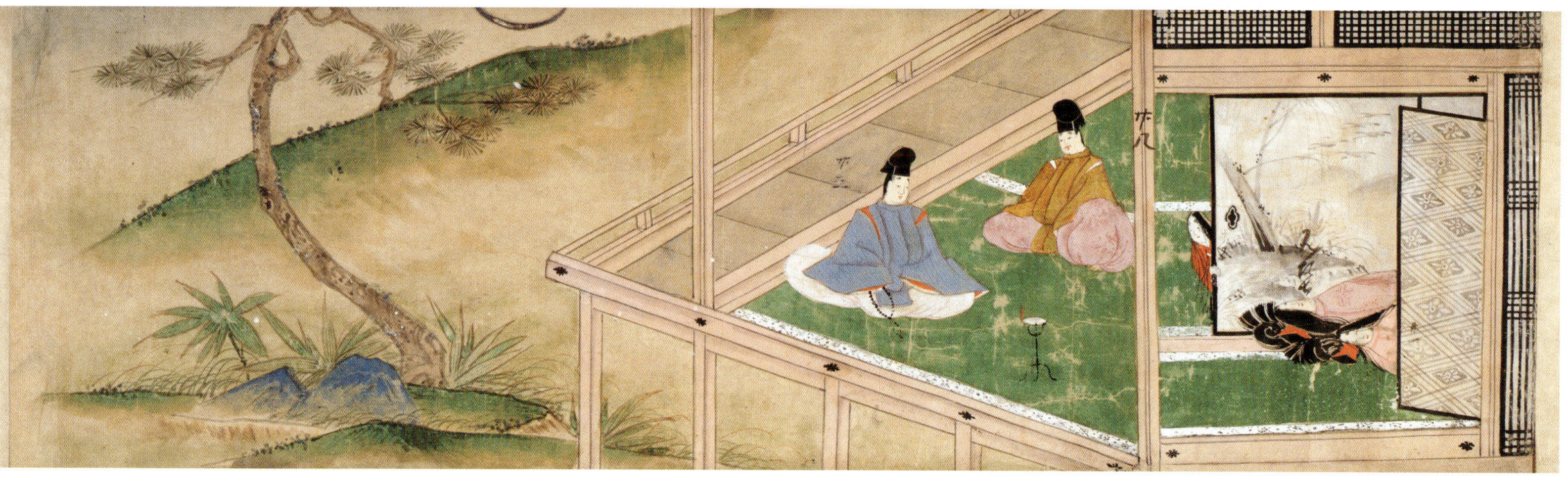

57 *A Wakeful Sleep* (*Utatane sōshi emaki*). Sixteenth century. One handscroll; ink and color on paper, 15.3 x 674.0 cm. National Institute for the Humanities, National Institute of Japanese Literature. Painting 3, Ishiyamadera scene.

therefore, the viewer traverses the Ishiyamadera landscape beginning with the view of the river in the upper right, then gazes over rolling hills, and passes temple structures and rock formations before arriving at the interior of the temple. A telling comparison can be found in painting 3 of the other polychrome handscroll of *A Wakeful Sleep* (fig. 57), in which the grounds of Ishiyamadera do not preface a view of the inside, thus rendering it a generic interior scene without a sense of the particularity of place.

In painting 4 the expanded exterior view generates narrative suspense. The wide expanse of blue water and mist bands ensures that while unrolling the scroll there will be a moment when the viewer witnesses nothing but the empty Seta Bridge over water. Resolution is further postponed by the appearance of the first boat carrying the Chūjō and his entourage, which precedes the boat with the couple. Many of the figures in this first boat direct their gazes toward the left and suggest visual interest in that direction, further arousing the viewer's curiosity, a convention borrowed from continuous narrative handscrolls. Courtly decorum is maintained through the avoidance of effects associated with the continuous mode such as flying objects, gesticulating figures, and an otherwise exaggerated commotion that enhances the sense of a field of vision in flux. Nevertheless, the switch from monoscenic to continuous presentation in *A Wakeful Sleep* ensures that the dynamism and drama accrue with each successive painting.

VISUALIZING A KARMIC BOND

Pictorial pacing and self-conscious classicizing accord well with what appears to be the overriding program of the scroll: a celebration of the Fujiwara family. *A*

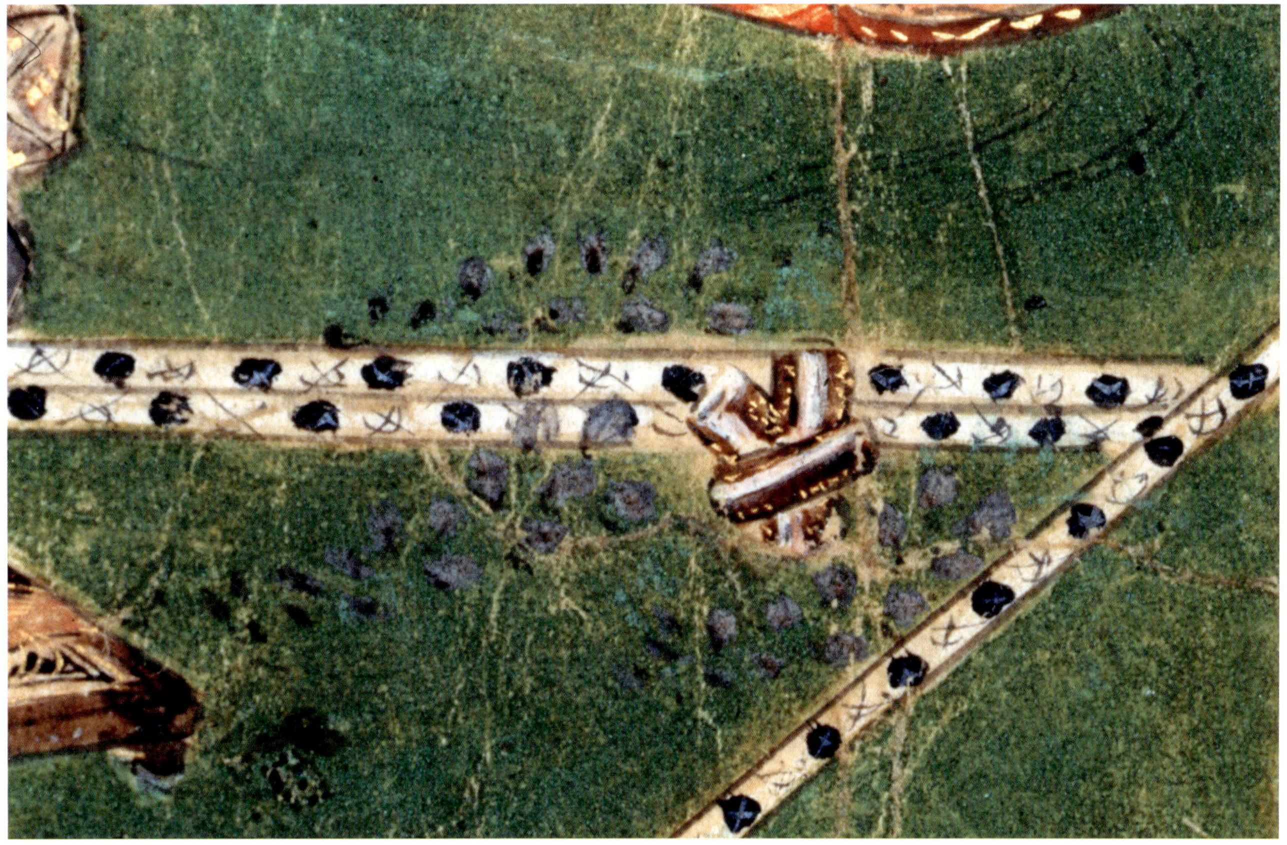

58 Tosa Mitsunobu, *A Wakeful Sleep*. Wisteria-wrapped letter, painting 1.

Wakeful Sleep is a tale of aristocratic matrimony that casts the couple's romance in the glow of Fujiwara prestige and imperial benevolence, all legitimated by the authority of the bodhisattva Kannon. This agenda is underscored in the fifth and final section of text, which reads as follows:

> The revered Kannon had led the couple to realize their long-standing karmic bond. They lived happily ever after, wanting for nothing, assisted by the excellence of the reign, and their legendary prosperity, which rivaled that of the Wisteria Leaves, extended even to their children and grandchildren.[44]

The couple's union is thus explicitly linked to a higher power, the bodhisattva Kannon, while its worldly success is linked to the imperial reign. Classical reference is found here as well, in the phrase "Wisteria Leaves" (*Fuji no uraba*), which refers to the chapter by that name in *The Tale of Genji*, in which Genji's glory reaches its peak when he is elevated to the status of a retired emperor, and when his son Yūgiri marries into the Fujiwara house of Tō no Chūjō and is promoted to the rank of counselor. In more general terms, however, the wisteria motif implies an exaltation of the Fujiwara clan, not only here but at the beginning of *A Wakeful Sleep*, when the man's letter mysteriously appears with sprays of wisteria (fig. 58).[45] The conspicuousness of wisteria motifs has even prompted one scholar to characterize the female character as a reincarnation of a Fujiwara patriarch, with her jump into the water and subsequent rescue a symbol of the family's renaissance.[46] In fact, there would have been little need for a renaissance, as the Fujiwara family still dominated court politics in the Muromachi period. The clan's five regent families (*gosekke*) maintained their grip on political power within the court hierarchy and clearly represented one constituency of the scroll. While most courtly romances were celebratory of the imperium, *A Wakeful Sleep* is distinguished by the supernatural sanctification of its subject.

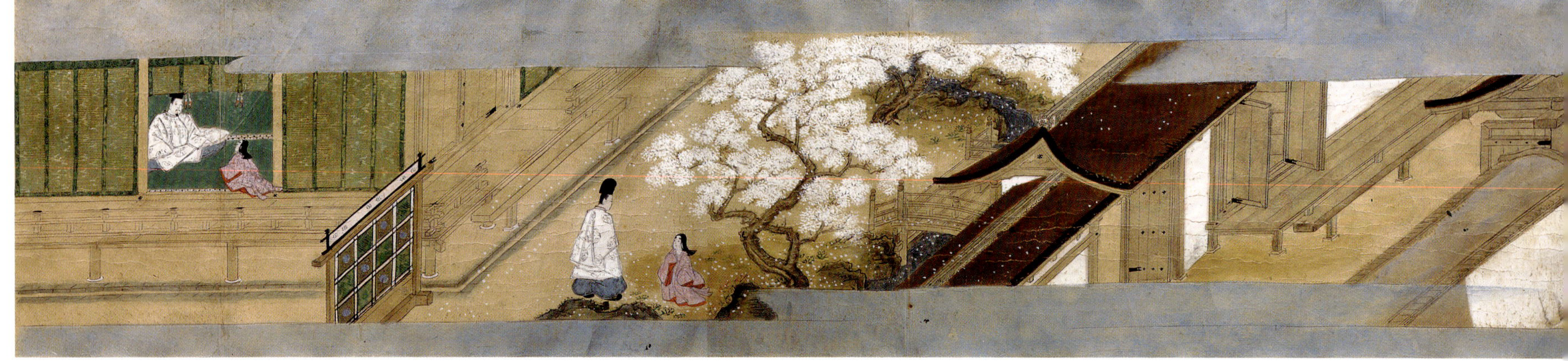

59 Tosa Mitsunobu, calligraphy by Sanjōnishi Sanetaka, *Legends of Kitano Tenjin* (*Kitano Tenjin engi emaki*). 1503. Three handscrolls; ink, color, and gold on paper. Kitano Tenmangū, Kyoto. Important Cultural Property. Scroll 1, painting 1.

The scroll skillfully merges the celebration of the Fujiwara lineage and the imperial reign with the Buddhist undercurrents that run throughout the tale, beginning with the first text. There we are told that "among the many tales of old, the account that follows is an extraordinary one" (*samazama no yo no mukashi monogatari ni wa ito fushigi naru koto mo haberu mono ka na*), thereby creating an air of mystery but also invoking a genre of Buddhist tales. The phrase "*fushigi naru koto*" (an extraordinary, or strange, thing) was often used to conclude supernatural tales (*reigendan*) about the Ishiyamadera Kannon, and its use here foreshadows the deity's role in the romance.[47] In the final line of text the narrator addresses the reader, stating that she would like to write more but that her intention was simply to record "the story of a couple brought together in an unusual dream through the manifestation of the Savior Bodhisattva's vow." According to the narrator's summation, the mysterious dream that united the couple, and by extension the other strange events as well (the couple's chance meeting at Ishiyamadera and the woman's miraculous rescue), were not random coincidences but, rather, manifestations of karmic causality. The profound karmic bond between the couple and the intervention of the bodhisattva in their reunion add an otherworldly sanctification to this idealized image of aristocratic union.

Mitsunobu's paintings augment the supernatural aura around the romance through a number of devices. The most conspicuous involves the multivalent motif of the cherry tree, the very presence of which suggests a miraculous meeting. The motif opens the scroll and leads the eye to the girl sleeping in her room. The anthropomorphized cherry tree that delivers an otherworldly being is not without precedent and is in fact directly alluded to in the third text section of *A Wakeful Sleep*. After the man fails to reappear in the woman's dreams, the woman's own desire for this elusive lover prompts her to recall a story about the daughter of Izumi Shikibu:

> When her lover Fujiwara no Norimichi ceased to call on her, Ko Shikibu passed the long empty months in melancholy. Suddenly he came to visit, and she was beside herself with joy. When it came time for him to depart, she stitched a thread on the sleeve of his cloak as a memento. By daylight, however, she saw the thread caught in a tree in the garden and realized that he had not really come. Her own excess of longing had summoned before her the image sheltered in her heart.

The text of *A Wakeful Sleep* quotes nearly in its entirety episode 26 from the thirteenth-century *setsuwa* collection *Tales of Present Times* (*Ima monogatari*), called "The Cherry Tree Lover" (*Sakuragi no koibito*).[48] As Abe Yoshitomi has pointed out, the allusion here seems to suggest that it is the spirit of the cherry tree in the girl's garden

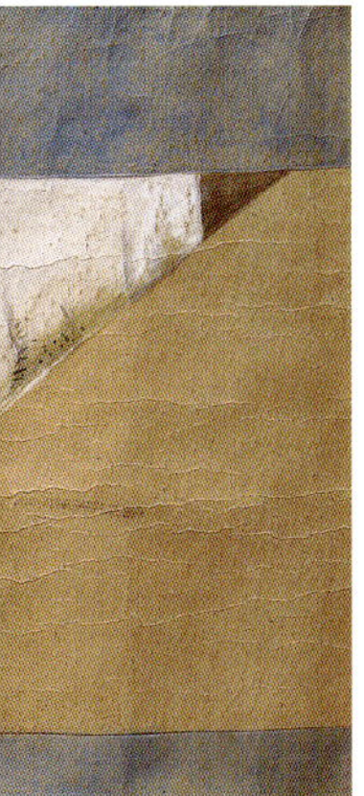

that generates her dream and conjures up the fantasy lover.[49]

The painted motif echoes similarly otherworldly moments in other handscrolls by Mitsunobu. He used the same motif as the backdrop for a mystical encounter in his rendition of *Legends of Kitano Tenjin* (1503) for the scene depicting the meeting between the courtier Sugawara no Michizane and his father, Sugawara Koreyoshi (fig. 59). According to legend, Michizane was not born but rather mysteriously appeared in Koreyoshi's garden as a small child. In the painting by Mitsunobu, the white cherry blossoms are in full bloom and spread over the gate and a small stream. They form a canopy over young Michizane's head as though presenting the boy to Koreyoshi. Like the flower petals falling down around him, the boy seems to have drifted down into the Sugawara garden.

Mitsunobu's first painting for *A Wakeful Sleep* similarly visualizes a connection between the cherry tree and the dream lover through its unique approach to representing the tree. The white branch of the cherry tree is painted to overlap with the green mat upon which the girl sleeps (extended as far as it can before overlapping with the building's posts) and seems to reach into her room, as if delivering the wisteria-wrapped letter lying in front of her (fig. 49). In the corresponding text, the girl hears the word "here" (*kore*) when she is offered the letter, unconnected to any human presence. The tree branch in the painting appears to have been deliberately anthropomorphized to suggest this strange delivery of the man's letter. This rendition contrasts with the ink-line version of *A Wakeful Sleep*, where the cherry tree remains confined to the exterior as an object for the woman's contemplation (fig. 60), or the other polychrome version, in which both the letter and the tree are at a distant remove from the woman (fig. 61).[50]

The second painting in Mitsunobu's scroll (figs. 1b and 52) continues to encourage a visual correspondence between man and tree. The man's position as he gazes down upon the sleeping girl resembles that of the white tree branch as it enters her room in the previous painting. Moreover, he is dressed in a white courtier's robe with a cherry blossom pattern, almost as if embodying the spirit of the cherry tree. The costume may represent a sartorial echo of Genji, as Mitsunobu used this particular costume frequently for his representation of the Shining One in his *Genji Album*. The use of the garment here may additionally allude to the erotic symbolism of the cherry blossom robe (*sakura no nōshi*) and its relationship to the eroticization of the hero as represented in Murasaki's novel.[51] A similar nuance appears in Mitsunobu's *Genji Album* in the illustration for chapter 8, "Under the Cherry Blossoms" ("Hana no en," fig. 62), depicting Genji's liaison with Oborozukiyo while at the home of his political rival, the minister of the right. In his cherry blossom cloak Genji steals into the room of Oborozukiyo, who is represented only by a curl of hair and a corner of robe. To Genji's right is another luminescent cherry tree, the branches of which parallel the movement of the lover advancing into the room of this Fujiwara woman (the wisteria tree in full bloom stands on the other side of the residence). The

60 *A Wakeful Sleep* (*Utatane sōshi*). Sixteenth century. One handscroll; ink on paper, 16.2 x (overall) 1108.8 cm. Freer Gallery of Art, Smithsonian Institution, Washington DC. Painting 1.

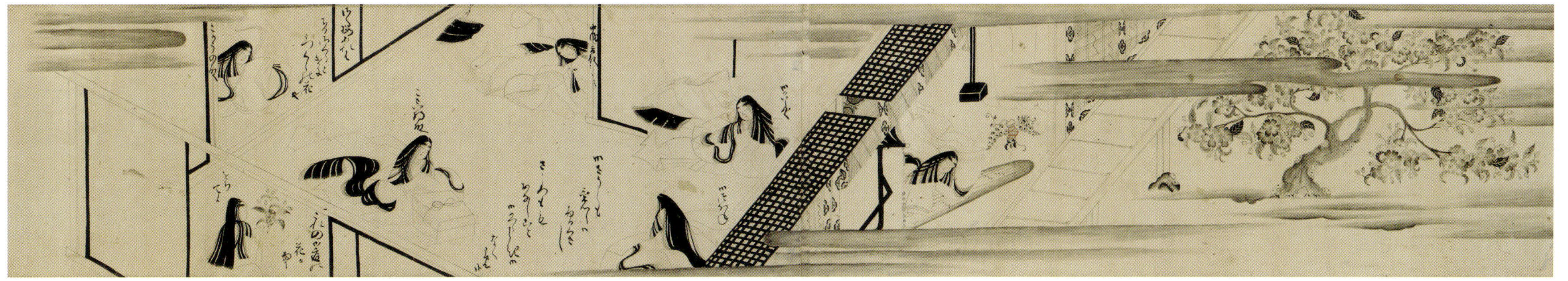

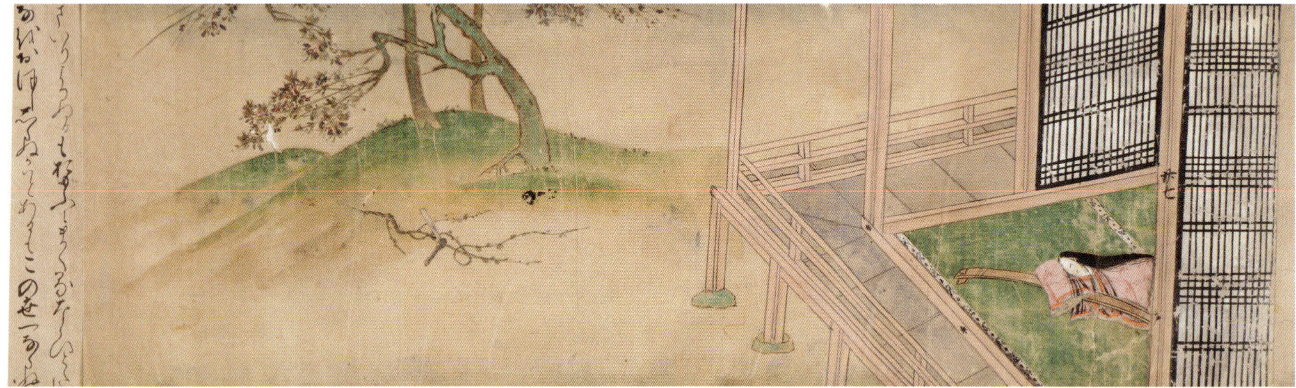

61 *A Wakeful Sleep*. National Institute of Japanese Literature. Painting 1.

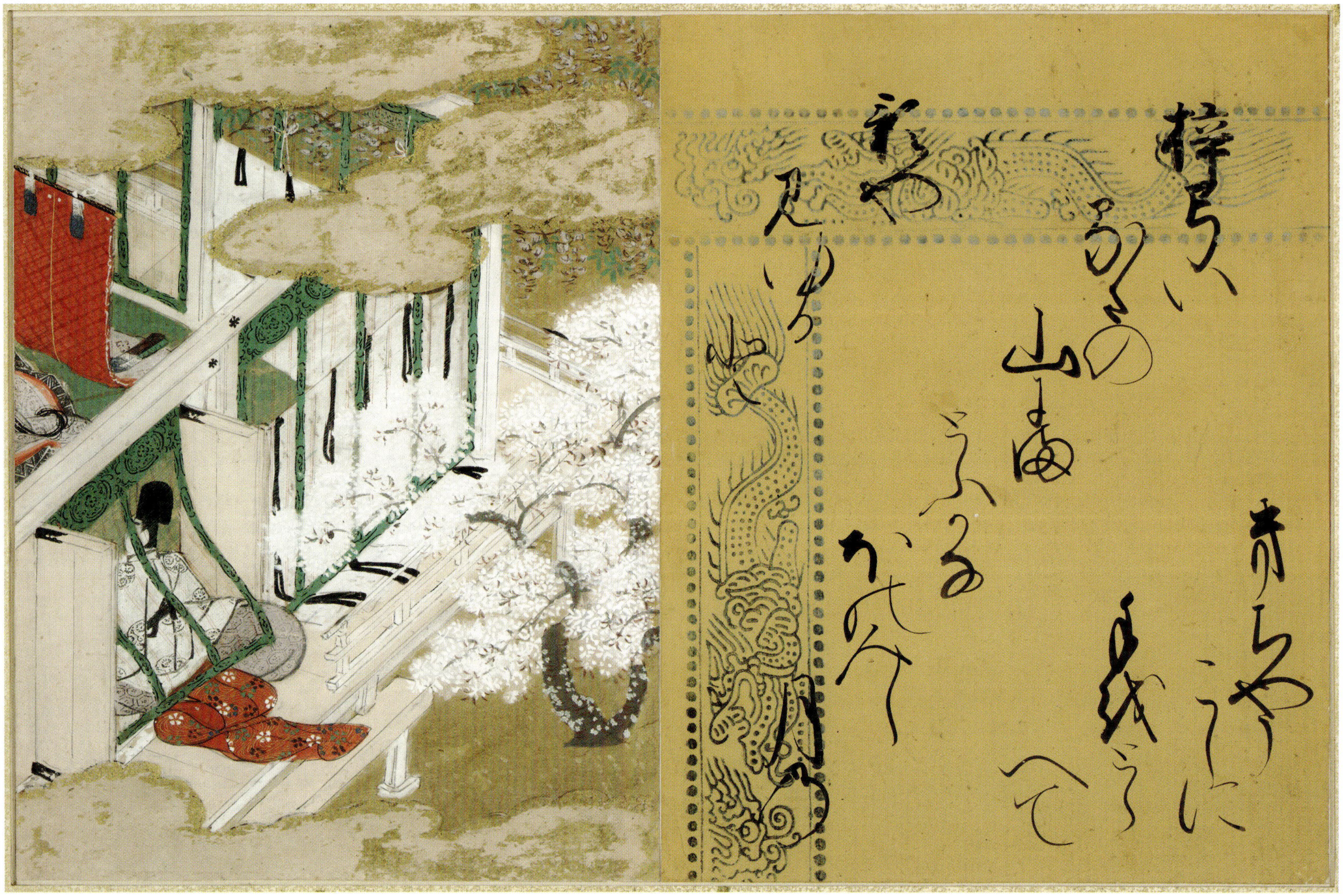

62 Tosa Mitsunobu, calligraphy by Konoe Hisamichi, *Tale of Genji Album*, 1509–10. Chapter 8, "Under the Cherry Blossoms" (*Hana no en*). Ink, color, and gold on paper. Harvard Art Museum, Arthur M. Sackler Museum, Bequest of the Hofer Collection of the Arts of Asia, 1985.352.8.B. Photograph by Katya Kallsen © President and Fellows of Harvard College.

single poem by Genji chosen to accompany this scene in the album enhances the sexual innuendo of the image:

Azusayumi	Flown like an arrow
Irusa no yama ni	Shot from a catalpa bow,
Madou kana	Lost on Irusa
Honomishi tsuki no	Longing for Moonset Mountain
Kage ya miyuru to	To betray the light I glimpsed.[52]

The juxtaposition of word and image encourages the viewer to liken Genji, as he does himself in the poem, to the shot arrow cloaked in the cherry blossom imagery. In *A Wakeful Sleep*, the dress cloak is paired with what were originally lavender-colored trousers, and the two colors would have visually reiterated the white of the cherry blossoms and the lavender of the wisteria in the previous painting.[53] The two paintings together suggest a conflation of the cherry tree, which delivers the letter and penetrates the girl's space with its branch, and the man, who enters her space from the same direction.

The paintings underscore the idea that this is no ordinary courtier visiting the woman. Besides the cherry tree, the man's visit is linked to another important element in the tale: the manifestation of the bodhisattva Kannon. Mashimo Miyako has suggested that, in addition to the tree personification of the girl's lover, it also represents the workings of Kannon.[54] She bases her argument on the importance of Kannon's role in the plot: the deity facilitates the girl's recovery from illness and the couple's meeting at Ishiyamadera, and his benevolent workings are explicitly mentioned in the epilogue. In Mitsunobu's paintings, the intrusion of the tree into the girl's room could be interpreted as Kannon delivering the man's letter and thus provoking the romance.

The last two paintings continue to emphasize a supernatural element in the couple's relationship. The paintings, by implying that the couple's eventual meeting was preordained, suggest their bond from another life, which the Buddha helped to extend. Certain pictorial devices help convey a sense of inevitability. The most effective is the "painting-within-painting" (*gachūga*), which opens up a space for metacommentary within the pictorial space. A striking instance can be found in painting 3 (fig. 63), in which the woman discovers the identity of the man in her dreams but realizes that she has no socially acceptable means of bringing about a real-life encounter. She then decides that her only recourse is to drown herself and encounter him in the next world. Painting 3 pictorializes this nonencounter by depicting the couple separated only by a sliding-door partition, with the man unaware of the woman's presence in the next room. In this split-screen composition, the viewer can visually access both rooms and project onto their inhabitants their respective psychological states—one pining after a mystery woman in his dreams, the other longing to meet her lover but tragically unable to do so. Yet even while both figures are thus separated, the mural décor in one of the rooms hints at the encounter to come. The minister of the left and his conversation partner sit in front of a folding screen of pine trees dotting the shoreline of a body of water on which two boats drift. The subject clearly foreshadows the scene in painting 4, in which the two men in their separate boats rescue the woman from the water. Even the parallel position of the two boats on the screen resembles the configuration of the two vessels in the final painting (fig. 1f). The backdrop not only hints at the ending but suggests its preordination.

The couple's otherworldly bond is most directly represented in painting 4 by the empty Seta Bridge, which stretches across the painting surface between light blue bands of mist (fig. 1e). Bridges are often used as symbols of the path to the afterworld or as liminal markers between earthly and otherworldly realms.[55] The prominence of the bridge in Mitsunobu's painting is strangely suggestive of the otherworldly forces uniting the couple in this scene. The final image, of the reunited couple in the boat, enthroned beneath a triangular roof, evokes a symbolic marriage (fig. 64). While the branch-covered roof of the boat in *A Wakeful Sleep* is unusual among medieval paintings, it does occasionally appear in images of temporary structures (*kariya*) built for the emperor or high-ranking members of the aristocratic class while on pilgrimages to temples or shrines (fig. 65).[56]

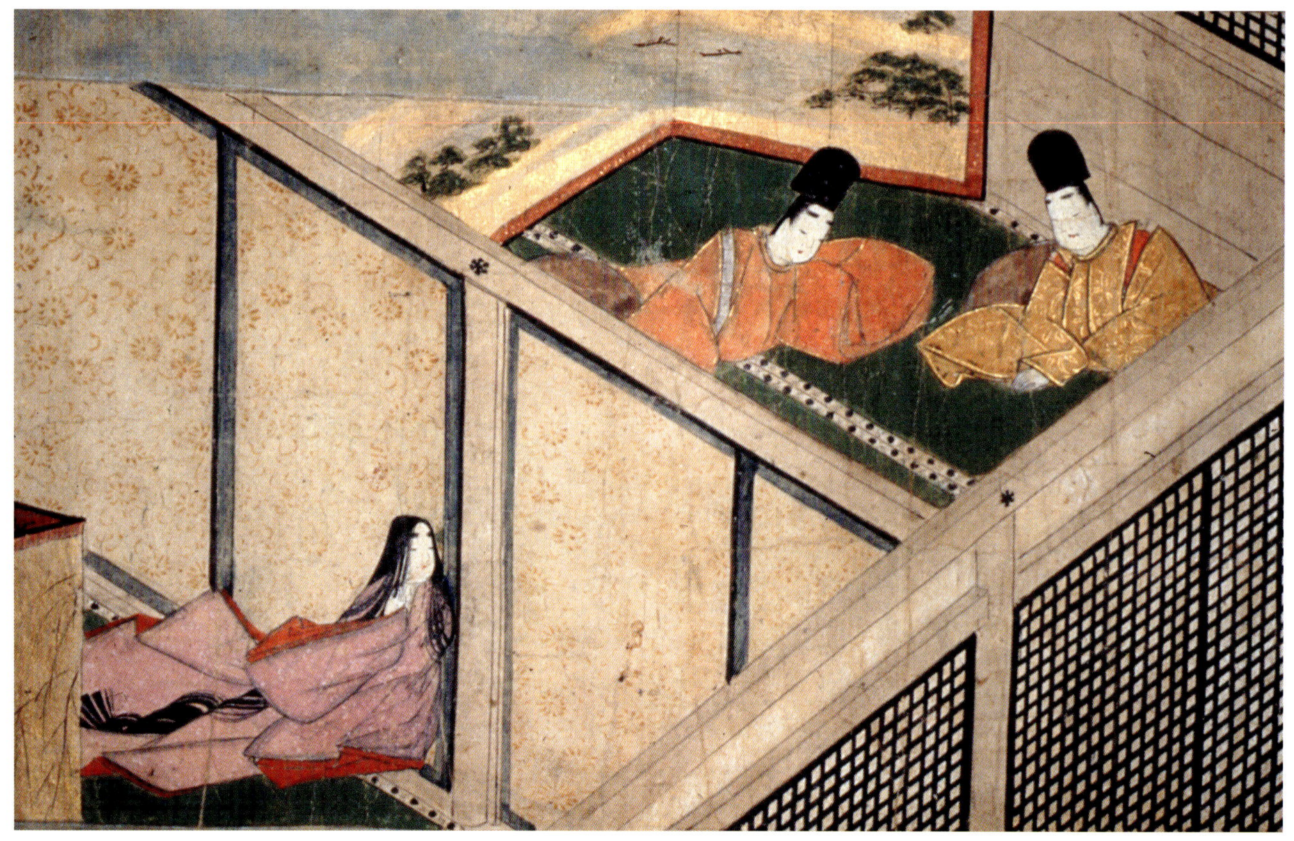

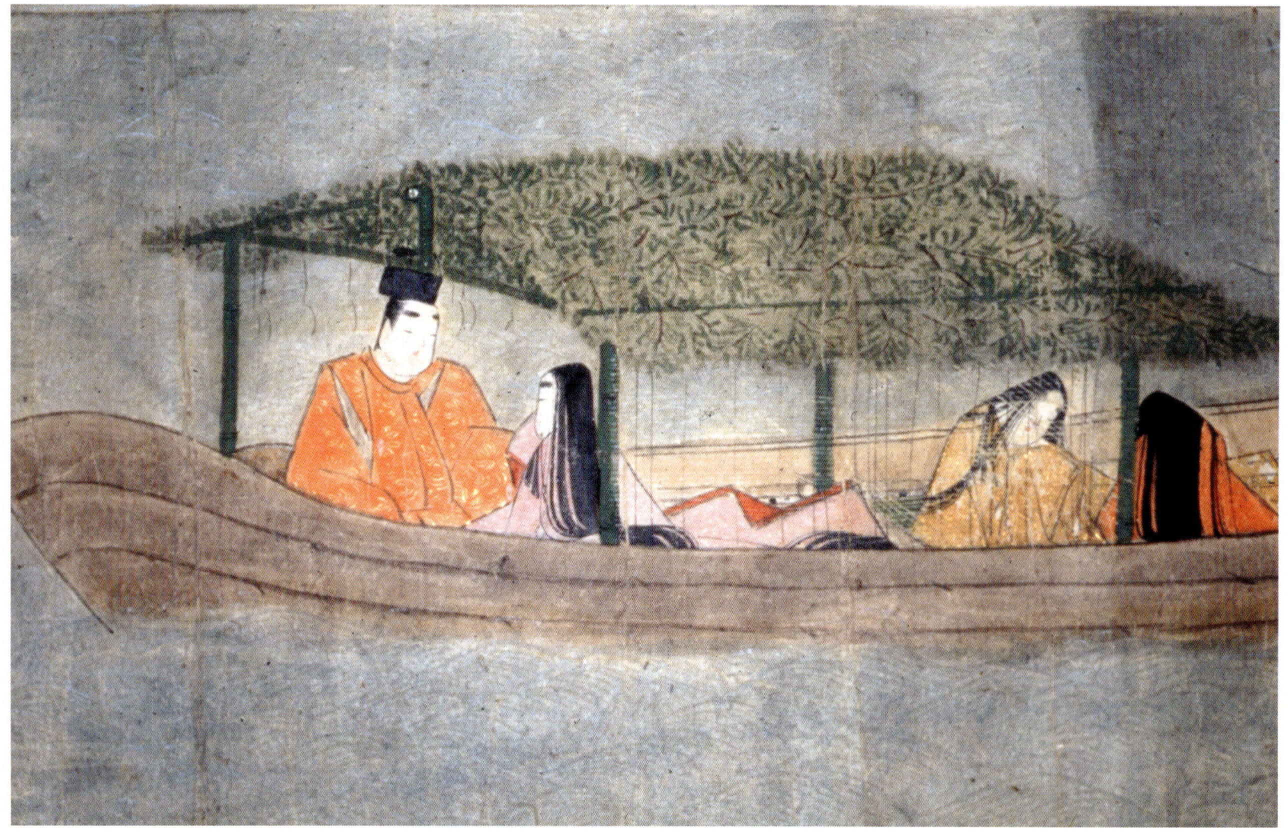

63 Tosa Mitsunobu, *A Wakeful Sleep*. Detail, painting 3.

64 Tosa Mitsunobu, *A Wakeful Sleep*. Detail, painting 4.

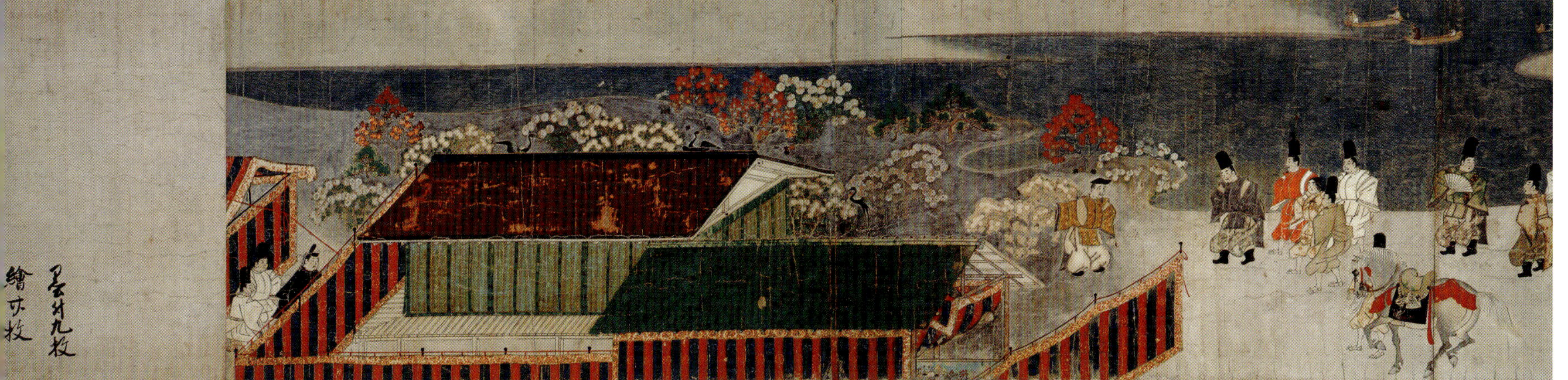

65 *Miraculous Origins of Ishiyamadera* (*Ishiyamadera engi emaki*). Early fourteenth century. One of seven handscrolls; ink and color on paper. Ishiyamadera, Ōtsu. Important Cultural Property. Detail, scroll 1.

By the fourteenth century, buildings with roofs covered in freshly cut pine branches evoked not only courtly elegance but ritual purity. In this regard, the boat in the Mitsunobu scroll, with its freshly cut, bright green foliage, may have conveyed the sanctity of a successful union between aristocrats.

THE FEMALE PROTAGONIST AND THE ROMANTIC IDEAL

One key to understanding the relationship between *A Wakeful Sleep* and its initial viewership is Mitsunobu's representation of the female protagonist as an ideal feminine type. Such an ideal was propagated most explicitly in the medieval period through instructional texts on feminine behavior called *kyōkun*. Although primarily known through Edo period examples, such as *Great Teachings for Women* (*Onna daigaku*), the genre began centuries earlier in Japan and several examples survive from the Muromachi period.[57] One has even been attributed to Sanjōnishi Sanetaka, apparently an epistle for his eldest daughter, Yasuko (b. 1480), upon the occasion of her marriage (to be discussed below).[58] Frequently the texts gather positive and negative models of feminine behavior, as in an instructional treatise in the form of a long poem (*nagauta*) attributed to Sōgi that contains sections on "the comportment of good wives" (*yoki nyōbō no mimochi*) and that of "bad wives" (*ashiki nyōbō no mimochi*).[59] The proper female etiquette espoused in these texts was often reinforced in Muromachi period literature in the characterizations of female protagonists. One clear-cut example is *A Tale of Two Nursemaids* (*Menoto no sōshi*), which embeds an admonitory epistle on feminine behavior within a comical tale of good and bad nursemaids and their respective young charges.[60]

Indeed, female etiquette primers and Muromachi courtly literature were more proximate textual genres than has previously been understood. The former instilled norms of behavior through anecdotal examples that could be of high literary quality, or at least pretensions, while the latter could mobilize fiction toward didactic aims. In some cases, this didactic purpose could be so well integrated into the narrative surface as to become thoroughly inconspicuous. *A Wakeful Sleep* falls into this category; its kinship to *kyōkun* is revealed through its invocation of female characters from the classical pantheon. The narrator's evaluation of Komachi's "trifling fancy" as opposed to the true devotion exhibited by the woman in *A Wakeful Sleep* already presents the protagonist as an exemplar of feminine commitment. Here Komachi, who was often characterized as a femme fatale during this period, is invoked as a foil.[61] The more complex invocation occurs toward the end of the tale in the form of Ukifune, the heroine of the final "Uji chapters" from *The Tale of Genji*, which I will address below. First, however, it is instructive to explore what new observations and insights can be

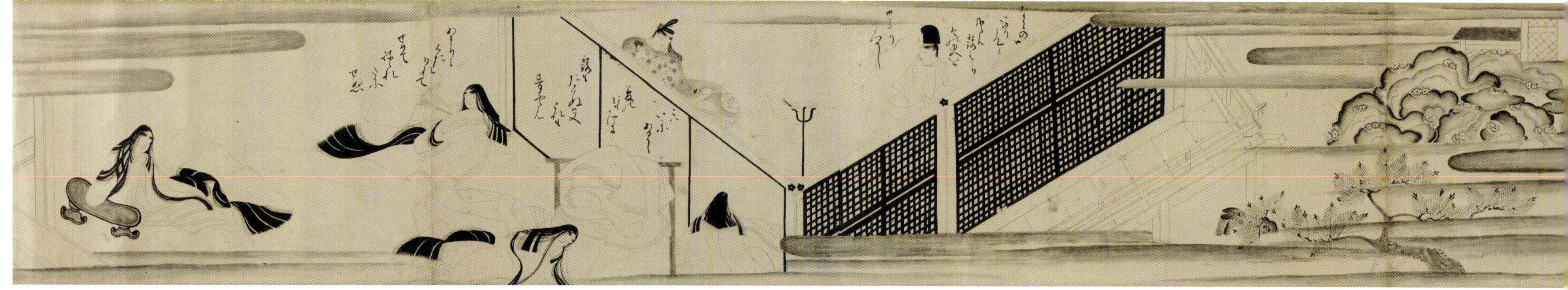

66 *A Wakeful Sleep*. Freer Gallery of Art, Smithsonian Institution, Washington, DC.

gained from the work when it is read and juxtaposed against the framework of a morality manual.

In this context, the heroine might be understood as a model of feminine and courtly restraint, in spite of (or perhaps because of) her role at the center of the action. Thus, while the plot revolves around the woman's openly expressed desire for her dream counterpart, most scenes depict her being *acted upon*. In the first two paintings in the scroll, the woman is asleep as things happen to her—the letter is delivered, and the courtier visits her in her dream. Only later, when the courtier describes the nature of his dreams in the Genji room at Ishiyamadera does the reader learn that she too has been paying the man nocturnal visits.

This record of genteel and understated, if not passive, comportment renders all the more shocking the breach of decorum visualized in painting 3 (fig. 63). There the protagonist catches a glimpse of her dream lover by peeking into the adjoining room:

His manner of speaking was identical to the man who had appeared in her dreams, her heart began to pound, and she desperately desired to see him. Her attendants were already fast asleep, exhausted from the long journey. The lamp had been extinguished, and light shone brightly from the next room. Peering in through the crack in the door, she saw an elegant man dressed in hunting garb sitting forlornly. He was identical in every respect to the man of her dreams. Thinking that she must be dreaming again, she listened on, suppressing the dark storms in her heart.

This passage represents a variation on the traditional literary device known as "peeking through the fence" (*kaimami*). Such scenes, ubiquitous in early courtly fiction, typically take place outside the space-time of everyday activity, most often in the middle of the night, and the character doing the spying, usually male, is often drawn toward a brightly lit interior that bathes the person inside with illumination.[62] Similarly, the woman here moves about the temple alone while her attendants sleep, recalling the behavior of a male, Genji-like character. Such freedom of movement and voyeurism on the part of a female subject were extremely rare in Japanese courtly fiction and could in fact mark a character intended for ridicule.[63]

The painting, however, plays a crucial role in reconciling what in this context amounts to a frank expression of sexual desire with an idealized protagonist by rendering ambiguous the act of looking. Though the text clearly describes her peeking through the opening, in the painting she sits up against the sliding door and faces toward the viewer, her eyes are turned slightly to the side, but she does not look directly at the men in the neighboring room. Indeed, from this odd angle, the figure directly in the line of the woman's vision would be the man's companion, the Chūjō, dressed in the yellow cloak, rather than the Sadaishō, who is positioned above and farther back in the room. This spatial indeterminacy is matched by a temporal one: the painting might depict the moment just before she gazes upon the man, when she hears the man's voice and desires to see him, or the moment just after, as she listens to the men's conversation and struggles with her longing to open the door.

The breach of convention here, however, is neutralized through pictorial means. Because of the angle at which the woman is depicted, the painted scene of her amorous espionage in *A Wakeful Sleep* has the odd effect of placing the scroll's viewer in the subject position of the peeking male in *kaimami* scenes. Unrolling the scroll from right to left, the viewer looks in on the girl to the left, echoing the conventional *kaimami* composition in which the man stands in the lower right looking toward the woman on the left. Such an arrangement can be found in several instances n the twelfth-century *Genji* scrolls, for example. All six *kaimami* scenes in Mitsunobu's *Genji Album* follow this pattern. The woman in *A Wakeful Sleep* becomes the object of the viewer's gaze as she sits frontally exposed, in a manner specific to *kaimami* convention. She is exposed, moreover, in a rather provocative way, dressed in the cherry blossom robe and captured in an emotional and excited state as she raises a hand to stroke her own hair.

Mitsunobu's *A Wakeful Sleep* transforms the female *kaimami* scene into a normative one. In the Mitsunobu version, the viewer may compare the woman's hair with the willow painted beside her on the folding screen, as a simile for female beauty. The pose of the woman encourages this comparison by directing the viewer's attention to her hair with her own touch. In ink-line illustrations of this story, the woman turns away from the viewer and gazes in the direction of the Sadaishō (fig. 66). All associations between the hair and the willow are gone, as the character is shown with her hair covered by a robe and seated beside a clothing rack rather than a folding screen. Both the ink-line version and Mitsunobu's painting provide an unobstructed view of the Sadaishō. In the ink-line version he is singled out through the decoration of his robe, and in Mitsunobu's painting his languorous posture captures perfectly the text's description of him as "sitting forlornly." Mitsunobu's painting thus offers both the male and the female figure up for the viewer's attention. It does so, however, by tempering the female *kaimami* scene to maintain the protagonist's status as an epitome of feminine virtue. The scroll painting captures instead the moment when the woman stops herself from entering the man's room: "Such forwardness was inappropriate for a woman, and she was forced to repress the urge."

The final painting continues to depict the restraint found in the previous three paintings. Only in this case the modesty of expression is all the more striking given the abundance of activity that takes place in the accompanying textual passage. The painting avoids, for example, representation of the heroine's dramatic jump off the Seta Bridge. Though vividly described in the text, Mitsunobu chose not to depict the woman's plunge and to show instead a bridge and river devoid of figures. This ellipsis is not due to a lack of precedent. Depictions of women jumping into rivers, usually in pursuit of men they desire, are not uncommon in Japanese painting, such as the Chinese maiden Zenmyō in *Lives of the Founders of the Kegan Sect*. In contrast to Zenmyō, however, the woman in *A Wakeful Sleep* does not aggressively pursue her lover—indeed, she does not pursue him at all—and ends up in his boat only when he retrieves her from the river. Her absence from her own would-be death scene not only diminishes her own agency but quiets what should be a highly dramatic and chaotic episode, punctuated by the attendant's screams for help as described in the accompanying textual passage.

The final depiction of the heroine in the scroll maintains this decorum. There she is in the boat of the dream man, with no hint of the unsightly image of her being pulled up by men "familiar with the ways of the water." Such self-censorship was not necessarily de rigueur in the courtly painting tradition. A notable example of such an image appears in *A Long Tale for an Autumn Night* (*Aki no yonaga monogatari emaki*), where a boy who leaps from the same Seta Bridge is vividly depicted in the process of drowning. Not only is no such scene painted in *A Wakeful Sleep*, but the woman, even after the ordeal of a suicide attempt and rescue, appears perfectly composed. Mitsunobu's painting shows a well-coiffed woman and in this regard closely follows the text, which describes how, miraculously, the woman's robes were completely dry when she was pulled from the water, and her hair had "nary a wisp astray." Yet Mitsunobu's selective fidelity to the textual passage means that pictorially her leap goes unacknowledged. This representational ambiguity simultaneously presents the woman as an ideal feminine type (reserved and inactive) while reinforcing the supernatural ambiance of the story. The omission also underscores the complexity of the relationship between paintings and text in *A Wakeful Sleep*. In portraying the heroine as a figure exemplary of feminine restraint, the paintings at times appear to conflict with the prerogatives of the story itself, which places more emphasis on the young woman as an active agent. On the other hand, the omission of the suicidal leap further suggests a parallel between the protagonist and perhaps the most famous female character in courtly fiction, Ukifune from *The Tale of Genji*.

The Ukifune chapter of *The Tale of Genji* ends with the eponymous protagonist looking down at the waters of the Uji River and contemplating suicide. When she next appears, in the "Writing Practice" (Tenarai) chapter, she has already been washed ashore and is being rescued by the bishop of Yokawa, who will send her to the nunnery at Ono. No description of Ukifune's actual jump into the water appears in the *Genji* text; rather, it is only implied by the description of the Uji River and is the object of speculation by other characters. Ukifune's actions go unrepresented, as do those of the heroine in *A Wakeful Sleep*. Through absence, then, the painting introduces one more presence. But in doing so, it only calls increased attention to a parallel latent in the text, in which the female character is associated with Ukifune in several places. The first parallel is suggested at the moment when the woman considers drowning herself. Like Ukifune, she weighs the gravity of the sin of dying before one's parent.[64] Ukifune worries about leaving her mother behind and sends her a final letter on the eve of her suicide attempt. The woman in *A Wakeful Sleep* sends her father a similar letter. Ukifune's suicide is also recalled when the young protagonist of the scroll walks toward the Seta Bridge: "Her heart composed, the girl walked calmly as a lamb to slaughter, yet the closer she drew to the bridge, the more foreboding the water seemed." The phrase "walking like a lamb to slaughter" (*hitsuji no ayumi*) is an expression taken from the *Nirvana Sutra* (*Nehangyō*)[65] but is here invoked to elicit comparison with how Ukifune feels as her attempted drowning nears: "Looking out over the river in the morning, she felt nearer death than a lamb on its way to the slaughter."[66] Thus does the woman in *A Wakeful Sleep* retrace Ukifune's shaky footsteps to the water's edge.

The two female characters, however, meet dramatically different fates. Ukifune is rescued after her suicide attempt and ends up living in the Ono nunnery, where she spends her days immersed in spiritual exercises and "writing practice." As Haruo Shirane has pointed out, after her rescue, Ukifune is "literally and figuratively reborn,"[67] having acquired a newfound will that differentiates her from her former self and other female characters in the novel. The scenes at the Ono nunnery depict her willfully avoiding male suitors, absorbed in her writing, and determined to become a nun. Some have suggested that Ukifune uses her writing as a means of self-expression; most of the poems that she composes in the chapter are not addressed to others but consist of an internal monologue, prompting an association with the female author of *Genji*.[68] In this way, the Ukifune character defies and transcends the expectations socially prescribed of her and represents an alternative ending to those usually allotted to women in courtly tales, that is to say, marriage, uneventful nunhood, or death.

Ukifune's would-be avatar in *A Wakeful Sleep* clearly does not live up to the independence of her predecessor, but she is not without the promise of a similar interiority. When she decides to look into the room in which Murasaki Shikibu is said to have authored *The Tale of Genji*, for example, she resembles momentarily Ukifune the writer. When she subsequently decides, like Ukifune, to drown herself, she is in a sense authoring her own future. While Ukifune found through her near-death experience a new life, literally as a writer, the woman in *A Wakeful Sleep*, having seen with her own eyes the men seated in Murasaki's room, in a sense gives up this role, and her suicide attempt results in a conventional end, marriage.

This conventional ending is pictorialized in the culminating image of the handscroll, in which the couple sits ensconced in the branch-covered boat. Yet this image ironically extends the Ukifune parallel, for throughout the history of *Genji*'s pictorial reception, a boat was the image most closely associated with the chapter.

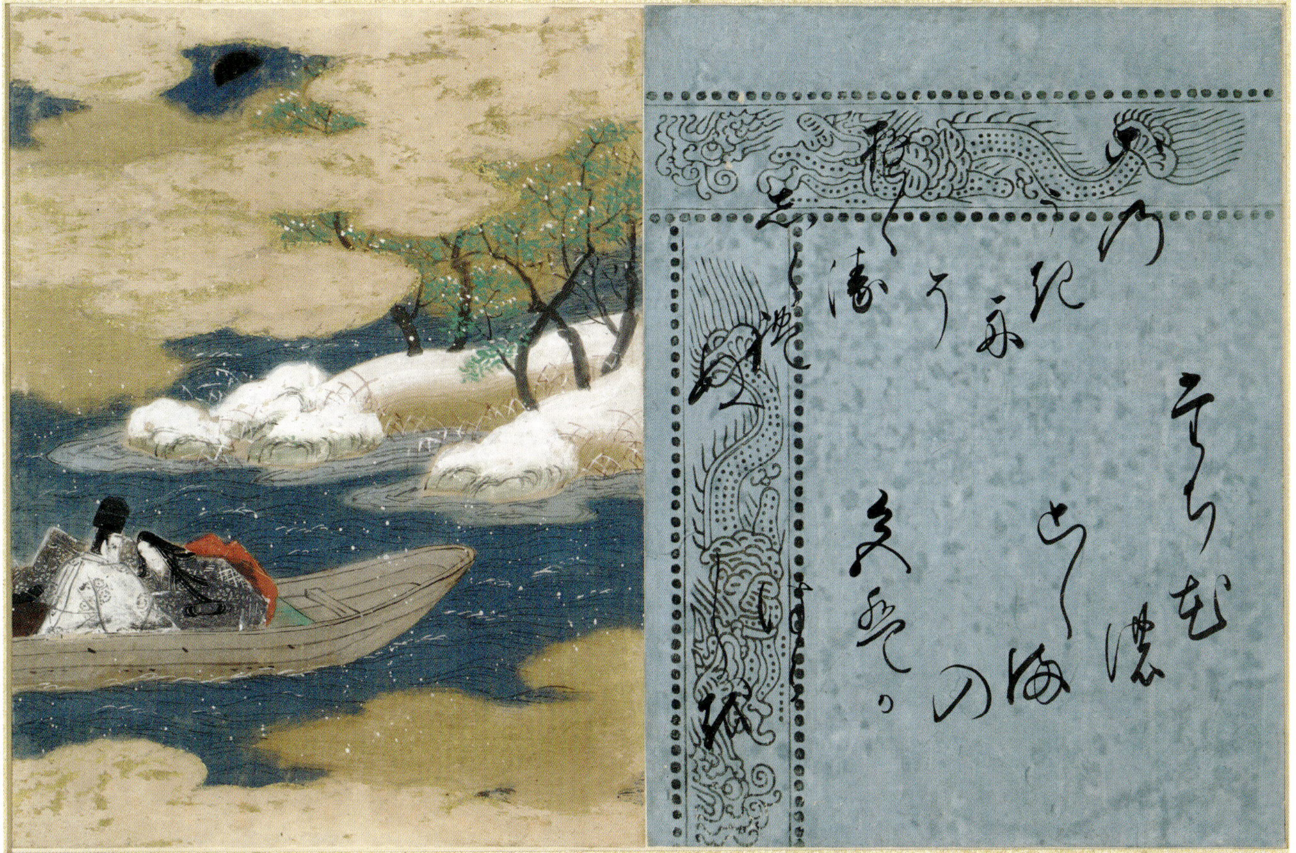

67 Tosa Mitsunobu, Tale of Genji Album. 1509–10. Chapter 51 "A Drifting Boat" (*Ukifune*). Ink, color, and gold on paper. Harvard Art Museum, Arthur M. Sackler Museum, Bequest of the Hofer Collection of the Arts of Asia, 1985.352.51.A. Photograph by Katya Kallsen © President and Fellows of Harvard College.

In *Genji,* the scene in question is the one in which Niou steals Ukifune away and takes her out boating on the river. The couple sequestered on a vessel floating down the Uji River became the most recognizable pictorial synecdoche for the chapter and was pictorialized many times over, including Mitsunobu's leaf from the *Genji Album* (fig. 67). In *Genji*, the boat scene represents an ideal image of romantic love from Niou's perspective, as described in the text: "The time was right, and so was the girl, and so was her poem: for him, at least, things could not have been more pleasingly arranged."[69] In *Genji*, however, the story goes on to undermine this romantic ideal through Ukifune's actions in the final chapters.[70] By ending with the boat scene, *A Wakeful Sleep* positions the idealized image of aristocratic union as the culminating one and can thus be understood as redactive with regard to *The Tale of Genji*. In effect, *A Wakeful Sleep* socializes the Ukifune character according to orthodox courtly norms of the medieval era. At the same time, this characterization based upon an earlier figure of great imagination and psychological complexity unsettles any attempt to understand the heroine one-dimensionally. The result is a figure marked by ambivalence, a passive-aggressive individual who is somehow not wholly subsumed by the prerogatives of lineage.

A WAKEFUL SLEEP AND ARISTOCRATIC MARRIAGE

In its matrimonial consummation, *A Wakeful Sleep* bears the marks of actual social practices of gender relations, family, and labor divisions operative within aristocratic society during the late Muromachi period, particularly that of *yometorikon* (literally, "take the bride"), or patrilocal marriage practice. Although examples of patrilocal marriage are found as early as the eleventh century, it did not become common among aristocrats until after the fourteenth century and was still in the process of being accepted around the time when *A Wakeful Sleep* was produced.[71] The story directly addresses the late-fifteenth-century aristocracy and its concerns surrounding this new form of union. Indeed, *A Wakeful Sleep* can be understood as an allegory of patrilocal marriage, in which a woman physically moves away from her father's house to the man's domain through marriage.

Because the production context of *A Wakeful Sleep* is undocumented, its earliest owners and readers cannot be identified for certain. But due to its stylistic association with Mitsunobu and by extension Sanetaka, the subject position it presupposes makes it likely that it was intended for someone like Sanjōnishi Yasuko, Sanetaka's eldest daughter, who was married to Kujō Hisatsune (1468–1530) in 1495. The marriage secured an immediate elevation in social circumstances, since the Kujō, as one of the select five Regent Houses (*gosekke*), were of a higher status than the Sanjōnishi.[72] Yasuko was now the wife of a future regent, and any male heirs she bore would likely occupy the position in the future; indeed, her son Kujō Tanemichi (1507–94) eventually became regent in 1533.[73] Moreover, although the Sanjōnishi family was related to the Fujiwara clan, the Kujō were one of only two families during the late medieval period—the other being the Konoe—who were directly descended from the Fujiwara regents of the Heian period and often supplied its titular heads. At the very least, the conspicuous wisteria imagery in *A Wakeful Sleep* would have had an unambiguous symbolic currency for this particular audience.

The possibility that *A Wakeful Sleep* was made for Yasuko, or someone like her, is meaningful to pursue as a way of understanding the complexities and ambiguities of its heroine. Yasuko receives relatively little attention in Sanetaka's diary, but one of the more detailed sequences of entries concerns the days leading up to her marriage. Yasuko was fifteen when she married the twenty-seven-year-old Hisatsune. Sanetaka describes his daughter's departure, which occurred on the twenty-fifth of the seventh month in 1495.[74] The negotiations concerning the union had concluded in the middle of the seventh month, and the Kujō family called for Yasuko on the day of the ceremony, sending six attendants and a carriage; she was allowed to take one female attendant from her own household. They departed in the evening and arrived that night and participated in what Sanetaka described as a secret ceremony. In keeping with custom, Sanetaka did not accompany his daughter and relies on hearsay in recording what took place at the Kujō residence. Apparently, over ten people came to the road to welcome her. Once inside, cups were raised in the newlyweds' honor five times, and much to Sanetaka's delight, the former regent Kujō Masamoto was in attendance. Sanetaka ends his entry by expressing what a wonderful event this was and his hopes for the couple's longevity.

Yasuko is a good candidate for the ideal reader of Mitsunobu's *A Wakeful Sleep*. As a teenage bride about to shoulder considerable responsibilities within a foreign household, including representing the Sanjōnishi name and bearing children, a picture scroll depicting a young female protagonist of similar status would have provided not only a subtle form of instruction but also a kind of aesthetic palliative for the difficulties that lay ahead. The female character in *A Wakeful Sleep* who ventures from home is adventurous (peeking into the *Genji* room) and strong willed (deciding to jump into the Seta River), but she is also filial, religious, and modest in demeanor (her self-restraint in approaching the man). By virtue of her relationship with a man ("as handsome as the shining Prince Genji") from her own social class, which she secures through a combination of self-assertion and restraint, the woman in the story acquires social and economic elevation above others. The tale thus holds out the promise of a similarly felicitous ending for its viewers and provides a visual counterpart to the words in the *Kana kyōkun* that congratulate its newly wedded reader, "you are truly blessed."[75] Someone like Yasuko may have seen herself in this image of a young woman who marries a Sadaishō, the same title as Hisatsune, her husband in real life. The charming images may have bolstered her belief in a social system that she was expected to support. They may have eased her departure from home and romanticized her impending relationship with her husband, distracting her from the more potentially frightening aspects of her new life.

A postscript to Yasuko's married life underscores the tremendous gaps that could open up between the aestheticized didacticism of the young heroine in *A Wakeful Sleep* and the lived reality of the new bride. Six months after her marriage, Yasuko's father-in-law and husband murdered one of the family's stewards, an aristocrat named Karahashi Arikazu, stabbing him to death in the Kujō home.[76] The court took stern action against this unusual incident of one aristocrat killing another, placing the family under house arrest.[77] Masamoto and Hisatsune had to cease their court service, and visits to the family were not allowed. As a result, Yasuko did not see her father or other family members for nearly two years after the incident, during which time she gave birth to her first child.[78] Apparently, the ideal circumstances of aristocratic life existed in the realm of representation only. The ambivalence in the protagonist of *A Wakeful Sleep* may ultimately reflect the fact that in the late medieval period cultural forms could no longer honestly conjure even the possibility of an ideal for Japan's aristocracy as they had during the time of Murasaki Shikibu. The decline in real terms of the material circumstances of court families had simply rendered unbridgeable the chasm between social reality and visions of the good life propagated in texts and images. The dreamlike quality of *A Wakeful Sleep* may to no small degree derive from the (acknowledged) irreality of its own propositions.

A Wakeful Sleep is paradigmatic of the way small scrolls participated in the cultural life of medieval Japan. It represents a specific pictorial interpretation of a recently authored short story that was circulating at the time. The tale itself, possibly authored by a woman at court, is a romance derived from the tradition of archaic romances (*giko*) of earlier centuries, radically pared down but overly classicized in a similar way. Although vaguely evocative of the heyday of courtly splendor and capped by a felicitous union, the tale itself comes across as ideologically noncommittal—it is preoccupied more with the formal tasks of classical allusion. Courtly women's literature of the period was not only a diversion, however, but in many ways about the recognition of its own sources, so that its readers were confirming and performing their own subjectivity. In this regard, the invocations of Ukifune are quite fitting. The fact that *A Wakeful Sleep*, in its essential incarnation as a short story, was a product of a literature by and for women is suggested by its ink-line scroll versions, in which ladies-in-waiting are incorporated actively into the story line, providing colorful commentary throughout.

Mitsunobu's version of *A Wakeful Sleep*, on the other hand, redirects the valence of the tale to the reigning prerogatives of the Fujiwara power structure. It does so not by appropriating and redesigning the story so much as by developing certain elements therein that were latent in the raw material but not overriding concerns, most prominently the celebration of the Fujiwara name, the otherworldly aura surrounding the union, and the presentation of the protagonists as exemplars of modesty and restraint. The result, as we have seen, is a conflicted work in which the supernatural is only incompletely naturalized and in which the female heroine is unconvincingly manipulated. The ambivalence in her characterization reflects the many models of representation that are folded into *A Wakeful Sleep*. In this regard, the work showcases the degree to which the small scroll could engender pictorial experimentation, for Mitsunobu draws on a wide array of traditional techniques of pictorial narrative but puts them to uses in unusual combinations to engineer an appropriate pictorial tone for the task at hand. Mitsunobu's paintings are, in effect, archaic in the same manner as their companion text. The pictorial pedantry ultimately serves a conservative agenda—but this was not always the case in Mitsunobu's *ko-e*.

THE JIZŌ HALL A PICTORIAL REBIRTH

4

Monk: "Since coming to this place I have experienced pleasure upon pleasure, but I long for my home."
Dragon woman: "I too have a body that cannot be free from suffering. You must pray for me."
—*The Jizō Hall*

It is difficult to imagine an object that embodies more perfectly the literary and visual sophistication of elite viewers in late-fifteenth-century Japan than *The Jizō Hall* (fig. 2). Illustrating the story of a young monk who ultimately achieves salvation after being temporarily led astray from the Buddhist path, the work exhibits a complex interweaving of story lines from diverse types of narratives, including tales of "strange marriages" (*kaikontan*), "Jizō miracles" (*Jizō reigendan*), and "wayward monks" (*hakaisō no shippaidan*). Moreover, the tale embeds within it two dissimilar and even antithetical perspectives: of a monk who attempts to redeem himself after succumbing to worldly temptation and of a dragon woman, who struggles to pursue her own salvation. On the surface the story concerns one monk and his redemption through the expedient means of the Buddha, but into this story is inserted another narrative, more subterranean, told from the point of view of the woman who leads the monk to his spiritual awareness. This chapter demonstrates how this remarkable shadowing of the main story line—and its concomitant twinning of contrasting protagonists—were achieved in pictorial terms and will discuss the implications of this form of layered representation for an understanding of the audience of *The Jizō Hall* and the medium of the small scroll.

Despite its generic complexity, scholars have tended to classify *The Jizō Hall* into one literary category or another.[1] While relying upon many of the tropes associated with specific types of tales mentioned above, it does not owe allegiance to any single one. Indeed, the categories cited by modern commentators are in some cases anachronistic and do not fully take into account the porosity of medieval tale culture. *The Jizō Hall* can be understood as manifesting a certain literary hybridity. This hybridity, however, needs to be explained in terms of the literary norms and expectations that were current at the time of its creation. As such, this chapter will argue for a revised taxonomy of medieval Japanese tale literature that will place in high relief the contours of this particular pictoliterary artifact. First and foremost within this taxonomy is the "account of rebirth" (*ōjōden*), which plays a central role in structuring the trajectory of the protagonist(s) in *The Jizō Hall*. I will also articulate how the paintings add layers of complexity to the work's intertextual character. Indeed, the unique combinatory logic of *The Jizō Hall* requires a sensitivity to the allusiveness of both its words and its images.

Previous studies have assumed that the story of *The Jizō Hall* predates Mitsunobu's late Muromachi handscroll despite the absence of any other recensions of the narrative.[2] For a variety of reasons to be elaborated upon below, it seems far more likely that *The Jizō Hall* narrative emerged in the late fifteenth century—that it was a tale newly authored and adapted for illustration as a picture scroll, rather than being an ancient work rerecorded or transcribed.[3] The creation of *The Jizō Hall* should be envisioned along the lines of the making of the *Clouds of Mt. Kōya* picture scroll described in chapter 2. In that case Sanetaka appears to have authored a short story to be illustrated as a small scroll at the request of the emperor, resulting in an entirely new literary and pictorial work. As we have already seen, Sanetaka was no mere scribe but was a wide-ranging author of new literary texts; in addition to short prose tales, his corpus includes a Nō libretto, a temple origin tale, and thousands of poetic compositions. Sanetaka's involvement in the creation of *The Jizō Hall*, elaborated upon below, provides an important context for understanding its literary density and multiple foundations. As in *Clouds of Mt. Kōya*, Sanetaka brushed the calligraphy for Mitsunobu's *Jizō Hall*. Judging from his involvement in other text-image projects, the scope of his work as calligrapher often included editing the text and assisting the artist in conceptualizing the images. *The Jizō Hall* proves to be no exception; a close reading of its narrative suggests the imprint of Sanetaka as editor and adapter.

The story can best be understood as an account of rebirth adapted and refitted into an entertaining illustrated narrative scroll. Although scholars have assumed that the genre of accounts of rebirth died out in the thirteenth century, it seems to have experienced a revival of sorts in the fifteenth century in the circle of Emperor GoTsuchimikado, who showed keen interest in the genre. Of direct relevance here is the fact that in 1498 he requested that Sanetaka copy a recently authored manuscript of "accounts of rebirth." After transcribing this text, Sanetaka was then asked to adapt a rebirth tale for illustration as a small scroll. Mitsunobu's *Jizō Hall* may be this illustrated scroll of 1498, but with no other details concerning the content of the tale, the identification remains conjectural.[4] Nevertheless, in managing the production of *The Jizō Hall* Sanetaka appears to have shaped the raw material of an account of rebirth into a short story for illustration in the small format. This process is best grasped when handscroll making is conceptualized in terms of a process tied to the literary and pictorial experimentations taking place with the *ko-e* format. Mitsunobu's paintings were an integral component of that experimentation, as his images for *The Jizō Hall* demonstrate.

Understanding *The Jizō Hall* narrative as a creative account of rebirth for imperial readers in the late fifteenth century clarifies some of the issues related to generic nonconformity, such as the conspicuous lack of pictorial emphasis on the bodhisattva Jizō in a tale that is set in a Jizō hall or the sense of dignity and respectability conveyed by the monk despite the tale's resemblance to more generic stories of wayward monks, whose protagonists are usually portrayed much less sympathetically. Finally, there is the ambiguous nature of the woman who takes the monk to her underwater abode. Despite the frequent appearance of such characters elsewhere, here she appears to demonstrate too much agency to be regarded as a mere tool of temptation. These characteristics, which render *The Jizō Hall* unfamiliar by the norms of the established genres of its time, succeed in generating a multiplicity of potential subject positions with which to engage and experience the scroll. This multiplicity, in turn, would have suited the prerogatives of a diverse group of male and female readers in imperial circles. Understood in this way, *The Jizō Hall* is an important example of the rise of intimate, small picture scrolls as an important mode of pictoliterary representation after the Ōnin War.

THE SCROLL AND THE STORY

The Jizō Hall, a single picture scroll currently in a private collection, consists of seven sections of text and seven sections of painting and measures 17.2 centimeters in height.[5] The calligraphy is in the familiar hand of Sanjōnishi Sanetaka.[6] Despite a late-seventeenth-century connoisseurial postscript (fig. 2r) by Kanō Tan'yū(1602–74) attributing the scroll to Tosa Mitsumochi (ca.1496–1559), later authenticators and modern scholars agree that the work is by Tosa Mitsunobu.[7] Although some areas of the paintings are well preserved with bright mineral pigments and thin lines of gold paint remaining, other parts have sustained considerable damage, and large patches of paper have entirely disappeared, leaving only the backing paper visible. All things considered, however, it is remarkable that the scroll has survived with all of its paintings and texts in their original order. And it is all the more fortunate because its texts preserve the only known version of *The Jizō Hall* story; in contrast to the other scrolls examined in this study, there are no other manuscript versions of the tale, illustrated or otherwise.

The Jizō Hall tells the story of an earnest young Buddhist monk who is affiliated with a temple in Echigo Province and who sets out to perform a one-thousand-day copying of *The Lotus Sutra*.[8] One day, as he is diligently transcribing the text in the Jizō Hall, a beautiful woman appears before him and offers to sponsor his sutra transcription (fig. 2a). The monk soon falls in love with her, and when he professes his feelings, she agrees to meet with him, but only after he has finished the important task at hand. At the ceremony marking the completion of the sutra transcription, the woman makes generous donations to the temple (fig. 2b), and afterward she begins meeting secretly with the monk, thus fulfilling her promise and his desire. Soon she suggests that he visit her home, which she explains lies beyond the sea (fig. 2c). As they stand at the edge of the shore, the monk hesitates, whereupon the woman provides him with a robe enabling him to walk on and under water. Arriving at the bottom of the sea, the monk gazes in disbelief at the palatial residence and the elegance of its inhabitants, who resemble "heavenly beings and the people of Tang" (*tennin moshi wa karabito*) (fig. 2e). He experiences "enjoyments beyond the realm of the ordinary" (*ima no keraku tada koto to mo oboezu*), prompting him to wonder if he has already been reborn as a Buddha (fig. 2f). With the passage of time, however, the monk begins to grow restless and becomes concerned that he has strayed from the Buddhist path. One night while sleeping with the woman, he notices that the hem of her garment resembles the tail of a snake (fig. 2g). Finally realizing that he has entered the Dragon Palace, the famous underwater lair of the Dragon King, the monk fears for his salvation and asks to return to his homeland (fig. 2h). The woman agrees but insists that first she must explain why she brought him here. She proceeds to inform the monk of the error of his desirous ways and brings out the sutra that he copied (fig. 2i). Instead of the sutra text, all that has been inscribed are the words "Quickly get this over with, I want to sleep with this woman, I want to sleep with her. I want this over with quickly, I want to sleep with her, want to sleep with her now" (*toku shihatete kono nyōbo to nebaya nebaya, toku shihatebaya, toku nebaya nebaya*), repeated countless times from beginning to end. Full of shame at having defiled the sutra transcription, the monk finally arrives at self-awareness and returns home dejected (fig. 2k). After he journeys back to the Jizō Hall, he falls asleep at the base of the statue of the bodhisattva Jizō, only to find himself transformed into a large snake (fig. 2l). He prays to receive the merciful intervention of Jizō, and soon the back of the snake splits open, allowing him to emerge intact in human form (fig. 2n). From then on the monk tries to resume his former life, but in speaking with his fellow monks, he learns that more than two hundred years have passed since he left for the Dragon Palace (fig. 2p). Shaken from the entire experience, he pursues his religious exercises with more diligence than ever, lives to be an old man, and eventually achieves rebirth in paradise (fig. 2q).

COMBINATORY LOGIC

The Jizō Hall draws upon a dizzying array of medieval storytelling patterns in crafting its own fable. Weaving together basic plotlines of Jizō and Kannon miracle tales in which those deities intercede on a devotee's behalf, humorous satires of monks who veer from the righteous path, didactic tales of human and nonhuman marriage, evil serpent women, or men whose greed or lust turns them into serpents, and the uncanny time lapse of the *Urashima Tarō* legend, the text resembles a tapestry of medieval tale literature. This quality suggests an author aware of and capable of incorporating the full horizon of fictional production of his time into his own composition.

Instead of wholly adhering to any one generic convention, the author of *The Jizō Hall* judiciously chooses from several and then recombines them into a seamless new narrative. Its success, however, is predicated upon the fact that no single one of its constituent borrowings overwhelms any other. In other words, generic identity is diluted to the point where just enough remains of any given tradition to trigger recognition by the viewer, but not enough for that element to become the main theme of the work. This moderation is greatly enabled by the scroll's pictorial images. A case in point is the work's relationship to the genre of "Jizō miracles" (*Jizō bosatsu reigendan*). While important elements from Jizō stories appear, the pictures deemphasize the bodhisattva's role, thus allowing for a more unaffiliated narrative. Accordingly, in an effort to reconstruct the tale's complex relationship to literary genres, the pages that follow will examine the scroll as a Jizō miracle tale, an errant-monk narrative, and an account of rebirth.

Miracles of Jizō

The Jizō Hall's setting, a small temple building housing an icon of Jizō, and its plot, which hinges upon the mercy of the bodhisattva in rescuing the protagonist, clearly draw upon a large corpus of tales recounting miracles associated with Jizō. Indeed, Edo period connoisseurs of the scroll, and twentieth-century scholars as well, determined that *The Jizō Hall* was simply a variant of a miraculous Jizō tale and thus gave the work its current title.[9] Jizō (or, in Sanskrit, Kṣitigarbha) is a bodhisattva of boundless compassion who assists the sentient beings of the Six Realms of existence during the long period between the death of the historical Buddha and the appearance of the future Buddha Maitreya, or Miroku. Jizō tales were compiled as early as the eleventh century in collections such as *Tales of Times Now Past* (*Konjaku monogatari shū*) and *Miracles of the Bodhisattva Jizō* (*Jizō bosatsu reigenki*).[10] Their popularity continued unabated throughout the medieval period, with numerous handscrolls of the subject dating from the thirteenth century onward.[11] In the fifteenth century, such scrolls circulated among the elite, were read out loud for the emperor, and were viewed privately by groups of courtiers.[12] Sanetaka and Mitsunobu themselves had previously, in 1487, collaborated on the *Miraculous Origins of Seikōji* (*Seikōji engi-e*), subtitled *The Roof-Thatching Jizō* (*yane-fuki Jizō*), a copy of which survives today.[13] As these numerous references and extant works attest, the Jizō miracle story was alive and well in the late fifteenth century, and the appearance of its narrative conventions in Mitsunobu's and Sanetaka's *Jizō Hall* scroll is not unexpected.

Yet *The Jizō Hall* departs so dramatically from the conventions of illustrated Jizō tales that it is difficult to imagine the scroll having been perceived as such by contemporary viewers. The most significant departure is the absence of Jizō himself in Mitsunobu's paintings.[14] A survey of extant illustrations of Jizō tales suggests that their dramatic appeal was predicated upon the

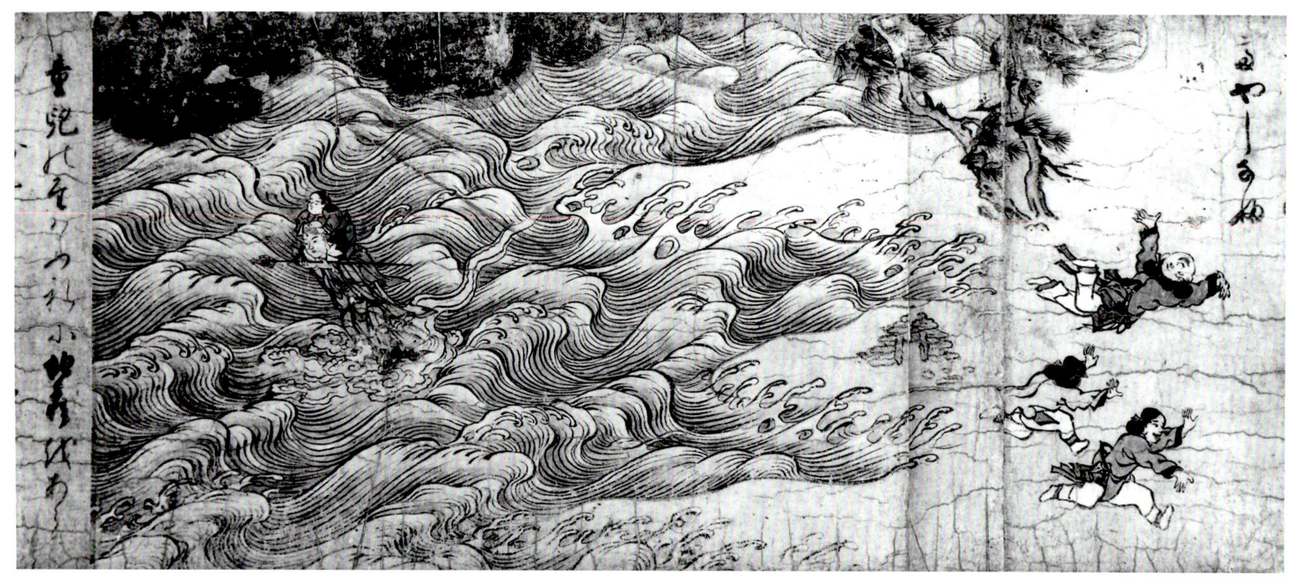

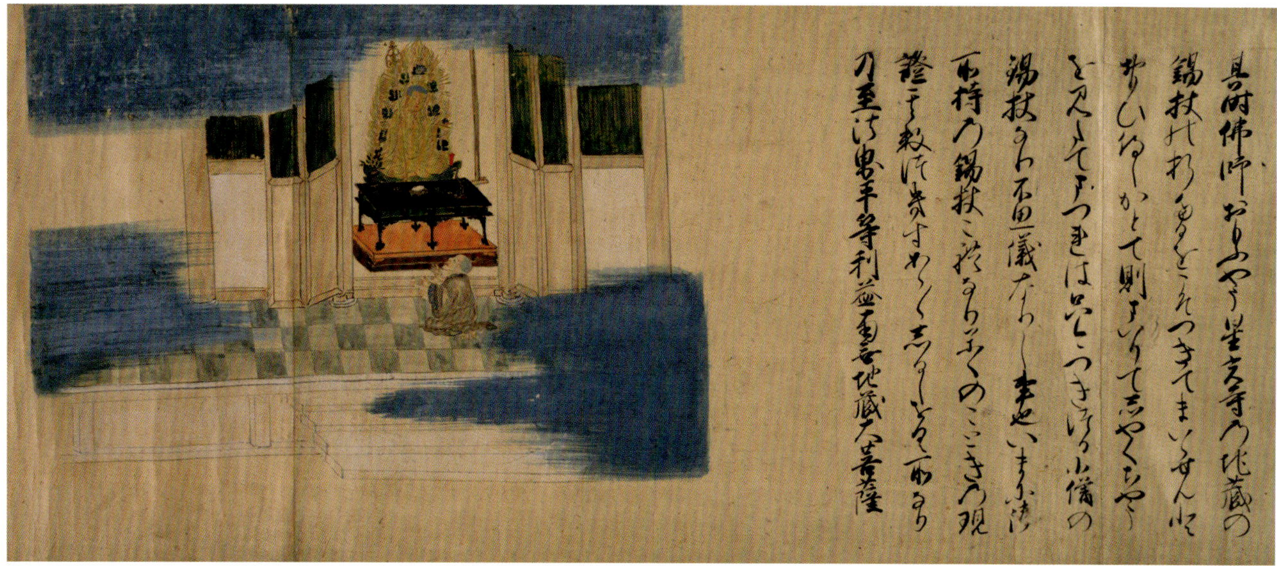

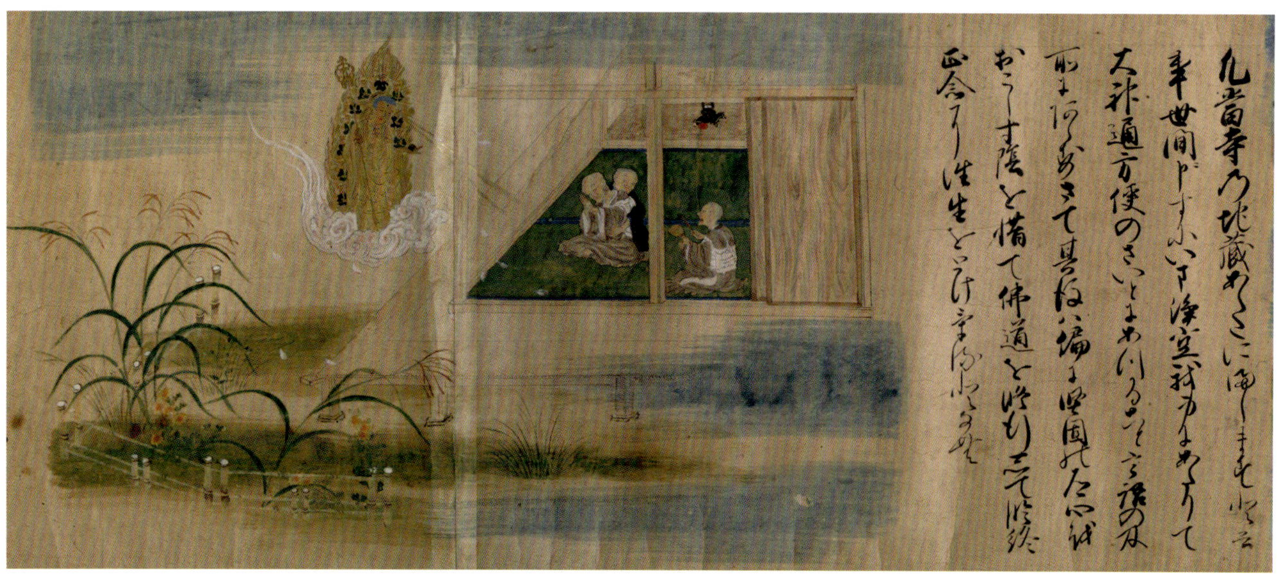

active presence of the bodhisattva. Much more than a static icon, in these scrolls Jizō commonly intervenes on behalf of devotees, as in the thirteenth-century scroll *Miracles of the Bodhisattva Jizō* (*Jizō bosatsu reigenki-e*), where in one dramatic scene he rescues from a tidal wave a young boy who had fashioned a small Jizō shrine out of seashells (fig. 68). In scrolls that illustrate legends about specific or well-known Jizō icons, their statues become animated, alight from their pedestals, and aid sentient beings caught in a variety of dire scenarios, literally pulling them up from the fires of hell or appearing in their dreams with staff, wishing jewel, and gilt mandorla. Such ambulatory icons usually return to their pedestals by the end of the scroll, where the concluding image depicts the statue prominently enshrined (fig. 69). Because of a close connection that developed between Jizō and the Buddha Amida in the medieval period, illustrated legends began to depict Jizō, instead of Amida, as the deity guiding devotees to the Pure Land at their moment of death (fig. 70).[15] The widespread belief that an encounter with a living Jizō signaled one's future rebirth into the Pure Land no doubt engendered the numerous pictorial encounters with Jizō that allowed handscroll viewers to experience salvation vicariously.

It comes as some surprise then that *The Jizō Hall* forgoes all opportunities to represent the deity that would later become its namesake. In the scroll's four separate scenes of the temple building, for example, only the base of the statue and its altar appear, thus denying even a partial view of the bodhisattva. Instead, bands of mist consistently veil the enshrined icon. Jizō's absence at the protagonist's moment of death also sets this small scroll apart from works such as *Miraculous Origins of Seikōji*, where the bodhisattva is the source of the golden rays that shine upon the worshiper being welcomed into the Pure Land. The golden rays in *The Jizō Hall* emanate from nothing but sky (fig. 2q). One might consider these proxy depictions as examples of less being more, wherein the absence of a full view of the bodhisattva adds to his mystery. Such subtlety was never a goal, however, of the numerous handscrolls from the thirteenth to fifteenth centuries made explicitly to praise Jizō and his miraculous powers.

Unlike such scrolls, *The Jizō Hall* was clearly not intended for proselytization or to help enhance the aura surrounding a given temple's treasured icon. Rather, it was a short-story small scroll intended for personalized reading experiences by laypeople. As such, it embodies one of the main features of the short-story small scroll: its focus on a small number of human protagonists and their trials and tribulations. Comparing this scroll to unillustrated Jizō tales further highlights the lack of concern in *The Jizō Hall* for the deity. Protagonists in tales from *Miracles of the Bodhisattva Jizō* and *Tales of Times Now Past* spend much of their time thinking of Jizō, praying to him, and hoping to see a living manifestation of him. No such preoccupation absorbs the monk in *The Jizō Hall*, and accordingly the bodhisattva's visual presence is downplayed.

A similar interweaving of a Jizō story line into a short-story small scroll occurs in *Tale of the Fox*, a small scroll produced in the circle of Mitsunobu.[16] Here an older monk lured into the lair of a shape-shifting fox woman is rescued by monks carrying staffs (the worldly manifestations of Jizō), who suddenly appear and trigger the woman's reversion to her true fox form (fig. 71). Upon encountering the bodhisattva, the woman's fox paw emerges from her sleeve, while in the background, her attendants, now foxes, scamper about in a frenzy. A revelation by the monk soon follows, as he comes to understand the delusional life he has been living. Both *Tale of the Fox* and *The Jizō Hall* use fantastical locales—the frightening fox den and the exotic Dragon Palace—and incorporate climactic scenes depicting lycanthropic

68 *Miracles of the Bodhisattva Jizō* (*Jizō bosatsu reigenki-e*). Late thirteenth century. One handscroll; ink and color on paper. Tokyo National Museum.

69 *Miraculous Origins of Seikōji* (*Seikōji engi-e*). Fifteenth century. Two handscrolls; ink, color and gold on paper. Tokyo National Museum. Important Cultural Property. Detail, scroll 2.

70 *Miraculous Origins of Seikōji* (*Seikōji engi-e*). Fifteenth century. Two handscrolls; ink, color and gold on paper. Tokyo National Museum. Important Cultural Property. Detail, scroll 2.

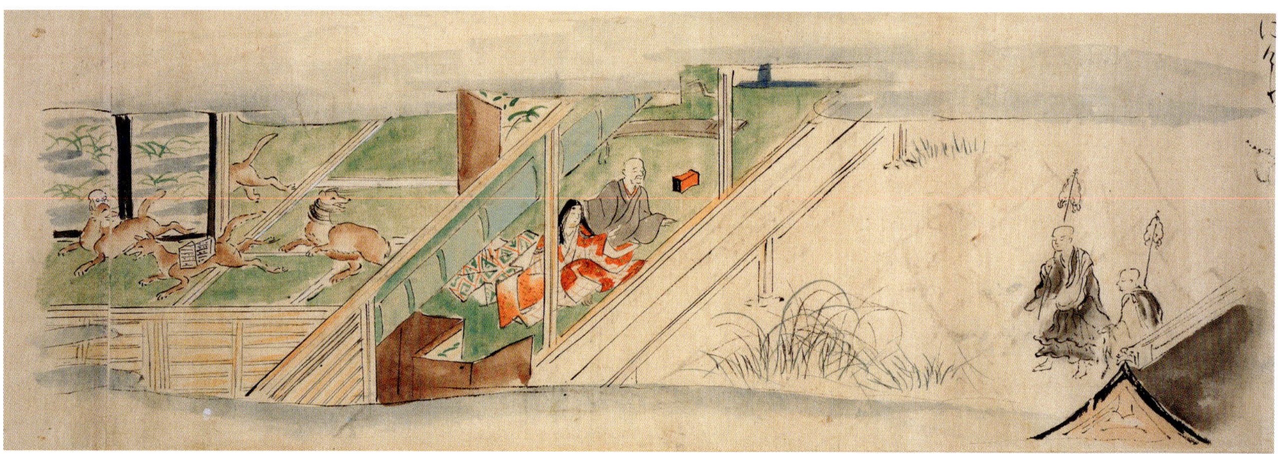

71 Kanō Tan'yū, *Tale of the Fox* (*Kitsune sōshi emaki*). Seventeenth century. Copy of fifteenth-century scroll. Department of Japanese Literature, Gakushūin University, Tokyo. Painting 5.

transformations to entertain the reader while emphasizing the personal revelations of their protagonists. *Tale of the Fox*, however, remains much truer than *The Jizō Hall* to the orthodoxy of Jizō tales; not only is Jizō represented pictorially, but the story ends with the man recounting the harrowing episode to his daughter, rather than showing a scene related to his rebirth. Even among small scrolls, *The Jizō Hall* is more complex and employs a unique pictorial ellipsis of Jizō to quietly fold the tradition of such miracle tales into itself.

The Errant Monk

Another type of medieval literature not only alluded to but willfully reworked in *The Jizō Hall* is that of "blunders of wayward monks" (*hakaisō no shippaidan*), modified here by defying convention and depicting a monk who is fully redeemed by the end of the tale. Although the category of the wayward-monk tale was not employed in the Muromachi period, the character of the errant holy man appears so frequently in medieval literature, and the commonalities between stories of this theme are so pronounced, that the category presents a useful framework for understanding *The Jizō Hall*.[17] A narrative pattern common to wayward-monk tales consists of the introduction of a dilemma generated by the protagonist-monk's sexual desire, the subsequent narrative development sustained by the character's fecklessness, and, in the end, the monk's humiliation and/or punishment as a result of his amorous exploits. These tales are most often comical, as the errant monk was recognized among medieval readers as an easy target for ridicule.

Two late medieval stories classified as wayward-monk tales, *The Useful Nun* (*Oyō no ama*)[18] and *Whispering Bamboo* (*Sasayakidake*), provide illuminating comparisons to *The Jizō Hall*. In the former, an old peddler woman referred to as a "nun" convinces an aging monk that he is perfectly justified in living out his days with a young wife, which she offers to procure for him. On the night of their betrothal, she tricks the monk (with the help of several cups of sake) into thinking that she herself is the young bride. The man does not realize his mistake until the next morning, and the story ends with the suggestion that the monk will spend the rest of his days in the company of this hideous old woman. *Whispering Bamboo* recounts the tale of a lecherous monk from Kuramadera who uses a hollow section of bamboo to whisper in the ears of a sleeping couple, tricking them into sending their beautiful young daughter to his mountain temple.[19] When the men transporting the girl to the monastery in a large chest fall asleep along the way, a nobleman's attendant finds her, replaces her with a mangy cow, and takes the girl to his master. A farcical scene ensues when the monk (unaware of the substitution) attempts to

embrace the agitated animal in his darkened bedchamber, mistaking the animal's tail for a woman's tresses and pledging vows of love amid the cow's bucking and leaping. Word gets out of the woman's miraculous transformation into a cow, which brings thousands of people, including bands of vicious warriors, to the temple. When the rightful owner of the cow appears and exposes the monk's evil deeds, the monk is publicly humiliated as the crowd erupts in thunderous laughter. Before those angered by the monk's egregious behavior can punish him themselves, a forceful storm carries him upward and leaves him for dead hanging upside down from a cypress tree. Thereafter he becomes an evil spirit and, eventually, the guardian deity of the mountain.

The Jizō Hall resembles these errant-monk tales to the extent that its plot turns upon the monk's desire for the woman, for which he is ultimately punished. The scroll also has its share of comedy, the moment of greatest hilarity being the revelation of the sutra-copying error. The reader learns of this blunder at the same time as the monk in the story, and the scene makes for a humorous climax midway through the tale. In that scene the woman informs the monk that instead of copying the sutra, he has transcribed his own lewd thoughts about her onto the sutra paper. The monk's crude language, quoted in the text of the picture scroll ("Quickly get this over with, I want to sleep with this woman"), comes as a surprise to both the monk and the scroll's reader, heightening the humor of the episode. For until that point, the reader may have considered the monk rather righteous for completing the one-thousand-day sutra copying and might have wondered, like the monk himself, if he had not been reborn in paradise as a reward for his diligence. The revelation of the error functions as a pivot point that explains the narrative events leading up to that moment, while making a mockery of the sutra-copying exercise and the monk's religious pretensions. The sacred scripture that he took such care not to defile in the first scene by donning the face mask, and that was celebrated so elaborately in the temple's "Ten Kinds of Offerings" (*jisshu kuyō*) ceremony, turns out to have consisted of nothing but lascivious words.

Derision toward the Buddhist clergy and its pretensions is common in wayward-monk tales. *Whispering Bamboo*, for example, sarcastically juxtaposes the exalted outward persona of the ritual-performing monk with the lewd and deceitful thoughts that occupy his mind. *The Useful Nun* pokes fun at individuals outside the clergy who profess to lifestyles of sincere Buddhist practice. The old woman in this story may be called a "nun" (*ama*), but she more closely resembles an itinerant saleswoman than a proselytizer.[20] The illustrations in a sixteenth-century picture scroll of this tale further characterize her as a peddler—her bundle containing her wares for trade appears prominently beside her in every scene (fig. 72). Meanwhile, in the depiction of the monk's hut, the accoutrements for the tea ceremony are displayed as conspicuously as the objects on his Buddhist altar, suggesting that he practices tea more intently than religion and is as serious a monk as the woman is a real nun.

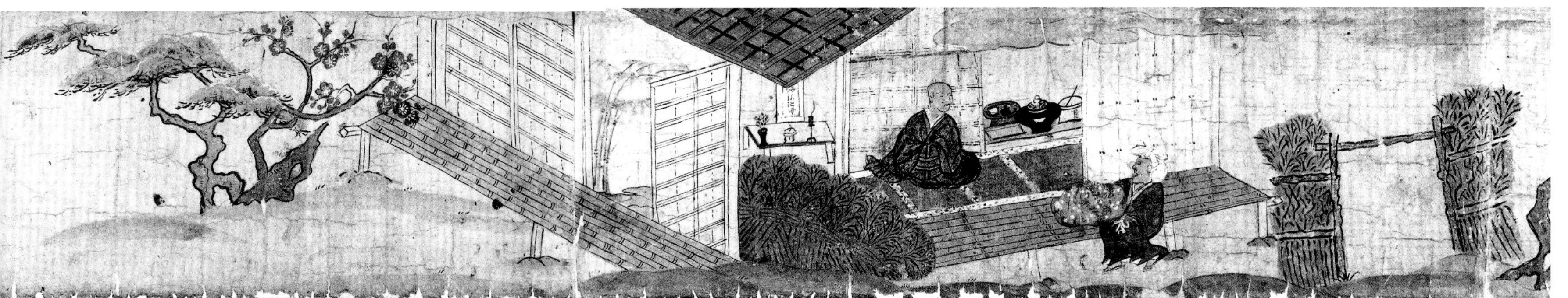

72 *The Useful Nun* (*Oyō no ama*). Sixteenth century. Two handscrolls; ink and color on paper; H. 14.8 cm. Suntory Museum of Art, Tokyo.

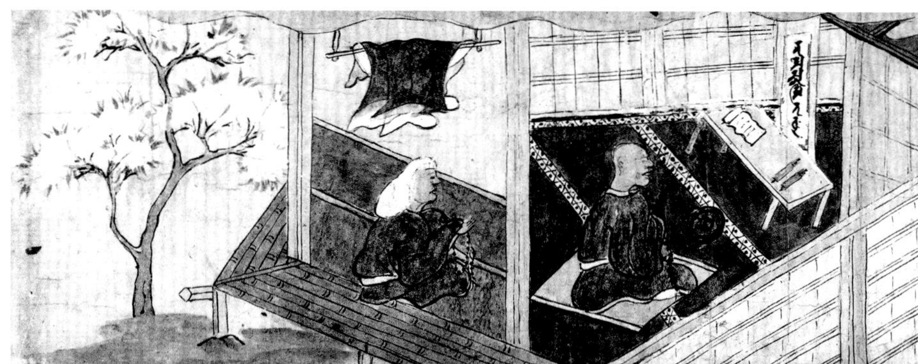

73 *The Useful Nun* (*Oyō no ama*). Sixteenth century. Two handscrolls; ink and color on paper; H. 14.8 cm. Suntory Museum of Art, Tokyo.

But while *The Jizō Hall* may employ some of the essential characteristics of the wayward-monk genre—the comical air, the portrayal of a gullible monk, the caricature of religious pretensions—it never offers a direct or sustained critique of the Buddhist establishment. Similar to the work's allusions to Jizō miracle tales, components of the wayward-monk tale here exhibit a restrained quality, particularly in the even-handed characterization of the monk. This impartiality is largely accomplished through the story's lack of the cunning characters that are de rigueur in more parodic tales, those who deliberately use their Buddhist robes to deceive others for personal gain. Unlike the monk of *Whispering Bamboo*, who perfidiously exploits the authority of his social position and preys upon the good intentions of a young girl's parents, the monk of *The Jizō Hall* deceives no one but himself. Moreover, he continues to appear well-meaning throughout the tale; although he allows his mind to wander during his Buddhist exercises, his later shock at witnessing the content of his own lustful thoughts indicates that he truly believed he was copying the sutra correctly. *The Jizō Hall* is in no way a cautionary tale about the shenanigans of deceitful priests.

A similar comparison can be made between female characters, with a woman who calculatingly deceives the gullible monk in *The Useful Nun* versus an ultimately benign dragon woman in *The Jizō Hall*. Both of these female characters are temptresses, and the picture scrolls introduce them in an identical way: in the initial scene of each scroll, they first approach their respective monks in the middle of religious exercises on exterior verandas. While the peddler woman seeks to satisfy her own desire for a husband, the woman in *The Jizō Hall* seduces the monk in order to lead him to enlightenment. The woman in *The Jizō Hall*, the reader later learns, approached the monk only to acquire a copy of *The Lotus Sutra* and pursued their sexual relationship only to teach the monk a lesson. She thus plays the familiar role of the bodhisattva who assumes the guise of a beautiful woman to lead a sinner to a higher spiritual awareness. Her depiction thus stands in stark contrast to the gritty portrayal of the peddler woman in *The Useful Nun*, who actually flirts with the convention of the dissembling female deity. Instead of encountering a beauty who later leads him to Buddhist enlightenment, the monk in *The Useful Nun* begins with an elderly woman and ends with one, with no hope that she might be a goddess in disguise.

The Useful Nun parodies the kind of tale that *The Jizō Hall* becomes by its conclusion, in which a monk ultimately achieves spiritual awareness through a dalliance with a beautiful woman. Much of the humor of *The Useful Nun* in fact derives from the potential hypocrisy of the idea of sex as an expedient means and seems to imply the absurdity of that narrative formula. In the last text and painting of *The Useful Nun*, for example, the priest wonders whether his predicament might in fact be the "seed of enlightenment" (*kore mo omoi satori no tane naran*).[21] The painting depicts the monk facing the altar with his back to the woman, as if desperately praying for her transformation into a bodhisattva (fig. 73). In contrast to *The Useful Nun*, *The Jizō Hall* takes its source texts and its own place within the *setsuwa* tradition more seriously. Though it plays with narrative genres and often changes their formulaic endings, it does so without undermining the didactic message of its prototypes.

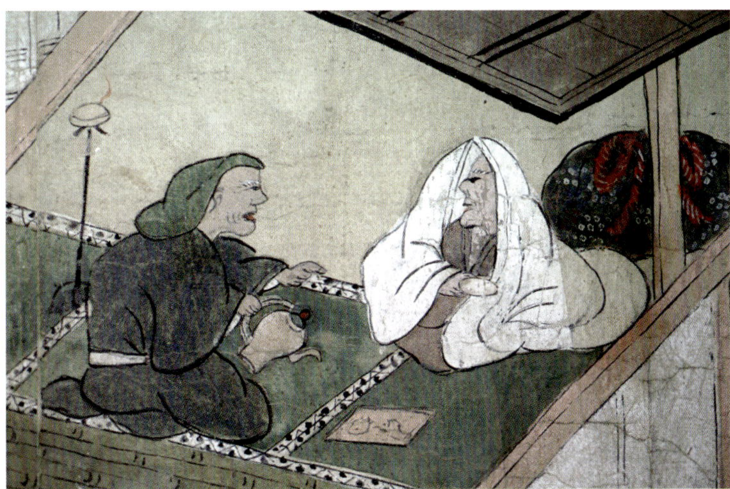

74 *The Useful Nun* (*Oyō no ama*). Sixteenth century. Two handscrolls; ink and color on paper. Suntory Museum of Art, Tokyo. Detail.

The contrast between *The Useful Nun* and *The Jizō Hall* extends to their respective modes of painting. The paintings of *The Useful Nun* are pictorial caricatures that match the exaggerated depiction of the characters found in the text and thoroughly undermine the Buddhist platitudes in which those characters speak. Their portraits belie their self-images. In the scene in which the monk mistakes the old nun for a young woman, for example, the figures are brusquely rendered (fig. 74): the lines delineating their faces consist of short segments executed with unevenly inked brushes, the eyes of the two characters in profile appear as though viewed from the front, and the pupils are ill-defined, consisting of dark smudges, while short vertical lines make up the eyebrows, to which thick white pigment has been added. While these characteristics may indicate the hand of an amateur, or at the very least a painter with much less polish than Mitsunobu, the rough style effectively conveys the humor of the tale and the degenerate state of monk and nun. The characters' mouths, although simply rendered, contain a touch of red between slightly parted lips that suggests that both characters may be toothless. And although the robe draped over the nun's head is meant to disguise her as a young woman, her white eyebrows, made conspicuous by the heavy white pigment blotchily applied, suggest that the monk is too easily taken in. The artist also deftly captured the appearance of the monk's aged body as he eagerly kneels before the woman pouring *sake*; his back is markedly hunched, and the white eyebrows and wrinkles around his mouth emphasize his advanced years. The looseness of the pictorial style and disregard for the politesse of normative painterly representation thus match the parodic nature of the text while encouraging the viewer to treat the main characters mirthfully. This differs from Mitsunobu's refined images, in which the figures maintain a robust respectability throughout the scroll.

Another important element that shapes period characterizations of the wayward monk is the representation of his age. In both *Whispering Bamboo* and *The Useful Nun* the monks are said to be elderly, which seems to have made their sexual exploits all the more comical.[22] The desire for beautiful young women on the part of such venerables leads to predictable conclusions; the monk in *The Useful Nun* suffers the fitting punishment of having to live out his days with an old woman instead of with the youthful bride he had coveted. In *Tale of the Fox* another man of the cloth is wizened as well, and the paintings bare his wrinkled body for the viewer to behold. In the context of the minimal depiction of nudity in medieval picture scrolls, the representation of the naked monk here registers unambiguously its parodic intent. In a scene in which the old man readies himself for his amorous liaison with the fox woman, he showers on the veranda (fig. 75), where his bony chest and sagging breasts are exposed to the viewer. Running the water through his hair, he appears to wash himself rather vigorously in anticipation of his rendezvous. To the left of the shower scene, the monk appears again, standing in the doorway, now fully clothed and in his priestly garb, ready for his meeting. The monk is exposed again in the sixth painting section of the scroll, after he realizes that everything he had experienced with the fox woman had been an illusion. The elegant mansion was nothing but a dilapidated old house littered with bones and trash, while the luxurious robe he thought he had donned turns out to have been a pathetic patchwork of waste paper (fig. 76). Donning nothing but these rags, the monk crawls on his hands and knees from beneath the decrepit building. A group of children heckle him as he exits the gate, whereupon a sympathetic passerby gives him a short robe to cover himself.

In contrast to all three of these tales, *The Jizō Hall* focuses on the amorous exploits of a youthful monk.[23] As he follows the woman to the undersea realm, he resembles one of the romantic heroes from tales such as *Urashima Tarō* rather than a stereotypical lecherous old monk.[24] The monk's relative youth at the beginning of *The Jizō Hall* even seems to render his actions more forgivable and his redemption at the end of the scroll more convincing. He ages before our eyes in the final two paintings of the scroll and in the last scene appears as a venerable old monk, purged of sexual desire. The monk is spared the public humiliation found in *Tale of the Fox* and *Whispering Bamboo*. There are no witnesses to his most embarrassing moments, such as the revelation of the sutra miscopying and his issuance from the serpent, which is said to have taken place in the middle of the night. Moreover, the narrator makes a point of saying that "no one made the connection that the monk had emerged from the snake" (*kono sō hebi no naka yori idetaru koto, sono toki wa shiritaru mono mo nakarikeri*). And because hundreds of years had passed when the monk encountered the other priests of the Jizō Hall, none of them realized it was he who had run off with the Dragon King's daughter. The narrator goes on to say that "later people began to understand" (*ato sama ni zo hito mo shiritari keru*), but this seems to imply a quiet acceptance. Thus, the monk in *The Jizō Hall*

75 Kanō Tan'yū, *Tale of the Fox* (*Kitsune sōshi emaki*). Seventeenth century. Copy of fifteenth-century scroll. One handscroll; ink and color on paper. Department of Japanese Literature, Gakushūin University, Tokyo.

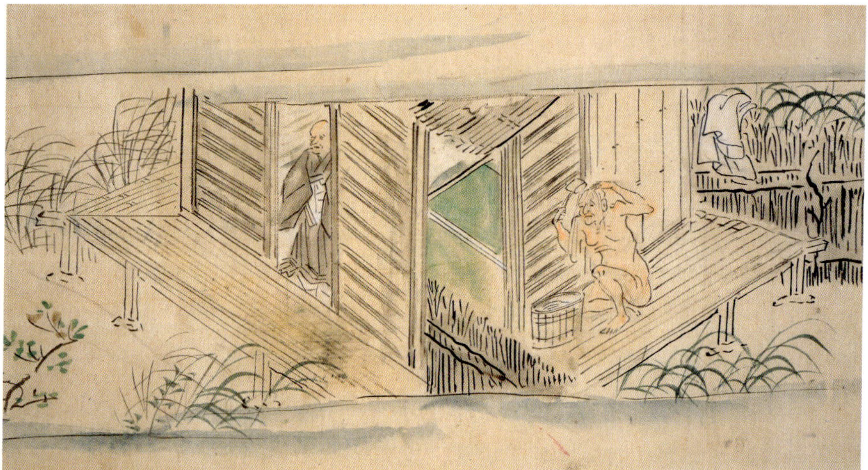

76 Kanō Tan'yū, *Tale of the Fox* (*Kitsune sōshi emaki*). Seventeenth century. Copy of fifteenth-century scroll. One handscroll; ink and color on paper. Department of Japanese Literature, Gakushūin University, Tokyo.

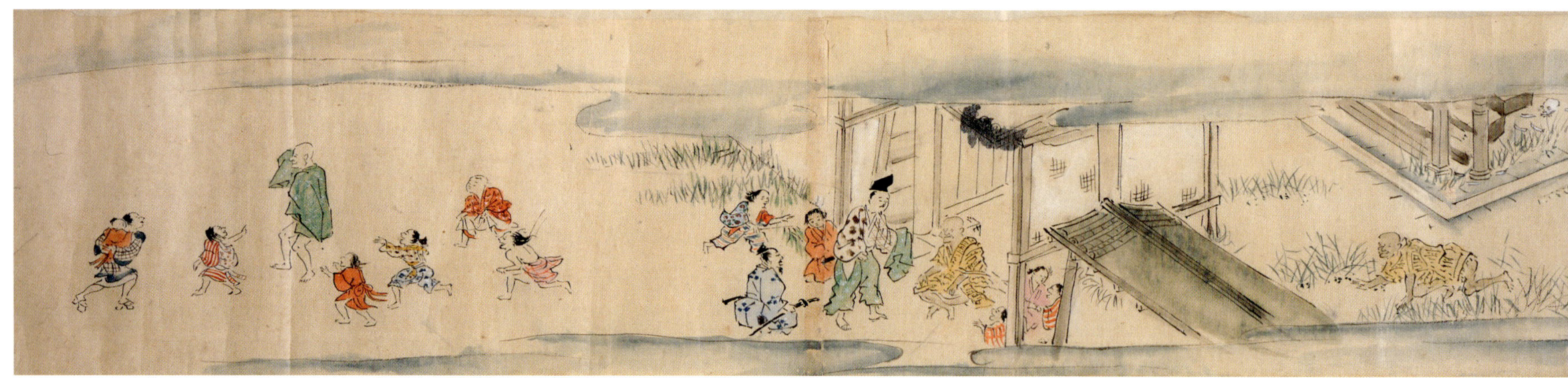

develops into a sympathetic protagonist by the end of the scroll, when he appears as an admirable old man whose awakened state is indicated by his seated posture, closely associated with immanent rebirth in paradise.

The Jizō Hall thus draws upon certain tendencies of errant-monk tales, such as their comedic episodes, and borrows as well from the figure of the gullible monk, but recuperates the protagonist's moral standing by the end of the tale. A full appreciation of the tale's accomplishment would be compromised by understanding it solely as a parody of the Buddhist clergy. While parody accounts for a measure of its appeal, and moments of real hilarity are found throughout, the primary narrative trajectory centers on the spiritual awareness gained through the expedient means of the dragon woman, ending with a didactic Buddhist message. The ending has a moral but does not moralize, differentiating it in a fundamental way from typical wayward-monk tales.

Accounts of Rebirth

Of the patterns of literary production that reverberate throughout *The Jizō Hall*, none is of greater importance than the *ōjōden*, or "account of rebirth." This story type designated brief narratives of paradisal attainment that were believed to have died out by the Muromachi period and have consequently not been an object of inquiry for scholars of the late medieval era, let alone commentators on *The Jizō Hall* or the small-scroll corpus. The neglect is not entirely unjustified: not only were compilations of these accounts thought to have died out by the thirteenth century (not to be revived until the seventeenth), but the majority of rebirth accounts are too short to be compared with tale literature, and "pictures of rebirth" (*ōjōden-e*) as a specific genre are all but unknown. As I will demonstrate, however, in the creative and revivalist milieu of GoTsuchimikado's court (r. 1464–1500), rebirth accounts and pictures of them were being created. A description of how *The Jizō Hall* incorporates elements of this genre will establish a foundation for the argument that *The Jizō Hall* was conceptualized as an account of rebirth made for the emperor. As in the case of other tale types, however, rebirth accounts provided less a narrative template than a set of organizational tactics and literary devices for the authorship of a small scroll. By leaving the main character anonymous, introducing multiple temporal registers, and presenting a nonsectarian view of rebirth, *The Jizō Hall* alters its source beyond recognition and achieves a pictoliterary story line of uncanny flexibility.

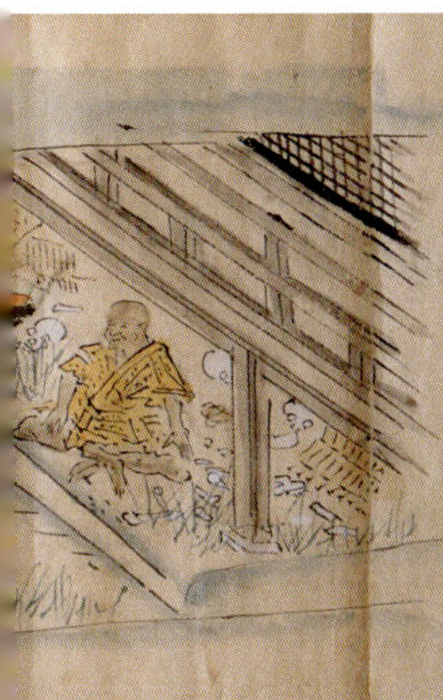

Accounts of rebirth consist of brief narratives of people believed to have been reborn into Amida's Pure Land. The genre flourished in the Heian period (794–1185), beginning with the earliest compilation of an *ōjōden* around 982, *A Record of Japanese Who Have Achieved Rebirth in Supreme Bliss* (*Nihon ōjō gokuraku ki*), and culminating in several prodigious collections from the early twelfth century.[25] The compilers were all laymen of the aristocratic class who aimed to encourage readers in their own endeavors toward rebirth; such Good Samaritanism undoubtedly improved their own fitness for this happy fate.[26] Compilations continued to appear in the thirteenth century, although they were largely by Buddhist monks with overtly sectarian agendas.[27] In a typical *ōjōden* the subject is introduced, his (or her) pious deeds or Buddhist devotions are enumerated, his death and its accompanying wondrous signs (purple clouds, strange fragrances, and heavenly music) are described, and the names of witnesses who vouch for the account's veracity are recorded. Rebirth is always the goal and climax of the account, and the stories often end with a description of the subject's posture at the time of death: seated, hands clasped in prayer or fixed in a mudra, facing toward the west, where Amida's Pure Land was understood to be located, and often in the process of chanting the name of the Amida Buddha (*nenbutsu*). The following account of rebirth from the *Shūi ōjōden* (1111), compiled by Miyoshi no Tameyasu (b. 1050), provides some idea of a typical *ōjōden* text:

Shimotsuke no Atsuse, Lieutenant of the Left Division of the Headquarters of the Inner Palace Guards, served as personal attendant and bodyguard to the emperor from his early youth through adulthood, yet never did he abandon his devotion

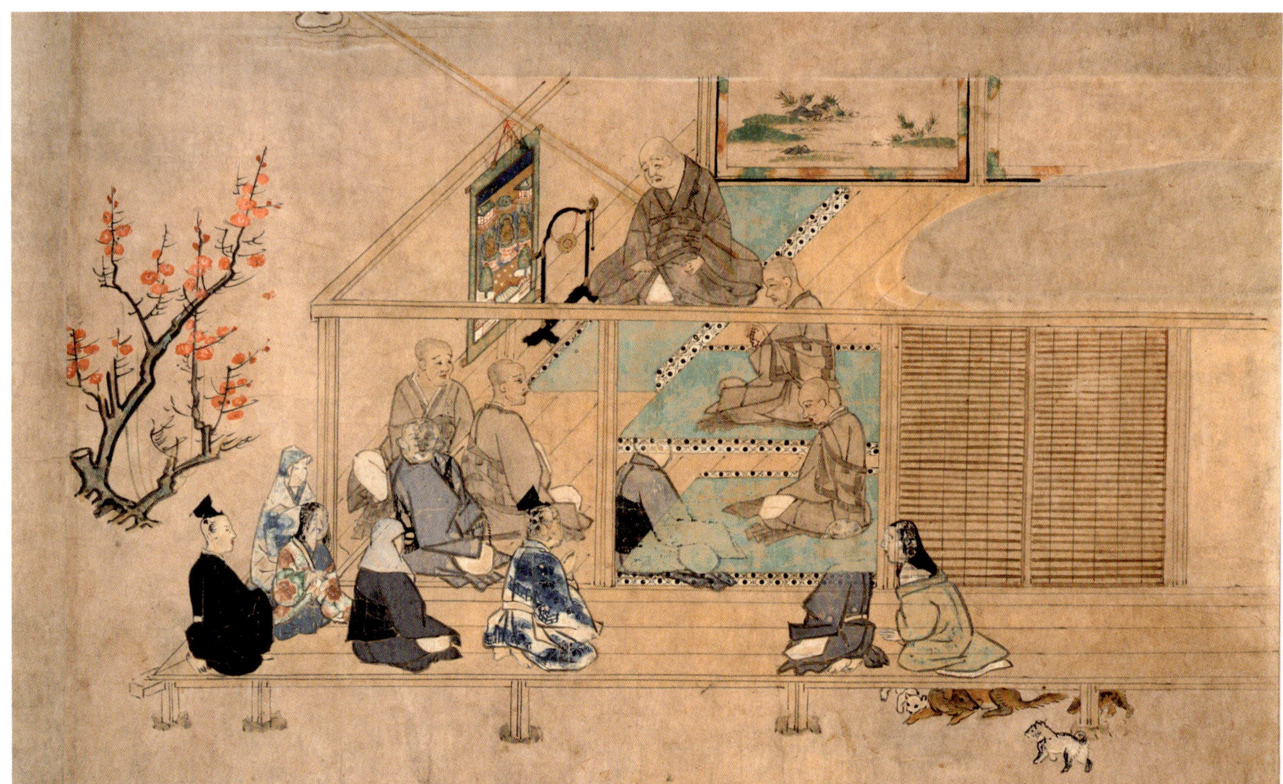

77 *Illustrated Life of Hōnen* (*Hōnen Shōnin eden*). Early fourteenth century. Forty-eight handscrolls; ink and color on paper. Chion'in, Kyoto. National Treasure. Detail, scroll 44.

to the *nenbutsu*. From his middle years onward, he was not begrudging of his own property and wealth, and constructed halls and buildings for Buddhist practices, and made copies of the Buddhist scriptures. After he left secular life his devotion increased all the more, and days followed upon nights as he completely forgot all endeavors apart from the *nenbutsu*.

On the fourteenth day of the first month of the lunar year of the second year of Eichō era [1096–97], he developed a slight illness. Immediately he bathed, and then, facing a sixteen-foot image of the Buddha Amida, he fastened a five-colored thread to the Buddha's hand, and holding the other end in his own hand, performed the *nenbutsu*. The following day he admonished his children and grandchildren and close attendants: "Today is the fifteenth day," he said. "You must not remain close by. You must not set my mind in disarray. Please do as I ask."

When the hour of the monkey arrived, there was a light from the direction of the southwest that illuminated his breast. Those nearby wondered at this, but when they looked outside the door, there was no sunlight whatsoever, but only dark clouds.

That day a woodcutter came out of the mountains and reported to those assembled: "There are strange clouds in the West," he said. "They have formed a layer that hangs like a blanket over this place. The clouds are of an unusual color. The reason I have come is to inform you of what I have seen."

After the evening sun set, and as the night grew still, seated properly with palms pressed together and facing the West, he ceased breathing.

After his breath had ceased, he remained as before, properly seated with palms pressed together. For several days the man's clothing at the spot where the brilliant light had shone upon it was all of a golden color. It did not change it in the least. Of those who witnessed this or heard of it, there was no one who was not filled with wonder.

A personal note: The place where his life came to an end was Ichijō Horikawa. The hall still exists today, and I myself have seen it.[28]

Although accounts of rebirth were not regularly pictorialized, illustrated biographies of eminent monks incorporated aspects of the genre into their paintings. Such is the case with *Illustrated Life of Hōnen* (*Hōnen Shōnin eden*, ea. fourteenth century), concerning the life and teachings of Hōnen (1133–1212), the founder of the Pure Land sect of Buddhism (*Jōdoshū*).[29] Consisting of forty-eight scrolls, it represents the most extensive handscroll project in the history of the format. The scrolls seek to document the efficacy of chanting Amida's name as a means to being reborn in the Pure Land, a cornerstone of the doctrine preached by Hōnen. Of the 235 scenes illustrated in the scrolls, 54 of them depict other individuals, many of them Hōnen's devoted disciples, achieving paradisal reincarnation at the moment of death. The *Hōnen* scrolls present an encyclopedic array of death scenes. The paintings usually depict a dying subject bathed in golden rays of light and surrounded by friends and followers, who witness the miraculous event. Postures at the moment of passing vary, with some people seated and some lying on their sides, and various paraphernalia are depicted to represent the moment of rebirth, such as hanging scrolls of the welcoming Amida or of paradise itself (fig. 77). Like their written counterparts, the numerous rebirths pictorialized in the *Hōnen* scrolls, presented one after another in vivid detail, were meant to persuade the viewer of the efficacy of the sect and its practices.

The Jizō Hall incorporates elements from both the narrative structure of written *ōjōden* and scenes of rebirth of the type found in the *Hōnen* scrolls. Indeed, its story opens much like a traditional account of rebirth, purporting to document the event by introducing its historical setting:

> At a time now past, in a place called Sugano in the province of Echigo, there was a mysterious Jizō Hall. And in this hall was a monk who had begun a one-thousand-day copying of *The Lotus Sutra* in accordance with the Law.[30]

But, in contrast to most accounts of rebirth, here the monk's name is not given. Although stories with an anonymous subject are known among earlier examples, most make a point of mentioning the lack of a name and note the monk's temple instead.[31] Thus, already at the outset, *The Jizō Hall* establishes a usefully ambiguous quality that oscillates (oddly) between the specificity of rebirth tales and the generic quality of other forms of fiction.

In contrast, the conclusion of *The Jizō Hall* adopts the framework of an account of rebirth through its provision of proof of lineage. The final seven lines of text 7 explain the tale's origins and reintroduce the place-name of Sugano in Echigo as the hometown of the monk who transmitted the story, the holy man Fumon. The final paragraph reads:

> This tale is found among stories collected from long ago. Sugano is the birthplace of the late monk of Tōfukuji, Mukan Chōrō Fumon Shōnin. The head of the snake is still there today; [Fumon Shōnin] saw it himself and related this to the Zen monk Kitayama Reigen Ryōshinbō.[32]

These two monks named at the end of the tale were well-known historical figures and no doubt familiar to the scroll's initial readers. Mukan Fumon (1212–91) was a prominent Zen monk and a disciple of Enni Ben'en (Shōichi Kokushi, 1202–80), the founder of the Kyoto Zen monastery Tōfukuji.[33] Fumon himself was the third abbot of Tōfukuji and the founder of the Zen monastery Nanzenji.[34] Fumon's birthplace was not Sugano, as *The Jizō Hall* text says, but he did spend his youth in Echigo Province.[35] The other person mentioned in the conclusion to *The Jizō Hall*, Kitayama Reigen Ryōshinbō, referred to as a "Zen monk" (*aru zensō*), was a disciple of Fumon whose biography was recorded in the *Record of the Transmission of the Flame in the Enpō Era* (*Enpō dentōroku*, 1678).[36]

The ending thus confirms the story's route of transmission, certified by invoking the authority of two Zen monks. Fumon, a priest with ties to Echigo, is reported to have actually witnessed the snake head while in the province and then reported it to Reigen. The verification of the oral transmission of the story recalls the documentary tenor of *ōjōden*. The calligraphy of the final paragraph sets it apart from the body of the text (fig. 2-0); all seven lines are indented, conveying visually that

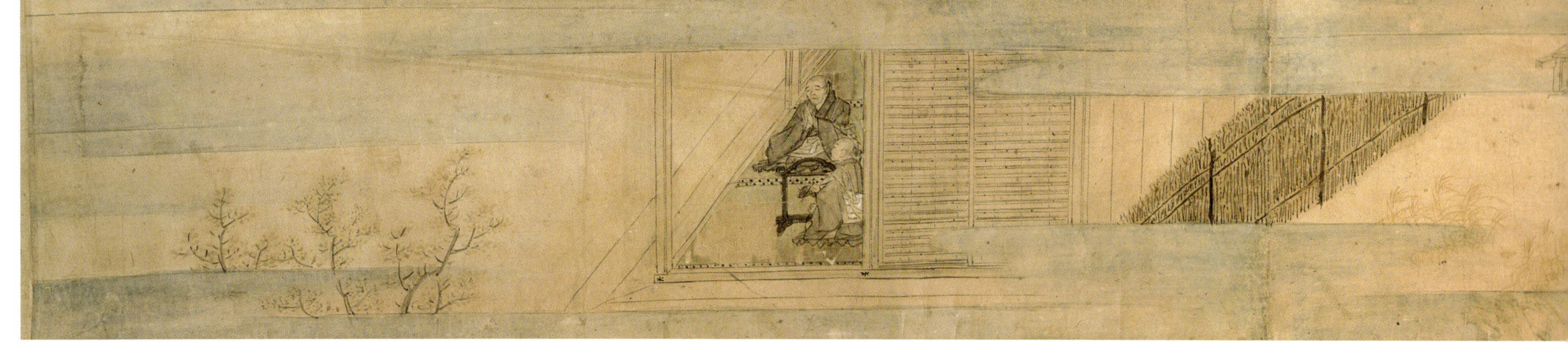

78 Tosa Mitsunobu, *The Jizō Hall* (*Jizōdō sōshi emaki*). Late fifteenth century. One scroll; ink, color, and gold on paper, 17.2 x 1578.4 cm. Private collection.

they are the words of someone outside the story. This distinction visually corresponds to the addenda seen in *ōjōden* compilations, which conclude with a line quite similar to the last line in *The Jizō Hall*, in which the narrator verifies, "The hall still exists today and I myself have seen it."

Unlike typical accounts of rebirth, which make a point of clearly identifying the date and timing of the rebirth, however, *The Jizō Hall* constructs multiple temporal layers that confound an understanding of when the events actually took place. Thus, the protagonist's seemingly brief sojourn in the Dragon Palace actually lasts over two hundred years. This temporal expansion creates a distant past within the confines of the narrative itself; the monk returns to the Jizō Hall and hears the events of his life spoken about as ancient lore. With no reign names given, nor any other indication of when the monk lived, the story becomes unmoored from the specific settings that so characterized earlier rebirth accounts.

Pictorially the final scene in *The Jizō Hall* evokes a typical scene of rebirth but pares it down to the bare essentials (fig. 78); it omits many of the motifs found in the *Hōnen* scrolls, such as the Amida paintings, some with strings attached and held by the dying subject to lead him into the next world. The lack of Buddhist images may have been meant to reflect the humble state of the Jizō Hall, as well as the lonely atmosphere in which the monk found himself, as mentioned in the text. The lone priest in the foreground, in contrast to the throngs of people depicted in the scenes of rebirth in the *Hōnen* scrolls, also conveys humility and isolation. The minimalization of motifs and figures in *The Jizō Hall* implies a different function from that of a work like *Illustrated Life of Hōnen*. The scenes of rebirth in the *Hōnen* scrolls instruct a viewer on the particulars of dying, both to elucidate the process and to verify the actuality of the events for the promotion of the sect. The individuals depicted were actual disciples of Hōnen, in keeping with the agenda of pictorial verification.

The Jizō Hall uses the *ōjōden* narrative structure to create an overarching framework for the tale but transforms the genre from within. Diverse literary formations, thus subsumed, are integrated in such a way so as to lead inexorably to the climax of rebirth. Rather than being a story about the miraculous powers of Jizō, *The Jizō Hall* portrays the journey of its protagonist from earnest practitioner to sinner to religious exemplar. And though the scroll exploits characterizations found in tales about errant monks, the monk in *The Jizō Hall* is differentiated from those in other tales by his lack of guile. Nevertheless, the use of a frame story allows the picture scroll to be seen as an illustration of cause and effect: it begins with the monk copying *The Lotus Sutra* for his own salvation and ends with the attainment of that goal. Although many elements have been borrowed from earlier traditions to reach this point, the tale's narrative thread appears to trace the karmic trajectory of one individual.

THE SHADOW PROTAGONIST

A careful reading and an even more careful viewing, however, indicate otherwise. The monk's ostensible foil in *The Jizō Hall*, the dragon woman, is more than simply a catalyst for her male counterpart's salvation and is arguably the more intriguing character in the story. An oblique rereading of the tale, focused on this female character, makes clear her status as a second protagonist. With a perspective thus sensitized brought to bear, the tale can be about the monk or the mysterious woman, the male spiritual aspirant or the female seductress, or both. Either can serve as the focus of the reader's identification or the vehicle for the exposition of Buddhist teaching. A close engagement with the text and images reveals that the woman in the tale is not simply the expedient means by which the monk achieves spiritual awareness but an autonomous character preoccupied with her own soteriological status. As such, she can be understood to tap into the concerns of late medieval readers, both men and women, anxious about the possibility of female rebirth in paradise. The definitive and auspicious closure to the monk's story only highlights the irresolution of the dragon woman's state, which consequently lingers in the mind. Much more than a one-dimensional character, the dragon woman is in fact an amalgamation of several fictional female types, all of which are an important part of her identity. In this way, as she changes guises in chameleon-like fashion, she comes to embody the intertextuality of the narrative itself, moving from seductress, to guardian deity, to Chinese maiden, to dragon woman, all the while alluding to a variety of tales that feature such feminine prototypes.[37]

The woman first appears in the standard role of the temptress, as signaled by her pose on the veranda of the monk's quarters in the first painting (fig. 79). Here a lady, simply dressed but aristocratic based on her grooming, leans toward the monk, who is absorbed in his sutra copying. In extending one hand toward him she assumes an assertive posture, at least by the standards of medieval picture scrolls. Yet this bearing also echoes that of other alluring sirens who have tempted unsuspecting monks and led them into regrettable situations, such as the beautiful messenger in *Tale of the Fox* (fig. 80). There the young woman who solicits this monk on behalf of the fox spirit assumes a virtually identical seated position, down to the solicitous hand softly touching the tatami border. Even the old woman in *The Useful Nun* strikes a similar pose when she first propositions the monk (fig. 72). In thus miming the comportment of other circulating examples of libertine women, the opening scene of *The Jizō Hall* establishes pictorially the promise of promiscuity in its female solicitor. But while these other female characters never transcend the role of the unchaste, the woman in *The Jizō Hall* emerges as a far more complex, multidimensional seductress.

79 Tosa Mitsunobu, *The Jizō Hall*. Detail, painting 1.

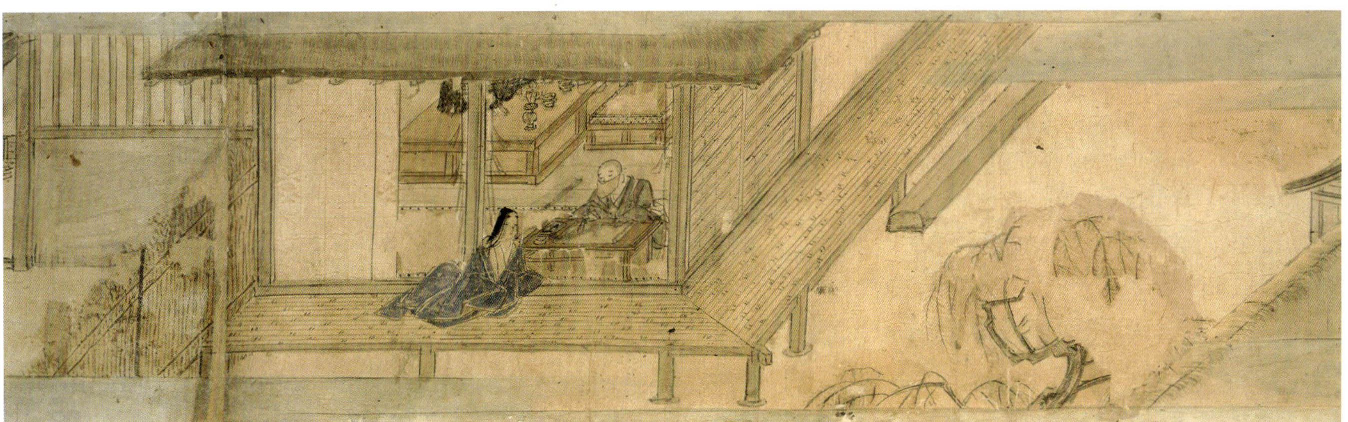

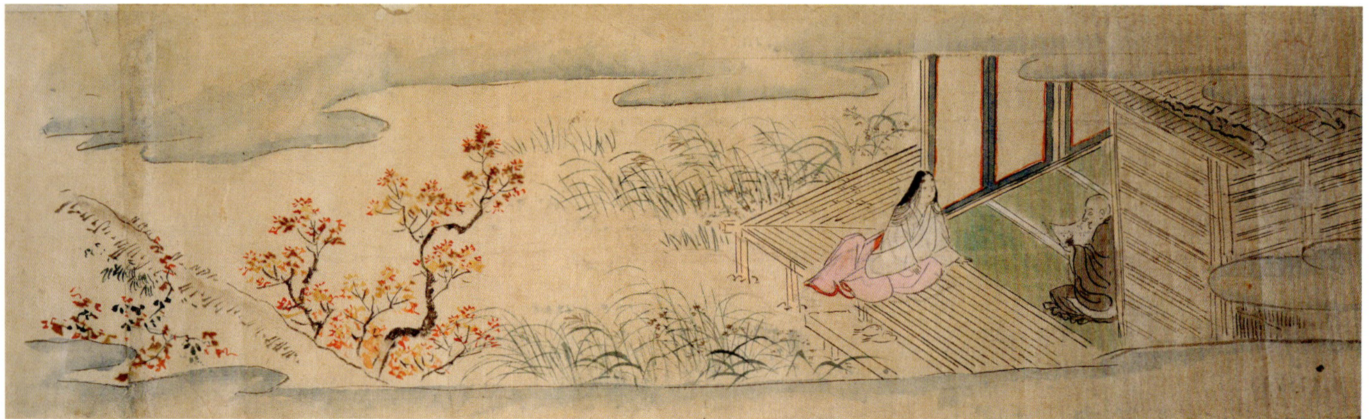

80 Kanō Tan'yū, *Tale of the Fox* (*Kitsune sōshi emaki*). Seventeenth century. Copy of fifteenth-century scroll. One handscroll; ink and color on paper. Department of Japanese Literature, Gakushūin University, Tokyo.

Already the second scene intimates unusual spiritual ambition on her part by describing her benevolence as akin to that of the "ten demons" (*jūrasetsu*), daughters of demons famously converted to Buddhism in the "Dharani" chapter of *The Lotus Sutra*, when she offers to provide financial assistance for the sutra copying.[38] These once-malevolent demon daughters vowed to use their own bodies to "protect those who accept and keep, read and recite, and put into practice" this sutra.[39] They came to be worshiped as protective female goddesses, and their images were sponsored by women and used for women's memorial services.[40] Likened in the text to those female guardians of the Dharma, in the second scene of *The Jizō Hall* the woman is depicted according to the pictorial iconography of the demon daughters (fig. 81). She is shown walking solemnly forward on the temple veranda carrying some of her donations for the "ten kinds of offerings" ceremony (*jisshu kuyō*), which traditionally concluded the one-thousand-day copying of the sutra (fig. 82).[41] Her upright, stately pose as she offers a tray of red- and gold-colored objects recalls similar painted instances of religious offering on the part of the demon daughters, such as Kyokushi (fig. 83), who is often found offering up an incense burner on a tray as she accompanies the bodhisattva Fugen.[42] More of the woman's generous offerings appear in a large chest

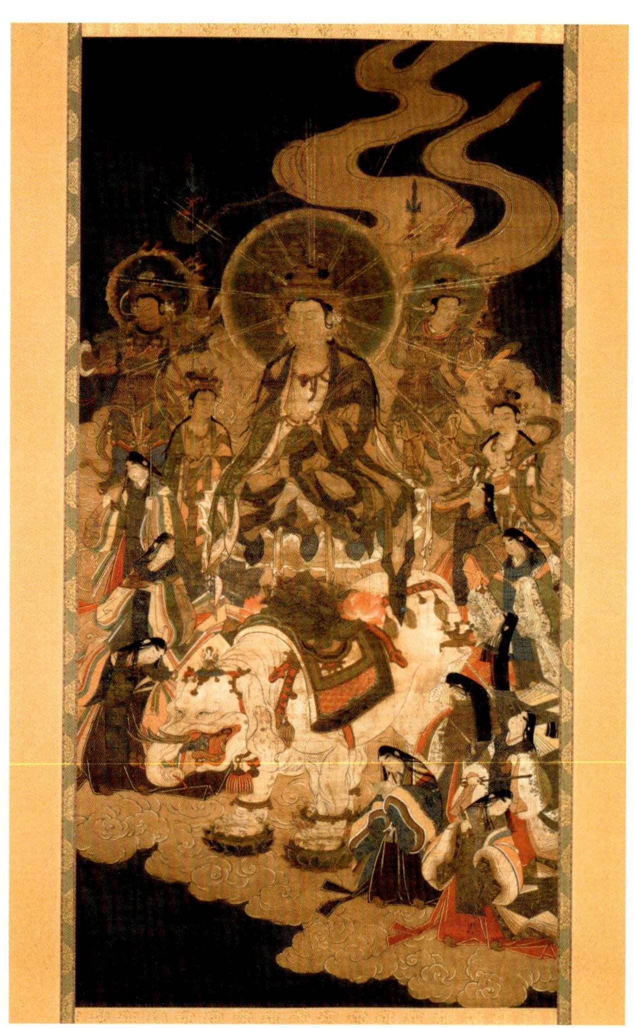

81 *Bodhisattva Fugen and the Ten Demon Daughters* (*Fugen Jūrasetsunyo zō*). Kamakura period. Hanging scroll; ink and color on silk. Nara National Museum. Important Cultural Property.

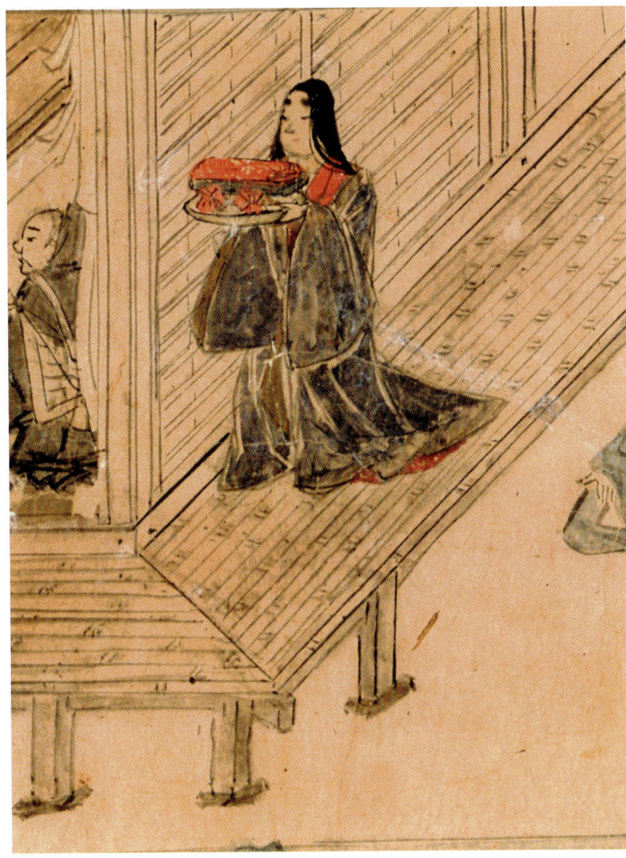

82 *The Jizō Hall* (right). Detail.

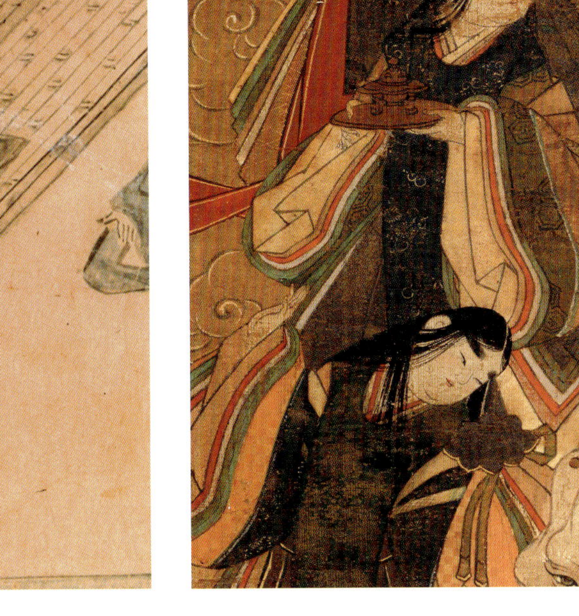

83 *Fugen Jūrasetsunyo* (left). Detail of fig. 81, Kyokushi.

beside her kneeling attendants, the cover of which lies open to reveal what appear to be patterned silks and embroidered brocades that are said to have helped transform the humble Jizō Hall into a magnificent temple. In pose, gesture, and action, then, the female benefactress is transformed into a guardian of the *Lotus Sutra* herself. The painting takes the text at its word.

By the third painting, the woman has undergone yet another transformation, this time emerging as an otherworldly nymph. Her portrayal here evokes enchanting sea creatures of ancient tales, such as the eighth-century tale *Urashima Tarō* and several Tang period (618–907) prose tales that relate encounters between young men and lithe goddesses of rivers, streams, and lakes.[43] In this instance, however, the change is sudden. In the first two paintings she appears as a highborn Japanese woman wearing a red undergarment and layered robes on top, with long black hair extending down the length of her back, like the beauties in courtly romances of old. But as soon as the pair enters the palace beneath the sea, she metamorphoses into what the monk describes as "a heavenly maiden" (*tennyo*). With her red hair ornament, upswept hairdo, and flowing scarf, she resembles representations of heavenly and/or Chinese maidens in East Asian painting more broadly (fig. 84). Her dress, and especially the looped braids atop her head, recall the elusive siren of the Song period handscroll *Nymph of the Luo River* (fig. 85).[44] Also evoked is the famous Chinese woman Zenmyō from the thirteenth-century Japanese picture scrolls *Lives of the Founders of the Kegon Sect* (fig. 86).[45] Even the colors of the woman's costume, an orange robe and a green scarf wrapped around her arms, are similar to Zenmyō's attire (fig. 87), no doubt a chromatic combination that was deemed appropriate for the exotica of both scrolls.

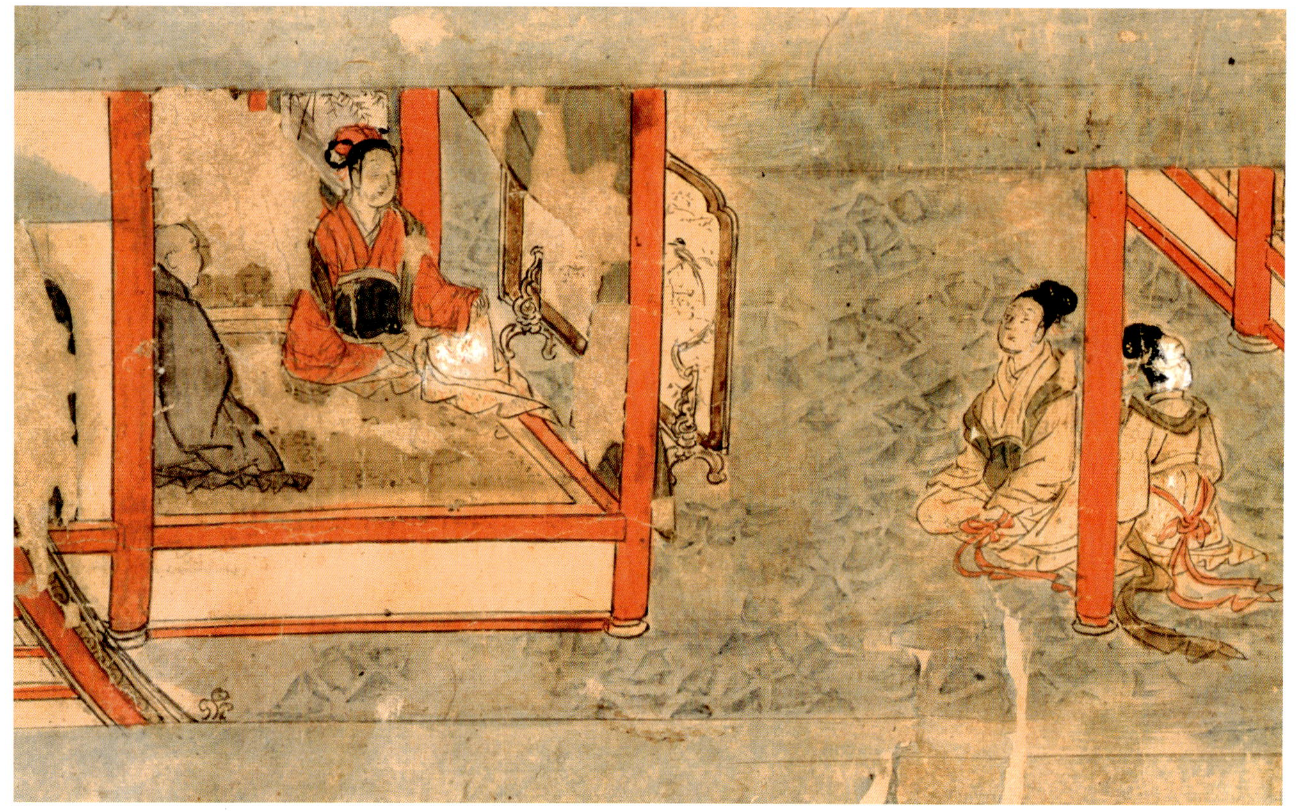

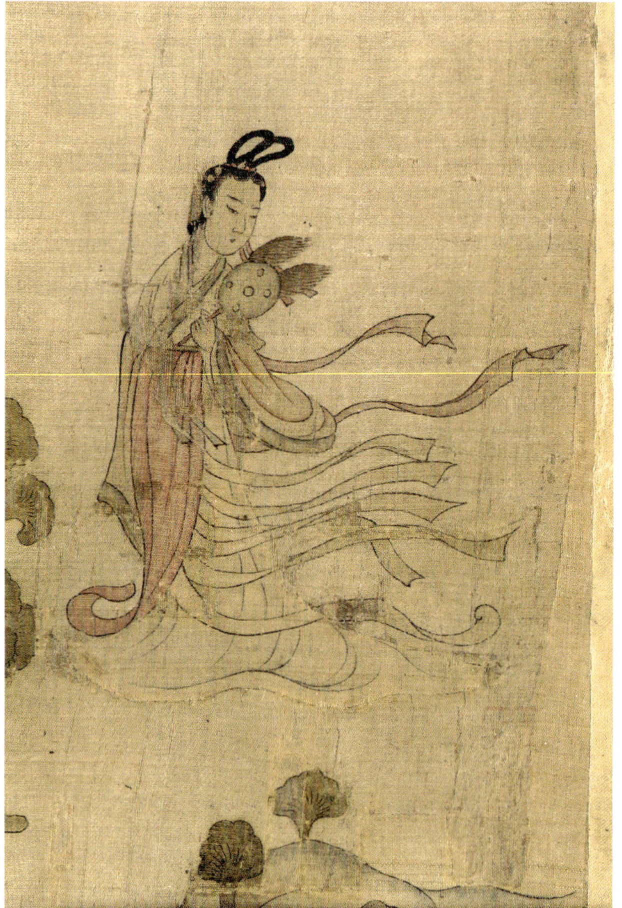

84 *The Jizo Hall*. Detail, painting 3.

85 *Nymph of the Luo River*. Traditionally attributed to Gu Kaizhi (ca. 344–ca. 406). Chinese, twelfth–thirteenth century. One handscroll, ink and color on silk, 29.7 x 896.1 cm. Freer Gallery of Art, Smithsonian Institution, Washington D.C. Gift of Charles Lang Freer. Detail.

It is at this point that the graceful and cosmopolitan image of the benefactress takes a turn for the supernatural. One night while sleeping with his paramour, the monk notices that the hem of her garment resembles the tail of a snake. Having already begun to harbor a sneaking suspicion that he may have entered the legendary underwater abode of the Dragon Palace, the monk's fears are confirmed by the sight of the scaly appendage. A deep anxiety overtakes him as he begins to wonder about his fate. At this point it becomes clear that the now-amphibian heroine is being cast in the mold of yet another common female paragon of medieval Japanese tale literature, that of the dragon woman. In fact, this serpentine character was commonplace in Chinese lore

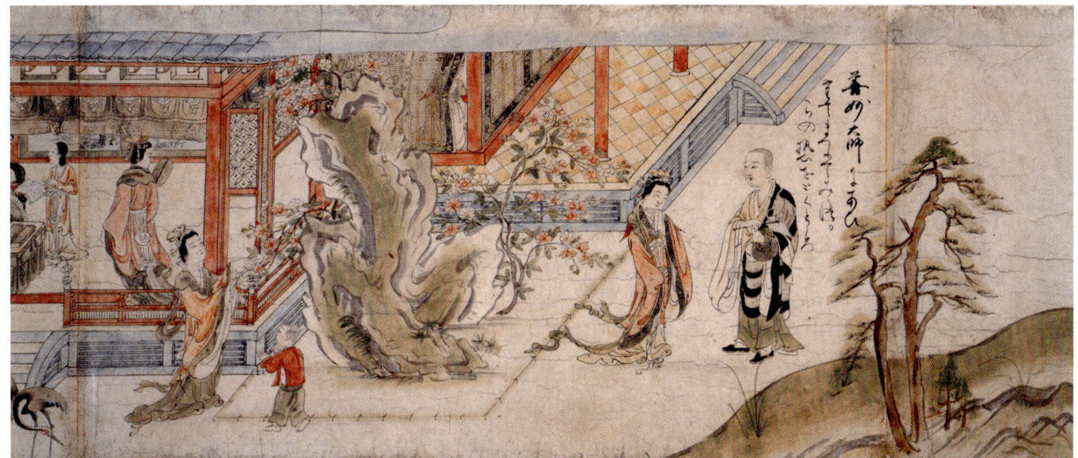

86 *Lives of the Founders of the Kegon Sect* (*Kegonshū sōshi eden*). Thirteenth century. Seven scrolls; ink and color on paper, H. 31.7 cm. Kōzanji, Kyoto.

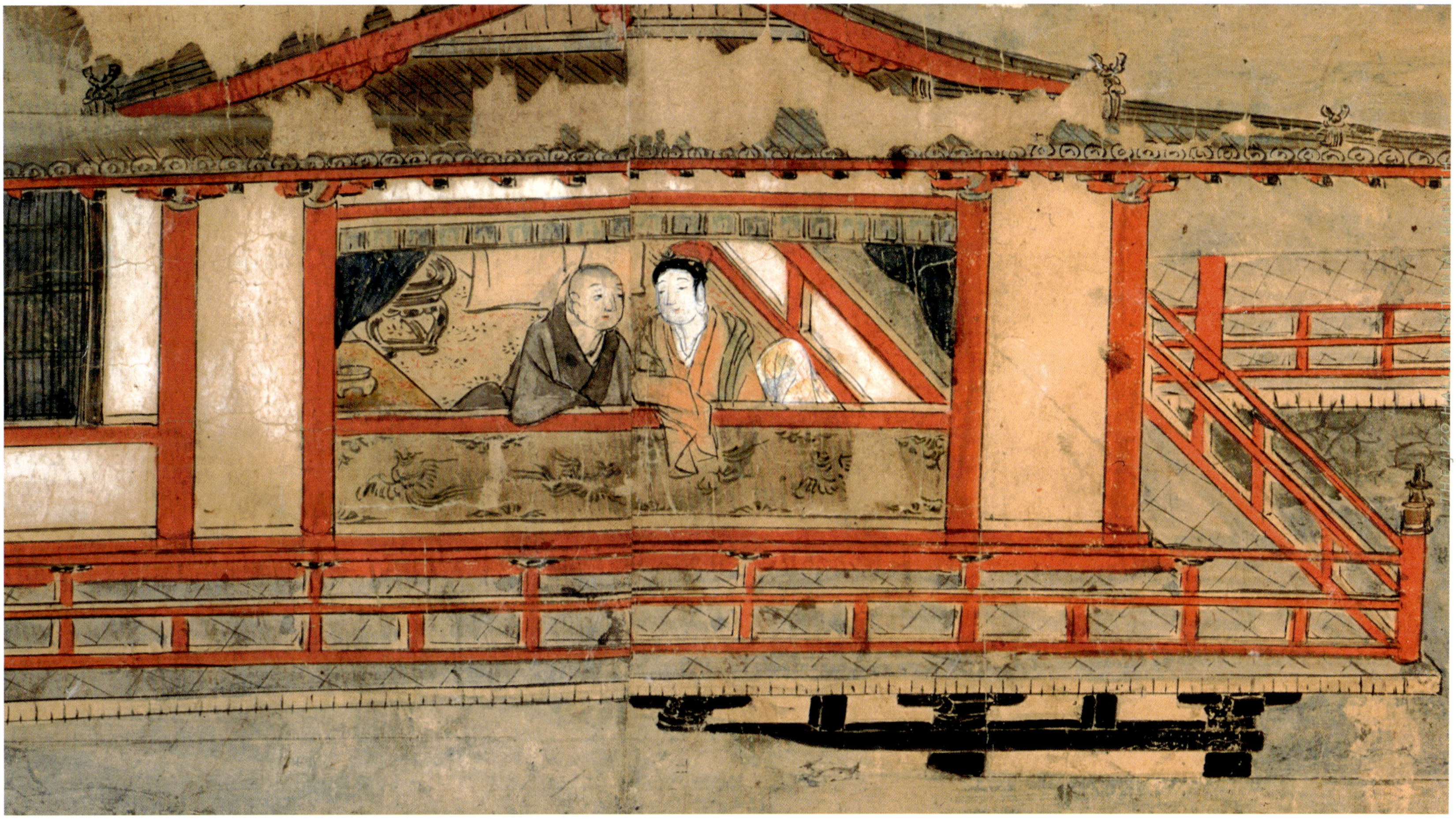

87 *The Jizo Hall*. Detail, painting 4.

from as early as the Tang period and could fulfill a whole range of literary functions, from seductress to savior. The mytheme of the serpent woman or, more precisely, what Fabio Rambelli calls "the semantic field of snake-serpent-dragon" represents an ambiguous presence, at once benign and ferocious.[46] Countless examples from Japanese literature demonstrate that the serpent woman, once her true nature is revealed and her rage is unleashed, can become a lethal threat to her lover. Such is the case for the monk on a pilgrimage to Kumano in *The Tale of Dōjōji*, an eleventh-century tale with an extant illustrated version roughly contemporary with *The Jizō Hall*.[47] There, when the monk protagonist parts ways with a woman who had fallen in love with him, she transforms into a fire-breathing snake and pursues him across land and water (fig. 88). Although he attempts to hide inside the bell of Dōjōji Temple, the serpent woman finds him, wraps herself around the bell, and spits flames of fire until the monk inside is burned beyond recognition (fig. 89).

Ultimately, however ferocious they may appear, such serpent women are usually subdued by the story's conclusion, revealing themselves to be an expedient means (*hōben*) of the Buddha, like undercover Buddhist operatives who direct sentient beings toward salvation. Such is the case with the frightening woman in *The Tale of Dōjōji* picture scroll, who in the end emerges as a catalyst of the monk's rebirth. After *The Lotus Sutra* is recited on the monk's behalf, both the woman and the monk reappear as heavenly beings seated on a cloud (fig. 90), while the text explains her predetermined role. Similarly, in *Lives of the Founders of the Kegon Sect*, Zenmyō undergoes a daunting serpentine transformation after being rejected by the monk Gishō (fig. 5), but ultimately she sacrifices herself to assist him. Transforming into a dragon, she escorts Gishō to his homeland and undergoes a second metamorphosis into a giant boulder

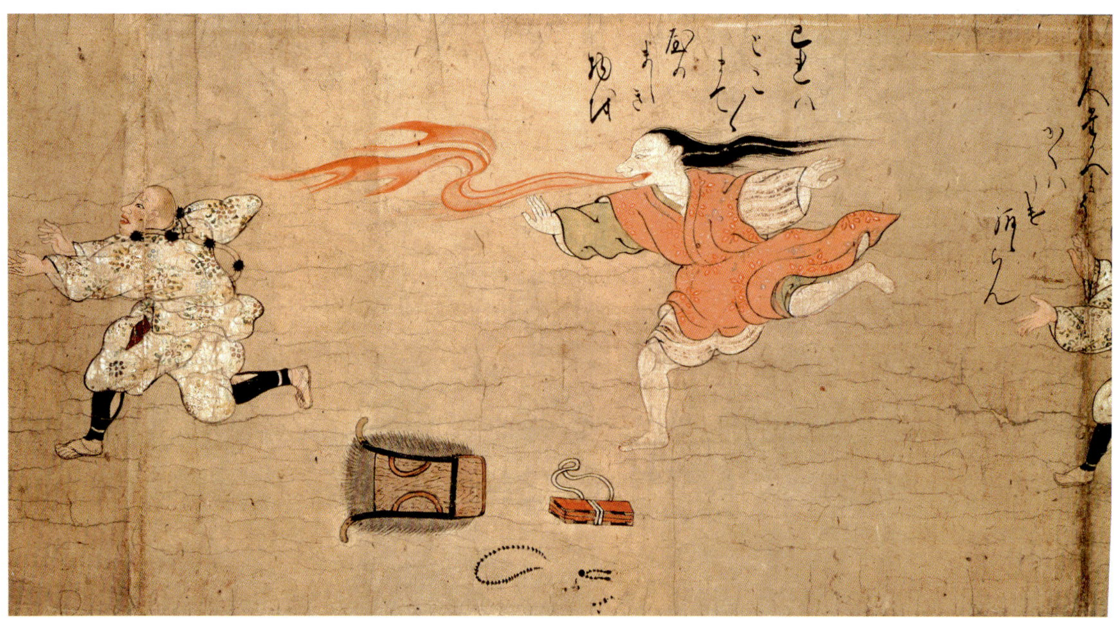

88 *The Tale of Dōjōji* (*Dōjōji engi emaki*). Sixteenth century. Two handscrolls; ink and color on paper. Dōjōji, Wakayama Prefecture. Important Cultural Property. Detail, scroll 1.

89 *The Tale of Dōjōji*. Detail, scroll 2.

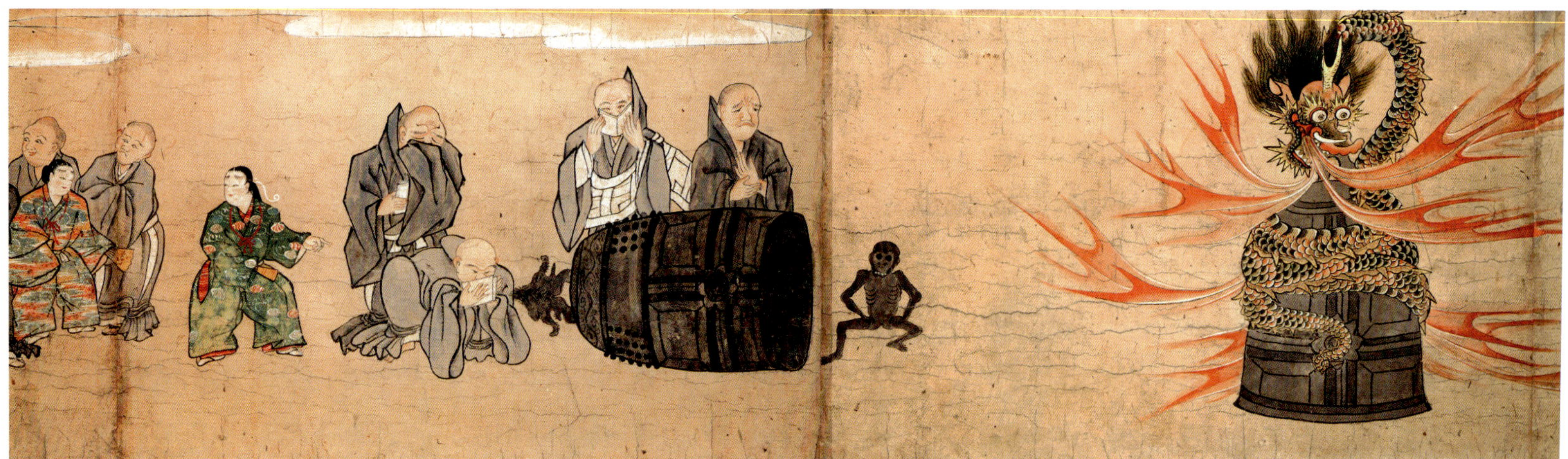

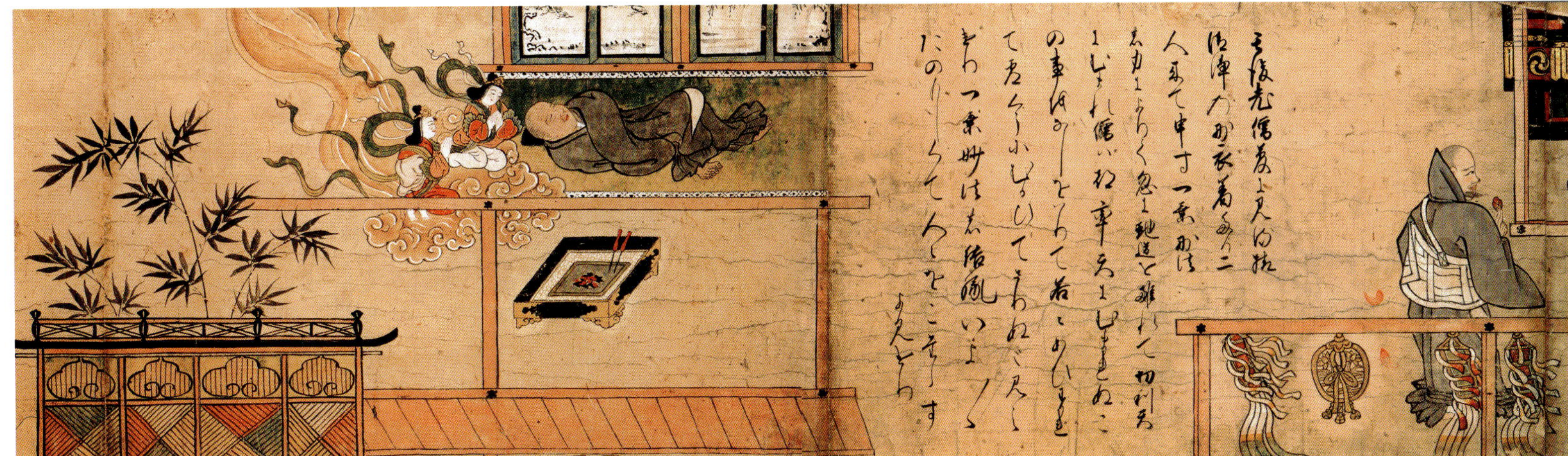

90 *The Tale of Dōjōji.* Detail, scroll 2.

that paves the way for Gishō to establish his own temple as well as the Kegon sect in Silla. In these stories the force of the serpent-feminine is harnessed to promote the spiritual advancement or religious goals of the male protagonists. The culmination of *The Jizō Hall* suggests that the woman in this instance fills just such a role. In this regard, the female character appears as the quintessential bodhisattva-like figure, who aids sentient beings in achieving enlightenment through some form of sacrifice. As in many other stories, the woman uses her sexual allure simply to direct the monk to the proper path and to expedite his salvation.

The woman in *The Jizō Hall* differs from those in other reptilian-transformation tales, however, in one striking way: she is not an anonymous serpent woman, a cold-blooded dragon queen, but in fact a daughter of the Dragon King; she calls to mind in particular the young Dragon Girl from the "Devadatta" chapter of *The Lotus Sutra*. In the medieval period, the Dragon Girl came to stand as a symbol of the possibility of female Buddhahood, despite the so-called five obstructions that women face.[48] Her enlightenment occurs when the bodhisattva Mañjuśrî appears before the Buddha and his disciples having just returned from preaching the sutra at the Dragon King's palace under the ocean. He reports having saved countless beings, among them the eight-year-old daughter of the Dragon King, whom he says achieved Buddhahood instantaneously. When one member of the group responds to this news with skepticism, the Dragon Girl suddenly appears before them to demonstrate her ability. The Buddha's disciple Sariputra says to her, "A woman's body is filthy, it is not a Dharma-receptacle. How can you attain unexcelled bodhi?"[49] She responds by offering up a precious jewel to the Buddha, who accepts it immediately. She then turns to the group and says, "With your supernatural power you shall see me achieve Buddhahood even more quickly than that!"[50] The members of the assembly then watch as she changes into a man, proceeds to the Spotless World of the South, takes a seat atop a jeweled lotus blossom, and attains awakening in the span of an instant. The chapter ends with the bodhisattvas looking on in silence and accepting the Dragon Girl's achievement, demonstrating both the facility of this female serpent-dragon and the power of *The Lotus Sutra* to redeem even the most marginalized beings.

The woman in *The Jizō Hall* evokes the Dragon Girl from *The Lotus Sutra*, first and foremost as a denizen of the Dragon Palace. The Dragon Palace became a complex topos in the medieval Japanese imaginary, at once a dark, watery underworld and a sacred realm of the Dharma, in some cases even associated with paradise. Certain sutras claimed it as the site where all sacred texts would be preserved between the death of the historical Buddha and the appearance of the future Buddha Maitreya.[51] Thus, in the fifth text in the scroll,

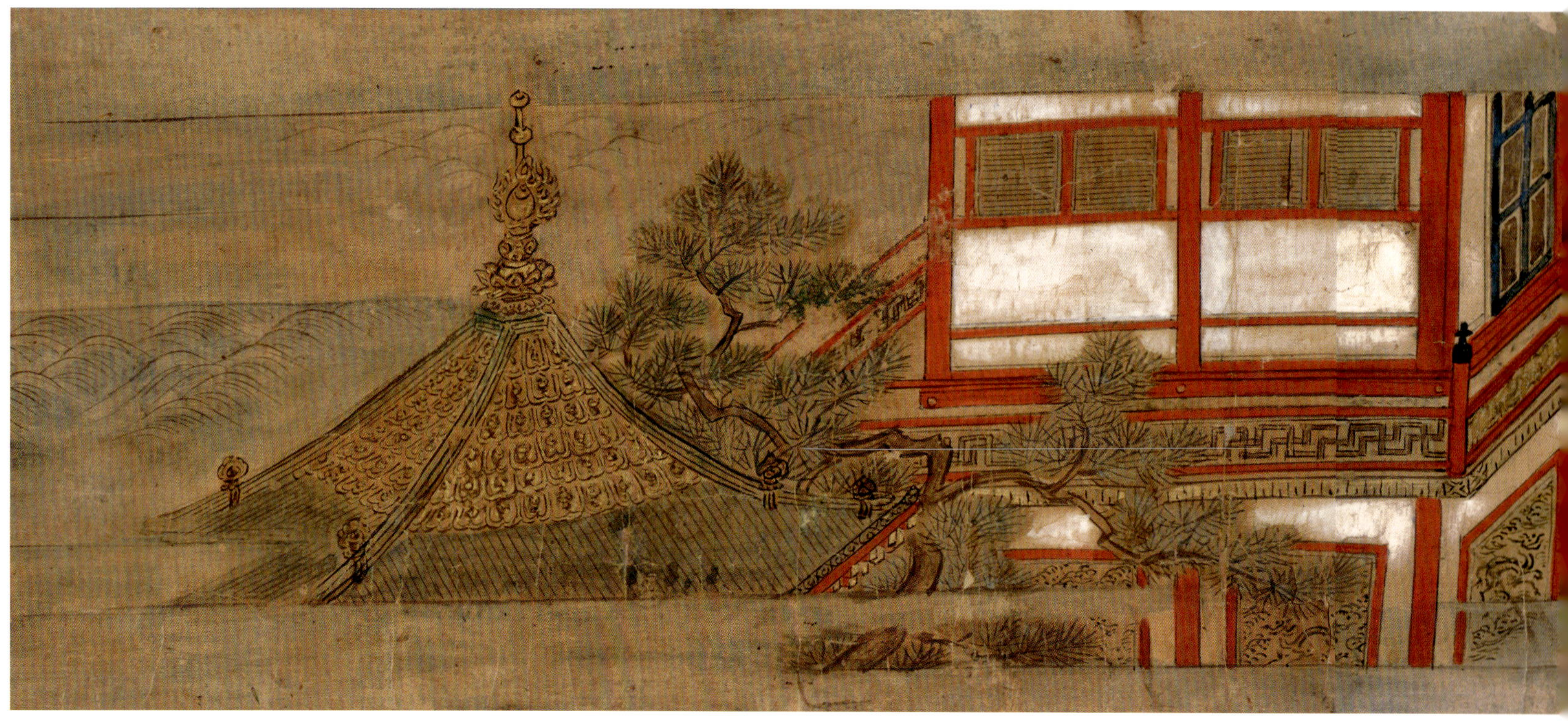

91 *The Jizō Hall.* Detail, painting 5, sutra repository.

after the monk confronts the woman with his desire to leave, she explains, "This palace contains a sutra repository preserving great numbers of sacred texts." And in the painting of the Dragon Palace that follows this passage (fig. 91), Mitsunobu includes buildings that communicate the site's function as Dharma archive to the viewer. Positioned at the end of a horizontal sequence of images that meanders through the rooms of the Dragon Palace, the image of the sutra repository leaves the viewer with an impression of the numinous quality of this aqueous realm. The building has an almost auratic presence, as it quietly hovers unoccupied between mist bands and the water below. Churning waves beneath the fantastical bridge lap up against the building's first floor, where the walls of each of its bays are emblazoned with images of dragons. Connoting another aspect of the Dragon Palace myth is the flaming jewel finial atop a pyramidal roof depicted to the left of the sutra repository. Certain Buddhist texts note that the Dragon King stored not only sutras but relics in his palace. Relics have long been associated with jewels, and countless texts describe the Dragon King as the possessor of the great wish-fulfilling jewel (*nyoi hōju*).[52] Mitsunobu seems to have strategically painted only the rooftop of this building, thus allowing for the juxtaposition of this unusually large jewel with the sutra repository building, reinforcing the idea of the Dragon Palace as the treasury of relics and sutras.

The precious jewel also recalls the Dragon Girl in *The Lotus Sutra*, whose presentation of the sacred gem to the Buddha and his quick acceptance of it figure prominently in her story. As Brian Ruppert has noted, the daughter of the Dragon King "has secret access to the treasure house of Buddhism, and so she can offer, in lieu of temporal merit accumulation, a gem that attests her capacity to attain enlightenment."[53] Documents from the medieval period also make clear the widespread understanding that the jewel the girl offered to the Buddha was in fact the wish-fulfilling jewel of the Dragon Palace.[54] The image of the enflamed gem in *The Jizō Hall* thus calls to mind the Dragon Girl and her gift to the Buddha, encouraging the reader to link the woman in the story to the mythical character. Like the Dragon Girl, the woman in the picture scroll seems to possess extra-

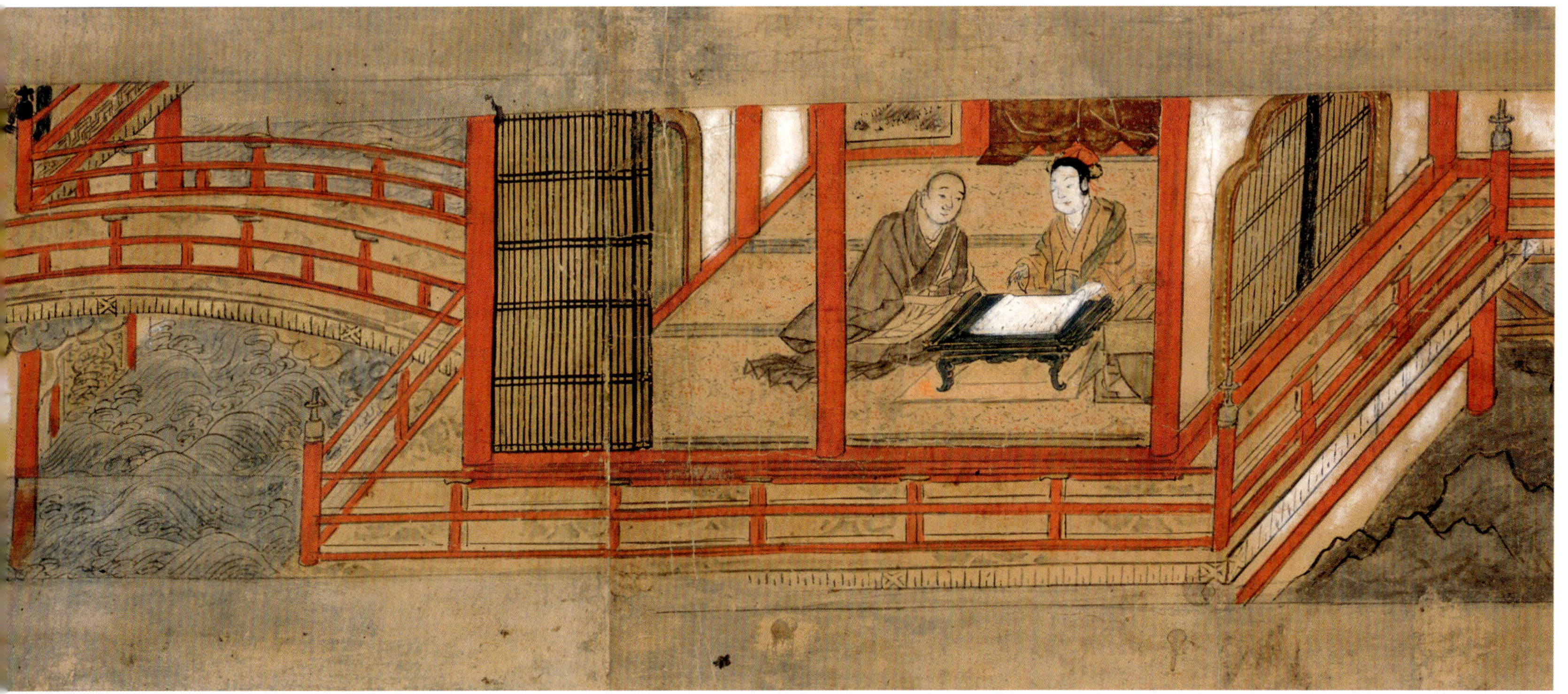

ordinary wisdom and also functions as the protector of the Buddhist teachings and the caretaker of the sutra repository. When she shows the monk the sutra that he had copied, she assumes the tone of a wise teacher as she tells him:

> In the beginning, when the sutra copying was planned in accordance with the Law and I humbly formed a connection with that noble endeavor, you began to have feelings for me, turning the Buddhist exercises into a mockery. . . . This palace contains a sutra repository preserving great numbers of sacred texts. Since in the beginning this sutra too aimed at according with the Law, I planned to place it among the others, but alas, it became a farce. . . . Quickly return to your homeland, practice sincerely, and finish the sutra copying according to the Law. . . . If you do these things, the farcical words you wrote will be transformed into a sutra of wonderful truths.[55]

Her statement makes it clear that in seeking out the monk she had simply been acting as caretaker of the sutra repository of the Dragon Palace, in search of yet another sacred text to safeguard below the waves during the dark age before the arrival of the future Buddha.

The monk alludes again to the Dragon Girl when he marvels at the pleasures of the palace and wonders if he has been "reborn as a Buddha in this very body" (*sokushin jōbutsu*). This term was closely associated in the medieval period with the Dragon Girl from the "Devadatta" chapter, as the phrase that described her instantaneous enlightenment.[56] The woman in *The Jizō Hall* here appears to be an adult avatar of the eight-year-old girl who achieved Buddhahood in *The Lotus Sutra*, but one who remains in need of spiritual intervention. In her parting words to the monk she explains her dilemma: "I too have a body that cannot be free from suffering. You must pray for me." The body entrapped in pain to which she refers alludes both to her female and to her nonhuman, dragon body, and the assertion indicates that she will remain in the Dragon Palace as an unsaved being after the monk's departure. In asking for the monk's prayers, however, she expresses faith in her soteriological potential, and thus of all similar beings, who with the proper intercession may achieve rebirth.

Given the prominence of the Dragon Girl in medieval culture as a symbol of female enlightenment, as well as the urgency of the woman's request to the monk to pray on her behalf, the growing agency assumed by the benefactress in *The Jizō Hall* introduces new wrinkles into what until this point was a fairly straightforward plot progression. From here, the story appears to become that of the dragon woman or, more precisely, proceeds in a manner in which the subjectivities of two separate protagonists, the monk and his seductress, are given equal billing, their stories advancing in tandem. Indeed, *The Jizō Hall* might even be read as the dragon woman's story, in which she is the protagonist who ventures out into the world seeking a righteous transcription *of The Lotus Sutra* for her own emancipation.[57] In this guise she represents the figure, widespread in medieval Japan, of the serpent woman who assumes human form to listen to a priest's sermon.[58] Her overtures to the monk on the veranda of his temple in the first painting could thus be viewed as an expression of longing to hear the sacred scripture. And as becomes clear, the woman's endeavor to hear the sutra and to form a karmic connection (*kechien*) with its transcription failed only when she pinned her hopes on an unworthy monk, a monk whose lust turned the sutra copying into a farce and who compromised her chances of Buddhahood. In other words, the scroll invites the viewer to contemplate what might have happened if the monk had properly carried out his copying and thus leaves open the possibility of this dragon woman's future salvation.[59]

As with a cleverly crafted optical illusion, then, the viewer is made to see double: the female devotee seeking salvation and the male priest saved by the mercy of Jizō. This simultaneity is achieved by taking preexisting and well-established literary and pictorial templates, breaking them down into their core components, and reassembling them as one entity in the picture scroll. While one of those templates was the serpent woman story, here it is uniquely conflated with imagery of the Dragon Girl from *The Lotus Sutra* and the Buddhist topos of the Dragon Palace. That conflation makes *The Jizō Hall* stand out among similar tales and suggests a production context in which the Dragon Girl was the focus of an unusual degree of interest.

As the pages that follow demonstrate, there is a strong likelihood that the context for *The Jizō Hall*'s production and viewership was the circle of the imperial court of GoTsuchimikado and his female attendants in the 1490s. But first it is important to further examine the characterization of the story's shadow protagonist. Because she represents a serpent woman character cast as a daughter of the Dragon King, she is differentiated in terms of social status from the woman who pursued the monk in the *Tale of Dōjōji*, a provincial widow of no particular distinction, as well as from Zenmyō, an apparently wealthy Chinese maiden but of ambiguous social circumstances.[60] As the princess of the undersea palace, on the other hand, the woman in *The Jizō Hall* is royalty. Her mythical status also connotes royal connections of an earthly kind; the Dragon King legend was always a serviceable metaphor for actual kingly power because of its focus on the sacred jewel or relics in general.[61] Thus, it is invoked as a representation of imperial authority in *The Tale of Genji*; in the imagery surrounding the Itsukushima Shrine and its related artworks sponsored by the Taira family in their attempt to possess the throne; in a fourteenth-century tale that describes the Byōdōin at Uji as the Dragon Palace and the regent Fujiwara no Yorimichi (990–1074) as the Dragon King.[62] Such connotations would not have been lost on readers of the fifteenth-century scroll, especially those who themselves were members of the imperial household.

Pictorially the benefactress of *The Jizō Hall* is depicted in such a way that she is clearly distinguished from the representation of other reptilian maidens in Japanese tale literature. Her character is always portrayed as elegant and refined. She consistently appears as a more authoritative figure than the monk, who, towered over physically, seems to shrink in her shadow, as when they are on the seashore about to depart for the underwater palace (fig. 2c). Upon arriving at her residence, the monk appears half hidden behind a pillar as the woman administers orders to a swarm of servants (fig. 2e). The woman's opulent surroundings—the elegantly appointed rooms outfitted with curtains and patterned carpets, the courtyard with scholar rocks, the vivid red posts and tiled roofs—could easily pass as a palace residence in the Chinese capital.

More important, the woman in *The Jizō Hall* never

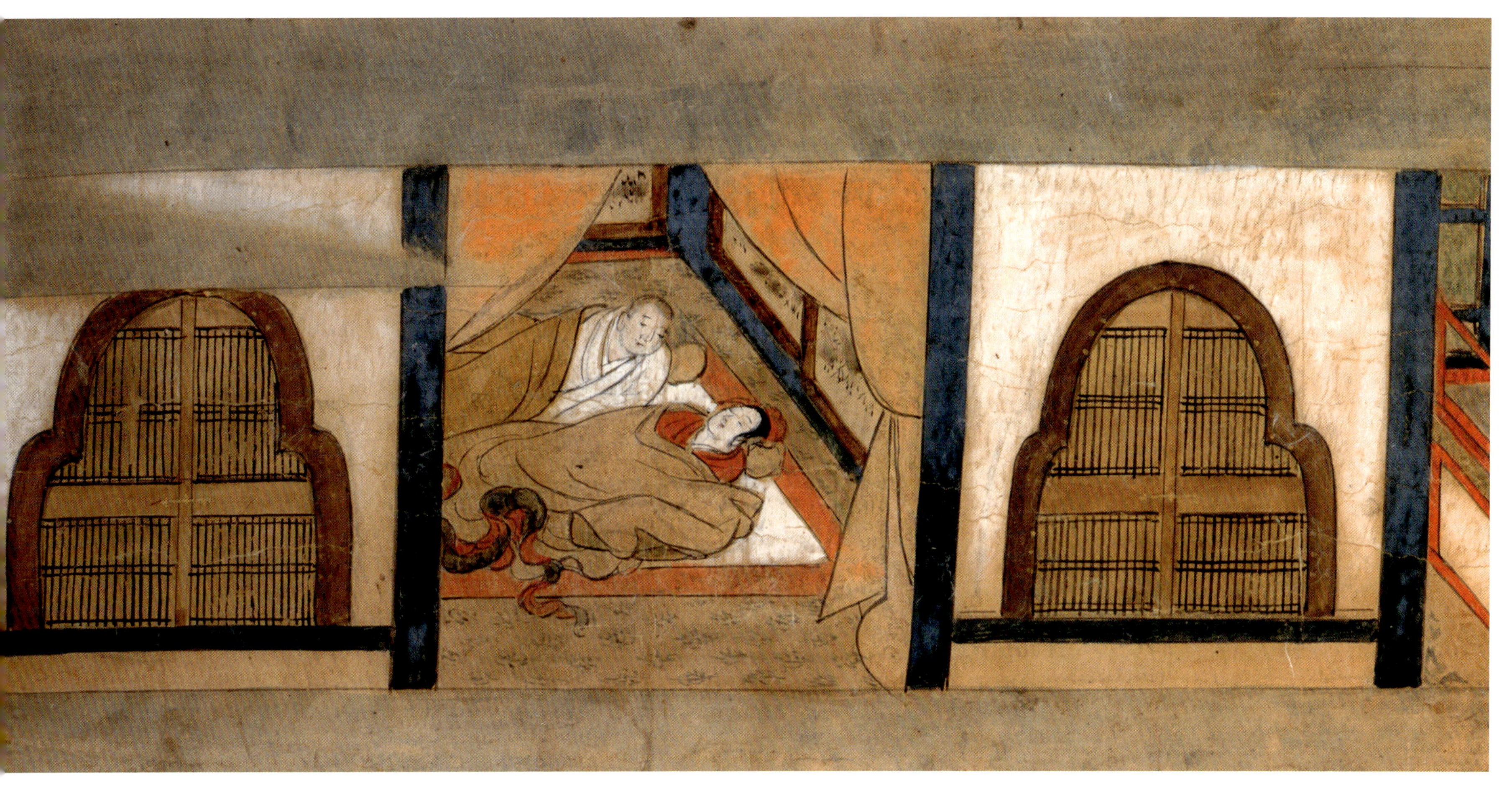

92 *The Jizō Hall.* Detail, painting 4.

appears lustful, and in fact seems to transcend desire. Her explanation of her initial encounter with the monk as a quest for a sutra to add to her repository suggests that their dalliance beneath the sea was not solely an issue of lasciviousness on her part. Far from it, the earnestness of her tone suggests an extracarnal sincerity that belies the scales on her body. Accordingly, the paintings minimize to the greatest extent possible the woman's reptilian identity, an artistic decision that is all the more striking considering that serpents were viewed as incarnations of desire. Upon discovery of her serpent-like tail, she is not represented as a large scaly creature, as are her colleagues in the *Dōjōji* and the *Kegon* scrolls, whose artists reveled in the depiction of the women's serpentine transformation. Rather, her tail remains difficult to detect and intriguingly ambiguous—it could easily be mistaken for a decorative twist of fabric peeking out from beneath her robes (fig. 92). In the conventional pattern of serpent woman tales, a prime opportunity for the woman's transformation comes at the moment of her rejection, when her jealousy becomes embodied by the metamorphosis into serpentine form. In contrast to this pattern, when the monk in *The Jizō Hall* confronts the woman with his desire to leave (fig. 93), she does not fly into a jealous rage or reveal her true form but instead calmly instructs him on how to return home and change his ways. With such a regal demeanor, untainted by obvious amphibious devolution, the benefactress emerges as a figure worthy of imperial emulation.

Ultimately, the woman's failure to achieve salvation leaves her with an inconclusive, undramatic, and even melancholy ending. The open-endedness of her fate is a far cry from the conclusion of the *Dōjōji* picture scroll, wherein the woman and man eventually achieve rebirth, or that of *Lives of the Founders of the Kegon Sect*, in which the woman's successive transformations bring the tale to a climactic conclusion. The happy closure of both works may reflect the fact that both were known to have been used for the purposes of proselytization and edification; Zenmyō's deeds even inspired a separate didactic text explicitly for the edification of women.[63] *The Jizō Hall*, in contrast, bears a more literary mood. The woman's salvation, while clearly a main theme, remains discretely in the background, in the shadow of the man's rebirth.

One way in which the discretion with regard to the woman's representation manifests itself in *The Jizō Hall* is in the inversion of the standard transformation of the female into a snake: the monk himself turns into a reptile upon returning to the Jizō Hall. Mitsunobu's depiction of the monk in his serpent form appears in two separate scenes, the first when he appears coiled up at the base of the temple's altar and scares away his fellow monks (fig. 21) and the second when he sheds his reptilian skin (fig. 94). The snake itself, a brown scaly creature with a long snout and a single horn on the top of its head, is thick and fleshy, convincingly capable of containing the body of the monk. It closely resembles the serpent that enwraps the monk Kenkei in *Miraculous Legends of Kiyomizudera*, painted by Mitsunobu in 1517 (fig. 95). The snake in *The Jizō Hall* is less agile, however, and its depiction captures wonderfully the ambiguity surrounding the nature of the monk's serpent body. Has he become the serpent, or has he been ensnared by one? The very image of the man-snake, in keeping with the literature of serpentine transformation, denotes punishment for acts of lust or greed. In *The Jizō Hall*, the monk's transformation into a snake and his subsequent emergence from the reptile thus graphically illustrate his transcendence of sin. By shedding this symbol of impurity, he becomes capable of the rebirth of the final scene. According to this understanding, the snake body was generated by the monk's own actions.

The very complexity of the dual transformation becomes evident only in this final scene, for the snake also seems to represent the residual impurities present in the body of the monk after his sexual encounter with the Dragon King's daughter. The text obliquely refers to this possibility when the monk contemplates his serpent form and thinks to himself, "he had been turning into a snake ever since he was cloaked in that brocade-like

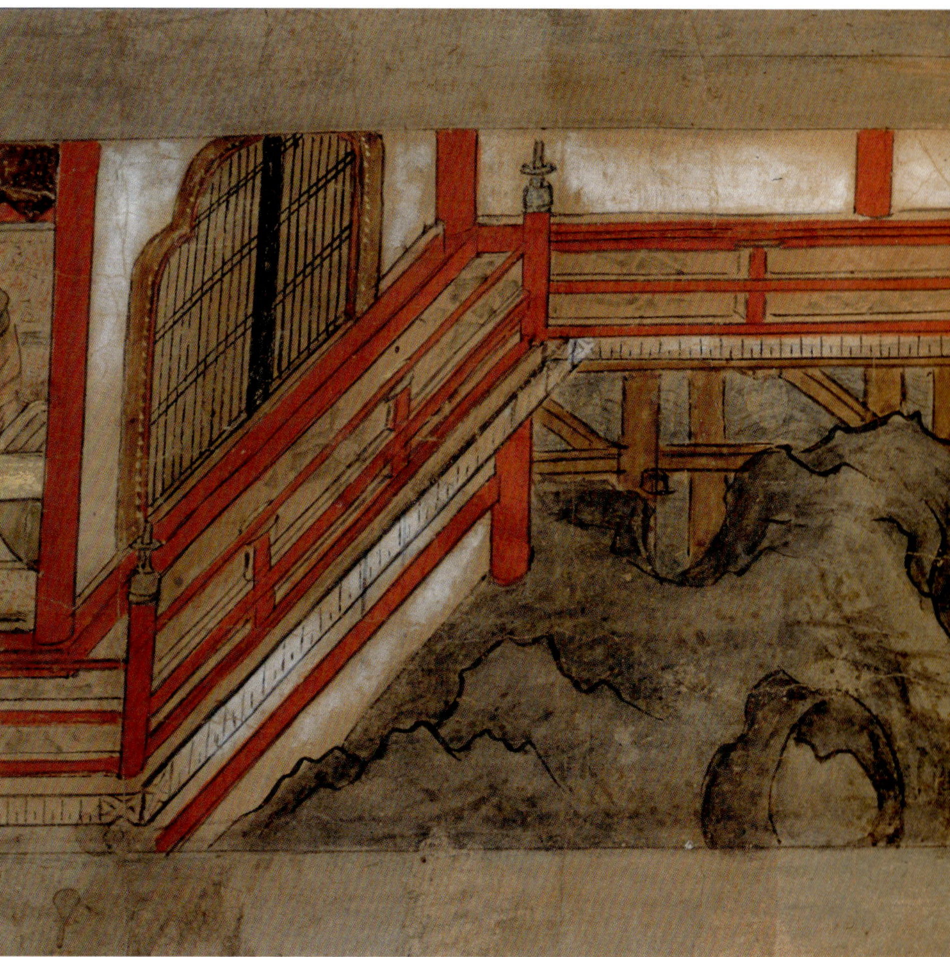

thing," the robe in which the woman wrapped him in order to traverse the sea. He thus shifts the responsibility onto the woman, whose reptilian body (and its metonymic counterpart, the "brocade-like thing") defiles him. He then sheds the snakeskin, in a way rehearsing the transformation of the Dragon Girl herself, who must cast off her female reptilian body for a male one before achieving Buddhahood. This transformation serves the goal of rebirth, as it purges the monk of his previous sins, but it also retains within it an echo of the dragon woman and her plight, the shadow protagonist's final appearance in the scroll.

AN IMPERIAL PAINTING

Several characteristics of *The Jizō Hall* that once seemed puzzling—its intertextual eclecticism that brings together a dizzying array of well-worn story lines, its incorporation of Dragon Girl imagery into a monk-meets-serpent-woman

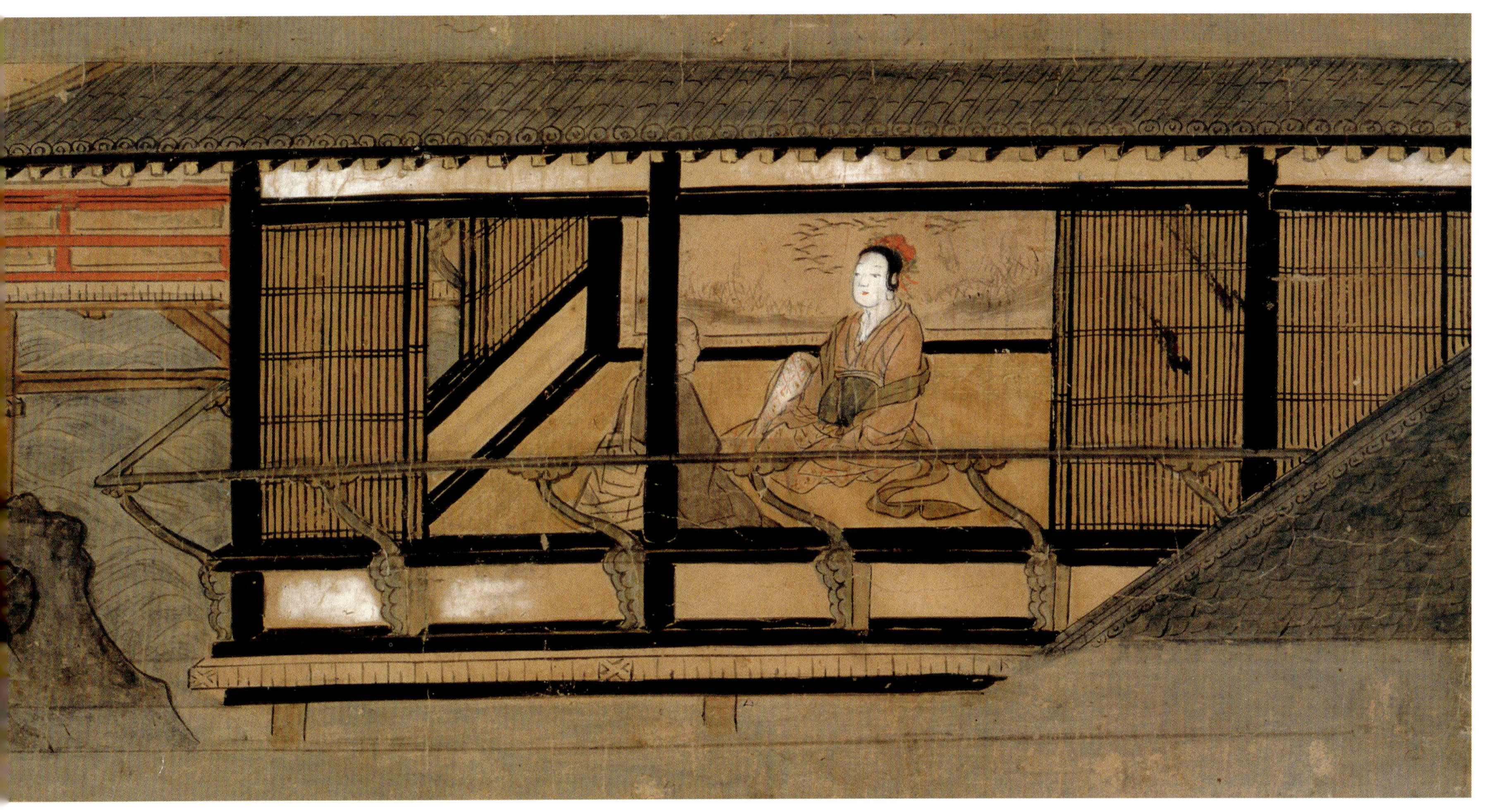

93 *The Jizō Hall.* Detail, painting 5.

tale, and its identity as an "account of rebirth" from a time when the genre was thought to have died out—all begin to make sense after examining the most plausible context for the scroll's production, the imperial court of GoTsuchimikado. The emperor and his ladies-in-waiting supervised the creation of a small-scroll *Account of Rebirth* (*Ōjōden ko-e*) in 1498, a project recorded in Sanjōnishi Sanetaka's diary. This *Account of Rebirth* and *The Jizō Hall* bear enough traits in common to suggest that they are one and the same work. Both are small-format scrolls with the same calligrapher, Sanetaka.[64] Both were most likely executed by Tosa Mitsunobu; although Sanetaka never mentions the painter of the 1498 scroll, Mitsunobu is the most likely candidate given his position as Painting Bureau director, his relationship to Sanetaka, and his earlier execution of a small scroll for the emperor, *Clouds of Mt. Kōya,* in 1474–79. Finally, both scrolls depict the same subject: rebirth (*ōjō*). At the very least, GoTsuchimikado's court, steeped in Pure Land belief, is the most likely environment out of which a scroll such as *The Jizō Hall* could have emerged. Before examining the 1498 small scroll and its relationship to *The Jizō Hall* in depth, a brief discussion of this religious context is in order.

GoTsuchimikado's interest in accounts of rebirth, and his desire to have one illustrated, developed out of his familiarity with Genshin's *Essentials of Rebirth* (*Ōjō yōshū*, 985). Although Genshin's text had always been accorded a prominent place in court culture, in the late fifteenth century it received renewed attention thanks to the influence of the Tendai monk and abbot of Saikyōji, Shinsei Shōnin (1443–95).[65] By all accounts an eloquent and charismatic man of the cloth, Shinsei was one of the emperor's closest religious advisers and began lecturing

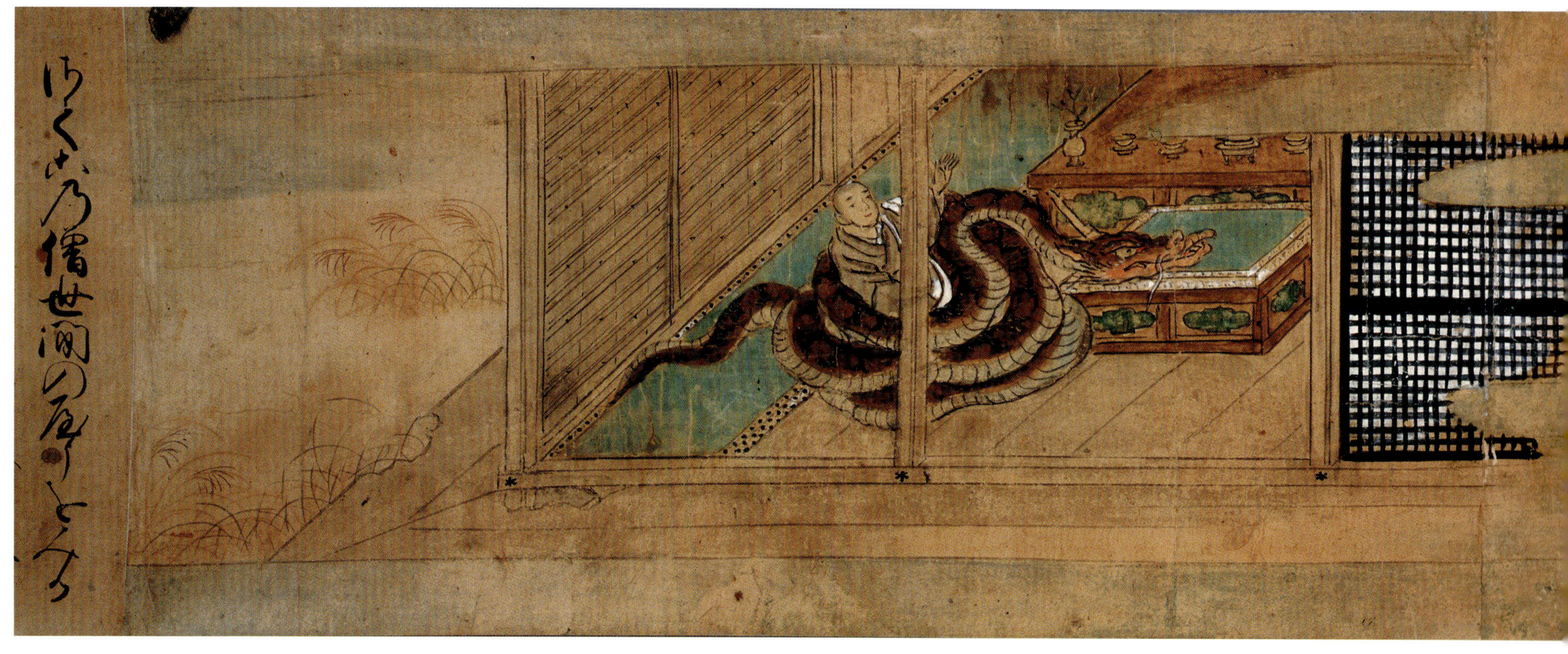

94 *The Jizō Hall.* Detail, painting 6.

on the *Essentials of Rebirth* at the palace in 1485, eventually also expounding on the text in the residences of prominent courtiers and elite warrior families.[66] He received the title of *shōnin* from the emperor after a subsequent lecture in 1486,[67] and in 1489 he conducted a five-day series of lectures to commemorate the death of the emperor's mother, Karakumon'in, which touched upon the "Devadatta" chapter of *The Lotus Sutra*, as well as Genshin's text.[68] *Essentials of Rebirth* was significant not only as a seminal text of Pure Land belief but also as a companion piece to the earliest compilations of *ōjōden*; while Genshin's work explicated the doctrinal theory of rebirth, compiled accounts brought its exposition to life with supposedly real-life examples.[69] *Essentials of Rebirth* even refers its readers to instances of rebirths in Japan as recorded in the *ōjōden* compiled by Genshin's contemporary Yoshishige no Yasutane.[70] It thus appears to have instigated new interest in the *ōjōden* genre in the late medieval period.

The revival of rebirth accounts in GoTsuchimikado's court has been overlooked by most modern commentators.[71] The most prominent example is *Record of the Account of Rebirth of Shinsei Shōnin* (*Shinsei Shōnin ōjōden ki*), which uses the format of the *ōjōden* to memorialize the life of Shinsei. Authored in 1495, the year of Shinsei's death, it recounts his biography and religious teachings and includes a vivid description of his death and rebirth.[72] GoTsuchimikado even makes an appearance in the monk's *ōjōden*, as the text describes the reigning emperor witnessing the purple clouds that appeared after Shinsei's death and declaring it a true instance of rebirth. Shinsei's biography contains several short accounts of the rebirths of his disciples, resembling thirteenth-century *ōjōden* that focused on individual monks and their followers, such as *Accounts of Rebirth at the Invocation of Amida's Name* (*Nenbutsu ōjōden*; ca. 1262–78) and its description of the deaths of seventeen of Hōnen's disciples.[73] Shinsei Shōnin's biography similarly emphasizes the salvation of his followers to demonstrate the efficacy of the monk's teachings.

Record of the Account of Rebirth of Shinsei Shōnin was apparently not an isolated example. Of special note is a new *ōjōden* recorded several years later, which GoTsuchimikado requested Sanjōnishi Sanetaka to copy. The manuscript had been compiled by a monk named

Seiun Shōnin.[74] Late one night in the eighth month of 1498, Sanetaka was called before the emperor, where he transcribed by lamplight Seiun's text concerning accounts of "recent people reborn into the Pure Land" (*kindai ōjō bito nado*).[75] Sanetaka calls the text Seiun's "new work" (*shinsaku*),[76] indicating that this was an *ōjōden* of recent vintage rather than a copy of a preexisting work from centuries earlier, and one that most likely recounted stories about individuals personally known by the compiler and his audience.

GoTsuchimikado not only desired a copy of Seiun's text, however, but also wanted it illustrated as a small-format handscroll, as subsequent entries in Sanetaka's diary make clear. As no previous *ōjōden* were illustrated, GoTsuchimikado's request was out of the ordinary. Perhaps the emperor was familiar with paintings from the locus classicus of *ōjō-e*, *Illustrated Life of Hōnen*, four scrolls of which he had viewed in 1476.[77] Perhaps he wanted to have his own personal image of a scene of rebirth because the reading of *ōjōden* was thought to improve one's chances for salvation by creating a connection between the reader and the successfully reborn individuals described in the accounts. *Ōjōden* were understood to have a personalized religious efficacy, for which a small scroll might have been especially well suited, given the intimacy of its mode of representation. Timing no doubt played a role as well in the emperor's decision to have his commission illustrated; in 1498 he was about to turn sixty, the average age of previous *ōjōden* compilers, and the completion of a sexagesimal cycle was traditionally a moment in one's personal timeline when preparations for death became important.[78] GoTsuchimikado seems to have been contemplating his own death, which in fact occurred just two years later.

The emperor may have commissioned a short-story small scroll based on one tale of rebirth extracted from Seiun's collection. The singling out of one story from a collection of tales for illustration as a small scroll was common, as the following chapter demonstrates. In this sense the commissioned scroll resembles other small scrolls that emerged from the milieu of Mitsunobu and Sanetaka. Although the fanciful nature of *The Jizō Hall* differentiates it from the overwhelming majority of *ōjōden*, it is not entirely without precedent. While traditional compilations of biographical accounts of people reborn in the Pure Land do not contain fantastical encounters between humans and nonhumans, or serpent transformations, such rebirth tales do appear in the *Miraculous Lotus Sutra Tales from Ancient Japan*

95 Tosa Mitsunobu, *Miraculous Legends of Kiyomizudera*. Dated 1517. Three handscrolls; ink and color on paper. Tokyo National Museum. Important Cultural Property.

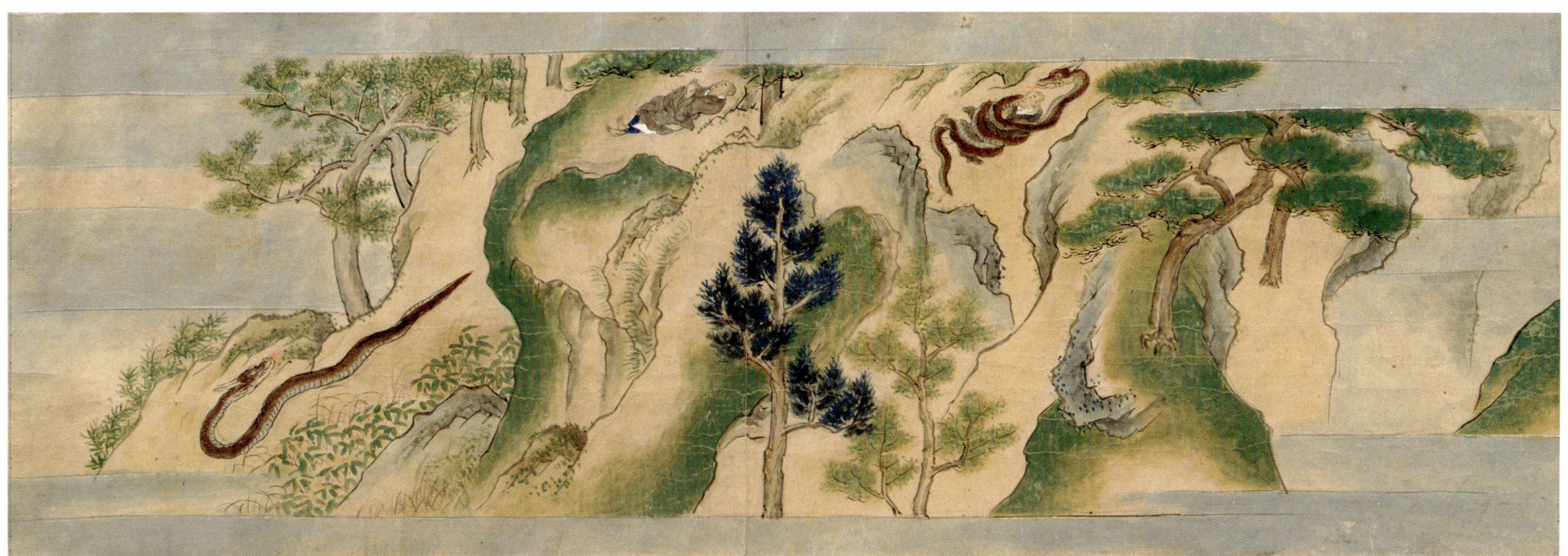

(*Dainihonkoku Hokkekyōgenki*, commonly known as the *Hokkegenki*), written by the Buddhist priest Chingen between 1040 and 1044.[79] All the stories in the *Hokkegenki* describe the power of *The Lotus Sutra*, but they conclude with the rebirth of the subject so frequently that contemporary readers considered them *ōjōden*.[80] Among the work's 129 stories, several describe people reborn as snakes because of their evil deeds in previous lives; they are saved only by hearing recitations of *The Lotus Sutra*. Three stories in the collection recall the plot of *The Jizō Hall*, in that unsuspecting men encounter demons, foxes, or serpents disguised as beautiful women.[81]

Compilers of more traditional biographical accounts incorporated tales from the *Hokkegenki* into their own compilations.[82] In such cases the stories were shortened to focus on the rebirth of the subject, and the role of *The Lotus Sutra* was de-emphasized (to highlight the invocation of Amida's name). Conversely, compilers of Buddhist tale (*setsuwa*) collections incorporated orthodox *ōjōden* into their collections, by transliterating the Chinese characters (*kanbun*) of the original accounts into the more accessible Japanese syllabary (*kana*) and rendering historically specific biographies into longer tales with more universal appeal. One chapter of the *Tales of Times Now Past*, for example, is devoted to *ōjōden*, but the accounts are longer than traditional ones and provide more psychological description, while adding explanatory comments about their conclusions.[83]

The Jizō Hall more closely resembles elaborate accounts of rebirth found in tale collections, such as *Tales of Times Now Past*, rather than straightforward biographical *ōjōden*. The text begins with the phrase "At a time now past" (*ima wa mukashi*), the same line with which all stories in *Tales of Times Now Past* begin, while the final paragraph claims that the story was "found among stories collected from long ago" (*furuki mukashi monogatari domo kakiatsumetaru naka ni mietari*). Both the opening and ending lines thus place the origin of the story somewhere in the distant past and situate it within the tradition of Buddhist tale literature. It defines itself as being part of this tradition not only through the phrasing mentioned above but also in its use of a script that mixes Chinese characters and the phonetic syllabary (*kana majiribun*) as opposed to the strict use of Chinese characters (*kanbun*) in *ōjōden*.

Given this preexisting tradition of editorial freedom, where compilers of rebirth tales could expand, condense, or reshape a biographical account into a more fanciful tale, Seiun's text too, even if it was of the more orthodox variety, could have undergone a literary transformation. In other words, one of Seiun's accounts could have become a tale not too dissimilar to *The Jizō Hall* without departing too radically from the approaches of previous compilers. Of crucial importance in this regard, however, was the degree to which Seiun's *ōjōden* was transformed through the process of its illustration as a picture scroll; the images had a metamorphic effect on the original story, while the new format of the small scroll necessitated that editorial changes be made to the text. As he had done many times before, the emperor put Sanjōnishi Sanetaka in charge of adapting the text for illustration. Roughly one month after first copying Seiun's manuscript for the emperor, Sanetaka notes that he was officially asked to write and submit the text for this *ōjōden* picture scroll, which he completed in four days.[84] Like other handscroll projects described in his diary, this one involved substantial back-and-forth between the patron and the calligrapher/editor. It was during this process that the parties involved had the opportunity to further transform Seiun's text and to determine how they wanted the illustrated version to look.

In addition to Sanetaka's diary entries, more details concerning his editorial role surface in a letter from GoTsuchimikado's female attendants preserved on the back of one of the sheets of his diary. It reads:

> Concerning the text for the picture scroll from the other day, you should write it as you see fit and bring it to the palace. As for the section of five and three,[85] you should leave it as it was in the original. Toward the end, in places where it is wordy and it is reasonable to pare it down, you should do so. As for the temporary cover, use the honorable court's paper enclosed herein and attach one more section to the end. You should remove any extremely thin parts.[86]

The letter suggests that Sanetaka had leeway to condense parts of the prose, while with other parts he was precisely instructed by the patron not to make changes. Sanetaka was also asked to rewrite one passage because the thinness of the paper (also mentioned in the letter) necessitated a new sheet.

The letter clearly indicates that Seiun's text was being modified and adapted for the small-scroll format, although the extent of that modification can only be imagined given the laconic prose of the letter and the diary entries. The random preservation of the letter as a piece of scrap paper, however, suggests that even more communication went on concerning the scroll, the traces of which no longer survive. These cryptic documents were undoubtedly fragments of a larger conversation, now lost, between Sanetaka, the emperor, and his female attendants concerning the scroll. Sanetaka made almost daily appearances at the palace, and the women's letters function as confirmations of, or supplements to, verbal instructions and discussions. Letters to and from the Tsuchimikado palace were delivered quickly to Sanetaka's residence in the Upper Capital (Kamigyō),[87] while Sanetaka's attendance at court meant that he had ample opportunity to discuss the content of the scroll.[88]

The palace letter also illuminates details that Sanetaka did not include in his daily record, such as the input he received from female attendants. As intimate companions to the emperor and administrators of the imperial household, the group of roughly six high-ranking women who saw to his daily needs may have had more to do with the production of this scroll than previously imagined.[89] While the female letter writers may have simply been scribes for GoTsuchimikado, taking dictation as he stated his wishes about the material problems of the scroll, the emperor likely left many details up to the women themselves. The attendants were highly educated women capable of managing the cultural decision making of the emperor, and indeed it was part of their regular duties to see to such matters. Far from cloistered within the palace walls, they were often more mobile than GoTsuchimikado himself[90] and were uniquely situated to communicate with Sanetaka in particular. One of the attendants in charge of internal palace affairs, known as Shin Dainagon no Suke, was Kajūji Fusako (d. 1518), the sister of Sanetaka's wife.[91] Yet another one of his wife's sisters, Kajūji Fujiko, served GoTsuchimikado's crown prince, the future emperor GoKashiwabara, acting as a constant companion to him since his youth.[92] During the month between Sanetaka's initial transcription of Seiun's manuscript and his brushing of the *Ōjōden* scroll's calligraphy, Fusako and Fujiko, as well as several other ladies of the imperial entourage, visited Sanetaka's residence to collect his wife, who joined them in a visit to Shin'nyodō Temple.[93] As on many other occasions, they conversed with Sanetaka and shared a drink before their departure, providing an opportunity to discuss any number of issues, including the content of the picture scroll in question.

Piecing together these sources of information, a possible scenario connecting the 1498 *Ōjōden* small scroll and the extant *Jizō Hall* begins to materialize in which Seiun's text was used as the raw material for this highly nuanced pictoliterary work. The process begins with Sanetaka copying the source text, compiled by Seiun Shōnin. One month later the palace sends word that they would now like the completed picture scroll calligraphy. Although Sanetaka makes no mention of the small-scroll text during the month between his copying of Seiun's manuscript and his brushing of the scroll's calligraphy, he may have worked on the text during that time by consulting with Mitsunobu, reconceptualizing the tale, dividing it into sections for illustration, or possibly transliterating the Chinese characters of the original into a mixture of syllabic script and characters. While the extant documents include only terse logistical directions regarding production, there may have been informal conversations between the emperor, Sanetaka, the ladies-in-waiting, and the artist. During this time, it is appealing to speculate that the image of the Dragon Girl of *The Jizō Hall* took her distinctive shape at the urging of the palace ladies or others in the group. And it is tempting to imagine that *The Jizō Hall* text with its episode beneath the sea was on Sanetaka's mind during a *renga* gathering held two days before completing the text of the *Ōjōden ko-e*, at which he composed a link that included the phrase "entering the sea."[94]

The result is a short story that expands the typical

ōjōden plot structure into an elaborate narrative tale that sidetracks a monk's path to salvation, taking him through a series of adventures, and the reader through a tour of literary genres. The story moves imperceptibly from religious tale, to comedy, to myth through an intricate web of allusions. In doing so, it manifests at select moments the erudition of its mediator. This tale also employs Buddhist terminology for comedic effect. When the monk contemplates the pleasure he has been enjoying at the woman's residence, for example, he wonders if he has already been "reborn as a Buddha in this very body" (*sokushin jōbutsu*). Coming from a monk who has just been described by the narrator as "uneducated, guileless, and completely lacking in good judgment," the words lose their serious doctrinal implications and imply that the feeling of "Buddhahood in this very body" may be equivalent to the feeling of an amorous encounter. Then there is of course the humorous moment when the monk is confronted with his miscopied sutra. Someone like Sanetaka would have been capable of embellishing the text with Buddhist allusions as well as humor. His engagement with comical or vulgar literary forms is clearly documented in the *Saishōsō*, his personal poetry collection, which contains nearly three hundred *kyōka* (comic verses).[95] Sanetaka also composed *haikai* (comic linked verse) with *renga* masters like Sōgi, Gensei, and Sōchō and avidly read and composed popular poems called *ko-uta* (literally "small songs").[96] It seems that Sanetaka was known for his authorial wit, as when in 1494 the imperial court asked him to write the judgments for a *kyōka* poetry competition.[97] Sanetaka was, in other words, well suited in terms of both erudition and sense of humor to craft a story like *The Jizō Hall.*

Still other elements of the story betray Sanetaka's imprint. The inclusion of two historical figures that are Zen monks, for example, is anomalous among accounts of Pure Land rebirth and suggests his handiwork. Specific reference to Fumon Shōnin, the third abbot of Tōfukuji, may have been motivated by a desire to link the tale to that monastery, where Sanetaka had particularly strong ties. Sanetaka was on close terms with one of the most prominent abbots of Tōfukuji, Ryōan Keigo (1425–1514), to whom his youngest son, Keiyō (1494–1526), was apprenticed in 1501.[98] In the same year, Sanetaka personally arranged for Emperor GoKashiwabara to inscribe a portrait of Fumon Shōnin (fig. 96), which survives today.[99] The inclusion of Fumon's name

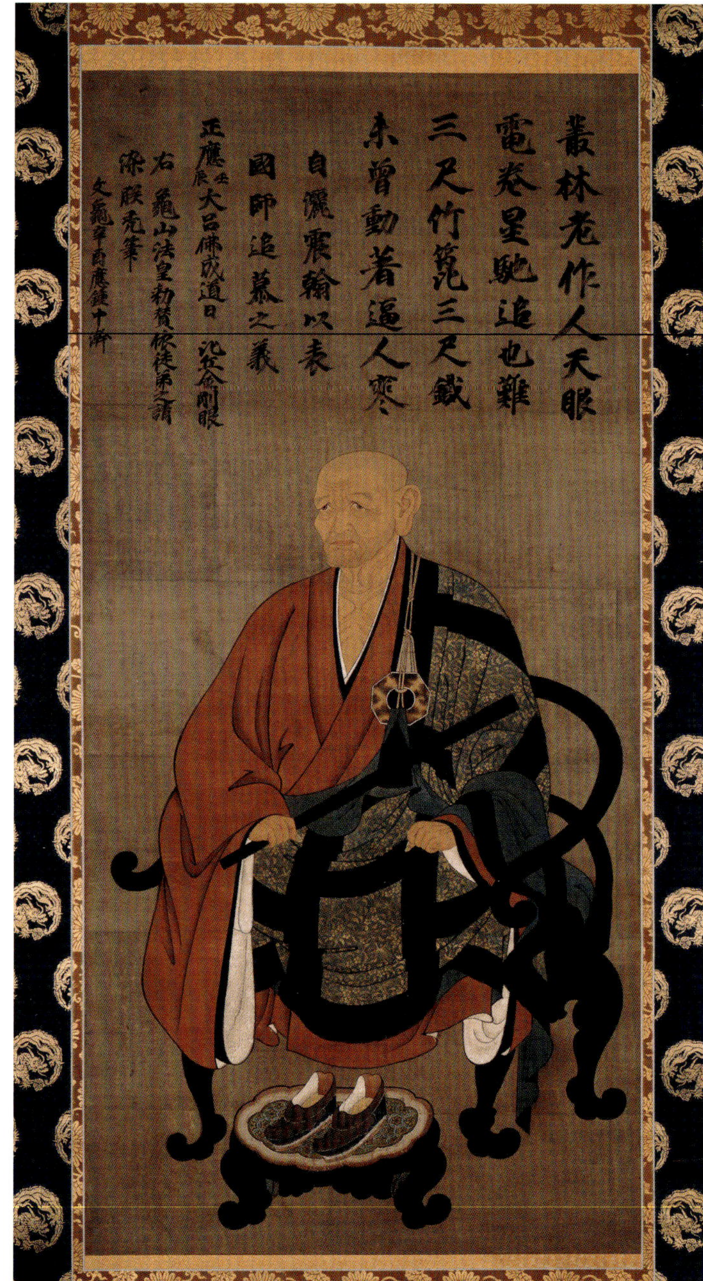

96 *Portrait of Mukan Fumon (Mukan Fumon Zenji shōzō.)* Inscribed by Emperor GoKashiwabara. Bunki 1 (1501). Hanging scroll; color on silk. Nanzenji, Kyoto. Important Cultural Property.

at the end of *The Jizō Hall* was no doubt inspired by Sanetaka's particularly close relationship with Tōfukuji in the late 1490s and early 1500s.

Sanetaka's sensibility mediated the ability of the scroll to accommodate a sexagenarian emperor and a group of erudite ladies-in-waiting. Perhaps other members of the inner imperial entourage were also beneficiaries of his editorial acumen. *The Jizō Hall* demonstrates the degree to which so much storytelling tradition, and so many literary strategies and moods, could be folded into a deceptively simple story line in the small-scroll format. But the registers into which this enfolding took place were as pictorial as literary. Visual devices and sleights-of-hand consistently provided the mechanism by which narrative adaptation and complexity could be generated, while paring down accompanying excerpts. It is in this sense that Mitsunobu the painter can be attributed a redactive role as well as an artistic one, a topic that will be explored in the next chapter.

BREAKING THE INKSTONE AN ACOLYTE TALE FOR A YOUNG SHOGUN

5

Namidagawa
araedo ochizu
hakanakute
suzuri no yue ni
someshi koromo wa

Though I shed a river of tears,
they do not come clean,
these robes stained black
by the inkstone

—*Breaking the Inkstone*

The tears being shed in the poem above are those of a retainer to a high-ranking courtier, and they are for the young son of the courtier, who has died because of the man's carelessness. The servant has destroyed his master's precious inkstone, a family heirloom that symbolizes the status of its owner as an erudite aristocrat. At the young boy's urging the man blamed the inkstone's destruction on the child and brought about his premature death; hence, the inkstone becomes the focus of his poetic lament and the symbol of the bond between them. The black robes of his poem, metaphorically stained by the ink of the broken inkstone, are the dark robes of the monk he will now become in order to pursue a life of Buddhist practice and prayer devoted to the boy's salvation. The relationship between the young man and the boy lies at the heart of *Breaking the Inkstone* and was one of the primary reasons this story was singled out for pictorial representation in the handscroll format.

Mitsunobu's *Breaking the Inkstone* of 1495 contains a colophon inscribed by its owner (fig. 3j), the young shogun Ashikaga Yoshizumi (1480–1511) and thus provides an opportunity to explore the inter-resonance between a painting's content and the social realities of its intended audience. The tragic tale pictorialized in the scroll takes on significantly new valences when viewed through the lens of its young owner's life, which suggests that small-format picture scrolls were intricately related—even customized—to the social circumstances of their owners. In the case of Yoshizumi, a youthful member of the military elite, those circumstances involved social bonds between men structured by a discourse of fealty and devotion. Thus, I will propose that it was the demonstration of an act of loyalty and self-sacrifice on the part of the young boy in *Breaking the Inkstone* that motivated the producers of the scroll to select this particular tale for illustration in the small-scroll format.

The meaning of the tale, however, extends well beyond any representation of loyalty and any didactic message that might be imparted. For that larger significance of the tale it is necessary to turn briefly to earlier interpretive frameworks for this story, namely the "tale compilation." For the most part, short tales (*setsuwa*) such as *Breaking the Inkstone* did not circulate as independent works in the late fifteenth century. Much like present-day short stories, which are rarely published individually but appear in compilations or magazines and literary journals, medieval tales were normally included within anthologies. Such compilations arrange the individual tales thematically and thus imply early interpretations of their perceived categorical meanings.

The earliest text version of *Breaking the Inkstone*, for example, appears in the early-twelfth-century anthology of over one thousand short stories known as *Tales of Times Now Past* (*Konjaku monogatari shū*), within a section containing sixteen stories of people who "renounce family ties" (*shukke*) and take Buddhist vows.[1] Its precise location in the collection and its relationship to its neighboring stories are revealing. The tale that precedes *Inkstone* tells of a falconer shocked into accepting the Buddhist path after seeing a vision of his wife and children as hunted prey, resembling the pheasants he himself has stalked and killed.[2] The tale immediately following concerns a courtier who, upon glimpsing the decaying corpse of his wife, is made painfully and instantly aware of the transience of the world and decides to take Buddhist vows.[3] The compiler of this twelfth-century anthology assumed an equivalence of affect between the inkstone-breaking story and these other episodes of religious awakening and accordingly inserted it between them.[4] As a didactic Buddhist tale, *Breaking the Inkstone* demonstrates the foolishness of attachment to worldly possessions and offers yet another example of a catalytic event, like viewing a decaying corpse, that might prompt withdrawal from the secular world, the event here being the death of an innocent child. The meaning of the tale was thus conditioned by its association with the generic category of the so-called renunciation tale as found in *Tales of Times Now Past.*

Authors of later variants of the inkstone-breaking tale redirected its powerful renunciatory message toward biographical ends, albeit the biography of a religious figure. These versions present the Buddhist monk who emerges at the end of the story (the former servant) as the main protagonist and apocryphally identify him as the famous tenth-century Buddhist monk Shōkū (907?–1007), an eccentric reciter of *The Lotus Sutra* and founder of the monastery and temple of Engyōji atop Mt. Shosha in Harima Province.[5] Thus, the servant who breaks the inkstone corresponds to the young Shōkū before he discovers the Buddhist path, and the death of the boy adds a poignant anecdote to the biographical narrative of the monk's spiritual journey. These versions also recount miraculous events from Shōkū's life, such as his legendary visit to a prostitute who suddenly transforms into the bodhisattva Fugen whenever he closes his eyes.[6] Again, the location in which these stories are found in the anthologies reveals a contemporary understanding of their ultimate message: in a collection called *Selected Stories* (*Senjūshō*, compiled 1250–82), the inkstone-breaking tale appears as one of many about famous holy men.[7] The tales in this collection convey Buddhist ideas about transience and impermanence, spiritual awakening, and the renunciation of worldly ties. In this context and with the additional episode about Shōkū's miraculous vision of the Buddhist deity, the story served as a component of religious hagiography.

Mitsunobu's small picture scroll of *Breaking the Inkstone*, however, represents a radical departure from versions of the tale found in earlier compilations. It was made and circulated independently, and from the perspective of anthologized versions, it was merely an extraction, disassociated from the logic of ordering that lent it categorical meaning. The isolation of *Breaking the Inkstone* reflects a significant development in the history of the reception of tale literature. As discussed in chapter 1, until the appearance of the small scroll, never before had the short story been matched with its own distinctive mode of illustration. The small picture scroll provided a vehicle for the dissemination of the short tale as an independent work, liberated from the interpretive framework of the literary compilation. Removed from its generic frame of either renunciation tale or hagiography, *Breaking the Inkstone* was opened to a wider range of interpretive possibilities on the part of its viewers/readers. That the artists and creators of this and other small scrolls felt similarly unrestrained is expressed through the citation of multiple literary and pictorial genres.

There is evidence to suggest, for example, that the creators of the 1495 picture scroll were familiar with both the renunciation story line of *Tales of Times Now Past* and the holy-man biography of *Selected Stories*; Mitsunobu's scroll is unique among all extant recensions of the tale in its combination of two key elements from both story lines that had previously remained isolated from one another: the boy's death in exile and the identification of the monk as the holy man Shōkū. The death in exile provides a scenario for the boy's ultimate scene of self-sacrifice and loyalty and his decision to remain true to his word even in the face of death. And yet this scroll identifies the servant as the holy man Shōkū, which is unusual; in every other version that links the story to the famous monk, the boy is not exiled but killed immediately, usually beheaded by his enraged father. The quick extermination of this character allows the focus of the narrative to shift immediately to the holy man, instead of providing a showcase for the young person's dutiful actions in exile. The inclusion of both elements in the picture scroll yields a unique rendition that combines a recounting of the monk's spiritual awakening with a compelling image of a virtuous young boy.

One is sensitized to the unique contours of *Breaking the Inkstone* only by allotting equal hermeneutic weight to the paintings. In ways unavailable to the brief and rudimentary texts in this scroll, the paintings cite other genres of illustrated narrative that infuse the story with rich overtones of meaning. Pictorial citation enables characterizations of the boy's virtue and his intimacy with the servant. As I will be demonstrate, Mitsunobu employed pictorial features associated with a genre of literature popular in the fifteenth century called "acolyte tales" (*chigo monogatari*), at the heart of which lie stories of intense spiritual, emotional, and romantic bonds between older monks and young male acolyte-attendants. Unlike the narratives enclosed within anthologies, *Breaking the Inkstone* uses pictorial citations to traverse generic boundaries. The referencing of the monk-acolyte genre, moreover, gives the scroll a seeming contemporaneity familiar to late-fifteenth-century viewers. The most important of those viewers was the shogun Yoshizumi, owner of the scroll. The latter part of this chapter will place the relationships depicted in the picture scroll between servant and boy, father and son, and master and servant in the context of specific homosocial relationships within the shogun's sphere; this will in turn suggest reasons for the receptivity to *Breaking the Inkstone* in the household of the young military leader.

In this chapter I aim to uncover the intricate resonances between the scroll's owner and the content of the scroll and thereby to understand the possible range of meanings this tale would have had for its initial audiences. This query is inseparable from the question of how the picture scroll conveys meaning. How are familial relationships, social hierarchies, and characteristics such as "virtue" represented at a specifically visual register? What are the precise mechanics of the scroll's pictorial citations? How does one articulate the mode of pictorial narration at work in these scrolls? Exploring this line of inquiry helps to define a semiotics of the small picture scroll, one that is predicated upon but also innovates upon a well-established picture scroll language developed throughout the four-hundred-year history of the narrative handscroll.

THE PICTORIAL LANGUAGE OF *BREAKING THE INKSTONE*

Four aspects of the narrative—transgression, virtue, death, and remorse—demonstrate the ways in which

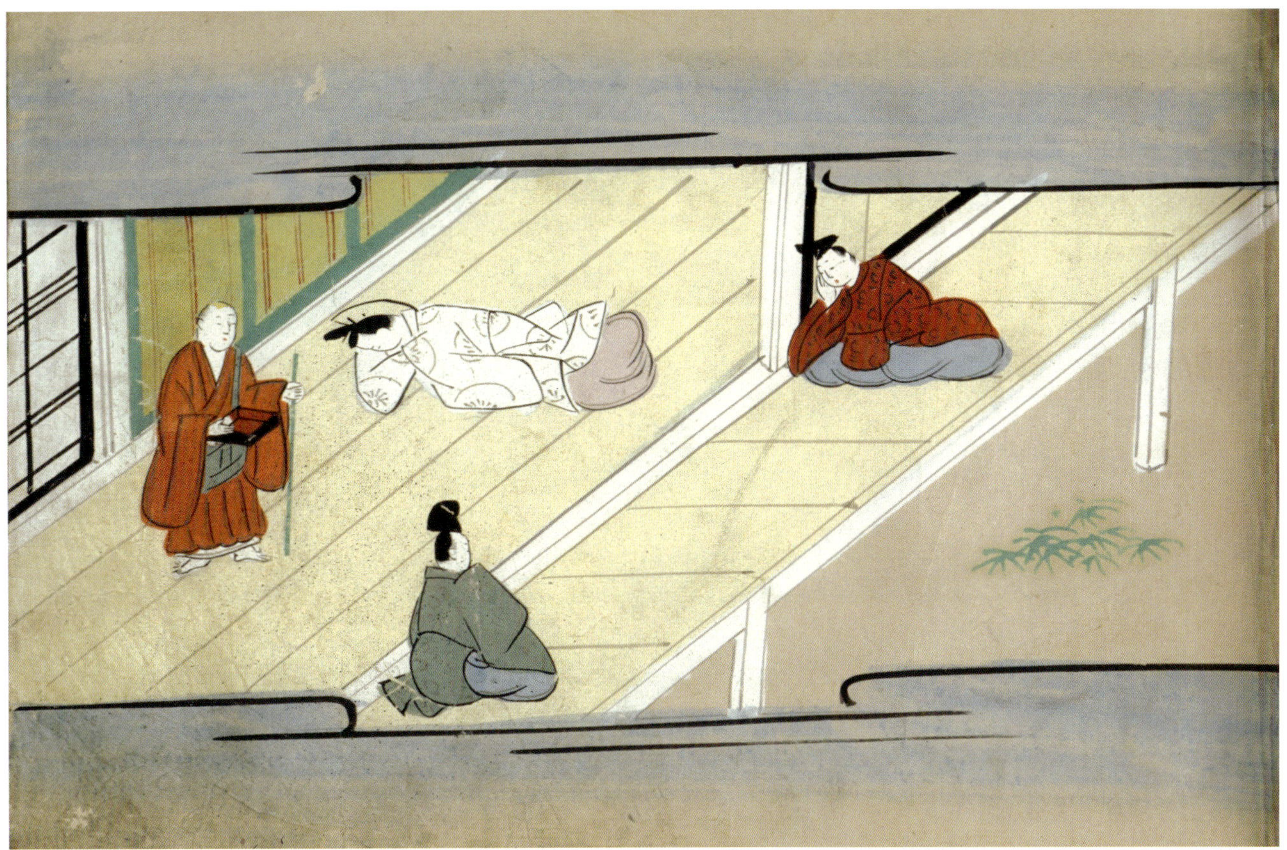

97 *Breaking the Inkstone* (*Nara e-hon Suzuriwari*). Muromachi period. Illustrated book, three vols.; 15.1 x 22.7 cm. Hiroshima University Library.

the characterization of the boy and his relationships were calibrated to the tale's newest audience. The specific visual strategies that help compose and engender the narrative are encapsulated by three techniques in particular: pictorial metonymy, architectural framing, and pictorial/generic citation. All of these techniques are premised upon the physical characteristics of the small-scroll format, in which multiple painted scenes could be viewed in quick succession, resulting in a pronounced contiguity between separate paintings. The three painting sections that constitute *Breaking the Inkstone* bear an implicit relationship to one another as images in a chronological sequence, and they also reference one another by showing, for example, slight variations of compositions that the viewer has already witnessed.

Representing the Transgression

Crucial to the narrative coherence of *Breaking the Inkstone* is the description of the inkstone, an object of such apparent significance that its destruction merited the banishment of a courtier's only son. Although the numerous versions of the tale cast the inkstone's importance in somewhat-different tones, some more political and others more supernatural, it is always linked to the figure of the father, the major counselor. Most frequently the inkstone is described as a family heirloom bestowed upon a great ancestor of the counselor by a god (*kami*), none other than Sumiyoshi, deity of poetry and resident god of the Sumiyoshi Shrine. One illustrated booklet of the tale from the Muromachi period devotes an entire illustration to the meeting between the god Sumiyoshi and the ancestor, who is identified as the legendary Fujiwara no Kamatari (614–69), founder of the Fujiwara clan (fig. 97). The inkstone granted to the counselor's forefather by Sumiyoshi has

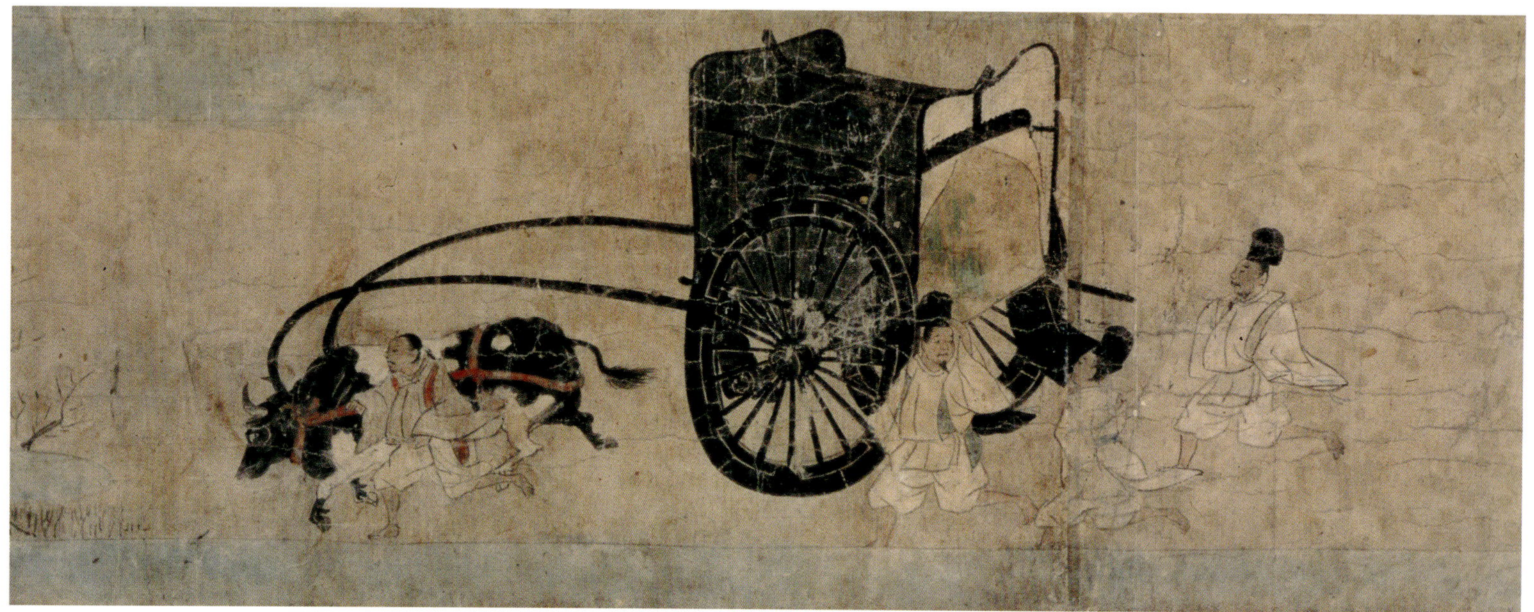

98 Tosa Mitsunobu, *Breaking the Inkstone* (*Suzuriwari sōshi*). Dated 1495. One handscroll; ink, color, and gold on paper. Hosomi Museum, Kyoto. Detail, painting 1.

protected the lineage and ensured its continued prosperity ever since. In this context, the father's wrath upon learning of the inkstone's destruction seems almost justifiable, as it portends the downfall of the family line.

The version of *Inkstone* found in the twelfth-century *Tales of Times Now Past* does not invoke a supernatural origin to convey the importance of this prized possession. This text tells of the father's intention to send the object along with his daughter to the imperial court in the hopes that she will win the favor of the emperor and advance the family's political fortunes, no doubt by becoming the mother of a crown prince and thus making the major counselor (here a minister of the left, *sadaijin*) the grandfather of an emperor. A description of the inkstone's physical appearance, the quality of the ink it produces, and the attentive care given to it by the father adds to the object's aura:

> The inkstone was not only beautiful, with its gold and silver decoration on a lacquered ground, but the consistency of its ink was unlike any other in the world. Among all the treasures in his daughter's dowry, the inkstone was the most precious. For this reason the minister never casually showed it to others, but kept it close at hand in a brocade bag tucked away inside a two-shelved shrine.[8]

In this version of the tale, the inkstone's reputation reaches the ears of the emperor, who expresses great interest. Thus, the inkstone is linked not only to the father but more importantly to the emperor, and to the potential future relationship between the minister's family and the imperial house.

In contrast to this buildup surrounding the inkstone prior to its destruction in virtually all extant versions of the tale, the text that accompanies the paintings in Mitsunobu's 1495 picture scroll makes no mention of the inkstone's origins or its significance and in fact never even uses the word "inkstone." The entire first text (fig. 3a), which spans less than a single sheet of paper, can be quoted in full:

> Once, while the major counselor was away at the imperial palace, a servant named Nakamichi opened this up and looked. Hearing the sound of a carriage, he carelessly rushed to put it away and broke it into three pieces. The young master of the house, just seven years old, asked the overwrought and sobbing servant what happened. After he explained, the young boy said, "You will be most certainly be severely punished. You must say that it was I who broke it."

Pictorial Characterization of the Virtuous Boy

A key to understanding the significance of *Breaking the Inkstone* for Yoshizumi lies in the narrative's focus on a virtuous young boy. Although the story pivots around an act of self-sacrifice and loyalty by the counselor's son, Mitsunobu's picture scroll places much greater emphasis than other versions on the representation of the child as an exemplar of virtue. This is evident in the first text and painting of the scroll, where the violation is staged in such a way that the boy appears unequivocally as an innocent party. In contrast, other versions of the story are vague on this account, and some go so far as to implicate the boy in the servant's transgression. Numerous examples depict the servant dropping the inkstone upon hearing the sound of the boy's footsteps approaching.[11] And in one version, it is the boy who tempts the servant to enter his father's study, where they rummage through his possessions. When they come upon the treasured inkstone, the boy urges the servant to remove it from its box so that they can both have a look.[12] As if to eliminate any such connection between the boy and the inkstone's destruction, Mitsunobu's picture scroll text states that the servant breaks the inkstone upon hearing the "sound of a carriage" (*kuruma no oto no shikereba*), referring of course to the counselor's vehicle returning from the imperial palace. The depiction of the carriage moving leftward toward the scene of the inkstone breaking thus sets the scroll and the story in motion (fig. 3b). The carriage functions in this instance as an acoustic sign that reverberates into the next scene, causing the servant to stumble forward, while at the same time signifying the presence of the major counselor. It demonstrates well the economy of small-scroll semantics; while invoking the authority of the handscroll tradition and making a specific allusion to the Michizane legend, it introduces the father to the crime and at the same time absolves the young boy of all responsibility and sets the stage for his characterization as an exemplary figure.

The boy's first appearance in the scroll occurs at the far left edge of the second scene (figs. 3c and 99), where his mere presence within the composition illustrates his willingness to take responsibility for the servant's crime. This particular painting folds two moments in time into a single frame. First comes the moment in which the servant, Nakamichi, has just allowed the precious object to slip from his grasp: he stumbles forward with the palm of his right hand facing down and his fingers spread wide; his upturned eyebrows convey a horrified expression as he looks down at the inkstone shattered into three pieces. Nakamichi appears again, slightly to the left of the broken inkstone, reflecting a later moment when his shock has turned to despair.[13] He kneels on the wooden floor in front of the major counselor's son, who appears at the far left of the scene seated upon green matting. The boy's placement within the composition is carefully considered and sets the tone for his figuration in the remainder of the scroll. Whereas the servant literally turns his back on the broken inkstone, the boy faces toward the shattered object, which lies directly in his line of vision. Thus staged, the boy seems to bear the burden of the broken inkstone with his small body, which marks the edge of the horizontal painting and punctuates the culmination of the leftward movement initiated by the speeding carriage at the beginning of the scroll. In this manner, Mitsunobu's opening painting is conceived in units of both short and long duration, visually generating linkages that are not explicit in the text.

The figural placement within the architectural frame, in addition to providing a visual counterpart to the child's verbal offer to take the blame for the broken inkstone, calls further attention to the boy's elevated social status as the young master of the house (*wakagimi*). In all other representations of this scene from the three illustrated books of *Breaking the Inkstone*, the object lies between the servant and the boy, who both look down upon the inkstone as if contemplating their mutual dilemma (fig. 102). Instead of representing the two figures as coconspirators, the boy's elevated position on the tatami in Mitsunobu's scroll suggests the child's social and moral elevation above the servant kneeling before him. As he appears to raise one sleeve to his face to wipe away his tears, the boy echoes the gesture and emotional state of the servant, a mirroring that portends his act of self-sacrifice on the servant's

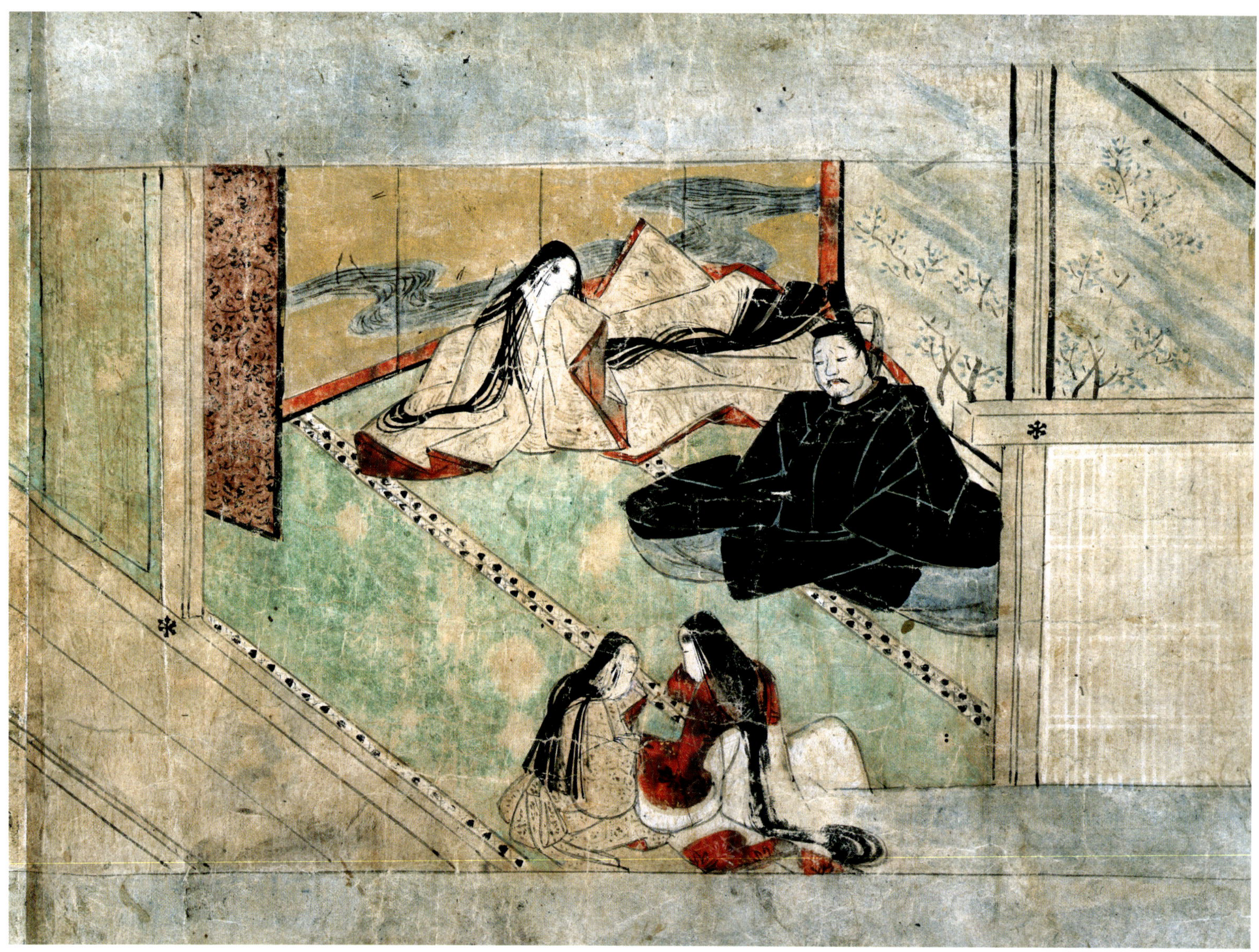

103 Tosa Mitsunobu, *Breaking the Inkstone*. Dated 1495. One handscroll; ink, color, and gold on paper. Hosomi Museum, Kyoto. Detail, painting 2.

behalf. In this regard, their parallelism visually conveys a *migawari*, literally an "exchange of bodies," in which a character will assume the burden of another character as an act of charity. That this exchange had religious overtones—the miraculous workings of deities were often enacted through such a substitution—only enhances the magnitude of the boy's act.

Painting 2 continues to emphasize the virtuous character of the boy by contrasting his behavior with that of the servant through a split pictorial composition (fig. 3d–e). The scenes may be viewed first in succession and then comparatively. In the first room, the counselor confronts Nakamichi, who lies about the incident and blames the broken inkstone on the boy. Nakamichi is shown kneeling on the floorboards facing the counselor with the three pieces of the inkstone displayed prominently on a bright red bag between them. To the left of this scene, over an interior partition of the house, the counselor appears in the act of banishing the boy, who tearfully accepts the punishment. The text of the scroll enables this presentation; in other versions of the tale (those that relate the biography of the monk Shōkū), the boy volunteers his guilt immediately after his father discovers the inkstone, thus obviating the servant's prevarication. Although the events clearly take place in succession, the two scenes may also be viewed simultaneously. Because of the split-screen effect created by the blown-off roof (*fukinuki yatai*) technique, the servant's cowardly act of lying and the boy's valorous display of bravery in the face of his father's castigation can be viewed side by side. Mitsunobu's painting manipulates the vectors of the architectural framework to juxtapose moral opposites, thereby illuminating the boy's virtue.

The traditional technique of removing the roof to allow an aerial and panoramic view of architectural interiors in Japanese handscrolls created opportunities for the mobilization of the various lines of the buildings to suggest and even structure the interrelational dynamic of characters found therein. But Mitsunobu's ability to calibrate to an unusual degree the emotional tenor of each character in *Breaking the Inkstone* merits close attention. In the scene of the boy's banishment, for example (fig. 103), the lines of the walls diagram the divisions that will occur between the individuals of the household. While the upper beam of a partition that juts out from the diagonal one separating the two adjacent rooms seems to end unnaturally in midair, it suggests a spatial division between the parents, who tilt their heads in toward each other as they look down upon the boy and nurse below. The line of the beam, if extended, would run directly between the parents and the child, creating an imaginary boundary that suggests their impending separation. The lines of the floor further accentuate the distance between the two groups and generate a visual sense of expulsion. The black-and-white borders of the tatami mats run in a sharp downward diagonal from left to right, appearing to force the boy and his nurse from the residence. With this banishment from his home the boy loses his social status; in the earliest version of the story he is sent to the home of his nurse, while in the scroll text he is exiled to a hut in Saga in the northwestern hills of Kyoto. Mitsunobu's painting portrays this excommunication visually by aligning the boy with his nurse in the same spatial sphere and using the diagonal lines of the floor to edge them toward the wooden floor of the veranda, the space usually occupied by the lowly servant.

The painted folding screen represents yet another architectonic element that conditions the emotional tenor of the scene. As already discussed in chapter 3, on *A Wakeful Sleep*, the depiction of a screen painting can function not only metonymically but metaphorically. Its subject helps fashion the interiority of the figure seated before it.[14] This is certainly the case in the scene of banishment in *Breaking the Inkstone*. As the *Konjaku* text tells us in an earlier recounting of this moment, the boy's mother is torn between the loss of her son and the obeisance she must show to her husband.[15] In Mitsunobu's painting, while its textual accompaniment lacks this description, the six-panel folding screen behind her openly projects the emotional turmoil that is conveyed only in modified form by the image of her hunching slightly forward with one sleeve raised to her face. The mother's head is juxtaposed against a blue river depicted on the golden screen, as though her crying had created a "river of tears" (*namida gawa*), a common literary trope that lends poetic sentiment to scenes of parting.[16] Closer inspection of the screen painting reveals two white cranes standing in the river with their beaks open as though crying out to each other across the river. Images of two birds calling to one another appear within large-scale paintings in the Muromachi period and in some instances could convey longing between mother and child.[17] In this particular scene in *Breaking the Inkstone*, the crying of the two birds echoes that of the mother and child separated from each other at opposite ends of the room.[18] In this way, the spatial emplotment of figures within the architecture, and even the mural décor, communicate the gravity and sorrow of the event and the boy's ability to nobly accept the sentence he receives from his father.

Death in Exile: A Filial Son and Dutiful Young Master

The culmination of the boy's act of compassion arrives in painting 2, which depicts his death in exile (fig. 3f). Architectural framing is again crucial in staging the emotional content of this scene, although it has necessarily been simplified. In the *Konjaku* text, the boy's refusal to reveal his own innocence and his

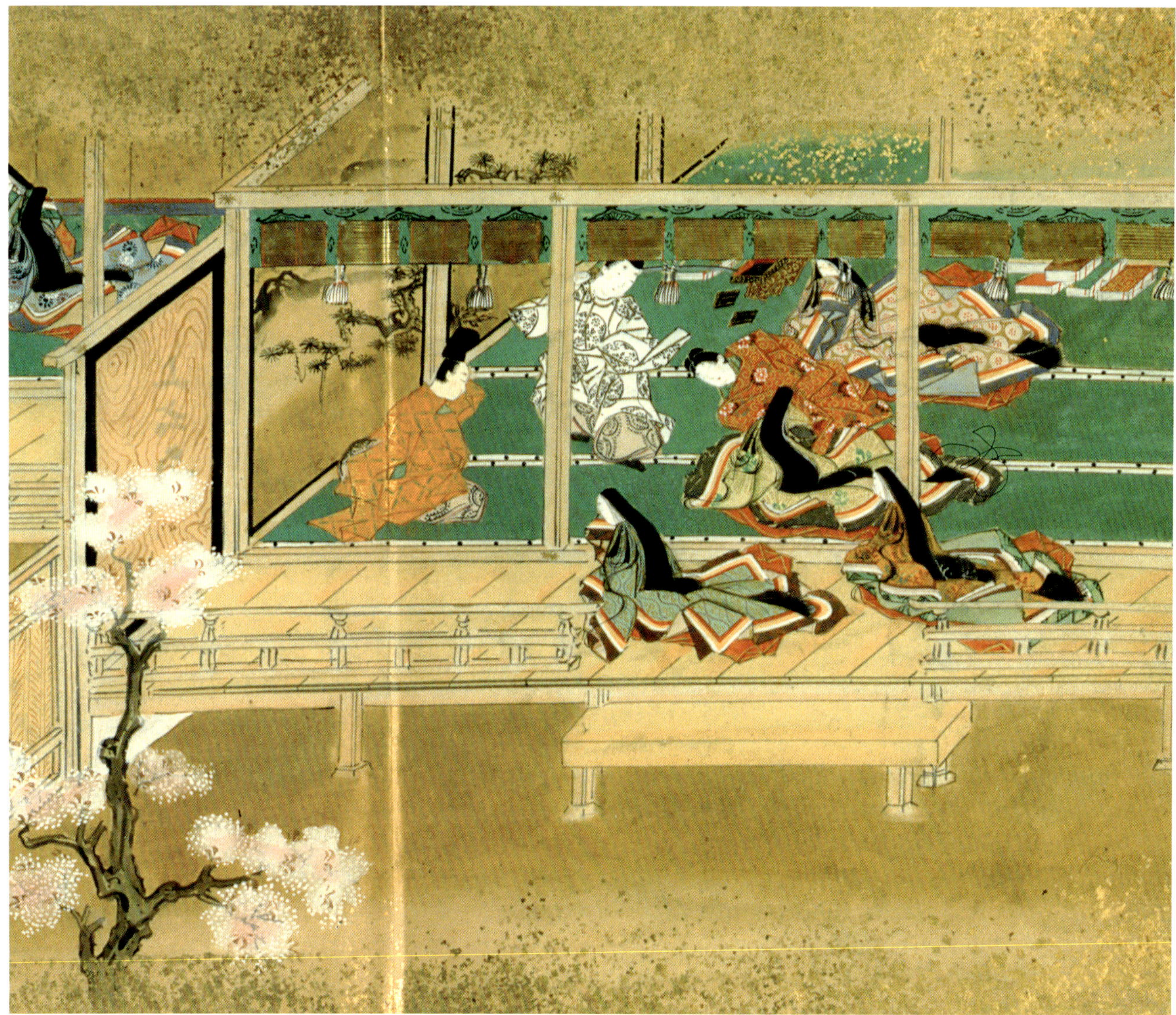

104 *Breaking the Inkstone* (*Suzuriwari*). Seventeenth century. Illustrated book, two vols.; 23.5 x 17.0 cm. Bibliothèque Nationale de France. Detail.

expressions of kindness toward his father on his deathbed present him as someone who remains loyal to Nakamichi and filial toward his parents. The final meeting between the boy and his parents provides the premise for an emotional representation of death marked by a poetic exchange. Although the texts in the picture scroll are brief, the artist and editor of the scroll seem to have based their rendition on the *Konjaku* version of the tale, the only one to include a scene of death in exile.

In every version of *Breaking the Inkstone* other than the picture scroll and the twelfth-century *Konjaku* text, the boy is not exiled but rather killed by the father immediately after the broken inkstone is discovered. One illustrated book of the story (fig. 104) renders this gruesomely by depicting the father raising his sword over his shoulder as the boy lies bundled in a robe before him, neck outstretched, the split inkstone just above visually foreshadowing his dismemberment. Yet another illustrated book shows the decapitation having already occurred (fig. 105), the broken inkstone here formally echoing or doubling the severed head and the bloody stump of the boy's neck. These images of the shattered inkstone and dismembered body placed side by side are in a cause-and-effect relationship and at the same time suggest an equivalence between the boy and the inkstone as two precious possessions of the father that have been destroyed.

Instead of this violence, however, the picture scroll follows the story line of the *Konjaku* version and recounts the boy's death from illness. In order to appreciate the extent of Mitsunobu's sensitive compression of pictoliterary expression here, it is necessary to describe the *Konjaku* death scene from which it takes its cue in some depth. The scenes of the boy's isolation in the twelfth-century text are heart-wrenching but also the most literary episodes of the tale; the characters compose poetry and exchange letters, while the narrator describes their emotions in detail. The poems composed by the boy reveal his fear and loneliness while separated from his parents for the first time and emphasize both his youthful innocence and his bravery:

Filled with fear over these unfamiliar surroundings, he passed the days in low spirits. One evening, looking extremely dejected, he recited to himself:

Kokoro kara	Though my heart led me
aretaru yado ni	to this ramshackle lodging where
tabine shite	I sleep as a traveler,
omoimo kakenu	my mind is filled
mono omoi koso	with unexpected thoughts.

How must his nurse have felt as she watched him muttering to himself.[19]

Later, after the boy falls ill, the nurse sends his mother another poem he composed, which reflects his longing for his parents:

Akenuru naru	Announcing the break of day,
tori no naku naku	the bird cries and cries,
madoro made	I wonder, do my parents know
ko wa kaku koso to	that I have spent the night thus,
shiru rame ya kimi	wakefully weeping?[20]

105 *Breaking the Inkstone* (*Suzuriwari*). Muromachi period. Illustrated book, three vols.; 16.2 x 23.7 cm. Katō Collection, Japan. Photograph by the author. Detail.

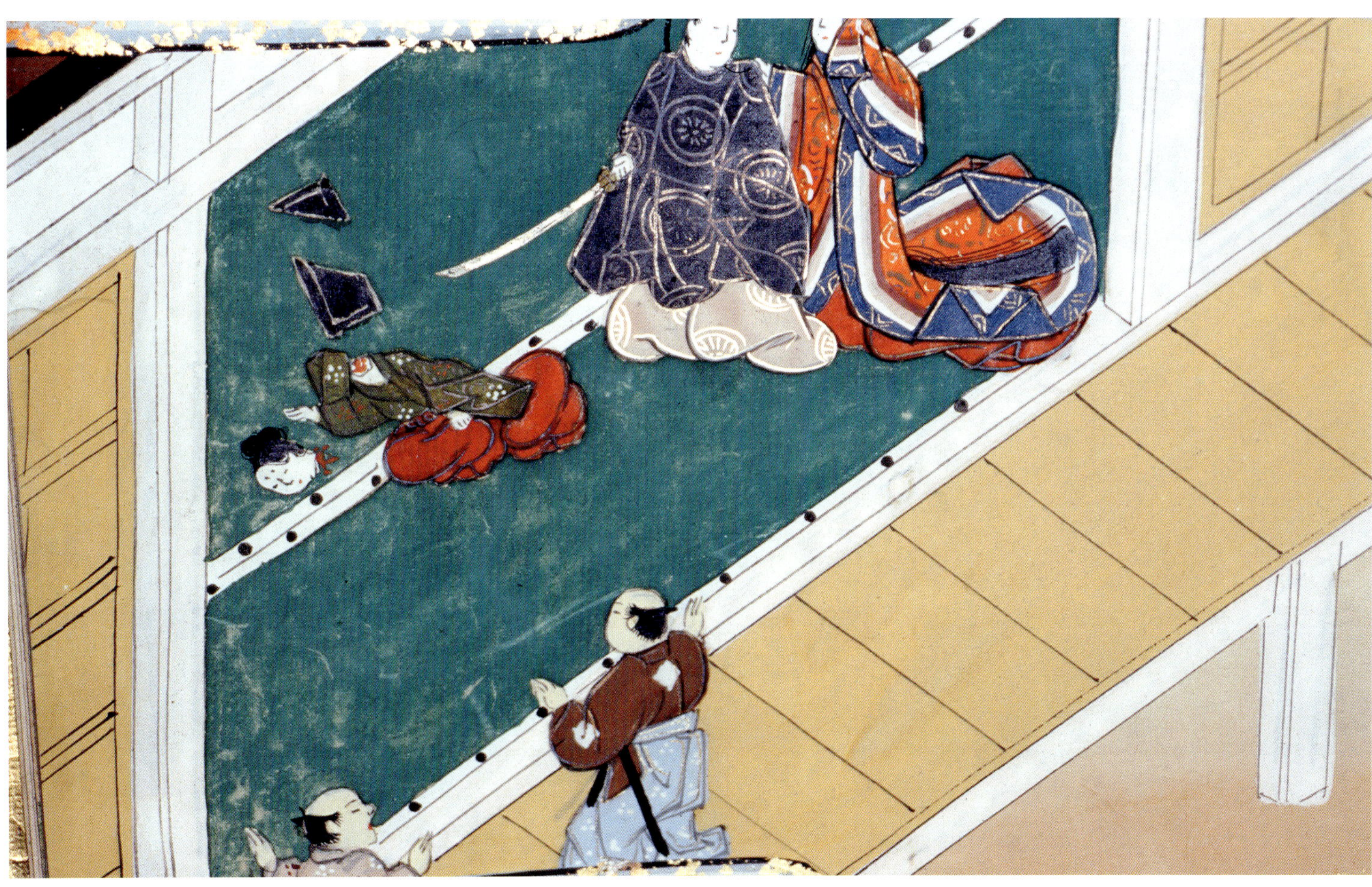

The poem reveals the boy's inability to blame his mother or father for his fate, as he wonders poignantly whether he even remains in their thoughts.

A poetic exchange also punctuates the scene of the boy's dying moments, when the father expresses his remorse for the first time:

Stepping down from the carriage, they approached the boy and saw him lying there, even nearer death than they had heard. Seeing him like this, the minister said, "Would even one hundred thousand inkstones made of gold and silver be worth this? I thought he was careless and sent him away in a fit of anger. What a pitifully wretched thing I have done! I must have been out of my mind to send this boy away." Feeling deep remorse he said:

Mutsugoto mo	Affectionate words,
nani ni ka wa sen	what use are they now?
kuyashiki wa	How tragic
kono yo ni kakaru	that in this world
wakare nari keri	we must make such a break.

Putting his face to the ear of the barely conscious boy, he said, sobbing, "Son, do you think me cruel?"

The boy whispered, "How could I possibly think that of my own parent?" The minister felt he had no way to respond. Unable to speak, he cried bitter tears of regret, but now there was nothing to be done. The young boy whispered:

106 Tosa Mitsunobu, *Breaking the Inkstone*. Dated 1495. One handscroll; ink, color, and gold on paper. Hosomi Museum, Kyoto. Detail, painting 2.

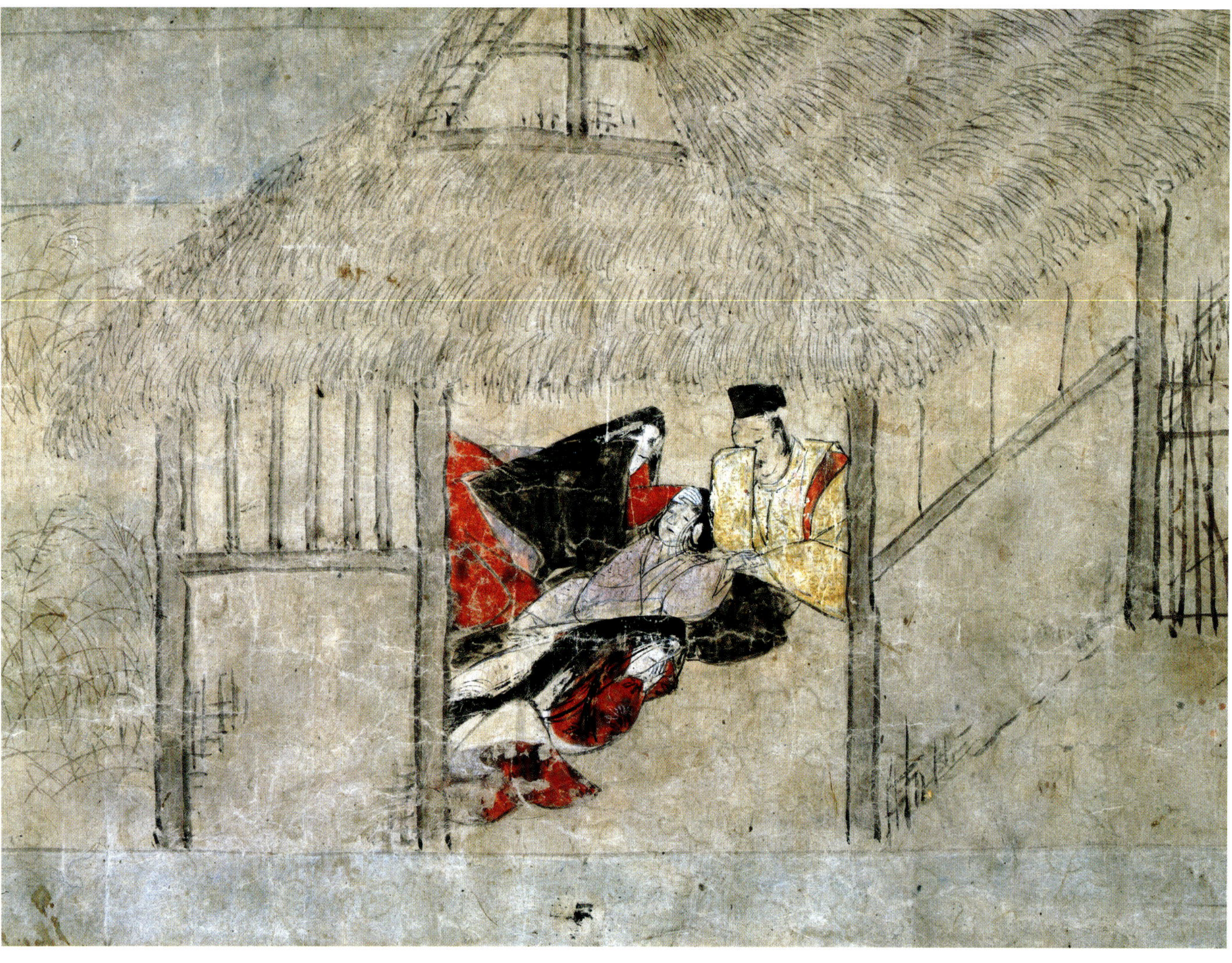

Tarachine no	When my father
itoishi toki ni	began to hate me,
kienamashi	I thought I would be better off dead,
yagate wakare no	and now at last, I have reached
michi to shiri seba	that final road of parting.[21]

Though seemingly in great pain, he called out the name of Amida ten times in a loud voice, then passed away. The heartbreak of the mother and father was beyond words. His long hair fell over his body, and his beautiful face wore a peaceful expression as if he were asleep. Seeing him like this his parents and nurse were crazed with an overwhelming sense of grief. A number of days passed, and the boy's body was buried according to custom. Since the nurse's house was so shabby, he was returned to his father's home, where Buddhist services began to be conducted.[22]

While this early version of the narrative paints a pathetic picture of the young boy's death and conjures up the sadness of his parents and nurse, the text of the fifteenth-century scroll contains a summary of the events so brief that when read without the images it appears callous. The scroll text sums up the boy's exile, sudden death, and parent's reaction in just a few short sentences:

On the dirt floor of a one-room hut in Saga, the nurse spread out a short robe. In no time it seemed as though the boy might be near death, at which point she sent word of the situation through a young child, and the mother and father came together. They grieved, but there was nothing that could be done.

The passage provides none of the poems found in the *Konjaku* anthology, no description of the boy's ordeal, no exchange between the boy and his father, and an extremely terse description of the parents' grief.

The scene in Mitsunobu's scroll, however, conveys some of the pathos of the earlier text through architectural framing: it differs from all other paintings in the scroll by offering only a small window through which to view the scene (figs. 3g and 106). The left post of the aperture-like opening has the effect of slowing down the flow of the visual narrative and creating an emphatic pause at this climactic scene. Every other scene in the scroll employs architectural frames that run along pronounced diagonal axes and ultimately help to propel the movement leftward, creating a high vantage point at a greater remove from the action. In the death scene, however, the presence of a roof forces the panoramic gaze to ground level as we peer into the house apparently straight on, through a square frame created by the posts of the structure and the line of the roof eave. The viewer is thus placed in the ground-level position of the spectators depicted around the counselor's carriage and who gesture toward the hut. This is the only instance in the scroll in which the act of spectatorship itself is represented, contributing to the caesura in the progression of the visual narrative. The viewer is encouraged to linger over the scene inside the hut, just as the depicted spectators do.

Within the cramped confines of the hut, the boy's white face is centered, doubly framed by the square opening and the hands and bodies that surround him. In pictorial terms, and with radical economy, it vividly evokes the deathbed scene in the twelfth-century text. The dying protagonist's long hair falls over his ears, his downturned eyes are shut, and his dark mouth appears slightly open, perhaps following the text's description of the boy's painful expression just before he dies. The image also captures the touching exchange of parting words, as described in the *Konjaku* text, when the father asks for exoneration; the conspicuously exposed ear of the boy and the glimpse of the father's mouth to the side of his raised sleeve are undoubtedly references to that whispered exchange.

In the scene of the boy's death the intrusive architectural lines—both depicted and imagined—that separated the individuals in the previous scene of banishment have disappeared, and within the small hut, the family resembles a unified grieving body. The father holds his son's hand, the mother touches his forehead, and the nurse is positioned virtually on top of the boy, as the bodies of all three characters encircle and merge with that of the boy. His passing momentarily reunites the family members until it serves its redemptive function and once again fragments the family, as each member leaves the household to devote himself or herself to Buddhist practice.

Remorse and Resolution

In contrast to the twelfth-century version of *Breaking the Inkstone*, in which only the servant entered a life of Buddhist practice, in Mitsunobu's handscroll the parents too renounce the secular world (fig. 3h). The third and final painting of the scroll begins with the back of a folding screen giving way to an image of the boy's nurse, gazing toward the next room, where the mother sits weeping. Her long flowing hair has been cut and she wears the dark robes of a nun while clutching Buddhist prayer beads. To the left, the father takes Buddhist vows and is having his head shaved by two priests, one with razor in hand, the other with hands clasped in prayer. Two white cloths cover the father's ears and a black lacquered bowl with gold details sits in front of him to collect the shaven hair. The father's mournful expression and hands pressed together in prayer convey the seriousness of the religious commitment he now undertakes in light of this tragedy of his own making. The scroll's ending, as opposed to that of other versions, emphasizes the parents' remorse and valorizes the boy's death by showing its power to move others to seek the Buddhist path.

Ultimately, however, this scene is penultimate to the culminating one (fig. 3j), which depicts Nakamichi, now a monk, praying for the boy's salvation. The first episode is effectively demarcated from that of the parents' home by a bucolic landscape (fig. 3i). Unrolling the scroll after the scene of the father's tonsure leads to emerging bands of mist at the top and bottom of the painting that multiply to cover much of the picture surface; the mists eventually trail off leftward over hills spotted with trees, clusters of autumn grasses, and two deer in the center looking leftward. This intervention of nature designates a shift in narrative time and setting, to the remote Mt. Shosha, a venerable mountain peak in Harima Province, where Nakamichi has secluded himself. The final scene in the handscroll depicts only one corner of the mountain temple (fig. 107). There the latticed door of the building opens to reveal the servant inside praying before an altar lined with gilded ritual vessels. His head completely shaved, Nakamichi now wears the robes and tunic of a monk. He kneels with his back to the viewer and his face in profile. With his palms together clasping his prayer beads he turns his head up toward the icon on the altar with his mouth slightly open as if in the middle of recitation. The pose of the kneeling servant here repeats that of the first painting of the scroll that showed the two figures in mirrored postures (fig. 99) and suggests that the former pairing has now been rendered eternal. Although physically absent, the boy still exists in the servant's thoughts, as the text of the scroll makes explicit by stating that Nakamichi devoted his life to praying for the boy. Retrospectively, the boy's sacrifice thus seems ultimately to have been made for the purpose of prompting the religious awakening of Nakamichi.

This aspect of *Breaking the Inkstone*, this apparent karmic bond between man and boy, recalls a number of "acolyte tales" (*chigo monogatari*), which usually center on an attachment between an older male priest and a young male acolyte that develops into an intensely emotional and ultimately spiritual bond over the course of the narrative. The most common ending of such tales involves the death of the young partner and the ensuing spiritual awakening and redemption of the elder monk. Such tales were frequently illustrated in picture scroll form and peaked in popularity during the Muromachi period, when they were read among a variety of social classes, including the emperor and aristocrats. By centering upon a sacrificial death that furthers the spiritual advancement of an older male protagonist, *Breaking the Inkstone* clearly evokes this literary genre, which is enhanced by Mitsunobu's pictorial citation of acolyte tale imagery.

BREAKING THE INKSTONE AS AN ACOLYTE TALE

Acolyte tales that focus on the unabashed allure of the young *chigo* seem to partake of a general appreciation of ephemeral beauty that was epitomized by the fleeting youthful appearance of boys. The convergence of this sentiment with Buddhist beliefs may seem counterin-

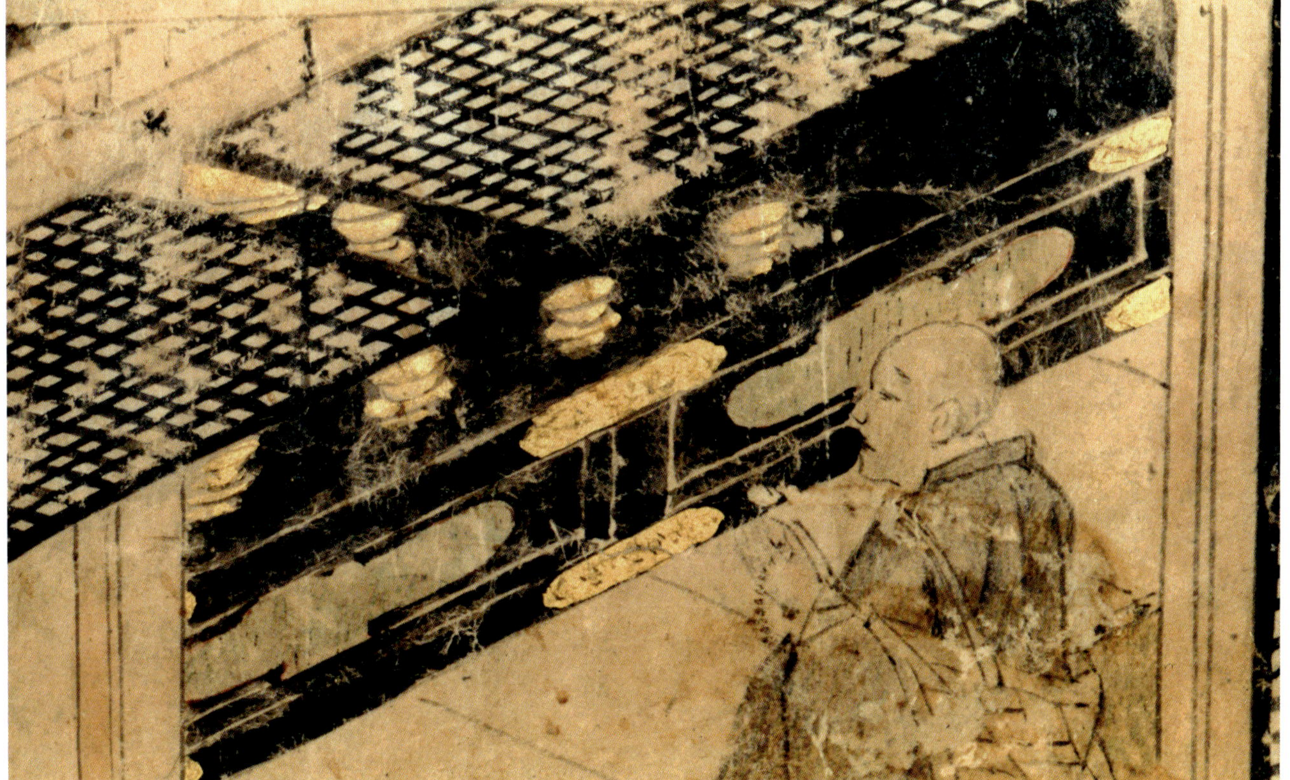

107 Tosa Mitsunobu, *Breaking the Inkstone*. Dated 1495. One handscroll; ink, color, and gold on paper. Hosomi Museum, Kyoto. Detail, painting 3.

tuitive but was in fact widespread; the beautiful youth seems to have been an embodiment of the transience of life and thus in literary tales could act as a device to provoke a heightened understanding of the illusory nature of the world.[23] Literary and pictorial descriptions of the boys who feature as the objects of desire in acolyte tales frame the ethereal beauty of the male youth in this manner. A classic example is the late-fourteenth-century handscroll *A Long Tale for an Autumn Night* (*Aki no yonaga monogatari*).[24] The figure who becomes the object of the monk's affection in this story is a young man of sixteen named Umewaka (literally "Plum Youth"). The monk first catches a glimpse of the boy standing between a profusion of cherry blossoms and a willow tree (fig. 108). The evanescence of cherry blossoms made them a long-standing symbol of ephemeral beauty, and here the juxtaposition of the boy and the flower is no coincidence. Meanwhile, the strands of a willow were a frequent metaphor for a woman's long, beautiful hair. The monk seems to acknowledge this comparison when he likens the boy's long hair to gracefully swaying sea grasses, recalling the billowing green branches of the tree.

Common physical characteristics of the *chigo* include a pale, white face, red lips, long hair tied in a ponytail, and bright-red garments, as can be seen in the depiction of Umewaka from *A Long Tale for an Autumn Night*. Similarly, the young man in *Legend of Kannon's Manifestation as a Youth* (*Chigo Kannon engi-e*), another illustrated acolyte tale from the late fourteenth century (fig. 109), is said to be "a youth of thirteen or fourteen, of complexion as pale as the moon."[25] He is described as wearing "over a purple underrobe . . . a garment of white silk and [split trousers] the color of fallen leaves [with] a bamboo ornament in his long sleek hair."[26] Many other examples can be cited to demonstrate that the *chigo* was a readily recognizable figure to contemporary viewers of illustrated tales. *Breaking the Inkstone* draws on the expectations of this figural type in the characterization of its own youthful protagonist.

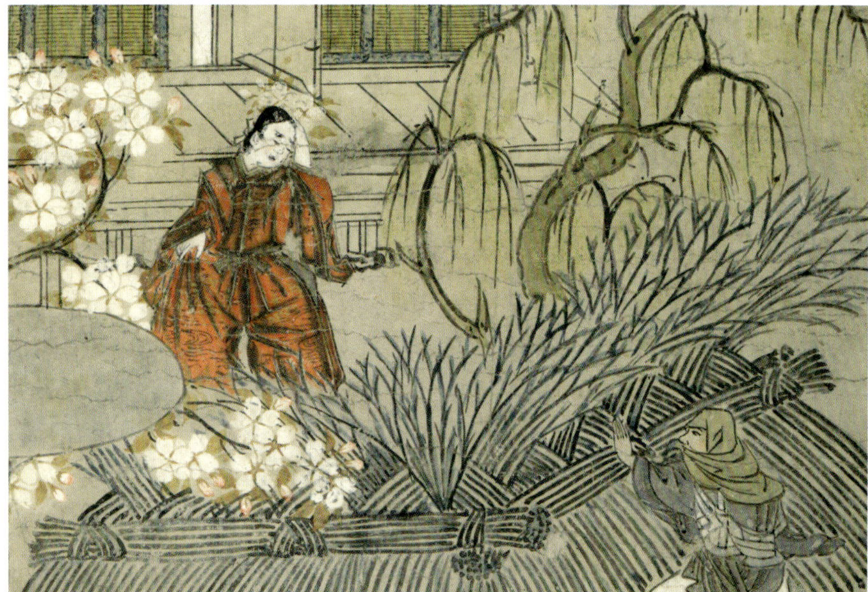

108 *A Long Tale for an Autumn Night* (*Aki no yonaga monogatari emaki*). Late fourteenth century. Three handscrolls; ink, color, and gold on paper. The Metropolitan Museum of Art, Purchase, Funds from various donors, by exchange, Fletcher Fund and Dodge Fund, 2002 (2002.459.1). Image © The Metropolitan Museum of Art, New York. Detail, scroll 1.

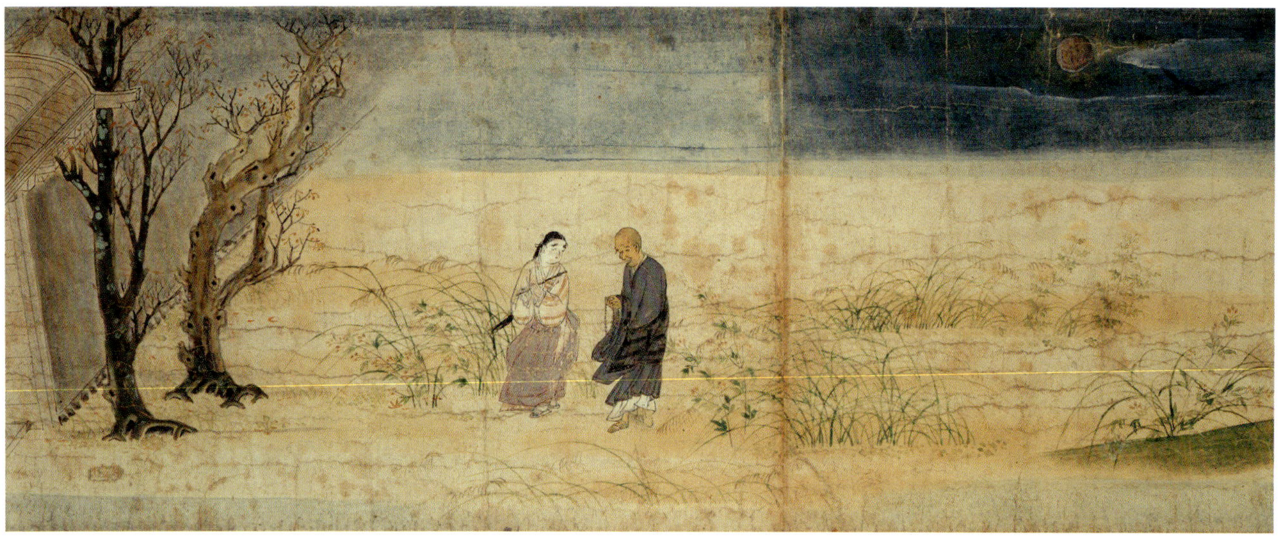

109 *Legend of Kannon's Manifestation as a Youth* (*Chigo Kannon engi-e*). Kamakura period, fourteenth century. One handscroll; ink and color on paper, H. 31.5 cm. Kōsetsu Museum of Art, Kobe. Important Cultural Property.

The young boy in *Breaking the Inkstone* bears a striking resemblance to contemporary representations of *chigo* in both text and image. Although there is no textual description of him in the text of Mitsunobu's scroll, the twelfth-century version of the tale, which as we have seen was most likely the primary source text for Mitsunobu's paintings, describes his appearance in some detail. The boy is introduced there as follows:

> The boy had a beautiful appearance and a generous heart. He was thirteen years old. By now he should have had his coming-of-age ceremony, but because there was such reluctance to cut his gorgeous hair, it had been delayed. Although he was just a young boy, he was wise beyond his years.[27]

Ironically, the description of his hair and the hesitation over its cutting recall the descriptions in classical narrative tales of the resistance young women experience when they attempt to cut their tresses to take Buddhist vows.

Hairstyles in elite circles were indeed codified and signified a person's age or stage in the life cycle. Soon

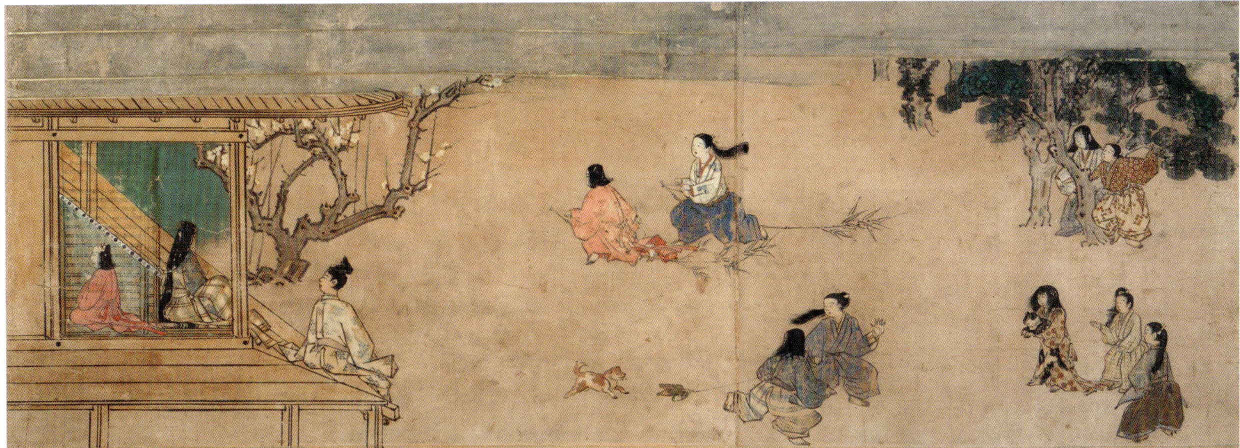

110 *Illustrated Life of Hōnen* (*Hōnen Shōnin eden*). Kamakura period, fourteenth century. Forty-eight handscrolls; ink and color on paper. Chion'in, Kyoto. National Treasure. Detail, scroll 1.

after birth, an infant's head was shaved, and continued to be shaven until the age of three, when the hair began to be grown out but was kept relatively short.[28] At the age of seven, children entered a new phase, in which they were referred to as *warawa;* this stage lasted from seven to fifteen years of age and was conceived of as a period, prior to a boy's coming-of-age ceremony, when he was no longer an infant and was making the transition to adulthood. Representations of boys in the *warawa* stage of childhood show them with their hair either cut at shoulder length and loose or long and tied back in a ponytail (fig. 110). The long hair of acolytes, also between the ages of seven and fifteen or sixteen, is uniformly depicted as tied back in a ponytail in medieval picture scrolls.

Mitsunobu emphasizes the boy's hair in *Breaking the Inkstone* by depicting it in a way that does not conform to any of the standards for length or style for young boys in fifteenth-century painting (fig. 111). The hair, which extends down his back and falls into delicate strands around his ears, is much too long to be worn loose in the *warawa* style, according to pictorial convention.[29] This seems to be the transitional or suspended appearance of a boy whose coming-of-age ceremony was deliberately delayed, but it also evokes the long tresses celebrated in acolyte tales. The boy in *Inkstone* thus appears to span the categories of *warawa* and *chigo*, with the loose locks of a child but of a length approaching that of an acolyte. The ambiguity here allows the boy to function as a young child while at the same time alluding to the figure of the acolyte.

The delaying of the boy's coming-of-age ceremony holds him in a state of suspended nonadulthood and situated outside male and female gender categories. The boy's appearance renders him ambiguous as to gender. Only the shorter length of his hair and the manner in which it cascades down his back in several strands distinguish the boy from the female nurse at his side. This ambiguity is combined with a certain youthful fragility to realize a sympathetic character of resonant appeal that also draws upon the acolyte tradition. He is shown weeping in two of the three paintings in which he appears, lending these scenes a sense of poetic tragedy, which frequently marks acolyte tales and emphasizes the bond between an elder monk and his acolyte.

Breaking the Inkstone alludes to acolyte tales most clearly, however, in its rendering of the boy's death. Scenes of cathartic passing often marked the dramatic pinnacle of works in this genre. A memorable example is found in a scene in *Legend of Kannon's Manifestation as a Youth,* where the beloved boy suddenly falls ill, leaving his master to grieve (fig. 112). An even more striking instance is found in *A Long Tale for an Autumn Night*, in the scene where Umewaka jumps from the Seta Bridge and drowns in the Seta River (fig. 113). This image of the deceased youth, with his head resting on the lap of the

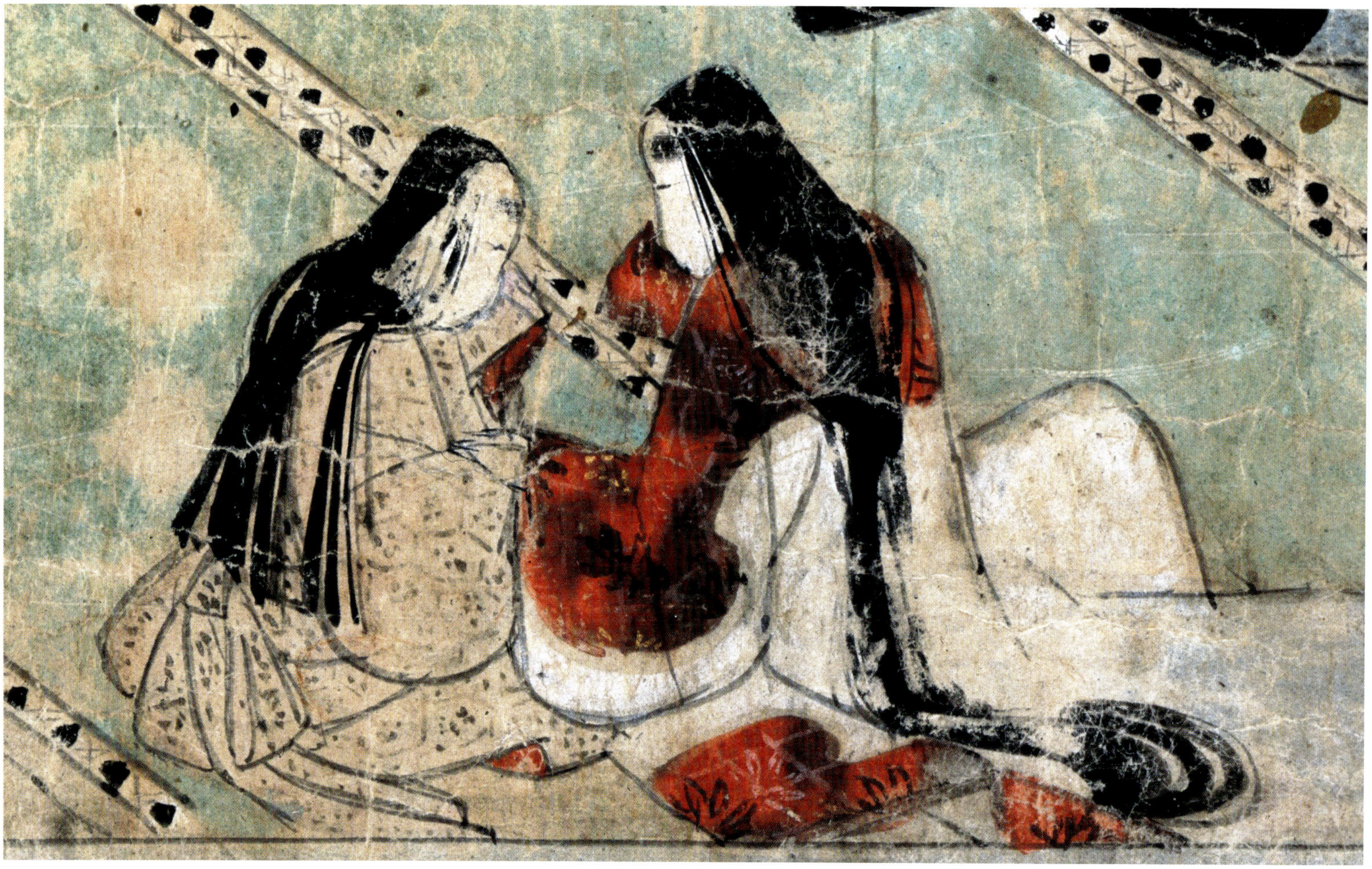

111 Tosa Mitsunobu, *Breaking the Inkstone*. Dated 1495. One handscroll; ink, color, and gold on paper. Hosomi Museum, Kyoto. Detail, painting 2.

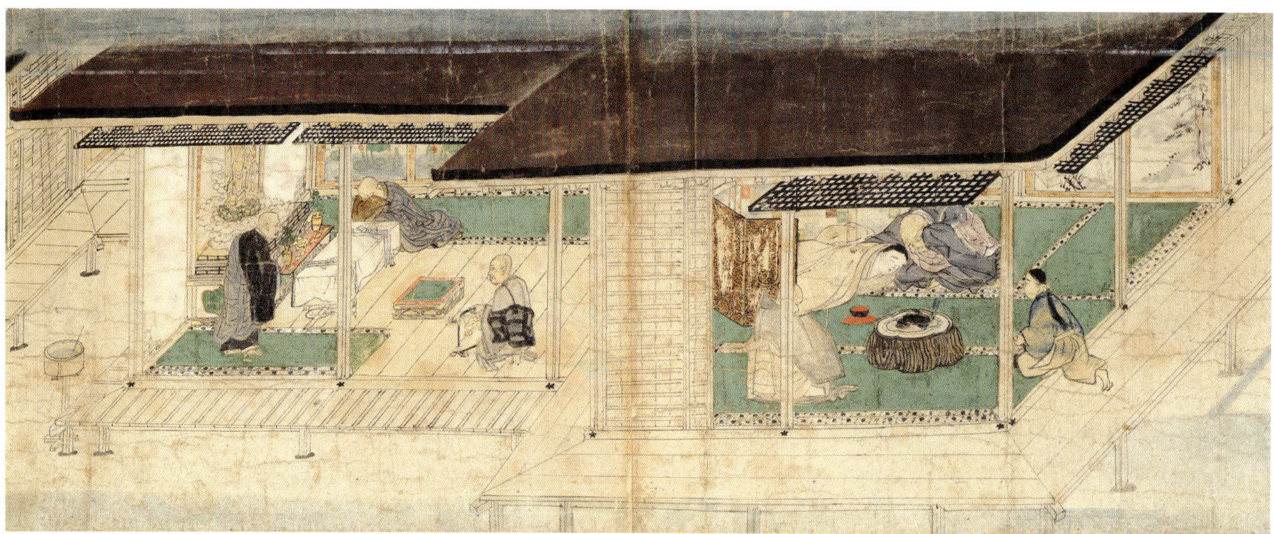

112 *Legend of Kannon's Manifestation as a Youth* (*Chigo Kannon engi-e*). Kamakura period, fourteenth century. One handscroll; ink and color on paper, H. 31.5 cm. Kōsetsu Museum of Art, Kobe. Important Cultural Property.

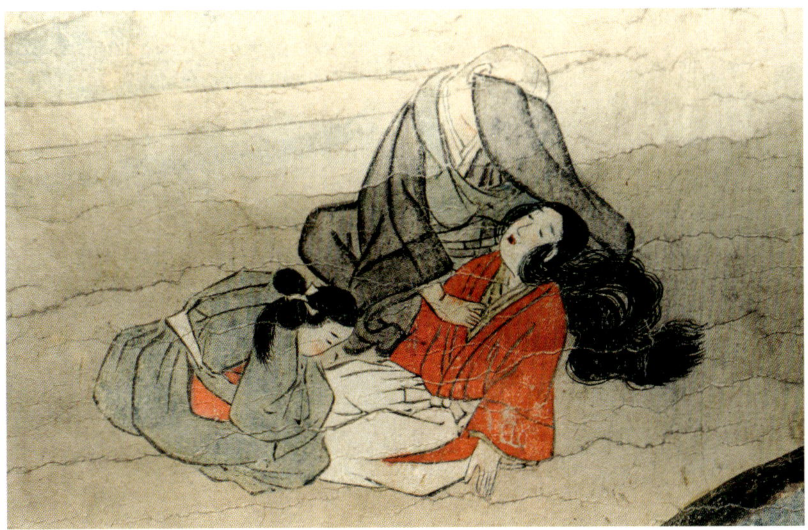

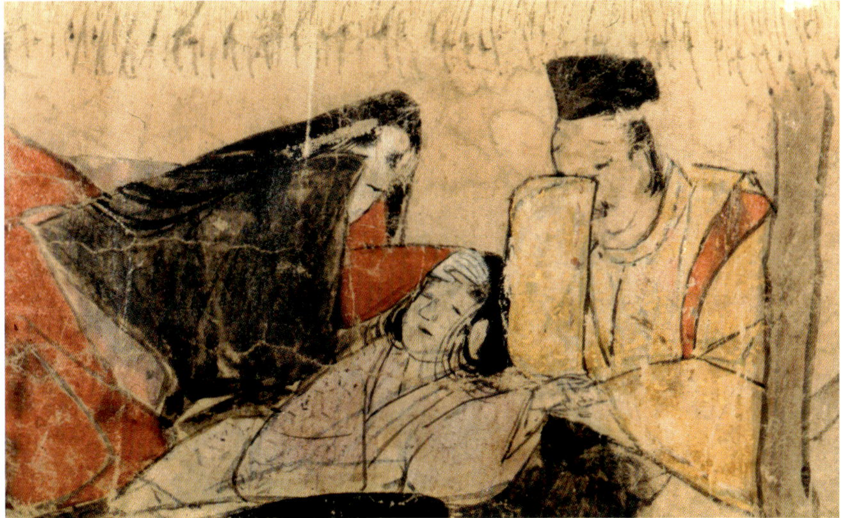

113 *A Long Tale for an Autumn Night* (*Aki no yonaga monogatari emaki*). Late fourteenth century. Three handscrolls; ink, color, and gold on paper. The Metropolitan Museum of Art, Purchase, Funds from various donors, by exchange, Fletcher Fund and Dodge Fund, 2002 (2002.459.3). Photograph by the author. Detail, scroll 3.

114 Tosa Mitsunobu, *Breaking the Inkstone*. Dated 1495. One handscroll; ink, color, and gold on paper. Hosomi Museum, Kyoto. Detail, painting 2.

priest and his long hair flowing around his body, closely resembles that of the figure in *Breaking the Inkstone* (fig. 114). The angle of the boys' bodies, their hair, which falls around their ears, and the bodies of their attendants lying at their feet are all revealingly similar.[30] While it is possible that Mitsunobu makes direct reference to the earlier handscroll in his rendition, the similarities may simply point to a common pool of poignant death scene templates for the acolyte genre. As such shared imagery shows, though all of these boys may be symbols of the ephemerality of life, through death they remain young and beautiful for eternity.

The majority of *chigo* tales and *Breaking the Inkstone* are differentiated, however, by highly dissimilar outcomes. In the former, the *chigo,* who ultimately leads the elder priests to spiritual awareness, most commonly reveal themselves to be earthly manifestations of the bodhisattva Kannon. Thus, the final climactic scene in the *Legend of Kannon's Manifestation as a Youth* depicts the bodhisattva Kannon emerging from the deceased boy's coffin (fig. 115). Such *chigo* are enlightened beings acting as earthly messengers of the Buddha and assume whatever guise necessary to recruit a person to the Buddhist path. The boy in *Breaking the Inkstone* evokes this aspect of the *chigo* but remains decidedly human throughout the tale. Nowhere in the accompanying text is the boy described as an incarnation of the Buddha, nor does he return after death to proclaim his successful rebirth, as happens in two illustrated manuscript versions of the tale. In one such illustration, the boy appears on a cloud in the arms of a monk (fig. 116), while in another a purple cloud materializes at the funeral to signify his rebirth (fig. 117). As a flesh-and-blood child rather than the manifestation of a Buddhist deity, the boy in the handscroll is unambiguously a human exemplar of virtuous behavior, someone who displays filial piety and remains loyal to an elder male figure who is not part of his family. Yet by evoking the imagery of boys from *chigo* tales, as well as divine boys as represented in Buddhist imagery, the paintings imbue the character with an otherworldly aura. *Breaking the Inkstone* thus bears a self-conscious relationship to the acolyte tale, one that was necessary to portray the relationship between a young boy and an older male figure in which the boy exhibits a loyalty that he is willing to maintain until death. Why this portrayal of extrafamilial loyalty was desired will become clear after examining the nature of the scroll's initial audience.

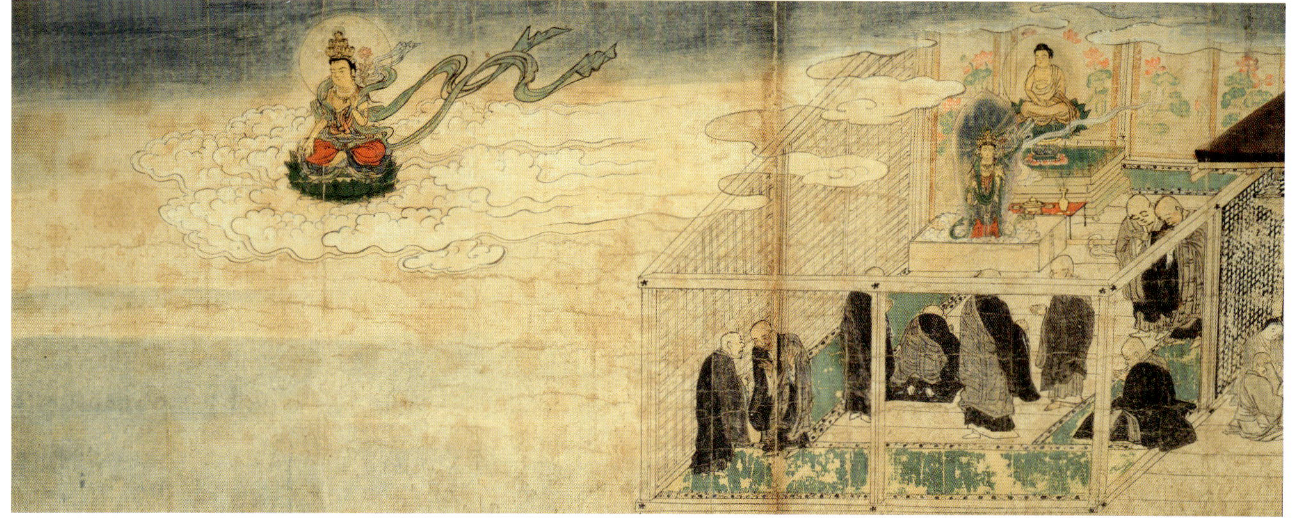

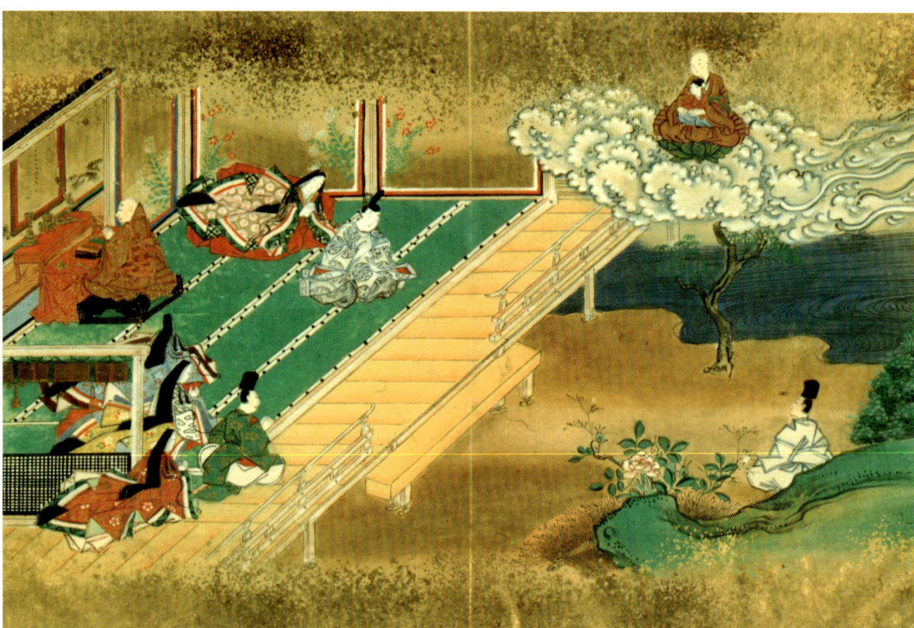

115 *Legend of Kannon's Manifestation as a Youth* (*Chigo Kannon engi-e*).

116 *Breaking the Inkstone* (*Suzuriwari*). Seventeenth century. Illustrated book, two vols.; 23.5 x 17.0 cm. Bibliothèque Nationale de France. Detail.

117 *Breaking the Inkstone* (*Nara e-hon Suzuriwari*). Muromachi period. Illustrated book, three vols.; 15.1 x 22.7 cm. Hiroshima University Library.

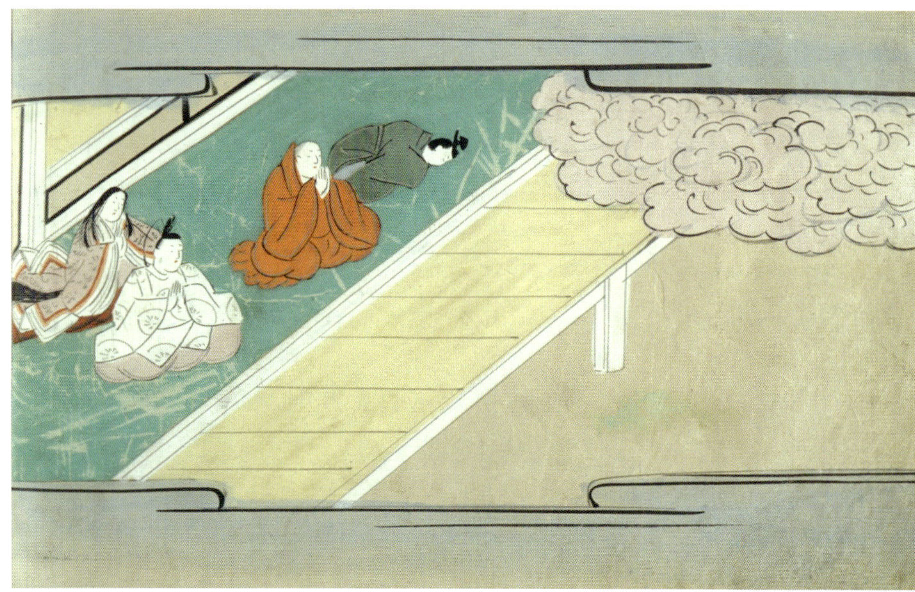

YOSHIZUMI AND HOSOKAWA MASAMOTO

Abutting the final painting of *Breaking the Inkstone* is a colophon (fig. 3k) inscribed by the scroll's owner, Ashikaga Yoshizumi (1480–1511), that reads: "Meiō 4 [1495] eleventh month, twenty-ninth day, Minamoto Yoshitaka." The Minamoto, or Genji, surname in the inscription denotes Yoshizumi's lineage among the Ashikaga shoguns, who claimed descent from the Seiwa Genji princely line and counted among their forebears the first shogun, Minamoto no Yoritomo (1147–99). Yoshizumi signed the scroll close to one year after having been officially appointed shogun, during which time he used the name Yoshitaka.[31] The political intrigue surrounding Yoshizumi's ascent to the position of shogun provides a crucial context for grasping the extreme figurations of piety, both filial and religious, in *Breaking the Inkstone*. The following précis of Yoshizumi's circumstances will usefully preface a discussion of the subject positions presupposed by the 1495 scroll. Yoshizumi was the nephew of the eighth shogun, Ashikaga Yoshimasa, the son of Yoshimasa's older brother Masatomo (1435–91), who was *bakufu* administrator (*horikoshi kubō*) of the Eastern Region (Kantō).[32] In 1487, Yoshimasa and his wife Hino Tomiko (1440–96) arranged for the seven-year-old Yoshizumi to move from his birthplace in Izu to Kyoto, where he would be educated but also readied as a potential successor to the shogunal seat should something happen to Yoshimasa's sole male heir, the ninth shogun Yoshihisa (1465–89). After arriving in Kyoto, Yoshizumi was placed in the care of Kōgen'in within the Zen Buddhist monastery of Tenryūji in Saga.[33]

Soon enough, the *bakufu* administrator was left without an heir to fill the position of shogun; Yoshihisa died while encamped with his men in Ōmi in 1489, and Yoshimasa died soon thereafter, in 1490, leaving Tomiko with considerable power in determining the next shogun. Initially, she put her full support behind Ashikaga Yoshitane (1465–1522), the son of Yoshimasa's brother Yoshimi (1439–91), and enabled his assumption of the realm's highest military office in 1490. Indicative of the political machinations of the age, however, Tomiko acted to ensure her political control over Yoshitane and his father, Yoshimi, by turning over the Ogawa palace (traditionally known as the residence of the military leader) to Yoshizumi in the same year.[34] By granting this young member of the Ashikaga lineage the residence, Tomiko sent a less-than-subtle message to Yoshitane and Yoshimi that Yoshizumi was also a rightful heir to the shogunate and could at any moment become a rallying symbol for anti-Yoshitane factions.[35] Clearly viewing this act as a threat, Yoshitane and Yoshimi destroyed the Ogawa palace, immediately triggering a plot by Tomiko and her allies to overthrow the shogun.[36]

Conspiring with Tomiko against Yoshitane was the longtime *bakufu* administrator Ise Sadamune.[37] Sadamune abruptly resigned his post as head of the *bakufu*'s Administrative Board (*mandokoro*), which he had held for over twenty years, after Yoshitane became shogun. He did so on the very day that Tomiko's intent to bestow the Ogawa residence on Yoshizumi became known, suggesting that they were taking steps together to overthrow the new shogun.[38] Sadamune's later prominent position within Yoshizumi's shogunate further suggests his earlier involvement in Yoshitane's ouster; Sadamune effectively ran the government for the teenage Yoshizumi and became one of the most influential men in the *bakufu*.

It was the warrior Hosokawa Masamoto (1466–1507), however, who was responsible for the military maneuvers against Yoshitane. Masamoto was the leader of the Keichōke branch of the Hosokawa, the members of which were powerful military governors (*shugo daimyō*) and long-standing retainers of the Ashikaga shoguns.[39] Their territories, which included the provinces of Settsu and Tanba, were concentrated in the Kinai region in the vicinity of Kyoto, and they became the only governors who remained in the capital after the dissolution of the *shugo* residential requirement in Kyoto that had been promulgated toward the end of the Ōnin War.[40] The Hosokawa wielded tremendous power over the shogunate, and the *bakufu* came to rely on their military prowess to suppress large-scale revolts that occurred in the capital.

In 1493 Masamoto orchestrated a violent coup d'état against Yoshitane, killing off most of the shogun's supporters and successfully installing the young Yoshizumi as the new military leader.[41] Masamoto then designated himself shogunal administrator (*kanrei*), a post that enabled him to control the military government from within the government structure itself. Although the coup was executed by the forces of Hosokawa Masamoto, Hino Tomiko and her confidant Ise Sadamune were most certainly coconspirators behind Yoshizumi's appointment. All of these individuals exploited the young Yoshizumi as a malleable figurehead, but Masamoto came to exert the most control over the young man once the coup had been carried out. He did this by secretly moving Yoshizumi into his own residence in the fourth month of 1493 and making it the shogun's official residence.[42]

One way that Masamoto asserted his control over Yoshizumi was to make him constantly aware of the instability of his position. The ousted shogun Yoshitane had survived the coup of 1493 and lived among supporters in the outer provinces and plotted his revenge; he thus posed a constant threat to Yoshizumi. On several occasions Yoshitane and his band of warriors attempted to attack the capital, but Hosokawa's forces were always successful in suppressing them.[43] An even greater worry for Yoshizumi than a straightforward attack by Yoshitane was the concern that his own allies might switch their allegiance to Yoshitane or other Ashikaga clan members. This included Hosokawa Masamoto himself, who began to make overtures to another young Ashikaga, Yoshitane's half brother Yoshitada (1479–1502), who had been allowed to reside in Kyoto after Yoshitane's removal.[44] Although Masamoto may never have seriously entertained the idea, Yoshitada was a useful pawn to keep the young shogun in check as he grew older and increasingly eager to exert his own political will. The threat of Yoshitada was eliminated in 1502 when Masamoto murdered the twenty-four-year-old, apparently on the order of Yoshizumi, who had dramatically sequestered himself at the temple Konryūji in Iwakura and refused to leave unless this potential rival was killed.[45]

Yoshizumi officially received the title of shogun in the first month of 1495, but in these early years Masamoto effectively ran the shogunate, earning the moniker "half-shogun" (*han-shogun*).[46] When Yoshizumi inscribed his name on *Breaking the Inkstone* less than one year later, he was thus still under the watchful eye of his administrator. Living in the same residence gave Masamoto the opportunity not only to control the reins of government but to shape the education of the fifteen-year-old shogun. *Breaking the Inkstone*, which highlights a male-male relationship deepened by the fidelity of the younger partner, seems like just the kind of story that Masamoto might have approved of Yoshizumi reading. And as we shall see, the scroll seems tailored—in ways both deliberate and subtle—to suit the situation and interests of its primary audience.

MASAMOTO, MOUNTAINS, AND MAGIC

As noted in the first part of this chapter, Yoshizumi's *Breaking the Inkstone* ends with what seems to be a reference to the holy man Shōkū. It does so by alluding to his renunciation story at the end of a tale that until that point most closely followed a version with no reference to the monk. Shōkū is never mentioned by name. The scroll text simply says that the servant Nakamichi took the tonsure and climbed Mt. Shosha, the mountain with which Shōkū is associated and on top of which he founded the temple Engyōji. Rather than Shōkū, then, the scroll text highlights the mountain. While the words "Shosha no yama" may have been enough to conjure in the mind of the reader the image of the holy man and the tale of his religious awakening, no other version of this story that alludes to Shōkū omits the monk's name. Although a seemingly minor detail, I will argue that this omission and the scroll's mention of Mt. Shosha open an important window onto the prerogatives of the work's makers, particularly Hosokawa Masamoto.

Mt. Shosha was far from a generic holy place in the minds of Masamoto, Ashikaga Yoshizumi, and the members of their circle. The names of the mountain and its founder were already in general circulation due to many legends associated with them.[47] Mt. Shosha was also the focus of imperial pilgrimage, and according to one account, Emperor Kazan (r. 984–86) secretly brought a painter with him on his pilgrimage in order to depict the countenance of the famous holy man;[48] during the visit, however, Shōkū caused a great tremor that brought the painter out of hiding and forced his brush to fall on the portrait, leaving a mark that perfectly replicated a mole on the holy man's face. Such miraculous legends about Mt. Shosha were disseminated not only in literary anthologies but also through oral transmission during the Muromachi period. Yoshizumi's Ashikaga forebears were patrons of the institutions of Mt. Shosha; the sixth shogun, Yoshinori, made the pilgrimage in 1432,[49] and Yoshimasa helped to rebuild the temple's Lecture Hall (*kōdō*) in 1463.[50] When the temple's five-story pagoda went up in flames in 1479,[51] and when its Nyoirin Kannon statue and Tahōtō pagoda burned in 1492, aristocratic diarists in both Nara and the capital took note.[52]

Shōkū's religious legacy, however, was not the only attraction that drew Masamoto/Yoshizumi to Mt. Shosha. Its location in Harima Province (Banshū), which was governed by Akamatsu Masanori (d. 1496), made it a key site in the geopolitical alliances that sustained the Yoshizumi regime. As the governor of Harima, Bizen, and Mimasaku provinces, and with powerful warrior families among his retainers, Masanori was a crucial ally for Masamoto. Masamoto guaranteed the Akamatsu clan's allegiance by arranging for his older sister, the former nun Dōshōin (b. 1461–64), to wed the widowed Masanori.[53] The blatantly strategic nature of the alliance was made clear when, just days after the betrothal was announced in the third month of 1493, Masamoto informed his retainers of the secret plan to oust the sitting shogun, Yoshitane.[54] The coup was successfully completed in the fifth month when the shogun Yoshitane was captured and brought to Kyoto by none other than Akamatsu Masanori.[55] Masanori died of illness in 1496, but Dōshōin remained in Harima Province, where she exerted unrivaled authority over the region, even prompting one scholar to characterize her as a "female daimyo."[56] When Yoshizumi himself was forced to flee Kyoto in 1508 after Masamoto's death, he turned to the Akamatsu clan and Dōshōin to protect his newborn son, the future shogun Yoshiharu (1511–50), who was raised in Harima Province.[57] The Akamatsu of Harima and Dōshōin were thus instrumental in installing Yoshizumi as shogun in 1495 and served as lifelong allies. Through this close relationship, Hosokawa Masamoto had a connection not only to Harima Province but to Engyōji on Mt. Shosha, since Akamatsu Masanori was an important lay patron of the temple.[58]

Beyond even these connections, however, Masamoto's attention to Mt. Shosha derived from its association with the practice of mountain asceticism (*shugen*), of which the shogunal administrator was a serious devotee.[59] Various networks of ascetic practice involving mountain pilgrimages and retreats became codified into a distinct religious order, Shugendō, sometime during the ninth or tenth centuries. It fits poorly into the received map of Japanese sectarian religions, eclectically drawing upon belief in *kami*, the Shingon and Tendai sects of Buddhism, and Daoism.[60] Practitioners, who were exclusively male, were known as *yamabushi*, literally "those who lie down in the mountains," or *shugenja*, "those who accumulate power" through austerities in the mountains.[61] These men performed periodic ritual climbs of sacred mountains to venerate deities and undertook prolonged stays, akin to retreats, during which they performed ascetic practices that culminated in the transmission of secret knowledge.[62] Women were prohibited from ascending Mt. Shosha in the late medieval period,[63] as was the rule for mountains that were designated *shugendō* centers, a female presence being contradictory to the avowed aims of escape from carnal desire and the practice of rigorous austerities. Because one of the primary goals of *shugen* practitioners was the acquisition of supernatural power, which could include the ability to exorcise demons, divine the future, heal illness, walk on swords and fire, and fly through the air, it was especially attractive to the military warlords of the Sengoku era.

Masamoto was widely believed by contemporaries to be immersed in these magico-religious practices. One eyewitness account from 1493 describes how Masamoto received instruction in *shugen,* or "the way of Tengu" (referring to mythical birdlike creatures with long noses), from the *yamabushi* Shisen'in Kōsen (active late fifteenth century) and how both men worshiped Minamoto no Yoshitsune (1159–89) at Kuramadera, the mountain temple where Yoshitsune was said to have learned magical swordsmanship from a *tengu* king.[64] Another Muromachi text describes Masamoto as a "practitioner of the magic arts and the ways of Atago, who wore the garb of a lay monk or a mountain ascetic (*yamabushi*)."[65] He was rumored to have used magic to fly and stand in midair, and "once when he was reading a sutra, a *dharani* [a mystic phrase] reverberated in response, making the hair of those watching stand on end."[66] Other sources, also of the period, reflect the mythologization of Masamoto among his contemporaries. A monk from Harima Province named Kūzen (active late fifteenth century) wrote that Masamoto was conceived when Prince Shōtoku flew into Masamoto's mother's mouth; Masamoto was thus widely viewed as Shōtoku's reincarnation.[67] Kūzen also explains Masamoto's special link to Mt. Atago, a center of *shugen* practice, relating that, when Masamoto was kidnapped at age twelve, an avatar of the deity enshrined there revealed his whereabouts in a dream.[68]

Such mythologization strongly suggests that references to Masamoto's *shugen* practices were prone to no small amount of hyperbole. Nevertheless, it is easy to understand Masamoto's commitment to Shugendō since it promised religious and supernatural empowerment and offered political opportunities through its networks of practitioners. In one instance, Masamoto and his men, dressed in the garb of *yamabushi*, traveled to the northern provinces in 1491 using the same Shugendō routes as the famous practitioner Dōkō (1465–1501).[69] While the practice of religious austerities may have been a main goal of the trip, another aim was to shore up support among the Uesugi clan, governors of Echigo Province, for the impending coup of 1493.[70] Useful alliances were made possible by a shared commitment to Shugendō, such as with the *yamabushi* Shisen'in Kōsen; in addition to acting as Masamoto's instructor in the

118 *Origins of Religious Austerities at Tsukiminedera* (*Tsukiminedera konryū shugyō engi emaki*). Dated 1495. Three handscrolls; ink, color, and gold on paper, H. 34.3 cm. Freer Gallery of Art, Smithsonian Institution, Washington, DC. Detail, scroll 2.

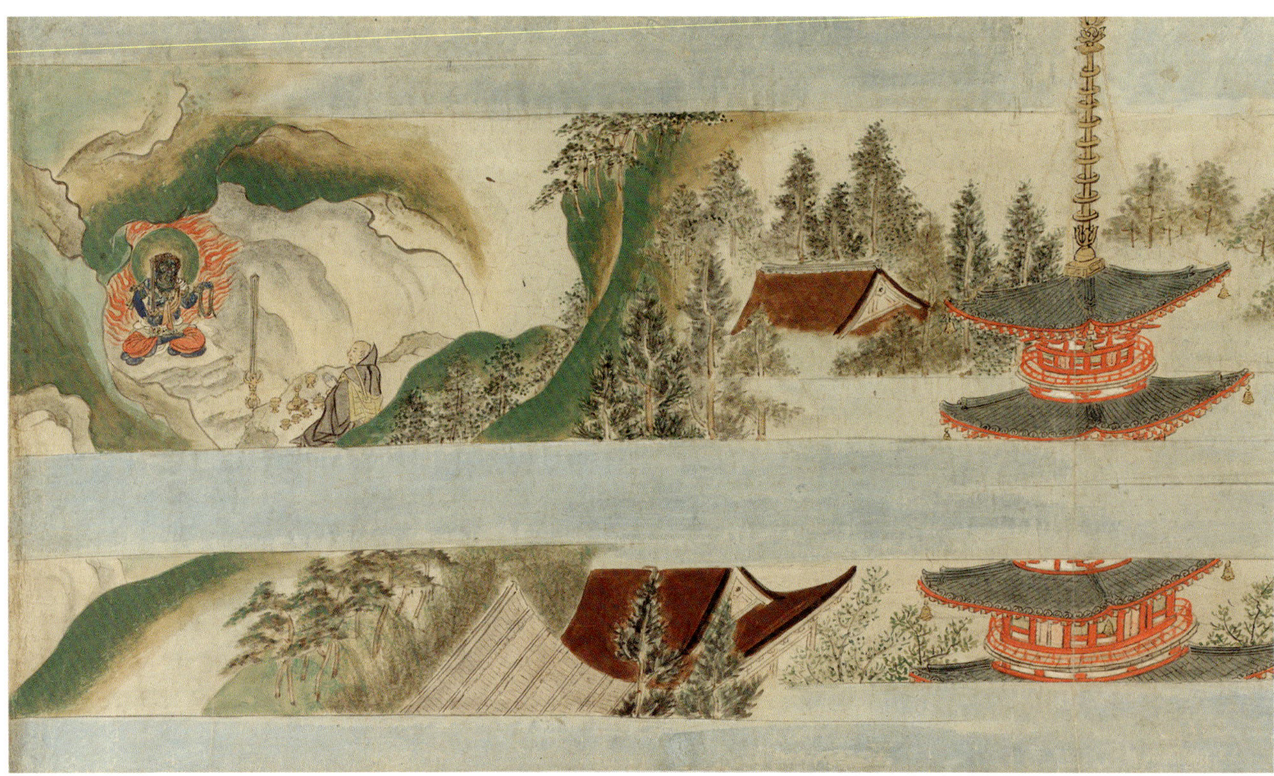

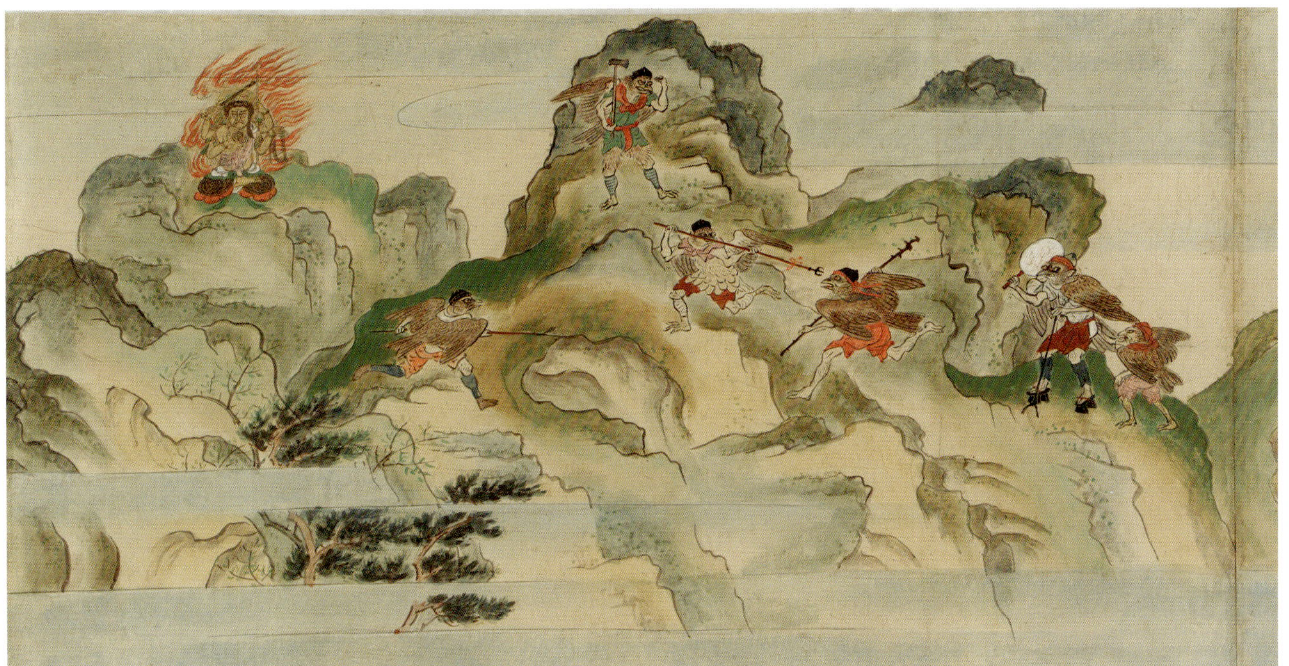

119 *Origins of Religious Austerities at Tsukiminedera* (*Tsukiminedera konryū shugyō engi emaki*). Dated 1495. Three handscrolls; ink, color, and gold on paper, H. 34.3 cm. Freer Gallery of Art, Smithsonian Institution, Washington, DC. Detail, scroll 2.

magical arts and as his attendant, Kōsen had personal connections to Aki Province that allowed Masamoto to monitor the powerful Ōuchi clan in the neighboring provinces of Suō and Nagato.[71] Finally, Masamoto's *shugen* practice and his donning of a *yamabushi* costume might have effectively allowed him to fashion himself as a feared warrior of supernatural powers.

The intertwined nature of Masamoto's interest in mountain asceticism and his political machinations are perfectly embodied in a handscroll project that he most likely commissioned in 1495, the same year that *Breaking the Inkstone* was created. *Origins of Religious Austerities at Tsukiminedera* (*Tsukiminedera konryū shugyō engi emaki*), also painted by Tosa Mitsunobu, relates the legends of a temple located in Settsu Province, one of the key home provinces of Hosokawa Masamoto.[72] The references to *shugen* practice are explicit in this scroll, ranging from the term *shugyō* in the title of the work to numerous details in the text and paintings.[73] In one episode (fig. 118), when the founding monk Nichira Shōnin prays to Fudō for the power to "subdue foreign lands" (*ikoku chōbuku*), a sword descends upon the altar and speaks:

"Above all, this sword is just like the Buddha in protecting those who pursue the ascetic practice in service to the Buddha, believing firmly in the tenets of the Shingon sect." The mountain was thus named Kenbi (Pommel of the Sword).[74]

The text sanctions *shugen* practitioners and describes their sacred protection by this magical sword, while the painting depicts the protagonist Nichira enacting a Fudō-centered ritual. The Shingon Buddhist deity Fudō Myōō (Acala) was the main focus of ascetic practice for the *shugenja*, who would attempt to identify spiritually with Fudō as a way to harness the deity's powers to subdue (*chōbuku*) evil spirits.[75] The image of Fudō as an object of worship in this scroll, and the appearance of the term *chōbuku* twice in the text, link the scroll unambiguously to *shugen* practice.

Another scene in the *Tsukiminedera* scroll (fig. 119) evokes the actual mountain setting of ascetic rituals by depicting a group of *tengu* dressed as *yamabushi* frolicking in the vicinity of Fudō on the sacred peak. Medieval commentators referred to *shugen* practice as the "way of *tengu*" (*tengu no hō*), and *tengu,* the supernatural, demon-

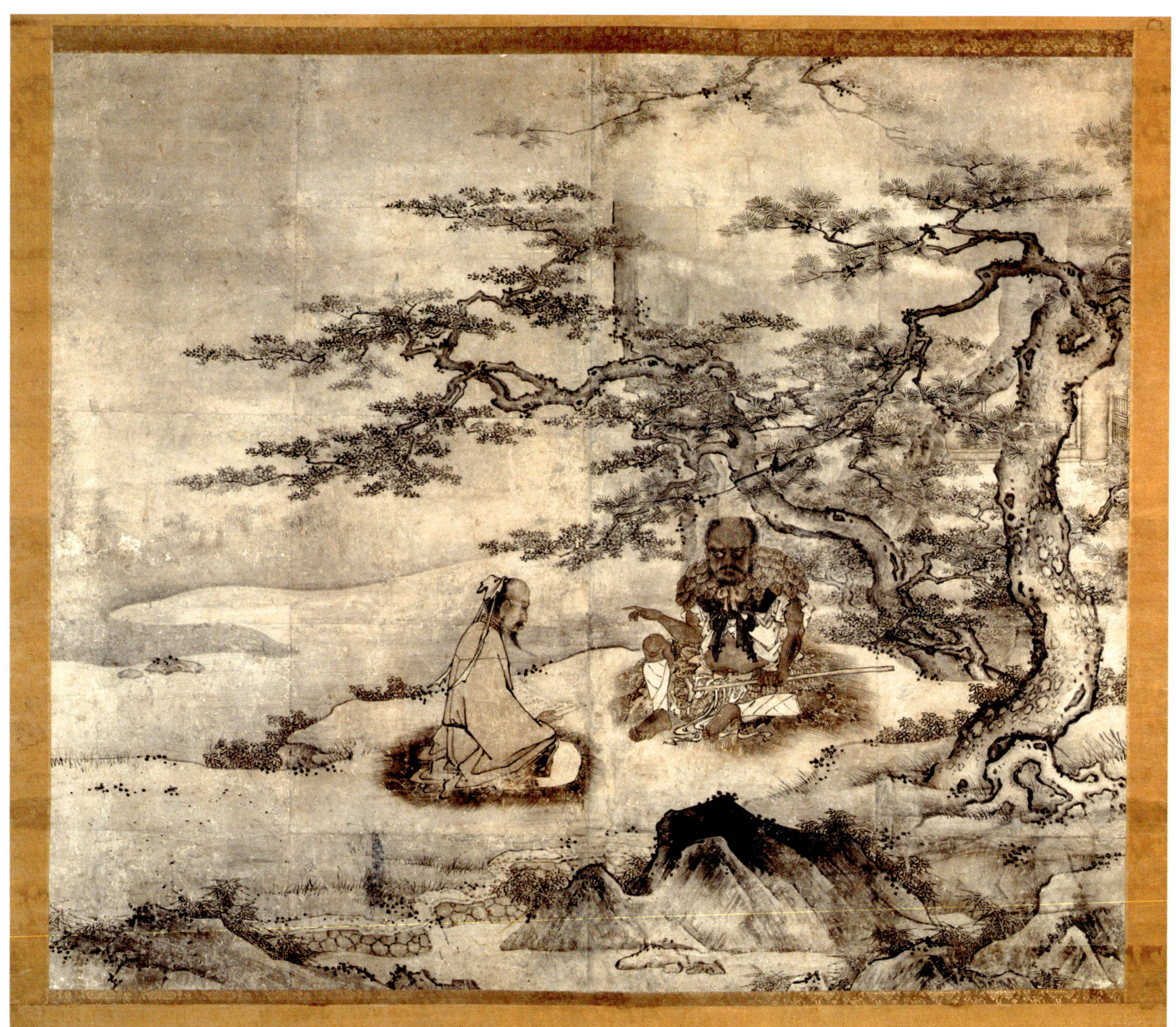

120 Attributed to Kanō Masanobu, *Zhongli Quan and Lü Dongbin*. Late fifteenth century. Partition painting now mounted as a hanging scroll; ink and light color on paper, 151.6 x 171.6 cm. Seigen'in Temple, Kyoto.

like creatures thought to inhabit mountains, was one nickname for *yamabushi*. The *Tsukiminedera* painting thus visualizes the imaginary world of *yamabushi*, upon which Masamoto drew as he sought to expand his political influence and military might. This *shugen*-inspired picture scroll is inextricably bound up with Masamoto's political aspirations, and it was likely offered to its namesake temple as a way of ensuring control of the unruly provinces and success over his rivals.

Masamoto's political ascendancy in the late 1480s and 1490s put him in a position to be a leading cultural patron in Kyoto. It is in this context that he engaged the leading painters in the capital, first and foremost Tosa Mitsunobu. But Mitsunobu was not the only painter to service the shogunal administrator. Masamoto commissioned partition paintings (*shōhekiga*) by another professional painter active in the capital, Kanō Masanobu (1434–1530), for his own residence, the Hall of First Pleasures (Yūshoken) in 1491 and a screen painting by the same artist for Daishin'in, a subtemple of Myōshinji that he helped found in 1492.[76] Although the paintings from Masamoto's residence do not survive, one panel from a set of wall paintings that originally adorned the walls of the Seigen'in, a subtemple of Ryōanji established by Masamoto in 1489, depicts a topic in keeping with the Shugendō-tinged character of his other projects, that of the Chinese warrior and immortal Lü Dongbin (fig. 120). In the painting, attributed to Kanō Masanobu, Lü Dongbin is bequeathed the secrets of Daoism from his master Zhongli Quan. Daoist elements exerted a great influence on Shugendō, and it is difficult to ignore the resemblance between the image of Lü Dongbin and that of an ideal *shugenja*. According to the hagiography of the Chinese immortal, Lü underwent various trials for the purpose of self-cultivation and the attainment of interior alchemy, all reminiscent of *shugen* austerities.[77] Lü was widely viewed as a peripatetic spirit who journeyed throughout China, and he was worshiped as a deity who used his sword and thunder magic to expel demons and heal diseases.[78] Paintings of Daoist immortals became a mainstay of Zen temple walls in the sixteenth century, but this slightly earlier example may be seen as a forerunner that reflects the idiosyncratic interests of Seigen'in's warrior patron. Masamoto's involvement in mountaineering and magic makes this Chinese warrior-immortal who possessed all the powers that the *shugenja* hoped to attain an intriguing self-image.[79]

Masamoto was undoubtedly drawn to the holy man of Mt. Shosha depicted in *Breaking the Inkstone* for similar reasons. Among the numerous legends that had accrued around Shōkū Shōnin, several cast him as a monk who embodied *shugen* ideals. He was said to have possessed supernatural powers, including the ability to travel "from Shosha to Mt. Hiei, a distance of thirty-five leagues, in a single moment."[80] One of earliest legends about the monk mentions that he was served by two boys (*gohō dōji*), protective deities frequently attached to holy men known for their practice of austerities.[81] Protective boy deities figure prominently in Shugendō lore as figures who guide ascetics into the mountains and who act as messengers for other deities.[82] Shōkū's boy attendants, Otomaru and Wakamaru, were avatars of Fudō and Bishamon, who possessed superhuman strength and the ability to fly.[83] Boy attendants commonly flank images and sculpture of Fudō, as well as those of En no Gyōja, the legendary seventh-century founder of the Shugendō sect. Shōkū, in this instance, was a holy man customized to Masamoto's fertile religious imagination.[84]

It is no coincidence that Masamoto's charge Yoshizumi was in the possession of a narrative scroll about a man who went to live on Mt. Shosha. The absence of Shōkū's name in the text somewhat muffles the reference but at the same time facilitates projections onto the story. The identity of the man who climbs Mt. Shosha can be understood as a type. Indeed, many of the characters are easily universalized, as so much abbreviation and variation have abstracted the tale into one that foregrounds an extrafamilial relationship between a young boy and an older male figure. The argument proposed here is that this abstraction lent itself to highly individuated readings of the Mitsunobu scroll. The boy protagonist, for example, would have had deep resonance for Ashikaga Yoshizumi, who like the boy in the story had been separated from his parents at the age of seven and sent away to Saga, where Kōgen'in was located.[85] In 1493 Yoshizumi was removed from the temple and brought into Masamoto's own home, where he signed his name to *Breaking the Inkstone* two years later. Masamoto, although officially a servant to Yoshizumi, was older and clearly in charge; in this sense, his relationship to the young shogun bears an uncanny resemblance to that of Nakamichi and the young boy. These personalized readings were not, however, predicated upon a direct correspondence between fictional characters and historical viewers but rather emanated from the ambiguous but dynamic space the scroll provided for envisioning complex and reciprocal bonds between the men in Masamoto's household.

BREAKING THE INKSTONE AND BONDS BETWEEN MEN

In order to gauge the dynamic of projection and individuation at issue, it is worth exploring further the homosocial bonds entangling the main characters involved in the production of *Breaking the Inkstone.* The personal allegiances that were so crucial to Masamoto's military strategies and political rise were always in danger of disintegration. In 1504, for example, Yakushiji Motokazu, Masamoto's retainer and deputy governor of Settsu Province, launched a traitorous rebellion against the shogunal administrator. The uprising was quickly suppressed and Motokazu was forced to commit suicide. Before cutting his stomach he composed a final death poem to be given to Masamoto:

> Hell is where my good master's house belongs.
> It is there that today I don the traveler's cloak.
> (*Jigoku ni wa yoki waga nushi no aru yado de*
> *kyō omoitatsu tabikoromo ka na*)
>
> In the final analysis, the shogunal administrator loves young boys [*wakashū*]; this should be read to expose him when he is with them.[86]

The motivations for Motoichi's act of treason, his hatred of Masamoto, and his desire to "expose his dreadfulness," seem to have stemmed from a looming threat that Masamoto was about to rescind the Settsu deputy governorship from the Yakushiji clan.[87] One commentator has suggested that the angry words directed at Masamoto betray a homosexual relationship between the shogunal administrator and his deputy.[88] Such an interpretation accords with the mainstream scholarly understanding of Masamoto's erotic life as based on "male love" (*nanshoku*).

Given Masamoto's resistance to marriage and his known proclivities for young men, it is tempting to read overtones of male love into the bond between servant and boy in *Breaking the Inkstone*. One twentieth-century reader to do so was the writer Yukio Mishima, who referred to this tale in his novel *Forbidden Colors* (*Kinjiki*, 1951–53). In the novel the main characters, a beautiful young man named Yūichi and an old writer named Shunsuke, visit the Sanbōin Hall of Daigoji Temple. The abbot shows them the sexually explicit fourteenth-century *Acolyte Scroll* (*Chigo no sōshi*), in which a manservant named Chūta engages in anal intercourse with a boy.[89]

> The pictures of male love [*nanshoku-e*] that followed the simple, frank text were filled with a pleasant, artless sensuality. As Yūichi studied excitedly every scene, Shunsuke's mind was drawn to the name of the man, Chūta, the very name of the retainer in "The Broken Inkstone." The innocent boy had taken the blame of the family retainer on himself. The strength of character that led him to keep silent even until death led one to imagine some kind of pact in the terse, simple description. As a result was not just the sound of the name Chūta—one given to the person fulfilling that particular function—enough to bring a dark smile to the faces of the men of that era?[90]

The character Shunsuke's words are spoken in the context of a midcentury novel intended to expose, among other things, the scope and qualities of contemporary homosexual society, hidden in plain sight. In other words, there is clearly a rhetorical purpose to having Shunsuke project onto *Breaking the Inkstone* a bond of male love between the boy and the older male figure.

Mishima's agenda aside, one wonders whether the servant in the handscroll version of *Breaking the Inkstone*—whose name, Nakamichi, could also be read Chūdō, a variant of Chūta—did not elicit a similar association at the time. As we have seen, *Breaking the Inkstone* alludes to the homoerotically charged genre of acolyte tales and is shadowed by it through formal similarities, not only in the boy's appearance. The trajectory of the plotline also encourages this association. As a rule, acolyte tales culminate in the death of the younger partner, and these stories affiliate homoerotic desire with premature death. Within the context of the story, the primary purpose of these deaths is to lead the older male partner to enlightenment. The same pattern of early death and religious awakening structures *Breaking the Inkstone*, whereby after the boy's demise the man spends the rest of his days praying for his young master's salvation, with the hopeful expectation of his own as well. The strong bond between them was directly expressed in a poem in the *Konjaku* version of the tale by the servant after he leaves his family to pursue a life of Buddhist practice:

Mumatama no	My jet black hair
kami o tamukete	I leave as an offering.
wakareji ni	I have decided
okureji to koso	to make our separate paths
omoitachinure	one.

The Mitsunobu version leaves this verse out, yet the potency of its sentiment infuses the final painting, which visually echoes the first painting in the scroll where the man faces the boy and their fate is sealed. Although physically absent, the boy will live on forever in the man's memory. And while the scroll never directly implies a sexual relationship between the servant and the boy, their deep bond suggests a dynamic of displaced homoerotic love, one that can find consummation only in death. Sexual content has thus been sublimated into a virtual elegy for a lost love.[91]

In conjunction with this sublimated homosocial desire, however, the tale exemplifies values promoted by members of the military class in this period, namely the notion of duty (*giri*). The concept of *giri* appears repeatedly in Muromachi period didactic texts and was taken up in particular by members of the military class as a way of cementing feudal alliances.[92] While narrative tales of later periods would explicitly link homoeroticism with loyalty, *Breaking the Inkstone* does not imply a physical relationship in places where it would have been possible. Rather, this fifteenth-century picture scroll might be thought of as an inchoate form of a homoerotic tale of loyalty between men (*nanshoku giri monogatari*), which would not be fully articulated within a warrior code of ethics until the Edo period. The irreducibility of the subtle interrelationships in this scroll ultimately transcends easy typological classification.

The ambiguity of the scroll's message is mediated by an awareness of its intended audience. An examination of the deep politics of Masamoto's circle, however, reveals that Yoshizumi was not the only youth in this environment anticipated by the tale of the broken inkstone. In addition to Yoshizumi, another young man was living in Masamoto's household, Hosokawa Sumiyuki (1489–1507), a person for whom the work may have had even more resonance. Having never married and never fathered a child of his own, Masamoto adopted Sumiyuki to be his future heir in 1491.[93] Just a few months before Yoshizumi inscribed his name on *Breaking the Inkstone*, the six-year-old Sumiyuki was formally brought into the service of Yoshizumi as Masamoto's heir and the shogun's designated future administrator.[94] The content, the elementary prose, and certain idiosyncrasies of the text all point to this young boy as another likely beneficiary of the scroll, an object that might even have been produced on the occasion of Sumiyuki's entrance into the household.

Breaking the Inkstone contains several parallels to Sumiyuki's own situation that are difficult to ignore, beginning with the equivalence of his own social status and the boy's in the story. Sumiyuki came, not from a military family, but from one of the loftiest aristocratic lineages at the time. His father, Kujō Masamoto (1445–1516), was a former regent (*kanpaku*), the highest possible position within the court hierarchy, the occupants of which were culled from a select group of noble lineages.[95] Like the boy in *Inkstone* with his major counselor (*dainagon*) father, Sumiyuki's father was of ministerial rank. Here too, the lack of onomastic specificity enables a more intimate engagement with the story line. While all other versions of *Breaking the Inkstone* make the major counselor a historical personage, the handscroll identifies him only as *dainagon*. As with "the man who climbed Mt. Shosha," which alludes to Shōkū but leaves him unnamed, this character lacks the final degree of specificity that would compromise more individuated experiences of the text. The boy's age represents one more liaison between Sumiyuki and the text. In no other version of *Breaking the Inkstone* is the boy said to be seven years old; most recensions say that he is ten years of age, while the twelfth-century *Konjaku* version, which was most influential for the handscroll, depicts him as thirteen.[96] Making the protagonist the same age as Sumiyuki (who would have been seven by the premodern Japanese counting method) creates an obvious additional solicitation for an empathetic response. One early-sixteenth-century narrative entitled *The Palace of Goblins* (*Tengu no dairi*) lists *Breaking the Inkstone* among a group of tales read by the seven-year-old protagonist in the story.[97] While this is a fictional list, it indicates that *Breaking the Inkstone* was considered suitable reading material for boys of Sumiyuki's age.

Indeed, the very syntax of the textual passages of the scroll suggests an accommodation to readers who have yet to reach full maturity. Their extreme abbreviation

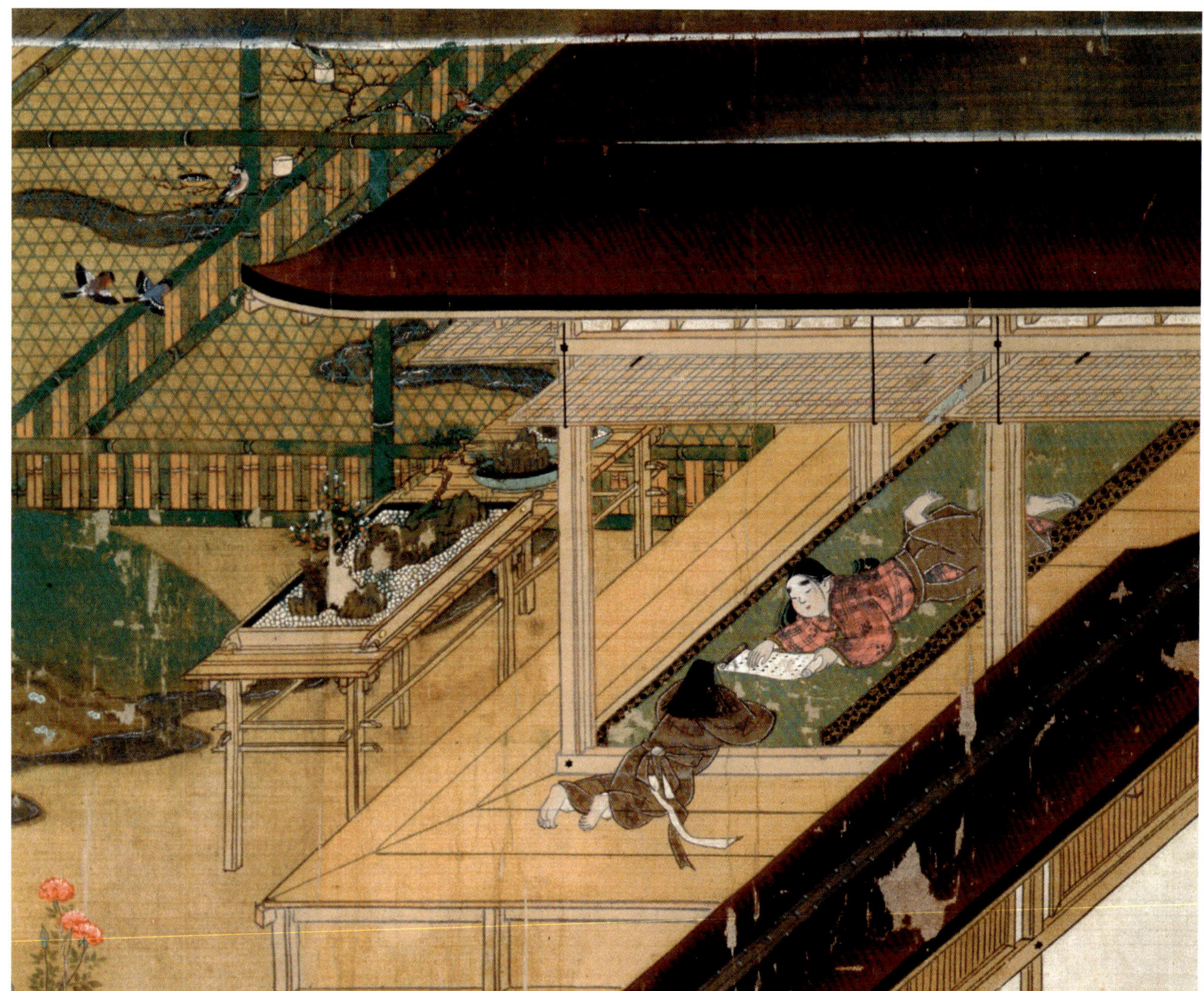

121 *Miracles of the Kasuga Deity* (*Kasuga Gongen kenki-e*). Dated 1309. Twenty scrolls; ink and color on silk, H. 41.0 cm. Museum of the Imperial Collections (Kunaichō Sannomaru Shōzōkan), Tokyo. Detail, scroll 5.

signals their likely role as performative or oral texts that were spoken in conjunction with a viewing of the paintings. The use of an unspecific pronoun in the crucial first line of the first passage, for example, seems to anticipate the presence of a raconteur reading the text out loud while gesturing to the paintings. Here, instead of the word for "shrine" (*zushi*), the text offers the pronoun "this" (*kore*): "Once, while the major counselor was away at the imperial palace, a servant named Nakamichi opened *this* up and looked." This opening line is cryptic unless we imagine someone pointing to the image of the large black shrine while reading the text aloud. Further demonstrating the oral nature of the handscroll text is its reliance on brief dialogic passages to move the narrative forward. These dialogues correspond closely to the conversations appearing to take place in the pictorial representations. In the second scene of painting 1 (fig. 3c), for example, the boy sits face-to-face with the servant while the text ends with his spoken words: "You will most certainly be severely punished. You must say that it was I who broke it." Similarly, the next two painting scenes of the major counselor's residence correspond to verbal exchanges recorded in the text. The texts here seem to function as scripts that, if read aloud, would have animated the paintings and the characters depicted within them. In the first, Nakamichi responds to the counselor's questions about the broken inkstone by stating: "the young master of the house was playing with it." And in the second exchange, the counselor appears in the process of banishing his son, while the scroll text quotes his angry reproach: "He is not my son, but one born of an enemy. He must be sent far away into the mountains."

Even the brief dialogues in the scroll text contain phrases of abbreviation that suggest opportunities for improvisatory elaboration by oral storytellers. After the inkstone is broken, for example, when the young boy asks Nakamichi what happened, he uses a phrase that literally means "such-and-such": "the servant explained that such-and-such happened" (*shika jika to kotaekereba*). While a longer narrative might have reiterated the event in the servant's own words, here it is conveyed through shorthand. Such truncated texts appear to have worked like cues, providing just enough information so that someone reading the scroll aloud could have elaborated on the events and filled in the dialogue with cadenzas of dramatic infill. In addition to pointing out pictorial elements in order to clarify the terse scroll text, a reader may have contributed details, elaborated themes, and related the story to the viewer's own life. Perhaps such instruction occurred in a leisurely fashion, as in the kind of scenario suggested by a frame from the early-fourteenth-century *Miracles of the Kasuga Deity* (*Kasuga Gongen kenki-e*) (fig. 121), which shows two boys lying on their stomachs, one clearly older than the other, reading and gesturing at a scroll. With its particular focus on a seven-year-old boy and its pared-down texts, *Breaking the Inkstone* could certainly have catered to a viewer just that age embarking on his reading and writing practice.

Less than two years after *Breaking the Inkstone* was made, one of Masamoto's retainers, a governor of Hyōgo Province named Hahakabe Masamori, requested that Sanetaka make two study books (*tehon*) for Sumiyuki to use for reading and writing practice.[98] This reference indicates the attention being paid to Sumiyuki's formal education by Masamoto's retainers, either at Masamoto's request or in an effort to curry favor with the powerful administrator and his young heir. It is a small step from here to imagining a similar interest in Sumiyuki's education assumed by Masamoto and/or Yoshizumi, who likely commissioned *Breaking the Inkstone* for him and possibly read the work with him.

In 1495 Sumiyuki and Yoshizumi entered into a relationship in which Sumiyuki's loyalty to the shogun would be crucial. Masamoto's desire to foster a kind of filial fraternity between them is manifest in the name, Sumiyuki, that he chose for his heir: it incorporates the second character from Yoshizumi's name in a show of solidarity.[99] Given the context in which the scroll was read, the homosocial reciprocity found in its illustrations seems to have informed and even conditioned its small and privileged readership. This was clearly not a one-way relationship but a symbiotic one, in which the valences that governed "real life" and the dynamics that structured the interrelationships among the dramatis personae of the fictional world mutually animated one another. Human bonds were calibrated by their literary counterparts and in turn determined the degree of emotional intensity that might be attributed to them.

To understand why the mutual slippage of art and life should not be dismissed too readily, one need look no further than the confines of Masamoto's household, where issues of loyalty and betrayal were a constant and seething concern. Yoshizumi's efforts to assert his power as shogun as he reached his twenties and his public disagreements with Masamoto have already been noted. But Sumiyuki, too, grew up surrounded by retainers eager to use him to replace Masamoto. This is exactly what happened in 1507, when Sumiyuki, aided by a group of retainers, assassinated Hosokawa Masamoto while seated in his bath.[100] Masamoto's reign of power, which began with the coup of 1493 in which he installed Yoshizumi as shogun, thus came to an end with another startling act of betrayal, this time on the part of his own adopted son. Against this violent backdrop, retroactively, the loyal boy in *Breaking the Inkstone* seems to embody more a fantasy of virtue than its exemplar, an embodiment of innocence lost.

EPILOGUE

Tosa Mitsunobu's death went unrecorded but is assumed to have taken place sometime early in the 1520s. An entry in the diary of Kanroji Motonaga, a longtime calligrapher-collaborator (see figs. 36–37), patron, and fellow versifier, mentions the painter's attendance at a morning meal Motonaga hosted late in the first month of 1521.[1] This reference to Mitsunobu's participation in what was an annual gathering to mark the New Year is one of the last vestiges of his activity in the archival record, after which only one reference to his attendance at a *renga* session in 1525 remains.[2] At Motonaga's New Year's gathering the following year, it is Mitsunobu's son Mitsumochi instead who makes an appearance.[3] From this point forward, Mitsumochi assumes the social trappings of his father: in 1523, he is secured in his ownership of the Okumosha estate, indicating that he was director of the Painting Bureau. In the years that follow, the coterie of aristocrats who regularly called upon the services of Mitsunobu—including Motonaga, Sanetaka, and Yamashina Tokitsugu, scion of a family with close relations to the Tosa—begin to refer to Mitsumochi simply as "Tosa" or by somewhat-more-elaborate titles such as "Tosa shōgen."[4] This was how the historical record marked the changing of generations in artisanal families. Given names and sobriquets may have been modified by a character, but the titles, social rituals, commissions, and institutional relationships all stayed largely the same and were dutifully chronicled in the same laconic manner. Mitsunobu had passed away, but the Tosa lived on.

In the case of Mitsunobu, it is nevertheless somewhat surprising that his passing was not recorded by any of his companion courtiers, many of whom kept daily memos on the affairs of their household and cultural circle, of which Mitsunobu was an occasional member. After all, by this time Mitsunobu had been the head of the Painting Bureau for over fifty years, through the reigns of two long-lived emperors, and was a veritable institution in his own right. He was a fixture in the cultural landscape of the capital and possessed the right of first refusal on many of the narrative painting projects promulgated therein. On the other hand, Mitsumochi and, increasingly, other painters were available to fulfill the very same tasks for which Mitsunobu had taken up his brush: Buddhist icons, mortuary portraits, folding screens, gift fans, and narrative handscrolls, even their small-format versions. Given the relative importance of familial, as opposed to individual, subjectivity in the social consciousness of the medieval Japanese elite, Mitsunobu's death did not represent the disruption in its cultural environment that a modern art historical sensibility would like to imagine. Mitsumochi was a dynamic and enormously capable craftsman, one deserving of more recognition in his own right; all told, he represented the Tosa brand with remarkable success. Yet the conditions under which small scrolls had emerged as a new and experimental pictoliterary medium had shifted imperceptibly.

Although the fate of the small scroll after the Mitsunobu era is, strictly speaking, beyond the purview of this study, this coda will chart some of the ways in which small scrolls developed in the middle decades of the sixteenth century and beyond. One significant motivation of the previous five chapters has been the thesis that the small scroll reached its apogee under the brush of Mitsunobu, although this efflorescence was just as attributable to his environment as it was to his abilities. What distinguished the medium in formal terms during this period was an uncanny calibration of pictorial expression to its text, as well as a condensation of expression that took advantage of all of the tricks of the handscroll trade—elision, framing devices, a savvy horizontality—along with a free and intimate borrowing from past exemplars of this tradition. These qualities infused simple stories with multiple dimensions, shadow plotlines, and rich semantic overtones. In the years and decades after Mitsunobu's passing, the resonant word-image relationship of small scrolls passed as well, or rather became diluted beyond recognition as the medium was dispersed into a variety of different kinds of representational pursuits. One need not be melancholic about this shift, as the new scrolls were brimming with their own unique appeal, which included earthy humor, sharp didacticism, and new configurations of visual amateurism. These were the qualities that characterized small scrolls in their next incarnations. In what follows I attempt to take the measure of this shift, to bring into sharper relief the legacy of Mitsunobu and his collaborators.

Although small scrolls may have achieved mature expression during Mitsunobu's day, they remained popular well into the sixteenth century. Mitsumochi is known to have made one for the shogun Ashikaga Yoshiharu, and scattered mention of others can be found. Emperor GoNara (1497–1557), furthermore, was known at one point to have nineteen small scrolls in his personal collection alone.[5] While some of these works surely dated from an earlier time, handed down from his father and grandfather, in all likelihood others were commissioned by him personally. More than anything, however, the embrace of small scrolls in the very late Muromachi period is attested to by the number of surviving works from this era, some of which can be reasonably placed within the known dates of Mitsumochi's activity, circa 1522–68. This does not mean, however, that Mitsumochi was the painter of most or even some of them. It is more likely that small scrolls of this time were produced by either dexterous amateurs from the aristocratic community or anonymous town painters. The latter group was also responsible for illustrating the so-called "Nara picture books" (*Nara ehon*) that circulated with increasing frequency over the course of the sixteenth century; indeed, the similarity in tone and content between these books and scrolls provides another foundation for their approximate dating. The primary historical context for this shift in the manufacture of small scrolls from elite artisanal studios to amateur and middlebrow professional painters is summarized in the overused but necessary term "popularization." On the one hand, aristocratic families continued to view the format as well-suited for short-tale literature and pedagogy, but these families increasingly took over responsibility for their creation, for reasons to be discussed below. On the other hand, a wider cross section of elite society (i.e., more merchants and warrior families) began to see the merits of smallish dimensions for custom-made storytelling. This expanded viewership reflected the ongoing diffusion of courtly practices to different niches of the social sphere. But the small scrolls fostered new modes of spectatorship and literary experience as well.

Before taking a closer look at the particulars, it is worth addressing the fate of the Tosa Studio during this period. As mentioned earlier, Mitsumochi's roster of clientele reads much the same as Mitsunobu's, only in updated form, listing the shrines, temples, scholar-aristocrats, and elite warriors of his day. Accordingly, his repertoire and commissions were not dissimilar to his forebear's either, spanning the gamut from large, polychrome origin legends for institutions like Taimadera to portraits of Ashikaga Yoshiharu to *Genji* screens (e.g., "The Clash of the Carriages") for the circle of Emperor Ōgimachi (1517–93). On the archival surface, Mitsumochi appears to have followed the pattern established in the previous generation, leaving a paper trail in the Tosa family documents and making the occasional cameo in the diaries of the privileged. Two notable contrasts between father and son in these sources are the far fewer references to estate income and a greater concentration on fan painting, to the point that in the 1550s and 1560s this appears to be the main studio specialty. Mentions of Mitsumochi in the diaries of the Yamashina (*Tokitsugu-kyō ki*) and palace ladies-in-waiting (*Oyudono no ue no nikki*) during these decades usually concern fans, which were often executed for a cash payment.[6] The sources undoubtedly point to Mitsumochi's inability to collect on the privileges of his rank and his concomitant reliance on the steady income from painted fans.

In the context of this study, however, the most significant difference between Mitsunobu and Mitsumochi is the fact that the latter is never mentioned engaging in communal poetic activity.[7] As chapter 2 demonstrated, linked-verse gatherings with his clients and peers was a mainstay of Mitsunobu's social calendar. Judging from his extant poems, the court painter was no court poet, but he could nevertheless string together metrically structured verse on an assigned theme and pass it along to the poet to his left with a fair measure of competence. This was all that was asked of him, and the benefits reaped could be considerable. Membership in a fraternity of men of letters ensured that social interaction could slide at any time into economic transaction. Just as importantly, knowledge of the poetic canon and occasional versifying provided Mitsunobu with special insights into the myriad ways in which his craft could complement and complicate literary expression. The most eloquent demonstration of this was the small scroll.

The reason for Mitsumochi's lack of recorded linked-verse activity, or for that matter of any engagement with the literary components of his painting commissions, is unclear. Like his father he maintained a relationship with Sanetaka and other scholar-aristocrats in Kyoto. Both Sanetaka and Konoe Hisamichi were calligraphers for his handscrolls. Others with whom he interacted were active in *renga* circles, such as the townsman Kawachiya Sōjin, who had Mitsumochi execute a portrait of the famous *renga* poet and disciple of Sōgi Botanka Shōhaku (1443–1527) in 1551.[8] In comparison to the previous generation, however, this Tosa painter seemed almost aliterary. It is tempting to attribute this diminishment of poetic fellowship to individual sensibility or personal disposition. Yet the more historically honest analysis would foreground the altered conditions of artistic practice in the capital instead.

Mitsunobu came of age during the cautious peace of the post–Ōnin War era, which in the long duration of the Warring States period ends up appearing reasonably stable. Undoubtedly, the old painter lived through many truly disruptive political shifts: most notably the coup of Hosokawa Masamoto (1493) and the battles among Hosokawa heirs (1507–8), which included three successive attempts at a coup. During his half century as head of the Painting Bureau, however, those he relied on for support remained in the capital. If anything, the dispersal of resident warriors from Kyoto back to their home provinces after the civil war, to focus on local governance, generated greater demand for Tosa products; the *Genji Album* (the Sue family) and the "Scenes in and around the Capital" screens (the Asakura family) are examples. Mitsumochi, on the other hand, had the misfortune of overseeing a painting studio during a qualitatively more unstable period, in a capital whose political fortunes endured protean and even kaleidoscopic transformation. His list of things seen and heard included the tense and dual administration of the realm under the Hosokawa and the Ashikaga during the 1520s; the rise and suppression of the Lotus uprising (1532–36); the occupation of the capital by Miyoshi Chōkei (1549–53); the assassination of Ashikaga Yoshiteru and interregnum under the deputies of Chōkei (1565–68); and finally, toward the end of his life, Oda Nobunaga's march into the capital (1568). Mitsumochi's most important patron, Ashikaga Yoshiharu, ran a shogunate-in-exile that for a time even roamed the countryside, with his official painter carrying out commissions from one stop to the next. It is not difficult to imagine, given these circumstances, that the immediate environment was no longer conducive to regular and joint partakings of poetry. This may be the main reason that Mitsumochi was unable to participate in linked verse.

Whatever the reasons for this difference in social activities between father and son, it clearly leaves an imprint on Mitsumochi's oeuvre. His paintings place a high premium on chromatic contrast and clarity of structure. As often noted, they bear a close resemblance to the work of his slightly older contemporary Kanō Motonobu (fig. 8), and influence may have been exerted in both directions between these two (not to mention the possibility of family ties).[9] In comparison, Mitsunobu's surfaces appear subdued, more yielding and soft-spoken. More important, the son's output appears less concerned with the challenge of finding a pictorial expression that corresponds to the text it is assigned to enhance. Instead, Mitsumochi seems to want to delineate a robust and autonomous painted equivalent to the text. My purpose here is not to provide a profile for Mitsumochi's painting style but only to establish the conditions for a changed relationship between the Tosa Studio and small-scroll production under his watch. We will never know what his interest was in the companion arts, but what is certain is that he brought it less to bear on his painting than did Mitsunobu. *Miraculous Origins of Hasedera* (fig. 12), the set of small scrolls he executed for Yoshiharu as a boy shogun, amply bear this out.

Thus, the Tosa's works are of diminished relevance to an analysis of small scrolls in the middle decades of the sixteenth century. And while erudite courtiers continued to take an interest in and patronize the production of handscrolls, the quality of their engagement with painters was measurably different from that of the Mitsunobu-Sanetaka collaboration. Literary expertise and classical learning continued to inform the production of painting, but they now manifested themselves in different ways. Men of letters oversaw the production of largely didactic rebus-pictures of *waka* poetry in small-scroll format. Aristocratic daughters such as the elusive Gyokuei, alleged author of the *Monochrome Tale of Genji Scrolls* in the Spencer Collection (fig. 27) and similar works, applied their impressive expertise to *The Tale of Genji* to introduce new variations into received pictorial iconography. The anonymous authors of the Nara picture books and related small scrolls focused on fantastic and entertaining stories that demanded of their accompanying paintings only that they stage the scenes in highly theatrical, festive, and emotive ways. This was the landscape of the small scroll in the era of the dispersed old guard and dispersed representational agendas.

Although the focus of this study is on small scrolls under the Mitsunobu regime, it is only fair to emphasize the sophistication of the new examples of small-scroll art. *Tale of the Chrysanthemum Spirit* (*Kiku no sei no monogatari*, also known as *Kazashi no himegimi;* fig. 122) offers a wonderful case.[10] It is an exemplar of the type of fantastic tale that often found expression in miniature handscrolls during the sixteenth century. A Minamoto "middle counselor" (*chūnagon*) and his wife, the daughter of a court minister, have a daughter who from a young age shows a special and intimate connection to the chrysanthemum; in the fall, she can be witnessed communing with a garden full of chrysanthemums

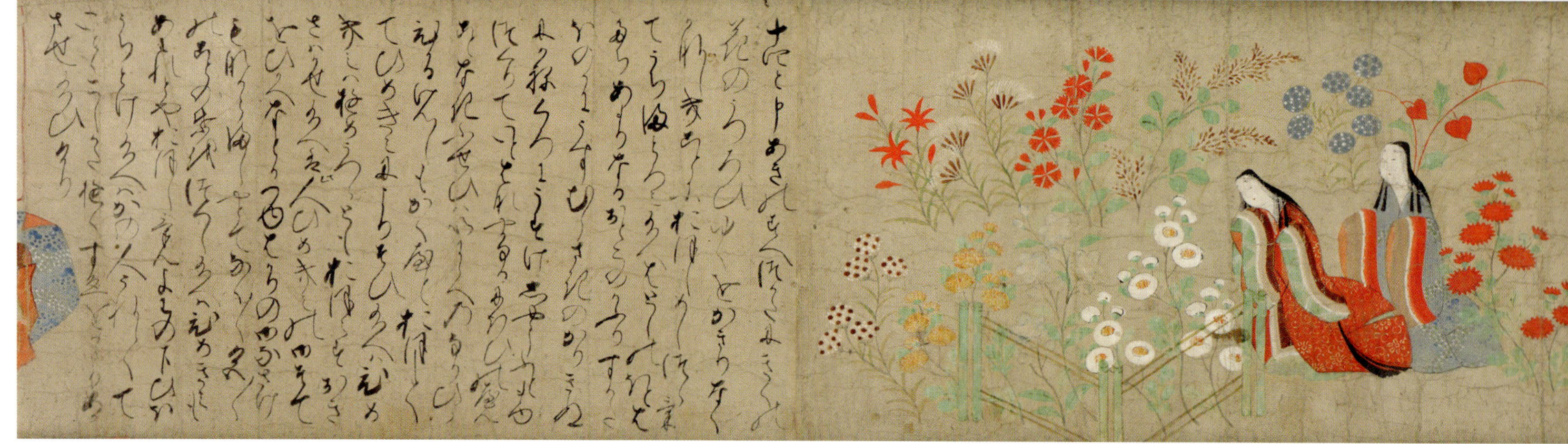

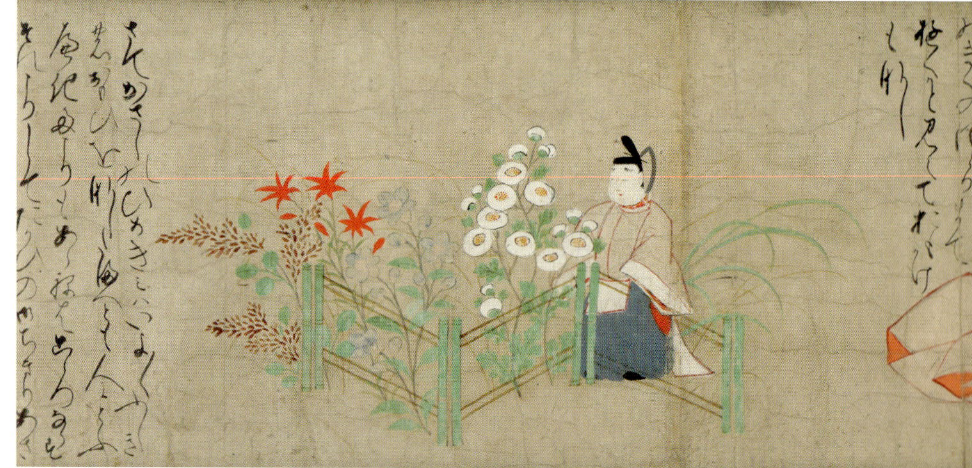

122 *Tale of the Chrysanthemum Spirit* (*Kiku no sei no monogatari; Kazashi no hime monogatari-e*). Muromachi period, sixteenth century. One handscroll; ink and color on paper, 17.2 x 748.7 cm. Harvard Art Museum, Arthur M. Sackler Museum, Bequest of the Hofer Collection of the Arts of Asia, 1985.469. Photograph by Katya Kallsen © President and Fellows of Harvard College.

(fig. 122a), growing inexpressibly sad when they inevitably wither away. One evening she is visited by a male courtier, the anthropomorphized spirit of a chrysanthemum (fig. 122b). Upon parting the next morning, the flower spirit promises they will meet again and disappears at the flowering hedge (fig. 122c). One day the emperor hosts a flower-picking contest and orders the middle counselor to provide chrysanthemums from his garden. That evening, the flower spirit returns to tell the daughter that this is the last evening they can meet and hands her what appears to be his hair wrapped in thin paper. He also tells her he has entrusted her with a child, whom she should regard as a surrogate for him. The daughter later gives birth to a baby girl, but she soon falls ill with longing and dies. The little girl, meanwhile, grows up to be a young woman of incomparable beauty who eventually marries the emperor and gives birth to a boy and a girl, much to the happiness of the middle counselor and his wife.

Artists contemporary with Mitsunobu, or in his studio, pictorialized similar tales, in which the "strange" matrimonial arrangements involved a crane and a rat. In those cases, however, the story conformed to the characteristics of the new short story described in chapter 1, with a clear (and brief) narrative progression, accelerated drive toward resolution, and a moral lesson, all encompassed by a unity of literary expression. In the case of *Tale of the Chrysanthemum Spirit*, however, the story line meanders and ends gloriously. Somewhere in its episodes is buried a moral concerning the rewards received by those who please the emperor, but even this theme takes a backseat to the supernatural elements of the tale. Most important of all, however, is that pictorially the scroll is as subdivided as its story. The tale unfolds over no fewer than twenty discrete units of text and image, a number that would have been unimaginable in *Tale of the*

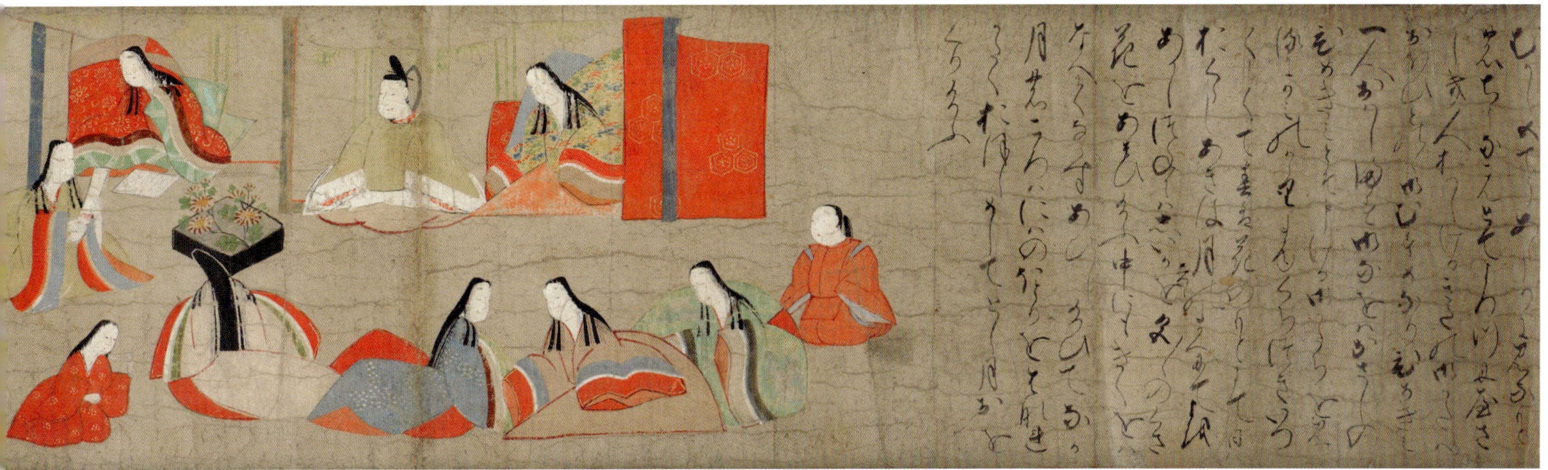

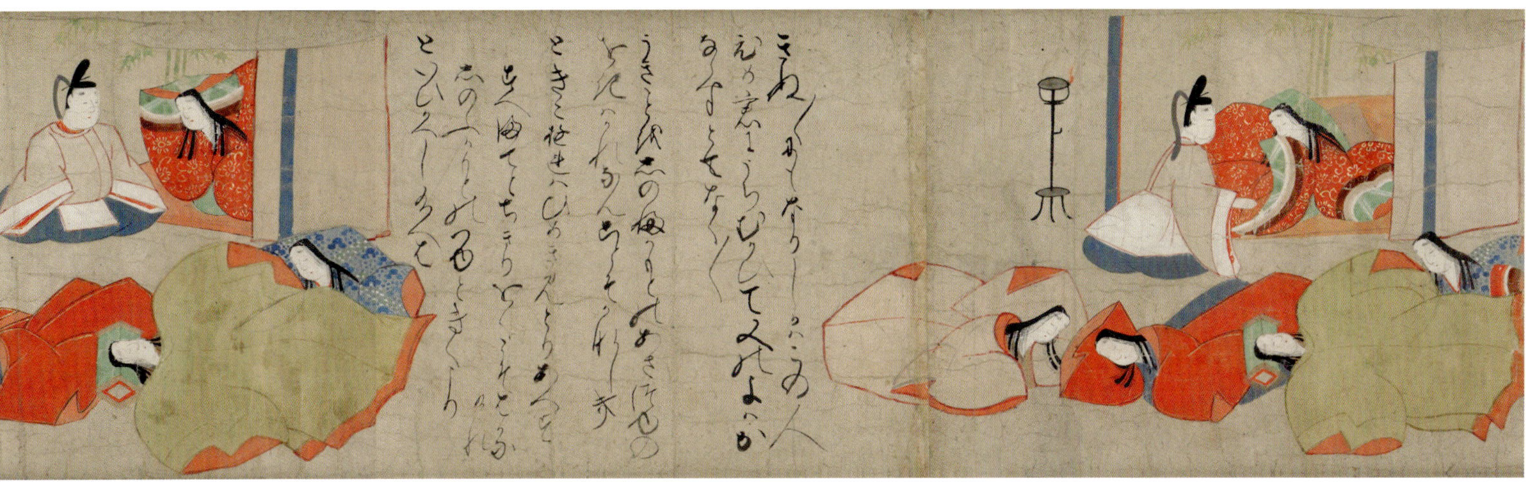

Rat. Not only does *Tale of the Chrysanthemum Spirit* lack a unity of pictoliterary expression, but it offers a fundamentally different way of experiencing narrative progression and the interplay between pictures and words. Its textual episodes and units of painting are freely painted on the same sheets of handscroll paper, sometimes higher and sometimes lower on the page, visually echoing the meandering nature of the story itself, as opposed to the expressive symmetries between word and image in small scrolls of the previous era.

The numerous ink-line (*hakubyō*) small scrolls contemporary to *Tale of the Chrysanthemum Spirit* scroll offer yet a different guise for the post-Mitsunobu development of this medium. Most of these scrolls address *The Tale of Genji* and were likely produced by women of the aristocracy, including reclusive nuns and ladies-in-waiting at court. Communities of these women long regarded the small-format handscroll as a site for the transmission of cultural information among themselves; this was especially the case for ink-line paintings, which were considered a privileged mode in which to pass on genealogies of information concerning classics such as *The Tale of Genji*. As opposed to the short-story tales pictorialized by Mitsunobu, however, the content of sixteenth-century *hakubyō* scrolls tended to take the form of pictorial commentary.

The abovementioned *Monochrome Tale of Genji Scrolls* in the Spencer Collection attributed to the nun Gyokuei provide a prime example (fig. 27). In a set of six scrolls, this work represents all fifty-four chapters of *The Tale of Genji* with one or more poetic or prose excerpts and one painting each. This format represented a visual distillation of the type of knowledge that aristocratic

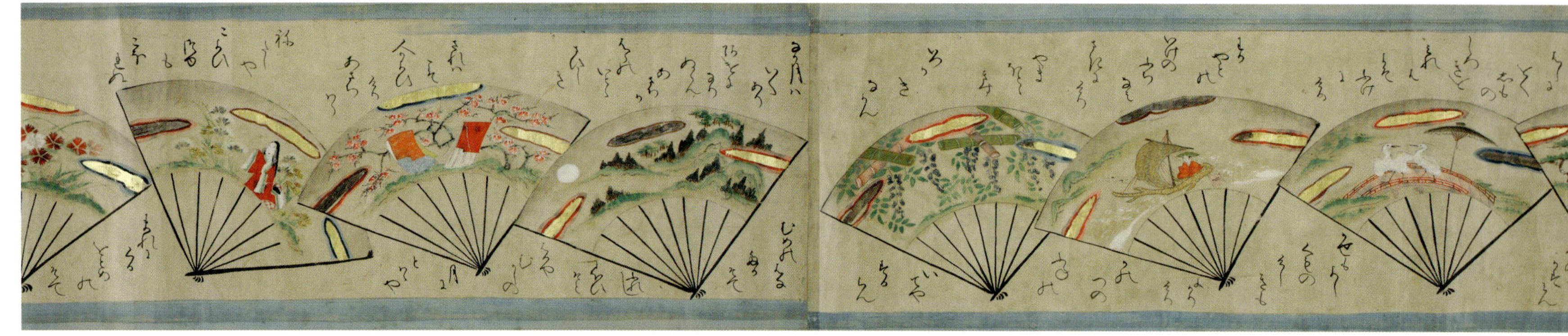

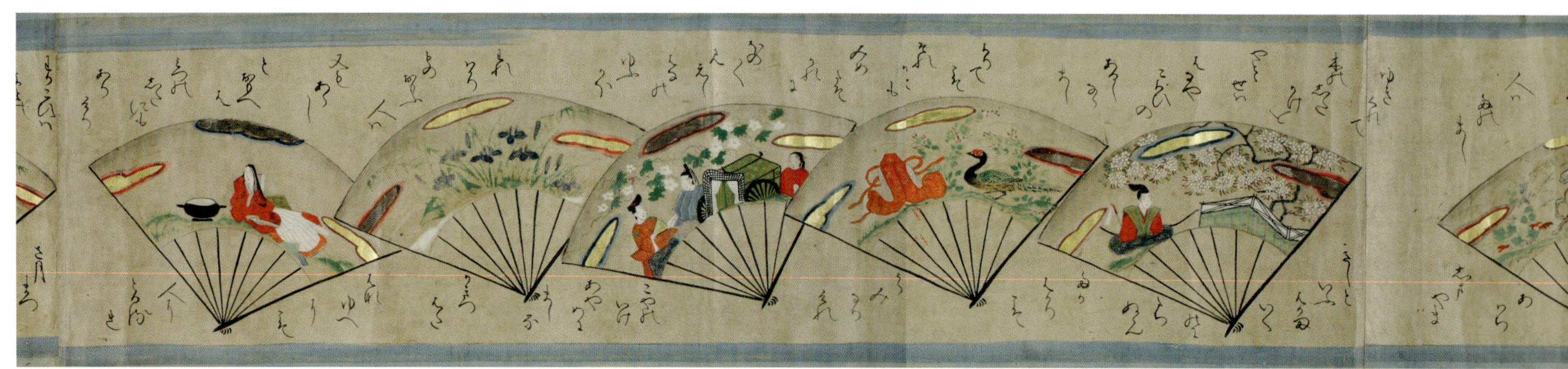

123 *Compendium of Fans* (*Ōgi no sōshi*). Muromachi period, late sixteenth century. One handscroll; ink and color on paper, 18.2 x 380 cm. National Institutes of the Humanities, National Institute of Japanese Literature.

women considered their privilege to know intimately. Far from consisting of rote memorization of the 795 poems in the tale, chapter titles, main characters, and primary events, however, this knowledge was centered on readerly habits and traditions of interpretation. Thus, the "Spring Shoots II" (Wakana II) chapter was reinterpreted in the *Genji Scrolls* with the Akashi nun as its protagonist, in a proactive identification of the self with characters of similar situation in Lady Murasaki's classic.[11] This kind of appreciation was carried out with great sophistication, however, and complexified every chapter of the novel. And it was conveyed in a pictorial shorthand that asserted the prerogatives of the *hakubyō* communities in the subtlest and most indirect of ways. Both the mannered pictorial awkwardness of this shorthand and its elaboration within the diminutive dimensions of the small scroll were important components of this visual mode, for it physically conveyed the sociopolitical status (the plain, modest materials, the amateur training) and thus the authenticity of its author. The communicative agenda here was far removed from the refined sensibility of a Mitsunobu small scroll.

Yet a third kind of small scroll in the mid–sixteenth century is the didactic-poetic small scroll, best exemplified by the phenomenon of "Compendium of Fans" (*Ōgi no sōshi;* fig. 123). These works consisted of a chain of poems inscribed across the leftward-progressing surface of a small scroll, accompanied in each instance by a picture of a folding fan that engaged the content of that poem. These pairings could manifest a wide range of engagements, anything from literal pictorial equivalents to clever rebus combinations to far more allusive painted ciphers that required invocations of verse to decipher properly. Whatever the arrangement, each pairing required the active participation of the viewer to comprehend and thus facilitated and was facilitated by expertise in the poetic canon. While the historical function and significance of "Compendium of Fans" scrolls are obscure, one likely hypothesis attributes

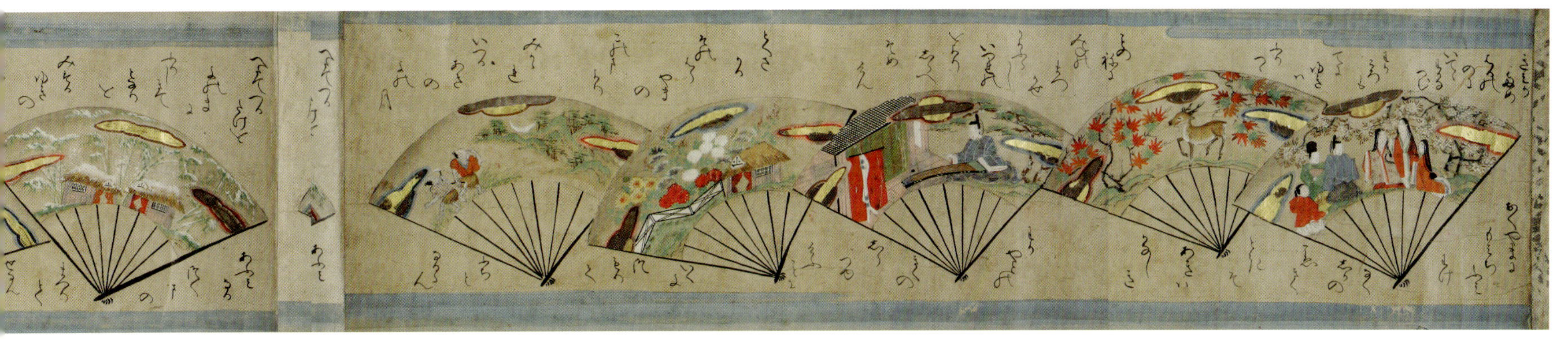

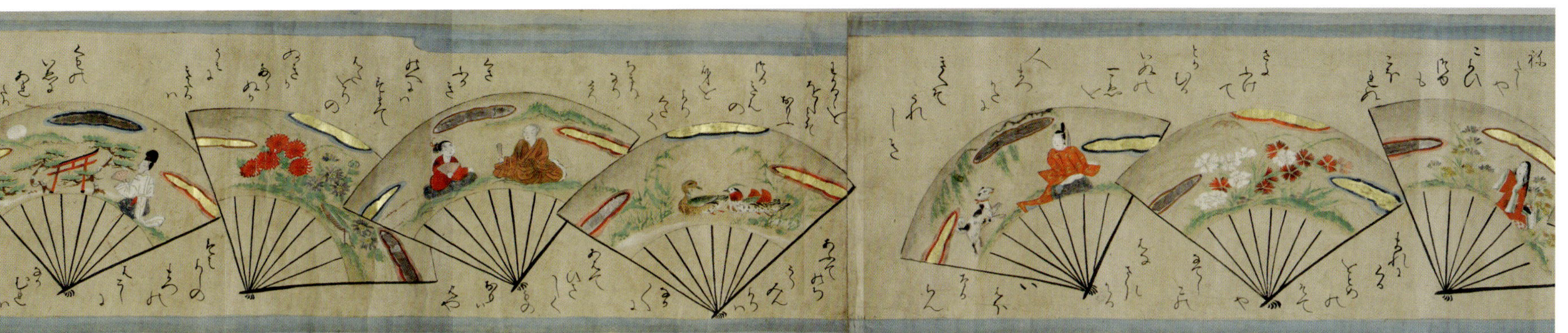

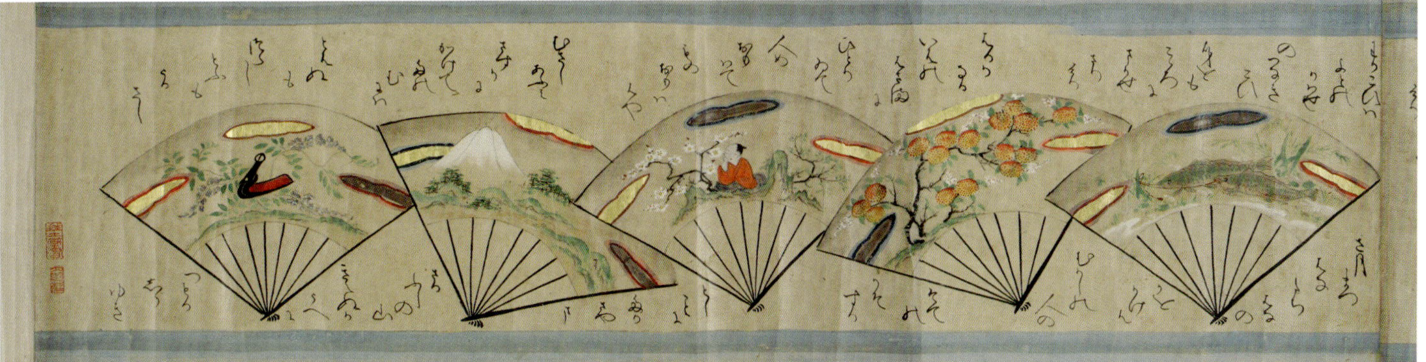

to them a mnemonic function.[12] Scrolls of this nature would have aided in the commitment to memory of strings of poems in anthologies popular at the time, such as the *New Collection of Ancient and Modern Poems* (*Shinkokinshū*).

The readership of warrior-poets for such small scrolls further demonstrates the changing nature of the man of letters who engaged painters in the execution of such works. In what seems like a transition to a new era, in 1525 (the likely year of Mitsunobu's death) Sanetaka brushed "poems for a small picture scroll" (*ko-e uta*) for a warrior named Wakatsuki Jirō (Kunisada), who had arrived from Yūzen bringing sea bream and other gifts for the courtier, and the two drank into the night.[13] According to the poet Sōchō (1448–1532), Wakatsuki had aspired to the poetic way, and the illustrated scroll with poems selected and brushed by the famous literatus was no doubt meant to help him in his endeavors.[14]

Didactic-poetic scrolls for young people, reminiscent of the small scrolls and booklets brushed by Sanetaka for the crown prince in the 1470s, also flourished in this era. Indeed, many of the poetry-centered small scrolls of the sixteenth century should be situated in the context of pedagogy and the *waka* culture at large in the late medieval and early modern era.[15] Because of their didactic nature, these scrolls were deemed most appropriately executed on smaller surfaces, but the dimensions did not necessarily influence the forms and representations.

The above examples by no means exhaust the uses to which small scrolls were put as the sixteenth century progressed, but they provide enough of a survey to suggest how they developed in the late Muromachi period. Even later, the growth of the publishing industry and the spread of printing inaugurated new conditions for the survival of the manuscript culture within which small scrolls had achieved maturity. These developments, however, are simply too far beyond the reach of this study to be considered here. Instead, this epilogue has simply attempted to provide a later vantage point from which to assess the art historical and cultural legacy of small scrolls of the late fifteenth and early sixteenth centuries. By now there should be no doubt of the continued vitality of the narrative handscroll medium throughout the medieval period and great suspicion of the accounts of decline ascribed to this art form in most surveys up to this point. The best small scrolls that emerged in the Mitsunobu environment tell a very different story. They delineate, if not an ascent or a maturation, then a mastery of visual tactics, all of the artifice that had become associated with representation in and on this peculiar surface.

The techniques embodied in earlier works created a rich universe of possibility with which ambitious cultural innovators experimented in the creation of a radically new pictorial form. In the process, the essence of the *emaki* format—its horizontality, its multidimensional matrimony of word to image—was tapped in the name of authentic cultural production. The richness of this essence was revealed in the simple discovery that a change of scale provided the opportunity not only to adjust formal ratios but to start over. For the members of Mitsunobu's circle, this starting over meant a shared view of the whole arc of a pictorial story, as well as a shared agenda concerning how to allow a viewer-reader to traverse this arc. This realization, and the many representational adjustments that came with it, turned the small scroll into a highly effective pictorial medium. Moreover, these new developments sharpen our understanding of the earlier *emaki* tradition as a whole. The history of the Japanese handscroll has yet to be written, but when it is, small scrolls deserve a large place therein.

APPENDIX TRANSLATIONS

A Wakeful Sleep (*Utatane sōshi emaki,* fig. 1), one handscroll, in National Museum of Japanese History, Chiba Prefecture. Translated by Virginia Skord as "A Tale of Brief Slumbers," in *Tales of Tears and Laughter* (Honolulu: University of Hawaii Press, 1991), based on the annotated edition of the text in Tajima Kazuo, annotator, *Utatane no sōshi*, in pt. 1 of *Muromachi monogatarishū*, vol. 54 of *Shin Nihon koten bungaku taikei,* ed. Ichiko Teiji et al. (Tokyo: Iwanami Shoten, 1989), 269–89. Reproduced with permission of the University of Hawaii Press.

TEXT 1

Utatane ni	In a brief slumber
koishiki hito o	I caught sight of my beloved
miteshi yori	and now I cling
yume chō mono wa	to each passing dream[1]
tanomisometeki	

Komachi's words express but a trifling fancy in comparison to the passion that rejects even life itself. Among the many tales of long ago is one extraordinary account of such a love.

The story I am about to tell occurred in the not-too-distant past. There was once a prominent minister well regarded at court. Of his many children born to several consorts, one son was the Master of the Crown Prince's Household; another younger son held the rank of prelate and was head priest of Ishiyama Temple. The Minister had but a single daughter, sister to the Prelate, whom he cherished beyond measure. He considered sending her to serve at court and had already begun making preparations for her presentation when he realized that she would be surrounded by a bevy of imperial consorts and ladies of the bedchamber. In such an atmosphere, even if she were to receive imperial favor, she would be subjected to fierce jealousy, and he feared lest she become withdrawn and sink into depression. As he vacillated over the decision, certain presentable suitors called with offers to marry and care for her, but he was reluctant to give his precious daughter to anyone at all.

Soon the girl blossomed into the full flower of maidenhood and radiated such an array of charms that she was a pleasure to behold. Her father treated her with special consideration, inviting ladies of excellent qualities to serve her. At times she lived happily, deriving amusements from the many diversions afforded by the spring flowers and autumnal foliage. Other times, however, the weight of her father's duties led him to neglect her, and, her mother having passed away, the girl perforce spent long hours in lonely idleness.

Near her rooms grew a late-blooming wild cherry tree, adorned with blossoms far outlasting those of other flowering trees. As the spring days slipped away, she found solace in these flowers and lamented their final descent to earth. One lonely afternoon, as the long rains gently fell and droplets ceaselessly pattered on the eaves, she left off her aimless plucking at the koto and lay down, falling off into a deep sleep.

Suddenly, it seemed that someone appeared before her, proffering a branch of flowering wisteria deeply fragrant despite the dew still clinging to it. Attached to the branch was a slip of paper tinted in the same pale lavender hue as the wisteria. Assuming that this lovely offering was a message from the Kamo Priestess,[2] the girl casually picked it up. In a man's hand was written:

Omoine ni	Yet more fleeting than a daydream
miru yume yori mo	from the slumbers of love—
hakanaki wa	the vision of another
yoso no omokage	a reality yet unknown.

The traces of ink were well modulated and the hand remarkable, revealing that the poem had been written by no ordinary person. She gazed at it with admiration, her heart in turmoil, wondering who might have sent it. This was a most unexpected dream!

TEXT 2

This vivid vision had been so beautiful and the traces of his brush so lovely that her heart was quite captivated, and she yearned to see more. She sat lost in bemused contemplation until night fell. Lamps were brought in, and she played at *go* with her attendant Chūnagon and nursemaid Ben. Though she tried to maintain interest in the game, she was wholly preoccupied by thoughts of the unknown man in that fleeting dream and overwhelmed by a sense of unreality. In a daze, she pulled over the movable curtain to take a brief nap.

There at her side was a figure wearing a soft courtier's robe layered over a crimson robe and trousers of pale lavender lined with green. The color and quality of his dress were so elegant and his fragrance so profoundly penetrating that she was quite entranced. They lay together with an intimacy of long association. When she cast a glance at his face, her heart throbbed wildly. So radiantly handsome and charming was he, possessed of such refinement and a host of appealing features, that he brought to mind the shining Prince Genji of tales of old. Indeed, the very sight of him led her to think that even a man could possess the proverbial hundred charms.[3] Mute in her agitation, tears streaming down, she tried to move away, but he grasped her hand and addressed her.

"The anguish of my love cannot but have moved you to pity—did you not even look at the faint traces of my brush? Your failure to respond caused me such distress that I was compelled to come. Do you not know the expression 'a slave to love'? The bonds linking a man and woman are not only of this life but are fated from past lives as well. So often in the past has unrequited longing led to terrible retribution! If you and I were to leave our love unconsummated in this world, it would wander aimlessly on the dark path to come. Would this not be a lamentable fate?"

He tearfully spoke on, though unable to pour out all that was in his heart. Somehow he seemed to know that she was not unmoved, though he could hardly hear her response. All too soon there came the faint sound of the cock's call of dawn. "The cock must be well accustomed to the resentment of departing lovers," she heard him say dispiritedly. Just one encounter could not possibly suffice for the full exchange of lovers' intimacies. Sensing something oppressing her, she looked up to see that the sun had risen high in the sky. With a sense of utter unreality, she arose, but was not at all herself.

TEXT 3

How terribly confusing was this dream arisen from slumbers beneath the spring blossoms! It had always been said that, in a love dream, the object of yearning appeared in one's own dream, but she had also heard that a soul could wander afar to visit the dreams of the beloved, as exemplified in the lines by Princess Shikishi, "the one I would see even in a dream."[4] What kind of dream had this been? Who had appeared before her? What unknown sender had offered these blossoms of affection? Should others realize that she was lying lovelorn in the shadows of the tree of laments, sleeves damp with tears, they would regard it as deeply sinful.

When her lover Fujiwara no Norimichi[5] ceased to call on her, Ko Shikibu[6] passed the long empty months in melancholy. Suddenly he came to visit, and she was beside herself with joy. When it came time for him to depart, she stitched a thread on the sleeve of his cloak as a memento. By daylight, however, she saw the thread caught in a tree in the garden and realized that he had not really come. Her own excess of longing had summoned before her the image sheltered in her heart.

Who was it that loved her both in dream and in reality? Although there was no way to communicate her longing to him, her heart remained in turmoil. "How did I sleep that night such as to see him?" she wondered as she lay on her lonely bed.[7] Her own fragrance wafting up served as the only reminder of that vision. She so yearned for him, and dwelled so constantly on him, that presently she completely lost her ability to distinguish reality from dream. The thought of anything else—even things she had previously liked—was distasteful to her. As time passed, she weakened and became increasingly distraught, unable so much as to glance at food. Deeply concerned, her father and attendants offered prayers and commissioned services for her recovery. Day and night the halls were filled with the commotion of rituals and sutra recitations, but she remained sunken in her own reveries. That her father should worry so on her behalf became to her a source of further anguish, and she grew even worse.

Shocked to hear of her condition, her brother the Prelate came to conduct services on her behalf. Some hope lay in the particularly effective vow of salvation for all sentient beings made by the Savior Kannon of Ishiyama; there had been much talk of the miracles she performed. He promised that the girl would make a pilgrimage to Ishiyama if her condition were sufficiently relieved to permit the journey. To everyone's vast relief, her health improved, most probably owing to the innumerable prayers on her behalf.

Soon she was making hurried preparations for a journey to Ishiyama. She chose to travel without carriage or fanfare, limiting her retinue to Chūnagon, her nurse, and four or five close attendants, for her petition was just as weighty as that of Lady Tamakazura, who had traveled on foot to Hatsuse Temple.

When she arrived she was impressed by the singular beauty of the place. From the foot of the cliffs stretched a moon-bathed expanse of rippling waves; the cliffs were covered by deep layers of moss—untold aeons must have passed since they were mere pebbles. The ancient garden was suffused with the silence of another world, and all the hardships of her journey were forgotten as she gazed at it. She prayed fervently and prostrated herself in supplication. Entreating that her many afflictions be vanquished, intoning loudly the prayer, "Thy great vow is as deep as the seas," she paid homage with all her soul.[8]

Late at night, she finally completed her worship. The room adjoining her own was said to have sheltered Murasaki Shikibu when writing *The Tale of Genji*, and the girl was curious to see this unusual place. Suddenly she heard a refined voice from within. It seemed that a certain general of the left [*sadaishō*] was summoning a middle captain [*chūjō*]. Then the voice of the Middle Captain responded.

"Why did you come here to pray when the annual court appointment ceremonies were nigh, when you had pressing obligations both public and private? I cannot but wonder why you have wet your sleeves in these autumnal dews to come here. It defies all reason! You have not told me the least thing about why we are here, and it pains me to feel such a gulf between us. It seems that you are atoning for some sin you have committed—please tell me," he entreated sadly.

"Well, you know that one should not speak of dreams at night," replied the General, "but you are so concerned, and there is no longer any point in concealing it. I have entrusted the Buddha with my prayers for a clear resolution to my longings."

His manner of speaking was precisely that of the man who had visited her dreams. Her heart was thrown into turmoil, and she was desperate for a glimpse of him. Her attendants were already fast asleep, fatigued from the long journey. The lamp had been extinguished, and light shone brightly from the next room. Peering in through the crack in the door, she saw an elegant man dressed in hunting garb sitting forlornly. He was identical in every respect to the man of her dreams. Thinking that she must be dreaming again, she listened on, suppressing the dark storms in her heart.

"In China and in Japan, people have been guided by dreams, one seeking on Fugan Plain,[9] another who readied a boat to set out for the shores of Akashi.[10] In these and other cases, their dreams have coincided with reality. At the end of the third month of last year, I received a poem, apparently from a woman, attached to a lovely branch of wisteria:

Tanome tada	I wake to find
omoiawasuru	our tryst but a reverie—
omoi ne no	would that dreams too
utsutsu ni kaeru	come back to life.
yume mo koso are	

Ever since then, we have visited each other nightly for almost two years. We have vowed the eternally fresh passion of intertwined branches of two trees and the ever-constant love of two birds sharing one wing. Throughout my service at court and in the privacy of my own affairs, through the beauty of the changing seasons, I have been living solely in the hope that my dreams might be realized. Consumed with the thought of it, I could attend to nothing else; I am no longer myself and have weakened in body and spirit. I have rested all hope on this pilgrimage."

The girl was profoundly moved to hear him alternately laughing and crying as he poured out his tale of love and sadness. This indeed was the dream she had seen and the reality behind it! She desperately longed to pull open the sliding door that separated them and to converse of their nightly pledges. Yet such forwardness was inappropriate for a woman, and she was forced to repress the urge.

She was at the end of her wits. Those ephemeral dreams had rendered her unable to forget him; now she had heard the same tale about dreams of love and seen the same face of her dreams. All this had come to an end as empty as the open sky, for there was no way to bridge the gap between them, even for a moment. She had no way of predicting his reaction should she burst in and pour out her raging emotions, so she was unable to speak out or go to his side. For her, this stolen glimpse must be their only encounter. Her only recourse lay in becoming a fisherwoman in the waters, trusting that the ever-flowing currents of love would unite them in the world to come. Thus she bravely resolved to die.

After her mother's death, she had relied solely on her father and looked to him for protection; he in turn had loved her dearly. Should she commit the grave sin of predeceasing her parent, somber skies must darken the path she would tread in the hereafter. As he awaited her return on the morrow, he would be unaware that the brief full tide of her life would soon recede—with what sorrow would he receive the tidings, and how he would mourn! Still her resolution wavered not. Sadly, she remembered those who had served her for so long and her friends at court—the Kamo Priestess, the Empress, the various imperial princes and princesses. Regrettably, shallow rumors would cling to her unhappy name in the wake of her death. Numerous considerations gave her pause, but her resolve was strengthened by the prospect of meeting her beloved in the world to come. She lit the lamp and wrote a letter to her father, her eyes so blurred by tears that she was barely able to see. "Do not grieve. Alas, the dews on the young clover of spring are fleeting, yet all must die in the end."

TEXT 4

Dawn finally broke. Chūnagon and the others read sutras, the girl's own faintly whispered prayers barely audible. As her attendants admired the dawn breaking over the waters and mountains, she reflected on their grief should they discover the slightest dewdrop of her heart's intentions. It was indeed sad, but she had been granted a glimpse of the reality behind her dream vision and the knowledge that his feelings mirrored hers. This had to be a manifest token of the Kannon's expedient means, a trustworthy guide to the world to come that lent her courage to face the end with serenity. Hoping that the sin of dying before her parent might prove to be a kind of inverse karma, she prayed that she and her beloved might share a lotus leaf in perfect nuptial harmony in the Pure Land. Though this was her own heart's desire, it was nonetheless very sad.

Her party hastened to depart before the sun rose higher. Her brother's wetnurse, now bent with age, lived close to the nearby Seta Bridge. She had implored them to come visit, saying, "I live so near to where you will be passing. It won't do to let this rare opportunity go to waste . . . if I could only see you. Please come—then you can continue your journey by carriage." For one with intentions such as hers, visiting a place near the water provided a good pretext.

Her heart composed, the girl walked calmly as a lamb to slaughter, yet, the closer she drew to the bridge, the more foreboding the water seemed. What retribution from another life had led her to the depths of this watery grave? Now that the moment of death was on her, she imagined her father's terrible desolation after his only daughter had departed the world before him. Among the many examples of sad events that flooded her mind was the line of verse, "I know not where I go in the hereafter . . . ,"[11] and she was obliged to brush away the torrent of tears coursing down her face lest someone remark them. In the middle of the bridge, she paused, wavered indecisively, then leaped into the waters below.

"What has she done!" screamed her nurse in shock, standing transfixed in utter horror. Unable to restrain her tears, lacking even the presence of mind to jump in after her, her only thought was somehow to rescue her mistress, and she screamed for help at the top of her lungs.

Just then there appeared an elegant boat bearing a number of gentlemen dressed in hunting costume, who wondered at her hysterical sobbing. Overjoyed to see them, the nurse wildly screamed out, "Someone has just jumped in. Can you help?" stamping her feet in the frenzy of her emotion. Moved by pity for her, they resolutely let down some men familiar with the ways of the water, who dragged up the girl.

That the girl should be rescued from the watery depths was indeed a true witness to the message of the Lotus Sutra. Miraculously, her robes bore not a trace of moisture, as if they had been dry for many a long year.

The boat bore none other than the General, who, having completed his seven days of prayer, was on his way home. After the lady had been safely bundled aboard, the General regarded her closely. She was not yet twenty years old, charming and innocent, with striking eyes and features that brought to mind a far-off white wreathed cherry in the misty dawn light. Her face was modestly averted, and her abundant hair spilled down luxuriantly, nary a wisp astray, filled with the dewy grace of a willow. He felt that his customary dream was but an ephemera compared to this glowing reality. They spoke together without tiring, as if they had known each other for years. One might expect that a woman of such tender years would be embarrassed at having been pulled up in this manner, but she felt not a trace of reserve, for this was the same man dear to her in her dream life.

TEXT 5

The love they shared was so strong that it flourished even in the darkness of a jet-black dream; how much more now that they were able to meet in reality! The revered Kannon had led the couple to realize their long-standing karmic bond. They lived happily ever after, wanting for nothing, assisted by the excellence of the reign, and their legendary prosperity, which rivaled that of the Wisteria Leaves, extended even to their children and grandchildren.[12]

I should like to write on further, but I intended to tell only the story of a couple brought together in a dream through the manifestation of the Savior Bodhisattva's vow, and I shall leave the embellishments to another. To ramble on further would be a waste of ink, so I shall put aside my brush.

The Jizō Hall (*Jizōdō sōshi emaki*, fig. 2), one handscroll, in a private collection. My translation is based on the unannotated transcription of the scroll text in Ichiko Teiji, ed., *Mikan chūsei shōsetsu,* vol. 3, Koten bunko, no. 53 (Tokyo: Koten Bunko, 1951).

TEXT 1

At a time now past,[13] in a place called Sugano in the province of Echigo, there was a humble Jizō hall.[14] And in this hall was a monk[15] who had begun a one-thousand-day copying of *The Lotus Sutra* in accordance with the Law.[16] The days and months passed quickly. Once, after about two years, while the monk was reverently reading aloud *The Lotus Sutra,* a beautiful woman dressed in gauzy white silk and possessing an air of refinement came to listen to the chanting of the sutra. After this had happened a number of times, the monk inquired, "Where are you from? One doesn't expect to find someone like you around here." The woman replied, "I live not too far from here. I would like to become a donor. What kinds of things do you need for these exercises? I shall give you something to express my goodwill." The monk said, "To form a sacred bond through these exercises would truly accord with the original intention of the Buddha. As for the donation, there are those who give horse saddles and the like and others who give silks and textiles. Still others send cash equivalent to the amount of rice they themselves would eat. Whether large or small your donation will not be refused." The woman said, "Then I shall become a sponsor of these services and prepare my offerings."

While fondly likening her benevolence to that of one of the ten demon daughters [*jūrasetsu*],[17] the monk came to feel a deep love for her. When he proclaimed this to the woman, she replied, "That is quite a simple thing. Complete the sutra copying in accordance with the Law, and afterward, I will meet with you." The monk was overcome with joy. Though his mind was elsewhere, he continued the exercises for the number of days vowed.

TEXT 2

When the one-thousand-day exercise was over and the time had come to make the "ten kinds of offerings,"[18] the woman came riding in a palanquin surrounded by a throng of attendants. The spectacle was truly awe inspiring. When the ceremony came to an end, she brought forward the objects intended as offerings, an innumerable number of things like gold and silver, jewels, figured silks, and embroidered brocades. The other monks received their share as well. Before long, the temple was rebuilt into a magnificent Great Hall in which to carry out Buddhist ceremonies.

After this, the monk met regularly and in secret with the woman. When she said, "This is not appropriate. Let me take you to where I live," the monk responded, "Yes, let's go," and he followed her. They went along together, just the two of them, until they arrived at the edge of the sea. When they were about to enter the sea, the monk finally said, "Hold on! Just how am I supposed to go in there?" "Well then, wear this," the woman said, covering him almost entirely in something that seemed like brocade. Thereupon, he had not the least trouble crossing the sea. The surface of the water became like dry land, and they set out for the distant offing. After a while they could no longer see land in any direction.

TEXT 3

Arriving at the bottom of the sea, the monk came upon a palatial complex of towers and monastic buildings. Elegant and refined, it was otherworldly. He felt as if he was looking at a Chinese painting; it was marvelous. Passing through the gate, the woman whom he had thought of as his own wife suddenly resembled a heavenly maiden. Numerous male and female attendants greeted them, announcing excitedly, "The princess is here." The lively scene was truly indescribable in its splendor. Everyone looked like heavenly beings or like the people of Tang, as though depicted in a painting. Amid such a welcome he felt as though he were someone else. It was like nothing he had experienced before; it was simply like a dream unfolding before his eyes.

TEXT 4

A holy man from a remote mountain temple, the monk was uneducated, guileless, and completely lacking in good judgment. Nevertheless, perhaps his training in the Law of Dharma, even if short-lived, had instilled in him a small amount of sense. As he passed the days and months in this place and contemplated his situation, he realized that the pleasure he now enjoyed was beyond the realm of the ordinary.[19] He wondered if in reward for his diligence in copying the sutra in accordance with the Law he had already become a living Buddha. But then again, he did not get the feeling that he had been born into the Buddha realm. Recalling that he had entered the sea, he had the sneaking suspicion that this might be some such place as the Dragon Palace, but he could not just come out and ask. If that were the case, what would be the result of his Buddhist practices?

He continued to contemplate these things when, one night while sleeping with the woman, he saw that the hem of her heavenly garment resembled the tail of a snake. Now there was no doubt in his mind; he had entered the Dragon Palace. He felt alienated from his surroundings and wondered what would become of him should he live like this until the end of his days. He thought anxiously of how he could shed this spell and return to the man he once was.

TEXT 5

The monk said to the woman, "Since coming to this place I have experienced pleasure upon pleasure, but I long for my home. How might I go about returning for a brief visit?"

The woman replied, "That is a simple thing. The answer lies within your heart. There is something that I have been meaning to tell you, and so I brought you here. The reason for all of this is as follows. In the beginning, when the sutra copying was planned in accordance with the Law and I humbly formed a connection with that noble endeavor, you began to have feelings for me, turning the Buddhist exercises into a mockery. I shall take out the very sutra that you wrote and show it to you. This palace contains a sutra repository preserving great numbers of sacred texts. Since in the beginning this sutra too aimed at according with the Law, I planned to place it among the others, but alas, it became a farce. Nevertheless, because of your initial diligent efforts, you were rewarded with this brief spell of pleasure. Because your thoughts strayed later on, however, you must now return to the evil path.[20]

"Quickly return to your homeland, practice sincerely, and accomplish the sutra copying according to the Law, and this time you should escape the cycle of birth and death. I too have a body that cannot be free from suffering. You must pray for me. If you do these things, the farcical words you wrote will be transformed into a sutra of wonderful truths. Make these practices that I have described your own and you will realize that the power of the Dharma is no empty matter."

Saying, "Here is the sutra that you wrote," she brought out a jeweled sutra box. The cover was removed and the strings untied, revealing what had been written. "Quickly get this over with, I want to sleep with this woman, I want to sleep with her. I want this over with quickly, I want to sleep with her, want to sleep with her now . . ." These words were the only ones written and they repeated countless times from beginning to end.

There was no reason to argue, for this was certainly written in his own hand. The monk felt dejected and ashamed beyond words. After it had been looked over, the sutra was returned to the treasure hall. Many people accompanied the monk to the edge of the sea to see him off. From there the monk returned to Sugano by himself.

TEXT 6

The monk returned to the Jizō hall. Though he thought that no time had passed since his departure, the building was completely dilapidated, looking nothing like it had in the past. Feeling distressed, he entered the hall and fell asleep using the altar seat as a pillow. Then a group of monks approached who seemed to be affiliated with the temple, one of whom suddenly entered the hall. When he saw the sleeping monk, he let out an exclamation before falling down on the spot and losing consciousness. "What is going on?" another monk said, as he too entered and then fainted. In this way three people expired. When the residents of the village hurriedly gathered to take a look, the sight that met their eyes was a huge snake about six or seven *jō*[21] long and two or three *shaku*[22] in diameter, coiled up and resting its head on the altar seat.

The monk awoke and wondered what was going on. He felt deeply disappointed upon realizing that he had been turning into a snake ever since he had been cloaked in that brocade-like thing. Weeping tears of regret he turned to Jizō, earnestly confessed the sins that had prevented him from following the Buddhist path and vowed to copy the sutra as prescribed by Buddhist Law. After he had repented for his shameful sins, in the middle of the night, the back of the huge snake suddenly broke open, and from it the monk emerged. To look upon the shed skin was a horrific experience beyond comparison. The cast-off shell of the snake lay there lifeless. Hearing of this, people from neighboring villages gathered at the site and witnessed the spectacle with a great deal of excitement. There was no one at that time, however, who knew that the monk had emerged from the snake.

TEXT 7

The monk looked at the world around him and realized there was not a single person that he knew from before. And with no one who seemed to recognize him, he felt as though he were encountering for the first time a world that was somehow lacking. He asked, "What happened to that monk called 'something-or-other,' who performed a sutra copying at this venerable hall in recent years?"

The temple monks replied that they had not heard of such a thing happening in recent years. When he gave them the approximate era, although they did not know exactly when it took place, they answered:

"Well, we heard about such a thing happening long ago. As many as two hundred years have passed since then. It is said that a monk became friendly with the daughter of the Dragon King and entered the sea. After that, this temple was rebuilt two or three times. Originally a temple of no connection,[23] thanks to that monk's cultivation of worldly fields and the training of monks we have continued like this until today."

Then the monk asked them how old they thought he looked, and they replied that he seemed to be about seventeen or eighteen. "How strange," he thought. He wanted to say, "I am that monk from long ago," and tell them his name, but it was not something that he could simply come out and say. Later on people came to understand. After that he devoted all of his energies to carrying out the explanation of *The Lotus Sutra* according to the Law. He wholeheartedly performed his exercises for attaining Buddhahood in the next world and did nothing else. After many years, he finally achieved rebirth.

This tale is found among stories collected from long ago. Sugano is the birthplace of the late monk of Tōfukuji, Mukan Chōrō Fumon Shōnin. The head of the snake is still there today; [Fumon Shōnin] saw it himself and related this to the Zen monk Kitayama Reigen Ryōshinbō.

B*reaking the Inkstone* (*Suzuriwari sōshi emaki*, fig. 3), one handscroll, Hosomi Museum, Kyoto. My translation is based on the transcription of the scroll in Umezu Jirō, "Suzuriwari emaki sono hoka: 'Ko-e' no mondai," *Kokka* 828 (1961): 97–104. Reprinted in Umezu, *Emakimono sōshi*, 285–97.

TEXT 1

Once, while the major counselor was away at the imperial palace, a servant named Nakamichi opened this up and looked. Hearing the sound of a carriage, he carelessly rushed to put it away and broke it into three pieces. The young master of the house, just seven years old, asked the overwrought and sobbing servant what had happened. After he explained, the young boy said, "You will most certainly be severely punished. You must say that it was I who broke it."

TEXT 2

When the major counselor took out the inkstone to look at it, as he did every day without fail, he was shocked to find it broken and asked Nakamichi. The servant appealed to the counselor by saying, "The young master of the house was playing with it." Outraged, the counselor said, "He is not my son, but one born of an enemy. He must be sent far away into the mountains." The boy's mother spoke up, but her words were unheeded, and the boy was accompanied only by his wet nurse. On the dirt floor of a one-room hut in Saga, the nurse spread out a short robe. In no time it seemed as though the boy might be near death, at which point she sent word of the situation through a young child, and the mother and father came together. They were full of sorrow, but there was nothing that could be done.

TEXT 3

And so the father and mother renounced the world. Nakamichi, who confessed, "In truth it was I who broke the inkstone," likewise shaved his head and climbed Mt. Shosha. He devoted himself in various ways to Buddhist practice and offered prayers that the young boy might attain Buddhahood. A very moving thing indeed.

B*reaking the Inkstone*, in *Tales of Times Now Past* (*Konjaku monogatari shū*). My translation is based on the edition annotated by Mabuchi Kazuo, Kunisaki Fumimaro, and Konno Tōru in vol. 22 of *Nihon koten bungaku zenshū* (Tokyo: Shōgakukan, 1972), 536–47.[24]

"A servant who breaks an inkstone takes the tonsure on account of a small child"

Long ago, during the reign of Emperor Murakami,[25] there was a man called the Koichijō Minister of the Left, whose name was Moromasa.[26] He was the fifth son of the regent known as Teishinkō (Upright and Faithful Lord).[27] He had one daughter, whom he loved dearly.[28] She had elegant looks and a warm heart, and her mother and father cherished her beyond measure.

The emperor heard about this girl and insisted that she become an imperial consort. Deciding to present her at court, the minister quickly set about making preparations. In arranging his daughter's dowry he exhausted his resources, racking his brain and doing everything he could to gather her toiletries and personal accessories. Among the objects was an inkstone box that was particularly wonderful. Inside was an inkstone, a priceless family heirloom that had been handed down for generations. Not only was the inkstone beautiful, with its gold and silver decoration on a lacquered ground, but the consistency of its ink was unlike any other in the world. Among all the treasures in his daughter's dowry, the inkstone was the most precious. For this reason the minister never casually showed it to others but kept it close at hand in a brocade bag tucked away inside a two-shelved shrine. The minister thought to himself, "I'll put it in its box on the day that she goes to the palace," and so it was not to be taken out but to remain safely stored away. The emperor too heard about this inkstone, and being inclined toward such objects, he inquired as to whether there really was such an inkstone. The minister thought it truly fortunate that he should possess this treasure and be able to place it in his daughter's dowry.

Employed in the minister's household was a young man whose appearance was not unkempt and who came from a passable family. The minister instructed him to clean up the minister's own quarters. As he cleaned every morning, the young man, who had himself dabbled in calligraphy, felt a great desire to see the inkstone that was stored away in the minister's shrine. One day the minister went to the palace, and his wife was off in her own rooms with her daughter giving her instructions on her robes. Some of the female attendants were with them, while others were in their own apartments, busy with preparations for the young lady's departure. With everyone thus away, the young man cleaning thought to himself, "If I were to secretly open it up now and look at the inkstone, who would know?"

He took the key out from beneath the inkstone box and opened the shrine. He removed the inkstone and looked at it. It was even more exquisite than had been rumored, and he was enchanted by it. Resting it in the palm of his hand, he raised it up and down. He had been looking at it for a while when he heard the sound of footsteps. As he rushed to put the inkstone back, he fumbled and dropped it. It was broken right in two. The man felt miserable and was unable to think. He shook like someone possessed, his vision dimmed, his heart raced, and tears flowed from his eyes as he sobbed uncontrollably. He wondered, "What will the minister say when he sees this, and what will become of me?" Can we even imagine how truly wretched he must have felt?

The person making the sound of the footsteps was the young master of the house. The boy had a beautiful appearance and a generous heart. He was thirteen years old. By now he should have had his coming-of-age ceremony, but because there was such reluctance to cut his gorgeous hair, it had been delayed. Although he was just a young boy, he was wise beyond his years. And when he saw that the attendant had broken the inkstone, that the man was dazed and confused and looked like someone on the verge of death, he was mortified. The boy asked him, "What is going on here?" but the man simply sobbed, unable to answer. The boy felt great pity for him. He picked up the broken inkstone, shut it back in the shrine the way it was, and turned the key. He then said to the attendant, "You need not agonize so much over this." And he instructed the man, "Say that the young master is the one who removed the inkstone to have a look and shattered it to pieces." When the man heard this, what must he have thought? He crawled away feeling truly overjoyed and grateful.

And yet the man felt terribly guilty. He told no one about the incident and went around in a daze. When the minister came home from the palace, he felt like taking out some of his things. When he opened the shrine, he saw that the inkstone had been removed from its bag and was broken perfectly in two. His vision dimmed when he saw this. He was shocked and unable to think. After taking a moment to control his rage, he questioned the female attendants. They replied that they knew nothing about it, but they said that "it must have occurred around the time when that young man comes to clean your room." The minister summoned the man and asked, "How was it that this inkstone was broken? Do you know anything about this?" The man's face changed color. He gathered up his sleeves and prostrated himself. The minister was an extremely short-tempered person, and with anger in his eyes he pressed him, "Speak up, mister!" In a trembling voice, the man could only twice mutter the words "the young master." The minister raised his voice and pressed him further, "What!? How?" The man continued, "He took it out, and while he was looking at it, he dropped it and broke it." The minister was silent for some time, then he said to the man, "Alright, now quickly get out! Get out!" The man groveled away.

The minister then entered the inner quarters and told his wife, "This broken inkstone is the boy's doing. He is not my son, but an enemy from a former life. That worthless creature, to think that I spent all of these years affectionately raising him," and he sobbed loudly. His wife wept when she heard this. All the ladies too clustered together and cried enough to bring misfortune upon them. It goes without saying that the boy's nurse was even more distraught. After a while the minister said, "I never want to lay eyes on that boy again. The bond between parent and child is such that perhaps we will cross paths in later years, but for now I do not want to see him. Quickly take him to his nurse's house and keep him there." Since the boy was being so furiously chased out, the nurse borrowed someone's carriage, and with a profound sadness in her heart, she gathered up some things without a moment's delay. She collected the weeping boy and they departed. Both the nurse and the young boy cried uncontrollably the entire way there.

Upon arriving at the nurse's house, the young boy saw that it was a small hut, terribly dilapidated and tiny. Filled with fear over these unfamiliar surroundings, he passed the days in low spirits. One evening, looking extremely dejected, he recited to himself:

Kokoro kara	Though my heart led me
aretaru yado ni	to this ramshackle lodging where

tabine shite	I sleep as a traveler,
omoimo kakenu	my mind is filled
mono omoi koso	with unexpected thoughts.[29]

How must his nurse have felt as she watched him muttering to himself. Because the young boy had such a beautiful heart, all of the members of the minister's household secretly came to visit him, shedding tears as they did so. In particular, the male attendants who had served him arranged among themselves to keep nightly watch over him.

When three or four days had passed, the young boy began to feel unusual and was overcome with fever. After three or four more days went by, it was clear that this was a serious illness. Greatly troubled, the nurse sent word to the boy's mother. The mother was shocked and told the minister, "Over these past three or four days the boy has caught fever and is suffering." Without showing any signs of grief, the minister said, "Such a fool as that, what use would he be even if he lived? If this should lead to his death, it would be a fortunate thing." The mother was beside herself with grief, and though she wanted to go and see her son, the minister was firm in his anger. The lamentable thing about being a woman was that she could not simply do as she wished and go to see the boy. The mother explained this in a letter and sent it to the nurse. The nurse read it at the boy's side, as he lay there listening.

After about seven days had passed, there was a day of strict taboos and no one came to visit. On that day, at around the hour of the boar [10 p.m.], the young boy was near death. Because of the strictness of the taboo, the nurse could not inform the boy's parents. At around the hour of the tiger [4 a.m.], thinking that perhaps the taboo had been lifted, she sent word to the boy's mother about his illness and impending death. She also wrote that the young boy seemed to have a deep love for his parents, but that he held back from saying so, and that knowing this was overwhelmingly sad for her. The boy then recited to himself:

Akenuru naru	Announcing the break of day,
tori no naku naku	the bird cries and cries.
madoro made	I wonder, do my parents know
ko wa kaku koso to	that I have spent the night thus,
shiru rame ya kimi	wakefully weeping?

Hearing him recite this in such a pained voice, she could bear it no longer, and she included the boy's poem with her own message.

The mother looked at the letter and cried and cried as she read both the nurse's note and the boy's poem aloud to the minister. Since this was a child he had truly cherished in the beginning, he said, "I thought he would be fine. If this is truly a serious illness, then this is a terrible tragedy. If so, we must go and see him." The shabbiness of their destination demanded that they travel discreetly. They rode together in one carriage, sobbing the entire way.

Stepping down from the carriage, they approached the boy and saw him lying there, even nearer death than they had heard. Seeing him like this, the minister said, "Would even one hundred thousand inkstones made of gold and silver be worth this? I thought he was careless and sent him away in a fit of anger. What a pitifully wretched thing I have done! I must have been out of my mind to send this boy away." Feeling deep remorse, he said:

Mutsugoto mo	Affectionate words,
nani ni ka wa sen	what use are they now?
kuyashiki wa	How tragic
kono yo ni kakaru	that in this world
wakare nari keri	we must make such a break.

Putting his face to the ear of the barely conscious boy, he said sobbing, "Son, do you think me cruel?"

The boy whispered, "How could I possibly think that of my own parent?" The minister felt he had no way to respond. Unable to speak, he cried bitter tears of regret, but now there was nothing to be done. The young boy whispered:

Tarachine no	When my father
itoishi toki ni	began to hate me,
kienamashi	I thought I would be better off dead,
yagate wakare no	and now at last, I have reached
michi to shiri seba	that final road of parting.[30]

Though seemingly in great pain, he called out the name of Amida ten times in a loud voice, then passed away. The heartbreak of the mother and father was beyond words. His long hair fell over his body, and his beautiful face wore a peaceful expression as if he were asleep. Seeing him like this his parents and nurse were crazed with an overwhelming grief. A number of days passed, and the boy's body was buried according to custom. Since the nurse's house was so shabby, he was returned to his father's home, where Buddhist services began to be conducted.

After the third of the weekly offerings had been made, the man who had cleaned for the minister, who had not been seen for days, approached.[31] Seeing that the man was wearing black mourning robes, the minister said to him, "That's strange. I didn't hear anything about you losing a parent. For whom do you wear mourning robes?"

The man lied prostrate before him and began weeping hysterically. Thinking this all the more strange, the minister asked, "What is wrong?" The man replied, "These robes are for the young master." The minister said, "What is this about? Why should you wear black robes, unlike all the other servants?" The man sobbed and said, "Hearing that your inkstone was so wonderful, I was overcome with desire to see it. When you were away at the palace, I secretly took it out, and while I was looking at it, I dropped it and broke it. When the young master came in and saw what a terrible state I was in, he said, 'Blame this on me. It is a terrible pity that you feel so bad about this. It will not be a serious matter if I take responsibility. If you take the blame, you will certainly be punished.' It is shameful, but because I wanted to escape my crime, that is the excuse I told you. I felt deeply regretful when the young master bore the punishment, and then when he passed away so soon afterward, I was beside myself with grief! Words are inadequate, so the least I can do is to wear these mourning robes." Sobbing, he composed the poem,

Namidagawa	Though I shed a river of tears,
araedo ochizu	they do not come clean,
hakanakute	these robes stained black
suzuri no yue ni	by the inkstone
someshi koromo wa	

There was no limit to his weeping.

When the minister heard this, he fell into an even deeper despair. He entered the inner rooms and sobbed as he told his wife, "The child did nothing wrong." And he explained the whole story. When the wife heard this, what grief must she have felt? The minister said, "This child was not an ordinary person. And that I should have punished him for this!" He felt profound remorse. Hearing all of this, what anguish the boy's nurse must have felt!

After that, the man disappeared without a trace. He had parents and a wife and children, who looked for him but never learned his whereabouts. Written on the wall of the servant's quarters were the words:

Mumatama no	My jet black hair
kami o tamukete	I leave as an offering.
wakareji ni	I have decided
okureji to koso	to make our separate paths
omoitachinure	*one.*

He immediately cut his hair and became a monk and set out to practice religious austerities. He was a man capable of deep compassion.

The parents and the nurse heard about this and felt an indescribable grief and love for the boy. Nevertheless, the father, mother, and nurse did not take Buddhist vows. Because the young man had been the recipient of the boy's kindness, he abandoned his family ties, earnestly pursued Buddhist practices, and prayed for the boy's rebirth. So it was said, and so it has been handed down.

NOTES

ABBREVIATIONS

CK	Kanroji Chikanaga, *Chikanaga-kyō ki*
CKH	Kanroji Chikanaga, *Chikanaga-kyō ki hoi*
KG	Fushimi Sadafusa, *Kanmon gyōki*
NK	Nakamikado Nobutane, *Nobutane-kyō ki*
SK	Sanjōnishi Sanetaka, *Sanetaka-kō ki*

INTRODUCTION

1 The term *emaki* dates to the mid-Edo period; in the medieval period picture scrolls were referred to by their subject title followed by the word *e* (picture) and the number of scrolls (*kan/maki*) in the set; thus, we find *Ishi Jizō e, ikkan* (picture of the Stone Jizō, one scroll). In this book, extant picture scrolls will be cited according to their most commonly known and easily searchable titles (e.g., *Shigisan engi emaki* or *Kasuga Gongen genki-e*).

2 The pictorial achievements of late-twelfth-century *emaki* are often attributed to the sponsorship of GoShirakawa. See Komatsu Shigemi, "Ōchō emaki to GoShirakawa-in," in *Genji monogatari emaki, Nezame monogatari emaki*, vol. 1 of *Nihon emaki taisei*, ed. Komatsu Shigemi (Tokyo: Chūō Kōronsha, 1977), 114–33.

3 *Engi*, often translated as "origins," is a Buddhist term that literally means "coming into existence by depending on other things," or "dependent origination," and it refers to the Buddhist notion of the interdependence of all things. See Inagaki Hisao, *A Dictionary of Japanese Buddhist Terms, Based on References in Japanese Literature* (Union City, CA: Heian International, 1989), 46.

4 *Engi* recording the origins of Buddhist institutions in Japan began to be written before the mid-eighth century; see Edward Kamens, *The Three Jewels: A Study and Translation of Minamoto Tamenori's "Sanbōe,"* Michigan Monograph Series in Japanese Studies, no. 2

(Ann Arbor: Center for Japanese Studies, University of Michigan, 1988), 87n49.

5 Mitamura Masako and Mitani Kuniaki have attempted to reconstruct one possible scenario for the production of the twelfth-century *Genji Scrolls,* involving a kind of group authorship; see Mitamura and Mitani, *Genji monogatari emaki no nazo o yomitoku* (Tokyo: Kadokawa Shoten, 1998). For the artifactual nature of the scrolls and their production, see Yukio Lippit, "Figure and Facture in the Genji Scrolls: Text, Calligraphy, Paper, and Painting," in *Envisioning The Tale of Genji: Media, Gender, and Cultural Production*, ed. Haruo Shirane (New York: Columbia University Press, 2008), 49–80.

6 References in medieval diaries to tales and picture scrolls being read and viewed in a communal setting will appear throughout this study. For a discussion of how the storytelling site influenced medieval tale literature, see Sasaki Kōji, "Chūsei bungaku ni okeru ba to seikaku," *Nihon bungaku* 36–2, no. 404 (1987): 40–49.

7 For a detailed study of one artistic response to the text, see Suga Miho, "Kitano Tenjin engi Mitsuoki bon no kōsatsu," *Kokka* 1209 (1996): 7–23.

8 Standard surveys include the following: Okudaira Hideo, *Emaki: Japanese Picture Scrolls* (Rutland, VT: C. E. Tuttle, 1962); Okudaira Hideo, *Narrative Picture Scrolls* (New York: Weatherhill, 1973); Dietrich Seckel, *Emakimono: The Art of the Japanese Painted Hand-Scroll* (New York: Pantheon Books, 1959); Akiyama Terukazu, *Emakimono* (Tokyo: Shōgakukan, 1968); Akiyama Terukazu, *Japanese Painting* (Geneva: Skira, 1972); Wakasugi Junji, *Emakimono no kanshō kiso chishiki* (Tokyo: Shibundō, 1995).

9 Akiyama Terukazu, "New Buddhist Sects and *Emakimono* (Hand-Scroll Painting) in the Kamakura Period," *Acta Asiatica* 20 (1971): 58–76; Akiyama Terukazu, "Emaki no hasshō to tenkai," in vol. 1 of *Nihon emakimono no kenkyū* (Tokyo: Chūō Kōron Bijutsu Shuppan, 2000), 1–68.

10 Karen Brock's study of picture scrolls produced and read within the circle of Prince Sadafusa (1372–1456) and his son Emperor GoHanazono (1419–70) captures the importance that aristocratic families and the imperial court attached to the possession of narrative scrolls in the late medieval period; see Brock, "The Shogun's 'Painting Match,'" *Monumenta Nipponica* 50, no. 4 (1995): 433–84.

11 I will touch on the role of court women in the production and reception of handscrolls in chapters 2 and 3; also see Melissa McCormick, "Genji no ma o nozoku: Hakubyō Genji monogatari emaki to nyōbō no shiza," trans. Maki Kaneko, in *Genji monogatari o yomitoku 1: Egakareta Genji monogatari*, ed. Kawazoe Fusae and Mitamura Masako (Tokyo: Kanrin Shobō, 2006), 101–29; Melissa McCormick, "Monochromatic Genji: The *Hakubyō* Tradition and Female Commentarial Culture," in *Envisioning The Tale of Genji*, 101–28. On the attribution of a *Genji* scroll in the *hakubyō* mode to a court lady in the service of Emperor GoTsuchimikado (1442–1500), see Miyakawa Yōko, "Hakubyō *Genji monogatari emaki:* GoTsuchimikado-in Kōtō no Naishi hitsu," *Kokusai Keiei Bunka Kenkyū* 6, no. 2 (March 2002): 143–84.

12 Known as *The Illustrated Life of Kōbō Daishi,* the scrolls owned by Tōji monastery are reproduced and discussed in *Kōbō Daishi gyōjō emaki no sekai: Eien e no hishō* (Kyoto: Tōji Hōbutsukan, 2000); Manabe Shunshō, "Kōbō Daishi gyōjō ekotoba no kaigaka," in *Kōbō Daishi gyōjō ekotoba*, vol. 6 of *Zoku Nihon emaki taisei,* ed. Komatsu Shigemi (Tokyo: Chūō Kōronsha, 1983), 78–109. For other versions of the *emaki,* see Umezu Jirō, "Kōbō Daishi gyōjō emaki no keifu," *Nihon bijutsu kōgei* 319 (1965): 38–42; Shinbo Tōru, "Kōbō Daishi den emaki nijū," in *Shinshū Nihon emakimono zenshū, bekkan 1: Zaigai hen,* ed. Shimada Shūjirō (Tokyo: Kadokawa Shoten, 1980), 3–10.

13 See *Tōdaiji daibutsu engi, Nigatsudō engi*, vol. 6 of *Zoku zoku Nihon emaki taisei,* ed. Komatsu Shigemi (Tokyo: Chūō Kōronsha, 1994).

14 In addition to the work of Karen Brock, cited above, recent articles by Takagishi Akira have begun to illuminate the breadth of activity of the Ashikaga shoguns in the production of handscrolls; see Takagishi Akira, "Muromachi dono emaki korekushon no keisei," *Bijutsushi* 155 (2003): 16–29.

15 Brock, "The Shogun's 'Painting Match.'"

16 Yoshiharu's version of the *Hasedera engi emaki* is the only extant "dependent-origin" (*engi*) tale illustrated as a *ko-e* and will be discussed in chapter 1, which surveys the works that survive in the small-scroll format. The six scrolls that make up this *engi* are

examined in Sakakibara Satoru, "Rokkan-bon 'Hasedera engi-e' shōkai," in *Kohitsu to emaki,* vol. 4 of *Kohitsugaku sōrin*, ed. Komatsu Shigemi (Tokyo: Yagi Shoten, 1994), 113–96.

17 Kamei Wakana, "'Kuwanomidera engi emaki' kenkyū," *Kokka* 1193 (1995): 3–21; revised and expanded in *Hyōshō to shite no bijutsushi: Muromachi Shōgun Ashikaga Yoshiharu to Tosa Mitsumochi no kaiga* (Kunitachi-shi: Brücke, 2003).

18 Masamoto's patronage of picture scrolls will be examined in chapter 5.

19 The three-scroll set painted by Kanō Motonobu (1477–1559) is currently in the Suntory Museum of Art, Tokyo. Sakakibara Satoru has demonstrated the connection between these scrolls and the political aspirations of the Hōjō clan; see Sakakibara, "Santorī Bijutsukan-bon 'Shuten dōji emaki' o megutte," pts. 1 and 2, *Kokka* 1076 (1984): 7–29 and *Kokka* 1077 (1984): 33–56.

20 Umezu Jirō, "Suzuriwari emaki sono hoka: 'Ko-e' no mondai," *Kokka* 828 (1961): 97–104. Small scrolls are entirely absent from the most authoritative scholarly compendia of *emaki*, the three series, totaling fifty-five volumes, edited by Komatsu Shigemi between 1977 and 1995: *Nihon emaki taisei*, 27 vols. (Tokyo: Chūō Kōronsha, 1977–79); *Zoku Nihon emaki taisei,* 20 vols. (Tokyo: Chūō Kōronsha, 1981–85); and *Zoku zoku Nihon emaki taisei,* 8 vols. (Tokyo: Chūō Kōronsha, 1993–95). Instead, small-format scrolls were set apart from these canonical picture scrolls and grouped with *otogi zōshi emaki* and *Nara ehon;* see, e.g., Okudaira Hideo, *Otogi zōshi emaki* (Tokyo: Kadokawa Shoten, 1982); Nara Ehon Kokusai Kenkyū Kaigi, ed., *Zaigai Nara ehon* (Tokyo: Kadokawa Shoten, 1981).

21 Umezu, "Suzuriwari emaki sono hoka," 103.

1 A BRIEF HISTORY OF SMALL SCROLLS

1 *Life of Prince Shōtoku*, now in a private collection in Kyoto, consists of ten scrolls that each measure 15.9 centimeters in height. Colophons at the end of scrolls 5 and 10 date the work to 1324 (Genkō 4).

2 Of the sixty-four paintings, seventeen are replacements executed in 1710 by Kanō Tsunenobu (1636–1713); see Ogushi Sumio, "Kiwamete yoku nita mittsu no Shōtoku Taishi emaki," *Kokka* 711 (1951): 219–27.

3 *Miraculous Origins of Hasedera*, now in the collection of Hasedera in Nara, measures roughly eighteen centimeters in height. The paintings are partially reproduced in Nara Kokuritsu Hakubutsukan, ed., *Shaji engi-e* (Tokyo: Kadokawa Shoten, 1975).

4 Sakakibara Satoru has argued persuasively that the scrolls were made for the shogun Ashikaga Yoshiharu (1511–50) around the year 1523 based on entries from the diary of Konoe Hisamichi (1472–1544) (the calligrapher of the scrolls), which discuss borrowing a three-scroll set from the temple apparently for the purpose of creating the *ko-e* version. See Sakakibara, "Rokkan-bon 'Hasedera engi-e' shōkai."

5 Once divided and owned by Matsunaga Jian (1875–1971) and the *Nihonga* artist Maeda Seison (1885–1977), the single scroll (16.1 x 625.4 centimeters) of *Heike Courtiers* is now in the Fukuoka Art Museum and consists of five texts and four paintings.

6 Like *Heike Courtiers*, *Recollections of In no Dainagon* was previously in the collection of Matsunaga Jian and is currently in the Fukuoka Art Museum. The set consists of two scrolls, each measuring 19.3 centimeters in height. The existence of an additional fragment found in an album of calligraphy samples suggests that originally the work may have contained at least one other scene. The fragment is reproduced and discussed in Tamura Etsuko, "In no Dainagon ni kansuru jakkan no kōsatsu," *Bijutsu kenkyū* 326 (1983): 1–16.

7 It is possible that paper sizes of early picture scrolls were deliberately chosen to suit the subject matter or function of a given handscroll, and that paper size could connote the genre of a work. Narratives of courtly romances and illustrations of female courtiers' diaries measured anywhere from twenty to twenty-five centimeters in height. In contrast, scrolls characterized by long, continuous paintings of action-driven narratives were composed on paper measuring over thirty centimeters in height. As might be expected, the most public scrolls, those meant to impress a large audience or communicate at a distance, utilized the largest paper sizes available. The *Mongol Invasions Scrolls* (ca. 1293), which recount the Japanese battles against the Mongol attacks of 1274 and 1281, measure roughly forty centimeters in height and are among the largest scrolls of the medieval period. The twenty scrolls

of *Miracles of the Kasuga Deity* (1309), at an average of forty-one centimeters, similarly project an imposing presence. The producers of *Legends of Kitano Tenjin* (*Kitano Tenjin engi emaki,* 1219) bypassed the size limitations of paper-making technology by turning standard paper sheets of fifty-one centimeters in width on their sides to create the tallest scroll set of the period. In a slightly different vein, scrolls of explicitly Buddhist subjects, such as the Heian period *Hells Scrolls* (*Jigoku zōshi*) and *Hungry Ghosts* (*Gaki zōshi*), employ paper of the same size as that used in Buddhist sutras, roughly twenty-five centimeters in height, perhaps announcing the Buddhist subject matter before the work was even unrolled.

8 Scholars have posited Fujiwara no Takafusa (1148–1209), a participant in some of the scenes in the scroll, as the narrator and possible author of the text; see Nakamura Yoshio, "Heike kindachi sōshi to Fujiwara Takafusa: Seigaiha no dan no shutten o chūshin to shite," in *Emakimono kotobagaki no kenkyū* (Tokyo: Kadokawa Shoten, 1982), 211–40. Another theory builds upon the idea of Takafusa as a popular protagonist in the Kamakura period, appearing as he does in the scroll *Lord Takafusa's Love Songs*, and attributes the work to an editor who incorporated lines from Takafusa's own writings into the scroll text of *Heike Courtiers*; see Kobayashi Kayoko, "Takafusa to iu imēji: 'Heike kindachi sōshi' to 'Takafusa kyō tsuya kotoba emaki,'" *Dōshisha kokubungaku* 56 (2002): 28–42. Kobayashi also suggests that this scroll and other texts that construct an image of Lord Takafusa as a lover may have been created roughly one hundred years after Takafusa's time, perhaps in the circle of Takafusa's granddaughter Lady Kitayama (1196–1302).

9 For this passage in English see chapter 10, section 11, of *The Tale of the Heike*, trans. Helen Craig McCullough (Stanford: Stanford University Press, 1988), 347–48.

10 The text of the scroll is transcribed in Tamura Etsuko, "In no Dainagon ni kansuru jakkan no kōsatsu."

11 Later connoisseurs identified the author-painter-calligrapher of the scroll to be the poet and GoDaigo supporter In no Dainagon Kazan'in Morokata (1301–32), an attribution that Tamura Estuko has supported based on a calligraphic comparison; see Tamura, "In no Dainagon ni kansuru jakkan no kōsatsu," 5–6.

12 See the entry for the fifth day of the ninth month of the fifteenth year of Bunmei (1483) (hereafter cited as Bunmei 15 [1483] 9.5), in Sanetaka's diary, *Sanetaka-kō ki* (hereafter cited as *SK*), vol. 1, pt. 2, 454. Sanetaka refers to the scrolls as "ink pictures" (*sumi-e*), one of the medieval terms for what are now called ink-line or, in Japanese, *hakubyō-e* (literally "white drawing pictures").

13 It is unlikely that the scrolls Sanetaka mentioned were the illustrated *Pillow Book* that survives in the Asano Collection as a single scroll measuring 25.5 centimeters in height and also dating to the fourteenth century. This extant work is thought to correspond to a set of scrolls noted in the diary of Prince Fushimi Sadafusa (1372–1456), *A Record of Things Seen and Heard* (*Kanmon gyoki*); see the entry for Eikyō 10 (1438) 12.3 in vol. 2 of the *Kanmon gyoki* (cited hereafter as *KG*), published in *Zoku gunsho ruijū hoi* 2, ed. Hanawa Hokiichi and Ōta Tōshirō, rev. ed. (Tokyo: Zoku Gunsho Ruijū Kanseikai, 1999–2000), 585. Sadafusa does not refer to the *Pillow Book* that he viewed as a *ko-e*.

14 Eikyō 3 (1431) 12.5 (*KG*, vol. 1, 621).

15 Tōin Kinkata authored *Chronology of Successive Emperors* (*Kōtairyaku*), *Historical Compendium* (*Rekidai saiyōshō*), and *Humble Gleanings* (*Shūgaishō*), the last an encyclopedia-like text, as well as his diary, *Entairyaku*, which was well known among diarists of the Muromachi period; see Hayashiya Tatsusaburō, *Nairan no naka no kizoku: Nanbokuchō ki "Entairyaku" no sekai* (Tokyo: Kadokawa Shoten, 1975), 151–58. Karen Brock places Sadafusa's reference to Tōin's *Activities of the Twelfth Month* scroll in the context of his interest in materials related to court ritual, knowledge of which he saw as a means to assert his identity in the face of political domination by the shogun Ashikaga Yoshinori (1394–1441); see Brock, "The Shogun's 'Painting Match,'" 451.

16 Komatsu, "Ōchō emaki to GoShirakawa-in," 118–19.

17 Although what remained of the Heian original was lost to fire in 1661, several copies were made. Among them, the recension in the Tanaka Collection by Sumiyoshi Jokei and Gukei from 1626 is thought to come closest to the originals and consists of sixteen scrolls that measure 45.3 centimeters in height. For reproductions, see Komatsu Shigemi, ed., *Nenjū gyōji emaki*, vol. 8 of *Nihon*

emaki taisei (Tokyo: Chūō Kōronsha, 1977).

18 The *Miraculous Origins of Mt. Shigi* tale appears as "The Holy Man from Shinano Province," story 65 in *Old Collection of Tales* (*Kohon setsuwashū*); see D. E. Mills, *A Collection of Tales from Uji* (Cambridge: Cambridge University Press, 1970), 286–91. For the Japanese text, see story 101 in Miki Sumito et al., eds., *Uji shūi monogatari, Kohon setsuwashū*, vol. 42 of *Shin Nihon koten bungaku taikei* (Tokyo: Iwanami Shoten, 1990), 196–202, 497–503. The *Major Counselor Ban* tale appears as story 114, "How the Major Counselor Ban Set Fire to the Ōten Gate," in Miki et al., *Uji shūi monogatari*, 242–45; and in Mills, *Collection of Tales from Uji*, 319–21.

19 *A Collection of Tales from Uji* contains, for example, nearly two hundred tales, while the *Old Collection of Tales* includes seventy.

20 The three *Miraculous Origins of Mt. Shigi* scrolls combined measure nearly thirty-six meters in length, while the *Major Counselor Ban* scrolls measure roughly twenty-six meters in total length. Both works are currently mounted as three-scroll sets, but this was not necessarily their original state. *Major Counselor Ban*, for example, is thought to have originally been mounted as a single scroll, based on an entry in Sadafusa's diary in which he mentions seeing the scroll, which was then in the possession of Hachiman Shrine in Wakasa Province; see Kakitsu 1 (1441) 4.26 (*KG*, vol. 2, 617); cited in Brock, "The Shogun's 'Painting Match,'" 474. For more on the *Shigi* scrolls in English, see Yoshiaki Shimizu, "The Shigisan-engi Scrolls, c. 1175," in *Pictorial Narrative in Antiquity and the Middle Ages*, ed. Herbert Kessler and Marianna Shreve Simpson, Studies in the History of Art, vol. 16 (Washington, DC: National Gallery of Art, 1985), 115–29; Karen L. Brock, "The Making and Remaking of *Miraculous Origins of Mt. Shigi*," *Archives of Asian Art* 45 (1992): 42–71.

21 Although currently mounted as four scrolls, *Minister Kibi's Trip to China*, like the *Major Counselor Ban* scrolls, is thought to have originally consisted of one scroll; it too is mentioned in Sadafusa's diary as having been in one scroll and in the possession of the Hachiman Shrine in Wakasa Province; see the previous note. For more on these scrolls in English, see Robert T. Paine, "The Scroll of Kibi's Adventures in China (*Kibi Daijin Nitto Ekotoba*), a Japanese Painting of the Late Twelfth Century Attributed to Mitsunaga," *Bulletin of the Museum of Fine Arts* 31 (1933): 359–75; Jan Fontein, "Kibi's Adventures in China: Facts, Fiction, and Their Meaning," *Bulletin of the Museum of Fine Arts* 66 (1968): 49–68; Edward J. Sullivan, "The *Kibi* and *Ban Dainagon* Scrolls: Two Masterpieces of *Emakimono* by Mitsunaga," *Marsyas* 17 (1975): 67–78.

22 For more on *Stories Selected to Illustrate Ten Maxims* and an English summary of the illustrated tale, see John Van Ward Geddes, "A Partial Translation and Study of the 'Jikkinshō'" (PhD diss., Washington University, St. Louis, 1976). For the Japanese text, see Asami Kazuhiko, ed., *Jikkinshō*, vol. 51 of *Shinpen Nihon koten bungaku zenshū* (Tokyo: Shōgakukan, 1997), 288–91.

23 The emperor's procession before arriving at Ono spans thirteen sheets of paper; his duplicate appearances in the courtyard of the former empress appear in paintings 1 and 3 in the scroll; for complete illustrations, see Komatsu Shigemi, *Sumiyoshi monogatari emaki, Ono no yukimi gokō emaki*, vol. 19 of *Nihon emaki taisei* (Tokyo: Chūō Kōronsha, 1978).

24 For reproductions, see Komatsu Shigemi, ed., *Nayotake monogatari emaki, Naomoto mōshibumi ekotoba*, vol. 20 of *Nihon emaki taisei* (Tokyo: Chūō Kōronsha, 1978).

25 *Stories Selected to Illustrate Ten Maxims,* section 10, entitled "One Should Seek to Develop Talent and Artistic Ability"; see Asami, *Jikkinshō*, 419–20.

26 This tale appears in *Tales Heard from Writers Old and New* (*Kokon chomonjū*); see Nishio Kōichi and Kobayashi Yasuharu, eds., *Kokon chomonjū,* vol. 59 of *Shinchō Nihon koten shūsei* (Tokyo: Shinchōsha, 1983), pt. 1, 33–34.

27 For complete illustrations, see Komatsu, *Nayotake monogatari emaki, Naomoto mōshibumi ekotoba*. The emperor is represented four times in this scroll, with his face hidden each time, a phenomenon in medieval painting discussed in Yamamoto Yōko, *Emaki ni okeru kami to tennō no hyōgen* (Tokyo: Chūō Kōron Bijutsu Shuppan, 2006), esp. 149–65.

28 Margaret Helen Childs describes how this Buddhist worldview comes to permeate medieval literature, and short fiction in particular, in her study of "revelatory tales" (*zangemono*), a subcategory of medieval fiction in which characters give firsthand accounts of tales of

sorrow or loss that led to religious awareness and commitment; see Childs, *Rethinking Sorrow: Revelatory Tales of Late Medieval Japan* (Ann Arbor: Center for Japanese Studies, University of Michigan, 1991), 1–28.

29 The very genre of the short story is thought to have been born with Poe's writing on the form, but as Charles May points out, Poe's ideas, particularly the idea of a "totality of interest," were indebted to writings on the German *nouvelle* by the poet and critic August Wilhelm Schlegel (1767–1845), among others; see May, *The Short Story: The Reality of Artifice* (London: Routledge, 2002), 108 (first published in 1995).

30 Quotation from Poe's review of *Zinzendorff, and Other Poems* by L. H. Sigourney, in *Southern Literary Messenger*, January 1836. Reproduced in James A. Harrison, ed., *The Complete Works of Edgar Allen Poe* (New York: AMS Press, 1965), vol. 8, 126. Cited in Charles E. May, *Edgar Allan Poe: A Study of the Short Fiction* (Boston: Twayne Publishers, 1991), 118.

31 See Susan Marie Rochette-Crowley, "Marginal Genre, Major Form: The Twentieth Century Short Story and Theories of the Marginal and Minor" (PhD diss., University of Wisconsin, Madison, 1994), 59, for a discussion of the novel and how the reader's relationship to a good novel is often described in terms of a "master-slave" rhetoric.

32 Poe made this statement in the context of a discussion of plot in a review of *Night and Morning: A Novel* by Edward Bulwer-Lytton, in *Graham's Magazine*, April 1841; reproduced in Harrison, *Complete Works of Edgar Allen Poe*, vol. 10, 117, 122; cited in May, *Edgar Allan Poe*, 120. An elaboration of this idea is found in his discussion of the prose tale in a review of *Twice-Told Tales* by Nathaniel Hawthorne, in *Graham's Magazine*, May 1842; reproduced in Harrison, *Complete Works of Edgar Allen Poe*, vol. 11, 106–9.

33 Susan Lohafer, *Reading for Storyness: Preclosure Theory, Empirical Poetics, and Culture in the Short Story* (Baltimore, MD: Johns Hopkins University Press, 2003), 168.

34 May, *Short Story*, 116, from a discussion of Boris Ejxenbaum's writings on the short story.

35 For a provisional list of small scrolls that date before 1600, see Melissa McCormick, "Tosa Mitsunobu's *Ko-e:* Forms and Functions of Small-Format Handscrolls in the Muromachi Period (1333–1573)" (PhD diss., Princeton University, 2000), 346–52.

36 Miya Tsugio, "Ashikaga Yoshihisa shoji 'Kitsune sōshi emaki' o megutte," *Bijutsu kenkyū* 260 (1968): 27–40. In a colophon to *Tale of the Fox*, the seventeenth-century connoisseurs Sumiyoshi Jokei (1599–1670) and Sumiyoshi Gukei (1631–1705) attributed the scroll to Tosa Mitsunobu, and several later scholars followed suit; see Umezu Jirō, "Suzuriwari sōshi sono hoka," in *Emakimono sōshi* (Kyoto: Hōzōkan, 1972), 289. For full-color reproductions of the fifteenth-century *Tale of the Fox* scroll paintings, see Yoshida Yūji, *Tosa Mitsunobu*, vol. 5 of *Nihon bijutsu kaiga zenshū* (Tokyo: Shūeisha, 1979), pls. 22–23.

37 This scroll is in the collection of the Kyoto National Museum and is discussed in Kanō Hiroyuki, "Tosa Mitsunobu hitsu 'Tsuru sōshi' ni tsuite," *Kyoto Kokuritsu Hakubutsukan Gakusō* 5 (1983): 85–110. A later copy is in the collection of the Freer Gallery of Art, Smithsonian Institution, and is the subject of Miya Tsugio, "Tsuru no sōshi," *Kobijutsu* 8 (1965): 115–17.

38 See Miya Tsugio, "Otogi-zōshi to Tosa Mitsunobu: Nezumi zōshi emaki kō," *Bijutsu kenkyū* 313 (1980): 1–18.

39 A widely used taxonomy of medieval literature is found in Ichiko Teiji, *Chūsei shōsetsu no kenkyū* (Tokyo: Tokyo Daigaku Shuppankai, 1955); for "tales of strange marriage," see 351–62.

40. Miyajima Shin'ichi pointed out the stylistic similarity of *Tales of the Heike* to *Tale of the Crane* while suggesting that the "brush strength" of this painter, or lack thereof, indicates "an artist past his prime" and thus an artist senior to Mitsunobu. See Miyajima Shin'ichi, *Kyūtei gadan shi no kenkyū* (Tokyo: Shibundō, 1996), 165.

41 Aizawa Masahiko, *Tosa Mitsunobu*, vol. 2 of *Shinchō Nihon bijutsu bunko* (Tokyo: Shinchōsha, 1998), unpaginated explanation for pl. 14. Miyajima Shin'ichi suggests that the scroll should be counted among Mitsunobu's extant works; see Miyajima, *Kyūtei gadan shi no kenkyū*, 164.

42 Members of the Ashikaga read scrolls by both artists; *Tale of the Fox* likely corresponds to a "Fox Scroll" seen by Sanjōnishi Sanetaka in 1497 that had previously been owned by the shogun Ashikaga Yoshihisa, as hypothesized in Miya, "Ashikaga Yoshihisa shoji 'Kitsune sōshi,'" 33–34. Ashikaga Yoshizumi owned *Breaking the*

Inkstone, painted by Mitsunobu.

43 Quoted by May, *Short Story*, 117.

44 Mito Nobue makes this point and suggests that the perspective varies in each of the scroll's paintings to correspond to the subtleties of the text. In the second painting, for example, objects are seen from the old nun's point of view, while in the third painting the perspective returns to the young woman in the form of a recollection; see Mito, "Dare ga miteiru kōkei na no ka? Otogi sōshi ni miru katari no shiten," in *Bijutsushika, ōi ni warau—Kōno Motoaki Sensei no tame no Nihon bijutsushi ronshū*, ed. Kōno Motoaki Sensei Taikan Kinen Ronbunshū Henshū Iinkai (Tokyo: Brücke, 2006), 287–307.

45 Miya Tsugio, "Nezumi sōshi emaki," in *Tenjin engi emaki, Hachiman engi, Amewakahiko sōshi, Nezumi no sōshi, Bakemono sōshi, Utatane sōshi,* suppl. vol. 2 of *Shinshū Nihon emakimono zenshū*, ed. Shimada Shūjirō (Tokyo: Kadokawa Shoten, 1981), 36.

46 *Finding Gems and Gaining the Flower* (*Shūgyoku tokka*), trans. J. Thomas Rimer and Yamazaki Masakazu, in *On the Art of the Nō Drama: The Major Treatises of Zeami* (Princeton: Princeton University Press, 1984), 137–40.

47 Umezu, "Suzuriwari emaki sono hoka."

48 The female and adolescent viewership of *ko-e* is commonly mentioned in museum exhibition labels and in books for general audiences, such as Wakasugi Junji, *Bijutsukan e ikō: Emaki o yomitoku* (Tokyo: Shinchōsha, 1998), 157.

49 The rituals and ceremonies that clearly demarcated stages in the life cycle in the premodern period are the focus of much recent scholarly attention; see, e.g., Fukutō Sanae and Kojima Naoko, eds., *Seiiku girei no rekishi to bunka: Kodomo to jendā* (Tokyo: Shinwasha, 2003). Historians of children and family life in premodern Japan seemed to have been less affected by the pervasive shadow of Philippe Ariès, who argued that an understanding of childhood as a separate stage of life requiring special needs did not exist before the eighteenth century; his *Centuries of Childhood: A Social History of Family Life*, trans. Robert Baldick (New York: Random House, 1962), was not translated into Japanese until 1980: *Kodomo no tanjō: Anshamu rejīmu-ki no kodomo to kazoku seikatsu,* trans. Sugiyama Mitsunobu and Sugiyama Emiko (Tokyo: Misuzu Shobō, 1980).

50 Christine Guth describes how the publisher Hasegawa Takejirō (1853–1936), well aware of Western literary genres and the rise of children's literature in Europe and America, launched a series of translations of traditional Japanese stories and marketed them to Western audiences as "small fairy tale books." See Christine M. E. Guth, "Hasegawa's Fairy Tales: Toying with Japan," *Res: Anthropology and Aesthetics* 53/54 (2008): 266–81. This deliberate and anachronistic association between ancient tales and children, mediated through miniature objects, is precisely what seems to have informed early studies of medieval *ko-e*. As Guth points out, however, even these nineteenth-century fairy tale books were collected and read, sometimes solely, by adults.

51 Barbara Ruch, "Origins of the Companion Library: An Anthology of Medieval Japanese Stories," *Journal of Asian Studies* 30, no. 3 (1971): 593–610. The term *otogi-zōshi* was first used in reference to the twenty-three stories in Shibukawa's *Companion Library* and others like them in 1890 by Sekine Masanao in his *Shōsetsushi kō* (Kinkōdō, 1890), 34. There he describes the stories as "having no significance other than being fairy tales for women and children"; quoted and cited in James T. Araki, "*Otogi-zōshi* and *Nara-ehon:* A Field of Study in Flux," *Monumenta Nipponica* 36, no. 1 (Spring 1981): 6.

52 Mary Elizabeth Berry, *Japan in Print: Information and Nation in the Early Modern Period* (Berkeley and Los Angeles: University of California Press, 2006).

53 Ishikawa Tōru examines folios and picture scrolls through the mid–Edo period and their interrelationship in *Nara ehon, emaki no seisei* (Tokyo: Miyai Shoten, 2003). Ishikawa has also pointed out the inappropriateness of the term *Nara ehon*, which falsely suggests a connection to the city of Nara or to the Buddhist artists (*ebusshi*) once located there, but suggests that its usage is too entrenched to discard; see his edited volume *Miryoku no Nara ehon emaki* (Tokyo: Miyai Shoten, 2006), 5–8. Peter Kornicki examines the persistence of manuscript production (which could easily be applied to *emaki*) in the age of print in "Manuscript, Not Print: Scribal Culture in the Edo Period," *Journal of Japanese Studies* 32, no. 1 (2006): 23–52.

54 Such reframing of content seems to stem from the emergence of publishing as what Berry calls a "mid-

market enterprise" that "made available to samurai and commoner constituencies goods previously available to elite communities through the labor of copyists" (*Japan in Print*, 29).

55 Mitsunobu's *ko-e* have been categorized as such in the most important reference work for picture scrolls: Miya Tsugio, Shinbo Tōru, and Yoshida Yūji, eds., *Kadokawa emakimono sōran* (Tokyo: Kadokawa Shoten, 1995). The most extended discussion of small scrolls as *otogi-zōshi emaki* appears in Okudaira, "Otogi zōshi emaki no keifu," in *Otogi zōshi emaki*, 3–30, esp. 22–23.

56 Examples of works dismissed until recently were several produced in the early fifteenth century, such as *Tale of Windfall* (*Fukutomi sōshi*) and *War of the Twelve Animals* (*Jūnirui kassen emaki*), both highly coded works full of political satire and erudite puns. James Ulak reconstructs much of the hidden meaning in the former in "'Fukutomi zōshi': The Genesis and Transmutations of a Medieval Japanese Scatological Tale" (PhD diss., Case Western Reserve University, 1994); and Sarah E. Thompson does the same for the latter in "The War of the Twelve Animals (*Jūnirui kassen emaki*): A Medieval Japanese Illustrated Beast Fable" (PhD diss., Columbia University, 1999).

57 Nicholas Orme, "Children and Literature in Medieval England," *Medium Aevum* 68 (1999): 218–46; cited in Daniel T. Kline, ed., *Medieval Literature for Children* (New York and London: Routledge, 2003), 5.

58 For a list of extant *Genji* small scrolls and more information on the *hakubyō* mode as a "nonprofessional" style, see McCormick, "Genji no ma o nozoku," 103; McCormick, "Monochromatic Genji."

59 The *Monochrome Tale of Genji Scrolls* in the Spencer Collection bear an inscription by the artist, who claims that the scrolls have been copied faithfully from the original. For more on this inscription and its possible author, see McCormick, "Monochromatic Genji"; also see Katagiri Yayoi, "Hakubyō Genji monogatari emaki ni okeru e to kotoba: Supensā-bon o chūshin ni," *Firokaria* 6 (1989): 88–114.

60 Sakakibara, "Rokkan-bon 'Hasedera engi-e' shōkai."

61 The colophon is transcribed in Ogushi, "Kiwamete yoku nita mittsu no Shōtoku Taishi emaki," 223.

62 In the colophon, dated to the nineteenth day of the seventh month of 1324, the work is referred to as a "five *sun*" (i.e., fifteen-centimeter) "main icon" (*honzon*) that together with "altar implements" (*gusoku*) were to be given to a person by the name of "Nyoikiku dono."

63 Considering the possible religious meaning of this scroll text's transcription, the lined paper, which is also used for sutra texts, may carry a religious connotation as well.

64 Eikyō 10 (1438) 11.27 (*KG*, vol. 2, 577).

65 Sadatsune's exact age here is unknown, but as the younger brother by the same mother of Emperor GoHanazono (1419–70), he could not have been more than seventeen years of age in 1438.

66 The term used is *hikyō*, which, according to the sixteenth-century Japanese-Portuguese dictionary *Nippo jisho*, can also mean "vulgar" or "base"; see entry for *fiqeō* in Doi Tadao et al., eds., *Hōyaku Nippo jisho* (Tokyo: Iwanami Shoten, 1980), 236.

67 Brock, "The Shogun's 'Painting Match,'" 463–65.

68 Over the course of two months in the year Bunmei 7 (1475), for example, Sanetaka acted as lecturer for a poetry gathering at the palace on 6.13 (*SK*, vol. 1, pt. 1, 86); viewed a three-scroll set of *Miraculous Origins of Zenkōji* (*Zenkōji engi-e*) on 7.17 and read it aloud at the palace the following day (*SK*, vol. 1, pt. 1, 91); and edited and added diacritical marks to the palace's copy of *Kokinshū* on 7.30 (*SK*, vol. 1, pt. 1, 93). Sanetaka viewed and copied the texts and inscribed the labels for various small picture scrolls on Bunmei 6 (1474) 2.9, 10.29, 11.5, Bunmei 8 (1476) 3.8, and Bunmei 11 (1479) intercalary 9.15 (see *SK*, vol. 1, pt. 1, 11, 30, 31, 151, 341).

69 Bunmei 6 (1474) 10.15 (*SK*, vol. 1, pt. 1, 28).

70 Bunmei 6 (1474) 9.28 (*SK*, vol. 1, pt. 1, 25). The small booklet (*ko-sōshi*) cited here probably refers to a bound volume rather than a scroll.

71 Bunmei 11 (1479) intercalary 9.23 (*SK*, vol. 1, pt. 1, 342). Sanetaka mentions that he submitted the scroll on the nineteenth day of the month and also notes that he had just received the paper (*orikami*) upon which he was to inscribe the poetic topics for Prince Katsuhito's poetry gathering to be held nine days later, on 9.28.

72 Sanetaka provided the poetic topics (*dai*) for the crown prince's gathering; he sent these to the palace on intercalary 9.23, five days before the event. They consisted of "fulling cloth in winter," "late autumn rain," and "love poems" (*SK*, vol. 1, pt. 1, 342). On the twenty-fifth of the month, the prince joined in a linked-verse gathering at the palace, and on the twenty-eighth, his

own poetry gathering was followed by the composition of twenty verses and a linked-verse session sponsored by the emperor that the prince attended. In the entries describing these events Sanetaka names the high-ranking courtiers who participated, demonstrating that these were official gatherings at which the young prince was making a formal appearance.

73 Yoshihisa borrowed the eleven small scrolls from Hosokawa Shigeyuki (1434–1511), provincial governor of Sanuki, and returned them all a few days later except for one about a "golden goose" (*Kari kin e*), which he held onto for further perusal. See the entry for Bunmei 13 (1481) 11.2 and 11.7 in the diary of Ninagawa Chikamoto (1433–88), *Ninagawa Chikamoto nikki*, reproduced in vol. 8 of *Dai Nihon shiryō* (Tokyo: Tōkyō Daigaku, 1927), pt. 13; cited by Takagishi Akira, *Muromachi ōken to kaiga: Shoki Tosa-ha kenkyū* (Kyoto: Kyoto Daigaku Gakujutsu Shuppankai, 2004), 326.

74 Miya, "Ashikaga Yoshihisa shoji 'Kitsune sōshi,'" 33–34. Miya reasons that Yoshihisa must have been relatively young when he owned the *Fox* scroll since he died at the age of twenty-five.

75 *Zoku gunsho ruijū* (Tokyo: Zoku Gunsho Ruijū Kanseikai, 1933), vol. 32, pt. 1, 263, discussed in Tabata Yasuko, "Chūsei no 'ie' to kyōiku," in *Nihon chūsei josei shiron* (Tokyo: Tōshobō, 1994), see esp. 198–99.

76 See the entries for Bunmei 8 (1476) 2.13 (*SK*, vol. 1, pt. 1, 146), where Sanetaka records reading from *A Collection of Tales from Uji* (*Uji shūi monogatari*) for the emperor.

77 Takahashi Nobuyuki, "Sanjōnishi Sanetaka: Chūō to chihō to no bunka kōryū," *Kokubungaku kaishaku to kanshō* 57, no. 3 (March 1992): 82.

78 For an excellent overview of medieval education, see Haruo Shirane, "Curriculum and Competing Canons," in *Inventing the Classics: Modernity, National Identity, and Japanese Literature*, ed. Haruo Shirane and Tomi Suzuki (Stanford: Stanford University Press, 2000), 220–49.

79 One example is the Tang Dynasty primer for children *Meng qiu* (746), which concisely names nearly six hundred historical or legendary personages from China's past, along with the deed or characteristic for which they are famous, expressed in four-character lines. Known as *Mōgyū* in Japanese, the text had made its way to Japan by the ninth century, where it was used not only as a textbook for aristocratic youth but as a sourcebook for Heian writers such as Sei Shōnagon in her *Pillow Book*. See Burton Watson's introduction to his translation, *Meng Ch'iu: Famous Episodes from Chinese History and Legend* (New York: Kodansha International, 1979), 10, 14n2.

80 *Azuma kagami*, Genkyū 2 (1204) 11.26, in vol. 32 of *Shintei zōho Kokushi taikei*, ed. Kuroita Katsumi (Tokyo: Yoshikawa Kōbunkan, 1932), 622. The twenty-scroll set was presented in an exceptional lacquered box with a *maki-e* design, much admired by the shogun. These picture scrolls illustrated the oldest written battle tale in Japan, *The Chronicle of Masakado* (*Shōmonki*), which described the battles fought against Taira Masakado, a warrior who, legend has it, attempted to conquer the Kantō region in the 930s.

81 *Azuma kagami*, Kangen 3 (1245) 10.11, in vol. 33 of *Shintei zōho Kokushi taikei*, ed. Kuroita Katsumi (Tokyo: Yoshikawa Kōbunkan, 1933), 354. The shogun Minamoto no Sanetomo was assassinated in 1219, leaving the shogunate without any Minamoto heirs to assume the position of shogun. This initiated a period in which members of the powerful Hōjō family, who served the shogunate as regents, came to dominate the military government, in part by installing young, malleable boys in the position of shogun. Yoritsugu and his father, Yoritsune, before him were two such puppet shoguns, culled from the Fujiwara in Kyoto.

82 Military tales were not the only type of picture scroll viewed by the shoguns. In 1232, for example, the fifteen-year-old shogun Fujiwara no Yoritsune (1218–56) viewed scrolls depicting an imperial procession during the reign of Emperor GoToba while the texts were read aloud. See *Azuma kagami*, Jōei 1 (1232) 1.4, in *Shintei zōho Kokushi taikei*, vol. 33, 113. The *bakufu* had defeated GoToba ten years earlier in the Jōkyū Disturbance of 1221, in which the former emperor attempted to overthrow the warrior government in the east. It is interesting to consider whether these scrolls, deliberately ordered from Kyoto, might have been shown to the young shogun as a kind of cautionary tale regarding imperial privilege and warrior authority.

83 Eishō 3 (1506), 11.11–12 (*SK*, vol. 4, pt. 2, 649). The handscrolls viewed by Sanetaka are thought to correspond to a set of three now in the Tokyo National Museum; see Komatsu Shigemi, ed., *Gosannen Kassen Ekotoba*, vol. 15 of *Nihon emaki taisei* (Tokyo:

Chūō Kōronsha, 1977).

84 Brock, "The Shogun's 'Painting Match.'"

85 Yoshihisa requested to see the *Myōe* scrolls in midproduction and was told to wait until their completion; see the entry for Bunmei 11 (1479) 4.12 from Hirohashi Kaneaki's diary, *Kaneaki-kyō ki,* in vol. 8 of *Dai Nihon shiryō* (Tokyo: Tōkyō Daigaku, 1926), pt. 11, 392; this entry, the *Myōe* scroll project, and the scroll exchange between the emperor and Yoshihisa are discussed in Takagishi, *Muromachi ōken to kaiga*, 322–26.

86 See above n. 73. The diarist who recorded this exchange, Ninagawa Chikamoto, clearly differentiated the scroll types through his use of the terms "large pictures" (*ō-e*) and "half-sized pictures" (*hangiri-e*), the latter being a less common fifteenth-century term for small scrolls that was apparently more attuned to paper height than the term *ko-e* was.

87 *Clouds of Mt. Kōya* (*Takano gumo-e*) and the "tale of rebirth" small scroll will be discussed in detail in chapters 2 and 3.

88 Kawakami Mitsugu, *Nihon chūsei jūtaku no kenkyū* (Tokyo: Bokusui Shobō, 1967), 173.

89 Ibid., 184–86. The new Tsuchimikado palace (completed in 1456) was abandoned for twelve years after the onset of the Ōnin War in 1467, when GoTsuchimikado and the crown prince took refuge in a number of temporary residences. The Small Palace remained in need of repair well after the imperial complex was reoccupied and was not thoroughly renovated until 1493 (ibid., 177).

90 Ibid., 181.

91 Bunki 2 (1502) 6.2 (*SK*, vol. 4, pt. 1, 22–23). Sanetaka first hears of the structure for sale on the second of the month, discusses it with Gensei (the go-between for the transaction) on the fourth, and purchases it and has it delivered on the sixth.

92 Bunki 2 (1502) 8.4 (*SK*, vol. 4, pt. 1, 47).

93 Sanetaka did in fact add a teahouse to his compound, one of many renovations that he began in the tenth month of 1524 (Daiei 4); see Haga Kōshirō, *Sanjōnishi Sanetaka* (Tokyo: Yoshikawa Kōbunkan, 1960), 194–96, for this and more on Sanetaka's interest in tea and his acquisition of tea bowls.

94 The reference is found in the "Decoration Section" (*Kazari shidai*) of the text. For an annotated transcription of the standard Tohoku University Library version, see Murai Yasuhiko, ed., *Kundaikan sōchōki, Okazari no sho,* vol. 1 of *Chanoyu no koten* (Tokyo: Sekai Bunkasha 1983), 98–101.

95 See the entries for Eishō 9 (1512) 3.13 and 5.21, the letter on the reverse of the entry for 5.21, and the entry for Eishō 17 (1520) intercalary 6.11 (*SK,* vol. 5, pt. 2, 623, 654, 727–28; and vol. 13, 386).

96 Sanetaka first receives the painting along with a decorated tray, an object that would have been placed in a decorative alcove with the painting. Moreover, several years later, in 1520, he exchanges the scroll for a polychrome Shaka painting to use for a Buddhist ritual, suggesting that the ink-line drawing was for semiprivate, nonritual use within a *zashiki* setting.

97 Itakura Masa'aki, "Chōu dai 'Geisan zō' (Taipei Kokyū Hakubutsuin) o meguru shomondai," *Bijutsushi ronsō* 17 (2001): 159–85; I thank Yukio Lippit for bringing this article to my attention.

98 Yamane Yūzō, "Ikebana to zashiki kazari," in vol. 2 of *Ikebana bijutsu zenshū* (Tokyo: Shūeisha, 1982), reprinted in Yamane Yūzō, ed., *Kadōshi kenkyū* (Tokyo: Chūō Kōronsha, 1996), 105–21.

99 Katagiri Yayoi, "Tosa-ha to ryōshi sōshoku—Daiōji-zō 'Genji monogatari nukigaki dankan' o megutte," *Museum* 465 (1989): 4–14. Mitsunobu's studio also executed underdrawing designs for tea ceremony kettles, such as one in the Fukuoka Art Museum; see Nakayama Kōichirō, "Ashiyagama shita-e zukan to Tosa Mitsunobu," *Museum* 531 (1995): 23–34.

100 Fifteenth-century diaries name Mitsunobu as the artist of handscrolls that no longer survive, such as *Miraculous Origins of Seikōji* (*Seikōji engi-e*, 1487), *Miraculous Origins of Kajūji* (*Kajūji engi-e*, 1512), and the small scroll *Clouds of Mt. Kōya* (*Takano gumo-e*, 1474–79), discussed extensively in chapter 2. Recently, another Mitsunobu-attributed handscroll, entitled *Tale of Shitamoe* (*Shitamoe monogatari-e*), has come to light; it illustrates a short story but is a standard-size work (31.1 centimeters in height) executed in the *hakubyō,* or ink-line, mode. If in fact it is by Mitsunobu, it would show that the division between large and small scrolls and subject matter was not absolute, with exceptions being made perhaps because of a patron's request or the mode of representation. For photographs of the scroll, see Shibunkaku, ed., *Shibunkaku kosho shiryō mokuroku*, vol. 18 of *Zenbon tokushū* (Kyoto: Shibunkaku, 2006), no. 197, 106–9.

2 THE CULTURAL MILIEU OF SANJŌNISHI SANETAKA AND TOSA MITSUNOBU

1 For an excellent overview of Sanetaka's life and literary activities, see H. Mack Horton, "Sanjōnishi Sanetaka," in *Medieval Japanese Writers*, ed. Steven D. Carter, Dictionary of Literary Biography, vol. 23 (Detroit: Gale Group, 1999), 247–60.

2 *SK*, vol. 2, pt. 2, 445–46.

3 Color reproductions of the scrolls can be found in Komatsu Shigemi, ed., *Zoku Nihon emaki taisei*, vols. 14–15 (Tokyo: Chūō Kōronsha, 1982). For a full English translation of the text, see Royall Tyler, *The Miracles of the Kasuga Deity* (New York: Columbia University Press, 1990).

4 The calligraphers were Takatsukasa Mototada (1247–1313) and his three sons Fuyuhira (1275–1327), Ryōshin (1277–1329), and Fuyumoto (1285–1309).

5 Although the scrolls were long thought to have been given to the shrine at the time that Kinhira wrote the preface in 1309, Suegara Yutaka has shown that they were dedicated after Kinhira's death in 1315 by his brother, the Kōfukuji monk Kakuen, who acted as editor of the scroll text; see Suegara, "'Kasuga Gongen genki-e' no hōnō o megutte," *Nihon rekishi* 695 (2006): 62–70.

6 After being dedicated to the shrine, the scrolls were lent to Kyoto only three times before the Edo period, once for a "picture match" (*e-awase*) sponsored by Ashikaga Yoshimitsu in the early fifteenth century, once for the 1490 viewing by Emperor GoTsuchimikado cited here, and once again in 1529 when they were requested by Emperor GoNara (Kyōroku 2.2.29); see Tyler, *Miracles of the Kasuga Diety*, 18; following Nagashima Fukutarō, *Nara bunka no denryū* (Tokyo: Meguro Shoten, 1951), 244–50.

7 In the entry for Entoku 2 (1490) 7.21, Sanetaka mentions receiving word from the emperor the day before (*SK*, vol. 2, pt. 2, 445).

8 Sanetaka's wife was one of Norihide's four daughters. Her sister Fusako was a high-ranking female attendant to Emperor GoTsuchimikado and may have facilitated the lending of the *Kasuga* scrolls to her father. Fusako was appointed to the position of *shin dainagon no suke* in 1485 and would have had substantial influence with the emperor by 1490; see entry for Bunmei 17.5.13 (*SK*, vol. 1, pt. 2, 593).

9 Entoku 2 (1490) 7.26 (*SK*, vol. 2, pt. 2, 447).

10 Miyakawa Yōko, *Sanjōnishi Sanetaka no kotengaku* (Tokyo: Kazama Shobō, 1995), 58. The entry in Sanetaka's diary concerning the birth of his fourth child and second daughter, known as Chacha, is at Entoku 3 (1491) 3.24 (*SK*, vol. 2, pt. 2, 573).

11 The platform, still in the shrine's possession, measures 42.3 x 197.8 centimeters and consists of six panels connected by hinges, with a paper surface and an embroidered mounting on the reverse. Images of the shrine grounds, from the shrine gate to Kasuga Mountain, executed in gold and silver paint decorate the platform's surface, while a wisteria (*fuji*) pattern (the symbol of the Fujiwara house) appears on the reverse. The dais thus announces in its very design the intimate relationship between the Fujiwara family and the Kasuga Shrine.

12 Brock, "The Shogun's 'Painting Match.'"

13 During the Ōnin War, GoTsuchimikado used the Muromachi palace of Ashikaga Yoshimasa as his temporary residence, but even this complex went up in flames in 1476, destroying virtually all of the imperial texts and musical instruments, as well as the belongings of Yoshimasa and his female attendants kept there. See the entry for Bunmei 8 (1476) 11.13, in the diary *Nagaoki Sukune ki*, reproduced in vol. 8 of *Dai Nihon shiryō*, ed. Tōkyō Daigaku (Tokyo: Tōkyō Daigaku, 1901), pt. 9, 110–11. The emperor was finally able to move back to his Tsuchimikado palace in the twelfth month of 1480; see Kaneko Kinjirō, "Sōgi and the Imperial House," trans. H. Mack Horton, in *Literary Patronage in Late Medieval Japan*, ed. Steven D. Carter (Ann Arbor: Center for Japanese Studies, University of Michigan, 1993), 68.

14 Miyakawa, *Sanjōnishi Sanetaka to kotengaku*, 1125.

15 Mitsunobu and Sanetaka's version of *Legends of Kitano Tenjin* was completed in 1503 and is currently in the possession of the Kitano Tenmangū in Kyoto. Photographs of only a few scenes from the three scrolls have been published. For a concise description of these and other Kitano Tenjin scrolls, see the entries by Yoshida Yūji in Miya, Shinbo, and Yoshida, *Kadokawa emakimono sōran*, 69–72, 97–99.

16 In a colophon at the end of the first scroll in the three-scroll set, Sanetaka writes that the work replaced the "old version" that had been lost. Meanwhile, a

colophon on the scroll from the Jōkyū version (subsequently recovered) testifies that it was once missing. See Yoshida in ibid., 97–99.

17 Sanetaka responded to the request for his "humble brush" by saying that his "hesitations were without limit, but that he would try his best," a more formal acceptance than usual. See the entry for Bunki 1 (1501) 8.26 (*SK,* vol. 3, pt. 2, 733). The references to his bathing (*gyōzui*) before each inscription appear in the entries for Bunki 3 (1503) 2.14, 2.17, 2.18, and 3.24 (*SK,* vol. 4, pt. 1, 97, 99, 112).

18 Many of these projects are well documented in Sanetaka's diary and will be touched upon in later chapters of this book, but a clear example of Sanetaka's coordinator role can be found in the entries on the production of the 1509–10 *Genji Album,* now in the collection of the Harvard Art Museum; see Melissa McCormick, "Genji Goes West: The 1510 *Genji Album* and the Visualization of Court and Capital," *Art Bulletin* 85, no. 1 (March 2003): 54–85. Sanetaka was by no means unique in acting in this capacity; the use of a coordinator, or coordinators, was a predominant mode of artistic production in medieval Japan; for more on this topic in the context of *Genji* painting, see Iwama Kaoru, "Genji-e seisaku ni miru kōdinētā to eshi," *Kyōto Shiritsu Geijutsu Daigaku bijutsu gakubu kenkyū kiyō* 34 (1989): 53–71. One of the first scholars to conceptualize this role in painting production, particularly for handscrolls, was Karen Brock; see "*Tales of Gishō and Gangyō:* Editor, Artist and Audience in Japanese Picture Scrolls" (PhD diss., Princeton University, 1984).

19 Bunki 1 (1501) 9.18 (*SK,* vol. 3, pt. 2, 740). For more details on the project and all of the relevant diary entries, see Quitman E. Phillips, *The Practices of Painting in Japan, 1475–1500* (Stanford: Stanford University Press, 2000), 113–17.

20 The preparatory drawings mentioned in Sanetaka's diary entry were most likely Takakane's original sketches for the *Kasuga* scrolls previously in the possession of an imperial princess who was known as "Narutaki dono" (she had entered the Narutaki nunnery) and who was the niece of Prince Fushimi Sadafusa; see Yoshida, *Tosa Mitsunobu,* 109. Sadafusa received the scrolls from his niece, and the next day the women in his household viewed them as the texts were read aloud; see the entries in Sadafusa's diary for Eikyō 10 (1438) 2.27, 28 (*KG,* vol. 2, 521–22). Karen Brock outlines how these sketches may have been handed down within the Fushimi branch of the imperial family in "The Shogun's 'Painting Match,'" 465–67. It is not clear when Sanetaka viewed the preparatory drawings, and no explicit mention is made of him viewing them with Mitsunobu in the diary, although it is conceivable that he may have shown them to the painter.

21 Shinbo Tōru states that the word *engi* does not appear in handscroll titles before the fifteenth century; see Shinbo, *Kitano seibyō-e no kenkyū* (Tokyo: Chūō Kōron Bijutsu Shuppan, 1994), 3–9. The titles of examples of the genre such as *Kegon engi emaki* tend to be later appellations.

22 Instances of Mitsunobu presenting or sending his "New Year's fan paintings" are recorded in *Oyudono no ue no nikki,* the diary of the female attendants to the emperor; see the entries for Meiō 3 (1494) 1.11 and Meiō 4 (1495) 1.6, in *Oyudono no ue no nikki,* 10 vols., *Gunsho ruijū hoi,* ed. Hanawa Hokiichi and Ōta Toshiro (Tokyo: Zoku Gunsho Ruijū Kanseikai, 1932–34), vol. 2, 355, 410. The fan presentations to the *bakufu* took place every year; see, for example, the first month of Eishō 13 (1516), in *Denchū mōshitsugu ki,* in *Gunsho ruijū,* ed. Hanawa Hokiichi (Tokyo: Zoku Gunsho Ruijū Kanseikai, 1959–60), vol. 407, *Buke-bu,* vol. 8, 260. The artist Awataguchi Minbu, a member of another Kyoto atelier, presented fans to the shogunate as well.

23 On these strategies, see Yukio Lippit, "The Birth of Japanese Painting History: Kano Artists, Authors, and Authenticators of the Seventeenth Century" (PhD diss., Princeton University, 2003).

24 Melinda Takeuchi takes up this subject in "Tosa Mitsunobu and the Afterlife of a Name," in *The Artist as Professional in Japan,* ed. Melinda Takeuchi (Stanford: Stanford University Press, 2004), 78–102.

25 The misattribution of the extant *Miraculous Origins of Seikōji* (*Seikōji engi-e*) in the Tokyo National Museum to Sanetaka and Mitsunobu (thought to be the scrolls originally executed in 1487) prevented scholars from clearly articulating the artist's style. Sakakibara Satoru proved definitively, however, that the calligraphy of the extant *Seikōji* scrolls is not by Sanetaka and that the paintings therefore should not be de facto attributed to Mitsunobu; see Sakakibara, "'Seikōji engi e' shiken," *Museum* 423 (1986): 4–26.

26 Tani Shin'ichi first analyzed Edo period texts on the Tosa School lineage in "Fujiwara Yukimitsu kō," in *Muromachi jidai bijutsu shiron* (Tokyo: Tōkyōdō, 1942), first published in *Bijutsu kenkyū* 87 (1939), and posited his own version of the lineage in *Nihon bijutsushi gaisetsu* (Tokyo: Tōkyōdō, 1948). The next three authors to tackle the subject offered slight variations on the relationships between early Tosa painters but are in general agreement that Mitsunobu descended from Yukimitsu; see Yoshida Yūji, *Tosa Mitsunobu*; Miyajima Shinichi, *Kyūtei gadan shi no kenkyū*. Most recently Takagishi Akira has proposed a new conceptualization of the lineage, envisioning a broad-based Tosa School that encompassed within it the Rokkaku Studio, the Kasuga Studio, and a line of painters who worked for the shogunate, or "*bakufu* painters" (*bakufu goyō*), but in which Fujiwara no Yukimitsu is still posited as the founder; see Takagishi, *Muromachi ōken to kaiga*.

27 Entry for Eishō 14 (1517) 11.27, in Nakamikado Nobutane, *Nobutane-kyō ki* (hereafter cited as *NK*), in vol. 45 of *Zōho shiryō taisei*, ed. Zōho Shiryō Taisei Keigyōkai (Kyoto: Rinsen Shoten, 1965), 317.

28 Nobutane states that the painting depicts figures present at the "Gathering at the Inner Chamber of the Imperial Residence" (*Chūden gyokai*) of Jōji 6 (1367) 3.29, described in chapter 40 of the *Chronicle of Great Pacification* (*Taiheiki*). See *Taiheiki*, ed. Hasegawa Tadashi, vol. 57 of *Shinpen Nihon koten bungaku zenshū* (Tokyo: Shōgakukan, 1998), 434–45.

29 Miyajima Shin'ichi argued that an entry in the diary of Tōin Kinkata (1291–1360), *Entairyaku mokuroku*, from Bunna 1 (1352) 9.16, concerning the newly designated *edokoro azukari* can only have referred to Yukimitsu, who according to records in the *Tosa House Documents* (*Tosa ke monjo*) received the title by at least 1355; see Miyajima, *Kyūtei gadan shi no kenkyū*, 109–10. Yukimitsu's court rank would have made him someone with whom Mitsunobu associated; he rose through a series of ranks that correspond closely to Mitsunobu's own pattern of ascension, going from *Sakon shōgen* to *Ukon shōgen, Gyōbu shōyū,* and eventually achieving the Fourth Rank.

30 Paintings for the Daijōe ceremony included folding screens depicting landscapes of the two provinces designated as the *yuki* and *suki* fields, the sacred rice fields from which the grain for the ceremony was offered. There were also three-dimensional models of mountains to which painters applied color. For more on the ceremony, including a brief explanation of the three-dimensional "symbolic mountain displays," see Robert S. Ellwood, *The Feast of Kingship: Accession Ceremonies in Ancient Japan* (Tokyo: Sophia University, 1973).

31 The name "Kasuga" first appears in the inscriptions on the reverse of *Legends of the Yūzū Nenbutsu Sect* (*Yūzū Nenbutsu engi emaki,* Seiryōji version, 1414), where one of the artists is identified as "Kasuga Fujiwara Yukihide," probably indicating the location of his studio on Kasuga Avenue. Scholars have suggested a sublineage of Tosa artists who inherited a studio near this Kasuga location: the studio of the fourteenth-century artist Fujiwara no Yukimitsu was thought to have been located one street north of Kasuga, on Nakamikado, while Tosa Mitsunobu's studio was located one street south, at the intersection of Oi and Takakura. Thus, the petition from the Kasuga Studio in 1466 is thought to have come from Mitsunobu. See Yoshida Yūji, "Kasuga edokoro no keifu," in *Tosa Mitsunobu,* 109. The document that mentions Yukimitsu's studio location is the *Iwashimizu Hachimangū kiroku*, Jōji 5 (1366) 4.19, where the artist is referred to as "Edokoro Nakamikado Echizen no kami Fujiwara Yukimitsu." Mitsunobu's studio location is mentioned in the *Daijōin jisha zōjiki* from 1477. See Fujiwara Shigeo, "'Daijōin jisha zōjiki' ni kisareta 'tenka edokoro,'" *Tokyo daigaku shiryō hensanjo fuzoku gazō shiryō kaiseki sentā tsūshin*, no. 22 (2003): 2–5.

32 Mitsunobu's petition is mentioned in the entry for Bunshō 1 (1466) 6.21 in Kanroji Chikanaga, *Chikanaga-kyō ki hoi* (hereafter cited as *CKH*), vol. 44 of *Zōho shiryō taisei,* ed. Zōho Shiryō Taisei Keigyōkai (Kyoto: Rinsen Shoten, 1965), 25. Kanroji Chikanaga (1424–1500) was appointed official messenger for GoTsuchimikado's Daijōe ceremony and recorded numerous details about the event in his diary, including the controversy over the painting commission.

33 The studio took its name from its location at the intersection of Rokkaku and Takakura avenues in the center of the city.

34 Bunshō 1 (1466) 6.21 (*CKH,* 25). Miyajima thinks the Kasuga Studio paintings referred to were by both

Fujiwara Yukihide and the next *edokoro azukari*, Tosa Mitsuhiro, as listed in the *Tosa ke den*; see *Kyūtei gadan shi no kenkyū* (1996), 149, 342–45.

35 Bunshō 1 (1466) 6.21 (*CKH*, 25–26). Yoshida Yūji and others have suggested that the painter for the 1383 (Eitoku 3) ceremony was Rokkaku Jakusai (d. 1424); see Yoshida Yūji, *Tosa Mitsunobu*, 107.

36 Bunshō 1 (1466) 6.22 (*CKH*, 26–28).

37 Bunshō 1 (1466) 8.6 (*CKH*, 51).

38 One *hiki* was roughly equivalent to 10 *mon* (coins) in the late fifteenth century, but the actual value of 5,000 *hiki* in 1466 is difficult to determine. To put the amount in context, Mitsunobu received a mere 50 *hiki* for painting thirty artificial flowers for a court ceremony in 1502; see the entry for Bunki 2.9.16 in the diary of Konoe Masaie (1444–1505), *Gohōkōin ki*, vol. 4, in vol. 8 of *Zoku shiryō taisei*, ed. Takeuchi Rizō (Kyoto: Rinsen Shoten, 1967), 136.

39 These additional payments, dating to Bunshō 1 (1466) 11.19 and 12.09 respectively, appear in a document entitled *Bunshō-do daijōe Kippuan*, the original manuscript of which in Chikanaga's hand is in the Kunaichō Shoryōbu (Imperial Household Archives and Mausolea Department). See Tanuma Mutsumi, "Muromachi bakufu zaisei no ichi danmen: Bunshō-do daijōe o chūshin ni," *Nihon rekishi* 353 (1977): 1–26; cited by Takagishi, *Muromachi ōken to kaiga*, 192, 419n34.

40 The document survives in the Tokyo National Museum among the *Tosa House Documents* (*Tosa ke monjo*), transcribed in Kimura Tokuei, ed., *Tosa monjo kaisetsu* (Tokyo: Iwai Kamejirō, 1935), 18–19; and in Yoshida Yūji, *Tosa Mitsunobu*, 101. Mitsunobu is referred to as "Lieutenant of the Bodyguards of the Right" (*Ukon shōgen Mitsunobu*).

41 According to Miyajima, the *edokoro azukari* appointment usually coincided with a new reign and with the Daijōe ceremony, making that commission a critical one for a painter's future. Based upon Tosa Hirochika's largesse toward Tosa Mitsunobu, Miyajima suggests that Hirochika was Mitsunobu's father and speculates that he deliberately took the tonsure between 1465 and 1468 so that his son could be designated *edokoro azukari* at the 1466 imperial accession; see *Kyūtei gadan shi no kenkyū*, 157. All other scholars of the Tosa School (Tani Shin'ichi, Yoshida Yūji, Aizawa Masahiko, and Takagishi Akira) believe that Mitsunobu's father was Tosa Mitsuhiro rather than Hirochika. Takagishi suggests that Hirochika was Mitsunobu's uncle and became his protector after Tosa Mitsuhiro's death; see Takagishi, *Muromachi ōken to kaiga*, 291–93.

42 The document from Bunmei 1 (1469) 11.28 is signed by the shogunal administrator Hosokawa Katsumoto, governor of Tanba Province, and is addressed to the *bakufu* administrator Naitō Motosada, deputy governor of Tanba Province; see Kimura Tokuei, *Tosa monjo kaisetsu*, 20–21. For a photograph of the document, see Yoshida, *Tosa Mitsunobu*, 100, fig. 4. Another document relating to the initial award of this estate dates to Bunmei 2 (1470) 1.11 and is addressed to a clan head in the province. The three documents cited thus far illustrate the chain of command in conferring Mitsunobu's title and land award, from emperor to shogun to *kanrei* (or *shugo* of the province in question) to *shugo-dai* and finally to local clan head. The confirmation process probably took less than five months.

43 A number of letters in the *Tosa House Documents* affirm Mitsunobu's rights to proceeds from the estate in Tanba and demand that the proceeds be turned over to him; see the documents dating to Bunmei 16 (1484) 12.29, 12.30, and Bunmei 17 (1485) 2.11, intercalary 3.1, and 4.4, transcribed in Kimura Tokuei, *Tosa monjo kaisetsu*, 22–29.

44 Bunmei 17 (1485) 4.4. Four separate documents, all signed by both Suwa Sadamichi and Kiyohara Hidekazu and addressed to four provincial families of Taki-gun (the Hatake, Nonogaki, Yamanouchi, and Nakazawa), describe a charge leveled by "Tosa taifu shōgen Mitsunobu" that the village heads and farmers have absconded with the yearly revenue due for land rent (*nengu*). The documents declare the *bakufu*'s order that the farmers be brought back to their lands and instruct the addressees to assist Mitsunobu's representative in the use of force against those who resist return; see Kimura Tokuei, *Tosa monjo kaisetsu*, 26–29. By the end of the month, Mitsunobu received a document jointly signed by the village heads and farmers of the estate that ostensibly marked the end of the conflict between Mitsunobu and the peasants who worked his land. The farmers agreed to give Mitsunobu 16 *koku* of rice from the annual yield, acknowledged their delinquency with back payments, and pledged to pay the amount due

that year promptly and fully; see Kimura Tokuei, *Tosa monjo kaisetsu*, 29–30 (see 31–34 for a related document). Hosomi Sueo calls this document an *ukejō*, a contractual agreement between the proprietor and peasants; Hosomi, *Tanba no shōen* (Tokyo: Meicho Shuppan, 1980), 39.

45 The *bakufu* informed the local residents and clan heads that the rights should be returned to Mitsunobu and the forged documents destroyed; see the letter dated to Eishō 3 (1506) 8.6, as well as letters from the *bakufu* from 10.28 and 4.12 of the same year. The imperial edict confirming Mitsunobu's rights is dated to Eishō 5 (1508) 9.3; see Kimura Tokuei, *Tosa monjo kaisetsu*, 49–53.

46 Except for the Okumosha and Kokubunji estates, all of the other properties from which Mitsunobu derived income appear only once in the documents; one estate's income was designated for a specific project to be produced by the *edokoro*.

47 Ibid., 58.

48 A document dated to Entoku 4 (1492) 5.25 and addressed to both the deputy governor and the local farmers confirms Mitsunobu's rights. A document dated to Bunki 3 (1503) 12.23 concerns the land being usurped. See ibid., 42–44, 49.

49 On Eishō 4 (1507) 11.18, the land was seized by someone called Izumihara; see ibid., 52–53. Kimura points out that Mitsunobu complained of unlawful actions by this same Izumihara in Bunki 3 (1503), which suggests that this was a continuing problem that the *bakufu* was ineffective in correcting.

50 The Buddhist sculptor *busshi* Kakuyū was awarded the income in Eishō 6 (1509); ibid., 55–56. According to Kimura, documents in the *Amenomorike monjo* show that the Kokubunji estate was a hereditary property in Kakuyū's family, first awarded by Ashikaga Yoshimitsu in Meitoku 4 (1393) 6.29 and subsequently confirmed by Yoshinori and Yoshimasa.

51 Eishō 8 (1511) 9.29; ibid., 58.

52 The documents also call attention to the peasant labor that supported the artistic projects in the capital, easily forgotten in art historical studies, while providing some record of resistance to this system.

53 In a letter dated Bumei 16 (1484) 12.30, Suwa Sadamichi states that he and the governor of Bitchū visited Hosokawa Masamoto, entreating him on Mitsunobu's behalf for the return of the Okumosha estate and finally receiving his consent. They inform Mitsunobu that he would soon receive an official directive; see ibid., 24.

54 Thirty verses by Sanetaka were included in the *New Tsukuba Collection*, a 1495 manuscript of which survives in his hand. For more on the compilation and sponsorship of this anthology, see Kaneko, "Sōgi and the Imperial House."

55 H. Mack Horton, *Song in an Age of Discord: "The Journal of Sōchō" and Poetic Life in Late Medieval Japan* (Stanford: Stanford University Press, 2002), 25. Horton's study vividly portrays the centrality of social networks in cultural interaction in this period.

56 The gathering, which took place on Kanshō 6 (1465) 12.14, is known through the manuscript of poems composed for the occasion, *One Hundred Verses Relating to Boat* (*Nani fune hyakuin*), cited in Iwasaki Yoshie, "Tosa Mitsunobu no bungei katsudō: Yōmei bunko zō 'Sanjusshu' ka to renga," *Gobun* (Osaka Daigaku) 47 (1986): 43–44. The manuscript, housed in the Japanese Literature Department, Hiroshima University, is fully transcribed in Etō Yasusada, *Sōgi no kenkyū* (Tokyo: Kazama Shobō, 1967), 23–26. The *fushimono*, or "topic," found in the titles of *renga* sequences, such as the word "boat" in this title, was an anachronistic element from earlier forms of *renga* and did not set the overall theme of the sequence; for a more thorough explanation, see Steven D. Carter's discussion of a solo sequence by Sōgi from 1492 in *The Road to Komatsubara: A Classical Reading of the Renga Hyakuin* (Cambridge, MA: Harvard University Press, 1987), esp. 117–18.

57 According to Iwasaki, the *renga* gathering took place in 1466 sometime before the fourth month. The manuscript from the event, *One Thousand Votive Verses for Kumano* (*Kumano hōraku senku*), is transcribed in *Zoku gunsho ruijū*, "Renga bu," vol. 17, pt. 1, no. 476, *Kumano senku*, 459–85; see Iwasaki, "Tosa Mitsunobu no bungei katsudō," 43.

58 Iwasaki, "Tosa Mitsunobu no bungei katsudō," 43.

59 In 1488, for example, Hino Tomiko (1440–96) commissioned from Mitsunobu the design for a sake cup and stand, a project that will be elaborated upon below.

60 McCormick, "Genji Goes West," 61.

61 The one thousand verses were divided into ten

sequences of one hundred verses; see *Kumano senku*, in *Zoku gunsho ruijū*, "Renga bu," vol. 17, pt. 1, 459–85, Mitsunobu poem on 471.

62 See the entry for Bunmei 18 (1486) 6.27 in Nakanoin Michihide's diary, *Jūrin'in Naifu ki*, in *Shiryō sanshū*, ed. Okuno Takahiro and Katayama Masaru (Tokyo: Zoku Gunsho Ruijū Kanseikai, 1972), 236. Michihide, whose younger brother was the celebrated poet and *renga* master Botanka Shōhaku (1443–1527), had an extensive knowledge of classical texts and Chinese and Japanese poetry and *The Tale of Genji*. In 1476 Michihide had actually given Mitsunobu instructions on painting the details of the costumes for a certain *Genji* project; see the documents on the reverse of Sanetaka's diary dating to Bunmei 8 (1476) 10.6–8, *Sanetaka-kō ki, Bunmei 8 nen fuyu shihai monjo* (*SK*, vol. 10, 156); cited by Aizawa, *Tosa Mitsunobu*, 87.

63 The term "*tamuke*" (parting gift), found in the second verse that Mitsunobu composed for Hosokawa Katsumoto's 1465 *renga* gathering ("many years have passed since our parting *waka*"; *Yamato kotoba no / tamuke iku toshi*), appears in the conspicuous final poem of the *Konjaku monogatari shū* version of *Breaking the Inkstone* (*Suzuriwari sōshi*), a text that Mitsunobu likely consulted when illustrating that story; for the manuscript transcription of the *renga* poems, see Etō, *Sōgi no kenkyū*, 26.

64 Sōgi hosted six out of eight of the poetry gatherings Mitsunobu attended in 1486, 1488, 1496, and 1500; see Iwasaki, "Tosa Mitsunobu no bungei katsudō"; or the annotated chronology of Mitsunobu in McCormick, "Tosa Mitsunobu's *Ko-e*," 362–72.

65 *SK*, vol. 2, pt. 2, 572. All of the poems composed at this gathering, as well as the names of the participants, are recorded in what may be the original manuscript transcribing the event, currently in the collection of the Yōmei Bunko (manuscript 775–71). Iwasaki Yoshie transcribed all of the poems and reproduced a photograph of the manuscript. The document shows that nineteen men participated in the gathering (Sanetaka identifies only seven high-ranking courtiers in his diary), including warriors, *renga* poets, Buddhist monks, and Mitsunobu, the only painter. Iwasaki also analyzed Mitsunobu's *waka*, showing that it is a patchwork of famous poems; see Iwasaki, "Tosa Mitsunobu no bungei katsudō," 44.

66 Meiō 2 (1492) 4.21, in vol. 4 of *Kitano Shake nikki*, ed. Takeuchi Hideo and Yamada Yūji, in *Shiryō sanshū* (Tokyo: Zoku Gunsho Ruijū Kanseikai, 1973), 73. On the Hitomaro offering ceremony, see Anne E. Commons, "The Canonization of Hitomaro: Paradigm of the Poet as God" (PhD diss., Columbia University, 2003), 144–92.

67 Sōgi was at the center of activity of the Kokinshū Secret Traditions (*kokin denju*) in the fifteenth century and officially transmitted the secrets to a chosen few, including Sanjōnishi Sanetaka and Konoe Masaie; see Miyakawa, *Sanjōnishi Sanetaka to kotengaku*, 670–82. For more on the function of Hitomaro portraits, see Sugimoto Yoshihisa, "Hitomaro zō shinkō to sono kyōju: Gosho denju to no kankei o chūshin ni," *Bijutsushi kenkyū* (Waseda daigaku bijutsushi gakkai) 36 (1998): 39–58.

68 Mitsunobu completed the handscroll on Eishō 9 (1512) 5.4 and attended the poetry gathering on Eishō 10 (1513) 4.8, as recorded in Kanroji Motonaga's diary, *Motonaga-kyō ki*, in *Shiryō sanshū*, ed. Haga Kōshiro (Tokyo: Zoku Gunsho Ruijū Kanseikai, 1973), 217, 233.

69 Tokitsuna's brother, Yamashina Sadanobu, died on Meiō 3 (1494) 7.30, at the age of nineteen, from wounds he suffered two days earlier when defending his home against intruders. Yamashina Tokikuni, the father of Tokitsuna and Sadanobu, prepared for the ceremony to mark his son's one-hundredth-day death anniversary and on 8.27 requested a portrait sculpture of Sadanobu from Susuki Mochikazu. The sculpture arrived from Rinshō'in and the *edokoro* applied the pigment on 11.09, the day before the ceremony. These events are recorded in Tokikuni's diary; see Yamashina, *Tokikuni-kyō ki*, vol. 5, ed. Toyoda Takeshi and Iikura Harutake, in *Shiryō sanshū* (Tokyo: Zoku Gunsho Ruijū Kanseikai, 1977), 118–19, 158.

70 The set of three handscrolls, now in the collection of the Tokyo National Museum, contains calligraphy by six aristocrats; in addition to Motonaga and Nobutane, the calligraphers were Konoe Hisamichi, Sanjō Saneyoshi, Sanjōnishi Sanetaka, and most likely Ichijōin Ryōyo. See Sakakibara Satoru, "Kiyomizudera engi shaken," in *Kiyomizudera engi, Shin'nyodō engi*, vol. 5 of *Zoku zoku Nihon emaki taisei,* ed. Komatsu Shigemi (Tokyo: Chūō Kōronsha, 1994), 127.

71 The references to this painting begin on Eishō 16 (1519)

5.9, when Nobutane asks Mitsunobu to use a painting owned by Sanetaka as his model. At that point Mitsunobu had already attended at least four *renga* sessions at Nobutane's residence, and he even led a gathering at the courtier's house on 6.16, ten days after the Amida painting was consecrated; see *NK,* vol. 3, in *Zōho shiryō taisei*, vol. 22, 254, 263.

72 On Tosa School Buddhist painting, in particular the numerous works by Tosa Yukihiro, see Takagishi, *Muromachi ōken to kaiga*, 195–247.

73 On the early history of the *gyakushu* ritual in the Heian and Kamakura periods, see Motoi Makiko, "Jūōkyō to sono kyōju: Gyakushu, tsuizen butsuji ni okeru shōdō o chūshin ni," *Kokugo kokubun* 67, no. 6 (1998): 22–33, and *Kokugo kokubun* 67, no. 7 (1998): 17–35.

74 Sanetaka wrote inscriptions on these paintings as he received them one by one after Mitsunobu had completed them; see the entries for Chōkyō 3 (1489) 8.18 and Entoku 1 (1489) 9.18 (*SK*, vol. 2, pt. 1, 294, 314). Seven of the extant Jōfukuji *Ten Kings* paintings bear labels that say they were painted for the emperor's "reverse-rites" ceremony that took place on Entoku 1 (1489) 12.23; the remaining three paintings have inscriptions identical to the other seven but bear the date Entoku 2 (1490) 5.14, roughly five months after the ceremony. See Umezu Jirō, "Futakumi no jūōzu: Yukimitsu to Mitsunobu no gaseki," *Bukkyō geijutsu* 36 (1958): 32–35. For an in-depth discussion of Mitsunobu's Ten Kings paintings, their relationship to the Yukimitsu set, a concise history of the genre, and background on the *gyakushu* rites, see Phillips, "Narrating the Salvation of the Elite: The Jōfukuji Paintings of the Ten Kings," *Ars Orientalis* 33 (2003): 121–45.

75 Entry for Chōkyō 3 (1489) 5.6, in *Oyudono no ue no nikki*, cited by Aizawa, *Tosa Mitsunobu*, 16.

76 Entry for Chōkyō 3 (1489) 5.7 (*SK*, vol. 2, pt. 1, 241).

77 It is unclear what kind of mandala was used and whether or not it was painted by Mitsunobu. Entoku 1 (1489) 12.23 (*SK*, vol. 2, pt. 1, 347–48).

78 Entoku 1 (1489) 12.14 (*SK*, vol. 2, pt. 1, 342–43). Sanetaka brushed the poem on the painting almost ten days before the ceremony.

79 The attribution to Mitsunobu is based on a record in the *Hanjūzanmai'in ki*, a short account of the Fushimi imperial-family temple, possibly written by Sanetaka's son, Kin'eda (1487–1563); the writer states that Tosa Mitsunobu painted the portrait and that the emperor himself drew his own face while looking in a mirror, thus creating a *kamigata*, or sketch, on which the artist would base his portrait; see *Gunsho ruijū*, vol. 24, 216–17. Later sources mention the portrait again, when it was worshiped on the anniversaries of GoTsuchimikado's death; see Tani Shin'ichi, *Muromachi jidai bijutsu shiron* (Tokyo: Tōkyōdō, 1942), 464, 470n71.

80 Konoe Masaie was one such mourner who burned incense before Karakumon'in's portrait and before one of the former emperor GoHanazono; see the entry for Chōkyō 2.5.27 in Masaie's diary, *Gohōkōin ki,* vol. 2, in vol. 6 of *Zoku shiryō taisei,* 212. Years later (Meio 5 [1496] 5.22, 5.26, 5.28) Sanetaka suggests Mitsunobu's painting of the emperor's mother as a model for Kanō Masanobu to use for his portrait of Hino Tomiko (1440–96). The funeral of Karakumon'in, whom Sanetaka refers to as *kokumo*, or "mother of the nation," took place on Chōkyō 2 (1488) 5.3 and is recorded in great detail in his diary.

81 For more on this portrait, see Iwahashi Koyata, "Tosa Mitsunobu no ichi isaku: GoEn'yū tennō shin'ei," *Bukkyō bijutsu* 16 (1930): 12–19.

82 In 1499 Sanetaka was asked by the chief priest of Unryū'in to request GoTsuchimikado's calligraphy for Mitsunobu's painting, seven years after its execution; see Meio 8 (1499) 4.20, 4.21, 4.27 (*SK*, vol. 3, pt. 2, 640–41, 644–45). The portrait is also mentioned in a letter to Sanetaka from the chief priest of Unryū'in on the reverse of the diary entries (*shihai monjo*) for Meio 8 (1499) 4.30–5.03 and in a *nyōbō* letter to Sanetaka on the reverse of the entry for 5.3 (*SK,* vol. 11, 492–93). Also see entry for Entoku 4 (1492) 4.28, in *Oyudono no ue no nikki*, vol. 2, 260.

83 See the entry for Entoku 2 (1490) 1.8, in *Oyudono no ue no nikki*, vol. 2, 130.

84 Meio 4 (1495) 6.8, in ibid., 435.

85 See Sawa Ryūken, "Muromachi shoki no Fugen enmei gazō to sono hissha: Takayoshi, Yukitada, Yukihide," *Bukkyō geijutsu* 11 (1951): 39–49.

86 See the entry for Bunki 2 (1502) 3.5 (*NK*, vol. 2, 15), cited by Aizawa, *Tosa Mitsunobu*, 90.

87 Tani Shin'ichi, "Mitsunobu hitsu Momonoi Naoakira zō zukai," *Kokka* 488 (1931): 213–14.

88 Nakanoin Michihide recommends Mitsunobu in a letter to his uncle, the priest Shuban (1416–83) of Ninnaji's Shinkōin subtemple, who was in charge of

having a portrait made of Honkaku Daishi Yakushin and had asked his nephew to suggest an artist; Bunmei 14 (1482) nen shihai monjo, on the reverse of dates 4.1–17, in *Jūrin'in Naifu ki*, 297.

89 Bunki 1 (1501) 10.4 (*SK*, vol. 3, pt. 2, 746).

90 The sketch was introduced by Tani Shin'ichi in "Sanetaka zō no kamigata: Tosa Mitsunobu kō hoi," *Bijutsushi* 17 (1955): 1–6. Also see Tokyo Daigaku Shiryō Hensanjo, ed., *Dai sanjū ikkai shiryō tenrankai reppin mokuroku: "Sanetaka-kō ki" to Sanjōnishi ke* (Tokyo: Tokyo Daigaku Shiryō Hensanjo, 1995).

91 Sanetaka brushed the calligraphy for *Miraculous Origins of Seikōji* by Tosa Mitsunobu, the drawings for which he describes as "magnificent"; see Bunmei 19 (1487) 2.29 (*SK*, vol. 1, pt. 2, 765). The version of *Miraculous Origins of Seikōji* (figs. 69, 70) now in the Tokyo National Museum is thought to be a slightly later copy of the scrolls by Mitsunobu and Sanetaka; see Sakakibara, "Seikōji engi-e shaken"; and n. 25 above.

92 Takagishi, *Muromachi ōken to kaiga*, 366–84.

93 Sanetaka's revenue from *shōen* estates was not always reliable, forcing him to turn to other sources of income, such as hiring out his brush inscribing everything from classic literary texts to *shōgi* gaming pieces or even resorting to such drastic measures as selling his prized copy of *The Tale of Genji*, for which he received 3,000 *hiki* in 1520; see Eishō 17.3.7 and 3.10 (*SK*, vol. 5, pt. 2, 706). For details on Sanetaka's household finances and their decline, see Haga Kōshirō, "Chūsei makki ni okeru Sanjōnishike no keizaiteki kiban to sono hōkai," *Nihon gakushiin kiyō* 13, no. 1 (1955): 23–63.

94 Eishō 1 (1504) 3.23 (*SK*, vol. 4, pt. 1, 249).

95 The popularity of Thirteen Buddhas paintings seems to be linked to the schedule of thirteen rituals that had to be performed after a person's death, which was tied ultimately to Ten Kings belief; see Tamura Ryūshō, "Jūsanbutsu zuzō to jūōzu honjibutsu: Shinkō shiryō no zuzōgaku," *Mikkyō zuzō* 4 (1986): 14–28.

96 Eishō 1 (1504) 5.15 (*SK*, vol. 4, pt. 1, 288).

97 Ibid., 328–29. The memorial services (*tsuizen*) took place on Eishō 1 (1504) 10.14, and in the evening sutras were offered and incense burned at the grave of Sanetaka's mother. Sanetaka's diary entry includes a "record of offerings" (*tsuizen mokuroku*), in which Mitsunobu's *Thirteen Buddhas* painting tops the list.

98 Eishō 3 (1506) 4.30 (*SK*, vol. 4, pt. 2, 542).

99 Eishō 5 (1508) 8.29 (*SK*, vol. 5, pt. 1, 91).

100 For more on their trip, see McCormick, *Genji Goes West*, 62–63.

101 Eishō 5 (1508) 9.5 (*SK*, vol. 5, pt. 1, 93).

102 Nakamikado Nobutane asked Mitsunobu to sketch the Amida (*Amida honzon*) owned by Sanetaka in the twelfth month of Eishō 5 (1508); recorded in a letter from Nobutane to Sanetaka found in the "documents on the reverse," *Eishō go nen fuyu shihai monjo*, 12.22–23 and 12.20–21 (*SK*, vol. 13, 139). In a letter preceding this one Nobutane asked Sanetaka to lend him an Amida painting that he had seen the other day at Sanetaka's residence so that he could show it to Mitsunobu to use as a model; see document on the reverse of 12.17–19 and 12.4–16 (*SK*, vol. 13, 138–39).

103 Eishō 6 (1509) 3.3 (*SK*, vol. 5, pt. 1, 170). Nakamikado Nobutane sent Sanetaka the new Amida painting by Mitsunobu (based on Sanetaka's own painting) for him to see, and Sanetaka found its "exalted countenance truly magnificent" (*makoto ni shushō no son'yō*).

104 While Sanetaka did inscribe labels on the *Ten Kings* paintings for Emperor GoTsuchimikado in 1489, he clearly did not act as an adviser for the project; when Sanetaka viewed the older set at the palace, he records that he was *told* the paintings were by Yukimitsu (using a word that conveys hearsay), thus implying that he was not an authority on the images and was not directing the project.

105 A good example of inscribers, or poets, receiving sketches of a painting in order to work on their texts is offered by the *Eight Views of the Xiao and Xiang* paintings that adorned the walls of Ashikaga Yoshimasa's Izumidono. Designs (*eyō*) were sent to the twelve monks charged with composing poems on *shikishi* to accompany the sliding-door paintings. Yoshimasa, the patron, saw the sketches and the poems before the project was finalized. See the entries for Chōroku 4 (1460) 12.7, 12.11, 12.12, and Kanshō 2 (1461) 1.12, 1.17, in vol. 1 of *Inryōken nichiroku*, ed. Tamamura Takeji and Katsuno Ryūshin (Kyoto: Shiseki Kankōkai, 1953), 280–82, 286.

106 See the entry for Chōkyō 2 (1488) 12.15 (*SK*, vol. 2, pt. 1, 178–79). The full entry also appears in Tani, *Muromachi jidai bijutsu shiron*, 468; and in Tokuda Kazuo, "'Ōgi no sōshi emaki' o megutte (josetsu)," *Kokugo kokubun ronshū* (Gakushūin Joshi Tanki Daigaku

Kokugo Kokubun Gakkai), no. 20 (1991): 91–92n37. Tokuda identified the two poems used in the design as from *Shinkokinshū*.

107 The poem appears in book 18 of *Shinkokinshū*, "Miscellaneous Songs," pt. 3, poem 1690. For the Japanese text, see *Shinkokinshū*, ed. Minemura Fumito, vol. 43 of *Shinpen Nihon koten bungaku zenshū* (Tokyo: Shōgakukan, 1995), 490.

108 The poetic inscription seems even more poignant in light of the twenty-four-year-old's death from illness while still in Omi, just one year later.

109 Sanetaka assisted on another design for a sake cup; he advised the commissioner of the project on the poem and its graphic relation to the pictorial design and brushed the calligraphy. The cup was to be used at a Nō performance at the shogunal residence; see the entry for Eishō 7 (1510) 4.26 (*SK*, vol. 5, pt. 1, 358).

110 Bunmei 6 (1474) 11.12 (*SK*, vol. 1, pt. 1, 32).

111 On Bunmei 7 (1475) 1.10, Sanetaka discussed the text with the emperor, and less than two weeks later, on 1.23, he was summoned to the palace to view the preparatory drawings by Mitsunobu; he notes that he spoke with the emperor late into the night, although the exact content of the discussion is unknown (*SK*, vol. 1, pt. 1, 45–46). Sanetaka met the emperor yet again, toward the work's completion, on Bunmei 11 (1479) 3.11 (*SK*, vol. 1, pt. 1, 306).

112 Like Sanetaka, Nakanoin Michihide (1428–94) was a renowned scholar and advised GoTsuchimikado on various matters of literature and court precedent. Michihide lectured on *The Tale of Genji* at the palace and read the work for the emperor; he also coauthored a Nō play with Sanetaka, and his advice was sought by other courtiers making scroll texts for the emperor. As we have seen, Tosa Mitsunobu had at least one discussion with him concerning *The Tale of Genji*.

113 Bunmei 7 (1475) 1.23 (*SK*, vol. 1, pt. 1, 46).

114 "Bunmei 11 nen haru natsu shihai monjo" (documents on the reverse of dates 3.11–14, 1479) (*SK*, vol. 10, 222–23).

115 Tokuda Kazuo, *Otogi-zōshi kenkyū* (Tokyo: Miyai Shoten, 1988), 83–129.

116 The texts appear on the reverse of the diary entries for Bunmei 7 (1475) 7.28–30 and 8.2 (*SK*, vol. 10, 75–84). Tokuda Kazuo discusses Sanetaka's activities as an author and attempts to decipher the meaning of these fragments in *Otogi-zōshi kenkyū*, 83–129.

117 See the entries for Bunmei 13.8.11–21 in the diary of Nakanoin Michihide, *Jūrin'in Naifu ki*, 72. The play was performed twenty-two years later at the shogunal palace of Ashikaga Yoshizumi in 1503; see the entry for Bunki 3.9.19 (*SK*, vol. 4, pt. 1, 182–83). Charo D'Etcheverry points out Sanetaka's unique decision to focus the plot of his *Sagoromo* play on the hero's imperial accession in "Cannibalizing Memory: Teika, Sanetaka, and Fujioka's Sagoromo," in vol. 1 of *Issues of Canonicity and Canon Formation in Japanese Literary Studies*, ed. Stephen D. Miller (West Lafayette, IN: Association for Japanese Literary Studies, Purdue University, 2000), 259–68.

118 To cite but one example, the palace owned a copy of *Selection of Tales* (*Senjūshō*, mid–thirteenth century), a collection of 121 anecdotes and parables concerning Buddhist revelations, renunciations, and stories on the theme of impermanence. Sanetaka wrote out the nine volumes of the work on Bunmei 11 (1479) 9 (shōgetsu).5 (*SK*, vol. 1, pt. 1, 331), and several years later, on Meiō 6 (1497) 9.27, he collated the palace's copy and made corrections (*SK*, vol. 3, pt. 2, 446). For a translation and introduction to the collection, see Jean Moore, "*Senjūshō:* Buddhist Tales of Renunciation," *Monumenta Nipponica* 41, no. 2 (1986): 127–74.

119 Bunmei 7 (1475) 7.18 (*SK*, vol. 1, pt. 1, 91). Sanetaka's familiarity with painted *engi* goes beyond these readings; he brushed the calligraphy for over eight picture scrolls of painted *engi* during his lifetime.

120 Bunmei 8 (1476) 2.13 (*SK*, vol. 1, pt. 1, 146). In the same year that he wrote *Clouds of Mt. Kōya*, Sanetaka read from *A Collection of Tales from Uji* (*Uji shūi monogatari*) for the emperor on five separate nights.

3 *A WAKEFUL SLEEP*

1 All translations from *A Wakeful Sleep* in this chapter are, with minor modifications, from Virginia Skord, trans., "A Tale of Brief Slumbers," in *Tales of Tears and Laughter* (Honolulu: University of Hawaii Press, 1991). For the complete translation of the tale by Skord, see the appendix.

2 *Kokinshū*, book 13 (Love Poems 3), poem 658, translated by Laurel Rasplica Rodd with Mary Catherine Henkenius in *Kokinshū: A Collection of Poems Ancient and Modern*

(Princeton: Princeton University Press, 1984), 238.

3 *Kokinshū,* book 12 (Love Poems 2), poem 552, translated by Rodd with Henkenius, in ibid., 208.

4 Abe Yoshitomi cites a reference in *A Wakeful Sleep* to a late-fourteenth-century poem from *New Collection of Ancient and Modern Poems Continued* (*Shinshoku kokinshū*, 1439), the last imperial *waka* anthology, to support a Muromachi date for the tale; see Abe, "Utatane sōshi ron: Fu, kōbun narabi ni chūkai, kō," *Kokubungaku kenkyū shiryōkan kiyō* 8 (1982): 88–90, 131; also see his subsequent article "Utatane sōshi: Denpon to sono chūkai hotei," *Gobun* (Nihon Daigaku) 73 (1989): 19.

5 On the ink-line scrolls, see Yonekura Michio, "Bosuton bijutsukan bon 'Utatane sōshi' ni tsuite," in *Shinshū Nihon emakimono zenshū*, suppl. 2, ed. Shimada Shūjirō (Tokyo: Kadokawa Shoten, 1981), 46–55. Yonekura introduced the Mitsunobu scroll in "Zuhan kaisetsu, Kokuritsu Rekishi Minzoku Hakubutsukan zō Utatane sōshi," *Bijutsu kenkyū* 352 (1992): 270–74.

6 Abe Yoshitomi transcribes the Mitsunobu scroll text and notes the differences found in other versions in "Utatane sōshi ron," 112–28; his later article does the same for three additional texts later brought to his attention; see "Utatane sōshi," 14–17.

7 The two ink-line scrolls also differ from other versions in their use of *kana* instead of Chinese characters in two places, their illustration of two extra scenes, and their approach to painting composition. For how these differences relate to authorship and readership, see McCormick, "Genji no ma o nozoku."

8 Abe Yoshitomi suggested that the Mitsunobu scroll text was copied from an earlier original, based upon an apparent scribal error (the name of Izumi Shikibu's daughter appears simply as "Shikibu no naishi" instead of "Koshikibu no naishi"), although he did not rule out the possibility that it is the original text; see Abe, "Utatane sōshi ron," 109.

9 Some scrolls of *A Wakeful Sleep* were left untitled; in his *Compendium of Old Tales* (*Komonogatari ruijishō*), Kurokawa Harumura (1799–1866) listed one handscroll version under the heading "Tale without a Name" (*Na-nashi monogatari*); see the reprint of Harumura's text in *Monogatari sōshi mokuroku zenhen*, ed. Yokoyama Shigeru and Kobashi Yorizō (Tokyo: Ōkayama Shoin, 1937), 106.

10 Mitsuoki became Painting Bureau director in 1654, a position unoccupied by a Tosa painter since the time of Mitsunobu and his son Mitsumochi (active ca. 1496–1559). Like his seventeenth-century Kanō School counterparts, Mitsuoki was an active connoisseur within the Edo period culture of authentication and attributed a number of works to his ancestor Mitsunobu in an effort to consolidate the Tosa School; for more on this phenomenon, see Takeuchi, "Tosa Mitsunobu and the Afterlife of a Name."

11 A copy of the story by Imadegawa Harusue (1539–1617), a court mediator for Toyotomi Hideyoshi, was entitled *Yumeji monogatari;* it no longer survives but was referenced in yet a later copy of the tale; see Matsubara Kazuyoshi, "Tawa sōsho 'Yumeji monogatari' honkoku to kaisetsu," *Kokubungaku* (Hiroshima University) 96 (1982): 44–53.

12 The female protagonist has heard that "a soul could wander far to visit the dreams of the beloved," alluding to a *Shinkokinshū* poem by Princess Shikishi about this kind of nocturnal travel; see Tajima Kazuo, annotator, *Utatane no sōshi*, in pt. 1 of *Muromachi monogatarishū*, vol. 54 of *Shin Nihon koten bungaku taikei*, ed. Ichiko Teiji et al. (Tokyo: Iwanami Shoten, 1989), 276; Skord, *Tales of Tears and Laughter,* 69.

13 Entry for Bunmei 6 (1474) 11.05 (*SK*, vol. 1, pt. 1, 31).

14 Tokuda, *Otogi-zōshi kenkyū*, 88. Abe Yoshitomi had previously discounted the connection, however, stating that the title "*Yumegatari*" would better suit a tale centered on the relating of dreams ("Utatane sōshi ron," 90). Abe's conclusion, however, seems to neglect the importance of the scene in *A Wakeful Sleep* in which the protagonist recognizes her lover when he tells his dreams to his friend at Ishiyamadera.

15 The *Yumegatari* reference appears in Michele Marra's English translation, "*Mumyōzōshi:* Introduction and Translation," *Monumeta Nipponica* 39, no. 4 (Winter 1984): 418.

16 Horton, "Sanjōnishi Sanetaka," 255.

17 Ibid., 255–56.

18 As Ōtsuki Osamu points out, post-*Genji* courtly narratives often begin with allusions to earlier *waka*, Chinese poems, *monogatari*, or diaries; see Ōtsuki, *Chūsei ōchō monogatari no kenkyū* (Tokyo: Sekai Shisōsha, 1993), 17.

19 For the origins of the term *giko monogatari*, see *Nihon koten bungaku daijiten* (Tokyo: Iwanami Shoten, 1984), vol. 2, 125. A more thorough and critical etymology is found in Robert Omar Khan, "'Ariake no Wakare': Genre, Gender, and Genealogy in a Late Twelfth-Century Monogatari" (PhD diss., University of British Columbia, 1998), 34–63.

20 Ōtsuki gives some examples of this negative usage in *Chūsei ōchō monogatari no kenkyū*, 15. Viewed as less important than Heian period tales, these medieval courtly narratives have been vastly understudied, with annotated texts only recently published in the series Ichiko Teiji et al., eds., *Chūsei ōchō monogatari zenshū* (Tokyo: Kasama Shoin, 1995–). In English see Charo B. D'Etcheverry, *Love after the "Tale of Genji": Rewriting the World of the Shining Prince* (Cambridge, MA: Harvard University Press, 2007).

21 Ōtsuki, *Chūsei ōchō monogatari no kenkyū*, 17.

22 Ichiko Teiji so characterized the tale while praising it as "an excellent medieval piece, rich with dreamy sentiment and full of elegant turns of phrase"; see Ichiko, *Chūsei shōsetsu no kenkyū*, 109.

23 Donald Keene provides useful synopses of these tales in *Seeds in the Heart: Japanese Literature from Earliest Times to the Late Sixteenth Century* (New York: Columbia University Press, 1999), 789–824.

24 Haruko occupied the position of *kōtō naishi*, a high-ranking secretary to the emperor; see Okuno Takahiro, *Kōshitsu gokeizaishi no kenkyū*, vol. 1 (Tokyo: Unebi Shobō, 1942), 479. Lee Butler discusses the various responsibilities of the *kōtō naishi* in the sixteenth century in *Emperor and Aristocracy in Japan, 1467–1680* (Cambridge, MA: Harvard University Asia Center, distributed by Harvard University Press, 2002), 50–56.

25 Ichiko Teiji, *Chūsei shōsetsu to sono shūhen* (Tokyo: Tokyo Daigaku Shuppankai, 1981), 125–26; Tonomura Nobuko, "Nyōbō bungaku no yukue," in *Jūgo jūroku seiki no bungaku*, vol. 6 of *Iwanami kōza Nihon no bungaku shi*, ed. Kuboto Jun et al. (Tokyo: Iwanami Shoten, 1996), 185.

26 Another woman active in monthly poetry gatherings in the late fifteenth century was Fuyuko, the wife of Sanjō Kin'atsu, minister of the right; see Itō Kei, "Sanjōnishi Sanetaka to waka, sono san," *Kokubungaku kenkyū* 35 (1966): 72; cited by Horton, "Portrait of a Medieval Marriage: The Domestic Life of Sanjōnishi Sanetaka and His Wife," in "In Memory of Marian Ury," special issue, *Japanese Language and Literature* 37, no. 2 (2003): 135.

27 Ichiko, *Chūsei shōsetsu to sono shūhen*, 125–26. The narrative is transcribed in Matsumoto Ryōshin, ed., *Muromachi jidai monogatari taisei*, *hoi* 2, vol. 10 (Tokyo: Kadokawa Shoten, 1988), 560–603.

28 Mashimo Miyako, "'Hanyū no monogatari' ron," in *Nihon bungaku no genfūkei*, ed. Fukuda Akira (Tokyo: Miyai Shoten, 1992), 249.

29 McCormick, "Monochromatic *Genji*."

30 Tokuda Kazuo sees works such as the *Lady Chūgū* as a bridge between *giko monogatari* and *otogi-zōshi* that deal with courtly subject matter; see Tokuda, *Otogi-zōshi jiten* (Tokyo: Tōkyōdō Shuppan, 2002), 341–42.

31 Wakita Haruko, "Sengokuki ni okeru tennō ken'i no fujō," pts. 1 and 2, *Nihonshi kenkyū*, no. 340 (1990): 1–27 and *Nihonshi kenkyū*, no. 341 (1991): 30–58.

32 Abe Yoshitomi, "Utatane sōshi ron," 138. Abe believes that the prominence of the wisteria motif, along with the multiple allusions to Fujiwara poets, indicates that the text was meant to exalt the Fujiwara clan. I will discuss this in greater detail below.

33 The Kamo Priestess (*sai'in*) refers to an imperial princess sent to serve at the Kamo Shrine. The last imperial princess to do so was the third daughter of Emperor GoToba (1180–1239), indicating that the story is probably set sometime before the Kamakura period.

34 Tajima Kazuo points out that this evocative passage, with its "rain droplets on the eaves" (*noki no tamamizu*) and the "loneliness of the long spring rains," recalls a poem by Gyōsei in the *Shinkokinshū* (ca. thirteenth century); see Tajima, *Utatane no sōshi*, 273n9.

35 When Yonekura Michio introduced *A Wakeful Sleep*, he tried to prove that Mitsunobu could have painted the scroll despite the presence of *tsukuri-e*-type paintings and even felt it necessary to rule out the possibility that different artists had executed the exterior and interior scenes; see Yonekura, "Zuhan kaisetsu," 273.

36 Murashige Yasushi, "Den Tosa Mitsunobu hitsu 'Matsu zu byōbu' ni tsuite," *Kokka* 1118 (1988): 30–41.

37 For this episode see Royall Tyler, trans., *The Tale of Genji* (New York: Viking, 2001), chap. 22, 414–19.

38 For a comprehensive account of female pilgrimage

in the Heian period, see Barbara Ambros, "Liminal Journeys: Pilgrimages of Noblewomen in Mid-Heian Japan," *Japanese Journal of Religious Studies* 24, nos. 3–4 (1997): 301–45.

39 Ibid., 337.

40 Sanetaka began brushing the calligraphy for this one scroll on Meiō 6 (1497) 10.11 (*SK*, vol. 3, pt. 2, 452). The first three of the seven scrolls that make up *Miraculous Origins of Ishiyamadera* are original and date to the early fourteenth century, but scrolls 4–7 are later replacements for lost volumes: scroll 5 (late fourteenth century), scroll 4 (1497), scrolls 6–7 (nineteenth century). Although the paintings in scroll 4 were long attributed to Mitsunobu, they clearly show another hand at work. Aizawa Masahiko believes they are by the same artist who executed the small scrolls *Tale of the Fox*, *Tale of the Crane*, and *Tales of the Heike*; see Aizawa, *Tosa Mitsunobu*, 10.

41 The twelfth-century *Miraculous Origins of Mt. Shigi* and *Genji Scrolls* exemplify, respectively, the continuous and monoscenic modes.

42 Sano Midori understands this mode to be one of the most salient characteristics of courtly narrative painting; see Sano, "Ōcho no bijutsu," in *Ōchō emaki to sōshoku kyō*, vol. 8 of *Nihon bijutsu zenshū,* ed. Nakano Masaki, Hirata Yutaka, and Sano Midori (Tokyo: Kōdansha, 1990), 153.

43 Ikeda Shinobu, "Heian jidai monogatari kaiga no hōhō—monogatari o yobikomu kaiga no dentō o kangaeru," in *Ōchō emaki to sōshoku kyō*, 175.

44 Adapted from Skord, *Tales of Tears and Laughter*, 77; for the Japanese text, see Tajima, *Utatane no sōshi,* 288.

45 The *fuji* motif often symbolized the Fujiwara family, as in the famous poem and its interpretation from episode 101 of the *Tales of Ise:*

Saku hana no	Longer than ever before
Shita ni kakururu	Is the wisteria's shadow—
Hito o ōmi	How many are those
Arishi ni masaru	Who shelter beneath
Fuji no kage kamo	Its blossoms!

"'What is the point of your poem?' someone asked. 'I was thinking about the Chancellor's brilliant career and the splendid accomplishments of other members of the Fujiwara family.'" See Helen Craig McCullough, trans., *Tales of Ise* (Stanford: Stanford University Press, 1968), 139; poem cited by Abe Yoshitomi, "Utatane sōshi ron," 138.

46 Abe Yoshitomi, "Utatane sōshi ron," 138.

47 Several stories concerning Kannon in fascicle 16 of *Tales of Times Now Past* contain this phrase; see, for example, story 18 about the Ishiyamadera Kannon in Mabuchi Kazuo, Kunisaki Fumimaro, and Inagaki Taiichi, eds., *Konjaku monogatari shū*, vol. 36 of *Shinpen Nihon koten bungaku zenshū* (Tokyo: Shōgakukan, 2000), 222.

48 For the Japanese text, see Kubota Jun et al., eds., *Ima monogatari, Takafusa shū, Tōzai zuihitsu*, in *Chūsei no bungaku* (Tokyo: Miyai Shoten, 1979), 145–46.

49 Abe Yoshitomi, "Utatane sōshi ron," 130.

50 The text of ink-line scrolls of *A Wakeful Sleep* in particular severs all connections between the cherry tree and the dream lover by omitting the line about Ko Shikibu stitching thread to the tree, enabling instead a reading of the cherry tree motif as a metaphor for female cultural production; see McCormick, "Tosa Mitsunobu's *Ko-e*," 186–201.

51 Kawazoe Fusae, *Sei to bunka no Genji monogatari—kaku onna no tanjō* (Tokyo: Chikuma Shobō, 1998), 70–85.

52 The translation is from Edwin A. Cranston, *Grasses of Remembrance*, vol. 2 of *A Waka Anthology* (Stanford: Stanford University Press, 2006), pt. B, 731.

53 Yonekura Michio believes that the trousers, now faded brown, were originally lavender, since colors of other motifs strictly accord with the textual description; Yonekura, "Zuhan kaisetsu," 271.

54 Mashimo, "'Hanyū no monogatari' ron," 249–51.

55 For the symbolic meaning of the bridge in Japanese art and literature, see, e.g., Amino Yoshihiko et al., eds., *Ama no hashi, chi no hashi*, vol. 2 of *Ima wa mukashi mukashi wa ima* (Tokyo: Fukuinkan Shoten, 1991); Melinda Takeuchi, "The Golden Link: Place, Poetry, and Paradise in a Medieval Japanese Design," in *Worlds Seen and Imagined: Japanese Screens from the Idemitsu Museum of Art,* ed. Kuroda Taizō et al. (New York: Asia Society, 1995), 31–53.

56 Fujiwara Shigeo, "'Kariya' shōkō: Matsu no ha o yane ni fuku koto," in *Emaki ni chūsei o yomu*, ed. Fujiwara Yoshiaki and Gomi Fumihiko (Tokyo: Yoshikawa

Kōbunkan, 1995), 101–45.

57 For more on the use of moral guides and the education of women in the Edo period, see Martha C. Tocco, "Norms and Texts for Women's Education in Tokugawa Japan," in *Women and Confucian Cultures in Premodern China, Korea, and Japan*, ed. Dorothy Ko et al. (Berkeley and Los Angeles: University of California Press, 2003), 193–218. *Kyōkun* for women roughly datable to the Muromachi period include *Sayo no nezame*, *Menoto no sōshi*, and *Mi no katami*. See fascicles 476–78 in vol. 17 of *Gunsho ruijū,* ed. Hanawa Hokiichi (Tokyo: Keizai Zasshisha, 1894).

58 The so-called *Kana kyōkun* is found in *Zoku gunsho ruijū*, vol. 32, pt. 2, 15–18; Itō Kei believes that Sanetaka wrote the instructions for Yasuko on Meiō 4.8.2, a few weeks after her marriage, when he received two reams of paper from his daughter and began "writing the letter himself." The text is also geared toward a new bride. See Itō Kei, "Kana kyōkun, Sōgi tanka nōto 1," *Wakashi kenkyūkai kaihō* 38 (1970): 14–17; Itō Kei, "'Kana kyōkun' kō—Muromachi jidai joryū bungaku ni karamete," *Chūsei bungaku* 16 (1971): 6–11.

59 The long poem attributed to Sōgi is appended to the *Kana kyōkun* attributed to Sanetaka; see Itō Kei, "'Kana kyōkun' kō."

60 See the English translation of this text in Skord, *Tales of Tears and Laughter*, 169–83.

61 On Komachi's characterization as a femme fatale in the medieval period, see Sarah M. Strong, "The Making of a Femme Fatale: Ono no Komachi in the Early Medieval Commentaries," *Monumenta Nipponica* 49, no. 4 (1994): 391–412.

62 On the structure of *kaimami* scenes, see Imai Gen'e, "Kodai shōsetsu sōsakujō no ichi shuhō—kaimami ni tsuite," *Kokugo to kokubungaku* 25, no. 3 (1948): 26–43; Hirota Osamu, "Genji ni okeru yōshiki to shite no kaimami," in *Kodai bungaku no yōshiki to kinō,* ed. Tsuchihashi Yukata (Tokyo: Ōfūsha, 1988).

63 Chino Kaori pointed out ingrained negative connotations of female *kaimami,* citing the example of the libidinous old woman in story 63 in *Tales of Ise*, derogatorily nicknamed Old Gray Hair (Tsukumogami) by Narihira; see Chino, "Mirareru onna to miru otoko: Koi no kōzu toshite no kaimami," in *Fikushon toshite no kaiga: Bijutsushi no me, kenchikushi no me,* by Chino Kaori and Nishi Kazuo (Tokyo: Perikansha, 1991), 96.

64 To compare the phrasing of the Japanese texts, see Tajima, *Utatane no sōshi,* 283; Abe Akio et al., eds., *Genji monogatari,* vols. 20–25 of *Shinpen Nihon koten bungaku zenshū* (Tokyo: Shōgakukan, 1994–98), vol. 6, 186.

65 Skord, *Tales of Tears and Laughter*, 79n23.

66 Edward G. Seidensticker, trans., *The Tale of Genji* (New York: Vintage Books, 1990), 1010.

67 Haruo Shirane, *The Bridge of Dreams: A Poetics of "The Tale of Genji"* (Stanford: Stanford University Press, 1987), 162.

68 Ōmori Junko, "Ukifune, Uta, Jendā: Hyōgen keishiki to shite no 'Tenarai' ni tsuite," in *Monogatari "onna to otoko,"* vol. 3 of *Shin monogatari kenkyū* (Tokyo: Yūseidō, 1995), 147–65.

69 Seidensticker, *Tale of Genji*, 991.

70 See Haruo Shirane, "The Uji Chapters and the Denial of Romance," in *Ukifune: Love in the "Tale of Genji,"* ed. Andrew Pekarik (New York: Columbia University Press, 1982), 113–38.

71 For a concise summary of the historiography of premodern Japanese marriage systems, see Hitomi Tonomura, "Re-envisioning Women in the Post-Kamakura Age," in *The Origins of Japan's Medieval World,* ed. Jeffrey Mass (Stanford: Stanford University Press, 1997), esp. 146–53.

72 Sanetaka's special connections to the emperor through his scholarship and his wife's family (her two sisters each served an emperor; the younger sister became the mother of Emperor GoNara) probably helped to secure the marriage; see Hara Katsurō, *Higashiyama jidai ni okeru ichi shinshin no seikatsu,* 6th ed. (Tokyo: Kōdansha Gakujutsu Bunko, 1994), 81. Concerning the prestige of the position of regent in the Muromachi period, see Steven D. Carter, *Regent Redux: A Life of the Statesman-Scholar Ichijō Kaneyoshi*, Michigan Monograph Series in Japanese Studies, no. 16 (Ann Arbor: Center for Japanese Studies, University of Michigan, 1996).

73 Yasuko's second son, Kyōjin (1498–1526), became the thirtieth *Daijōin monzeki*, superintendent of Kōfukuji in Nara. Thus, in the end, her descendants prospered even beyond what is claimed for the protagonists in *A Wakeful Sleep*, her children achieving the two premier positions within the Fujiwara hierarchy, regent and Kōfukuji superintendent.

74 Meiō 4 (1495) 7.25 (*SK*, vol. 3, pt. 1, 96).

75 *Kana kyōkun*, in *Zoku gunsho ruijū*, vol. 32, pt. 2, 15.

76 Meiō 5 (1496) 1.8 (*SK*, vol. 3, pt. 1, 152). The murder occurred on the seventh of the first month, in the evening. Apparently, discord had developed between Kujō Masamoto and Arikazu, who were cousins, ever since Masamoto refused to reimburse Arikazu for paying his court dues.

77 Sanetaka condemned the crime but expressed dismay over the punishment, which he felt showed a lack of respect for the rank and stature of the Kujō family. For a more detailed account of the crime and punishment, see Kanroji Chikanaga's diary, entries for Meiō 5.23–25 (*CK*, vol. 3, 281–83).

78 Sanetaka records seeing his granddaughter (Kujō *himegimi*) for the first time on Meiō 6 (1497) 2.11 (*SK*, vol. 3, pt. 2, 405).

4 *THE JIZŌ HALL*

1 Miya Tsugio provided an exhaustive survey of the text's various *setsuwa* allusions but concluded that it was best viewed as a "Jizō miracle tale" corresponding to its current title; see Miya, "'Jizōdō sōshi' ni tsuite," *Kokka* 851 (1963): 5–25. Ichiko Teiji interpreted the story as a "wayward-monk tale" in *Chūsei shōsetsu no kenkyū*, 146. Nitta Seiji argued that the diversity of genres incorporated into *The Jizō Hall* is its most distinguishing characteristic but claimed that it is essentially concerned with the "attainment of buddhahood" (*jōbutsu*) and, specifically, the redemption of serpents; see Nitta Seiji, "'Jizōdō sōshi' shiken," *Chūsei, kinsei bungaku kenkyū* 5 (1971): 33.

2 An implicit bias against Muromachi literature and narrative painting has often resulted in the assumption that high-quality works must be copies of earlier texts or paintings. Even Miya Tsugio in "'Jizōdō sōshi' ni tsuite" first assumed that both the text and the paintings were copied from a lost Kamakura period handscroll, but later he changed his position and argued that *The Jizō Hall* painting compositions, because of their similarity to those of the fifteenth-century *Tale of the Fox* scroll, must be original creations by Mitsunobu; see Miya Tsugio, "Ashikaga Yoshihisa shoji 'Kitsune sōshi emaki' o megutte," *Bijutsu kenkyū* 260 (1968): 33.

3 *The Jizō Hall* concludes by claiming that the story is "found among a collection of ancient tales." While this suggests that the work is an old one, predating the production of the handscroll, there are several reasons to doubt the sincerity of this statement, as will be discussed below. Moreover, no such story appears in any extant collection of tales, nor are there precedents for tales as complicated as this one among extant *setsuwa* collections.

4 Yoshida Yūji pointed out a possible connection between the *Ōjōden ko-e* recorded in Sanetaka's diary and the extant *Jizō Hall* in *Tosa Mitsunobu*, 102; more recently, Sakakibara Satoru suggested a direct correspondence between the two scrolls in a footnote but did not pursue the topic; see Sakakibara, "Kiyomizudera engi shiken," 133, 138n28.

5 Previously the scroll was in a private collection in Ishikawa Prefecture, and before that, it was owned by the Maeda family. The scroll appeared in a 1939 catalog of the Maeda family collection, *Sonkeikaku Bunko kokusho bunrui mokuroku*, as mentioned by Ichiko Teiji in *Mikan chūsei shōsetsu*, vol. 3, Koten bunko, no. 53 (Tokyo: Koten Bunko, 1951), 12–13; and Miya, "'Jizōdō sōshi' ni tsuite," 5.

6 Sakakibara Satoru identified Sanetaka as the calligrapher of *The Jizō Hall* through a meticulous stylistic comparison with firmly documented examples of his writing; see Sakakibara, "'Seikōji engi e' shiken," *Museum* 423 (1986): 21, 25n18.

7 Tan'yū's inscription reads "Painted by Tosa Gyōbu-taifu Mitsumochi" (*Tosa Gyōbu-taifu Mitsumochi hitsu*). The inside and outside of the lid of the scroll's box also bear attributions to Mitsumochi and Shōyō'in (Sanetaka's name after taking the tonsure 1516). Attributions to Mitsunobu appear in *Yamato nishiki*, edited by Sumiyoshi Hiroyuki (1755–1811); and the catalog of old paintings and attributions *Kōko gafu* (1910–11), in Kurokawa Mamichi, ed., *Kurokawa Mayori zenshū*, vol. 2 (Tokyo: Kokusho Kankōkai, 1910), 66–67. Miya Tsugio attributed *The Jizō Hall* to Mitsunobu despite Tan'yū's attribution to Mitsumochi; see Miya, Shinbo, and Yoshida, *Kadokawa emakimono sōran*, 421.

8 For a complete translation of the text see the appendix.

9 Yamashina Genkan put forward this idea in *Zuga ichiran* (1846); see his notation included in *Kokō gafu*, in Kurokawa Mamichi, *Kurokawa Mayori zenshū*.

The earliest reference to *The Jizō Hall* title appears in the eighteenth century, in *Yamato nishiki*, edited by Sumiyoshi Hiroyuki (1755–1811), in a listing of picture scrolls by Tosa Mitsunobu; see Miya, "'Jizōdō sōshi' ni tsuite."

10 For a translation of seven tales from *Miracles of the Bodhisattva Jizō* as well as a useful summary of the history of Jizō worship in Japan, see Yoshiko Kurata Dykstra, "Jizō the Most Merciful, Tales from Jizō Bosatsu Reigenki," *Monumenta Nipponica* 33, no. 2 (1978): 179–200.

11 Important studies of illustrated Jizō tales include Manabe Kōsai and Umezu Jirō, eds., *Jizō bosatsu reigenki ekotobashū*, Koten bunko, no. 118 (Tokyo: Koten Bunko, 1957); Manabe Kōsai, ed., *Jizō bosatsu no kenkyū* (Kyoto: Fuzanbō Shoten, 1960); and the articles on illustrated Jizō tales in the three books of Umezu Jirō's collected essays, *Emakimono sōkō* (Tokyo: Chūō Kōron Bijutsu Shuppan, 1968); *Emakimono zanketsu no fu* (Tokyo: Kadokawa Shoten, 1970); and *Emakimono sōshi* (Kyoto: Hōzōkan, 1972).

12 Fushimi Sadafusa records seeing Jizō scrolls in 1437 and again in 1438; on the latter date he viewed a six-scroll set of *Miracles of the Bodhisattva Jizō* (*Jizō genki-e*) in the collection of the Ashikaga shogun; see his diary entry for Eikyō 10 (1438) 6.7 (*KG*, vol. 2, 548). Karen Brock has pointed out that the shogun Yoshinori sent these Jizō scrolls along with a doctor to Sadafusa's son, Emperor GoHanazono, who had suddenly taken ill; Brock, "The Shogun's 'Painting Match,'" 471. In 1474 GoTsuchimikado had the courtier Kanroji Chikanaga read aloud from a five-scroll set of *Miracles of the Bodhisattva Jizō*; see the diary entry for Bunmei 6 (1474) 3.27 (*CK*, vol. 1, 170). Sanetaka viewed a two-scroll set of *Jizō of Mibudera* (*Mibu Jizō engi-e*) in 1490 and a single scroll entitled *The Stone Jizō* (*Ishi Jizō-e*) the following year; see the entries for Entoku 2 (1490) 9.23 (*SK*, vol. 2, pt. 2, 480) and Entoku 3 (1491) 8.11 (*SK*, vol. 2, pt. 2, 618). The extant *Mibu Jizō engi-e* (1486) may correspond to the scroll Sanetaka viewed, as suggested by Wakasugi Junji in Miya, *Kadokawa emakimono sōran*, 182. It was also in the late fifteenth century that many Jizō-related texts were copied and preserved for posterity; the oldest extant copy of *Miracles of the Bodhisattva Jizō* dates from this time, while the only complete copy of *Miracles of the Bodhisattva Jizō Picture Scroll Text* (*Jizō bosatsu reigenki ekotoba*), which served as the basis for several picture scrolls, dates to 1491; see Manabe Kōsai, *Jizō bosatsu no kenkyū*, 65–93.

13 Bunmei 19 (1487) 2.29 (*SK*, vol. 1, pt. 2, 765). The *Miraculous Origins of Seikōji* in the Tokyo National Museum, once thought to be the original handscroll by Mitsunobu and Sanetaka from 1487, is now considered a close copy made soon afterward by a different artist and a different calligrapher. See Sakakibara, "'Seikōji engi e' shiken."

14 Miya Tsugio ("Ashikaga Yoshihisa shoji 'Kitsune sōshi emaki' o megutte," 147) suggested that Jizō's absence was the result of an artistic aversion on Mitsunobu's part rather than, as I am suggesting, related to an understanding, unconscious or not, of the story's identity as something other than a Jizō miracle tale.

15 Dykstra, "Jizō the Most Merciful," 186–87.

16 The details of this scroll's relationship to Mitsunobu were discussed in chapter 1. The narrative found in the picture scroll *Tale of the Fox* is thought to have been based on a story in *Tales of Times Now Past*, in which the family of the man who has been lured away by foxes carves a statue of the bodhisattva (Kannon in this version), which comes to life and rescues the man; see Mabuchi Kazuo, Kunisaki Fumimaro, and Konno Tōru, eds., *Konjaku monogatari shū*, vol. 2, vol. 22 of *Nihon koten bungaku zenshū* (Tokyo: Shōgakukan, 1972),244–45; Marian Ury, *Tales of Times Now Past* (Berkeley and Los Angeles: University of California Press, 1979), 103. My figure 71 is from a seventeenth-century copy of the scroll by Kanō Tanyū, now in the collection of the Department of Japanese Literature at Gakushūin University, Tokyo.

17 Ichiko Teiji considered *The Jizō Hall* first and foremost a wayward-monk tale because of the importance of a miscopied sutra to the plot; see Ichiko, *Chūsei shōsetsu no kenkyū*, 142–46.

18 Virginia Skord translates this tale as "The Errand Woman" in her *Tales of Tears and Laughter*, 205–20, though she suggests the more literal title of "The Useful Nun" as an alternative. Skord's translation is based on the annotated text of an illustrated booklet published in Ichiko Teiji and Noma Kōshin, *Kanshō Nihon koten bungaku*, vol. 26 (Tokyo: Kadokawa Shoten, 1976), 51–93. The oldest version of the text appears in the sixteenth-century small-format scroll in the Suntory Museum of Art, Tokyo; see Okudaira,

Otogi zōshi emaki, 193–97.

19 See Frederick Kavanaugh's translation "An Errant Priest: *Sasayaki Take*," *Monumenta Nipponica* 51, no. 2 (1996): 219–44, based on the annotated Muromachi period text found in Shimazu Hisamoto and Ichiko Teiji, eds., *Zoku otogi-zōshi* (Tokyo: Iwanami Shoten, 1956), 83–111. Kavanaugh notes the tale's antecedents, which can be found in tale compilations as early as *Collection of Sand and Pebbles* (*Shasekishū*, ca. 1280) and *Miscellaneous Collection* (*Zōdanshū*, 1306); see Kavanaugh, "Errant Priest," 223.

20 Skord suggests that the woman in the story resembles a "*suai onna*, a trader of dry goods and clothing who sometimes engaged in prostitution," and that the term *ama* was "used quite loosely to designate a range of single women, from ordained, tonsured nuns to itinerant proselytizers and even prostitutes" (*Tales of Tears and Laughter*, 205).

21 Ibid., 219; Okudaira, *Otogi zōshi emaki*, 197.

22 The monk in *Whispering Bamboo* is "a revered ascetic of sixty-seven years" (Kavanaugh, "Errant Priest," 232); while the monk in *The Useful Nun* attempts to hide his age by telling the old woman, "I am not quite forty. I have suffered great hardships living in these conditions and consequently have become haggard. I probably appear over sixty" (Skord, *Tales of Tears and Laughter*, 211).

23 When the monk returns to his temple at the end of the tale, he asks his fellow monks how old he appears and they tell him "seventeen or eighteen" (see the translation for text 7 of *The Jizō Hall* in the appendix).

24 In a more explicit reference to the *Urashima Tarō* tale, the monk experiences a time lapse upon returning to the Jizō Hall, when he is told that over two hundred years have passed since his departure.

25 *Nihon ōjō gokuraku ki* and two other influential *ōjōden*, *Zoku honchō ōjōden* (1101) and *Shūi ōjōden* (1111), are published in Inoue Mitsusada and Ōsone Shōsuke, eds., *ōjōden, Hokkegenki*, vol. 7 of *Nihon shisō taikei* (Tokyo: Iwanami Shoten, 1974). Frederic J. Kotas provides thoroughly annotated English translations of select accounts from these collections, as well as an excellent discussion of the history and structure of *ōjōden* in Japan; see Kotas, "*Ōjōden:* Accounts of Rebirth in the Pure Land" (PhD diss., University of Washington, 1987).

26 In his preface Yoshishige no Yasutane, the compiler of *Nihon ōjō gokuraku ki*, states that his purpose is to strengthen others' resolve; see the translation by Richard Bowring, in "Preparing for the Pure Land in Late Tenth-Century Japan," *Japanese Journal of Religious Studies* 25, nos. 3–4 (1998): 232. For the Japanese text, see Inoue and Ōsone, *Ōjōden, Hokkegenki*, 11.

27 See Kotas, "*Ōjōden,*" 185–97. One complete *ōjōden* and two fragmented texts survive from this period. Both *Accounts of Rebirth on Mt. Kōya* (*Kōyasan ōjōden*, 1187) and *Accounts of Rebirth at Mii* (*Mii ōjōden*, 1217) (partially extant in an Edo period copy) focus exclusively on the rebirths of monks from a single monastery, with the latter containing a less-than-subtle anti-Enryakuji stance that reflects the famous animosity between Onjōji (Miidera) and Enryakuji. For the text of *Mii ōjōden,* see Tajima Kazuo, Komine Kazuaki, and Harima Mitsutoshi, eds., "Kyōrin Bunko-bon *Mii ōjōden* honkoku to kenkyū," in *Chūsei bungaku shiryō to ronkō* (Tokyo: Kasama Shoin, 1978), 559–91. The third post-Heian *ōjōden*, *Accounts of Rebirth at the Invocation of Amida's Name* (*Nenbutsu ōjōden*, ca. 1262–78), contains seventeen biographies, all of the subjects of which are devotees of Hōnen; the text is in Ienaga Saburō, "Kanazawa Bunko-bon *Nenbutsu ōjōden* kō," in *Chūsei Nihon bukkyō shisōshi kenkyū*, rev. and enlarged ed. (Kyoto: Hōzōkan, 1976), cited in Kotas, "*Ōjōden,*" 218n40.

28 *Shūi ōjōden*, vol. 2, tale 18, translated in Kotas, "*Ōjōden,*" 472–75. For the Japanese, see Inoue and Ōsone, *Ōjōden, Hokkegenki*, 337–38.

29 Several versions of *Illustrated Life of Hōnen* (*Hōnen Shōnin eden*) exist, but the most comprehensive is the set of forty-eight scrolls, a designated National Treasure, in the collection of Chion'in, Kyoto. Although undated, it was likely made to commemorate the one-hundredth death anniversary of Hōnen in 1312; see Komatsu Shigemi, "'Hōnen Shōnin eden' sōkan," in vol. 3 of *Zoku Nihon emaki taisei,* ed. Komatsu Shigemi, 122–67.

30 Ichiko, *Mikan chūsei shōsetsu,* vol. 3, 182.

31 As in *Shūi ōjōden,* vol. 3, tale 11: "In the district of Kii, in the province of Hizen there was a place of Buddhist practice named Komatsudera. There was a holy man whose name has been lost to us." For an entire translation of the story, see Kotas, "*Ōjōden,*" 505–7.

32 Ichiko, *Mikan chūsei shōsetsu,* vol. 3, 192–93.

33 Miya, "'Jizōdō sōshi' ni tsuite," 12. Also see Martin Collcutt, *Five Mountains: The Rinzai Zen Monastic Institution in Medieval Japan*, Harvard East Asian

Monographs, no. 85 (Cambridge, MA: Harvard University Press, 1981), 47.

34 Fumon's biography appears in the eighteenth-century collection of monk's biographies compiled by Mangen Shiban (1626–1710), the *Honchō kōsōden* (1702), which draws from previous biographies such as the *Genko shakusho* (fourteenth century). He was invited by Emperor Kameyama (1249–1305) to turn his detached palace into Nanzenji, and the emperor and courtiers became his followers in Zen Buddhism. A few years after his death, between 1303 and 1306, he received the posthumous name Busshin Zenji, and in 1323 he was named Daimin Kokushi by imperial decree. See fascicle 22 of *Honchō kōsōden*, pt. 1, in *Dai Nihon bunko, Bukkyō hen,* ed. Wada Toshihiko (Tokyo: Shun'yōdō, 1935), 357–60.

35 His actual birthplace was in Shinano Province (present-day Nagano), but he moved to Echigo Province with his mother at age seven, entered the temple Shōenji at age thirteen, and later lived at two temples there, Kehōji and Anrakuji. Thus, it is likely that he would have been commonly associated with Echigo Province; see *Honchō kōsōden*, 360.

36 *Enpō dentōroku,* compiled by Mangen Shiban, is reproduced in vol. 69 of *Dai Nihon bukkyō zensho, Shidenbu*, ed. Suzuki Gakujutsu Zaidan (reprint, Tokyo: Kankō Suzuki Gakujutsu Zaidan, 1972), 248. Reigen appears under the heading of followers of Chōraku.

37 Karen L. Brock finds a similar allusiveness in the representation of Zenmyō from *Lives of the Founders of the Kegon Sect:* Zenmyō appears as seductress, Song Chinese maiden, and protector of the Dharma. See Brock, "Chinese Maiden, Silla Monk: Zenmyō and Her Thirteenth-Century Japanese Audience," in *Flowering in the Shadows: Women in the History of Chinese and Japanese Painting*, ed. Marsha Weidner (Honolulu: University of Hawaii Press, 1990), 185–218. As will be discussed below, representations of Zenmyō, in turn, may have provided a pictorial model for the woman in *The Jizō Hall.*

38 For the "Dharani" chapter, see Leon Hurvitz, trans., *Scripture of the Lotus Blossom of the Fine Dharma* (New York: Columbia University Press, 1976), 320–24.

39 Ibid., 323.

40 Nicole Fabricand-Person argues for the connection between female patrons and the demon daughter theme in "Demonic Female Guardians of the Faith: The Fugen Jūrasetsunyo Iconography in Japanese Buddhist Art," in *Engendering Faith: Women and Buddhism in Premodern Japan,* ed. Barbara Ruch (Ann Arbor: Center for Japanese Studies, University of Michigan, 2002), 343–82.

41 *The Lotus Sutra* itself came to be referred to as "the ten offerings ceremony sutra" (*jisshu kuyō no kyō*); see *Sōgō Bukkyō daijiten,* ed. Sōgō Bukkyō Daijiten Henshū Iinkai, 3 vols. (Kyoto: Hōzōkan, 1987), vol. 2, 1124. The ten offerings consisted of flowers, incense, ornaments, powdered incense, unguent, burning of incense, canopies and banners, robes, dancing and music, and the joining of one's hands in worship; see Inagaki, *Dictionary of Japanese Buddhist Terms,* 159.

42 Fabricand-Person explains the iconography of each individual demon daughter and discusses the origins and development of the combined "ten demon daughters and Fugen" theme in "Demonic Female Guardians."

43 Carmen Blacker notes the serpentine nature of the woman in *Urashima Tarō* in "The Snake Woman in Japanese Myth and Legend," in *Collected Writings of Carmen Blacker* (Tokyo: Edition Synapse; Richmond, Surrey: Japan Library, 2000), 40–50 (first published in J. R. Porter and W. M. S. Russell, eds., *Animals in Folklore,* 1978). Edward H. Schafer surveys Chinese reptilian goddesses in *The Divine Woman: Dragon Ladies and Rain Maidens in T'ang Literature* (Berkeley and Los Angeles: University of California Press, 1973).

44 The scrolls in the Freer Gallery of Art, Smithsonian Institution, along with other versions, are discussed in Pao-chen Chen, "The Goddess of the Lo River: A Study of Early Chinese Narrative Handscrolls" (PhD diss., Princeton University, 1987); also see Wai-yee Li, "Dream Visions of Transcendence in Chinese Literature and Painting," *Asian Art* 3, no. 4 (1990): 53–78.

45 Karen Brock makes the point that, although Zenmyō is supposed to be a Tang maiden, her costume clearly alludes to representations of women and deities from Song Dynasty paintings; Brock, "Chinese Maiden, Silla Monk," 195–97.

46 Fabio Rambelli, "Serpents, Women, and the Quest for the Original Condition: Body, Gender and Salvation in Japanese Buddhism," paper presented at Stanford University, March 2000. Rambelli also discusses the ambiguity of feminine deities, including Kannon,

Benzaiten, and Kisshōten, all of whom were endowed with both benevolent and violent natures.

47 For a translation of the picture scroll text and an original interpretation of the work, see Virginia Skord Waters, "Sex, Lies, and the Illustrated Scroll: The *Dōjōji Engi Emaki*," *Monumenta Nipponica* 52, no. 1 (1997): 59–84.

48 A relatively large body of scholarship examines the reception and interpretation of the story of the Dragon Girl and the notion of female enlightenment in premodern Japan; see Nishiguchi Junko, *Onna no chikara: Kodai no josei to bukkyō* (Tokyo: Heibonsha, 1987), esp. 104–12; Yoshida Kazuhiko, "Ryūnyo no jōbutsu," in *Sukui to oshie*, ed. Ōsumi Kazuo and Nishiguchi Junko, vol. 2 of *Shirīzu josei to bukkyō* (Tokyo: Heibonsha, 1989), 45–91, also translated and adapted by Margaret H. Childs as "The Enlightenment of the Dragon King's Daughter in *The Lotus Sutra*," in *Engendering Faith*, ed. Ruch, 297–324; Edward Kamens, "Dragon-Girl, Maidenflower, Buddha: The Transformation of a Waka Topos, 'The Five Obstructions,'" *Harvard Journal of Asiatic Studies* 53, no. 2 (1993): 389–442.

49 Hurvitz, *Scripture of the Lotus Blossom of the Fine Dharma*, 201.

50 Ibid.

51 Hubert Durt, *Problems of Chronology and Eschatology*, Italian School of East Asian Studies Occasional Papers 4 (Kyoto: Italian School of East Asian Studies, 1994), 73, cited by Rambelli, "Serpents, Women, and the Quest for the Original Condition."

52 A *jataka* tale found in *The Three Jewels* (*Sanbōe*, 984), for example, tells of an Indian prince (the Buddha in a former life) who visits the Dragon Palace in the ocean to acquire the wish-fulfilling jewel possessed by the Dragon King; see Kamens, *Three Jewels*, 118–22.

53 Brian D. Ruppert, *Jewel in the Ashes: Buddha Relics and Power in Early Medieval Japan* (Cambridge, MA: Harvard University Asia Center, distributed by Harvard University Press, 2000), 203.

54 Ibid., 204. Ruppert cites the twelfth-century *Abridged History of Japan* (*Fusō ryakki*) compiled by the Tendai monk Kōen (d. 1169), which makes this connection between the wish-fulfilling jewel and the one offered by the Dragon Girl.

55 For the Japanese text, see Ichiko, *Mikan chūsei shōsetsu*, vol. 3, 192–93.

56 Saichō (767–822) was responsible for disseminating the concept of *sokushin jōbutsu*, which he discussed in terms of its relationship to the Dragon Girl's enlightenment story; see Paul Groner, "The *Lotus Sutra* and Saichō's Interpretation of the Realization of Buddhahood with This Very Body," in *The Lotus Sutra in Japanese Culture*, ed. George Tanabe and Willa Tanabe (Honolulu: University of Hawaii Press, 1989), 53–74.

57 Tanaka Takako makes this point in a literary context, but I would emphasize instead the dualistic nature of the narrative; see Tanaka, *"Akujo" ron* (Tokyo: Kinokuniya Shoten, 1992), 192–93.

58 Bernard Faure, *The Power of Denial: Buddhism, Purity, and Gender* (Princeton: Princeton University Press, 2003), 323, 398n132.

59 Tanaka, *"Akujo" ron*, 192–93.

60 Tanaka Takako argues persuasively that Zenmyō surroundings in the thirteenth-century picture scroll signify a brothel: she appears to reside near a seaport in an upscale residence that is occupied only by women, including one seated at a desk with brush in hand who appears to be the "madam" of the establishment; see ibid., 214–20.

61 The connection between imperial power and jewel/relic possession is explored in Tanaka Takako, "Uji no hōzō: Chūsei ni okeru hōzō no imi," in pt. 2 of *Gehō to aihō no chūsei* (Tokyo: Sunagoya Shobō, 1993), 115–47; and Ruppert, *Jewel in the Ashes*.

62 Tanaka, "Uji no hōzō," 126–32. For the relationship between Taira Kiyomori, the Dragon King/Palace conceit, and imperial aspirations, see Kajitani Ryōji, "Heike nōkyō zakkan," *Rokuon zasshū* (Bulletin of the Nara National Museum) 2, no. 3 (2001): 73–94.

63 The didactic function of the commentary on this scroll and its likely female audience, the nuns at Zenmyōji, are discussed in Brock, "Chinese Maiden, Silla Monk."

64 As previously noted, Sakakibara Satoru confirmed Sanetaka's hand in *The Jizō Hall* scroll in "'Seikōji engi e' shiken."

65 The official reading of his name, as given by the temple he founded, Saikyōji, is, as here, "Shinsei," but he is more commonly known as "Shinzei"; see Takenuki Genshō, ed., *Zusetsu Nihon bukkyō no rekishi, Muromachi jidai* (Tokyo: Kōsei Shuppan, 1996), 134–35.

66 Shinsei's lecture on Genshin's text is mentioned in the diary of the female attendants at the imperial court,

entry for Bunmei 17 (1485) 12.08; see *Oyudono no ue no nikki*, vol. 1, 428; and in the diary of Kanroji Chikanaga, *CK*, vol. 42, 261. Cited in Tendai Shinseishū shūgaku kenkyūjo, ed., *Yakuchū Shinsei Shōnin ōjōdenki*, vol. 36 of *Mie-ken gōshi shiryō kai sōsho* (Ōtsu: Mie-ken Gōshi Shiryō Kankōkai, 1972), 425.

67 Reference to Shinsei's lectures appears in the entry for Bunmei 18 (1486) 5.27 (*SK*, vol. 1, pt. 2, 682–83). To mark the conferral of the title, GoTsuchimikado brushed a "Shinsei Shōnin" name-scroll, later inscribed by GoKashiwabara in 1492, which survives at Saikyōji; see Ōtsu Shi Rekishi Hakubutsukan, ed., *Saikyōji to Tendai Shinseishū no hihō* (Ōtsu: Ōtsu Shi Rekishi Hakubutsukan, 1994), 22, pl. 7.

68 The series began on Chōkyō 3 (1489) 3.23 as recorded in the *Oyudono no ue no nikki, SK, NK, and CK.*

69 Kotas, "*Ōjōden,*" 68–69.

70 For more on the historical relationship between Genshin and Yasutane, see Bowring, "Preparing for the Pure Land."

71 Inoue and Ōsone, *Ōjōden, Hokkegenki*, 712. Kotas has attributed the disappearance of rebirth accounts to the widespread belief in the single *nenbutsu*, as propagated by Hōnen and Shinran, which deemphasized the need for lifelong religious devotion that *Ōjōden* readers were supposed to emulate; see Kotas, "*Ōjōden,*" 198–99. This hypothesis is contradicted, however, by the thirteenth-century *Nenbutsu ōjōden* about the rebirths of Hōnen's disciples, later pictorialized in countless versions of *Illustrated Life of Hōnen*.

72 The version of *Record of the Account of Rebirth of Shinsei Shōnin* that survives today was copied in 1526 by a disciple of Shinsei named Seion and is reproduced and annotated in Tendai Shinseishū shūgaku kenkyūjo, *Yakuchū Shinsei Shōnin ōjōdenki.*

73 See n. 27.

74 No information about the monk Seiun survives, and to my knowledge he does not make another appearance in Sanetaka's diary. He may have been one of Shinsei's disciples, many of whom took the "sei" character as the first character in their own names, such as Seion (the copyist of Shinsei's biography) and Seizen (the second abbot of Saikyōji). Seiun's relationship to Shinsei would help explain how the text came into GoTsuchimikado's possession.

75 Entry for Meiō 7(1498) 8.27 (*SK*, vol. 3, pt. 2, 553).

76 Entry for Meiō 7 (1498) 9.27 (*SK*, vol. 3, pt. 2, 565).

77 Sanetaka records viewing the four scrolls with the emperor; see the diary entry for Bunmei 8 (1476) 6.11 (*SK*, vol. 1, pt. 1, 165).

78 All of the compilers of extant Heian and Kamakura period *ōjōden* were around age sixty and had either taken the tonsure or would do so soon after they had created their texts.

79 Inoue and Ōsone, *Ōjōden, Hokkegenki*; and, in translation, Yoshiko Kurata Dykstra, *Miraculous Tales of the Lotus Sutra from Ancient Japan* (Honolulu: University of Hawaii Press, 1987).

80 Kotas, "*Ōjōden,*" 207.

81 The stories, "A Government Official of Higo Province," "A Fox on Suzaku Avenue," and "An Evil Woman of the Muro District of Kii Province" (the Dōjōji Tale), appear in the third volume of *Miraculous Lotus Sutra Tales from Ancient Japan* and in *Tales of Times Now Past*; see Dykstra, *Miraculous Tales of the Lotus Sutra,* 128–29, 142–43, 145–46.

82 Twenty of the accounts in Miyoshi no Tameyasu's *Shūi ōjōden* derive from tales found in the *Hokkegenki.*

83 Fifty-four *ōjōden* make up fascicle 15 of *Tales of Times Now Past,* which contains Buddhist tales from Japan; see Mabuchi, Kunisaki, and Konno, *Konjaku monogatari shū,* vol. 2, 37–173.

84 Three entries in the main part of Sanetaka's diary describe the brushing of the picture scroll text: Meiō 7 (1498) 9.24, 9.27, and 9.28 (*SK*, vol. 3, pt. 2, 564–65).

85 The meaning of these numbers is unclear. Perhaps they referred to sections (*dan*) 3 and 5 of the scroll text, or perhaps they were meant to be read as 3×5 (in other words, 15). The fifteenth day of the month figures prominently in tales of rebirth as the most common date for death and rebirth, apparently in reference to the date of the nirvana of Sakyamuni Buddha (Kotas, "*Ōjōden,*" 271); also see the account from the *Shūi ōjōden* quoted in full earlier in this chapter. Although this is purely speculative, a reference to "fifteen" in this letter could be shorthand for the scene of rebirth.

86 The undated letter was sent before 9.26, since it appears on the back of diary entries dating between 9.26 and 9.28; see *SK*, vol. 11, 447.

87 The Sanjōnishi mansion at Mushanokōji and Imadegawa avenues burned down two years later in 1500 in

a fire that consumed 20,000 homes in the capital. The family then moved to Muromachi Avenue, close to the Tsuchimikado palace at Higashinotōin and Tsuchimikado avenues, where Sanetaka remained for the rest of his life; see Haga, *Sanjōnishi Sanetaka*, 107–8.

88 It was not unusual for Sanetaka to receive written thanks on the same day for work submitted that day; a second undated letter from the female attendants acknowledges the emperor's receipt and approval of the picture scroll text, while also referring to a poetry gathering to be held at the palace the following day, an event that Sanetaka recorded in his diary on 9.29. Thus, the thank-you letter can be dated to 9.28, the same day that Sanetaka turned over his work to the emperor; see *SK*, vol. 11, 448.

89 Although dozens of women worked at the imperial palace, roughly twelve were in the immediate service of GoTsuchimikado, and around six of these women held ranks and positions that entitled them to write letters on the emperor's behalf. For more on the ranks and duties of imperial palace women, see Okuno, *Kōshitsu gokeizaishi no kenkyū*; Okuno Takahiro, *Sengoku jidai no kyūtei seikatsu* (Tokyo: Zoku Gunsho Ruijū Kanseikai, 2004), 125–38; Wakita Haruko, "Kyūtei nyōbō to tennō," in *Nihon chūsei joseishi no kenkyū: Seibetsu yakuwari buntan to bosei, kasei, seiai* (Tokyo: Tokyo Daigaku Shuppankai, 1992), 232–81; Lee Butler, *Emperor and Aristocracy in Japan, 1467–1680: Resilience and Renewal* (Cambridge, MA: Harvard University Asia Center, distributed by Harvard University Press, 2002), 50–56.

90 The highest-ranking women would on occasion make official visits to temples as imperial representatives in place of the emperor; see Wakita, *Nihon chūsei josei shi no kenkyū*, 262–63.

91 Sanetaka describes Fusako's appointment to the position of *naishi no suke* (assistant handmaid) as a felicitous event and notes that she went immediately to the palace to undertake her duties; see the entry for Bunmei 17 (1485) 5.13 (*SK*, vol. 1, pt. 2, 593). Women of the *naishi no suke* class were equivalent to *kugyō*, or senior nobles, and usually held the fourth or fifth court rank, although they could rise as high as the second or third rank and achieve even greater social success by bearing a crown prince. Some of the specificities of late medieval female ranks are discussed in Kuwayama Kōnen, "Muromachi jidai ni okeru kuge nyōbō no koshō," *Joseishigaku* 6 (1996): 1–12. Also see William H. McCullough and Helen Craig McCullough, trans., *A Tale of Flowering Fortunes* (Stanford: Stanford University Press, 1980), vol. 2, 820–23, for translations and definitions of women's positions at the Heian court.

92 Okuno, *Sengoku jidai no kyūtei seikatsu*, 128. Fujiko eventually rose to the position of *shin dainagon no suke* during GoKashiwabara's reign, gave birth to the future emperor GoNara (1496–1557), and owned her own home next to Sanetaka's residence. Sanetaka mentions construction on Fujiko's house, which she probably did not live in until after GoKashiwabara's death in 1526; see the entry for Kyōroku 5 (1532) 3.4 (*SK*, vol. 14, 311), cited in Wakita, *Nihon chūsei josei shi no kenkyū*, 265, 266n15.

93 In the entry, Fujiko is referred to as "Achacha," her name while attendant to crown prince Katsuhito (GoKashiwabara); see Meiō 7 (1498) 9.16 (*SK*, vol. 3, pt. 2, 560).

94 Sanetaka records his own verse as well as the lines of the emperor and the crown prince; see the entry for Meiō 7 (1498) 9.25 (*SK*, vol. 3, pt. 2, 564). Sanetaka's seventeen-syllable verse, an "upper half" (*moto noku*) of a *renga* contribution, reads:

Aki no [hi]	On an autumn day
nyūkai tōku	entering the sea distantly
kari nakite	the cry of wild geese

95 See Itō Kei's introduction to *Saishōsō*, in *Chūsei waka shū Muromachi hen*, vol. 47 of *Shin Nihon koten bungaku taikei*, ed. Itō Kei et al. (Tokyo: Iwanami Shoten, 1990), 417–70.

96 At least one such poetic gathering with Sōgi and other *renga* poets involved quite a bit of sake and much laughter in response to the poems; see the entry for Meiō 8 (1499) 3.15 (*SK*, vol. 3, pt. 2, 628–29). This and other entries related to comic verse are discussed in Tokuda Kazuo, "Sanjōnishi Sanetaka no 'zoku'—Sanetaka kō-ki ni miru bungei no ichisokumen," *Kokubungaku kaishaku to kanshō* 50, no. 8 (1985): 38–45.

97 Iwasaki Yoshie, "Muormachi-ki no fūzoku emaki—'Sanjūniban' 'Shichijūichiban' no seiritsu, kōsei, eishatachi," *Kobijutsu* 74 (1985): 55. Iwasaki has linked this imperial *kyōka* match to the extant *Poetry*

Match of Different Professions in Thirty-two Rounds (*Sanjūniban shokunin uta-awase*, 1494), a text full of puns and witticisms that contains at least one poem composed by Sanetaka, found in his posthumously published poetry collection *Setsugyokushū*.

98 In 1496, Sanetaka suggested Ryōan for the position of lecturer for an important ceremony held at the imperial palace, which, according to Miyakawa Yōko, may have been part of Sanetaka's preparations for his son's later acceptance as Ryōan's disciple; see Miyakawa, *Sanjōnishi Sanetaka to kotengaku*, 81.

99 Bunki 1 (1501) 10.3 (*SK*, vol. 3, pt. 2, 687). The extant portrait of Fumon with GoKashiwabara's inscription and the date of "Bunki 1, middle of the 10th month," must be the painting mentioned in Sanetaka's diary. Ryōan Keigo accompanied Sanetaka to the palace when the courtier requested the emperor's calligraphy for the portrait. This was one of many favors that Sanetaka performed for the Tōfukuji abbot, who was responsible for the well-being of his beloved youngest son. For more on Ryōan Keigo, see Asakura Hisashi, *Juzan Eisō, Shūzan Tōki: Zenrin no kizokuka no yōsō* (Osaka: Seibundō, 1990), 405.

5 *BREAKING THE INKSTONE*

1 Mabuchi, Kunisaki, and Konno, *Konjaku monogatari shū*, vol. 2, 536–47; all subsequent citations of this story are to this edition. Since this version of the tale figures prominently in the later discussion of the scroll, a full English translation is included in the appendix, along with that of the scroll text. The sixteen renunciation tales in *Konjaku* are the subject of William Michael Kelsey, "Didactics in Art: The Literary Structure of *Konjaku Monogatari-shū*" (PhD diss., Indiana University, 1976). Translations of four of these stories also appear in William Michael Kelsey, "*Konjaku Monogatari-shū:* Toward an Understanding of Its Literary Qualities," *Monumenta Nipponica* 30 (1975): 121–50.

2 For an English translation, see Ury, *Tales of Times Now Past*, 121–24; Kelsey, "Didactics in Art," 333–37.

3 For an English translation, see Kelsey, "Didactics in Art," 346–48.

4 The compiler probably transcribed a story already in circulation. Kelsey has pointed out that the language of this tale suggests that it might have been in oral, as well as written, circulation; see ibid., 212–13.

5 The characters for "Shosha" mean "write" or "copy," which probably inspired the compiler of *Selected Stories* (*Senjūshō*) to connect the temple's founder and the inkstone-breaking story in the thirteenth century; see Miyoshi Shūichirō, "Suzuriwari setsuwa tsūkan: 'Konjaku monogatari shū' kara bangai utaibon 'Suzuriwari' made," *Kokugo kokubungaku* (Fukui Daigaku) 30 (1991): 45.

6 For more on this story, as well as Shōkū's famous poetic encounter with Izumi Shikibu, see Hayashi Masahiko, "Chūsei ni okeru Shōkū Shōnin setsuwa ni tsuite," *Chūsei bungaku* 17 (1972): 8–14.

7 See chapter 10, story 58, in Nishio Kōichi, ed., *Senjūshō*, Iwanami Bunko 6746–49 (Tokyo: Iwanami Shoten, 1970), 190–95. A colophon to one recension of the *Senjūshō* reveals that it was copied from a manuscript dated to 1459, indicating that this collection was in circulation close to the time of Mitsunobu's *Breaking the Inkstone*. For background on *Senjūshō*'s redactions, dating, and authorship, as well as a translation of several tales, see Moore, "*Senjūshō*."

8 *Konjaku monogatari shū*, 537.

9 For the Japanese text, see *Suzuriwari*, in Yokoyama Shigeru and Matsumoto Ryūshin, eds., *Muromachi jidai monogatari taisei*, 13 vols. (Tokyo: Kadokawa Shoten, 1973–87), vol. 7, 656.

10 All versions of *Breaking the Inkstone* except the *Konjaku monogatari shū* and 1495 picture scroll versions describe the father as the grandson of Tokihira and call him Tokitomo. Hashimoto Naoki has suggested that the prevalence of myths about Michizane's wrathful spirit in the medieval period probably inspired this particular story line of *Breaking the Inkstone*; see Hashimoto, "Nara ehon 'Suzuriwari' to Shōkū Shōnin," *Senriyama bungaku ronshū*, March 1982, 21. Miyoshi Shūichirō elaborates upon the significance of the Michizane myth in the Hiroshima text in "Suzuriwari setsuwa tsūkan."

11 The boy's footsteps cause the servant to drop the inkstone in the versions found in *Tales of Times Now Past* (*Konjaku*), *Selected Stories* (*Senjūshō*), and the *Suzuriwari* illustrated book in a private collection in Japan.

12 This is the version in the illustrated book in the Hiroshima University Library; for the text see *Suzuriwari*, in Yokoyama and Matsumoto, *Muromachi jidai monogatari taisei*, vol. 7, 658.

13 This double depiction of Nakamichi is an example of

the pictorial device found in some narrative picture scrolls called "different time, same scene" (*iji dōzu*).

14 Wu Hung has analyzed this pictorial strategy at length in the context of Chinese paintings in *The Double Screen: Medium and Representation in Chinese Painting* (Chicago: University of Chicago Press, 1996).

15 After the boy is exiled, the narrator of the *Konjaku* text states: "The mother was beside herself with grief, and though she wanted to go and see her son, the minister was firm in his anger. The lamentable thing about being a woman was that she could not simply do as she wished and go to see the boy." See the full translation of this text in the appendix.

16 The phrase a "river of tears" appears in the *Konjaku* version of *Inkstone* in a poem composed by the servant while grieving after the young boy's death; it is quoted as the epigraph to this chapter. The wave pattern of the woman's robe may also reiterate the allusion to a "river of tears." While robe patterns do not always convey meaning in narrative paintings, there are important examples that do, such as in *Twelve Animals of the Zodiac* (*Jūnirui emaki*), where specific motifs on the robes serve as visual puns or represent the attributes associated with their animal-wearers. Kuroda Hideo discusses this briefly in a roundtable discussion with Chino Kaori and Tokuda Kazuo; see Kuroda, "Otogi zōshi no parareru wārudo," *Kokubungaku* 39, no. 1 (1994): 6–29, esp. 21–23.

17 Ogawa Hiromitsu reads the crane scroll in Muqi's Daitokuji triptych as an image of maternal love and separation in "Mokkei—kotenshugi no hen'yō (jō)," *Bijutsushi ronsō*, no. 4 (1988): 95–113.

18 Another poem found in the twelfth-century version of *Inkstone* illustrates the convention of equating a crying bird with a crying child. While in exile, the young boy composes a poem that uses the "singing," or "crying" (*naku*), of a bird at dawn to describe his own sleepless night spent thinking of his parents and weeping until daybreak.

19 *Konjaku monogatari shū*, 541–42. The translation of this poem is adapted from Kelsey, "Didactics in Art," 341.

20 *Konjaku monogatari shū*, 543.

21 The translation of this poem is adapted from Kelsey, "Didactics in Art," 344.

22 *Konjaku monogatari shū*, 543–45.

23 See William MacDuff, "Beautiful Boys in *Nō Drama:* The Idealization of Homoerotic Desire," *Asian Theatre Journal* 13, no. 12 (1996): 248–58.

24 Reproduced in Okudaira, *Otogi zōshi emaki*, 45–58. For an English translation, see Margaret H. Childs, "Chigo Monogatari: Love Stories or Buddhist Sermons?" *Monumenta Nipponica* 35, no. 2 (1980): 127–51.

25 "The Story of Kannon's Manifestation as a Youth" is translated by Margaret H. Childs in *Partings at Dawn: An Anthology of Japanese Gay Literature*, ed. Stephen D. Miller (San Francisco: Sunshine Gay Press, 1996), 31-35. Color reproductions of this scroll are published in Komatsu, *Nihon emaki taisei*, vol. 24.

26 Childs, "Story of Kannon's Manifestation as a Youth," 32.

27 *Konjaku monogatari shū*, 539.

28 Children between infancy and the age of seven were called *chigo*, literally "nursing children," not to be confused with acolytes, who were also called *chigo;* see Katō Osamu, *"Chigo" to "warawa" no seikatsu shi: Nihon no chūko no kodomotachi* (Tokyo: Keiō Tsūshin, 1994), 125.

29 Additional pictorial examples are found in Kuroda Hideo's compilation of images of children in medieval handscrolls: *"Emaki" kodomo no tōjō: Chūsei shakai no kodomozō*, in *Rekishi hakubutsukan shirīzu* (Tokyo: Kawade Shobō Shinsha, 1989).

30 Emperor GoHanazono viewed the picture scroll *A Long Tale for an Autumn Night* in 1438 according to an entry in the *Kanmon gyoki*, cited in Brock, "The Shogun's 'Painting Match,'" 471. In 1475 Sanetaka records reading *A Long Tale for an Autumn Night* aloud to the imperial prince Fushimi Kunitaka (1456–1532); see diary entry for Bunmei 7.11.10 (*SK*, vol. 1, pt. 1, 117). These references verify the circulation of this picture scroll in the fifteenth century in Kyoto, where Mitsunobu and his patrons would have either heard about it or seen it personally.

31 Yoshizumi was officially appointed shogun on Meiō 3 (1494) 12.27. He took the name Yoshitaka on Meiō 2 (1493) 6.19, changing it from Yoshitō, which he had assumed just two months before; the final name change to Yoshizumi occurred on Bunki 2 (1502) 7.21. For more details on Yoshizumi's names and court ranks, see Kokushi Daijiten Henshū Iinkai, ed., *Kokushi daijiten*, vol. 1 (Tokyo: Yoshikawa Kōbunkan, 1979), 173.

32 For general background on Yoshizumi and his family, see Katsumata Shizuo, "Tsūshi jūgo-jūroku seiki no Nihon: Sengoku no sōran," in vol. 4 of *Chūsei*, vol. 10

of *Iwanami kōza Nihon tsūshi* (Tokyo: Iwanami Shoten, 1994), 3–57, esp. 11–16.

33 Diaries and documents at this point refer to Yoshizumi as "Kōgen'in Seikō," or *kasshiki*, a term for a young boy living and being educated at a temple.

34 See the entry for Entoku 2 (1490) 5.18, in Konoe, *Gohōkōin ki*, vol. 2, vol. 6 of *Zoku shiryō taisei* (Tokyo: Rinsen Shoten, 1967), 334.

35 Tomiko had reasons to be anxious. She had clashed with Yoshimi, who opposed the appointment of her son Yoshihisa as Yoshimasa's successor, and one of her close allies, Ise Sadachika (1417–73), was exiled for plotting to assassinate Yoshimi, an event referred to as the "Bunshō era coup" (*Bunshō no seihen*; 1466, ninth month). See Yamada Yasuhiro, *Sengokuki Muromachi Bakufu to shōgun* (Tokyo: Yoshikawa Kōbunkan, 2000), 12.

36 For the various diary accounts of the destruction of the Ogawa palace, see *Dai Nihon shiryō,* vol. 8 (Tokyo: Tokyo Daigaku Shuppankai, 1995), pt. 36, 257–59.

37 Ise Sadamune's father, Ise Sadachika (1417–73), had served as tutor to the young Yoshimasa when he ascended to the position of shogun at fourteen, and Sadachika became director of the *bakufu*'s Administrative Board. By Sadamune's time, the Ise had occupied powerful bureaucratic positions within the Ashikaga *bakufu* for over one hundred and fifty years, since the early days of the Ashikaga shogunate in the fourteenth century; see Morita Kyōji, *Ashikaga Yoshimasa no kenkyū,* vol. 3 of *Nihon shi kenkyū sōkan* (Osaka: Izumi Shoin, 1993), 27–28.

38 Sadamune's antagonisms with Yoshitane's line extended from the prior generation; his father, Sadachika, had been expelled from the *bakufu* for a brief time for his involvement in a plot to assassinate Yoshimi in 1466. See Yamada, *Sengokuki Muromachi Bakufu to shōgun*, 12.

39 For a detailed discussion of the political alliances of the Hosokawa clan and their geographical power in the post-Ōnin and Bunmei eras, see Suegara Yutaka, "Hosokawa-shi no dōzoku rengō taisei no kaitai to kinai ryōgokuka," in *Chūsei no hō to seiji*, ed. Ishii Susumu (Tokyo: Yoshikawa Kōbunkan, 1992), 141–231.

40 Yamada, *Sengokuki Muromachi Bakufu to shōgun*, 108–9.

41 Known as the "Meiō period coup d'état" (*Meiō no seihen*), the overthrow is considered a watershed event that marks the onset of the Warring States period. Hosokawa Masamoto is seen as the embodiment of "the low overturning the high" (*gekokujō*), a condition that has been said to characterize the late fifteenth and early sixteenth centuries. Mary Elizabeth Berry vividly describes the events surrounding Masamoto's coup, as well as one contemporary observer's account of Yoshitane's capture, in *The Culture of Civil War in Kyoto* (Berkeley and Los Angeles: University of California Press, 1994), 45–50.

42 Masamoto's secret transfer of Yoshizumi is noted in the entry for Meiō 2 (1493) 4.21, in *Kitano Shake nikki*, vol. 4, 73. Formal recognition of Yoshizumi's living at Masamoto's house occurs one week later when his name is changed from Kōgen'in Seikō to Yoshitō and he is elevated to the Junior Fifth Lower rank; see, e.g., the entry for Meiō 2.4.28 in *CK*, vol. 3, 235.

43 Yoshitane finally regained his title as shogun in 1508, and Yoshizumi was forced to flee the capital. The rise of Yoshitane and his supporters Ōuchi Yoshioki (1477–1528) and Hosokawa Takakuni (1484–1531) marks a new era in Kyoto rule and cultural patronage, which resulted in the production of Tosa Mitsunobu's *Genji Album* (1509–10), commissioned by an Ōuchi retainer, Sue Saburō; see McCormick, "Genji Goes West."

44 Yoshitada, who was just a year older than Yoshizumi, remained in Kyoto after the coup, went into the service of the shogun, and was adopted by the courtier Konoe Masaie; see the entry for Meiō 3 (1494) 4.21 in Masaie's diary, *Gohōkōin ki*, where he is referred to as Jissōin; cited by Yamada, *Sengokuki Muromachi Bakufu to shōgun*, 89.

45 Yamada uses this episode, among others, to argue against the image of Yoshizumi as a puppet shogun, at least in his later years; see Yamada, *Sengokuki Muromachi Bakufu to shōgun*, 88–91. Sanetaka records Yoshizumi's departure for Iwakura on 8.4, Masamoto's murder of Yoshitada on 8.5, and the shogun's return to the capital on 8.6, after having received an imperial decree; see the entry for Bunki 2 (1502) 8.5 (*SK,* vol. 4, pt. 1, 47–48).

46 Michael Solomon, "The Dilemma of Religious Power: Honganji and Hosokawa Masamoto," *Monumenta Nipponica* 33, no. 1 (1978): 57.

47 For the various stories related to Shōkū Shōnin, see Hayashi, "Chūsei ni okeru Shōkū Shōnin setsuwa ni tsuite."

48 The story appears in the *setsuwa* anthology *Stories Heard from Writers Old and New* (*Kokon chomonjū,* 1254) in fascicle 11, "Painting" (*gazu*); see Nishio and Kobayashi, *Kokon chomonjū,* pt. 2, 29–30.

49 On Eikyō 4 (1492) 6.3, a member of the Akamatsu clan, governors of Harima, informed Mansai Jugō (1378–1435), political adviser to the shogun, that Yoshinori would visit Mt. Shosha during his trip to Hyōgo to check on the *karafune bugyō*, the newly created office to oversee the Ming tally trade ships. Yoshinori's trip took place during the eighth month of that year. See Mansai's diary, *Mansai Jugō nikki* (Kyoto: Rokujō Kappan Seizōjō, 1920), 470.

50 See the entries for Kanshō 4 (1463) 12.25 and 26, in *Inryōken nichiroku*, vol. 1, 441–42n51. The pagoda was struck by lightning on the first day of the first month of 1479 (Bunmei 11); for the various responses recorded in contemporary diaries, see *Dai Nihon shiryō*, vol. 8 (Tokyo: Tokyo Daigaku Shiryōhensanjo, 1926), pt. 11, 203–4.

52 Entoku 4 (1492) 2.22, in *Inryōken nichiroku*, vol. 5, 2229. The fire devastated the temple, destroying its main icon of Nyoirin Kannon, which was said to be carved from living wood. The *Inryōken* diarist blames the devastation on impure things that he has heard have been occurring at the temple, including women living on the premises. In 1495 the icon was recarved from the same wood and enshrined in the main hall known as the Maniden, rebuilt that year, suggesting that fund-raising efforts may have put the temple in people's minds that year.

53 Imatani Akira, "Akamatsu Masanori kōshitsu, Dōshōin-ni Hosokawashi no kenkyū: Chūsei ni okeru josei kenryokusha no keifu," *Yokohama Shiritsu Daigaku ronsō: Jinbun kagaku keiretsu* 46, nos. 1–3 (1995): 299–326.

54 Ibid., 302–3. The engagement was announced on 3.11, and the plans for the coup to install Yoshizumi as shogun were relayed to Masamoto's retainers by 3.20.

55 See the entries for Meiō 2 (1493) intercalary 4.18 and 19 in the diary of Konoe Masaie (1444–1505), *Gohōkōin ki,* vol. 3, 89; cited in Imatani, "Akamatsu Masanori kōshitsu," 304.

56 Imatani, "Akamatsu Masanori kōshitsu," 301.

57 Yoshiharu was born the same year that Yoshizumi died in exile in Ōmi Province, but Yoshizumi made sure that the infant was secretly sent to live with Dōshōin and Akamatsu Yoshimura (the adopted son of Masanori); see Nagae Shōichi, *Miyoshi Nagayoshi*, no. 149 of *Yoshikawa Kōbunkan Jinbutsu sōsho* (Tokyo: Yoshikawa Kōbunkan, 1968), 41.

58 Documents related to Akamatsu patronage of Engyōji are transcribed in Zoku Gunsho Ruijū Kanseikai Henshūbu, "Harima kuni Shoshazan engi (shinpo)," *Shigaku bungaku* 2, no. 3 (1959): 28–29.

59 Gorai Shigeru, ed., *Kinki reizan to shugendō*, vol. 11 of *Sangaku shūkyō shi kenkyū sōsho* (Tokyo: Meicho Shuppan, 1978), 314–15.

60 For more on Shugendō in English, see Miyake Hitoshi, *Shugendō: Essays on the Structure of Japanese Folk Religion* (Ann Arbor: Center for Japanese Studies, University of Michigan, 2001).

61 Paul L. Swanson, "Shugendō and the Yoshino-Kumano Pilgrimage: An Example of Mountain Pilgrimage," *Monumenta Nipponica* 36, no. 1 (1981): 55.

62 Miyake, *Shugendō*, 61.

63 Gorai, *Kinki reizan to shugendō*, 323n57.

64 This account of Masamoto's activities at Kuramadera was told by Karahashi (Sugawara) Arikazu (1448–96) to Kujō Hisatune (1468–1530); see the entry for Meiō 3 (1494) 9.24 in Hisatsune's diary, *Gojigen'in-dono gyoki*, in vol. 2 of *Kujō-ke rekisei kiroku*, in *Zushoryō sōkan,* ed. Kunaichō Shoryōbu (Tokyo: Kunaichō Shoryōbu, 1990), 148; cited in Morita Kyōji, *Sengokuki rekidai Hosokawashi no kenkyū,* vol. 5 of *Nihon shi kenkyū sōkan* (Osaka: Izumi Shoin, 1994), 26–27. Arikazu was a retainer of the Kujō family who was killed by Kujō Masamoto and his son Hisatsune just two years after this entry; this incident is discussed in chapter 3 of this book in the context of Sanjōnishi Yasuko's marriage to Hisatsune.

65 *Ashikaga kiseiki*, in vol. 13 of *Kaitei shiseki shūran*, ed. Kondō Heijō and Kondō Keizō (Tokyo: Kondō Kappanjo, 1902), 144; cited in Solomon, "Dilemma of Religious Power," 56.

66 *Ashikaga kiseiki*, 144; Solomon, "Dilemma of Religious Power," 56.

67 *Kūzen-ki*, in *Rennyo Shōnin Gyōjitsu*, ed. Inaba Masamaru (Kyoto: Hōzōkan, 1948), 33; cited by Solomon, "Dilemma of Religious Power," 56. Kūzen was a disciple of Rennyo (1415–99).

68 *Kūzen-ki*, 33; Solomon, "Dilemma of Religious Power," 56.

69 Suegara Yutaka, "Hosokawa Masamoto to Shugendō: Shisen'in Kōsen o chūshin ni," *Harukanaru chūsei* 12 (1992): 67. The monk Dōkō of Shōgoin in Kyoto was the elder brother of Regent Konoe Masa'ie; for more on his 1486 trip, see Miyake, *Shugendō*, 25.

70 Suegara, "Hosokawa Masamoto to Shugendō," 67.

71 Ibid., 64–66.

72 Takagishi Akira has argued compellingly for Hosokawa Masamoto as the patron of this scroll; see Takagishi, *Muromachi ōken to kaiga*, 345–84.

73 Gorai Shigeru pointed out the Shugendō influence on this scroll in "Tsukiminedera engi emaki to sangaku shūkyō," in suppl. vol. 1 of *Shinshū Nihon emakimono zenshū*, ed. Shimada Shūjiro (Tokyo: Kadokawa Shoten, 1980), 37–42.

74 The English translation is adapted from Takashi Katsuki, "The Origin of the Founding of the Geppōji (Geppōji konryū shugyō engi)," *Oriental Art* 16, no. 3 (1970): 250. For the Japanese text, see Shimada, *Shinshū Nihon emakimono zenshū*, suppl. vol. 1, 51.

75 Takagishi Akira has suggested that the term *ikoku chōbuku*, "subduing of foreign lands," likely refers to Masamoto's aspirations to overthrow the Ōuchi clan, with whom the Hosokawa were competing for control of overseas shipping rights; see Takagishi, *Muromachi ōken to kaiga*, 381–82.

76 Yamamoto Hideo, "Chūgoku koji jinbutsu zu, Ōsen Keisan san," *Kyōto Kokuritsu Hakubutsukan Gakusō* 12 (1990): 88–96.

77 Paul R. Katz, *Images of the Immortal: The Cult of Lü Dongbin at the Palace of Eternal Joy* (Honolulu: University of Hawaii Press, 1999), 57.

78 Ibid., 162.

79 I would therefore place Masamoto's interest in *shugen* slightly earlier than does Suegara, who attributes it to Kōsen's influence after Kōsen's return to the capital in 1494; see Suegara, "Hosokawa Masamoto to shugendō," 64.

80 The description appears in the late-fourteenth-century chronicle *Taiheiki,* chapter 11; see Yamashita Hiroaki, ed., *Taiheiki,* vol. 2, vol. 38 of *Shinchō Nihon koten shūsei*, ed. Yamashita Hiroaki (Tokyo: Shinchōsha, 1980), 155.

81 Carmen Blacker, "The Divine Boy in Japanese Buddhism," *Asian Folklore Studies* 22 (1963): 77.

82 Miyake, *Shugendō*, 117.

83 For more on *gohō dōji* in general, and Shōkū's attendants in particular, see Koyama Satoko, *Gohō dōji shinkō no kenkyū* (Kyoto: Jishōsha Shuppan, 2003), esp. 122–30.

84 If Masamoto had not been aware of Shōkū's legends before, he could have heard of them during his travels to Harima, from his sister Dōshōin, her husband Akamatsu Masanori, or the courtier Hashimoto Kinnatsu (1454–1538), the part-time resident of Harima and lay patron of Shoshazan who executed the calligraphy of the *Tsukiminedera* scroll; for more on Hashimoto and his possible relationship to Masamoto, see Takagishi, *Muromachi ōken to kaiga*, 366–70.

85 Yoshizumi's handscroll of *Breaking the Inkstone* is the only version of the tale to specify that the boy in the story was exiled to Saga, a locale in the hills to the west of Kyoto, where Yoshizumi lived for over five years. Yoshizumi was an orphan by 1491; after the death of his father, Ashikaga Masatomo, his mother and younger brother were killed by another one of Masatomo's sons, who apparently coveted the position of *bakufu* administrator of the Eastern Region; for more on this incident, see Suegara, "Hosokawa-shi no dōzoku rengō taisei," 199.

86 Motokazu's last words were reported by Kujō Hisatsune in a letter to his father, Kujō Masamoto, recorded in Masamoto's diary on Eishō 1 (1504) 11.11; see *Masamoto-kō tabi hikitsuke*, in vol. 1 of *Nihon shi shiryō sōkan,* ed. Chūsei Kuge Nikki Kenkyūkai (Osaka: Izumi Shoin, 1996), 337–38; cited in Chūsei Kuge Nikki Kenkyūkai, ed., *Sengokuki kuge shakai no shoyōsō*, vol. 2 of *Nihon shi kenkyū sōkan* (Osaka: Izumi Shoin, 1992), 255. A vivid description of Motokazu's rebellion and its violent suppression by Masamoto's forces begins Elizabeth Berry's book *Culture of Civil War in Kyoto*, 1–4.

87 Suegara, "Hosokawa-shi no dōzoku rengō taisei," 200.

88 Morita, *Sengokuki rekidai Hosokawashi no kenkyū*, 42.

89 This handscroll exists in the collection of Sanbōin; for a partial English translation of the scroll, see Gary P. Leupp, *Male Colors: The Construction of Homosexuality in Tokugawa Japan* (Berkeley and Los Angeles: University of California Press, 1995), 40–46.

90 The translation is adapted from Yukio Mishima, *Forbidden Colors*, trans. Alfred H. Marks (New York: Knopf, 1968), 184; for the Japanese text, see Yukio Mishima, *Kinjiki*, vol. 5 of *Mishima Yukio zenshū*, ed. Saeki Shōchi et al. (Tokyo: Shinchōsha, 1974), 253.

91 The preponderance of the death of boys in acolyte

tales and its relationship to medieval conceptualizations of homosocial desire deserve further study; the tradition bears an uncanny similarity to that of homoerotic literature in Renaissance Europe, particularly in the form of the pastoral elegy; see Stephen Guy-Bray, *Homoerotic Space: The Poetics of Loss in Renaissance Literature* (Toronto: University of Toronto Press, 2002).

92 In *Mirror of Society* (*Sekyōshō*), a Muromachi period text that records the daily schedule of young boys being educated at temples, the reading of "tales of duty" (*giri monogatari*) appears on the list of afternoon activities; see Tabata, *Nihon chūsei josei shiron*, esp. 197–203.

93 See the entry for Entoku 3 (1491) 2.13 in *Gohōkōin ki*, vol. 2, 375.

94 See the entry for Meiō 4 (1495) 8.25 in *Gōhōkōin ki*, vol. 3, 211.

95 More than a few courtiers were mystified over this adoption. In the *Gōhōkōin ki* entry for Entoku 3 (1491) 2.13, Konoe Masaie called it "unprecedented" and "inexplicable." It also angered Hosokawa clan members and retainers, who had expected Masamoto to select an heir from within their own ranks, which he later did by adopting a second son, Hosokawa Sumimoto (1489–1520) in 1503. For the political motivations behind Hosokawa Masamoto's adoption of Sumiyuki, see Ienaga Junji, "Horikoshi kubōfu metsubō no saikentō," *Sengoku shi kenkyū* 27 (1994): 1–10; and for the possible reasons that motivated Kujō Masamoto to relinquish his son to Masamoto, see Morita, *Sengokuki rekidai Hosokawashi no kenkyū*, 47–48.

96 On *Breaking the Inkstone* recensions and a chart of their variations, including the boy's age, see McCormick, "Tosa Mitsunobu's *Ko-e*," 37–40.

97 Matsumoto, *Muromachi jidai monogatari taisei*, *hoi* 2, 293–316.

98 Meiō 7 (1498) 3.20 (*SK*, vol. 3, pt. 2, 510). The first book consisted of the "Naniwa Bay" (Naniwazu) and "Asaka Mountain" (Asakayama) poems, which the *kana* preface to the *Kokinshū* calls "the mother and father of poetry and the texts with which one begins writing practice" (*uta no chichi haha no yo nite zo, tenarau hito no hajime ni mo shikeru*); see *Nihon kokugo daijiten,* vol. 15 (Tokyo: Shōgakukan, 1975), 292. The second text was an excerpt from *The Tale of Genji*, selections of the tale presumably chosen by Sanetaka as the most fundamental for a young person's early education.

99 Sumiyuki's name was changed in 1504 at the time of his coming-of-age ceremony; before that he was called Sōmeimaru. The ceremony is noted in the entry for Eishō 1 (1504) 12.10 (*NK,* vol. 2, 84), cited in Morita, *Sengokuki rekidai Hosokawashi no kenkyū*, 48–49.

100 Sumiyuki was nineteen and Masamoto forty-two at the time. Sanetaka heard about the assassination the night that it occurred, Eishō 4 (1507) 6.23 (*SK*, vol. 4, pt. 2, 742). For more on the retainers who assisted Sumiyuki, see Morita, *Sengokuki rekidai Hosokawashi no kenkyū*, 44–46.

EPILOGUE

1 See the entry for Eishō 18 (1521) 1.22 in Kanroji Motonaga, *Motonaga-kyō ki*, 292. Mitsunobu's painting projects for and with Motonaga were discussed in chapter 2.

2 Aizawa Masahiko wonders whether this "Mitsunobu" who attended a *renga* session sponsored by Konoe Taneie on 9.21 of 1525 was the artist; see Aizawa, *Tosa Mitsunobu*, 93. Iwasaki Yoshie believes, however, that the reference is indeed to the court painter and that he probably died in 1525; see Iwasaki, "Tosa Mitsunobu no bungei katsudō," 42.

3 Daiei 2 (1522) 1.19, in Kanroji Motonaga, *Motonaga-kyō ki*, 301.

4 For a complete list of Mitsumochi's activities and contemporary references to him, see Kamei, *Hyōshō to shite no bijutsushi*, 274–79.

5 The emperor received a request for scrolls from the shogun Yoshiharu and sent thirteen *ko-e* and then another six. See the entry for Tenbun 4 (1535) 2.29 in *GoNara Tennō shinki*, cited by Yoshida Yūji, *Tosa Mitsunobu*, 102.

6 Kamei, *Hyōshō to shite no bijutsushi*, 66.

7 Ibid.

8 The portrait was probably made for the twenty-fifth death anniversary of Shōhaku, and thus while Mitsumochi was living in Sakai; see Miyajima Shin'ichi, *Tosa Mitsunobu to Tosa-ha no keifu*, no. 247 of *Nihon no bijutsu* (Tokyo: Shibundō, 1986), 26–28.

9 Although Edo period commentators claimed a link between the Tosa and Kanō families during Mitsumo-

chi's era, Kamei Wakana refutes this and examines the biases of these texts in "Muromachi jidai no Tosa-ha o meguru gensetsu—jendā no shiten kara no bunseki," *Kenkyū nenpō,* no. 43 (Gakushūin Daigaku Bungakubu) (1997): 1–20.

10 For the text, see *Kazashi no himegimi*, ed. Ichiko Teiji, in pt. 1 of *Muromachi monogatarishū*, vol. 54 of *Shin Nihon koten bungaku taikei*, ed. Ichiko Teiji et al. (Tokyo: Iwanami Shoten, 1989), 291–309.

11 McCormick, "Genji no ma o nozoku"; McCormick, "Monochromatic Genji."

12 Yasuhara Makoto, *"Ōgi no sōshi" no kenkyū: Asobi no geibun* (Tokyo: Perikansha, 2003).

13 Daiei 5 (1525) 10.14 and 15 (*SK*, vol. 6, pt. 2, 55). Wakatsuki was a retainer of Hosokawa Takakuni (1484–1531), who had taken control of the military government, along with Ōuchi Yoshitaka, in 1508.

14 Sōchō mentions Wakatsuki's poetic ambitions after recounting his tragic, though heroic, death in battle in 1526; see Sōchō, *The Journal of Sōchō*, trans. and annotated by H. Mack Horton (Stanford: Stanford University Press, 2002), 131–32.

15 Tomoko Sakomura demonstrates how a poetry-centered tale called *The Forty-two Debates* (*Shijūni no monoarasoi*), often illustrated in the small format, could function as a didactic text for young people, specifically for the sons and daughters of the Yamashina and Hosokawa families; she also argues for the pervasiveness of *waka* in the visual culture of the period. See Sakomura, "Pictured Words and Codified Seasons: Visualizations of Waka Poetry in Late Sixteenth and Early Seventeenth Century Japan" (PhD diss., Columbia University, 2007).

APPENDIX. TRANSLATION

1 *Kokinshū,* no. 553, by Ono no Komachi.

2 The Kamo Priestess (*sai'in*) refers to an imperial princess sent to serve at the Kamo Shrine. The last imperial princess to do so was the third daughter of Emperor GoToba (1180–1239), indicating that the story is probably set sometime before the Kamakura period.

3 The phrase "hundred charms" (*mono no kobi*) derives from a description of Yang Kuei Fei in the "Song of Everlasting Sorrow"; see Skord, *Tales of Tears and Laughter*, 77n3.

4 Shikishi's poem is found in the *New Collection of Ancient and Modern Poems* (*Shinkokinshū*), Love Poems 2, poem 1124. Skord translates it as follows: "Lamenting for the one/I would see even in a dream/my sleeves of evening/drenched with tears" (*Yume nite mo/miyuran mono wa/nagekitsutsu/uchinuru yoi no/sode no keshiki wa*); see Skord, *Tales of Tears and Laughter*, 78n6.

5 Fujiwara Norimichi (999–1025) was the son of Fujiwara Michinaga (966–1027).

6 Ko Shikibu no Naishi (999–1025) was the daughter of Izumi Shikibu (b. 976?).

7 This is an allusion to a poem from the *Collection of Ancient and Modern Poems* (*Kokinshū*), Love Poems 1, poem 516: "Night after night/I shift my pillow around/how did I sleep that night/that I saw him in my dreams?" (*Yoi yoi ni/makura sadamen/kata mo nashi/ika ni neshi yo ka/yume ni mienu*); see Skord,*Tales of Tears and Laughter*, 78n9.

8 This quotation from chapter 25 of *The Lotus Sutra* concerns the limitless compassion of the bodhisattva Kannon.

9 *Fugan no ya* is a legendary spot in China where Emperor Yin was led by a wise man in a dream to find his loyal minister who helped him save the realm; see Skord, *Tales of Tears and Laughter*, 78n16.

10 I have translated the phrase *fune o mōke haberu tameshi* as "another who readied a boat," which Skord omits. The line clarifies the reference to the Akashi lay priest (Akashi nyūdō) from *The Tale of Genji*, who fatefully sails from Akashi to Suma and meets Genji, his future son-in-law.

11 This is an allusion to a poem written on her sickbed by Ko Shikibu no Naishi: "What shall I do?/I know not where I go/along the path I walk/before my parents" (*Ika ni sen/ikubeki kata mo omoezu/oya ni sakidatsu/michi oo shiraneba*). In *Kokon chōmonjū*, vol. 5. See Skord, *Tales of Tears of and Laughter*, 79n24.

12 Adapted slightly from Skord, *Tales of Tears and Laughter*, 77, to include the Wisteria Leaves (*Fuji no uraba*) phrase.

13 The tale begins with the phrase *ima wa mukashi*, the conventional opening for every tale in the *Konjaku monogatari shū*. See Marian Ury's translation of the *Konjaku monogatari shū* in *Tales of Time Now Past*.

14 The word for "humble" (*ayashi*) can also mean "mysterious," which here might have helped set the stage for the strange events about to unfold.

15 Literally "holy man" (*hijiri*), this term could be an epithet for an itinerant monk, but here it seems to have been used as a generic term for a monk without priestly rank.

16 A "sutra copied according to the Law" (*nyohō kyō*) was a term used exclusively for *The Lotus Sutra*.

17 *Jūrasetsu* refers to the ten female daughters of demons mentioned in chapter 26 of *The Lotus Sutra*, as discussed in chapter 4 of this study.

18 The *jisshu kuyō*, a ceremony of "ten kinds of offerings" to the Buddha, commemorates the end of a copying of *The Lotus Sutra*, so that the sutra itself is sometimes referred to as the *jisshu kuyō no kyō*; see *Sōgō Bukkyō daijiten*, vol. 2 (Hōzōkan, 1987), 1124. The ten offerings mentioned in *The Lotus Sutra* consist of flowers (*ke*), incense (*kō*), ornaments (*yōraku*), powdered incense (*makkō*), unguent (*zukō*), burning of incense (*shōkō*), canopies and banners (*sōgai dōban*), clothes (*ebuku*), dancing and music (*gigaku*), and the joining of one's hands in worship (*gasshō*); see Inagaki, *Dictionary of Japanese Buddhist Terms*, 159.

19 The word for pleasure here is *keraku*, which by using the same characters as *Kerakuten*, or "Creating Enjoyment Heaven," may refer to this heaven in the realm of desire (*yokkai*) where every pleasure is attainable at will.

20 *Akudō* is the human realm of the endless cycle of life and death.

21 Twenty meters; one *jō* is equivalent to three meters.

22 Ninety centimeters.

23 *Muen* can mean "unrelated to the Buddha," or "objectless."

24 The story is the ninth in fascicle 19 of the *Konjaku monogatari shū*. A previous translation is by Michael Kelsey in "Didactics in Art," 338–46. I adapted his phrasing for two of the poems that appear toward the end of the tale.

25 Emperor Murakami reigned from 946 to 967.

26 Fujiwara Moromasa (920–69), also known as Morotada, became minister of the left in 969, after the exile to Kyūshū of Minamoto Taka'akira, who previously held the position. Legend had it that Morotada masterminded Taka'akira's exile, and that Morotada's own death several months after his appointment as minister of the left was the result of retribution by Taka'akira's vengeful spirit.

27 Fujiwara Tadahira (880–949) became regent in 941. He was the great-grandfather of Fujiwara Michinaga and known as the founding ancestor of the main Fujiwara line.

28 This may refer to Hōshi (d. 967), Fujiwara Moromasa's daughter who became a junior consort (*nyōgo*) to Emperor Murakami in 958. She was known as the Sen'yōden consort and was famous for her beauty.

29 Adapted from Kelsey's translation of the poem in "Didactics in Art," 341.

30 Adapted from Kelsey's translation of the poem in ibid., 344.

31 According to Buddhist funerary practices, offerings (*tsuizen*) were to be made every seven days for a total of forty-nine days after a person's death.

BIBLIOGRAPHY

Abe Akio, Akiyama Ken, Imai Gen'e, and Suzuki Hideo, eds. *Genji monogatari.* 6 vols. Vols. 20–25 of *Shinpen Nihon koten bungaku zenshū.* Tokyo: Shōgakukan, 1994–98.

Abe Yoshitomi. "Utatane sōshi: Denpon to sono chūkai hotei." *Gobun* (Nihon Daigaku) 73 (1989): 13–20.

———. "Utatane sōshi ron: Fu, kōhon narabi ni chūkai, kō." *Kokubungaku kenkyū shiryōkan kiyō* 8 (1982): 85–139.

Aizawa Masahiko. "Ninagawa Chikamoto zō kamigata ni tsuite—Tosa Mitsunobu kankei no shōzōga shiryō." *Museum* 444 (1988): 4–10.

———. *Tosa Mitsunobu.* Vol. 2 of *Shinchō Nihon bijutsu bunkō.* Tokyo: Shinchōsha, 1998.

Akiyama Terukazu. "Amewakahiko sōshi emaki o meguru shomondai: Jōkan zuyō no shinshutsu o ki ni." *Kokka* 985 (1975): 9–25.

———. *Emakimono.* Tokyo: Shōgakukan, 1968.

———. "Emaki no hasshō to tenkai." In *Nihon emakimono no kenkyū,* vol. 1, 1–68. Tokyo: Chūō Kōron Bijutsu Shuppan, 2000.

———. *Genji-e. Nihon no bijutsu,* no. 119. Tokyo: Shibundō, 1976.

———. *Japanese Painting.* Geneva: Skira, 1972.

———. "New Buddhist Sects and *Emakimono* (Hand-Scroll Painting) in the Kamakura Period," *Acta Asiatica* 20 (1971): 58–76.

———. *Ōchō kaiga no tanjō: Genji monogatari o megutte.* Tokyo: Chūō Kōronsha, 1968.

Ambros, Barbara. "Liminal Journeys: Pilgrimages of Noblewomen in Mid-Heian Japan." *Japanese Journal of Religious Studies* 24, nos. 3–4 (1997): 301–45.

Amino Yoshihiko et al., eds. *Ama no hashi, chi no hashi.* Vol. 2 of *Ima wa mukashi mukashi wa ima.* Tokyo: Fukuinkan Shoten, 1991.

Araki, James T. "*Otogi-zōshi* and *Nara e-hon*: A Field of Study in Flux." *Monumenta Nipponica* 36, no. 1 (Spring 1981): 1–20.

Ariès, Philippe. *Centuries of Childhood: A Social History of Family Life*. Trans. Robert Baldick. New York: Random House, 1962.

Asakura Hisashi. *Juzan Eisō, Shūzan Tōki: Zenrin no kizokuka no yōsō*. Osaka: Seibundō, 1990.

Asami Kazuhiko, ed. *Jikkinshō*. Vol. 51 of *Shinpen Nihon koten bungaku zenshū*. Tokyo: Shōgakukan, 1997.

Ashikaga kiseiki. In vol. 13 of *Kaitei shiseki shūran*, ed. Kondō Heijō and Kondō Keizō. Tokyo: Kondō Kappanjo, 1902.

Azuma Kagami. Vols. 32–33 of *Shintei zōho Kokushi taikei*, ed. Kuroita Katsumi. Tokyo: Yoshikawa Kōbunkan, 1932–33.

Berry, Mary Elizabeth. *The Culture of Civil War in Kyoto*. Berkeley and Los Angeles: University of California Press, 1994.

———. *Japan in Print: Information and Nation in the Early Modern Period*. Berkeley and Los Angeles: University of California Press, 2006.

Blacker, Carmen. "The Divine Boy in Japanese Buddhism." *Asian Folklore Studies* 22 (1963): 77–88.

———. "The Snake Woman in Japanese Myth and Legend." In *Collected Writings of Carmen Blacker*, 40–50. Tokyo: Edition Synapse; Richmond, Surrey: Japan Library, 2000. First published in J. R. Porter and W. M. S. Russell, eds., *Animals in Folklore* (1978)

Bowring, Richard. "Preparing for the Pure Land in Late Tenth-Century Japan." *Japanese Journal of Religious Studies* 25, nos. 3–4 (1998): 221–57.

Brock, Karen L. "The Case of the Missing Scroll: A History and Reconstruction of Tales of Gishō and Gangyō." *Archives of Asian Art* 41 (1988): 6–31.

———. "Chinese Maiden, Silla Monk: Zenmyō and Her Thirteenth-Century Japanese Audience." In *Flowering in the Shadows: Women in the History of Chinese and Japanese Painting*, ed. Marsha Weidner, 185–218. Honolulu: University of Hawaii Press, 1990.

———. "The Making and Remaking of *Miraculous Origins of Mt. Shigi*." *Archives of Asian Art* 45 (1992): 42–71.

———. "The Shogun's 'Painting Match.'" *Monumenta Nipponica* 50, no. 4 (1995): 433–84.

———. "*Tales of Gishō and Gangyō:* Editor, Artist and Audience in Japanese Picture Scrolls." PhD diss., Princeton University, 1984.

Butler, Lee. *Emperor and Aristocracy in Japan, 1467–1680*. Cambridge, MA: Harvard University Asia Center, distributed by Harvard University Press, 2002.

Carter, Steven D., ed. *Literary Patronage in Late Medieval Japan*. Ann Arbor: Center for Japanese Studies, University of Michigan, 1993.

———. *Regent Redux: A Life of the Statesman-Scholar Ichijō Kaneyoshi*. Michigan Monograph Series in Japanese Studies, no. 16. Ann Arbor: Center for Japanese Studies, University of Michigan, 1996.

———. *The Road to Komatsubara: A Classical Reading of the Renga Hyakuin*. Cambridge, MA: Harvard University Press, 1987.

Chen, Pao-chen. "The Goddess of the Lo River: A Study of Early Chinese Narrative Handscrolls." PhD diss., Princeton University, 1987.

Childs, Margaret H. "Chigo Monogatari: Love Stories or Buddhist Sermons?" *Monumenta Nipponica* 35, no. 2 (1980): 127–51.

———. *Rethinking Sorrow: Revelatory Tales of Late Medieval Japan*. Ann Arbor: Center for Japanese Studies, University of Michigan, 1991.

———, trans. "The Story of Kannon's Manifestation as a Youth." In *Partings at Dawn: An Anthology of Japanese Gay Literature*, ed. Stephen D. Miller, 31–35. San Francisco: Sunshine Gay Press, 1996.

Chino Kaori. "Hidakagawa sōshi emaki ni miru dentō to sōzō." *Kinko sōsho* 8 (Tokugawa Reimeikai) (1981): 831–69.

Chino Kaori and Nishi Kazuo. *Fikushon to shite no kaiga: Bijutsushi no me, kenchikushi no me*. Tokyo: Perikansha, 1991.

Chino Kaori, Ikeda Shinobu, and Kamei Wakana. "Hābādo Daigaku Bijutsukan zō 'Genji monogatari gajō' o meguru shomondai." *Kokka* 1222 (August 1997): 54–85.

Chūsei Kuge Nikki Kenkyūkai, ed. *Sengokuki kuge shakai no shoyōsō*. Vol. 2 of *Nihon shi kenkyū sōkan*. Osaka: Izumi Shoin, 1992.

Collcutt, Martin. *Five Mountains: The Rinzai Zen Monastic Institution in Medieval Japan*. Harvard East Asian Monographs, no. 85. Cambridge, MA: Harvard University Press, 1981.

Commons, Anne E. "The Canonization of Hitomaro: Paradigm of the Poet as God." PhD diss., Columbia University, 2003.

Cranston, Edwin A. *Grasses of Remembrance*, pt. B. Vol. 2 of *A Waka Anthology*. Stanford: Stanford University Press, 2006.

Dai Nihon shiryō. Ed. Tōkyō Daigaku. Tokyo: Tōkyō Daigaku, 1901–.

Daijōin jisha zōjiki. Ed. Tsuji Zennosuke. Vols. 26–37 of *Zōho zoku shiryō taisei*, ed. Takeuchi Rizō. Kyoto: Rinsen Shoten, 1978.

D'Etcheverry, Charo. "Cannibalizing Memory: Teika, Sanetaka, and Fujioka's Sagoromo." In vol. 1 of *Issues of Canonicity and Canon Formation in Japanese Literary Studies*, ed. Stephen D. Miller, 259–68. West Lafayette, IN: Association for Japanese Literary Studies, Purdue University, 2000.

———. *Love after the "Tale of Genji": Rewriting the World of the Shining Prince*. Cambridge, MA: Harvard University Press, 2007.

Doi Tadao et al., eds. *Hōyaku Nippo jisho*. Tokyo: Iwanami Shoten, 1980.

Dykstra, Yoshiko Kurata. "Jizō the Most Merciful, Tales from Jizō Bosatsu Reigenki." *Monumenta Nipponica* 33, no. 2 (1978): 179–200.

———. *Miraculous Tales of the Lotus Sutra from Ancient Japan*. Honolulu: University of Hawaii Press, 1987.

Ellwood, Robert S. *The Feast of Kingship: Accession Ceremonies in Ancient Japan*. Tokyo: Sophia University, 1973.

Enpō dentōroku. In vol. 69 of *Dai Nihon bukkyō zensho, Shidenbu*, ed. Suzuki Gakujutsu Zaidan. Reprint, Tokyo: Kankō Suzuki Gakujutsu Zaidan, 1972.

Etō Yasusada. *Sōgi no kenkyū*. Tokyo: Kazama Shobō, 1967.

Fabricand-Person, Nicole. "Demonic Female Guardians of the Faith: The Fugen Jūrasetsunyo Iconography in Japanese Buddhist Art." In *Engendering Faith: Women and Buddhism in Premodern Japan*, ed. Barbara Ruch, 343–82. Ann Arbor: Center for Japanese Studies, University of Michigan, 2002.

Faure, Bernard. *The Power of Denial: Buddhism, Purity, and Gender*. Princeton: Princeton University Press, 2003.

Fontein, Jan. "Kibi's Adventures in China: Facts, Fiction, and Their Meaning." *Bulletin of the Museum of Fine Arts* 66 (1968): 49–68.

Fujiwara Shigeo. "'Kariya' shōkō: Matsu no ha o yane ni fuku koto." In *Emaki ni chūsei o yomu*, ed. Fujiwara Yoshiaki and Gomi Fumihiko, 101–45. Tokyo: Yoshikawa Kōbunkan, 1995.

———. "'Daijōin jisha zōjiki' ni kisareta 'tenka edokoro.'" *Tokyo daigaku shiryō hensanjo fuzoku gazō shiryō kaiseki sentā tsūshin*, no. 22 (2003): 2–5.

Fukutō Sanae and Kojima Naoko, eds. *Seiiku girei no rekishi to bunka: Kodomo to jendā*. Tokyo: Shinwasha, 2003.

Fushimi Sadafusa (1372–1456). *Kanmon gyoki*. 2 vols. In *Zoku gunsho ruijū hoi* 2. Ed. Hanawa Hokiichi and Ōta Tōshirō. Rev. ed. Tokyo: Zoku Gunsho Ruijū Kanseikai, 1999–2000.

Geddes, John Van Ward. "A Partial Translation and Study of the 'Jikkinshō.'" PhD diss., Washington University, St. Louis, 1976.

Gorai Shigeru, ed. *Kinki reizan to shugendō*. Vol. 11 of *Sangaku shūkyō shi kenkyū sōsho*. Tokyo: Meicho Shuppan, 1978.

———. "Tsukiminedera engi emaki to sangaku shūkyō." In *Shinshū Nihon emakimono zenshū*, ed. Shimada Shūjirō, suppl. vol. 1, 37–42. Tokyo: Kadokawa Shoten, 1980.

Gotō Michiko. "'Ie' ni okeru josei no nichijō to yakuwari—chūsei kōki no kaku kaisō o megutte." In *Onna to otoko no jikū—Nihon joseishi saikō*, vol. 3 of *Onna to otoko no ran—chūsei*, ed. Okuno Haruko. Tokyo: Fujiwara Shoten, 1996.

Groner, Paul. "The *Lotus Sutra* and Saichō's Interpretation of the Realization of Buddhahood with This Very Body." In *The Lotus Sutra in Japanese Culture*, ed. George Tanabe and Willa Tanabe, 53–74. Honolulu: University of Hawaii Press, 1989.

Gunsho ruijū. Ed. Hanawa Hokiichi (1746–1821). 20 vols. Tokyo: Keizai Zasshisha, 1893–94.

Gunsho ruijū. Ed. Hanawa Hokiichi (1746–1821). 29 vols. Tokyo: Zoku Gunsho Ruijū Kanseikai, 1959–60.

Guth, Christine M. E. "Hasegawa's Fairy Tales: Toying with Japan." *Res: Anthropology and Aesthetics* 53/54 (2008): 266–81.

Guy-Bray, Stephen. *Homoerotic Space: The Poetics of Loss in Renaissance Literature*. Toronto: University of Toronto Press, 2002.

Haga Kōshirō. "Chūsei makki ni okeru Sanjōnishike no keizaiteki kiban to sono hōkai." *Nihon gakushiin kiyō* 13, no. 1 (1955): 23–63.

———. *Higashiyama bunka no kenkyū*. Tokyo: Kawade Shobō, 1945.

———. *Sanjōnishi Sanetaka. Jinbutsu soshō*. Tokyo: Yoshikawa Kōbunkan, 1960.

Hanjūzanmai'in ki. In vol. 18 of *Gunsho ruijū*. Tokyo: Gunsho Ruijū Kanseikai, 1932.

Hara Katsurō. *Higashiyama jidai ni okeru ichi shinshin no seikatsu*. 6th ed. Tokyo: Kōdansha Gakujutsu Bunko, 1994.

Harrison, James A., ed. *The Complete Works of Edgar Allen Poe*. New York: AMS Press, 1965.

Hashimoto Naoki. "Nara ehon 'Suzuriwari' to Shōkū Shōnin." *Senriyama bungaku ronshū,* March 1982, 1–23.

Hayashi Masahiko. "Chūsei ni okeru Shōkū Shōnin setsuwa ni tsuite." *Chūsei bungaku* 17 (1972): 8–14.

Hayashiya Tatsusaburō. *Nairan no naka no kizoku: Nanbokuchō ki "Entairyaku" no sekai.* Tokyo: Kadokawa Shoten, 1975.

Hirota Osamu. "Genji monogatari ni okeru yōshiki to shite no kaimami." In *Kodai bungaku no yōshiki to kinō,* ed. Tsuchihashi Yutaka. Tokyo: Ōfūsha, 1988.

Honchō kōsōden. 2 vols. In *Dai Nihon bunko, Bukkyō hen,* ed. Wada Toshihiko. Tokyo: Shun'yōdō, 1935.

Horton, H. Mack. "Portrait of a Medieval Japanese Marriage: The Domestic Life of Sanjōnishi Sanetaka and His Wife." In "In Memory of Marian Ury." Special issue, *Japanese Language and Literature* 37, no. 2 (2003): 130–54.

———. "Sanjōnishi Sanetaka." In *Medieval Japanese Writers,* ed. Steven D. Carter, 247–60. Dictionary of Literary Biography, vol. 23. Detroit: Gale Group, 1999.

———. *Song in an Age of Discord: "The Journal of Sōchō" and Poetic Life in Late Medieval Japan.* Stanford: Stanford University Press, 2002.

Hosomi Sueo. *Tanba no shōen.* Tokyo: Meicho Shuppan, 1980.

Hurvitz, Leon, trans. *Scripture of the Lotus Blossom of the Fine Dharma.* New York: Columbia University Press, 1976.

Hyōgo Kenritsu Rekishi Hakubutsukan, ed. *Shoshazan Engyōji.* Himeji-shi: Hyōgo Kenritsu Rekishi Hakubutsukan, 1986.

———, ed. *Shoshazan Engyōji.* Himeji-shi: Hyōgo Kenritsu Rekishi Hakubutsukan sōgō chōsa hōkokusho, 1988.

Ichiko Teiji. *Chūsei shōsetsu no kenkyū.* Tokyo: Tokyo Daigaku Shuppankai, 1955.

———. *Chūsei shōsetsu to sono shūhen.* Tokyo: Tokyo Daigaku Shuppankai, 1981.

———, ed. *Mikan chūsei shōsetsu.* Vol. 3. Koten bunko, no. 53. Tokyo: Koten Bunko, 1951.

Ichiko Teiji and Noma Kōshin, eds. *Kanshō Nihon koten bungaku.* Vol. 26. Tokyo: Kadokawa Shoten, 1976.

Ichiko Teiji et al., eds. *Chūsei ōchō monogatari zenshū.* Tokyo: Kasama Shoin, 1995–.

Ienaga Junji. "Horikoshi kubōfu metsubō no saikentō." *Sengoku shi kenkyū* 27 (1994): 1–10.

Ienaga Saburō. "Kanazawa Bunko-bon *Nenbutsu ōjōden* kō." In *Chūsei Nihon bukkyō shisōshi kenkyū.* Rev. and enlarged ed. Kyoto: Hōzōkan, 1976.

Ikeda Hiroshi, ed., *Chūsei kinsei dōkashū.* Koten bunko no. 180. Tokyo: Koten Bunko, 1962.

Ikeda Shinobu. "Heian jidai monogatari-e no ichi kōsatsu—'onna-e' kei monogatari-e no seiritsu to tenkai." *Tetsugaku kaishi,* no. 9 (Gakushuin Daigaku Tetsugakkaihen) (1985): 37–61.

———. "Heian jidai monogatari kaiga no hōhō—monogatari o yobikomu kaiga no dentō o kangaeru." In *ōchō emaki to sōshoku kyō,* vol. 8 of *Nihon bijutsu zenshū,* ed. Nakano Masaki, Hirata Yūtaka, and Sano Midori. Tokyo: Kodansha, 1990.

Imai Gen'e. "Kodai shōsetsu sōsakujō no ichi shuhō— kaimami ni tsuite." *Kokugo to kokubungaku* 25, no. 3 (1948): 26–43.

Imanishi, Junko. "The Geppōji-Engi Scrolls in the Freer Gallery of Art." Master's thesis, Columbia University, 1981.

Imatani Akira. "Akamatsu Masanori kōshitsu, Dōshōin-ni Hosokawashi no kenkyū: Chūsei ni okeru josei kenryokusha no keifu." *Yokohama Shiritsu Daigaku ronsō: Jinbun kagaku keiretsu* 46, nos. 1–3 (1995): 299–326.

Inaba Masamaru, ed. *Rennyo Shōnin Gyōjitsu.* Kyoto: Hōzōkan, 1948.

Inagaki Hisao. *A Dictionary of Japanese Buddhist Terms, Based on References in Japanese Literature.* Union City, CA: Heian International, 1989.

Inoue Mitsusada and Ōsone Shōsuke, eds. *Ōjōden, Hokkegenki.* Vol. 7 of *Nihon shisō taikei.* Tokyo: Iwanami Shoten, 1974.

Inryōken nichiroku. See Kikei Shinzui.

Ishikawa Tōru, ed. *Miryoku no Nara ehon emaki.* Tokyo: Miyai Shoten, 2006.

———. *Nara ehon, emaki no seisei.* Tokyo: Miyai Shoten, 2003.

Ishizuka Kazuo. "Takamatsunomiya goshozō 'Utatane sōshi.'" In *Chūsei bungaku: Shiryō to ronkō,* ed. Ijichi Tetsuo, vol. 109 of *Kasama sōsho.* Tokyo: Kasama Shoin, 1978.

Itakura Masa'aki. "Chōu dai 'Geisan zō' (Taipei Kokyū Hakubutsuin) o meguru shomondai." *Bijutsushi ronsō* 17 (2001): 159–85.

Itō Kei. "'Kana kyōkun' kō—Muromachi jidai joryū bungaku ni karamete." *Chūsei bungaku* 16 (1971): 6–11.

———. "Kana kyōkun, Sōgi tanka nōto 1." *Wakashi kenkyūkai kaihō* 38 (1970): 14–17.

———, ed. *Saishōsō*. In *Chūsei waka shū Muromachi hen*, vol. 47 of *Shin Nihon koten bungaku taikei*, ed. Itō Kei et al., 417–70. Tokyo: Iwanami Shoten, 1990.

———. "Sanjōnishi Sanetaka to waka, sono san." *Kokubungaku kenkyū* 35 (1966): 69–83.

Itō Yūko. *Fuji no koromo monogatari emaki* (*Yūjo monogatari emaki*) *ei'in, honkoku, kenkyū*. *Kasama sōsho*, vol. 296. Tokyo: Kasama Shoin, 1996.

Iwahashi Koyata. "Tosa Mitsunobu no ichi isaku: GoEn'yū tennō shin'ei." *Bukkyō bijutsu* 16 (1930): 12–19.

Iwama Kaoru. "Genji-e seisaku ni miru kōdinētā to eshi." *Kyōto Shiritsu Geijutsu Daigaku bijutsu gakubu kenkyū kiyō* 34 (1989): 53–71.

Iwasaki Yoshie. "Muormachi-ki no fūzoku emaki—'Sanjūniban' 'Shichijūichiban' no seiritsu, kōsei, eishatachi." *Kobijutsu* 74 (1985): 50–70.

———. "Tosa Mitsunobu no bungei katsudō: Yōmei bunko zō 'Sanjūsshu' ka to renga." *Gobun* (Osaka Daigaku) 47 (1986): 34–46.

Joseishi sōgō kenkyūkai, eds. *Nihon josei shi*, vol. 2 *Chūsei* 2. Tokyo: Tokyo Daigaku Shuppankai, 1982.

Kadokawa Nihon Chimei Daijiten Hensan Iinkai. *Kadokawa Nihon chimei daijiten*. Vol. 15, *Niigata-ken*. Tokyo: Kadokawa Shoten, 1989.

Kajitani Ryōji. "Heike nōkyō zakkan." *Rokuon zasshū* (Bulletin of the Nara National Museum) 2, no. 3 (2001): 73–94.

Kamei Wakana. *Hyōshō to shite no bijutsushi: Muromachi Shōgun Ashikaga Yoshiharu to Tosa Mitsumochi no kaiga*. Kunitachi-shi: Brücke, 2003.

———. "'Kuwanomidera engi emaki' kenkyū." *Kokka* 1193 (1995): 3–21.

———. "Muromachi jidai no Tosa-ha o meguru gensetsu—jendā no shiten kara no bunseki." *Kenkyū nenpō*, no. 43 (Gakushūin Daigaku Bungakubu) (1997): 1–20.

Kamens, Edward. "Dragon-Girl, Maidenflower, Buddha: The Transformation of a Waka Topos, 'The Five Obstructions.'" *Harvard Journal of Asiatic Studies* 53, no. 2 (1993): 389–442.

———. *The Three Jewels: A Study and Translation of Minamoto Tamenori's "Sanbōe."* Michigan Monograph Series in Japanese Studies, no. 2. Ann Arbor: Center for Japanese Studies, University of Michigan, 1988.

Kaneko Kinjirō. "Sōgi and the Imperial House." Trans. H. Mack Horton. In *Literary Patronage in Late Medieval Japan*, ed. Steven D. Carter, 63–93. Ann Arbor: Center for Japanese Studies, University of Michigan, 1993.

Kanō Einō (1631–97). *Honchō gashi*. Annotated by Kasai Masa'aki, Sasaki Susumu, and Takei Akio. In *Yakuchū Honchō gashi*. Kyoto: Dōbōsha Shuppan, 1985.

Kanō Hiroyuki. "Tosa Mitsunobu hitsu 'Tsuru sōshi' ni tsuite." *Kyoto Kokuritsu Hakubutsukan Gakusō* 5 (1983): 85–110.

Kanroji Chikanaga (1424–1500). *Chikanaga-kyō ki 1–3*. Vols. 41–43 of *Zōho shiryō taisei*, ed. Zōho Shiryō Taisei Keigyōkai. Kyoto: Rinsen Shoten, 1965.

———. *Chikanaga-kyō ki hoi*. Vol. 44 of *Zōho shiryō taisei*, ed. Zōho Shiryō Taisei Keigyōkai. Kyoto: Rinsen Shoten, 1965.

Kanroji Motonaga (1457–1527). *Motonaga-kyō ki*. In *Shiryō sanshū*, ed. Haga Kōshirō. Tokyo: Zoku Gunsho Ruijū Kanseikai, 1973.

Kasashima Tadayuki. "Hābādo Daigaku Bijutsukan zō 'Genji monogatari gajō' kotobagaki no shofū to seisaku nendai." *Kokka* 1222 (1997): 53.

Katagiri Yayoi. "Hakubyō Genji monogatari emaki ni okeru e to kotoba: Supensā-bon o chūshin ni." *Firokaria* 6 (1989): 88–114.

———. "Tosa-ha to ryōshi sōshoku—Daiōji-zō 'Genji monogatari nukigaki dankan' o megutte." *Museum* 465 (1989): 4–14.

Kataoka Yoshimichi, ed. *Saikyōji no rekishi to jihō*. Ōtsu: Saikyōji, 1989.

Katō Osamu. *"Chigo" to "warawa" no seikatsu shi: Nihon no chūko no kodomotachi*. Tokyo: Keiō Tsūshin, 1994.

Katsuki, Takashi. "The Origin of the Founding of the Geppōji (Geppōji konryū shugyō engi)." *Oriental Art* 16, no. 3 (1970): 237–51.

Katsumata Shizuo. "Tsūshi jūgo-jūroku seiki no Nihon: Sengoku no sōran." In *Chūsei*, vol. 4, 3–57. Vol. 10 of *Iwanami kōza Nihon tsūshi*. Tokyo: Iwanami Shoten, 1994.

Katz, Paul R. *Images of the Immortal: The Cult of Lü Dongbin at the Palace of Eternal Joy*. Honolulu: University of Hawaii Press, 1999.

Kavanaugh, Frederick. "An Errant Priest: *Sasayaki Take*." *Monumenta Nipponica* 51, no. 2 (1996): 219–44.

Kawakami Mitsugu. *Nihon chūsei jūtaku no kenkyū*. Tokyo: Bokusui Shobō, 1967.

Kawazoe Fusae. *Sei to bunka no Genji monogatari—kaku onna no tanjō*. Tokyo: Chikuma Shobō, 1998.

Kazashi no himegimi. Ed. Ichiko Teiji. In pt. 1 of *Muromachi monogatarishū*, vol. 54 of *Shin Nihon koten bungaku taikei*, ed. Ichiko Teiji et al., 291–309. Tokyo: Iwanami Shoten, 1989.

Keene, Donald. *Seeds in the Heart: Japanese Literature from Earliest Times to the Late Sixteenth Century*. New York: Columbia University Press, 1999.

Kelsey, William Michael. "Didactics in Art: The Literary Structure of *Konjaku Monogatari-shū*." PhD diss., Indiana University, 1976.

———. "*Konjaku Monogatari-shū*: Toward an Understanding of Its Literary Qualities." *Monumenta Nipponica* 30 (1975): 121–50.

Khan, Robert Omar. "'Ariake no Wakare': Genre, Gender, and Genealogy in a Late Twelfth-Century Monogatari." PhD diss., University of British Columbia, 1998.

Kikei Shinzui (d. 1469) and Kisen Shūshō (d. 1493). *Inryōken nichiroku*. Ed. Tamamura Takeji and Katsuno Ryūshin. 5 vols. Kyoto: Shiseki Kankōkai, 1953–54.

Kimura Masanori, Shirahata Yoshi, Tsuchida Naoshige, et al., eds. *Kagerō nikki Makura no sōshi*. Vol. 6 of *Zusetsu Nihon no koten*. Tokyo: Shūeisha, 1979.

Kimura Tokuei, ed. *Tosa monjo kaisetsu*. Tokyo: Iwai Kamejirō, 1935.

Kitano Shake nikki. Ed. Takeuchi Hideo and Yamada Yūji. 7 vols. In *Shiryō sanshū*. Tokyo: Zoku Gunsho Ruijū Kanseikai, 1972–2001.

Kline, Daniel T., ed. *Medieval Literature for Children*. New York and London: Routledge, 2003.

Kobayashi Kayoko. "Takafusa to iu imēji: 'Heike kindachi sōshi' to 'Takafusa kyō tsuya kotoba emaki.'" *Dōshisha kokubungaku* 56 (2002): 28–42.

Kobayashi Tadao. "Kinko shōsetsu Suzuriwari no seiritsu ni kansuru ichi kōsatsu." *Kokugo bungaku* 25 (1956): 28–35.

Kōbō Daishi gyōjō emaki no sekai: Eien e no hishō. Kyoto: Tōji Hōbutsukan, 2000.

Kokushi Daijiten Henshū Iinkai, ed. *Kokushi daijiten*. 15 vols. Tokyo: Yoshikawa Kōbunkan, 1979–97.

Komatsu Shigemi, ed. *Gosannen Kassen Ekotoba*. Vol. 15 of *Nihon emaki taisei*. Tokyo: Chūō Kōronsha, 1977.

———, ed. *Kohitsu to emaki*. Vol. 4 of *Kohitsugaku sōrin*. Tokyo: Yagi Shoten, 1994.

———, ed. *Nayotake monogatari emaki, Naomoto mōshibumi ekotoba*. Vol. 20 of *Nihon emaki taisei*. Tokyo: Chūō Kōronsha, 1978.

———. *Nenjū gyōji emaki*. Vol. 8 of *Nihon emaki taisei*, ed. Komatsu Shigemi. Tokyo: Chūō Kōronsha, 1977.

———, ed. *Nihon emaki taisei*. 27 vols. Tokyo: Chūō Kōronsha, 1977–79.

———, ed. *Nihon no emaki*. 20 vols. Tokyo: Chūō Kōronsha, 1987–88.

———. "Ōchō emaki to Goshirakawa-in." In *Genji monogatari emaki, Nezame monogatari emaki*, vol. 1 of *Nihon emaki taisei*, ed. Komatsu Shigemi. Tokyo: Chūō Kōronsha, 1977.

———, ed. *Sumiyoshi monogatari emaki, Ono no yukimi gokō emaki*. Vol. 19 of *Nihon emaki taisei*. Tokyo: Chūō Kōronsha, 1978.

———, ed. *Zoku Nihon emaki taisei*. 20 vols. Tokyo: Chūō Kōronsha, 1981–85.

———, ed. *Zoku Nihon no emaki*. 27 vols. Tokyo: Chūō Kōronsha, 1990–93.

———, ed. *Zoku zoku Nihon emaki taisei*. 8 vols. Tokyo: Chūō Kōronsha, 1993–95.

Konoe Masaie (1444–1505). *Gohōkōin ki*. 4 vols. Vols. 5–8 of *Zoku shiryō taisei*, ed. Takeuchi Rizō. Kyoto: Rinsen Shoten, 1967.

Kornicki, Peter. "Manuscript, Not Print: Scribal Culture in the Edo Period." *Journal of Japanese Studies* 32, no. 1 (2006): 23–52.

Kosugi Keiko and Jacqueline Pigeot, eds. *Yokobue, Suzuriwari*. Koten bunko no. 492. Tokyo: Koten Bunko, 1987.

Kotas, Frederic J. "*Ōjōden:* Accounts of Rebirth in the Pure Land." PhD diss., University of Washington, 1987.

Koyama Satoko. *Gohō dōji shinkō no kenkyū*. Kyoto: Jishōsha Shuppan, 2003.

Kubota Jun et al., eds. *Ima monogatari, Takafusa shū, Tōzai zuihitsu*. In *Chūsei no bungaku*. Tokyo: Miyai Shoten, 1979.

Kugyō bunin. Vols. 53–57 of *Shinchō zōho kokushi taikei*, ed. Kuroita Katsumi. Tokyo: Yoshikawa Kōbunkan, 1936.

Kujō Hisatsune (1468–1530). *Gojigen'in-dono gyoki*. In vol. 2 of *Kujō-ke rekisei kiroku*. In *Zushoryō sōkan*, ed. Kunaichō Shoryōbu. Tokyo: Kunaichō Shoryōbu, 1990.

Kujō Masamoto (1445–1516). *Masamoto-kō tabi hikitsuke*. In vol. 1 of *Nihon shi shiryō sōkan*, ed. Chūsei Kuge Nikki Kenkyūkai. Osaka: Izumi Shoin, 1996.

Kuroda Hideo. *"Emaki" kodomo no tōjō: Chūsei shakai no kodomozō*. In *Rekishi hakubutsukan shirīzu*. Tokyo: Kawade Shobō Shinsha, 1989.

Kuroda Hideo, Chino Kaori, and Tokuda Kazuo. "Otogi zōshi no parareru wārudo." *Kokubungaku* 39, no. 1 (1994): 6–29.

Kurokawa Harumura (1799–1866). *Chitei sōsho yōmoku*. In vol. 9 of *Zoku shiseki shūran*, ed. Kondō Heijō. Tokyo: Kondō Shuppanbu, 1930.

———. *Komonogatari ruijishō*. In *Monogatari sōshi mokuroku zenhen*, ed. Yokoyama Shigeru and Kohashi Raizō. Tokyo: Ōkayama Shoin, 1937.

Kurokawa Mamichi, ed. *Kurokawa Mayori zenshū*. 6 vols. Vols. 27–32 of *Kokusho kankōkai sōsho*. Tokyo: Kokusho Kankōkai, 1910–11.

Kuwayama Kōnen. "Muromachi jidai ni okeru kuge nyōbō no koshō." *Joseishigaku* 6 (1996): 1–12.

Kyoto Shiritsu Geijutsu Daigaku Fuzoku Toshokan, ed. *Shōzō funpon* 1. In vol. 1 of *Tosa ha kaiga shiryō mokuroku*. Kyoto: Kyoto Shiritsu Geijutsu Daigaku Sōritsu Hyakujūnen Kinen Jigyō Jitsugyō Iin Kai, 1990.

Leupp, Gary P. *Male Colors: The Construction of Homosexuality in Tokugawa Japan*. Berkeley and Los Angeles: University of California Press, 1995.

Li, Wai-yee. "Dream Visions of Transcendence in Chinese Literature and Painting." *Asian Art* 3, no. 4 (1990): 53–78.

Lippit, Yukio. "The Birth of Japanese Painting History: Kano Artists, Authors, and Authenticators of the Seventeenth Century." PhD diss., Princeton University, 2003.

———. "Figure and Facture in the Genji Scrolls: Text, Calligraphy, Paper, and Painting." In *Envisioning The Tale of Genji: Media, Gender, and Cultural Production*, ed. Haruo Shirane, 49–80. New York: Columbia University Press, 2008.

Lohafer, Susan. *Reading for Storyness: Preclosure Theory, Empirical Poetics, and Culture in the Short Story*. Baltimore, MD: Johns Hopkins University Press, 2003.

Mabuchi Kazuo, Kunisaki Fumimaro, and Inagaki Taiichi, eds. *Konjaku monogatari shū*. 4 vols. Vols. 35–38 of *Shinpen Nihon koten bungaku zenshū*. Tokyo: Shōgakukan, 1999–2000.

Mabuchi Kazuo, Kunisaki Fumimaro, and Konno Tōru, eds. *Konjaku monogatari shū*. 4 vols. Vols. 21–24 of *Nihon koten bungaku zenshū*. Tokyo: Shōgakukan, 1971–76.

MacDuff, William. "Beautiful Boys in *Nō Drama:* The Idealization of Homoerotic Desire." *Asian Theatre Journal* 13, no. 12 (1996): 248–58.

Manabe Kōsai, ed. *Jizō bosatsu no kenkyū*. Kyoto: Fuzanbō Shoten, 1960.

Manabe Kōsai and Umezu Jiro, eds. *Jizō reigenki ekotobashū*. Koten bunko, no. 118. Tokyo: Koten Bunko, 1957.

Manabe Shunshō. "Kōbō Daishi gyōjō ekotoba no kaigaka." In *Kōōbō Daishi gyōjō ekotoba*, vol. 6 of *Zoku Nihon emaki taisei*, ed. Komatsu Shigemi, 78–109. Tokyo: Chūō Kōronsha, 1983.

Mansai Jugō (1378–1435). *Mansai Jugō nikki*. Kyoto: Rokujō Kappan Seizōjō, 1920.

Marra, Michele. "*Mumyōzōshi*: Introduction and Translation." *Monumenta Nipponica* 39, no. 2 (Summer 1984): 115–45; 39, no. 3 (Autumn 1984): 281–305; 39, no. 4 (Winter 1984): 409–34.

Mashimo Miyako. "'Hanyu no monogatari' ron." In *Nihon bungaku no ei*, ed. Fukuda Akira, 243–70. Tokyo: Miyai Shoten, 1992.

Mass, Jeffrey, ed. *The Origins of Japan's Medieval World: Courtiers, Clerics, Warriors, and Peasants in the Fourteenth Century*. Stanford: Stanford University Press, 1997.

Matsubara Kazuyoshi. "Tawa sōsho 'Yumeji monogatari' honkoku to kaisetsu." *Kokubungakukō* (Hiroshima University) 96 (1982): 44–53.

Matsumoto Ryūshin, ed. *Muromachi jidai monogatari taisei, hoi* 2. Tokyo: Kadokawa Shoten, 1988.

May, Charles E. *Edgar Allan Poe: A Study of the Short Fiction*. Boston: Twayne Publishers, 1991.

———. *The Short Story: The Reality of Artifice*. London: Routledge, 2002. First published in 1995.

McCormick, Melissa. "Genji Goes West: The 1510 *Genji Album* and the Visualization of Court and Capital." *Art Bulletin* 85, no. 1 (March 2003): 54–85.

———. "Genji no ma o nozoku: Hakubyō Genji monogatari emaki to nyōbō no shiza." Trans. Maki Kaneko. In *Genji monogatari wo yomitoku 1: Egakareta Genji monogatari*, ed. Kawazoe Fusae and Mitamura Masako, 101–29. Tokyo: Kanrin Shobō, 2006.

———. "Hābādo bijutsukan zō 'Genji monogatari gajō' to *Sanetakakōki* shosai no 'Genji-e shikishi.'" *Kokka* 1241 (1999): 27–28.

———. "Monochromatic Genji: The *Hakubyō* Tradition and Female Commentarial Culture." In *Envisioning The Tale of Genji: Media, Gender, and Cultural Production*, ed. Haruo Shirane, 101–28. New York: Columbia University Press, 2008.

———. “Tosa Mitsunobu’s *Ko-e:* Forms and Functions of Small-Format Handscrolls in the Muromachi Period (1333–1573).” PhD diss., Princeton University, 2000.

McCullough, William H., and Helen Craig McCullough, trans. *A Tale of Flowering Fortunes*. 2 vols. Stanford: Stanford University Press, 1980.

McCullough, Helen Craig, trans. *The Tale of the Heike*. Stanford: Stanford University Press, 1988.

———, trans. *Tales of Ise*. Stanford: Stanford University Press, 1968.

McKelway, Matthew Philip. *Capitalscapes: Folding Screens and Political Imagination in Late Medieval Kyoto*. Honolulu: University of Hawaii Press, 2006.

Miki Sumito et al., eds. *Uji shūi monogatari, Kohon setsuwashū*. Vol. 42 of *Shin Nihon koten bungaku taikei*. Tokyo: Iwanami Shoten, 1990.

Miller, Stephen D., ed. *Partings at Dawn: An Anthology of Japanese Gay Literature*. San Francisco: Sunshine Gay Press, 1996.

Mills, D. E. *A Collection of Tales from Uji*. Cambridge: Cambridge University Press, 1970.

Mishima, Yukio. *Forbidden Colors*. Trans. Alfred H. Marks. New York: Knopf, 1968.

———. *Kinjiki*. Vol. 5 of *Mishima Yukio zenshū*, ed. Saeki Shōichi et al. Tokyo: Shinchōsha, 1974.

Mitamura Masako and Mitani Kuniaki. *Genji monogatari emaki no nazo o yomitoku*. Tokyo: Kadokawa Shoten, 1998.

Mito Nobue. “Dare ga miteiru kōkei na no ka? Otogi sōshi ni miru katari no shiten.” In *Bijutsushika, ōi ni warau—Kōno Motoaki Sensei no tame no Nihon bijutsushi ronshū*, ed. Kōno Motoaki Sensei Taikan Kinen Ronbunshū Henshū Iinkai, 287–307. Tokyo: Brücke, 2006.

Miya Tsugio. “Ashikaga Yoshihisa shoji ‘Kitsune sōshi emaki’ o megutte.” *Bijutsu kenkyū* 260 (1968): 27–40.

———. “‘Jizōdō sōshi’ ni tsuite.” *Kokka* 851 (1963): 5–25.

———. “Nezumi sōshi emaki.” In *Tenjin engi emaki, Hachiman engi, Amewakahiko sōshi, Nezumi no sōshi, Bakemono sōshi, Utatane sōshi*. Suppl. vol. 2 of *Shinshū Nihon emakimono zenshū*, ed. Shimada Shūjirō, 34–39. Tokyo: Kadokawa Shoten, 1981.

———. “Otogi sōshi emaki: sono gafū to kyōjusha no seikaku.” *Kokubungaku* 22, no. 16 (1982): 74–82.

———. “Otogi-zōshi to Tosa Mitsunobu: Nezumi zōshi emaki kō.” *Bijutsu kenkyū* 313 (1980): 1–18.

———. “Tsukiminedera konryū shugyō engi ni tsuite.” In *Kōbō Daishi den emaki, Yūzū Nenbutsu engi-e, Tsukiminedera konryū shugyō engi*. Suppl. vol. 1 of *Shinshū Nihon emakimono zenshū, bekkan* 1, ed. Shimada Shūjirō, 29–36. Tokyo: Kadokawa Shoten, 1980.

———. “Tsuru no sōshi.” *Kobijutsu* 8 (1965): 115–17.

———. “Yatori Jizō engi ni tsuite.” *Bijutsu kenkyū* 298 (1975): 197–208.

Miya Tsugio, Shinbo Tōru, and Yoshida Yūji, eds. *Kadokawa emakimono sōran*. Tokyo: Kadokawa Shoten, 1995.

Miyajima Shin’ichi. *Kyūtei gadan shi no kenkyū*. Tokyo: Shibundō, 1996.

———. “Tokyo Kokuritsu Hakubutsukan hokan jūyō bunkazai Momonoi Naoakira zō ni tsuite.” *Museum* 450 (1988): 12–18.

———. *Tosa Mitsunobu to Tosa-ha no keifu*. No. 247 of *Nihon no bijutsu*. Tokyo: Shibundō, 1986.

Miyakawa Yōko. “Hakubyō *Genji monogatari emaki:* GoTsuchimikado-in Kōtō no Naishi hitsu.” *Kokusai Keiei Bunka Kenkyū* 6, no. 2 (March 2002): 143–84.

———. *Sanjōnishi Sanetaka to kotengaku*. Tokyo: Kazama Shobō, 1995.

Miyake Hitoshi. *Shugendō: Essays on the Structure of Japanese Folk Religion*. Ann Arbor: Center for Japanese Studies, University of Michigan, 2001.

Miyoshi Shūichirō. “Suzuriwari setsuwa no keifū—bangai utaibon ‘Suzuriwari’ (Nōken-bon) no hankoku to sono ichi zuke.” *Jin’ai kokubun* (Jin’ai Joshi Tanki Daigaku Kokubungakkai Kikanshi) 8 (December 1990).

———. “Suzuriwari setsuwa tsūkan: ‘Konjaku monogatari shū’ kara bangai utaibon ‘Suzuriwari’ made.” *Kokugo kokubungaku* (Fukui Daigaku) 30 (1991): 39–48.

Moore, Jean. “*Senjūshō:* Buddhist Tales of Renunciation.” *Monumenta Nipponica* 41, no. 2 (1986): 127–74.

Morita Kyōji. *Ashikaga Yoshimasa no kenkyū*. Vol. 3 of *Nihon shi kenkyū sōkan*. Osaka: Izumi Shoin, 1993.

———. *Sengokuki rekidai Hosokawashi no kenkyū*. Vol. 5 of *Nihon shi kenkyū sōkan*. Osaka: Izumi Shoin, 1994.

Motoi Makiko. “Jūōkyō to sono kyōju: Gyakushu, tsuizen butsuji ni okeru shōdō o chūshin ni.” *Kokugo kokubun* 67, no. 6 (1998): 22–33; 67, no. 7 (1998): 17–35.

Murai Yasuhiko, ed. *Kundaikan sōchōki, Okazari no sho*. Vol. 1 of *Chanoyu no koten*. Tokyo: Sekai Bunkasha, 1983.

Murashige Yasushi. “Den Tosa Mitsunobu hitsu ‘Matsu zu byōbu’ ni tsuite.” *Kokka* 1118 (1988): 30–41.

Nagae Shōichi. *Miyoshi Nagayoshi*. No. 149 of *Yoshikawa Kōbunkan Jinbutsu sōsho*. Tokyo: Yoshikawa Kōbunkan, 1968.

Nagashima Fukutarō. *Nara bunka no denryū*. Tokyo: Meguro Shoten, 1951.

Nakamikado Nobutane (1442–1525). *Nobutane-kyō ki*. 3 vols. Vols. 22 and 44–45 of *Zōho shiryō taisei,* ed. Zōho Shiryō Taisei Keigyōkai. Kyoto: Rinsen Shoten, 1965, 1967.

Nakamura Yoshio. "Heike kindachi sōshi to Fujiwara Takafusa: Seigaiha no dan no shutten o chūshin to shite." In *Emakimono kotobagaki no kenkyū,* 211–40. Tokyo: Kadokawa Shoten, 1982.

Nakanoin Michihide (1428–94). *Jūrin'in Naifu ki*. In *Shiryō sanshū*, ed. Okuno Takahiro and Katayama Masaru. Tokyo: Zoku Gunsho Ruijū Kanseikai, 1972.

Nakayama Kōichirō. "Ashigayama shita-e zukan to Tosa Mitsunobu." *Museum* 531 (1995): 23–34.

Nara Ehon Kokusai Kenkyū Kaigi, ed. *Zaigai Nara ehon*. Tokyo: Kadokawa Shoten, 1981.

Nara Kokuritsu Hakubutsukan, ed. *Shaji engi-e*. Tokyo: Kadokawa Shoten, 1975.

Narazaki Muneshige. "Tsukiminedera konryū shugyō engi." *Kokka* 783 (June 1957): 177–82.

———. "'Utatane sōshi' jō, ge." *Kokka* 786 (September 1957): 275–81; no. 787 (October 1957): 337–41.

Nihon kokugo daijiten. 20 vols. Tokyo: Shōgakukan, 1973–77.

Nihon koten bungaku daijiten. Tokyo: Iwanami Shoten, 1984.

Nishiguchi Junko. *Onna no chikara: Kodai no josei to bukkyō*. Tokyo: Heibonsha, 1987.

Nishio Kōichi, ed. *Senjūshō*. Iwanami Bunko 6746–49. Tokyo: Iwanami Shoten, 1970.

Nishio Kōichi and Kobayashi Yasuharu, eds. *Kokon chomonjū*. Pts. 1 and 2. Vols. 59 and 76 of *Shinchō Nihon koten shūsei*. Tokyo: Shinchōsha, 1983, 1986.

Nitta Seiji. "'Jizōdō sōshi' shiken." *Chūsei, kinsei bungaku kenkyū* 5 (1971): 33–42.

Ogawa Hiromitsu. "Mokkei—kotenshugi no hen'yō (jō)." *Bijutsushi ronsō,* no. 4 (1988): 95–113.

Ogushi Sumio. "Kiwamete yoku nita mittsu no Shōtoku Taishi emaki." *Kokka* 711 (1951): 219–27.

Okudaira Hideo. *Emaki: Japanese Picture Scrolls*. Rutland, VT: C. E. Tuttle, 1962.

———. *Narrative Picture Scrolls*. New York: Weatherhill, 1973.

———. *Otogi zōshi emaki*. Tokyo: Kadokawa Shoten, 1982.

Okuno Takahiro. *Kōshitsu gokeizaishi no kenkyū*. 2 vols. Tokyo: Unebi Shobō, 1942 (vol. 1); Tokyo: Chūō Kōronsha, 1944 (vol. 2).

———. *Sengoku jidai no kyūtei seikatsu*. Tokyo: Zoku Gunsho Ruijū Kanseikai, 2004.

Ōmori Junko. "Ukifune, Uta, Jendā: Hyōgen keishiki to shite no 'Tenarai' ni tsuite." In *Monogatari "onna to otoko,"* vol. 3 of *Shin monogatari kenkyū*. Tokyo: Yūseidō, 1995.

Ono Akitsugu. "Oroshiuri ichiba to shite no Todo uoichi no hattatsu." *Rekishi chiri* 65, no. 5 (1935): 465–90; 65, no. 6 (1935): 601–32.

———. "Sanjōnishike to Echigo aosoza no katsudō." *Rekishi chiri* 63, no. 2 (1934): 1–32.

Ōtsu Shi Rekishi Hakubutsukan, ed. *Saikyōji to Tendai Shinseishū no hihō*. Ōtsu: Ōtsu Shi Rekishi Hakubutsukan, 1994.

Ōtsuki Osamu. *Chūsei ōchō monogatari no kenkyū*. Tokyo: Sekai Shisōsha, 1993.

Oyudono no ue no nikki. 10 vols. In *Gunsho ruijū hoi*, ed. Hanawa Hokiichi and Ōta Toshiro. Tokyo: Zoku Gunsho Ruijū Kanseikai, 1932–34.

Paine, Robert T. "The Scroll of Kibi's Adventures in China (*Kibi Daijin Nitto Ekotoba*), a Japanese Painting of the Late Twelfth Century Attributed to Mitsunaga." *Bulletin of the Museum of Fine Arts* 31 (1933): 359–75.

Phillips, Quitman E. "Narrating the Salvation of the Elite: The Jōfukuji Paintings of the Ten Kings." *Ars Orientalis* 33 (2003): 121–45.

———. *The Practices of Painting in Japan, 1475–1500*. Stanford: Stanford University Press, 2000.

Pollack, Griselda. "Modernity and the Spaces of Femininity." In *Vision and Difference: Femininity, Feminism, and Histories of Art*. London and New York: Routledge, 1988.

Rambelli, Fabio. "Serpents, Women, and the Quest for the Original Condition: Body, Gender and Salvation in Japanese Buddhism." Paper presented at Stanford University, March 2000.

Rimer, J. Thomas and Yamazaki Masakazu, trans. *On the Art of the Nō Drama: The Major Treatises of Zeami*. Princeton: Princeton University Press, 1984.

Rochette-Crowley, Susan Marie. "Marginal Genre, Major Form: The Twentieth Century Short Story and Theories of the Marginal and Minor." PhD diss., University of Wisconsin, Madison, 1994.

Rodd, Laurel Rasplica, with Mary Catherine Henkenius, trans. *Kokinshū: A Collection of Poems Ancient and Modern*. Princeton: Princeton University Press, 1984.

Ruch, Barbara. "Origins of the Companion Library: An Anthology of Medieval Japanese Stories." *Journal of Asian Studies* 30, no. 3 (1971): 593–610.

Ruppert, Brian D. *Jewel in the Ashes: Buddha Relics and Power in Early Medieval Japan*. Cambridge, MA: Harvard University Asia Center, distributed by Harvard University Press, 2000.

Sakakibara Satoru. "Kiyomizudera engi shaken." In *Kiyomizudera engi, Shin'nyodō engi*, vol. 5 of *Zoku zoku Nihon emaki taisei*, ed. Komatsu Shigemi, 118–39. Tokyo: Chūō Kōronsha, 1994.

———. "Rokkan-bon 'Hasedera engi-e' shōkai" (1992). In *Kohitsu to emaki*, vol. 4 of *Kohitsugaku sōrin*, ed. Komatsu Shigemi, 113–96. Tokyo: Yagi Shoten, 1994.

———. "Santorī Bijutsukan-bon 'Shuten dōji emaki' o megutte." Pts. 1 and 2. *Kokka* 1076 (1984): 7–29; *Kokka* 1077 (1984): 33–56.

———. "'Seikōji engi e' shiken." *Museum* 423 (1986): 4–26.

Sakomura, Tomoko. "Pictured Words and Codified Seasons: Visualizations of Waka Poetry in Late Sixteenth and Early Seventeenth Century Japan." PhD diss., Columbia University, 2007.

Sanetaka-kō ki. Shomei sakuin. Ed. Doi Tetsuji. Tokyo: Zoku Gunsho Ruijū Kanseikai, 2000.

Sanjōnishi Sanetaka (1455–1537). *Sanetaka-kō ki*. Ed. Takahashi Ryūzo. 13 vols. Reprint, Tokyo: Zoku Gunsho Ruijū Kanseikai, 2000–2002.

Sano Midori. "Ōcho no bijutsu." In *ōchō emaki to sōshoku kyō*, vol. 8 of *Nihon bijutsu zenshū*, ed. Nakano Masaki, Hirata Yutaka, and Sano Midori. Tokyo: Kōdansha, 1990.

Sasaki Kōji. "Chūsei bungaku ni okeru ba to seikaku." *Nihon bungaku* 36–2, no. 404 (1987): 40–49.

Sawa Ryūken. "Muromachi shoki no Fugen enmei gazō to sono hissha: Takayoshi, Yukitada, Yukihide." *Bukkyō geijutsu* 11 (1951): 39–49.

Schafer, Edward H. *The Divine Woman: Dragon Ladies and Rain Maidens in T'ang Literature*. Berkeley and Los Angeles: University of California Press, 1973.

Seckel, Dietrich. *Emakimono: The Art of the Japanese Painted Hand-Scroll*. New York: Pantheon Books, 1959.

Seidensticker, Edward G., trans. *The Tale of Genji*. New York: Vintage Books, 1990.

Seikadō Bunko Bijutsukan, ed. *Muromachi no kaigaten: Shigajiku, byōbu, shōhekiga*. Tokyo: Seikadō Bunko Bijutsukan, 1996.

Shibunkaku, ed. *Shibunkaku kosho shiryō mokuroku*. No. 197. Vol. 18 of *Zenbon tokushū*. Kyoto: Shibunkaku, 2006.

Shiga Tadashi. *Josei kyōiku shi*. Tokyo: Fukumura Shuppan, 1968.

Shimada Shūjirō, ed. *Shinshū Nihon emakimono zenshū*. 30 vols., 2 suppl. vols. Tokyo: Kadokawa Shoten, 1975–81.

Shimatani Hiroyuki. "Kiyomizudera no kotoba o megutte." In *Kohitsu to emaki*, vol. 4 of *Kohitsugaku sōrin*, ed. Komatsu Shigemi. Tokyo: Yagi Shoten, 1994.

Shimazu Hisamoto and Ichiko Teiji, eds. *Zoku otogi-zōshi*. Tokyo: Iwanami Shoten, 1956.

Shimizu, Yoshiaki. "The Rite of Writing: Thoughts on the Oldest *Genji* Text." *Res* 16 (1988): 54–63.

———. "The Shigisan-engi Scrolls, c. 1175." In *Pictorial Narrative in Antiquity and the Middle Ages*, ed. Herbert Kessler and Marianna Shreve Simpson, 115–29. Studies in the History of Art, vol. 16. Washington, DC: National Gallery of Art, 1985.

Shinbo Tōru. *Kitano seibyō-e no kenkyū*. Tokyo: Chūō Kōron Bijutsu Shuppan, 1994.

———. "Kōbō Daishi den emaki nijū." In *Shinshū Nihon emakimono zenshū, bekkan 1: Zaigai hen*, ed. Shimada Shūjirō, 3–10. Tokyo: Kadokawa Shoten, 1980.

Shinkokinshū. Vol. 43 of *Shinpen Nihon koten bungaku zenshū*, ed. Minemura Fumito. Tokyo: Shōgakukan, 1995.

Shirane, Haruo. *The Bridge of Dreams: A Poetics of "The Tale of Genji."* Stanford: Stanford University Press, 1987.

———. "The Uji Chapters and the Denial of Romance." In *Ukifune: Love in the "Tale of Genji,"* ed. Andrew Pekarik, 113–38. New York: Columbia University Press, 1982.

Shirane, Haruo, and Tomi Suzuki, eds. *Inventing the Classics: Modernity, National Identity, and Japanese Literature*. Stanford: Stanford University Press, 2000.

Skord, Virginia. *Tales of Tears and Laughter*. Honolulu: University of Hawaii Press, 1991.

Sōchō (1448–1532). *The Journal of Sōchō*. Trans. and annotated by H. Mack Horton. Stanford: Stanford University Press, 2002.

Sōgō Bukkyō daijiten. 3 vols. Ed. Sōgō Bukkyō Daijiten Henshū Iinkai. Kyoto: Hōzōkan, 1987.

Solomon, Michael. "The Dilemma of Religious Power:

Honganji and Hosokawa Masamoto." *Monumenta Nipponica* 33, no. 1 (1978): 51–65.

Strong, Sarah M. "The Making of a Femme Fatale: Ono no Komachi in the Early Medieval Commentaries." *Monumenta Nipponica* 49, no. 4 (1994): 391–412.

Suegara Yutaka. "Hosokawa Masamoto to Shugendō: Shisen'in Kosen o chūshin ni." *Harukanaru chūsei* 12 (1992): 64–69.

———. "Hosokawa-shi no dōzoku rengō taisei no kaitai to kinai ryōgokuka." In *Chūsei no hō to seiji*, ed. Ishii Susumu, 141–231. Tokyo: Yoshikawa Kōbunkan, 1992.

———. "'Kasuga Gongen genki-e' no hōnō o megutte." *Nihon rekishi* 695 (2006): 62–70.

Suga Miho. "Kitano Tenjin engi Mitsuoki bon no kōsatsu." *Kokka* 1209 (1996): 7–23.

Sugimoto Yoshihisa. "Hitomaro zō shinkō to sono kyōju: Gosho denju to no kankei o chūshin ni." *Bijutsushi kenkyū* (Waseda daigaku bijutsushi gakkai) 36 (1998): 39–58.

Sugiyama Mitsunobu and Sugiyama Emiko, trans. *Kodomo no tanjō: Anshamu rejīmu-ki no kodomo to kazoku seikatsu*. Tokyo: Misuzu Shobō, 1980.

Sullivan, Edward J. "The *Kibi* and *Ban Dainagon* Scrolls: Two Masterpieces of *Emakimono* by Mitsunaga." *Marsyas* 17 (1975): 67–78.

Swanson, Paul L. "Shugendō and the Yoshino-Kumano Pilgrimage: An Example of Mountain Pilgrimage." *Monumenta Nipponica* 36, no. 1 (1981): 55–84.

Tabata Yasuko. *Nihon chūsei josei shiron*. Tokyo: Tōshobō, 1994.

Taiheiki. Ed. Hasegawa Tadashi. 4 vols. Vols. 54–57 of *Shinpen Nihon koten bungaku zenshū*. Tokyo: Shōgakukan, 1994–98.

Tajima Kazuo, annotator. *Utatane no sōshi*. In pt. 1 of *Muromachi monogatarishū*, vol. 54 of *Shin Nihon koten bungaku taikei*, ed. Ichiko Teiji et al., 269–89. Tokyo: Iwanami Shoten, 1989.

Tajima Kazuo, Komine Kazuaki, and Harima Mitsutoshi, eds. "Kyōrin Bunko-bon *Mii ōjōden* honkoku to kenkyū." In *Chūsei bungaku shiryō to ronkō*, 559–91. Tokyo: Kasama Shoin, 1978.

Takagishi Akira. "Muromachi dono emaki korekushon no keisei." *Bijutsushi* 155 (2003): 16–29.

———. *Muromachi ōken to kaiga: Shoki Tosa-ha kenkyū*. Kyoto: Kyoto Daigaku Gakujutsu Shuppankai, 2004.

———. "'Tsukiminedera konryū engi emaki' kara 'Daikakuji engi emaki' e—emaki no chūsei to kinsei." In *Settsu Amazaki Daikakuji shiryō 1*, ed. Takaigishi Akira, 64–84. Geppōsan Daikakuji, 2005.

Takahashi Nobuyuki. "Sanjōnishi Sanetaka: Chūō to chihō to no bunka kōryū." *Kokubungaku kaishaku to kanshō* 57, no. 3 (March 1992): 82–90.

Takahashi Tōru. *Monogatari to e no enkinhō*. Tokyo: Perikansha, 1991.

Takenuki Genshō, ed. *Zusetsu Nihon bukkyō no rekishi, Muromachi jidai*. Tokyo: Kōsei Shuppan, 1996.

Takeuchi, Melinda, ed. *The Artist as Professional in Japan*. Stanford: Stanford University Press, 2004.

———. "The Golden Link: Place, Poetry, and Paradise in a Medieval Japanese Design." In *Worlds Seen and Imagined: Japanese Screens from the Idemitsu Museum of Art*, ed. Kuroda Taizō et al., 31–53. New York: Asia Society, 1995.

———. "Tosa Mitsunobu and the Afterlife of a Name." In *The Artist as Professional in Japan*, ed. Melinda Takeuchi, 78–102. Stanford: Stanford University Press, 2004.

Tamura Etsuko. "In no Dainagon ni kansuru jakkan no kōsatsu." *Bijutsu kenkyū* 326 (1983): 1–16.

Tamura Ryūshō. "Jūsanbutsu zuzō to jūōzu honjibutsu: Shinkō shiryō no zuzōgaku." *Mikkyō zuzō* 4 (1986): 14–28.

Tanaka Takako. "*Akujo*" *ron*. Tokyo: Kinokuniya Shoten, 1992.

———. *Gehō to aihō no chūsei*. Tokyo: Sunagoya Shobō, 1993.

Tani Shin'ichi. "Fujiwara Yukimitsu kō." In *Muromachi jidai bijutsu shiron*. Tokyo: Tōkyōdō, 1942. First published in *Bijutsu kenkyū* 87 (1939).

———. "Mitsunobu hitsu Momonoi Naoakira zō zukai." *Kokka* 488 (1931): 213–14.

———. *Muromachi jidai bijutsu shiron*. Tokyo: Tōkyōdō, 1942.

———. *Nihon bijutsushi gaisetsu*. Tokyo: Tōkyōdō, 1948.

———. "Sanetaka-zō kamigata: Tosa Mitsunobu kō hoi." *Bijutsushi* 17 (1955): 1–6.

———. "Tosa Mitsunobu kō." In *Muromachi jidai bijutsu shiron*. Tokyo: Tōkyōdō, 1942. First published in *Bijutsu kenkyū* 100 (1940): 115–29; 101 (1940): 156–69; 103 (1940): 207–21.

———. "Tosa Yukihiro kō." *Bijutsu kenkyū* 127 (1942):275–84; 128 (1943): 8–14.

Taniguchi Noriko. "Suzuriwari ni kansuru ichi kōsatsu:

Hiroshima daigaku seiritsu o chūshin ni." *Otani joshi dai kokubun* 23 (1993): 229–40.

Tanuma Mutsumi. "Muromachi bakufu zaisei no ichi danmen: Bunshō-do daijōe o chūshin ni." *Nihon rekishi* 353 (1977): 1–26.

Tendai Shinseishū shūgaku kenkyūjo, ed. *Yakuchū Shinsei Shōnin ōjōdenki*. Vol. 36 of *Mie-ken Gōshi shiryō sōsho*. Ōtsu: Mie-ken Gōshi Shiryō Kankōkai, 1972.

Thompson, Sarah E. "A *Hakubyō* 'Genji Monogatari Emaki' in the Spencer Collection." Master's thesis, Columbia University, 1984.

———. "The War of the Twelve Animals (*Jūnirui kassen emaki*): A Medieval Japanese Illustrated Beast Fable." PhD diss., Columbia University, 1999.

Tocco, Martha C. "Norms and Texts for Women's Education in Tokugawa Japan." In *Women and Confucian Cultures in Premodern China, Korea, and Japan*, ed. Dorothy Ko et al., 193–218. Berkeley and Los Angeles: University of California Press, 2003.

Tokuda Kazuo. *Egatari to monogatari. Imēji rīdingu sōsho*. Tokyo: Heibonsha, 1990.

———. "'Ōgi no sōshi emaki' o megutte (josetsu)." *Kokugo kokubun ronshū* (Gakushuin Joshi Tanki Daigaku Kokugo Kokubun Gakkai), no. 20 (1991): 69–92.

———. *Otogi-zōshi jiten*. Tokyo: Tōkyōdō Shuppan, 2002.

———. *Otogi-zōshi kenkyū*. Tokyo: Miyai Shoten, 1988.

———. "Sanjōnishi Sanetaka no 'zoku'—Sanetaka-kō ki ni miru bungei no ichisokumen." *Kokubungaku kaishaku to kanshō* 50, no. 8 (1985): 38–45.

Tokyo Daigaku Shiryō Hensanjo, ed. *Dai sanjū ikkai shiryō tenrankai reppin mokuroku: "Sanetaka kōki" to Sanjōnishi ke*. Tokyo: Tokyo Daigaku Shiryō Hensanjo, 1995.

Tokyo Daigaku Shiryō Hensanjo, ed. *Shiryō sōran*. Tokyo: Shiryōhensanjo, 1936–.

Tonomura, Hitomi. "Re-envisioning Women in the Post-Kamakura Age." In *The Origins of Japan's Medieval World: Courtiers, Clerics, Warriors, and Peasants in the Fourteenth Century*, ed. Jeffrey Mass, 138–69. Stanford: Stanford University Press, 1997.

Tonomura Nobuko. "Nyōbō bungaku no yukue." In *Jūgo, jūroku seiki no bungaku*, vol. 6 of *Iwanami kōza Nihon bungaku shi*, ed. Kuboto Jun et al., 177–98. Tokyo: Iwanami Shoten, 1996.

Tyler, Royall. *The Miracles of the Kasuga Deity*. New York: Columbia University Press, 1990.

———, trans. *The Tale of Genji*. New York: Viking, 2001.

Ulak, James Thomas. "'Fukutomi zōshi': The Genesis and Transmutations of a Medieval Japanese Scatological Tale." PhD diss., Case Western Reserve University, 1994.

Umezu Jirō. "Den Tosa Mitsunobu hitsu 'Heike monogatari emaki.'" *Bijutsushi* 35 (1960): 95–99. Reprinted in *Emakimono sōshi*, 298–326.

———. *Emakimono sōkō*. Tokyo: Chūō Kōron Bijutsu Shuppan, 1968.

———. *Emakimono sōshi*. Kyoto: Hōzōkan, 1972.

———. *Emakimono zanketsu no fu*. Tokyo: Kadokawa Shoten, 1970.

———. "Futakumi no jūōzu: Yukimitsu to Mitsunobu no gaseki." *Bukkyō geijutsu* 36 (1958): 32–35.

———. "Ishiyamadera engi-e kō." *Bijutsushi* 6 (1952). Reprinted in vol. 22 of *Shinshū Nihon emakimono zenshū*, ed. Shimada Shūjirō, 3–13; and in *Emakimono sōko*, 429–49.

———. "Kōbō Daishi gyōjō emaki no keifu." *Nihon bijutsu kōgei* 319 (1965): 38–42.

———. "Shoki no Yūzō nenbutsu engi ni tsuite." *Bukkyō geijutsu* 37 (1958): 1–27. Reprinted in *Emakimono sōko*, 337–73.

———. "Suzuriwari emaki sono hoka: 'Ko-e' no mondai." *Kokka* 828 (1961): 97–104. Reprinted in *Emakimono sōshi*, 285–97.

———. "Tenjin engi emaki: Tsuda-bon to Mitsunobu-bon." *Bijutsu kenkyū* 126 (1942): 225–32. Reprinted in *Emakimono sōko*, 391–428.

Ury, Marian. *Tales of Times Now Past*. Berkeley and Los Angeles: University of California Press, 1979.

Wakasugi Junji. *Bijutsukan e ikō: Emaki o yomitoku*. Tokyo: Shinchōsha, 1998.

———. *Emakimono no kanshō kiso chishiki*. Tokyo: Shibundō, 1995.

Wakita Haruko. *Nihon chūsei joseishi no kenkyū: Seibetsu yakuwari buntan to bosei, kasei, seiai*. Tokyo: Tokyo Daigaku Shuppankai, 1992.

———. "Sengokuki ni okeru Tennō ken'i no fujō." Pts. 1 and 2. *Nihonshi kenkyū*, no. 340 (1990): 1–27; no. 341 (1991): 30–58.

———. "Women and the Creation of the 'Ie' in Japan: An Overview from the Medieval Period to the Present." Trans. David P. Phillips. *U.S.-Japan Women's Journal, English Supplement,* no. 4 (1993): 83–105.

Waseda Daigaku Toshokan. *Muromachi monogatarishū*.

Vol. 8 of *Waseda Daigaku zō, Shiryō eiin sōsho, Kokusho hen*. Tokyo: Waseda Daigaku Shuppanbu, 1987.

Waters, Virginia Skord. "Sex, Lies, and the Illustrated Scroll: The *Dōjōji Engi Emaki*." *Monumenta Nipponica* 52, no. 1 (1997): 59–84.

Watson, Burton. *Meng Ch'iu: Famous Episodes from Chinese History and Legend*. New York: Kodansha International, 1979.

Weidner, Marsha, ed. *Flowering in the Shadows: Women in the History of Chinese and Japanese Painting*. Honolulu: University of Hawaii Press, 1990.

Wu Hung. *The Double Screen: Medium and Representation in Chinese Painting*. Chicago: University of Chicago Press, 1996.

Yamada Yasuhiro. *Sengokuki Muromachi Bakufu to shōgun*. Tokyo: Yoshikawa Kōbunkan, 2000.

Yamamoto Hideo. "Chūgoku koji jinbutsu zu, Ōsen Keisan san." *Kyoto Kokuritsu Hakubutsukan Gakusō* 12 (1990): 88–96.

Yamamoto Yōko. *Emaki ni okeru kami to ten no hyōgen*. Tokyo: Chūō Kōron Bijutsu Shuppan, 2006.

Yamane Yūzō. "Ikebana to zashiki kazari." In vol. 2 of *Ikebana bijutsu zenshū*. Tokyo: Shūeisha, 1982. Reprinted in Yamane Yūzō, ed., *Kadōshi kenkyū* (Tokyo: Chūō Kōronsha, 1996), 105–21.

Yamashina Tokikuni (1452–1502). *Tokikuni-kyō ki*. Ed. Toyoda Takeshi, Tanuma Mutsumi, and Iikura Harutake. 8 vols. In *Shiryō sanshū*. Tokyo: Zoku Gunsho Ruijū Kanseikai, 1969–95.

Yamashina Tokitsugu (1507–79). *Rekimei dodai*. In vol. 29 of *Gunsho ruijū, Zatsu bu*. 3d ed. Tokyo: Gunsho Ruijū Kanseikai Taiyōsha, 1943.

Yamashita Hiroaki, ed. *Taiheiki*, vol. 2. Vol. 38 of *Shinchō Nihon koten shūsei*, ed. Yamashita Hiroaki. Tokyo: Shinchōsha, 1980.

Yasuhara Makoto. *"Ōgi no sōshi" no kenkyū: Asobi no geibun*. Tokyo: Perikansha, 2003.

Yokoyama Shigeru and Kobashi Yorizō, eds. *Monogatari sōshi mokuroku zenhen*. Tokyo: Ōkayama Shoin, 1937.

Yokoyama Shigeru and Matsumoto Ryūshin, eds. *Muromachi jidai monogatari taisei*. 13 vols. Tokyo: Kadokawa Shoten, 1973–87.

Yonehara Masayoshi. *Sengoku bushi to bungei no kenkyū*. Tokyo: Ofūsha, 1976.

Yonekura Michio. "Bosuton bijutsukan bon 'Utatane sōshi' ni tsuite." In *Shinshū Nihon emakimono zenshū*, suppl. 2, ed. Shimada Shūjirō, 46–55. Tokyo: Kadokawa Shoten, 1981.

———. "Zuhan kaisetsu, Kokuritsu Rekishi Minzoku Hakubutsukan zō Utatane sōshi." *Bijutsu kenkyū* 352 (1992): 270–74.

Yoshida Kazuhiko. "The Enlightenment of the Dragon King's Daughter in *The Lotus Sutra*." Trans. and adapted by Margaret H. Childs. In *Engendering Faith: Women and Buddhism in Premodern Japan*, ed. Barbara Ruch, 297–324. Ann Arbor: Center for Japanese Studies, University of Michigan, 2002.

———. "Ryūnyo no jōbutsu." In *Sukui to oshie*, ed. Ōsumi Kazuo and Nishiguchi Junko, 45–91. Vol. 2 of *Shirīzu josei to bukkyō*. Tokyo: Heibonsha, 1989.

Yoshida Yūji. "Ishiyamadera engi-e nanakan no rekitei." In *Ishiyamadera engi*, vol. 18 of *Nihon emaki taisei*, ed. Komatsu Shigemi. Tokyo: Chūō Kōronsha, 1978.

———. "Seikōji engi-e kō: Tosa Mitsunobu no shoki gafū kaisei o megutte." *Tezukayama Gakuin Daigaku kenkyū ronshū* 11 (1976): 161–76.

———. *Tosa Mitsunobu*. Vol. 5 of *Nihon bijutsu kaiga zenshū*. Tokyo: Shūeisha, 1979.

Zoku gunsho ruijū. Ed. Hanawa Hokiichi et al. 37 vols. Tokyo: Zoku Gunsho Ruijū Kanseikai, 1923–66.

Zoku Gunsho Ruijū Kanseikai Henshūbu. "Harima kuni Shoshazan engi (shinpo)." *Shigaku bungaku* 2, no. 3 (1959): 12–29.

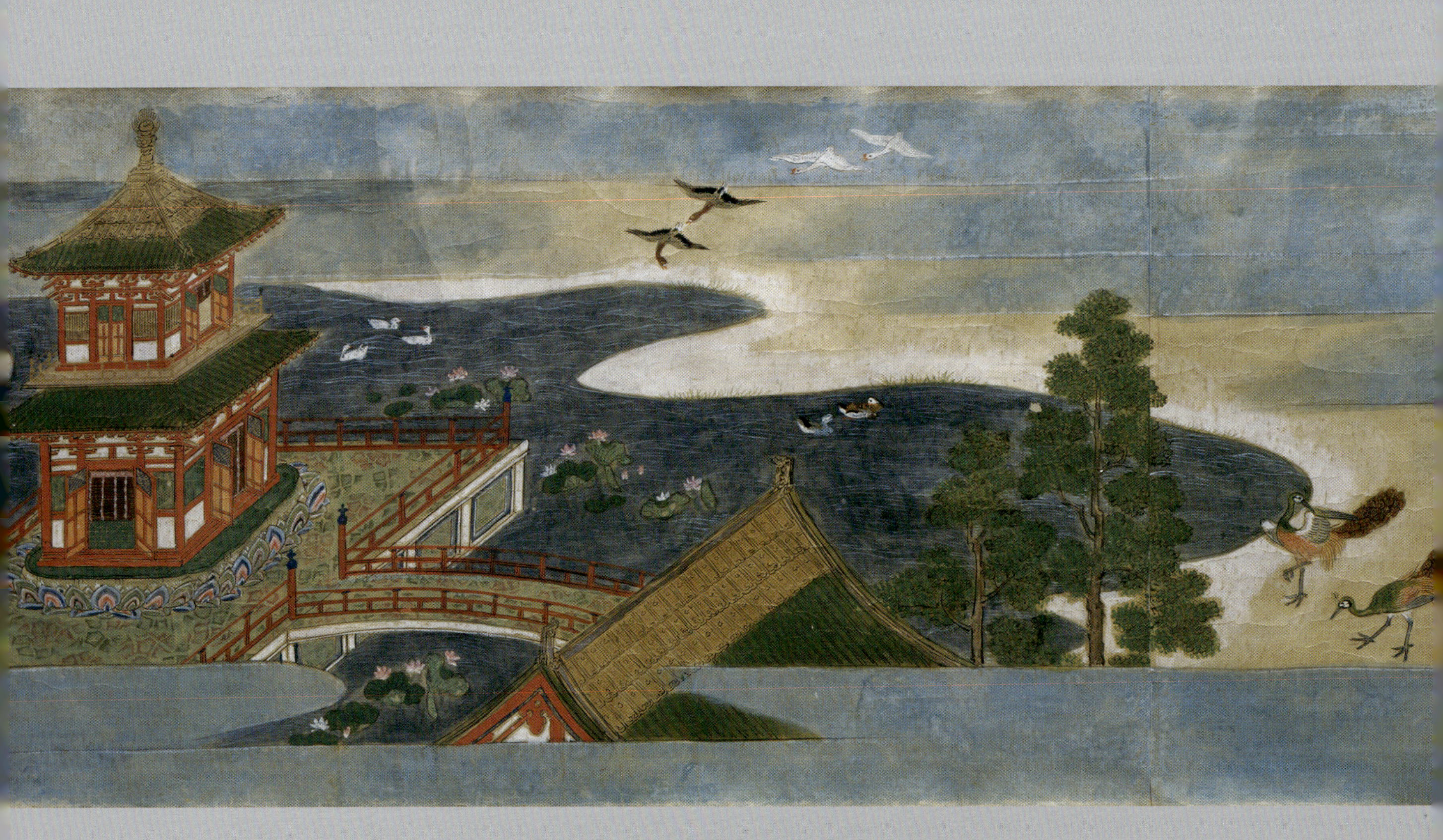

ILLUSTRATION CREDITS

Photographs and the permission to use them were generously granted by the present owners as noted in the captions. The Kyoto National Museum provided the photographs for figures 2, 5, 24, 39, 45, 55, 65, 77, 78, 79, 82, 84, 86, 87, 91, 92, 93, 94, 96, 110, 120; the Nara National Museum provided the photographs for figures 10, 11, 12, 28; and images for figures 34, 37, 38, 40, 46, 47, 48, 68, 69, 70, 95 were provided by the Tokyo National Museum, Image: TNM Image Archives, Source: http://TnmArchives.jp.

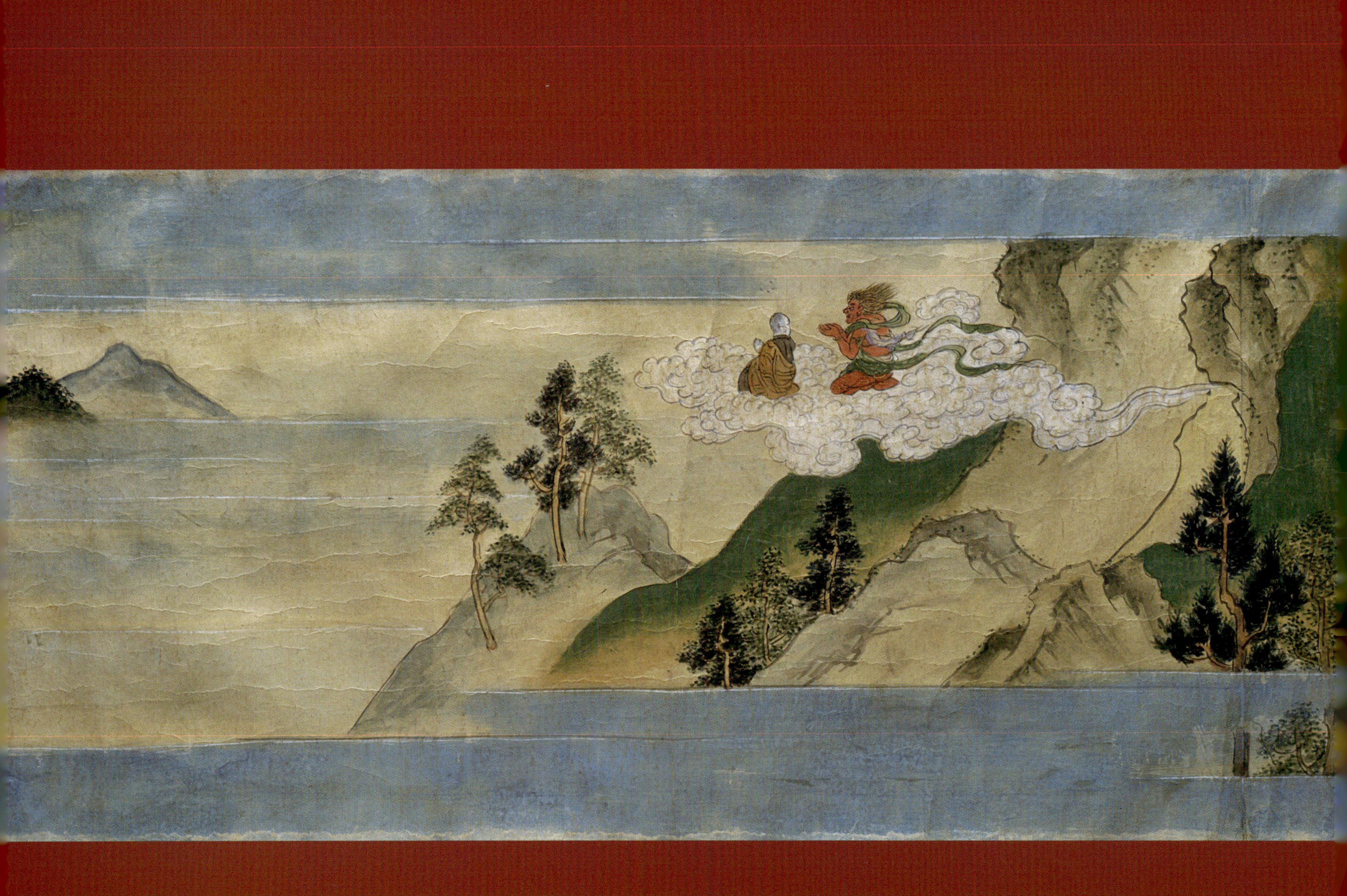

INDEX

Page numbers in *italic* refer to figures.